THE CAMBRIDGE HISTORY OF THE NATIVE PEOPLES OF THE AMERICAS

VOLUME I:

North America

THE CAMBRIDGE HISTORY
OF THE NATIVE PEOPLES OF
THE AMERICAS

VOLUME I: NORTH AMERICA
Edited by Bruce G. Trigger and Wilcomb E. Washburn

VOLUME II: MESOAMERICA
Edited by R. E. W. Adams and Murdo MacLeod

VOLUME III: SOUTH AMERICA
Edited by Stuart Schwartz and Frank Salomon

THE CAMBRIDGE HISTORY OF THE NATIVE PEOPLES OF THE AMERICAS

VOLUME I

NORTH AMERICA

PART 1

Edited by

Bruce G. Trigger
McGill University

Wilcomb E. Washburn
Smithsonian Institution

CAMBRIDGE
UNIVERSITY PRESS

Published by the Press Syndicate of the University of Cambridge
The Pitt Building, Trumpington Street, Cambridge CB2 1RP
40 West 20th Street, New York, NY 10011-4211, USA
10 Stamford Road, Oakleigh, Melbourne 3166, Australia

© Cambridge University Press 1996

First published 1996

Printed in the United States of America

Library of Congress Cataloging-in-Publication Data
North America / edited by Bruce G. Trigger, Wilcomb E. Washburn.

p.   cm. – (Cambridge history of the Native peoples of
the Americas)

Includes bibliographical references and index.

ISBN 0–521–34440–9

1. Indians of North America–History.   2. Eskimos–History.
I. Trigger, Bruce G.   II. Washburn, Wilcomb E.   III. Series.

E77.N62   1996

970.004'97–dc20   95-46096
                                                                              CIP

A catalog record for this book is available from the British Library.

Volume I: North America   ISBN   0-521-34440-9 hardback   complete set

Volume I: North America, Part 1   ISBN   0-521-57392-0

Volume I: North America, Part 2   ISBN   0-521-57393-9

Volume II: Mesoamerica   ISBN   0-521-35165-0

Volume III: South America   ISBN   0-521-33393-8

CONTENTS

Part 1

CONTENTS

Part 2

ILLUSTRATIONS

PART 1

PART 2

EDITORIAL PREFACE

The North America volume of the *Cambridge History of the Native Peoples of the Americas* traces the history of the indigenous peoples living north of the Rio Grande from their earliest appearance in the New World into the 1990s. In the tradition of Cambridge histories, it seeks primarily to synthesize existing knowledge rather than to present the results of original research or to pioneer innovative approaches to the study of Native American history. Yet realizing this seemingly modest goal has been a formidable undertaking, lending credence to critics of the project who suggested that it might be premature and impossible to bring to completion. This volume draws upon the results of research by many generations of historians, anthropologists, archaeologists, physical anthropologists, linguists, and Native cultural specialists. Nevertheless, partly as a result of biases that only now are beginning to be understood, much about Native history remains poorly known among professional scholars. The co-editors were selected to represent some of the diversity within the multidisciplinary field of Native American history. One editor is an American historian, the other a Canadian anthropologist. Their political views are also quite different. By helping to ensure that a wide range of viewpoints receive serious attention, these divergences have been sources of strength rather than weakness in editing this work.

The present volume does not attempt to compete with the multivolume *Handbook of North American Indians,* or with many excellent monographs, in presenting a series of "tribal histories." Ethnic identities have shifted significantly over time in North America, as they have done in other parts of the world. Thus they do not provide a particularly useful framework for considering other important aspects of Native North American history, such as changing ecological adaptations, responses to European diseases and settlement, or the gradual development of a pan-Indian identity. In order to provide more flexible coverage, an approach has been adopted in which thematic concerns define some chapters, while regional coverage defines others.

Today no historical study can (or should) avoid self-reflection. Chapters 1 and 2 examine changing Native views of their history and the views of non-Native historians. These chapters put existing literature relating to Native American history into perspective and establish the nature, limitations, and biases of our current state of knowledge. This is followed by Chapters 3 to 5, which use mainly archaeological data to trace the history prior to European contact of hunter-gatherers (including the earliest inhabitants of North America), the development of agricultural societies in the East and the Southwest, and the emergence of stratified societies in the Mississippi Valley after A.D. 800. As the content of these chapters makes clear, this ordering does not constitute the imposition of a unilinear evolutionary scheme on this material; it merely reflects the historical order in which such societies initially appeared.

Chapter 6 surveys the nature of contact between Europeans and Native Americans in the sixteenth century, including the extent and impact of European diseases introduced at this period. This was a time when enduring European settlement was not yet established outside of Florida. Chapters 7 to 11 examine what happened to Native peoples from about 1600 to the 1880s in those parts of North America that were extensively settled by newcomers of European and African origin prior to the end of the nineteenth century. Two chapters are devoted to the Eastern Woodlands and one each to the Great Plains, the Southwest and California, and the Northwest Coast. Each chapter examines the role played by Native peoples in facilitating European settlement and the various strategies, ranging from alliance to prolonged conflict or avoidance, by which these groups sought to cope with and benefit from a European presence. These chapters also document how European demographic expansion and growing economic competitiveness made it ever more difficult for Native peoples to determine their own destinies. Chapter 12 explores the experience of the Native peoples living in all these regions from 1880 to 1960, a period when their common experience of Euro-American domination and reservation life, combined with improved communication, led Native leaders to forge a new collective identity as Indians that complemented and empowered their older ethnic identities.

Chapters 13 and 14 trace the history from earliest European contact until modern times of the Native peoples of the Northern Interior and Arctic regions of North America, including Greenland. These were areas where, until after 1945, Euro-American and Euro-Canadian settlement was minimal and where Native peoples preserved a considerable degree of political autonomy. A final chapter, by one of the co-editors, offers a personal evaluation of trends in Native North American life since 1960, a period that has seen Native people increasing in numbers and retaking ever more control of their political, economic, and cultural life. Despite continuing problems of poverty, unemployment, and dependency, especially in northern regions, these developments belie the once firmly held belief of Euro-Americans that Native people would either become physically extinct or disappear into the North American melting pot. Despite its optimism, this chapter clearly indicates the changing but persistent external pressures with which Native people still must contend.

While the topics to be covered in each chapter were decided by the co-editors, authors enjoyed complete freedom to interpret their material as they thought best. It was not easy to recruit authors for these chapters. Native American studies is a field characterized by intense specialization, with many scholars, both professional and amateur, focusing not merely on single peoples but on specific aspects of their cultures. It is not difficult to find specialists to write about Cherokee warfare, Hopi ritual, or seventeenth-century Huron history. But to find individuals able and willing to generalize on a regional or continental scale is far more difficult. The co-editors were fortunate to be able to assemble a team of young, middle-aged, and senior scholars, who could complete the demanding chores that were assigned them. Some undertook this work on short notice when prior authors were unable to write or finish their papers. Each chapter stretched the synthesizing abilities of its authors to a considerable degree. Despite generous page allowances, great concision, selection, and generalization were required in order to provide balanced coverage. While some thematic overlap between chapters was necessary, every effort has been made to eliminate simple duplication. The production schedule of collective works, as is too well known, is determined by the speed of the slowest contributor. The co-editors thank those authors who met their deadlines for patiently enduring the unconscionable delays caused by a few authors who were less prompt.

This book is written at a time when postmodern views encourage relativism and alternative histories. It is frequently maintained that every group, and indeed every individual, perceives the past differently and that there is no way to judge one version of the past to be more authentic than another. The co-editors recognize the value of alternative histories. Histories written from a feminist or minority viewpoint complement mainline studies and ultimately make possible more rounded syntheses. In North America, ethnohistory played an important pioneering role in the development of the study of minority histories.

Nevertheless, the co-editors do not accept the extreme relativist argument that alternative views of history are incommensurate and that each must be accepted on its own terms. Historical interpretations can be judged not only according to their degree of internal logical coherence (this even most extreme relativists accept), but also according to their correspondence with factual evidence. Not all histories are equally consistent, nor do they stand up equally well when tested against the growing body of documentation that historians and anthropologists have at their disposal. Anyone or any group has the right to author histories, and many do so, consciously or unconsciously, in ways that promote their own interests. Yet professional historians have a responsibility to subject all interpretations to scholarly analysis. As more historical data become available, the possibility of subjective factors wholly determining interpretations diminishes.

This publication probably marks the end of an era in Native North American historical studies. Native American history and culture were studied first by amateur and then by professional anthropologists and historians, all but a few of whom were of European descent. Their work was grounded in evolutionary and romantic stereotypes. Native peoples were viewed as illustrating what earlier stages in the development of European culture had been like and as being on their way to cultural and probably biological extinction as a result of the spread of European civilization. Whether denigrated as cruel and uncivilized or portrayed as noble savages, Native peoples were treated as essentially belonging to the past.

Over the past forty years, researches by ethnohistorians mainly of European descent have revealed the mythical status of such views by documenting the important role that Native peoples have played, and continue to play, in North American society. The accumulation of a vast body of data relating to Native Americans both before and after the arrival of Europeans has provided a sound basis for a new understanding of Indian history. In particular, ethnohistorians have realized that indigenous societies are enduring and sometimes flourishing, and rarely disappear, even under the most adverse conditions. In this way, they have discovered for themselves what has long been obvious to Native peoples. These studies not only have revealed many more details about aboriginal history but also have transformed the understanding that nonaboriginal specialists and an increasing segment of nonaboriginal North Americans have of their own history.

This new attitude became especially evident during the commemoration of the quincentenary of Columbus's arrival in the New World. In 1992, the main emphasis was not on celebrating the achievements of Europeans, as it had been in 1892, but on coming to terms with the lasting suffering that European diseases and colonization had inflicted on the Native peoples of the western hemisphere. Encouraged by a new historical understanding, fewer Euro-Americans are associating living Native peoples with the past or viewing them as existing outside the social fabric and power structures of North America's national societies. In democratic societies, knowledge that helps to dispel unfounded prejudices held by majorities about minorities is of no small importance.

The co-editors are acutely aware that this history of Native Americans has been written by Euro-Americans and Euro-Canadians. This was not for the lack of a desire or effort to recruit Native American authors. Yet, despite a growing number of Native Americans who are writing about their past, the professional study of Native American history remains largely the domain of historians and anthropologists of European descent. While Native people have played the major political role in challenging the image that other North Americans have of them, nonaboriginal historians and anthropologists have been working to dispel myths that their predecessors helped to create.

It is essential that more Native people who are interested in studying their past should become professional historians and anthropologists, so that their special insights and perspectives can contribute to the study of Native history. Just as the barrier between Native and non-Native history was replaced by a symbiotic relation once Euro-American scholars realized that Native people had played a significant role in shaping North American society since 1492, so the distinction between professional anthropologists and historians on the one hand and Native people on the other should give way to disciplines in which Native people play an increasingly important role. Such collegiality will mark the beginning of a new phase in the study of Native history.

Especially in Canada there is a growing tendency to designate Native groups by the names they apply to themselves. Sometimes this amounts to little more than a spelling change, as when Micmacs are called Mi'kmaq. But it also involves calling Montagnais Innu, Hurons Wendat, Nootkas Nuu-chah-nulth, and the people Euro-Canadians call Ojibwas and Euro-

Americans call Chippewas Anishinabe. Despite the merits of this practice and the respect that it implies for Native people, consistent use of such terminology at this time would prove confusing to an international readership that is familiar with the conventional names that Europeans have applied to these groups. Hence the co-editors have decided to retain the ethnic names and spellings utilized in the *Handbook of North American Indians,* while noting in brackets self-designations where groups who are now using these names first receive substantial mention. The usage we have adopted is little different from referring to España as Spain or Deutschland as Germany. Following Native preference and common usage, however, the modern Eskimos of Canada are regularly referred to as Inuit; those of Alaska as Eskimos. An analogous policy is applied to personal names: King Philip is preferred to Metacom and Sitting Bull to Ta-Tanka-I-Yotank.

In conformity with general usage, the term Iroquoian refers to any Indian group speaking an Iroquoian language, while Iroquois is restricted to members of the Five (later Six) Nations: Senecas, Cayugas, Onondagas, Oneidas, Mohawks, and Tuscaroras. Likewise, Algonquian refers to any group speaking an Algonquian language, while Algonquin applies specifically to a series of Algonquian-speaking bands living in and near the Ottawa Valley.

In response to complaints from historians, most notably James Axtell, that referring to collective members of indigenous groups in the singular is an ethnocentric and "nonsensical convention left over from the nineteenth century" (*The Invasion Within* [New York, 1985], xi), in this volume such groups are called Hopis, Hurons, and Utes, just as people normally speak of Germans, Italians, and Russians. Inuit is already a plural. The term prehistory is also eshewed on the grounds that it unduly segments the continuum of Native history and may falsely imply that Native peoples did not have true history prior to the arrival of Europeans. This does not mean, however, that authors do not recognize a significant difference between history based almost exclusively on archaeological evidence and that based on a mixture of texts and archaeological data or on textual evidence alone. The term tribe is also avoided except as it is used as an administrative term by the U.S. government. Finally, the co-editors have followed Francis Jennings in avoiding inherently racial expressions such as Whites, Red people, and Blacks, except as they appear in specific historical usage or as statistical categories. While it is impossible and probably counterproductive to try to keep abreast of all the latest fashions in politically correct terminology, these conventions seemed particularly important.

The co-editors wish especially to thank Frank Smith for his help in editing this volume. His contributions have gone well beyond commissioning and overseeing the production of this volume and warrant his being considered a third co-editor. They also thank Camilla Palmer, Production Editor, and David Anderson, copyeditor, for the care they have taken in guiding this manuscript through press. Trigger wishes to thank Professor Toby Morantz, McGill University, for her helpful advice at many stages in the editing of these papers.

Even a history of this size cannot cover every aspect of Native American history and in this respect it is bound to disappoint readers searching for particular facts. Nevertheless, it provides the first comprehensive history of the Native peoples of North America from earliest times to the present. It offers readers an opportunity to observe how Native peoples have dealt with the environmental diversity of North America and have responded to the different European colonial regimes and national governments that have established themselves in recent centuries. It also provides a chance to begin to compare how Native peoples have fared in Canada, the United States, and Greenland. It is hoped that it will long be a useful guide for readers around the world who are interested in the history of these peoples and will constitute a permanent record of the state of knowledge in this field in the mid-1990s, as well as a benchmark against which future progress can be measured.

1

NATIVE VIEWS OF HISTORY

PETER NABOKOV

On January 2, 1971, a fieldworker for the Doris Duke Oral History Project was collecting narratives in Tuba City, Arizona. To warm up one conversation the interviewer opened John McGregor's *Southwestern Archaeology* (second edition) to page 114 and through an interpreter asked an elderly Navajo man what he thought of a map of North America with swooping arrows indicating the routes supposedly walked by Paleo-Indian peoples after they crossed over the Beringia Land Bridge to populate the continent.

When he couldn't get a straight answer his translator begged for patience, "he's telling it little by little," then added, "it doesn't sound very little to me though." The interpreter and informant put their heads together. "He said that he would like to tell you," the translator explained, "but . . . he will be punished for it . . . I mean the medicine, he can't tell how it works . . . he said that if he told all his secrets like that he would fall to pieces. . . ."

As for the migration routes from Western Alaska down into North America, "He said, 'that maybe some other guys came over like that, but us Navajos came a different way'." At this the old man launched into what sounded like contradictory origin stories. One was a fragmentary narrative in which cicada-like insects "won this world for us, won this land here, the reservation" after crawling up through the earth's underlayers. The second account had white corn kernels, "actually the mother of the Navajo tribe," and the sun, "the father," talking together, with Navajos born from the corn kernel's underarms. With that the old man clammed up.

Trying another tack, the interviewer queried about a second illustration, on page 129, which charted a chronological sequence of stone projectile points originating from Arizona's Desert Culture. Again the interpreter and elder huddled together, and again the translator spoke, somewhat apologetically: "He says that . . . this isn't true. Whoever wrote it, just thinks about it, just thinks about it . . . and just makes up a theory about it . . . ." As for who actually chipped those Folsom and Clovis arrowheads? "The horny toads carved it, he said that he has never seen them make it, but some of these old men that he is telling about, they have seen it. . . ."

Finally the translator delved into the old man's reticence. "He says there are too many people that might know secrets like that, [that] is why the young generation, they are kind of breaking up the tradition, breaking up like that. By keeping the secret for such a long time, that now . . . the Navajo nation is the biggest nation in the world, well not the world, but in the United States."[1]

What can be gleaned from this intriguing round over views of the past? Navajo and Euro-American modes of communicating what is significant about distant origins appear to be genres passing in the night. The vested interests which underwrite any culture's historical points of view or social memories stand, in this instance, at cross purposes. The archaeologist's fetish for temporal chronology faces the Navajo's diehard allegiance to his people's religious, aesthetic, and moral symbols. But the stalemate extends to historians as well. "Several scholars actually boasted to me," recalled ethnographer Ernest S. Burch, Jr., after researching Inupiat Eskimo history, "that they do not believe what Native Elders have told them . . . Ironically, but perhaps appropriately, many Natives do not believe archeological, historical, or ethnographic accounts of traditional life — when made by Euroamericans — unless they are corroborated by the oral testimony of elders."[2]

So often the practices and products of written history and spoken myth are presented as irreconcilable — the latter only appropriate in face-to-face exchanges during socially or ritually approved circumstances, the former available to any strangers who can read them whenever they can find the time. The sorts of "power" embodied in the two discourses also appear incompatible. While both history and myth indoctrinate with their own "truth claims," non-Indian history does so with the credibility of "two or more sources."

[1] From transcript of Tape #761, pp. 1–10, interview conducted on January 2, 1971 for the Doris Duke Oral History Project, Special Collections, University of New Mexico, Albuquerque, New Mexico.
[2] Ernest S. Burch, Jr., "From Skeptic to Believer: The Making of an Oral Historian," *Alaska History* 6(1) (1991).

Through the process which the old Navajo dismisses as "just" thinking, the late nineteenth-century Western ideal of a scientific history requires the systematic amassing and sequencing of facts in order to reconstruct a contingent account. It shuns hypothesis, and, as Peter Novick writes, it has been "scrupulously neutral on larger questions of end and meaning."[3] Even though this fact-founded, value-free, and narrative-driven notion of history gave way in the twentieth century to a more analytical approach which searched for causal explanations and incorporated social history, quantitative history, and ecological context, its building blocks remained the culturally neutral facts which are discovered and verified according to canons founded on the scientific model.

Not so myth. In the formal understanding of most Indian traditions, its accountings bypassed factual verification and deflected critical analysis. Its stories were supernaturally determined and humanly unquestioned. However much generations of Indian storytellers might reformulate myths "behind the scenes," as it were, their truths were represented as if inscribed in the stars, on a firmament above the fictions and nonfictions created by human agency.

Other defining characteristics are often added to discussions of Indian *ways of history*. Navajo storytelling probably shares with that of the plains-dwelling Arikaras — highlighted by scholar Douglas R. Parks — some of the following features: (1) a lessened concern with dates and historical periods, reflecting more what Parks calls "timelessness," and the frequent "displacement" of narrative elements, which allows actors from historical anecdotes, for example, to merge with or be projected into more mythic or sacred narratives; (2) a related "nondevelopmental" organization of historical narratives (an informant once told Parks that the most appropriate typology of Arikara myths and legends was by the categories of animal-beings they featured); (3) a focus on the "interpersonal," even when events of high moment are related; (4) a concern with narrative accuracy through careful attention to "oral repetition"; (5) and finally, the element of humor, which Indian narrators often see as adding critical performative spice to narratives about almost any time.[4]

Some of these contrasts in Native American and non-Indian scientific concepts of history also appear in Loretta Fowler's comments on historical

[3] Peter Novick, *That Noble Dream: The "Objectivity Question" and the American Historical Profession* (New York and Cambridge, 1988), 37.
[4] Douglas R. Parks, *Traditional Narratives of the Arikara Indians: Stories of Alfred Morsette: English Translations,* vol. 3, Studies in the Anthropology of North American Indians (Lincoln, Nebr., 1991).

consciousness among the Wind River Arapahos of Wyoming. She heard the Arapahos criticizing anthropological approaches to their history, which focused upon structural relationships and ecological variables, as missing the point. Her consultants argued that academics possessed no credentials for entering the ceremonial, social, and oratorical realms where their history found its form and motivation. To Fowler, "Arapahoes see their history as a mythological process, which operates as a conceptual framework for interpreting and shaping social action and which is not necessarily related to events as recorded by observers."[5]

This reminder of the profoundly religious role of history-making and history-perpetuating in many Indian societies helps us better to understand the reluctance to talk by the old Navajo from Tuba City. For American Indian "mythistory"[6] is often cloaked with the protective sanction of sacred utterance. To speak it promiscuously or publicly can be perilous, since its stories remain imbued with the powerful forces that originally created the world, and that can still destroy it. Handling such power therefore entails following the rules, and in Navajo culture such "taboos" abound. For this increasingly uneasy Navajo traditionalist, internal sirens were warning that those powers will know if he dares to call up the mythic past, as through the words of a magical formula, without good reason. Our sense of the exclusive, esoteric nature of this kind of history, and its symbiotic relationship to Navajo land tenure, only sharpens as the Doris Duke interviewer trespasses on Navajo intellectual and spiritual space. Not by their Treaty of 1864, but rather by "keeping the secret for such a long time," we are told, has the Navajo nation become the largest reservation in the United States. At the center of that "secret" are the narratives that bind together accounts of Navajo origins, ancient events, and eventual destiny.

As for Indian hesitation about sharing cultural information with Euro-Americans, perhaps "history" itself should be added to the list of scarce "limited goods" whose unequal distribution in face-to-face peasant societies, says anthropologist George Foster, produces cycles of envy and envy-deflecting practices — and in multi-cultural contexts, one might add, xenophobia and a craving for secrecy.[7] For some of today's American Indian

[5] Loretta Fowler, *Arapahoe Politics, 1851–1978: Symbols in Crises of Authority* (Lincoln, Nebr., 1982), 236.

[6] William H. McNeill, *Mythistory and Other Essays* (Chicago, 1986).

[7] George Foster, "Peasant Society and the Image of the Limited Good," *American Anthropologist* 67 (1965).

cultural leaders, increasingly anxious over their people's shrinking intellectual heritage, the "history" which on its face seems social, political, and safe for public recounting often gets formally reglossed as "religious property" so as to safeguard it from appropriation by prying outsiders.

But if this old Navajo won't divulge his people's private mythic past, one might well ask, within the proper cultural setting which individuals can, and when? The assignment and training for the role of traditional Indian "historian" certainly varied by people and time period. However, it can be expected that in these societies, where everyone observed an individual's personality at close range, a child's propensity for remembering, recording, and narrating might be noticed and encouraged early. Pima Indians stayed alert to youngsters who demonstrated an aptitude for recollecting traditions. When they matured into recognized Native historians eligible to engage in the male-only "smoke talk" of history-recounting, wrote Frank Russell, "the boys are regularly sent [to them so] that they may listen for four nights to the narratives of how the world was made and peopled: whence the Pimas came and how they struggled with demons, monsters, and savage enemies."[8] There could also be self-selection for the role, as intellectually gifted or prophetically inclined individuals carved out "historian" roles for themselves, or fate might offer a blinded or crippled individual this outlet for his sedentary, marginalized condition.

In the case of the Navajos, designated ritual "singers" (*hataalii*) were expected to recite their sacred mythistories with scrupulous attention to memorized detail during ceremonial occasions, which did not prevent generations of other Navajo narrators either from modernizing folktales involving supernatural beings, or from offering historical recollections of more secular, reservation times. Among the Ojibwa (Anishinabe) Indians of the Great Lakes, the duties of ritual priest and of historian – the *kanawencikewinini,* meaning "preserve man," the individual who "read" the mnemonics scratched into sacred birchbark scrolls – were collapsed into a single role.[9]

As for "when" Indian history came to life, along with somber ritual occasions there were numerous semiformal opportunities for transmitting accountings of the past. Among the Arikaras one might hear historical narratives during family get-togethers, when the delegates of different

---

[8] Frank Russell, *The Pima Indians,* 26th Annual Report of the Bureau of American Ethnology, 1904–1905 (Washington, D.C., 1908), 206.

[9] Thomas Vennum, Jr., "Ojibwa Origin-Migration Songs of the *Mitewiwin,*" *Journal of American Folklore* 91 (1978), 753.

peoples gathered to negotiate or reminisce, or when a youth was prompted by an elder (often a grandparent) to bring food to an uncle in exchange for personal instruction. Evenings were normally the preferred time for tale-telling, with winter (between first snowfall and first ice breakup) the appropriate season[10] (lest, in many Indian traditions, you lay yourself open to poisonous snakebite).

Along with chanting their mythic narratives of primordial history, Navajo medicine men also portrayed them, in sequences of stylized dry (sand) paintings during multiday curing ceremonies. Over a series of five or nine nights they sat patients in the very center of these multimedia, ritual settings so as to restore them to the sanctioned and secure sense of wholeness, health, and beauty, or *hozho,* that core concept which Navajos equate with the idealized, balanced cosmos.[11] Through these ceremonies Navajos drew upon the innate powers of that "secret" history which the old man from Tuba City was reluctant to share, but on these occasions it was for culturally sanctioned purposes of physical and psychological restabilization.

COMPARING CULTURAL VIEWS OF HISTORY

When outsiders contrast the historical orientations and world-views of preindustrial, oral cultures like those of Native Americans with post-traditional, modern societies, they frequently polarize them into ideal types. Not uncommonly this tendency is also an effective rhetorical device for assessing one's own society; as social critic Richard Rodriguez has observed, "[American] Indian memory has become the measure against which America gauges corrupting history when it suits us."[12]

Thus to religious historian Mircea Eliade, "traditional" society adhered to "cyclical time, periodically regenerating itself," which stood in opposition to "the other modern [notion], that of finite time, a fragment."[13] To cyclical time Eliade attached moral superiority, as it was "sacred" and "exemplary," whereas finite time was profane and degenerative, with history itself practically tantamount to "suffering."[14]

[10] Parks, *Traditional Narratives of the Arikara Indians,* 113–116.
[11] Gary Witherspoon, *Language and Art in the Navajo Universe* (Ann Arbor, Mich., 1977).
[12] Richard Rodriguez, "Mixed Blood, Columbus's Legacy: A World Made *Mestizo,*" *Harper's Magazine* 283 (November 1991), 49.
[13] Mircea Eliade, "The Yearning for Paradise in Primitive Tradition," in *Myth and Myth-making,* ed. H. A. Murray (New York, 1960), 112.
[14] Mircea Eliade, *The Myth of Eternal Return* (New York, 1954), footnote 97.

Bringing this home to North America, his European colleague Åke Hultkrantz wrote, "in contrast to Western cultures, Native Americans conceive of time not in linear, but in cyclical form . . . an eternally recurring cycle of events and years."[15] From a more economic perspective, the writer John Berger has viewed the operative dichotomy as between "mirror opposites," by which he means the "cultures of progress," which can envisage future expansion, and the "cultures of survival," for whom the future remains "a sequence of repeated acts of survival."[16] Nor have social scientists been able to resist this convenient reductionism: "history to them ['primitive peoples']," wrote Stanley Diamond, "is the recital of sacred meanings within a cyclic as opposed to linear perception of time. The merely pragmatic event, uninvolved with the sacred cycle, falls outside history, because it has no importance in maintaining or revitalizing the traditional forms of society."[17] In anthropologist Claude Lévi-Strauss's more sophisticated rendering of the dichotomy, his famous "cold" and "hot" societies, historical consciousness looms again as the defining factor:

The "cold" societies which we call "primitive" are not that way at all, but they wish to be. They view themselves as primitive, for their ideal would be to remain in the state in which the gods or ancestors created them at the origin of time. Of course this is an illusion, and they no more escape history than other societies. But this history, which they mistrust and dislike, is something they undergo. The hot societies – such as our own – have a radically different attitude toward history. Not only do we recognize the existence of history, we make a cult of it . . . We internalize our history and make it an element of our moral conscience.[18]

The popularizer of American Indian metaphysics Jamake Highwater unleashes a string of such dichotomies for distancing "primal" societies like Indians from "Western" ones like that of Anglo-Americans. For him, Indians are to Euro-Americans as holistic:linear; static:dynamic; atemporal: temporal; communal:individualistic; experiential:"formal, emotional, or decorative"; and of course, "spiritual":profane.[19]

Would that human cultures could be compartmentalized and compared so efficiently. More likely such a spewing of binaries does disservice to both its cultural oppositions. For even within the theoretical positions of

---

[15] Åke Hultkrantz, *Native Religions of North America: The Power of Visions and Fertility* (San Francisco, 1987), 32.

[16] John Berger, *Pig Earth* (New York, 1979), 204–5.

[17] Stanley Diamond, *In Search of the Primitive* (New Brunswick, 1974), 203.

[18] Claude Lévi-Strauss and Didier Eribon, *Conversations with Claude Lévi-Strauss*, trans. Paula Wissing (Chicago, 1991), 125.

[19] Jamake Highwater, *The Primal Mind: Vision and Reality in Indian America* (New York, 1981).

non-Indian, Euro-American society one finds both extremes: strident religious fundamentalism, ascribing talismanic sanctity and historical incontrovertibility to sacred texts, seated across the debating table from radical relativists, like historian Hayden White, who eagerly undermine all their discipline's objectivist claims by exposing the culturally predetermined models of aesthetics and morality that underwrite Western historical chronicles.[20]

Nonetheless, the rhetorical convenience of drawing philosophical lines in the sand remains irresistible, and the drive to dichotomize has even infiltrated American Indian public policy. When U.S. government consultants compared religious traditions in an explanatory report mandated by the American Indian Religious Freedom Act of 1978,[21] "world" religions were labeled as "commemorative" because they presumably fixated on "sacred events" and historical individuals. "Tribal" peoples, on the contrary, practiced "continuing" religions, which were untraceable to a historical "event or founder." Unfortunately, as David White has noted, this sharp division would delegitimize many syncretized American Indian spiritual expressions which are documentably "historical" creations.[22]

It is ironic that despite abundant examples of religious syncretism within Navajo society since their pre-Spanish incorporation of Pueblo symbols, the old Navajo exegete in my opening vignette revealed himself just as split-minded as non-Indian intellectuals when it came to contrasting the historical consciousness of pre- and postliterate peoples. With his close association between human "thinking" and "writing" in the Anglo-American approach negatively compared with the absolutist seal of approval accorded his own sacred myths, we also detect an echo not only of Lévi-Strauss's "hot" and "cold" distinction, but also of the structuralist's famous aside that myths might autonomously do a culture's "thinking" on their own.

Nor was this Navajo man alone in his cultural critique. Again and again, Native Americans have weighed the relative merits of spoken and written traditions. "I am very glad to demonstrate to you that we also have books," explained Waihusiwa, the Zuni storyteller, to Frank Hamilton Cushing, "only they are not books with marks in them, but words in our

---

[20] Hayden White, *Metahistory: The Historical Imagination in Nineteenth-Century Europe* (Baltimore, 1973) and *Tropics of Discourse: Essays in Cultural Criticism* (Baltimore, 1978).

[21] *American Indian Religious Freedom Report*, P. L. 95–34, Federal Agencies Task Force, U.S. Department of the Interior, Washington, D.C. (1979).

[22] David R. M. White, "Native American Religious Issues . . . Also Land Issues," *Wassaja, The Indian Historian* 13(3) (1980), 39–44.

hearts, which have been placed there by our ancients long ago, even so long ago as when the world was new and young, like unripe fruit."[23] In describing an Acoma man's conversion in a dream to Christianity, the anthropologist Leslie A. White says the man found himself standing before a God who was dressed like a "successful American Indian business-man." The deity told him that while the Bible let Euro-Americans into heaven, the traditional "prayer stick" remained the Indian's "key to para-dise."[24] Many Indian people continue to resent the fact that the narratives they feel to be their true, one-and-only "history," Euro-American scholars with readier access to book publishers and school classrooms often demote as "folklore." Ignoring his own commitment to the printed word, Lakota writer Luther Standing Bear foreshadowed their complaint:

stories were the libraries of our people. In each story, there was recorded some event of interest or importance, some happening that affected the lives of the people. There were calamities, discoveries, achievements, and victories to be kept. The seasons and the years were named for principal events that took place . . . a people enrich their minds who keep their history on the leaves of memory. Countless leaves in countless books have robbed a people of both history and memory.[25]

NARRATIVE GENRES AND HISTORICAL CONSCIOUSNESS

Despite the tendency toward dichotomous thinking when scholars con-trast other cultures from an academic distance, fieldworkers on the ground have grown aware that the spectrum of American Indian narratives, behav-iors, and symbols which carry any information faintly deemed "historical" actually falls on any number of different points between the idealized poles of chronology (history) and cosmology (mythology). Comprehending the meanings of the past through Indian eyes and narratives requires one to pay close attention to the diversity of ways in which among different Indian peoples temporal "phasings" and historical "commentaries" can extend backwards into primordial eras and forward to embrace remem-bered individuals and recent events.

A close look at Indian languages reveals few monolithic notions of the past. While the Navajo elder from Tuba City gave precedence, in the

---

[23] Frank Hamilton Cushing, *Zuni Folk Tales* (New York, 1901), 92.
[24] Leslie A. White, *The Acoma Indians*, Forty-Seventh Annual Report of the Bureau of American Ethnology, 1929–1930 (Washington, D.C., 1932), 32.
[25] Luther Standing Bear, *Land of the Spotted Eagle* (New York, 1933), 27.

strained circumstances of an interview with an insistent stranger, to a concept of history which seemed the antithesis of how Euro-Americans construe former happenings, an oft-used Navajo term for the past, *atk'idaa,* literally means "on top of each other," or more loosely, "experiences or events stacked up through time," which sounds like a fair description of the direct historical approach of any Anglo archaeologist. At the same time, this generously inclusive term, *atk'idaa,* draws in, according to Kenneth J. Pratt, "events in terms particular to an individual's recall or personal opinion," oral tradition relating people and places in remote as well as recent times, and the "major source of healing power for serious illness," thereby returning us to the more sacred, privileged sense of the word stressed by the old man from Tuba City.[26]

Indian oldtimers and intellectuals alike often grumble that grouping their indigenous histories under cover terms like "mythology" and "folklore" suggests falsehood and simple-mindedness and furthers the stereotype that they had no sense of history. "I want you to know that this is not one of the fairy stories I am telling you, but a fact," said a Kutenai elder named Abraham Wolf Robe to Harry Holbert Turney-High in 1939 before relating a legend. "It is real history," he insisted.[27] Yet it has been largely anthropologists, folklorists, and linguists whose interest in Native genres of oral tradition has turned up those embedded and indigenous theories of history which have been variously characterized as "traditional history,"[28] "folk history,"[29] "ethno-ethno history,"[30] or "historicity," which anthropologist Emiko Ohnuki-Tierney prefers to "historical consciousness" in order to avoid the implication that "how people think of and experience their history is always conscious," and which she defines as the "collective understanding of history."[31]

An awareness that such metahistories might lurk within nonliterate traditions has taken time to sink in. In 1952 historian Bernard DeVoto, no great believer in Indian historicity per se, nonetheless confessed that

[26] Kenneth J. Pratt, "Some Navajo Relations to the Past," in *Papers from the Third, Fourth, and Sixth Navajo Studies Conferences,* ed. June-el Piper (Window Rock, Ariz., 1993).

[27] Harry Holbert Turney-High, "Two Kutenai Stories," *Journal of American Folklore* 54(213–14) (1941), 191.

[28] E. E. Evans-Pritchard, "Anthropology and History," in *Social Anthropology and Other Essays* (Glencoe, Ill., 1962).

[29] Charles Hudson, "Folk History and Ethnohistory," *Ethnohistory* 13 (1966).

[30] Raymond D. Fogelson, "On the Varieties of Indian History: Sequoyah and Traveller Bird," *Journal of Ethnic Studies* 2 (1974).

[31] Emiko Ohnuki-Tierney, ed., *Culture through Time: Anthropological Approaches* (Stanford, Calif., 1990), 19.

"American historians have made shockingly little effort to understand the life, the societies, the cultures, the thinking, and the feeling of the Indians."[32] Over thirty years ago Fred Eggan hoped that "The future writers on Indian history will give us the other side of the coin emphasizing the Indian's view of his world."[33] Five years later Charles Hudson suggested that "the analysis of a society's folk history should proceed hand in hand with an analysis of that society's world-view or belief system."[34] More recently, commenting on Raymond Fogelson's analysis of a Cherokee legend concerning a precontact rebellion against a religious elite, Robert A. Brightman urged, "some of us should be writing or recording Indian historical consciousness of Indian religious history."[35]

But that "recording" also requires an understanding as to how Indians reformulated their historicities in the light of the socio-political realities of five hundred years of Indian–Euro-American interaction, as Bernard S. Cohn has emphasized:

To study Australian aborigines, or American Indians, or Indian villagers without locating them in relation to the colonial structures which were or are the central social fact of their lives – without paying attention to the traders, the missionaries and administrators, and to the whole process by which the indigenous peoples become incorporated in various fashions into the capitalist and socialist economies – is to trivialize the experience of the natives.[36]

Pursuing those goals entails a radical step beyond what one might call even the most ‘enlightened "ethnohistory," in which non-Indian documents are screened so as to "depict Indians as active agents in our mutual past," in the words of ethnohistorians James A. Sandos and Larry E. Burgess.[37] For Calvin Martin only offered half the solution when he wrote in 1978 that "ethnohistory offers a belated means of resolving the dilemma of the bifurcated Indian – the Indian of anthropology and the Indian of history."[38] The present essay concerns the necessary next step into the

---

[32] Quoted in J. K. Howard, *Strange Empire* (New York, 1952), 8.

[33] Fred Eggan, "Anthropological Approaches to Ethnological Cultures," *Ethnohistory* 8(1) (1961), 8.

[34] Hudson, "Folk History and Ethnohistory," 64–5.

[35] Robert Brightman, "Towards a History of Indian Religion: Religious Changes in Native Societies," in *New Directions in American Indian History*, ed. Colin G. Calloway (Norman, Okla., 1988), 238.

[36] Bernard S. Cohn, "History and Anthropology: The State of Play," *Comparative Studies in Society and History* 22 (1980), 218.

[37] James A. Sandos and Larry E. Burgess. " 'White Man Got No Dreaming': Willie Boy in Ethnohistorical Perspective," 32. Paper presented at the Annual Meeting of the American Society for Ethnohistory, D'Arcy McNickle Center for the History of the American Indian, Newberry Library, Chicago, Illinois, November 2–5, 1989.

[38] Calvin Martin, "Ethnohistory: A Better Way to Write Indian History," *Western Historical Quarterly* 9(1) (1978), 56.

conceptual frontier that is Native American historical philosophy. It argues for braiding the metahistorical frameworks that produce American Indian narratives into future writing of richer, more culturally nuanced, and many-voiced accountings for Indian pasts — prior to, during, and possibly even after, if one is to take Indian prophecy seriously, their relations with Euro-Americans.

THE DYNAMICS OF MYTH

As with the "culture area" concept in American Indian social anthropology which parcels the continent into broad ecological domains occupied by culturally similar peoples, the generic Myth/Legend/Folktale trinity in American Indian folklore is a clumsy but helpful outsider's tool for distinguishing traditional narratives. As we shall see, each of these gross categories can be a repository for some kind of Indian historicity. As folklore scholar William Bascom has highlighted their main features, *myths* are sacred narratives which involve nonhuman characters, take place in a different or earlier world, and are regarded by the societies which hold them dear as absolute truth; *legends* are regarded as secular or sacred, transpiring in today's world and featuring human characters, and are considered factual and often historical; *folktales* are secular narratives, generally occurring out of place and time, involving human and nonhuman characters, and are regarded as fictional stories with high entertainment (and educational, though Bascom underplays this) value.[39]

Applying Bascom's scheme calls for fine-tuning, from people to people and language to language. For some Indian traditions seem to have produced fewer types of folklore, others more, and narrative hybrids are still emerging. Refining and localizing Bascom's genres also calls for a second look at the functional roles of different narratives in Indian culture. We must realize that when tough times made Indians draw upon their oral traditions for support and reassurance, the formal properties of each of these genres could bend to the task. Even American Indian mythologies, perhaps more muscle-bound and conventional than legends or folktales, present ample evidence of their ability to adjust to rapidly changing external circumstances.

Before launching into the numerous senses of Indian history reflected in myth, legend, and tale, we might hunt for them first in narrative genres

[39] William Bascom, "The Forms of Folklore," *Journal of American Folklore* 78 (1965).

recognized by Indians themselves, a task which quickly proves to be insepa-rable from the search for culturally specific notions of "time." Among the Koyukans of interior Alaska, for instance, it is stories from *Kk'adonts'idnee,* or the "Distant Time," which explain both the origins and behavioral patterns of all "beings" – biological, botanical, geologic, even climatic.[40] In some cases temporal categories double as cover terms for indigeneous genres, as with the Zuni term *chimiky'ana'kowa,* or "The Beginning," refer-ring to the genesis narratives they regard as historical truth.[41]

Among the Tillamooks of Oregon, according to Elizabeth Jacobs, the temporal trajectory covered three successive time spans: the "myth age," the "era of transformations," and the "period of true happenings."[42] Grouped in the first were original creation events that bestowed life to all things. The second era witnessed the stuff of recreative drama, as a "trickster-transformer" being conquered monsters, molded topography, and fashioned the distinct ethnic groups we know today. Only in the third period came what non-Indians relegate to their "history," when named human ancestors took part in known events in specific locations. While the same tripartite division held for Nunamiut Eskimos studied by Nicho-las J. Gubser, their time frames were somewhat vaguer: *Itchaq amma,* the real ancient, almost timeless days before any known ancestors, *Ipani,* recent times, within living memory of individuals today, *Ingalagaan,* the indistinct period in between. Interestingly enough, Nunamiut generally positioned their "true history" (*koliaqtuaq*) in the first, ancient era, while their "imaginative stories" (*unipquaq*) were consigned to recent times.[43]

To illustrate what one might term the "encompassing tendency" of mythic thought, by which it almost instinctively extends its proprietory reach over multiple time frames, let anthropologist Frederica de Laguna explain the word *cagun,* a key concept in the historical thought of the Tlingits of the Northwest Coast:

It has been claimed with justice that every people live their own myths, that is, that their conduct in the present reflects what they believe their past to have been, since that past, as well as the present and the future, are aspects of the "destiny" in which they exhibit themselves as they think they really are. The Tlingit them-selves sense this and use the term "ha (our) cagun" for the origin and destiny of their sib [or, of their clan, both terms meaning all descendants through the male

[40] Richard Nelson, *Make Prayers to the Raven* (Chicago, 1983), 16–19.

[41] Dennis Tedlock, *Finding the Center: Narrative Poetry of the Zuni Indians* (New York, 1972), xvi.

[42] Elizabeth D. Jacobs, *Nehalem Tillamook Tales,* University of Oregon, Monographs in Anthropology no. 3 (1959), ix.

[43] Nicholas J. Gubser, *The Nunamiut Eskimos: Hunters of Caribou* (New Haven, Conn., 1965).

or female line of a single human or supernatural ancestor], including the totemic animal or bird encountered by their ancestors and the powers and prerogatives obtained from it, as well as their own place in the universe and the ultimate fate of their unborn descendants.[44]

By underscoring the claims to ultimate truth which most traditional societies accord to myths, Bascom was trying to rescue them from their demotion in colloquial speech — "Oh, it's just a myth." Along with the requirement that Indian myths encompass through patterning all events of the past, present, and future, their second, less-studied survival mechanism is to permit internal tinkering and add-ons. Investigating what Raymond Firth has called this "plasticity of myth" entails appreciating the "created" and "contingent" factors embodied in a dynamic comprehension of what culture does for participants who live in time. Loosening up old attitudes about the relative conservatism of myths does not necessarily mean that they become impoverished by responding to changing historical circumstances, nor, as P. van Baaren has noted, that they automatically "become secularized when a certain myth is in the process of losing its [original] function."[45] On the contrary, myth in this proactive mode, while betraying "adaptability to new situations and challenges," actually demonstrates its power as a sacralizing, truth-decreeing strategy. Indeed, a striking range of creative leeway in the reformulation of mythology is evidenced across Native North America.

According to Fred Eggan, writing in 1967, "The Hopi Indians [of Arizona] are still creating myths."[46] To illustrate he compared two accounts of a bloody clash between Hopis and Navajos in the mid-1850s, narrated over forty years apart. For the older rendition, which Eggan comments is deficient in chronological specifics — "always a weak point in Pueblo accounts" — the details of observed events were remarkably detailed and "accurate," as if brought close through a telescope. In the later version, the telling fell into another, more mythic, narrative canon, as if seen far away through a telescope turned the other way around. New motivations for triggering events were attributed, generalized ways of Hopi behavior were

---

[44] Frederica de Laguna, *The Story of a Tlingit Community: A Problem in the Relationship between Archeological, Ethnological, and Historical Methods*, Bulletin 172, Bureau of American Ethnology (Washington, D.C., 1960), 202.

[45] P. van Baaren, "The Flexibility of Myth," *Studies in the History of Religions* 22 (1972), 199 (reprinted in *Sacred Narrative: Readings in the Theory of Myth*, ed. Alan Dundes [Berkeley, Calif., 1984]).

[46] Fred Eggan, "From History to Myth: A Hopi Example," reprinted in *Essays in Social Anthropology and Ethnology*, The University of Chicago Studies in Anthropology, Series in Social, Cultural, and Linguistic Anthropology, no. 1 (Chicago, 1975), 297.

sanctioned, the story chartered basic cultural and territorial divides between Hopis and Navajos, and hence "the account is on its way to becoming tradition and myth." Eggan proffered this test case to persuade other American Indian scholars that the cautious sieving of mythologizing narratives and their controlled comparison — separating generic affirmations of cultural themes from "the historical events embedded in them" — could reveal "a good deal about Hopi [or American Indian] history and character, and help us to understand the changes they have undergone."[47]

It is not uncommon to find Indian stories, like those told by the late Okanagan narrator from British Columbia Harry Robinson, which incorporate the origin of Europeans into their creation accounts. According to Robinson, "God" left a primordial pair of twins with a piece of paper on which was written the knowledge of how to live forever. Laying it on a rock, he warned them not to peek. When the younger one stole the paper, and God asked him where it was, he first professed ignorance. Commented Robinson,

now today, that's the White man . . . And that's why the White man can tell a lie more than the Indian. Then God told the younger one he might as well read the paper, as it would be his power source for all time. But God warned, "That paper . . . it's going to show you how you going to make it back here. But not right away. Long time from now . . . (But) you're going to lose a lot of people."[48]

When the "progressive" shopkeeper and Native entrepreneur Edward P. Hunt, of New Mexico's Acoma Pueblo, recited an origin myth whose memorization was integral to his initiation as a sacred clown, the twins who engendered humankind were female.[49] More to our point, while one of the girls, Iatiku, became the "mother of all Indians," the other, Nautsiti, revealed some curiously non-Indian traits. The Christianized narrator has her always desiring more than her fair share, displaying a lighter skin color, a roughness with plant life, a tendency toward solitariness, a liking for metal, and a weakness for temptation by a snake. Eventually she disappears toward the east — where other Keresan accounts state unequivocally that she became a man and "father of the Whites."[50]

Among the Three Affiliated Tribes of North Dakota, the Mandan tale-

[47] Ibid., 313.

[48] Harry Robinson, compiled and ed. Wendy Wickwire, *Nature Power: In the Spirit of an Okanagan Storyteller* (Seattle, 1992), 14.

[49] Matthew W. Stirling, *Origin Myth of Acoma and Other Records*, Bulletin 135, Bureau of American Ethnology (Washington, D.C., 1942).

[50] Franz Boas, *Keresan Texts*, vol. 8, part 1 (Publications of the American Ethnological Society), 221.

teller John Brave's account of how Lone Man and First Creator made the
world also references Euro-American society. First Creator, the omnipotent,
initially makes "white man's cattle"; their horns are so crooked their eyes are
obstructed, their testicles so heavy they walk bow-legged. Save those beasts
for later, advises Lone Man, for now make buffalo for the Indians. After First
Creator approves of the rest of Lone Man's natural creations, they find red-
headed maggots in a wolf carcass. Neither takes responsibility for those, and
Lone Man removes them to the other side of a lake. "In the days to come," he
decrees, "they'll have intelligence." And narrator Brave comments, "when
you see white men, some of whom have red heads, they are descendants of
those maggots. And today these white men are very intelligent, as it was
promised. Today they are doing everything, even all those things which
seem impossible." The selection ends with his digression on the relative
powers of this creative pair. It is actually Lone Man, Brave points out, who
"long ago" was God, and then he provides a wonderful glimpse of why he is
so sure: "Whenever he saw some children around the village, he always
wiped their noses. For Lone Man was kind-hearted." On the other hand,
First Creator seemed in Brave's imagination more akin to the Euro-
American's God, "always the one who fooled people."[51]

Such narratives show Indians improvising on traditional plot lines to
incorporate historical events. The plasticity of mythic composition is such
that it can loop its revisionist reach backwards in time so as to embrace
those broad epochs the French historian Fernand Braudel termed the
"longue durée." One way Indian traditions accomplish this is by sanctifing
the temporal dimension of its mythic narratives. Among the Tewa people
of northern New Mexico, writes Alfonso Ortiz, "an expression frequently
used in Tewa oral traditions is 'when it has been four times,' which is used
to convey both a sense of time and a sense of space simultaneously . . .
There is so much of this four of this, and four of that [spans of days or
travels] that this is obviously not history in the sense that we as scholars
understand it."[52] When events took place outside the landscape demarcated by their four sacred mountains, units of twelve were the norm
"because in the Tewa genesis the migration from the northern boundary of
the Tewa world to the present Tewa villages took place in twelve steps."[53]

---

[51] Douglas R. Parks, A. Wesley Jones, and Robert C. Hollow, *Earthlodge Tales from the Upper Missouri: Traditional Tales of the Arikara, Hidatsa, and Mandan* (Bismark, N.D., 1978), 67–71.
[52] Alfonso Ortiz, "Some Concerns Central to the Writing of 'Indian' History," *The Indian Historian* 10(1) (1977), 19.
[53] Ibid.

So it was in Plains Indian stories that everything from vision quests to battle charges to getting sacred medicines to work required three tries before success arrived on the fourth.

Mythic reformulations can be driven by a variety of motivations. Under ordinary circumstances they strive to bring the historically contingent into conformity with the eternally cosmic. Where they address cross-cultural tensions, they sometimes deliver frontal attacks, as with the Copper Eskimo story of the woman who copulated with dogs and gave birth to the first Europeans.[54] Read closely, however, others prove to be riddled with more subtle detonations of what we might call reverse "cultural critique," wherein one society offers oblique, often derogatory commentary or comparisons with another, generally giving itself the upper hand or casting itself in the better light. For users only, these absolutist renditions of the preordained history of Native and European relations strive to negate or co-opt change. Their traditional claims to community credulity and allegiance buy time while they attempt to balance the retooling of plots and transformation of characters with their recommitment to traditional values.

Still, the dangers of potential disenchantment cannot be underestimated. Cosmogenic myths can never wholly be transformed into historical manifestos, nor can their truth-claims metamorphose into matters of personal opinion. Tragic as it may be, the language structures which carried them from one generation to another can become functionally extinct, and many nuances and resonances of a culture's propelling narratives can become lost for good. Finally, irreversible upheavals in a society's economic or ecological underpinnings can render traditional myths largely irrelevant as charters for a people's viable institutions.

THE POWERS OF PROPHECY

Prophecy is a subset of mythic narrative by which Indian tradition assumes a sort of predestined superiority over historical events yet to come. "If myth anchors the present in the past," Percy Cohen has written, "then prophecy anchors it in the future."[55] By its claim that the future is theirs to know and outsiders' to find out, prophecy offers Indians an important conceptual weapon in the power struggles between indigenous and invasive worldviews. They can stay a step ahead of the history which volatile interaction

---

[54] "Those Who Became White Men," in Knud Rasmussen, *Intellectual Culture of the Copper Eskimo,* 5th Thule Expedition, vol. 9 (Copenhagen, 1932), 240–1.

[55] Percy Cohen, "Theories of Myth," *Man* (1969), 351.

with Europeans has kicked into accelerated motion. Folklorist Jarold Ramsay has coined the term "retroactive prophecy" to highlight "one of a numerous set of native texts, some mythological and others historical or personal, in which an event or deed in pre-Contact times is dramatized as being prophetic of some consequence of the coming of whites."[56] Selecting stories from the Pacific Northwest, Southwest, and Great Basin which demonstrate "contact-era mythopoetic invention," Ramsay underscored their emphasis on the dire consequences of European contact: epidemics, liquor, money, armies, laws, missionaries, schools, and more.

Such forecastings abound across Native America. Along the New England seaboard these "reformulations of indigenous knowledge," as William S. Simmons characterizes the process, were also ways by which Indian converts to Christianity reconciled their Native birth with their spiritual rebirth through "introducing Christian themes to their pre-European past."[57] The stories explained the origin of black-faced people with tight curly hair, water that burnt your throat and made you feel like you were flying, and pots that didn't smash into sherds when dropped. Indian soothsayers dreamt of floating islands with puffy white panels and sticks that spat fire. When they actually first saw ships, these Native New Englanders only had their prophecies verified – or recomposed, for their initial impression was indeed of walking or floating islands, with billowing clouds affixed to upright trees, whose banks discharged thunder and lightning.[58]

It was volcanic activity in the Cascade Mountains in the late eighteenth century which alerted a Spokane prophet from the far west to a "different kind of men . . . who will bring with them a book and will teach you everything, and after that the world will fall to pieces."[59] More recently, the Zuni "grandfathers" from New Mexico expressed forebodings of coming decay, when "Drinkers of dark liquids will come upon the land, speaking nonsense and filth . . . Population will increase until the land can hold no more . . . The tribes of men will mix . . . Then our possessions will turn into beasts and devour us whole."[60]

---

[56] Jarold Ramsay, "Retroactive Prophecy in Western Indian Narrative," in *Reading the Fire: Essays in the Traditional Indian Literatures of the Far West* (Lincoln, Nebr., 1983), 153.

[57] William S. Simmons, "Of Large Things Remembered: Southern New England Legends of Colonial Encounters," in *The Art and Mystery of Historical Archaeology* (CRC Press, 1992), 323.

[58] Ibid., 319.

[59] Quoted in Jarold Ramsay, "Retroactive Prophecy in Western Indian Narrative," 153.

[60] The Zuni People, trans. Alvina Quam, *The Zunis: Self Portrayals by the Zuni People* (Albuquerque, N.M., 1972), 3.

An equally bleak prediction climaxes a Jicarilla Apache tale of the great flood: "At the end of the world these people who travel with their eyes are going to come back and go to all directions . . . For the telephone and telegraph are not going to be here any more. They are all going to burn. Next time the earth will be destroyed by fire."[61] Again, according to Ramsay, "The myths of such native groups, it is clear, had always served to uphold the people's world view *as a continuum,* by accommodating real and imagined changes in their world" and hence are "formally consistent with their mythological view of what we call history."[62]

Along with their swift reflex for recasting cosmic origins in the light of historical contingencies, the oracular gaze of prophecy also peers into the distance, even to the end of time. Such foretellings are a trademark of the authority over history assumed by many American Indian revitalization prophets. One of the most famous was Smohalla, a Wanapum (Sahaptin) of the Columbia Plateau, who warned in the mid-1880s that "when God is ready, he will drive away all the people except the people who have obeyed his laws . . . All the dead men will come to life again; their spirits will come to their bodies again. We must wait here, in the homes of our fathers, and be ready to meet them in the bosom of our mother."[63] This sort of prophetic "post-history" is often part of a collective ideology, as among the Dunne-zas, a Canadian Subarctic people studied by anthropologist Robin Ridington. Their original *Naachin* or Dreamer was a messianic figure who blazed the "trail to heaven" and lived to tell about it. For his followers, those experiences were frequently routinized into liturgy for a Nativistic congregation who followed his blend of new Christianized ideas and old-style prophecies of terrible cataclysms, redemptive ethnic reunions, and settled accounts ahead.[64]

Behind nearly all these reformulations, one could argue, still lay the old historical agenda of mythic thought to assure its constituents, as already witnessed with the Tlingits, that in Lévi-Strauss's words "the future will remain faithful to the present and to the past."[65] The same basic message was communicated to the late-nineteenth-century fieldworker Frank Hamil-

---

[61] Morris Opler, *Myths and Tales of the Jicarilla Apache Indians,* Memoirs of the American Folklore Society 31 (New York, 1938), 113.

[62] Ramsay, *Reading the Fire,* 163.

[63] Major J. W. MacMurray, "The Dreamers of the Columbia River Valley in Washington Territory," *Transactions of the Albany Institute* 11 (1887), 248.

[64] Robin Ridington, *Trail to Heaven: Knowledge and Narrative in a Northern Native Community* (Iowa City, Iowa, 1988).

[65] Claude Lévi-Strauss, "When Myth Becomes History," in *Myth and Meaning* (New York, 1978), 43.

ton Cushing after his unsuccessful attempt to purchase for the Smithsonian Institution ceremonial objects from the Hopis of Arizona's Oraibi Pueblo: "They gave me in substance their myth of creation which for the sake of clearness I have given rather as a myth than as an infuriated argument, interspersed with the most insulting messages to Washington."[66]

HISTORY AND GEOGRAPHICAL MEMORY

The credibility of mythic accountings for ancient happenings is frequently reinforced by rooting their events in visible, and visitable, corners of the landscape. Indeed, Vine Deloria, Jr., sees the preeminence of topography over chronology as diagnostic of Indian historicity overall:

The contrast between Christianity and its interpretation of history – the temporal dimension – and the American Indian tribal religions – basically spatially located – is clearly illustrated when we understand the nature of sacred mountains, sacred hills, sacred rivers, and other geographical features sacred to Indian tribes. The Navajo, for example, have sacred mountains where they believe they rose from the underworld. Now there is no doubt in any Navajo's mind that these particular mountains are the exact mountains where it all took place. There is no beating around the bush on that. No one can say when the creation story of the Navajo happened, but everyone is fairly certain where the emergence took place.[67]

We may recall that the old Navajo at the outset of this essay used narrative to legitimize the Navajo claim not only to time, but also to space: "this world . . . this land here, the reservation." It seems practically a natural reflex for Navajos to project this "geographization" of their history through the ages, back to that primordial zone termed by the scholar of Navajo religions Karl W. Luckert the time of "pre-human flux." According to Luckert, Navaho chantways depict their mythic progenitors pursuing game in the same circular journeys which provided prototypical hunting routes for early Navajos to follow, all the way from British Columbia down to the American Southwest.[68]

Their hundreds of sacred places convert the Navajo topography, according to Sam and Janet Bingham, who have studied Navajo subsistence ecology, into something "like a book. A wise person can look at the stones

[66] Esther S. Goldfrank, "The Impact of Situation and Personality on Four Hopi Emergence Myths," *Southwestern Journal of Anthropology* 4 (1948), 244.

[67] Vine Deloria, Jr., *God Is Red* (New York, 1973), 138.

[68] Karl W. Luckert, *The Navajo Hunter Tradition* (Tucson, Ariz., 1975).

and mountains and read stories older than the first living thing . . . and since the first people made homes on the land, many people and many tribes have come and gone. The land still remembers them, however, and keeps . . . the things they left behind."[69] Among the southern California Chumashes, according to Travis Hudson and Georgia Lee, a similar consciousness obtained: "sites must clearly have served to connect the greater community with the past. Their specific location within the community served as a 'story display' of their past and present within the total realm of the universe."[70]

Special natural places often situate Native American narratives of creation, such as the travertine dome along a tributary of the Little Colorado where Hopis claim to have emerged from a series of underworlds, or the convergence of Turtle Creek and the wide Missouri in central North Dakota, which Hidatsa mythology identifies as the landing spot for a sacred arrow bearing their thirteen clans from an above-world. Sites like these could be magnets for seasonal religious pilgrimages and more personal, nostalgic journeys of renewal. Sometimes stories retain knowledge of a hidden landscape, for even when the visible topography has changed beyond recognition, old narratives rooted in them can retain their memory. That was what linguist Sally McLendon discovered when she drove an Eastern Pomo narrator around northern California. McLendon was shown specific places where the Pomo myths she was hearing had actually taken place, "despite the fact that none of the significant landmarks remained."[71]

One's personal history might be similarly grounded, as Tom Ration remembers of his fellow Navajos, "Long ago it was traditional custom to return to one's birthplace now and then and roll in the earth there."[72] At life's end one might return to remembered ground, as Thomas Jefferson recalled migrant Indians periodically revisiting a burial mound on his Virginia property, leaving offerings and prayers. Or as old Crows of central Montana, such as the great medicine man Big Ox might yearn, "Although

[69] Sam and Janet Bingham, *Between Sacred Mountains: Navajo Stories and Lessons from the Land* (Tucson, Ariz., 1984), 1.

[70] Travis Hudson and Georgia Lee, "Function and Symbolism in Chumash Rock Art." Paper presented at the Annual Meetings of the Southwestern Anthropological Association, Santa Barbara, March 1981, and the Society for American Archaeology, San Diego, April 1981, 25.

[71] Sally McLendon, "Cultural Presuppositions and Discourse Analysis: Pattern of Presupposition and Assertion of Information in Eastern Pomo and Russian Narrative," in *Linguistics and Anthropology,* ed. Muriel Saville-Troike (Washington, D.C., 1977), 163.

[72] Quoted in Peggy V. Beck and Anna L. Walters, *The Sacred: Ways of Knowledge, Sources of Life* (Tsaile, Ariz., 1980), 334.

he was travelling all over the country, he made the last request that he shall be returned to the place that he was born . . . And this is again the custom among the Crows. In the old days that people who have deceased were buried close to where they were born."[73]

Former village locations could exert a similar pull on the emotions of social groups, as Alfred C. Bowers recalls Hidatsa Indians from North Dakota telling him that "It was the custom of many families to return to living sites and to point out to the younger people the depressions of lodges where certain relatives had lived, their graves, or earth rings on the prairies where various ceremonies such as the *Naxpike* or Wolf ceremonies were held."[74] Other Plains peoples also erected stone cairns and still revisit them periodically to commemorate noteworthy battles where their heroes, whose names are still passed on from generation to generation, triumphed or fell in battle.

Where Indian stories involved the particular pedigrees of social units such as clans, lineages, or corporate "houses" whose boundary markers and distinctiveness within the larger polity had to be constantly maintained, a heightened concern for historical detail was bolstered by this keen sense of place. That seems to be the case with Navajo stories of clan movements and Hopi clan narratives related to the fate of ancient villages, and like-wise with the chronicles of aristocratic Northwest Coast families, whose "histories and laws were taught with stern accuracy" as to when, how, and where the heraldic crests displayed on their totem poles and house facades were acquired.[75]

Storied locations created a "topographic mnemonic" for the migration narratives of entire peoples, as with the stopping places and place names associated with epic relocations of the Creeks, Arikaras, Kiowas, and Crows. Some Indian peoples juggle both creation and migration mythic scenarios, notably the eastern Choctaws. Outside present-day Philadel-phia, Mississippi, they revere two separate sites, a mile and a half apart, at the headwaters of the Pearl River. Both are known as Nani Waiya. Their migration narrative reaches its ultimate destination at an old Woodland Period earthwork, which they dubbed as the "mother mound." But the Choctaws also have a creation story, linked to a natural hill, on whose

---

[73] Quoted in Peter Nabokov and Larry Loendorf, *Every Morning of the World: Ethnographic Resources Study of the Bighorn Canyon National Recreation Area*, National Park Service, National Forest Service, Bureau of Land Management (1994), 105.

[74] Alfred C. Bowers, *Hidatsa Social and Ceremonial Organization*, Bureau of American Ethnology, Bulletin 194 (Washington, D.C., 1963), 2.

[75] *We-gyet Wanders on* (Saanichton, B.C., 1977), 73.

south side is a cave from which their first people emerged. This way the Choctaws – whose ethnogenesis some scholars argue to be a seventeenth-century synthesis of two or even more groups – offer double protection for their territorial claims, as both incoming "chosen people" and aboriginal "first people."

Sometimes the landscape itself became the slate on which Native rock artists painted (pictographs) or incised (petroglyphs), what M. Jane Young terms "metonyms of narrative," symbols which more or less indelibly locked mythistoric accounts to place – often blessing and empowering the very spots where these events were said to transpire.[76] Rock art has been hypothesized to record both precontact historical processes, such as the innovative Katcina Cult which entered Pueblo country in the early fourteenth century,[77] and postcontact events, with Navajos painting priests wearing cross-emblazoned tunics on horseback in Canyon del Muerto, or Makahs carving a three-masted schooner on the rocks at Ozette on the Washington State coast.

For contemporary Indian narrators this geographic anchoring of community narratives remains a strength as well as a challenge. Says Leslie Marmon Silko, the Laguna Pueblo author of a memoir appropriately entitled *Storyteller:*

One of my frustrations is that unless you're involved in this, in these stories, in this place, you as a reader may not get it. I have to constantly fight against putting in detail and things that would be too tedious for the "outsider." At the same time I have to have some sort of internal integrity in the piece . . . In describing places and directions, there are stories that identify the place. These kinds of things make condensing a problem. It all depends on how much you want to make your stories acceptable to communities outside this one.[78]

LEGENDS AND ORAL TRADITIONS

So far this essay has stressed "narrative truth" over "historical truth," to borrow a distinction from Donald P. Spence.[79] Spence's point is that while psychoanalysis says it uncovers the latter, its real significance only unfolds in the former. History faces the same conundrum; how much of it is received

[76] M. Jane Young, *Signs from the Ancestors: Zuni Cultural Symbolism and Perceptions of Rock Art* (Albuquerque, N.M., 1988).

[77] See Polly and Curtis F. Schaafsma, "Evidence for the Origins of the Pueblo Katchina Cult as Suggested by Southwestern Rock Art," *American Antiquity* 39 (1974).

[78] Leslie Marmon Silko, "A Conversation with Leslie Marmon Silko," *Sun Tracks* 3(1) (1976), 31.

[79] Donald P. Spence, *Narrative Truth and Historical Truth* (New York, 1982).

structure and story and how much is documentary and original? Yet this is not to imply that American Indian oral traditions have nothing to contribute to our knowledge of what might have actually occurred in the past. The era of named people and remembered events is the territory of a second broad category of American Indian oral narrative, dubbed by folklorists as legend, which moves closer in "reality" and "time" to our present day. Indian legends are generally less secure and more contested than myths in terms of the consensus they arouse among listeners. As William S. Simmons eloquently characterizes this category of legends, some of whose core plots he documented as bridging 350 years of continuous retelling within remnant Indian communities in southern New England:

Legend conveys one generation's interpretations to the next. Through legend people select some experiences and not others for retelling. They depict these experiences in terms of motifs and symbols that are available to them at that time. These may come from ancestral tradition or from external sources to which one has been exposed. Legends float through a twilight between what may really have happened and what people believe to have happened. Although they are a collective phenomenon, no two individuals tell them in the same way. Through legend, place names and events are pressed into stories that have a life of their own.[80]

Within the legend-to-tradition spectrum implied here, we find heated scholarly debates over the potential utility of Indian oral tradition to non-Native notions of history. Earlier in this century, objectivist sticklers like anthropologist Robert H. Lowie saw minimal historical value in Indian oral traditions; a skepticism more recently expressed by the northern Plains anthropologist John C. Ewers: "the origins and ages of most of these traditions are unknown, and their contents are susceptible to elaboration, contradiction, or distortion with each mouth-to-ear transmission. They offer no reliable substitute for the written word."[81]

Other scholars, however, most notably ethnohistorians, contend that even the collective memories of acculturated Indian communities can "complement" written reconstructions of the past. For legends clearly fall into that time zone which collective memories almost touch, and which can feed into written history through guarded use of the sorts of corroborative techniques which Jan Vansina has worked out for African oral his-

---

[80] William S. Simmons, "The Mystic Voice: Pequot Folklore from the Seventeenth Century to the Present." Paper prepared for The Mashantucket Pequot Historical Conference, October 23–4, 1987, Norwich and Ledyard, Connecticut, 2.

[81] John C. Ewers, "When Red and White Men Met," *Western Historical Quarterly* 2(3) (1971), 136.

tory.[82] In 1959, for example, after Gordon M. Day listened to what St. Francis Abenakis from northern New England had to say about the destruction of their village by Rogers' Rangers in 1759, he felt confident in pinpointing exactly where the houses stood in which named individuals were killed, explaining why the Abenaki casualties were far fewer than reported, and hypothesizing on the precise identity and personal motivations behind the informer of the impending attack.[83] What preserved the accuracy of this Abenaki oral history were not any "fixed form" procedures, whereby information is scrupulously transmitted via memorized speeches or genealogical recitations of the sort delivered during public performances, chiefly investitures, or funerary rituals. Something about the intrinsic importance of their content to Abenaki sense of identity apparently safeguarded them for 200 years.

That was also what Andrew O. Wiget concluded after comparing Hopi narratives related to the Pueblo Revolt against their colonizers in 1680 with Spanish documents concerning the same momentous event.[84] Dividing his evaluative criteria into accuracy (1) of motivation, (2) of detail, and (3) of sequencing of events, Wiget concluded that the Native oral testimony preserved with emotional specificity Hopi resentments against the cruel and capricious behavior of the Spanish priests. In their details, the architectural shape of the Spanish friary, the number of priests killed, and the uprising's actual date, the Hopi stories were also on the mark – after 300 years. Third, Wiget found the chain reaction of events – from priests' arrival and early authoritarianism, to forced-labor construction of Oraibi, Awatovi, and Schungopavi missions, to increasing indignities climaxing with the planning and fulfillment of the attack – to square with the Spanish versions. Encoded in Hopi narratives was also "a statement of shared values, represented by shared symbols," which, at the same time, contained a high degree of durability and reliability. Admitting that some details were clearly collapsed, Wiget resisted giving priority to the search for factual accuracy over that for historical meanings. For him it remained crucial to avoid reducing some narrative elements to literalness and elevating others to myth if the "truth of the Hopi" were to be rescued from the "distortion of Western categories."[85]

[82] Jan Vansina, *Oral Tradition as History* (Madison, Wis., 1985).
[83] Gordon M. Day, "Oral Tradition as Complement," *Ethnohistory* 19 (1972).
[84] Andrew O. Wiget, "Truth and the Hopi: An Historiographic Study of Documented Oral Tradition Concerning the Coming of the Spanish," *Ethnohistory* 29 (1982).
[85] Ibid., 197.

Scrutinizing Winnebago stories from the Great Lakes region of a century later, Paul Radin was convinced that Indian legends could weld together dissynchronous elements.[86] His test case, a Native version of the French "discovery" of the Winnebagos, opened with a curiously objective profile of traditional Winnebago society's defining characteristics, good and not-so-good, which Radin considered the more recently composed part of the narrative (although from his excerpt, even it appears cobbled together from disparate mythic elements). From external evidence, however, Radin judged the narrative's second, more historical, portion, which dealt with the founding of the mixed-blood Decora dynasty, to transmit historical data over two centuries old with considerable accuracy. His conclusion alluded to the narrative's vested interest, which was less one of chronological accountability than, in essence, chartering the Decoras as a quasi-mythic lineage and celebrating the compounded French-Siouan benefits they bequeathed upon generations of Winnebago people.

The north-central Woodlands also afford an object lesson in how different self-interests often underlie European and Indian historical accountings for the same event. When their story of first contact with the French in 1715 is related by certain Chipewayans of Fort Chipewayan, Alberta, it is immediately personalized.[87] Unlike the Western account, the key protagonist is not an anonymous "slave woman" but a character we come to know, by the name of Fallen Marten. As socio-linguists Ronald and Suzanne Scollon point out, the two narratives underscore contrasting frames of value. In an impersonal voice, the English version stresses the economic and historical benefits of contact. But the more conversational and intimate Indian account stresses the argument between Crees and Chipewayans over credit for first discovering the possessions-bearing French (an interesting switch on the European race to claim the New World's natural resources).

The Native story also underscores the Indian woman's temporary alienation, as she trades with the French her knowledge of the terrain for access to their alluring goods and finally undergoes a psychologically stressful homecoming. Almost an ur-text for a new subgenre, what one could dub the Indian "reintegration ordeal" among one's own people, subsequent

---

[86] Paul Radin, "Reconstruction from Internal Evidence and the Role of the Individual," in *The Method and Theory of Ethnology: An Essay in Criticism* (South Hadley, Mass., 1987).

[87] Ronald Scollon and Suzanne B. K. Scollon, *Linguistic Convergence: An Ethnography of Speaking at Fort Chipewayan, Alberta* (New York, 1979).

generations of her people might well empathize and identify with this bitter foretaste of divided loyalties. Whereas the European story focused on the courage of early European traders in confronting the frozen wilderness, and on the riches to be gained from a new frontier market, the Native version stressed that it was Fallen Marten's bravery which "found the Frenchman," and that she imperiled her sense of identity to bring her people "knives, pails and everything."

When Catherine McClellan examined Alaskan Indian and European contact through Indian memories she initially looked for Native verifications to non-Indian accounts.[88] Where discrepancies occurred – as with Indians asserting that the famous explorer Robert Campbell had an Indian wife – she let them stand, leaving open the possibility that Native voices often yield behind-the-woods tips about the secret lives of historical figures. At the same time she was struck that "both the Tlingit and the Athabaskans have what appears to be a high tolerance for discontinuity in time;" their myth-time was able to coexist with either the present or the recent past.[89] That further clarified for her how some Native accounts of the 1898 Gold Rush could credit both a European prospector and his Indian associate with finding the precious mineral, while others had gold originating from an Indian encounter with the mythic Wealth Woman, thus conjoining their indigenous genres of "long ago stories" and "true stories."

Far to the south, the Catawabas of the Carolinas could agree on historical premises with their non-Indian neighbors but differ on their consequences. The Anglo-American version of their shared past had the Catawbas representing the amicable side of the friendly-hostile dichotomy – by which Euro-American Carolinians divide all Indians – to such a degree that the Indians freely turn over all their lands without thought of compensation (the same subtext as that of America's national Thanksgiving). Conversely, however, the Catawaba accounts portray their ancestors being too nice to "avaricious, grasping" Euro-Americans, who display utter ignorance of the etiquette of proper reciprocity. Indeed, observes Charles Hudson, until 1962 when Catawaba chiefs annually appealed to the state legislature for aid, they invariably prefaced their request with stern reminders of these unrequited kindnesses.[90]

---

[88] Catherine McClellan, "Indian Stories about the First Whites in Northwestern America," in *Ethnohistory in Southwestern Alaska and the Southern Yukon,* ed. Margaret Lantis (Lexington, Ky., 1970).

[89] Ibid., 116.

[90] Hudson, "Folk History and Ethnohistory," *Ethnohistory* 13 (1966).

Even in the absence of new data, an appreciation for Indian historicity can open up clichéd legends for reinterpretion. Reexamining one iconic "historical myth" – the "Indian princess" Pocahantas saving the life of colonist Captain John Smith – Margaret Williamson teased out a plausible story of two cultures vying to assimilate each other. She suggests that this was an example of events which are, as Marshall Sahlins has put it, "externally induced but indigenously orchestrated."[91] Perhaps the Powhatan Indians perceived Smith as a *werowance,* or sacred being, from a faraway people. And perhaps, using customary Native strategies such as adoption and arranged marriage, their chief manipulated his daughter's union so as to bring the powerful, auspicious Europeans under his confederacy's fold for political and economic gain.[92]

The study of Western Apache oral genres caused linguist Keith Basso to stumble upon a type of historical narrative utterly new to him, the *'agodzaahi,* "historical tale." Their settings were only two or three generations removed from the present, they were almost anecdotal in brevity, and usually described someone violating Apache norms, and the high cost of doing so. They featured formulaic opening and closing lines which precisely tied the accounts to known Apache places. Like a parable, their purpose was to "shoot" their moral into their human targets, and alter their behavior by provoking them to "replace" themselves, as Basso's consultants phrased it. These stories preserved the underlying "why" of historical action rather than its particular "what." They brought the "where" into the moral equation so as to create a landscape replete with ethical resonances for their membership of Apache listeners.[93]

NATIVE HISTORY THROUGH ORATORY

Native senses of history often come to life during highly formalized events that involve speech-making. Among today's Tlingits of Alaska the oratory delivered during memorials for the dead is replete with references to physical heirlooms, including masks, crest symbols, and dance regalia, known collectively as *at.óow.* These symbolically charged items, in turn,

---

[91] Marshall Sahlins, *Islands of History* (Chicago, 1985), viii.

[92] Margaret Holmes Williamson, "Pocahontas and Captain John Smith: Examining a Historical Myth," *History and Anthropology* 5(3–4) (1992).

[93] Keith H. Basso, " 'Stalking With Stories': Names, Places and Moral Narratives among the Western Apache," in *Text, Play and Story: The Construction and Reconstruction of Self and Society,* ed. Edward M. Bruner (Washington, D.C., 1984).

evoke the *shuka,* the generations of owner-descendants – the "ones who had gone before" – as well as the unborn, those who remain "ahead." One by one, family members stand up to enumerate their pedigrees of animal and human ancestors, traceable through these tangible emblems. The speeches serve many purposes – affirming the Tlingit sense of historical continuity, providing therapy for mourners, and integrating all social subsets within the community.[94]

Other Indian oratory draws upon quasi-mythic chronologies which were proclaimed from memory with seasonal regularity. This was how Cherokee Keetowah society speakers preserved their *Eloh',* the account of a long-ago migration across a vast sea to North America by their people's original seven clans. As seldom happened when oral tradition was committed to print, the written version which appeared in a bilingual Oklahoma newspaper in 1896 strove both to "presentize" the mythic and legendary past by establishing first causes for Cherokee existence and experience, and to "futurize" it by emphasizing the Cherokees' predestined spiritual strength and success as a historical society.[95]

Outside closed circles of Indian speakers and listeners, the protocols of diplomatic encounters between Native Americans and Euro-Americans produced volumes of Indian oratory, a boon to students of Indian historicity and a goldmine for later anthologizers. These negotiations often saw Indians prefacing their remarks with coded references to inherited rights and with chartering narratives that were frequently bewildering to their impatient Euro-American counterparts. At the Medicine Lodge Treaty negotiations of 1867, for instance, "Each speaker [first] told the history of his people and explained the Indian rapport with nature," writes historian Donald Fixico, "stating that his and his people's lives were affected by the coming of the white man."[96]

Sometimes Indian speeches were heard far from their homelands. When the Hopi leader Yukeoma from the "hostile" Pueblo of Hotevilla traveled to Washington, D.C., for a parley with President Howard Taft in March 1911, his intent was to alert the bureaucratic world to the gospel according to Hopis, as conveyed in his people's predestinatory

[94] Nora Marks Dauenhauer and Richard Dauenhauer, eds., *Haa Tuwunaaqu Yis, for Healing Our Spirit: Tlingit Oratory* (Seattle, 1990).

[95] Howard L. Meredith and Virginia E. Milam, "A Cherokee Vision of Eloh'," *The Indian Historian* 8(4) (1975).

[96] Donald L. Fixico, "As Long as the Grass Grows . . . The Cultural Conflicts and Political Strategies of United States–Indian Treaties," in *Ethnicity and War,* ed. Winston A. Van Horne and Thomas V. Tonnesen (Madison, Wis., 1984), 140.

narratives of origin. The scene sounds almost surreal. Normally in bare feet and a Union suit, for his White House appearance Yukeoma showed up at Pennsylvania Avenue in his homespun ceremonial Antelope Priest attire. President Taft, suffering from pinkeye, listened from behind dark glasses. Yukeoma opened his plea against schooling with talk of the "days of the medicine men, before the paleface took away from us the things that were ours." After Taft insisted on Hopi children walking in the Euro-American's way, a subdued Yukeoma had a second conference, this time with Commissioner of Indian Affairs Robert G. Valentine. Here he spoke at greater length about Hopi prophecies, the emergence from the underworld of two brothers, and the inscribed stones given by the Red Headed Spirit to the Hopis as proof of their right to their land "and that is why he don't want the civilized way," said the interpreter.[97] For this traditionalist, myth was the first, last, and only diplomatic argument a Hopi could advance. If it went unheeded, his people's prophecies would then warn Euro-Americans of the ultimate price.

FOLKTALES AS VESSELS OF HISTORICITY

The American Indian *folktale,* customarily seen as a vehicle for fanciful yarns about ribald animals, seems an unlikely conveyor of historical information. While anthropologist Robert Lowie's eyebrow would have risen at William Bascom's suggestion that "myths" were regarded as factual, and he would have remained scornful of any contribution "legends" might offer toward reconstructing chronology, he would have applauded Bascom's denial of any truth-value to folktales. Lowie expressed near-contempt at the suggestion that Native traditions had anything to offer history. As he wrote in 1915: "I cannot attach to oral traditions any historical value whatsoever under any conditions whatsoever,"[98] and as he reiterated in his presidential address to the American Folk-Lore Society two years later, "Indian tradition is historically worthless, because the occurrences, possibly real, which it retains, are of no historical significance; and because it fails to record, or to record accurately, the most momentous happenings."[99]

Yet a closer look at the examples, which are mostly folktales, that

---

[97] Katherine C. Turner, *Red Men Calling on the Great White Father* (Norman, Okla., 1951), 203.
[98] Robert H. Lowie, "Oral Tradition and History," *American Anthropologist* 17 (1915), 598.
[99] Robert H. Lowie, "Oral Tradition and History," *Journal of American Folklore* 30 (1917), 165.

Lowie summoned for his uncharacteristically strident statements suggests that he had little interest or eye for Indian historicity. Dismayed that the Lemhi Shoshones of Idaho, whom he visited in 1906, failed to recollect Lewis and Clark's visit, Lowie complained that he could only turn up two versions of "a purely mythical story" involving a contest between an Iron-Man, "father of the white people," whose home was on the water, and Wolf, "father of the Indians," who lived underground. Their competition involved who was faster at making guns. First Wolf used Indian tobacco to stupify his opponent, after which came the actual gun-making race, won by Wolf — other versions climax with Wolf showing Iron-Man he can take away the sun and plunge the world into darkness as well, or the smoke making Iron-Man choke to death on his own vomit. When Shoshones related these stories to Lowie at the turn of the twentieth century their population strength, political and religious rights, and sense of confidence had hit rock bottom. What possible interest had they in contributing to the archives of disinterested fact-finding? In their creative imaginations, at least, their contender, Wolf, could use their power, tobacco, to best the Euro-American at his own game — making metal things that killed.[100]

If Lowie viewed Shoshone narratives as deficient in hard chronology, he disdained Assiniboine accounts of obtaining horses and encountering the first Europeans in which their mythic culture-hero played the pivotal role. In his boat of five moose hides, the Assiniboine culture-hero, Iktumni, descended the Saskatchewan River and met Europeans on an island, bringing back the cloth garments he obtained through trade with them.[101] The whole encounter was rendered as a meaningful action of Assiniboine initiative, with Europeans almost under quarantine while the Indians assimilated their wares. This must have been a comforting narrative for a powerless people, and constituted a vital record of "attitudinal history" for scholars to come.

In such narratives the historical freight, borne by familiar metaphors, motifs, and plotlines, made no bones about its subjective function: the restoration to conceptual equivalence, if not preferability or even supremacy, of Indian worldviews. From the Native perspective, history was no more an objective property than was status or charisma. The playing field of these stories, to which Lowie seemed willfully oblivious, was the con-

---

[100] Robert H. Lowie, *The Northern Shoshone* (New York, 1909).
[101] Robert H. Lowie, *The Assiniboine* (New York, 1909).

test for cultural hegemony. For Indians the symbols highlighted in them were their subversive weapons of last resort, by means of which power relations were fought for the high stakes of cultural prestige and self-esteem. Tobacco, horses, iron, waters, cosmic undergrounds become counters in a game of who's on top – politically, territorially, ethically, spiritually, psychologically.

If we combine the observation that, of all folk genres, the tale enjoys the readiest responsiveness to shifting socio-economic conditions, with the fact that most American Indian folklore was elicited during decades of dizzying change, the suggestion that historical commentaries and value judgments might be encoded into this body of oral literature does not seem far-fetched. Often couched in seemingly innocent, entertaining forms, featuring tricksters, culture-heroes, evil monsters, and other familiar characters whose supernatural antics seem outside historical time, these commentaries could remain subversive and retain their pragmatic references. Indian listeners might take them on two levels, relishing the improvisations on traditional plots, while absorbing their parable-like morals regarding ethnically appropriate behavior and cross-cultural comparison.

According to religious historian Kenneth Morrison, "a seemingly 'lost' dimension of colonial history emerges from the evolution of [northeastern Algonquian Indian] stories as they gradually accommodated selective elements of Christian cosmology."[102] His examples are folktales of the Abenaki, Maliseet, and Micmac peoples of northern New England and eastern Canada, among whose traditional personages were Gluskabe, a trickster-hero, and cannibal giant or *Windigo* figures, frightening entities of devilish, humanoid, and beastlike appearance, who were actually possessed human beings. In one Windigo tale the man who becomes a cannibal giant is "healed" not by his own people, but by a Catholic priest. To explain the transformation, Morrison draws a structural comparison between the Indians' admiration for French Jesuits and the traditional function of their benevolent trickster-hero, Gluskabe – whom some Algonquians came to consider Jesus Christ's first created being. Morrison's deep reading of the interplay of Christian and Algonquian religious symbols explicates the "subtle gives and takes of a mutual spiritual acculturation" which, he argues, has been

[102] Kenneth M. Morrison, "Towards a History of Intimate Encounters: Algonkian Folklore, Jesuit Missionaries, and Kiwakwe, The Cannibal Giant," *American Indian Culture and Research Journal* 3(4) (1979), 53.

"largely underexplored because of a long-standing devaluation of folk-loric sources."[103]

From America's opposite shore Indian folklore played upon negative reflections of Euro-American society, according to Madronna Holden. She perceived "the most traditional of native tales and native mythical figures being used to respond to particular historical situations." Holden's inter-pretation of Trickster and Transformer tales from the Coast Salishes of the Pacific Northwest revealed hidden messages condemning missionaries and employers.[104] Here the traditional "Transformer" protagonist was lam-pooned as Jesus Christ, who arrogantly set about to "make people straight." When he found Indians walking on their hands, he set them rightside up, and proudly announced from village to village, "I am the one who is straightening everybody out."[105] His busybodying behavior be-comes cumulatively hilarious, the irony thick as smoke. Other Salish tales stated more didactically the clear superiority of Indian lifeways: "Though white people overwhelm us, it is Moon that has placed us here, and the laws we are bound to obey are those established by Moon in the ancient time."[106]

But it is those indirect, loaded critiques which delight Holden. From debunkings of missionaries they excoriate the Euro-American's obsession with material possessions, as in the Transformer tales where the alien work ethic produces tools so "hungry for work" that they must constantly be fed "wood chips and meat." They also call attention to a kind of mass produc-tion which dehumanizes people by making them part of a machine. The new boss, Raven, extends a fishtrap across a river using linked-together human beings instead of lashed poles. Ever the protector of Indians (and humanity in general), Moon frees the exhausted, drenched Natives, and warns Raven, "Never do this again . . . These people here are human beings."[107]

A subtler form of cross-cultural admonition is found in European tale-types reworked by generations of Indian taletellers. A Potawatomi exam-ple has an Indian boy named P'teejah ("petit Jean") exploiting the Old World motif of the "magic table cloth" for a novel spin on the power of material culture. Meeting a starving European soldier, the boy's tablecloth

---

[103] Ibid., 63.
[104] Madronna Holden, "Making All the Crooked Ways Straight: The Satirical Portrait of Whites in Coast Salish Folklore," *Journal of American Folklore* 89 (1976).
[105] Ibid., 274.
[106] Ibid., 276.
[107] Ibid., 283.

miraculously produces food for him. Then the soldier exhibits his magic
hat which creates more soldiers on command, and he offers to trade it for
the tablecloth. At first the boy resists, but then capitulates, calls forth the
soldiers, and orders them to retrieve his tablecloth. According to folklorist
Alan Dundes, who elicited the tale from a Kansas storyteller named Bill
Mzechteno, the story shows the Indian wielding control over the Euro-
American's artifacts for a change, offering him whiskey when the magic
tablecloth unfurls, then using his own possession to defeat him in a
variation on the traditional Indian shaman's duel.[108] The tale might not be
chronologically situated, but it is historically incisive where power relations are concerned, and its aim is practically to reverse history, which, we
may recall, is also what Eliade claimed to be the express design of mythic
consciousness.

Some Indian stories may embody a more Westernized, documentary
component. That was the supposition of archaeologist W. D. Strong after
he heard from Naskapi Indian hunters of northeastern Labrador in the
1930s how their culture hero and trickster story cycle featured large-
headed, long-trunked, big-toothed monsters who were eventually slain by
their trickster hero. Normally a tough-minded scientist who only concocted chronologies of bygone Indian eras from hard evidence dug out of
the ground, Strong took pains to distinguish these "historical traditions"
from other "myths of observation" he found in the literature, which were
the result, he believed, of Indians "rationalizing" into story form their
exposure to huge fossil bones. Strong credited the accounts he personally
heard from Indian lips as being possibly "a dim but actual tradition of the
time when the mammoth lived in North America."[109]

Strong's open-mindedness would find favor with the literalist reading of
Indian mythology advanced by the prolific American Indian intellectual
Vine Deloria, Jr., who has proposed that Indian references to ancient
cataclysms, supernovas, and volcanic eruptions "might be simply the
collective memories of a great and catastrophic event through which people came to understand themselves and the universe they inhabited."[110]

But again, any Indian "memories" about such distant times are bound to
be more interesting as commentary than documentation. What intrigued

---

[108] Alan Dundes, "The Study of Folklore in Literature and Culture: Identification and Interpretation," *Journal of American Folklore* 78 (1965).

[109] William Duncan Strong, "North American Indian Traditions Suggesting a Knowledge of the
Mammoth," *American Anthropologist* 36 (1934), 87.

[110] Deloria, *God Is Red*, 154.

Robert Brightman about Missinippi Cree historical lore he collected during fieldwork in northwestern Manitoba was its depiction of earlier, autochthonous "races." These included the crude "ancient people," also known as "hairy-heart beings" (*mimiditihisiwak*), and another group of territorial precursors whom Brightman describes as the "xenophobic dwarves" (*mimikwisiwak*). In the Cree stories featuring these mysterious beings Brightman detected an evolutionary bias. For the "hairy ancients" were associated with retrograde primitivism; to Crees they were technologically inferior, stupid, and monstrous. To Brightman they fit into "a characteristically [Cree] progressivist conception of human history," that defies those glib stereotypes about primitive man's cyclical, ahistorical view of the world.[111]

On the other hand, the prophetic gifts of the dwarves filled Crees with awe, admiration, and gratitude. If the mere mention of "hairy ancients" constituted a negative assessment of earlier ages, stories of the dwarves, keepers of the old ways who are said to withdraw from today's noisy, overcrowded, and polluted environment, identified with invasive Euro-American society, constituted a negative critique of modernity, overpopulation, and development. To Brightman, Cree historical consciousness actually juggled three separate storylines for contrasting the "past" with the "present." The first dramatized the growing improvement of human society over its cruder antecedents; the second, which Brightman drew from ethnohistorical sources which preserved Cree accounts about the introduction of trade goods, stressed the duplicity of traders and suggested that original Cree technology was equally efficient, and Indians before the trade period healthier and more vigorous; the third scenario, featuring the dwarves, constituted a more emphatic indictment of the ills of modern life and affirmed the superiority of traditional Cree lifeways. "Cree historical thought explores," writes Brightman, "both the virtues and the defects of the past and the present . . . From one perspective the past is vanishing, while from the other it advances to encompass the present."[112]

NATIVE HISTORY THROUGH RITUAL

Without half trying, some Indian religious ceremonies seem to have fit the Indian requirements for "doing history" — honoring and preserving their pasts by representing them through symbolic regalia and expressive perfor-

---

[111] Robert Brightman, "Primitivism in Missinippi Cree Historical Consciousness," *Man* 25 (1990), 119.
[112] Ibid., 125–6.

mances. Interested in how traditional peoples represent and reconnect with their heritage, Paul Connerton has argued that "if there is such a thing as social memory, we are likely to find it in commemorative ceremonies."[113] In American Indian religious schemes, these "commemorative" features are often enmeshed within a mythologizing narrative, the intent of which is to recharter a geographically removed or politically reformulated ethnic constituency.

Within the *mitewiwin* ceremonies conducted by Ojibwas of the Upper Great Lakes region, for example, ritual dramaturges planted numerous references to their origin-migration history. Especially precise were the prayers and songs which described historical journeys around Lake Superior. This sacred body of water was also represented by the floorspace of the bark-covered ceremonial enclosure, around which celebrants circulated in solemn procession. According to Thomas Vennum, Jr., who studied *mite* rites in exacting detail, "Portions of the origin tale were reenacted symbolically by the candidate in initiation rituals, and the journey to the west finds its parallel in the new member's 'path of life,' which originates in the sudatory [sweat bath] located to the east of the medicine lodge (*mitewikan*), leads into the lodge, 'passes through' it (Ojibwa terminology for initiation), and emerges from the western exit."[114]

Vennum's major discovery was the geographical precision of the *mite* song corpus. Ojibwas anchored their collective past to sequences of specific "resting places" on the epic journey of mythologized forebears. The sites seemed like giant footsteps, such as "Lake of Eddying Waters" (Lake St. Clair) and "long rapids" (Sault Ste Marie); the songs recalled the travels of Ojibwa forebears to a "homeland," at once legitimizing territorial claims and indoctrinating new members by having them dramatize that history in ritual.

Among the Crow Indians of Montana traces of a similar historical reenactment underlay adoption rituals for their sacred Tobacco Society (*basussua*). A Plains Indian hunting people who readily admit to having split off from the Hidatsas, a Middle Missouri farming people, the Crow explanation departs from scholarly stories as to why, when, and how this took place. In their collective memory — recently sanctioned as the official version supplied in printed bilingual texts for classroom use — it was the harmonious vision-quests of two brothers rather than a

---

[113] Paul Connerton, *How Societies Remember* (Cambridge, 1989), 71.
[114] Vennum, "Ojibwa Origin-Migration Songs of the *Mitewiwin*," 754.

squabble between the wives of opposing clan leaders over food distribution that led to the momentous split. One brother was given the corn, fathering the Hidatsa people. The other received sacred tobacco seeds, shepherding his migratory people on a grand tour of the Plains until reaching the Bighorn Mountain heartland where they coalesced as the Crows. During the Tobacco Society adoption ceremonies, the play of symbols and ritual processions recapitulated what anthropologist Sherry Ortner might term this "key scenario" for an indigenous narrative of Crow ethnogenesis.[115]

In discussing Navajo historicity, a tribal scholar and his non-Navajo collaborator boldly propose the Crows' "ceremonial discourse" to be something like an indigenous counterpart to Euro-American "history."[116] Their efforts at reconstructing a "developmental schematic of Navajo history" almost defiantly ignores cross-cultural contact. Instead they hypothesize a tentative sequence for the precontact succession of various Navajo ritual "Ways." Beneath the long-term trajectory of the Navajos' history, during which they detect a shift from "patriarchy" to "matriarchy," their argument for the relative conservatism in Navajo historical thought concludes with a profile of "stasis" which is at odds with conventional anthropological wisdom, which has branded Navajos as "adaptive, flexible, ever changing." The focus of "Navajo history," in their view, consists of this people's struggle to live outside the West's "obsessive fix on improvement, progress and perpetual change."[117]

In recent times more public, newsworthy commemorations have tested Native inventiveness to memorialize historical incidents without compromising their status as either singular, unrepeatable "events" or inextricable pieces of predictable, reassuring "structure." An example was the ingenious format which Pueblo Indians devised for observing the three-hundredth anniversary of the Pueblo Revolt of 1680. Influenced by the American Bicentennial festivities of 1976, they reenacted the relay runner network which had secretly linked the rebellious pueblos along the Rio Grande and those in Arizona for a synchronized uprising on the very same day in August 1680. Closer inspection of the participating pueblos revealed that each had its own agenda, most notably the Hopis. They

---

[115] Peter Nabokov, "Cultivating Themselves: The Inter-Play of Crow Indian Religion and History," Ph.D. dissertation, University of California, Berkeley (Anthropology), 1988.
[116] James C. Faris and Harry Walters, "Navajo History: Some Implications of Contrasts of Navajo Ceremonial Discourse," *History and Anthropology* 5 (1990).
[117] Ibid., 10.

revived a Bear Clan legend about one of their women, pregnant, who was removed to a place of refuge just after the 1680 revolt so as not to contaminate the infant with bloodshed and prevent his baptismal presentation to the sun twenty days later. With Bear Clan runners taking the lead in the "Tricentennial Run," the events were conflated so as to transform the 1980 anniversary into an ad hoc ritual for cultural self-determination and renewal.[118]

On the other hand, it was the traditional Lakota death wake, *washigila*, or "wiping the tears," which provided a prototype for the Bigfoot Memorial Ride (on horseback) that was synchronized for the hundredth anniversary of the killings at Wounded Knee Creek.[119] For four years prior to December 15, 1990, the Big Foot Riders undertook the 322 mile trek from Cheyenne River to Pine Ridge, South Dakota. Named for *Si Tanka*, or Big Foot, the leader of the contingent of Ghost Dancers who were mercilessly killed in 1890, the horsemen were accompanied by runners as well. The rhetoric which emerged from this ritual-in-the making honored the endurance of the commemorators (much as relatives commiserate with the suffering pledgers in a modern Lakota Sun Dance), their efforts to complete the proper mourning, and their recommitment to Lakota values.

NATIVE HISTORY REFLECTED THROUGH THINGS

The material culture Indians made and used provides an unexpected window into various American Indian kinds of history. In order to recover long-term changes in the Indian past, archaeologists compare Indian-crafted weapons, tools, and ornaments and their contexts in order to demonstrate cultural change over time and diffusion of cultural ideas over space. Yet, for their part, Indian cultures have not been blind to the profound associations between the material world and their many different pasts. Old relics which have been sanctified through their ties to earlier times often hold numinous or sentimental significance. These can include ancestral bones carried in portable ossuaries, communal medicine bundles, traveling shrines, and outmoded styles of domestic architecture transformed into religious spaces because of their link to older, more mythically connected days. Examples range from old southwestern pithouses that were built as ceremonial *kivas* after people resided in multistoried, domes-

---

[118] Peter Nabokov, *Indian Running* (Sante Fe, N.M., 1987).

[119] Charmaine White Face Wisecarver, "Wounded Knee: Mending the Sacred Hoop," *Native Peoples* (spring 1990).

tic room clusters to the earlier-style rectangular Mandan earthlodge which was retained as their *Okipa* ceremonial lodge long after most Mandans moved into the later, circular domestic earthlodges arranged around a common plaza.

A second way that historical interactions can be "read" from Indian material culture is related to those shorter time frames of intense cross-cultural interaction which the French historian Fernand Braudel refers to as "the conjuncture," spanning ten to a hundred years or so. From the earliest trade transactions between American Indians and Euro-Americans, what people wore, the tools they used, and how they adorned themselves registered historical changes and altered value systems. The speed and intensity with which their material, social, and political lives were transformed by glass beads, cloth, metal wares, and the like provide "implicit documentation" concerning their history.

The institutionalization of Western trade goods soon linked the Kwakiutl (Kwakw*aka*'wakw) peoples of British Columbia to the "world system" of trade in the Pacific rim. What an anthropological historian of the colonial period like Marshall Sahlins wishes to stress is how their selective adaptation of trade goods, such as Hudson Bay Blankets or metal pots and pans, served to elaborate their ceremonial potlatching and enhance the preexisting Kwakiutl cosmology.[120] Similar historical data come from Calvin Martin's inventive study of how a simple copper pot was "Indianized" by the Micmacs (Mi'kmaqs) of Nova Scotia. Apart from its utilitarian function, its historically bounded cultural "lives" included its highly valued role in the colonial exchange economy, its key place in ceremonial life as a burial vessel, its animated "life" as a "member" of the overarching belief system, and its circumstantial impact in altering older settlement patterns, which had been constrained by the need to find the proper wood to carve into food bowls.[121] Martin also might have mentioned the new historical "life" accorded those old-fashioned wooden bowls, for although they dropped from common usage, they acquired heightened prestige as self-consciously "traditional" feast dishes, only brought out on extra special occasions.

Other items were made by Indians explicitly to record historical events or memorable transactions of the brevity termed by Braudel as

---

[120] Marshall Sahlins, "Cosmologies of Capitalism: The Trans-Pacific Sector of 'The World System'," in *Culture/Power/History: A Reader in Contemporary Social Theory,* ed. N. B. Dirks, G. Eley, and S. B. Ortner (Princeton, N.J., 1994).

[121] Calvin Martin, "The Four Lives of a Micmac Copper Pot," *Ethnohistory* 22 (1975).

"surface oscillations." Most of these were *mnemonic* devices, memory aids which kept oral recitations on track during public presentations of a political, social, or religious nature. Some were more private possessions, such as the "string balls" that Yakima girls begin winding in childhood from strands of dogbane bark, attaching dentalium shells, glass beads, and colored cloth, and tying thousands of knots to them as their experiences accumulated, each a reminder of the moments of their lives. Upon their death the balls might be hung near their graves or buried with them.[122]

The symbols scratched into Great Lakes birchbark scrolls associated with the *mitewiwin,* or Grand Medicine Society, were decoded by initiated specialists. According to Thomas Vennum, Jr., the pictorial "migration charts" were cross-referenced to "song scrolls" and constituted an Ojibwa priest's library," which allowed him to "retain knowledge of the Ojibwa past . . . a reference text for the geohistory of his people."[123]

What sounds like a very old mnemonic device enabled the earthlodge-dwelling Arikaras of the Missouri River to recollect their genesis narrative, telling of the creator, Nishanu Natchitak, and his intermediary, Mother Earth. The item was a sheaf of thirty-four thin sticks which an old Arikara priest named Four Rings preserved in a sacred bundle. Arranging the sticks in six piles around a firepit in late summer 1924, Four Rings moved from pile to pile, each stick enabling him to conjure up for ethnographer Melvin R. Gilmore a scene in the creation of his people's complex cosmology, their value system, their early history, and their cultural destiny.[124]

With the coming of the horse and increased intergroup feuding it also became customary among Plains Indians for men to portray their battle exploits with pictographic figures on shirts, robes, and even tipi covers. An early example of these "partisan histories" came to light after Lewis and Clark collected a Mandan painted buffalo robe depicting a fight between horsemen believed to have taken place about 1797. In 1832 the painter, George Catlin, copied another Mandan robe on which the host to visiting Europeans, Chief Four Bears (Mato Tope), had illustrated his

[122] J. D. Leechman and M. R. Harrington, "String Records of the Northwest," *Indian Notes and Monographs,* series 2, 16 (New York, 1921).
[123] Vennum, "Ojibwa Origin-Migration Songs of the *Mitewiwin,*" 760.
[124] Melvin R. Gilmore, "The Arikara Book of Genesis," *Papers of the Michigan Academy of Science, Arts and Letters* 12 (1929).

twelve greatest battle exploits, including one hand-to-hand combat with a Cheyenne.

It is not clear if such early, individual "brag robes" of Plains warriors preceded the community records painted by Plains Indian chroniclers which were collected by travelers and ethnographers shortly afterwards. Known as *waniyetu yawapi,* or "winter counts," to the Dakotas, *sinaksin,* or "picture-writing," to the Blackfeet, their series of images were a visual "shorthand," highlighting the notable event of a given year. Although a collective diary, they were generally the work of self-appointed historian-artists. Starting at the center, the symbols might spiral outward, with each standing for, as a Sioux named Good Wood put it, "Something put down for every year about their nation."[125] Among the oldest winter counts on record was one by a Lakota, Baptise Good, which its mixed-blood "author" began with the year 1779. Like most winter counts, it made a point of commemorating the year 1833 by showing a slew of falling stars to represent the meteor shower which astonished Indians everywhere that winter.

Instead of attempting a complete "historical" record, these visualizations summarized, in Vine Deloria, Jr.'s phrase, "the psychic life of the community."[126] Yet, while Deloria may be correct that they ignore a people's "continuous subject matter," they can document personal chronologies, as Marion Smith learned by extracting census data from a Mandan example. "History to the Mandan," she concluded, "seems to be composed in large part of a set of interlocking life histories remembered in terms of a relatively few criteria such as birth, initiations, war deeds, supernatural displays, place in council, chieftainship and death."[127] For evaluating the candidacy of any event for representation, Smith believed the Mandan pictorialist, not unlike Western historians, looked to its impact upon a notable individual. Thus the Custer wipeout was illustrated as "Long-hair was killed by the Sioux."

Jogging the memory with such aids was not limited to the Plains. Among the Pimas of Arizona are found two-foot-long, notched "calendar sticks," which Frank Russell prefers to characterize as "annals," since their "Chronologic sequence is subordinated to narrative."[128] One stick harkens

---

[125] Helen H. Blish, "Dakota Histories and Historical Art," in *A Pictographic History of the Oglala Sioux* (paintings by Amos Bad Heart Bull) (Lincoln, Neb., 1967), 23.

[126] Deloria, *God Is Red,* 112.

[127] Marion Smith, "Mandan History as Reflected in Butterfly's Winter Count," *Ethnohistory* 7 (1960), 202.

[128] Frank Russell, "Pima Annals," *American Anthropologist* 5 (1903), 76.

back to 1833; another, still owned by the Covered Wells village, opens with the 1841 killing of three Papagos by Mexicans, includes marks standing for the reprisals and counter-raids, and continues with yearly symbols (some blank to indicate "nothing unusual"), abruptly ending in 1936, the year "the reservation was divided into eleven districts and those districts fenced."[129]

Among the Iroquois peoples oratorical aids appear to have achieved a greater complexity. Like the Pimas, they had sticks, or "condolence canes," made of walnut, carved with pictographs and fitted with tiny birchwood pegs, which were referenced to the roll call of chiefs who had founded the Confederacy of the Five Nations. During elaborate installation rituals for new leaders, who bore the names of the original chiefs, these canes assisted the oral recollections of their names, titles, and clan affiliations. Actually the canes represented two forms of mnemonic systems: the pictographs showing such items as a claw hammer or a log house were, according to William Fenton, "not the clues to titles but rather reflect the interpretations current among nineteenth-century Iroquois ritual leaders"; the arrangement of pegs, however, was an older device, probably dating back to the origin of the Confederacy.[130]

But if such carved canes assisted in calling up critical specifics of Iroquois oratory, an even more potent and sacred mnemonic aid of the Iroquois stood for deeper themes and meanings in their public discourse. That is the contention, at least, of Iroquois scholar and linguist Michael Foster, based upon his study of *wampum,* the record-keeping devices which joined with the canes in abetting collective memory. Among the Iroquois, these straps and strings of shell beads, popularly known as "*wampum* belts,*"* became material embodiments of "pledges or records of matters of national or international importance," in the words of Arthur C. Parker, an Iroquois himself and a trained anthropologist.

Strung on deer sinew, the tubular beads were both white, sliced from the central spine of a whelk shell, and purple, cut from hearts of quahog shells. At the highest diplomatic level, presentation of these belts formalized the allegiance of subsidiary tribes to the Iroquois Confederacy, while for everyday formalities "they regard no message or invitation, be it of what consequence it will, unless attended or con-

---

[129] Papago Tribe, *The Papago Reservation and the Papago People* (n.d.).

[130] William N. Fenton, "Field Work, Museum Studies, and Ethnohistorical Research," *Ethnohistory* 13 (1–2) (1966), 81.

firmed by belts or wampum, which they look upon as we our letters, or rather bonds."[131]

The belts also assisted historical recollection: "The interpretation of these several belts and strings brought out," wrote Lewis Henry Morgan, "in the address of the wise-man, a connected account of the occurrences at the formation of the confederacy. The tradition was repeated in full, and fortified in its essential parts by reference to the record contained in these belts."[132] Indeed, they were often helpless without this visual shorthand; during a treaty proceeding some Indians at Carlisle, Pennsylvania, had to reschedule their deliberations because someone "have mislaid some Strings, which has put their speeches into Disorder; these they will rectify, and speak to you in the Afternoon."[133]

But Michael Foster's interpretation of wampum's meanings probes deeper. While most non-Indian explanations have the belts functioning "retrospectively," as a way to call up past events, his Iroquois consultants suggested that they operated more "prospectively," as a means for organizing present, and even future, events. In contrast (or in cooperation) with the pictographs carved onto Condolence Canes which helped to order Iroquois speech-events, the simple metaphoric designs – the colored bands and linked stick figures – on the beaded belts served as a sort of conceptual code which enabled their users to evaluate the current status and desired direction of alliances between Indians and Indians or Indians and Euro-Americans.[134]

Other items of Indian manufacture appear to have actually aided and abetted a sort of resistance to history. Forms of ceremonial regalia, magical wearing apparel, and special architectural motifs were crucial to the "new" Indian religious movements that sought to combat or offset the imposition of Euro-American lifeways. Best known are the muslin and hide shirts and dresses of the Plains Indian Ghost Dance. The supernatural power of the crows, stars, dragonflies, and cedar trees emblazoned on them were intended to restore the old Indian cosmos which was under grave attack. In the beliefs of more militant Nativists, the garments were believed to deter bullets.[135]

Most revitalization movements featured distinctive apparel, from the

[131] Sir William Johnson in 1753, quoted in Lewis Henry Morgan, *League of the Ho-dé-no-sau-nee, or Iroquois* (Rochester, N.Y., 1851), 121.

[132] Ibid., 125.

[133] B. Sheehan, "Paradise and the Noble Savage," *William and Mary Quarterly* 26 (1969), 351.

[134] Michael K. Foster, "Another Look at the Function of Wampum in Iroquois-White Councils," in *The History and Culture of Iroquois Diplomacy,* ed. Francis Jennings (Syracuse, N.Y., 1985).

[135] *I Wear the Morning Star,* exhibition catalog (Minneapolis, 1976).

uniform-cut frock coats of the Faw Faw Movement among the Otos,[136] to the Bole Maru banners, dresses, and head dresses inspired by the California Pomo prophetess Essie Parrish.[137] In addition, the California Ghost Dance spawned new architectural forms, such as the voluminous earthlodges dreamt of by the Wintu prophet Norelputus,[138] which were eclipsed by the redwood-shingled ceremonial roundhouses that are still an icon of Native California traditionalism today.

Certain high-profile forms of material culture played a singular role in Indian history, enshrouded with much the same sort of near-sacred status accorded a European royal scepter or the original parchment of the Declaration of Independence preserved in Washington. Displayed or used on formal occasions, these "documents" – whether notable or even individually named wampum belts, collective medicine bundles, key clan possessions, or famous clan houses – were often personified. It is commonly this category of unique, exemplary items which star in today's controversies over the repatriation of museum materials.

How modern Indians self-consciously represent the past is also part of the connective tissue between material culture and history. Many twentieth-century Indian artists have been commissioned to depict historical events from before the advent of photography – new imagings of the Trail of Tears, the Navajo Long Walk, even the Gallup Intertribal Ceremonial. Usually a benign portrayer of his people's katcina dances, when the dean of Hopi painters, Fred Kabotie, was commissioned for a Hopi entry during America's bicentennial, he changed his tune. In Kabotie's realistic depiction of his people's war of independence, the Pueblo Revolt of 1680, a Catholic priest is shown hanging from the Oraibi church rafters, while on the roof Hopis tear apart its cross prior to putting the building to the torch.

As showcasers of Indian material culture, constantly revising their explanatory contexts, museums are also responsive to heated debates over historical and cultural representation. At a tribal museum like the *Ned Hatathli Cultural Center Museum* at Navajo Community College in Tsaile, Arizona, the Native emphasis on emergence out of underworlds by mythic supernaturals is given equal play alongside the non-Navajo archaeological

---

[136] David Wooley and William Waters, "Waw-No-She's Dance," *American Indian Art Magazine* 14(1) (1988).

[137] Clement W. Meighan and Francis A. Riddell, *The Maru Cult of the Pomo Indians: A California Ghost Dance Survival,* Museum Paper no. 23 (Los Angeles, 1972).

[138] Cora Du Bois, *The 1870 Ghost Dance,* University of California Publications, Anthropological Records 3(1) (1939).

story, thereby "exhibiting the debate." In Connecticut, the Institute of American Indian Studies premised its summer 1990 exhibition, "As We Tell Our Stories: Living Traditions and the Algonkian Peoples of Indian New England," on the theme of cultural continuity. Its message that "we are still here" explicitly countered the older museum habit of exhibiting artifacts from Indians "who were here."

Revisionist approaches to Indian history have reached the uppermost echelons of American popular culture. The prevailing mandate of the Smithsonian Institution's new National Museum of the American Indian, according to Director W. Richard West, Jr., is "to describe a non-European view of the world" by employing "the first person voice of the Indian peoples to communicate it."[139] Its flagship exhibit, the *Pathways of Tradition* show at New York City's U.S. Custom House, conspicuously omitted dates in its labels. "When you start pegging dates to items in the collection," explained Director West, "it connects to a linear timeline. We want to get away from that perspective."[140] The show's curator, Rick Hill, added, "What we are looking at in this show is not art as an evolutionary process but how ideas and beliefs remain strong through time."[141]

INDIAN HISTORY WRITTEN BY INDIANS

Much as Indian storytellers steered their narratives between the constraints of inherited genres and historical contingency, so two centuries of writing by Indian authors have produced admixtures of personal testimony, oral history, and angry polemic. Mission-educated converts were the first Indian writers, ranging from the "father of modern Native American literature," Samson Occom, a Mohegan from New England who became a well-known Presbyterian missionary, to Pablo Tac, a Luiseno convert to Catholicism from southern California, who wrote a youthful autobiographical memoir.

Sometimes their early writings were shaded with the same irony as oral narratives. The Pequot Indian Methodist minister William Apes conducted historical research, but interlarded his memoirs cum chronicles with bitter humor. "I could not find [the word "Indian"] in the Bible," Apes wrote, "and therefore concluded that it was a word imported for the

---

[139] Quoted in the *Washington Post*, November 23, 1992.
[140] Quoted in the *Wall Street Journal*, November 17, 1992.
[141] Quoted in the *New York Times*, November 15, 1992.

special purpose of degrading us. At other times, I thought it was derived from the term *in-gen-uity*."[142]

Other early Indian writers were never able to dovetail the different canons of oral tradition and written history. In 1852 a mixed-blood Chippewa (Ojibwa) legislator from Minnesota named William W. Warren converted his people's narratives into a "tribal history." His first language being his mother's Ojibwa, Warren sat rapt at the feet of elderly storytellers. But his first book opened with an apology for the fact that "Through the somewhat uncertain manner in which the Indians count time" the two people's "dates" might differ. Warren forced his blend of historical and cultural information into a linear, European model of chronological development.[143]

A similar ambivalence over the compatibility of Indian and European historical discourses weakened the writings of Warren's fellow Ojibwa nonfiction authors in Canada, George Copway and Peter Jones, as well as those of the Tuscarora, David Cusick. In his "history," Copway broached the idea of a single combined Indian nation, but his entrapment between the Euro-Canadian and Indian worlds, according to fellow Chippewa author Gerald Vizenor, estranged him: "he could only remember in printed words at a great distance from the oral tradition. Those who remained at the treeline noticed his transformation from totem to titles since his conversion. At the end of all his speeches, letters, and political ideas, his books, he must have been alone."[144] And while Peter Jones castigated Euro-Canadian culture for the evils besetting his people, he skimpily profiled Ojibwa culture and wound up, again in Vizenor's words, "separated from traditional cultures in his narrative posture" and seldom removing "the black robe of religious conversion from his prose."[145]

One little-known Indian scribe who creatively blended two cultural modes of historical narration was an Oglala Sioux named George Sword from Pine Ridge. His career covered being a horse-riding warrior against enemy peoples in his youth to becoming an elderly Episcopal deacon and tribal judge. While his autobiographical narrative opened with a genealogy and listing of personal war deeds, it was couched in the third person so as to declare its public, more generally historical function, according to

[142] William Apess, *On Our Own Ground: The Complete Writings of William Apess, a Pequot,* edited and with an introduction by Barry O'Connell (Amherst, Mass., 1992), li.

[143] William W. Warren, *History of the Ojibways,* Collections of the Minnesota Historical Society, vol. 5 (Minneapolis–St. Paul, 1885), 26.

[144] Gerald Vizenor, "Three Anishinaabeg Writers," in *The People Called Chippewa: Narrative Stories* (Minneapolis, 1984), 63.

[145] Ibid., 72.

scholar Raymond J. DeMallie. Yet the text switched into the first person wherever the responsibility for historical veracity was placed upon quoted eyewitnesses or historical chiefs. Much like a typical Plains Indian winter count, "Clearly, the important category for Sword's history is the event," says DeMallie, whether they were personal war deeds or collective experiences. Moreover, according to DeMallie, "The narrative is told as a series of episodes without drawing connections between them, suggesting the factors that underlay them, or any making moral judgement about them. Causality is generally implied by an indefinite third-person form: 'they decided,' 'it will happen.' "[146]

On the other hand, Cherokee doctor and chronicler Emmett Starr skirted the problem of reconciling Indian and non-Indian historical approaches by bequeathing literate Cherokees his rich compilations of genealogies, laws, and property transfers. This "legislative history" served the Cherokee fight against assimilationists and the "two gun [non-Indian] historians" sympathetic to them.[147] By Starr's day, Cherokee literacy was a good three-generations old, thanks to the establishment in 1828 of the *Cherokee Phoenix,* a weekly newspaper that published in the Cherokee syllabary and launched the era of Indian journalism.

But the Cherokees were not the only Native nation to put their own language into a unique script, to adapt print journalism to their needs, and to try to tell their history their own way. Native peoples as diverse as the Micmacs of Newfoundland, the Yaquis of the Southwest, and the Aleuts of Alaska invented their own writing systems. Between 1826 and 1924, Indian communities founded at least fifty newspapers, while today they number in the hundreds. And the American Indian autobiography, perhaps their earliest literary expression, continued to evolve.

After the personalized renditions of ethnic history emerging from early-nineteenth-century Indian writings, journalists and friends began eliciting autobiographies from Indians. But even when notables like Black Hawk (1882), Geronimo (1906), Plenty Coups (1962), or even Charles Eastman (1902) described their lives, they followed no Great Man theory of history. Quite the contrary, their common inclination was to underscore how their careers epitomized their peoples' ideals. "The 'wild' Indian," writes the

---

[146] Raymond J. DeMallie, " 'These Have No Ears': Narrative and the Historical Method," typescript of shortened version of paper delivered at the 1992 annual meeting of the American Society for Ethnohistory, Salt Lake City, Utah, November 10–11.

[147] Rennard Strickland and Jack Gregory, "Emmett Starr, Cherokee, 1870–1930," in *American Indian Intellectuals,* ed. Margot Liberty (St. Paul, Minn., 1978), 108.

Osage Indian scholar Carter Revard of these autobiographies, with tongue in cheek at the adjective, "was tied to land, to people, to origins and way of life, by every kind of human ordering we can imagine." "History," "Myth," and "Identity" were not "three separate matters, here, but three aspects of one identity."[148]

As if in resistance to such "structured" self-representations, when anthropologists of the culture-and-personality school began to elicit more exacting life-histories of representative Indians, such as the Winnebago Crashing Thunder (1926), the Chiricahua Apache "Chris" (1969), the Hopi Don Talayesva (1942), and the Navajo Left Handed (1938), these protagonists were encouraged to divulge uncensored transcripts of their everyday lives. Since high-visibility "history" rarely intervened upon their careers, the relative unrepresentativeness of their experiences could be compared against the collective ethnographic profiles of their societies. Discrepancies might provide new insights into the leeway individuals enjoyed, and reveal how their singular identities emerged from negotiations between group norms, personal predilections, and chance events.

Beginning in the 1960s, a new form of Indian-authored history emerged. Produced by tribes or Indian organizations, some were collections of transcribed oral histories, others were written by appointed tribal representatives. Criticized for lacking conventional academic accountability, they were nonetheless a far cry from the antiquated histories of Native groups acidly critiqued by anthropologist James Clifton. Issuing from non-Indian, old-fashioned academic historians, the scholarly sins of that "obsolete paradigm," according to Clifton, included unfamiliarity with Native languages, no acknowledgement of specific Indians as historical actors, perpetuating stereotypical terminology and recycling trite clichés, overreliance on dated, secondary sources, and a failure to extract from primary documents "Native American views, tactics, sentiments, and strategies in dealing with Americans."[149] For the subsequent generation of non-Indian academic historians, however, the resurgence in the 1960s of higher ethnohistorical standards at least placed Indian-centered histories, if not yet Native philosophies of history, at center stage.

When Indians began relating their own histories in their own way,

---

[148] Carter Revard, "History, Myth, and Identity among Osages and Other Peoples," *Denver Quarterly* 14(4) (winter 1980), 97.

[149] James A. Clifton, "The Tribal History – An Obsolete Paradigm," *American Indian Culture and Research Journal* 3(4) (1979), 90.

sometimes they benefited from outside support, as when tobacco heiress and philanthropist Doris Duke earmarked five million dollars for gathering American Indian oral history. Between 1967 and 1972, hundreds of taped conversations with Indian elders were cataloged in seven regional centers across the United States. Not unlike the Works Progress Administration oral histories amassed during the 1930s under federal government auspices, the sessions followed loose checklists, and once a tribal elder talked there was meager follow-up questioning. The Duke Oral History Project yielded only two anthologies, one from the Great Lakes/Plains, *To Be An Indian: An Oral History* (1971), and another from the Pueblo of Zuni, *The Zuni: Self Portrayals* (1972), which provided an interesting glimpse at how one Indian people's history still charted its unique path between cosmological mythology and chronological history.

At the same time, tribally produced, sometimes bilingual works such as *The Way It Was, Inaku Iwacha: Yakima Legends* (1974), edited by Virginia Beavert; *Noon Nee-Me-Poo (We, the Nez Perces): Culture and History of the Nez Perces* (1973), edited by Allen P. Slickpoo, Sr.; and, among the numerous tribally published Navajo histories, *Dinetah: Navajo History, II* (1983), edited by Robert A. Roessel, Jr., resurrected forgotten regional events and neglected local heroes and stressed the persistence of tribal institutions.

Meanwhile individual Indian historians weighed in with nonfiction chronicles that ranged from the highly secular and impersonal to the intensely spiritual, compensatory, and polemical. Sometimes the Native authors seemed under tight monitoring by their ethnic constituency, as with Byron Nelson's account of Hupa political and economic interactions with the Euro-American invaders of northwestern California.[150] Nelson's conspicuous avoidance of such sensitive topics as worldview and ceremonial life left some readers perplexed about what beat at the heart of the Hupa cultural continuity he extolled. At the other end of the spectrum were Basil Johnston's oral history retellings of Ojibwa traditional histories, which almost flaunted their absence of genre distinctions or chronological benchmarks.[151] Readers had to take at face value well-told renditions whose subject matter spanned the exploits of *Nanabo'zho,* the ahistorical trickster, to reminiscences of living members from Johnston's southern Ontario reserve.

Directly confronting the dissonance between Indian and European-style historical approaches, a bold Canadian Indian scholar, the Huron

[150] Byron Nelson, Jr., *Our Home Forever: A Hupa Tribal History* (Hoopa, Calif., 1978).
[151] Basil Johnston, *Ojibway Heritage* (New York, 1976) and *Moose Meat and Wild Rice* (Toronto, 1978).

(Wendat) Georges E. Sioui, espoused an "autohistory" to tackle "the study of correspondences between Amerindian and non-Amerindian sources."[152] As polemic his Indianized history traced the influence of Native American values in the culture at large and argued for replacing the evolutionary bias, which Sioui perceived as the flawed foundation of Western historiography, with the Indian's devotion to the "sacred circle of life" and its stress on the mutual interdependence of living things. As exemplar, his study rehabilitated the writings of Baron de Lahontan, a neglected seventeenth-century European eyewitness to the positive philosophical and religious values of Huron life, and surveyed the ecological and territorial history of his own Huron people so as to "safeguard the right of an Amerindian group to territories denied it by traditional non-Amerindian history."[153]

The literalist claims often underlying the freeform assemblage of legends, reminiscences, myths, and editorializing found in many collectively and singly authored histories of Native groups were defended by Jemez Pueblo historian Joe Sando. If Western history couldn't bring mythic narrative and Indian ideas of primordial creation in situ into its paradigms, Sando suggested that it might at least grant them equal time or parallel plausibility:

> If we accept Native North American oral history . . . then we can start with the ancient people who have been in North America for many thousands of years and still allow for European and Mediterranean colonists to strengthen or boost the developing culture. This appears to be what the indigenous people have been saying in their oral history. But later Europeans with their "proof positive" and "show me" attitudes have prevailed, and remain largely unwilling to consider, much less to confirm, native creation accounts.[154]

This position was not without its critics, such as Wilcomb E. Washburn, who was dissatisfied with the Nez Percé tribal history's vague use of the editorial "we" instead of clear authorship, its disregard for footnotes and other canons of scholarly accountability, its thin-skinned rejection of received terms such as "skirmish," and its reluctance to discuss religious factionalism.[155] From the Indian perspective, however, the challenge of

---

[152] Georges E. Sioui, *For an Amerindian Autohistory: An Essay on the Foundations of a Social Ethic* (Montreal, 1992).
[153] Ibid., 82.
[154] Joe S. Sando, *Nee Hemish: A History of Jemez Pueblo* (Albuquerque, N.M., 1982), 2.
[155] Wilcomb E. Washburn, Review of *Noon Ne-Me-Poo (We, the Nez Percés): Culture and History of the Nez Percés* (1973), in *Idaho Yesterdays: The Quarterly Journal of the Idaho Historical Society* 18(2) (summer 1974).

these new publications was not to play by old rules, but to forge new literary genres altogether. Contrary to Washburn, Lévi-Strauss became quite enthused by these written "continuation[s] of mythology." After reading some Northwest Coast examples he discovered "that the opposition . . . between mythology and history . . . is not at all a clear-cut one, and that there is an intermediary level."[156] By close study of these Indian-authored works, Lévi-Strauss concluded, "the gap which exists in our mind to some extent between mythology and history can probably be breached by studying histories which are conceived as not at all separated from but as a continuation of mythology."[157]

The two positions also crossed swords in Gail Landsman and Sara Ciborski's study of the controversy that erupted in northern New York State in 1987 when state educators commissioned a new resource guide for Indians in the schools. According to them, "the restless, impermanent quality of the foundation of [Iroquois] historical discourse" collided with an "objectivist history" that traded in " 'fixed rules and eternal verities,' " leaving no room for "the concept of negotiated representations of history."[158]

As fiction by American Indians also became popular in the 1970s, incorporating Native historicities appeared high on their list of artistic goals. The part-Flathead author D'Arcy McNickle was among the first to tackle the weight of the past upon the Indian future. In *Wind from an Enemy Sky* (1978), he summed up a lifetime's experience in government work, university teaching, and popular writing on Indian Affairs. His tale of a dam threatening a northwestern river brought the Indian mythological sense — embodied in a sacred medicine bundle appropriated by a New York museum — into direct conflict with the Euro-Americans' determination that nothing can stave the rush of progress. McNickle saw only cultural conquest and tragedy ahead for the values that underlie the traditional Indian sense of history.

On the other hand, Leslie Silko's *Ceremony* (1977), while a gritty depiction of dysfunctional life along Navajoland's border towns, underscored the adaptive ability of Indian cosmological beliefs. Her protagonist, a deeply disturbed World War II veteran, finds psychological recovery through the updated myths and revitalized "ceremonies" of a medicine

---

[156] Lévi-Strauss, *Myth and Meaning*, 40.
[157] Ibid., 43.
[158] Gail Landsman and Sara Ciborski, "Representation and Politics: Contesting Histories of the Iroquois," *Cultural Anthropology* 7 (1992), 443.

man whose fixed ethnic identity is less important than his skill at responding to breaking events.

Other prominent Indian writers have produced historical fiction, with James Welch, in *Fools Crow* (1986), successfully dramatizing late-nineteenth-century Blackfeet history through a conventional plot structure but methodically piling up details and motivations no outsider could intuit. From the northeastern plains, Louise Erdrich produced a three-novel epic of North Dakota Indian history[159] which fleshed out a multigenerational kinship chart whose blended racial identities yielded in the nineteenth century a brand new tribe, the Turtle Mountain Chippewas, a new language, *Michif,* and one might argue, new cultural and emotional structures which called for Erdrich's more daring literary risks with narrative and dialect in order to bring them to life. But Indian writers can get into hot water for playing too innovatively with their peoples' traditions. The experimental novel *Seven Arrows* by a self-identified Cheyenne author[160] drew criticism for desecrating Cheyenne tradition. At the same time, Vine Deloria, Jr., championed the book, "because an Indian dared to break out of the genre in which people had put Indian literature, and just say, 'I'm going to write a story that destroys chronological time, that intersperses humans and animals, that violates the standards of white society for writing about Indians.'"[161] If anyone picked up Deloria's gauntlet, it would seem to be the prolific Chippewa writer Gerald Vizenor. Insofar as historical writing is concerned, his career has run the gamut from an Emmet Starr–like responsibility for compiling tribal documents (1964) to his particular brand of Indian journalism which blends "instant history" (1984) with ironic short fiction that satirically targets all who might appropriate Indian narrative genres.

Perhaps the most imaginative Indian harmonizing of the contrasting discourses of Indian and Euro-American history is N. Scott Momaday's *The Way to Rainy Mountain* (1969). In a single, disarmingly slight prose collage, this Kiowa Indian poet self-consciously accepted the challenge of orchestrating the seemingly incompatible genres of personal autobiography, objective history, and ethnic tradition. When Momaday won the

---

[159] Louise Erdrich, *Love Medicine* (New York, 1984), *Beet Queen* (New York, 1986), *Tracks* (New York, 1988).

[160] Hyemeyohsts Storm, *Seven Arrows* (New York, 1981).

[161] Steve Crum, "A Conversation with Vine Deloria," in *Suntracks: An American Indian Literary Magazine,* no. 4 (Tucson, Ariz., 1978), 87.

Pulitzer Prize for *House Made of Dawn* (1968) in 1969, he had already written an earlier manuscript entitled *The Journey of Tai-Me* which experimented with a multivocal approach to the story of Kiowa ethnogenesis. Blending different typographies, line drawings (by his father Al Momaday), and rapid cutting between multiple verbal styles which differentiated his mythic, historical, tribal, and personal voices, Momaday swung freely back and forth in time to make his separated paragraphs read like an epic. Published under the title of *The Way to Rainy Mountain,* the book managed to depict Kiowa culture-history as both contingent and predestined; it blazed a trail for one kind of modern Indian history which might realize the past-in-the present on paper, but in the old Indian way.

This essay has joined with the distinguished historian H. Stuart Hughes's "vision of history" which stresses "the central importance of symbols in establishing common values of a given culture . . . The symbol conveys the implicit principles by which the society lives, the shared understanding of assumptions which require no formal proof."[162] In any search for Native people's historical consciousness we must realize that it has almost certainly undergone transformations, the "plasticity" of which Hughes also describes in his piece.

But we do recognize recurrent imperatives. The different Indian senses of the past are rarely random strings of unrelated, existential happenings. Usually they are structured in ways that highlight selected cultural meanings and preferable social processes, representing them through the medium of well-worn symbols. In these "histories," moreover, high value is placed upon the maintenance of Indian conceptual autonomy over time, in as consistent and reassuring a fashion as possible. Sometimes this requires tinkering with the "facts," and calls for retroactive enhancement in order for that history to make sense in Indian terms and to pass on essential meanings distilled from collective experience. Sometimes it swings between neighborhood gossip and lofty visions in order to personalize the past, to bring it in tune with an inherited worldview, to warn about moral consequences so as to have maximum impact on the "history of the future." While these and more freedoms to "make history" are commonly found in Indian traditions they do not necessarily mean that the academic sense of historical accuracy is jettisoned in the process. Indians have coexisted in many conceptual domains; their historical traditions have seen few incompatibilities between the world of facts and that of dreams.

---

[162] H. Stuart Hughes, *History as Art and as Science: Twin Vistas on the Past* (Chicago, 1975), 80.

Generally what remains of utmost importance to Indian historians has been psychological persistence, social congruence, spiritual independence, and perpetuation of core values – in short, the continuing Native American acculturation of time and space. For outsiders who complain this is not playing fair, Indians might well ask to be shown the cultural historicity – often bearing catch phrases such as "force majeure," "Third Reich," "divine right of kings," "manifest destiny," "Frontier Thesis," the Monroe Doctrine, or a fledgling president's first "Hundred Days" – which is not underwritten by similar vested interests. One might even argue that the didacticism of Indian narratives and histories is only more transparent and straightforward.

Twice in this essay the verb "bequeathed" has been used to characterize how Indian historians often consider their calling. Perhaps the analogy to material inheritance has heuristic value in communicating the senses of property and responsibility that are often found in Indian notions of history. Conceiving of the past as a collective dowry, which subsequent generations must maintain in high repair, as a sort of cultural capital from which they can draw ideological and spiritual interest, helps us understand why Indian history must stay receptive to synthesis, accretion, and refurbishment.

Without the opportunity for Indian peoples to tell their historical experiences in their many different ways, and without the burden upon non-Indian American historians to somehow weave Native historicities into the bedrock of their accounts, the fullness of the American experience will remain unwitnessed and alternative visions for its future unrevealed.

BIBLIOGRAPHIC ESSAY

To date there are no book-length surveys of the diversity of historical consciousnesses among Native North American peoples. One collection of essays on writing Indian history (*The American Indian and the Problem of History,* Oxford, 1987), which Calvin Martin edited to forefront revisionist or experimental approaches from a cross section of scholars dealing with Indian-Euro-American relations, hints more strongly than most collections of Indian historical essays at the differences between Indian and non-Indian ways of relating and using the past.

But Martin's preoccupation with exposing metaphysical and ethical gaps in prevailing concepts of Indian history ignores the fact that, as Alfonso Ortiz reminds us in a pioneering essay on the topic, "There is simply not *the* Indian viewpoint in the writing of history. Each tribe, band, community has its own sovereign history, and these histories do not intersect except in the case of contiguous or neighboring peoples" ("Some Concerns Central to the Writing of 'Indian' History," *The Indian Historian* 10 [1], 1977, 17).

The general neglect of such diversity, even of Indian historicity in general, was underscored by Mildred Mott Wedel and Raymond J. DeMallie when they complained of a 1975 ethnohistory of the Lower Brule Sioux, "The main portion of the book deals entirely with white-oriented history of the reservation, without considering any of the cultural dynamics that, from the Indian point of view, make up the real story of the reservation experience" ("The Ethnohistorical Approach" in *Anthropology of the Great Plains,* ed. W. Raymond Wood and Margot Liberty [Lincoln, Nebr., 1980], 119). Another far-seeing historian who has called for the incorporation of "native agency" into reconstructions of Indian-Euro-American relations is Frederick E. Hoxie ("The Problem of Indian History," *Social Science Journal* 25 [4], 1988).

In a useful collection of mini-essays by Indian and non-Indian historians, "Papers on Indian Historiography" (*Meeting Ground: Center for the History of the American Indian* 2 [1], Chicago, 1975), the Native scholar David Beaulieu offers an alternative way of considering this multiplicity of ways in which Native peoples account for the past: "The pluralistic model, however, is a decidedly European one, which could be described as a tree with many different branches, the idea of variations on a common theme. . . . There is, however, at least one other model, a model which is decidedly Native American, which can be described, as Ruth Roessel [a Navajo historian] does, as a forest of many different and varied trees. This model necessarily recognizes the legitimacy of independent tribal historiographies at the same time as it recognizes the Euro-American tree with all its branches" (17).

One admirable attempt to outline traditional Indian modes of conveying past events is Mary Jane Schneider's chapter "Indian History: Concepts and Methods" (in *North Dakota Indians: An Introduction,* Dubuque, Iowa, 1986). Another is found in Douglas R. Parks's introductory chapter to his *Traditional Narratives of the Arikara Indians: Stories of Alfred Morsette: English Translations* (Studies in the Anthropology of North American Indians, vol. 3, Lincoln, Nebr., 1991).

A scholar who has continually emphasized the need for an approach he calls American Indian "ethno-ethnohistory," or "anthropological ethnohistory," which explores how Indian peoples structure their pasts, is Raymond D. Fogelson. He coined the term in his "On the Varieties of Indian History: Sequoyah and Traveller Bird" (*Journal of Ethnic Studies* 2, 1974), and then applied it in his exploration of the notion that the Bering Strait migration might have gone the other way ("A Final Look and Glance at the Bearing of Bering Straits on Native American History," in *The Impact of Indian History on the Teaching of United States History* (Occasional Paper in Curriculum Series, D'Arcy McNickle Center for the History of the American Indian, Newberry Library, Chicago, 1986). This heretical idea of some Indian origins to Old World cultures is echoed by Lakota author Vine Deloria, Jr., in his "Afterword" to *America in 1492: The World of the Indian Peoples before the Arrival of Columbus,* ed. Alvin M. Josephy, Jr. (New York, 1992).

A few scholars, mostly anthropologists, have devoted long-term fieldwork to historical subjects from the Native point of view. Working in the Plains, Loretta Fowler derived a fresh understanding of Arapaho cultural persistence by examining their account of key tribal institutions (*Arapahoe Politics, 1851–1978: Symbols in Crises of Authority,* Lincoln, Nebr., 1982), while among the Gros Ventres she provided a completely alternative understanding of the time depth of social and symbolic activities (*Shared Symbols, Contested Meanings: Gros Ventre Culture and History, 1778–1984,* Ithaca, N.Y., 1987). One monumental treatment of a single tribe's epic history from the unique perspective of historian, Christian priest, and Cheyenne Sun Dance priest is Peter J. Powell's two pairs of two-volume histories, *Sweet Medicine: The Continuing Role of the Sacred Arrows, the Sun Dance, and the Sacred Buffalo Hat in Northern Cheyenne History* (Norman, Okla., 1969) and *People of the Sacred Mountain: A History of the Northern Cheyenne Chiefs and Warrior Societies, 1830–1879* (San Francisco, 1981).

Working in the Southwest, Peter Whiteley combined the techniques of meticulous ethnohistorical research with regard for Native cultural processes and historical dynamics in his study of the early twentieth-century founding of the Hopi village of Bacavi (*Deliberate Acts: Changing Hopi Culture through the Oraibi Split* [Tucson, Ariz., 1988]). But folk history can reach deeper into the past. Fifty-nine years ago two Pima Indians gave archaeologist Julian Hayden a creation narrative which linked their history to prehistoric Hohokam times, which editor Donald Bahr then supplemented with other Pima and Papago versions (*The Short, Swift Time of Gods on Earth,* Berkeley, Calif., 1994).

Since historical accounts were often elicited from Indians as part of their people's folklore, scholars from that discipline have been forerunners in studying the Native past from the Indian perspective. Early examples dealt with ethnic migrations, such as Albert S. Gatschet's *A Migration Legend of the Creek Indians with a Linguistic, Historic and Ethnographic Introduction* (Philadelphia, 1884). Examining blends of Native and European tradition is Jarold Ramsay, whose essays on "retroactive prophecy" and biblical influences on Indian mythology from the western United States are included in his *Reading the Fire: Essays in the Traditional Indian Literatures of the Far West* (Lincoln, Nebr., 1983). A marvelous project exhuming both the historical changes encased in eastern Indian folklore and its role in ethnic persistence is William S. Simmons's *Spirit of the New England Tribes: Indian History and Folklore, 1620–1984* (Hanover, N.H., 1986).

Other works that have sieved myths, folktales, and legends for alternative sources of historical interpretation include David M. Pendergast and Clement W. Meighan's "Folk Traditions as Historical Fact: A Paiute Example" (*Journal of American Folklore* 72, 1959); Frederica de Laguna's "Geological Confirmation of Native Traditions, Yakutat, Alaska" (*American Antiquity* 23, 1958); William C. Sturtevant's "Chakaika and the 'Spanish Indians' " (*Tequesta* n. 13, 1953); Richard A. Gould's "Indian and White Versions of 'The Burnt Ranch Massacre' " (*Journal of the Folklore Institute* 3, 1966); Beatrice A. Bigony's "Folk Literature as an Ethnohistorical Device: The Interrelationships between Winnebago Folk Tales and Wisconsin Habitat" (*Ethnohistory* 29 [3], 1982); and Douglas R. Parks's "An Historical Character Mythologized: The Scalped Man in Pawnee and Arikara Mythology" (in *Plains Indian Studies,* ed. Douglas H. Ubelaker and Herman J. Viola [Washington, D.C., 1982]).

Examining American Indian folklore for its preservation of what might be called "attitudinal history" and subversive survival strategies are Richard M. Dorson ("Ethnohistory and Ethnic Folklore," *Ethnohistory* 8 [1], 1961); Kenneth M. Morrison ("Towards a History of Intimate Encounters: Algonkian Folklore, Jesuit Missionaries, and Kiwakwe, The Cannibal Giant," *American Indian Culture and Research Journal* 3 [4], 1979); and Madronna Holden ("Making All the Crooked Ways Straight: The Satirical Portrait of Whites in Coast Salish Folklore," *Journal of American Folklore* 89, 1976).

With their discipline's bent for peeling back ideological strata, it is not surprising that historians of religion have weighed in with studies of Native pasts embedded in Indian rituals. While Karl W. Luckert found evidence of older Navajo culture in their mythology and ceremonial chants

(*The Navajo Hunter Tradition,* Tucson, Ariz., 1975), Armin W. Geertz looked at prophecy's evolving role in contemporary Hopi society (*The Invention of Prophecy: Continuity and Meaning in Hopi Indian Religion* [Berkeley, Calif., 1994]).

Almost none of the works mentioned so far would exist without American Indian translators, mediators, and co-authors, whose credit and identities have too long been neglected. New biographical profiles of Native scholars who collaborated on various projects related to Indian history include *American Indian Intellectuals,* ed. Margot Liberty (St. Paul, Minn., 1978), *Being and Becoming Indian: Biographical Studies of North American Frontiers,* ed. James A. Clifton (Chicago, 1989), and *Between Indian and White Worlds: The Culture Broker,* ed. Margaret Connell Szasz (Norman, Okla., 1994).

When Indians began writing down their history, starting in the eighteenth century, they did so in their own way, sometimes in their own syllabaries. For information on indigenous alphabets see Willard Walker ("Native American Writing Systems," in Charles A. Ferguson and Shirley Brice Heath, eds., *Language in the USA* [Cambridge, 1981]). Some historical material appeared in Indian-authored newspapers and periodicals; for useful summaries of the long tradition of Indian journalism see James and Sharon Murphy's *Let My People Know* (Norman, Okla., 1981); James P. Danky and Maureen E. Hady's *Native American Periodicals and Newspapers 1828–1982: Bibliography, Publishing Record, and Holdings* (Westport, Conn., 1984); and Daniel F. Littlefield, Jr., and James W. Pairns's *American Indian and Alaska Newspapers and Periodicals, 1826–1924* (Westport, Conn., 1984).

Another useful source of historical points of view has been the genre of American Indian autobiography. For the fullest listing of these life-history materials see H. David Brumble III, *An Annotated Bibliography of American Indian and Eskimo Autobiographies* (Lincoln, Nebr., 1981). This material has also attracted a more literary analysis of content; for such modern studies on the relations among Indian autobiography, identity, myth, and history, see Brumble's *American Indian Autobiography* (Berkeley, Calif., 1988) and Arnold Krupat, *For Those Who Come after: A Study of American Indian Autobiography* (Berkeley, Calif., 1985).

In both nonfiction and fiction, contemporary Indian writers continue to struggle with writing, preserving, and analyzing their own histories in their own ways, sometimes in conscious resistance to popular or academic non-Native canons. As David Rich Lewis has written, "I make this distinction between 'academic' history because native peoples always have and always will create and pass down their own oral traditions, their own histories. Folklorists have been responsible for capturing most of that material for non-Indian audiences, but increasingly, native peoples are recording and presenting it themselves, especially in the form of autobiography and modern literature. 'I believe stories are encoded in the DNA spiral,' writes Joy Harjo [noted Native American poet], 'and call each cell into perfect position.' " ("Still Native: The Significance of Native Americans in the History of the Twentieth-Century American West," *Western Historical Quarterly* 24 [2], 1993, 226). One Native American writer who during a prolific career has constantly experimented with new genres of Nativistic historical writing is Gerald Vizenor, from his documentary compilation, *Escorts to White Earth: 1868 to 1968* (Minneapolis, 1968) through his *The People Named the Chippewa: Narrative Histories* (Minneapolis, 1984).

For a comprehensive descriptive overview of Indian writing, with plentiful citations on Indian historians and histories of Indian peoples, see A. LaVonne Brown Ruoff, *American Indian Literatures: An Introduction, Bibliography Review and Selected Bibliography* (New York, 1990). Based on his experiences as an educator and bibliographer, Duane K. Hale has produced a practical handbook for Indian groups interested in producing their own community chronicles, *Researching and Writing Tribal Histories* (Grand Rapids, Mich., 1991).

2

NATIVE PEOPLES IN EURO-AMERICAN
HISTORIOGRAPHY

WILCOMB E. WASHBURN AND BRUCE G. TRIGGER

The greatest problem confronting scholars in researching the history of
Native Americans is that the written sources for that history derive largely
from the non-Native side and are subject to the distortions, misconcep-
tions, biases, and ignorance that are generally associated with history seen
from an external cultural perspective. Moreover, the nature of those biases
and distortions has varied over the centuries, so that the data from which
the historian must draw need to be interpreted with an understanding of
those changes. In addition, Native American history shares all the problems of history in general, which, as the British historian Christopher Hill
has observed, is rewritten by every generation, not because the past has
changed but because each generation asks different questions about it.[1] As
a result, historical writing often reveals as much about historians and their
social milieu as it does about the objects of their study.

Our knowledge of American Indian history does not depend only on
written sources. Oral history, although full of pitfalls, has demonstrated
that even through the veil of centuries the Native American past can
sometimes be recaptured by the diligent and sensitive researcher. Archaeology is providing increasingly sophisticated evidence about indigenous
societies from the earliest appearance of human beings in the New World
until the beginning of written records. For more recent times it supplements in many important ways the historical record of changes in Native
life as well as providing new insights into specific events, such as the
Battle of the Little Bighorn.[2] Nevertheless, the interpretation of archaeological data has limitations and biases that are no less significant than
those of written records. Efforts to draw historical inferences from ethnographic and linguistic data continue to suffer from major methodological

---

[1] J. E. C. Hill, *The World Turned Upside Down* (Harmondsworth, 1972), 15.
[2] *Past Worlds: The Times Atlas of Archaeology* (London, 1988), 45.

problems. Yet, when each data source is studied separately, a comparison of their findings can help to overcome the biases and deficiencies that are inherent in each of them.[3]

Finally, Native American scholars have made their appearance, and share with non-Native ones the burden and opportunity of interpreting the past history of both groups. It is appropriate that the responsibility for understanding the past is now coming to be shared jointly by these two groups because, from the moment of contact between the original inhabitants of the continent and the "second comers," each group has shaped the history of the other and no history of either that ignores the relationship with the other can accurately portray the past. Anthropological attempts to isolate the Native lifestyle from the influence of the non-Native, and thereby achieve the assumed purity of an "ethnographic present" account, free of outside influence and the corruption of change, have now been abandoned.[4] Historians and anthropologists alike recognize that Indians and non-Indians are caught up in a process of historical change that is rapid and endless and that there can be no isolation of one group from the other.

FIFTEENTH-CENTURY PRECONCEPTIONS, CONCEPTIONS, AND ACCOUNTS

The discovery of new peoples beyond the bounds of the Old World was anticipated and foreshadowed in the period just prior to the Great Age of Discovery. Travelers' tales, the rediscovery of Europe's classical past with its diverse stereotypes of alien groups, and contemporary accounts of exotic cultures in Africa and Asia provided Europeans with a preview of the unknown peoples to be met beyond the western bounds of their continent. The peoples anticipated by the discoverers included the exquisite damask-coated mandarins of China, the powerful warriors of "gold-roofed Japan," and the nearly naked inhabitants of the off-shore Asiatic islands in the "Sea of the Indies," all reported by Marco Polo. Other models of the exotic were provided by the dark Natives of the Canary Islands in the Atlantic, subdued by Spain, the kingdoms of sub-Saharan Africa discovered by Portuguese coastal explorations in the fifteenth century, the mysterious "skraelings"

---

[3] This multidisciplinary approach was pioneered by Edward Sapir, *Time Perspective in Aboriginal American Culture* (Ottawa, 1916); for a modern statement of its theoretical basis, see George P. Murdock, *Africa: Its Peoples and Their Culture History* (New York, 1959), 1–42.

[4] B. G. Trigger, "Ethnohistory and Archaeology," *Ontario Archaeology* 30 (1978), 17–24; Trigger, "Archaeology and the Ethnographic Present," *Anthropologica* 23 (1981), 3–17.

encountered by the Norse in Greenland and Vinland in the tenth and eleventh centuries, and the fabulous men with heads in their chests, or one-legged men, described by Sir John Mandeville.

With such a variety of humanity and near-humanity to expect in newly discovered realms, it is not surprising that, even before they reached the American mainland, the late-fifteenth-century European explorers groped for understanding and indulged in speculation about the character of the Native inhabitants of the Americas. The image of the "noble savage" began to be fashioned at this time. This image emphasized as much the initial innocence and generosity of the Native peoples of the New World as their nakedness, characteristics that were constantly noted by Columbus and the explorers who followed him. It must not be overlooked that the friendly reception reported by most early explorers had its roots in cultures in which propitiatory gestures were expected to turn aside superior power and acts of sharing and generosity were expected to elicit equivalent gestures on the part of others. Yet the acts of such cultures, which stressed group solidarity rather than calculations of individual benefit, morally impressed newcomers whose daily life was the antithesis of such an ethic.

Because subsequent contact between Europeans and Native Americans quickly changed the character of the relationship between them, it is important to isolate those cases of undoubted first contact in order to assess the historical truth of that initial contact. Columbus reported that

In order that they would be friendly to us – because I recognized that they were people who would be better freed [from error] and converted to our Holy Faith by love than by force – to some of them I gave red caps, and glass beads which they put on their chests, and many other things of small value, in which they took so much pleasure and became so much our friends that it was a marvel. Later they came swimming to the ship's launches where we were and brought us parrots and cotton thread in balls and javelins and many other things and they traded them to us for other things which we gave them, such as small glass beads and bells. In sum, they took everything and gave of what they had very willingly.[5]

This idyllic scene was repeated in the first contacts of many other early explorers, including Amerigo Vespucci, Goncalo Coelho, Pedro Álvares Cabral, Ferdinand Magellan, Giovanni da Verrazzano, and Sir Francis Drake. The reports usually note that the generosity of the Indian men included offers of Indian women to the Europeans. The impact of such generosity, combined with the dazzling display of naked bodies, on Europe-

---

[5] Oliver Dunn and James E. Kelley, Jr. (eds.), *The Diario of Christopher Columbus's First Voyage to America, 1492–1494 Abstracted by Fray Bartolome de las Casas* (Norman, Okla., 1989), 65.

ans brought up in the harsh restrictions of Old World society can well be imagined. Could the idyll have lasted? That is a matter for others to debate. Suffice it to say that the innocence of this New World Garden of Eden (an image actually used by Columbus) was soon to experience its evil serpent, when the weakness of the Native Americans attracted the avarice and stimulated the cruelty as well as the lust of the Europeans. Again Columbus's words record the ominous observation: "They do not carry arms nor are they acquainted with them, because I showed them swords and they took them by the edge and through ignorance cut themselves. They have no iron."[6]

One need not dwell on the tragic consequences of innocence and weakness in such a world. The actions of the men Columbus left at La Navidad following the wreck of one of his ships was a tale at once shameful and distressing to those who hoped the marriage of the Old and the New Worlds would be happy and legitimate. The enslavement, rape, and killing that followed provides a sad chapter in Caribbean and world history. The Spanish depopulated some of the islands by slave raids, destroyed (when European diseases did not) the great majority of Indians in others, and established institutions (of *repartimiento* and *encomienda*) that were at once destructive of the Natives and corrupting to the Spanish. Not for nothing did the friar Bartolomé de las Casas speak of the Spanish actions as "the destruction of the Indies" – that is the destruction of the wealth of the Indies: its people.[7]

At the same time other early explorers and commentators drew upon different preconceptions to denigrate the Indians as thralls of the devil, lustful hairy men, and brutal cannibals who had lost their primeval knowledge of God; or as ignorant people who lived in terror of the elemental forces of nature. The debate about whether Native Americans represented the innocent childhood of humanity or were the products of degeneration would continue into the nineteenth century.

SIXTEENTH-CENTURY REPORTS AND INTERPRETATIONS OF NATIVE AMERICANS

The sixteenth century belonged to the Iberian powers: Spain and Portugal. England, France, the Netherlands, and other European powers looked on enviously and fearfully, and made efforts to compete with the Spanish and Portuguese, but their efforts were episodic and largely unsuccessful in

[6] Dunn and Kelley, 67, entry for October 11, which includes the events of October 12.
[7] Bartolomé de las Casas, *Brevissima relacion de la destruycion de las Indias* (Seville, 1552).

comparison. Yet observers from many European countries left important accounts relating to the Native Americans.

The Spanish accounts of the Native Americans are the most conflicting in character and tone. The reason was the intertwining of the material interest of Spain and its moral conscience. Both motives, in the persons of kings, queens, priests, soldiers, merchants, and scholars, caused the Native Americans to be seen in different and often conflicting terms. Perhaps the most basic division was that highlighted in the debate at Valladolid in 1550–51 between the colonist-turned-friar Bartolomé de las Casas and the stay-at-home scholar Juan Ginés de Sepúlveda. While both the justification of Spanish rule in the Indies and the licitness of Spanish actions were at issue in the debate, the justification of each position rested on a differing conception of the Native inhabitants. Were Natives endowed with the same humanity as the Spanish, were their souls immortal despite their ignorance of the Christian message? Were their rights to their lands and persons inviolable, except as the result of faults meriting just wars and justifiable coercion? Las Casas answered with a thunderous "yes," and most of his life was devoted to attempting to save and preserve the Natives from the rapacity and violence of his fellow countrymen. Sepúlveda, following Aristotle, asserted that all humanity did not share equal abilities or rights and that there were some whose nature destined them to be slaves. The Indians of the newly discovered lands, he argued, were of this character and Spain was justified in making war upon them and coercing them as a father might correct his children. Spain, he believed, might ignore the customary usages obtaining among "civilized" countries in order to introduce Christianity and "civilization" into such a world.

The power of morality in Spain in the sixteenth century should not be overlooked or dismissed as hypocritical posturing intended only to promote the material interests of the Crown or of Spanish settlers in the New World. The king's advisers were, in fact, concerned that actions taken by the king's servants and subjects not outrage the royal conscience. Las Casas was able to shape Spanish policy and, indeed, papal policy, not only by the force of his arguments and the energy of his person but because of the genuine moral concern of the sovereigns. Other religious figures, such as the Dominican Bernardino de Minaya, joined Las Casas in what one scholar has called the "struggle for justice" in Spanish America.[8] Minaya, who broke with Francisco Pizarro in Peru when the latter said that he had

---

[8] Lewis Hanke, *The Spanish Struggle for Justice in the Conquest of America* (Philadelphia, 1949).

come to Peru to take the Incas' gold, not to save the Peruvians, traveled to Rome and was able to obtain from Pope Paul III a papal bull, *Sublimis Deus,* granted June 9, 1537, rejecting the assertion that "the people of whom We have recent knowledge should be treated as dumb brutes created for our service, pretending that they are incapable of receiving the catholic faith." Rather, the bull asserted, "We . . . consider . . . that the Indians are truly men and that they are not only capable of understanding the catholic faith, but according to our information, they desire exceedingly to receive it."[9] Despite such papal pronouncements, despite the efforts of other theologians like Francisco de Vitoria, and despite the "New Laws" that the Spanish crown issued to regulate, in accordance with justice and morality, the Spanish presence in the New World, the actual behavior of Spanish soldiers and settlers rarely coincided with the norms set by the king.

One does not have to adopt a Marxist or even a materialist point of view to note that self-interest played a significant role in distorting Spanish descriptions of the Native inhabitants of the New World. But what is the nature of the distortion? Were those, like Sepúlveda, who described the Indians as little more than brutes and beasts of the fields, given to shocking sins against nature and lascivious sexual behavior, rationalizing their own prejudices or, in the case of settlers who never committed their thoughts to paper, their own self-interest? On the other hand, were those who sought to save and defend the Indians, like Las Casas, exaggerating and distorting the true character of the Indians in the other direction, making them appear to be innocent lambs unjustly threatened by Spanish wolves?

Not all religious figures saw the Indians as did Las Casas. The Dominican Tomas Ortiz, for example, provided the Council of the Indies in 1525 with the following description:

On the mainland they eat human flesh. They are more given to sodomy than any other nation. There is no justice among them. They go naked. They have no respect either for love or for virginity. They are stupid and silly. They have no respect for the truth, save when it is to their advantage. They are unstable. They have no knowledge of what foresight means . . . They are incapable of learning. Punishments have no effect upon them. Traitorous, cruel, and vindictive, they never forgive. Most hostile to religion, idle, dishonest, abject, and vile, in their judgments they keep no faith or law . . . Liars, superstitious, and cowardly as hares. They eat fleas, spiders, and worms raw, whenever they find them. They

---

[9] Quoted in Wilcomb E. Washburn, *Red Man's Land/White Man's Law* (New York, 1971, and new edition, Norman, Okla., 1995), 13.

exercise none of the humane arts or industries. When taught the mysteries of our religion, they say that these things may suit Castilians, but not them, and they do not wish to change their customs . . . The older they get the worse they become . . . I may therefore affirm that God has never created a race more full of vice and composed without the least mixture of kindness or culture . . . We here speak of those whom we know by experience. Especially the father, Pedro de Cordoba, who has sent me these facts in writing . . . the Indians are more stupid than asses and refuse to improve in anything.[10]

Francisco de Vitoria, holder of the *prima* chair of theology at Salamanca University, published, in 1526, his lectures *On the Indians Lately Discovered*. Vitoria denied the calumny that the Indians were of unsound mind:

This is clear because there is a certain method in their affairs, for they have polities which are orderly arranged and they have definite marriage and magistrates, overlords, laws, and workshops, and a system of exchange, all of which call for the use of reason; they also have a kind of religion . . . Accordingly I for the most part attribute their seeming so unintelligent and stupid to a bad and barbarous upbringing, for even among ourselves we find many peasants who differ little from brutes.[11]

The interpretation and reinterpretation of Spanish accounts of the American Indians continue unabated to this day. Indeed, during the commemoration of the quincentenary of the Columbus voyages the controversy, particularly in the United States, intensified. Organizations established to celebrate the Spanish character of the discoveries openly asserted that one of their hopes for the 1992 celebrations was to remove "the black legend" of Spanish cruelty from American textbooks.[12] Las Casas, because of his fiery publications denouncing Spanish atrocities in the Indies, has for several centuries been accused of blackening the name of Spain without justification by exaggerating the number of Indians killed by the Spanish and the atrocious manner in which they were treated. Yet no defender of Spanish actions in the New World is willing to say what numbers of Indians murdered would validate Las Casas's indictment. Would it be 100,000 Indians? 1,000,000? 10,000,000? It is unlikely that passions on this subject will cool, particularly since Las

---

[10] Quoted in ibid., 8.

[11] Quoted in ibid., 9–10.

[12] The elimination of the concept of the "black legend" from textbooks was one of the stated purposes of the National Hispanic Quincentennial Commission, 810 1st Street, N.E., Suite 300, Washington, D.C. 20002. The executive director of the commission during the quincentennial was Elaine Coronado.

Casas was so unwilling to find excuses for Spanish behavior. His linking of his role as defender of the Indians and historian was made clear in his will, in which he asserted that he wrote his histories so that if God ever destroyed the Spanish nation for its crimes against the Indians, people would know why.[13]

Portuguese accounts of first and early contacts, while less extensive than the Spanish ones, parallel them in many ways. When Pedro Álvares Cabral, on his way to India in 1500, accidentally sighted Brazil, a scene took place which matched that of Columbus on San Salvador. That scene was reported by Pero Vaz de Caminha in a letter to King Manoel I. The same innocence of the Natives, their ignorance of iron, their assumed eagerness to accept Christianity and European ways, their generosity, their nakedness, and their sexual desirability, were all duly noted. Amerigo Vespucci, the Florentine who sailed to Brazil the year after Cabral, reported similar characteristics among the Natives of the new land.

Numerous non-Portuguese provided accounts of the Natives of Brazil, among them Paulmier de Gonneville, a French captain from Normandy, who spent many months among the Carijos of southern Brazil in 1503–04 and again in 1505. Captain Thomas Aubert and Jean d'Ango were other Frenchmen who not only described, but brought back, Brazilian Indians to France, where they participated in such dramatic events as the city of Rouen's welcome to Henri II and Catherine de' Medici when they visited the city in 1550. An artificial Brazilian village was set up for the occasion, peopled by Native Brazilians and French sailors dressed to resemble the Natives.

As the French and the Tupinambas became not only trading partners but also allies against the Portuguese, a respectful reciprocal relationship was created that has been seen as providing a useful model for later relations between French and Indians in North America.[14] This relationship included sending French boys to live with the Brazilians and learn their languages and ways of life. Other Frenchmen, some survivors of the abortive French attempts to settle Brazil, added to the favorable picture of the Native Brazilians. Among them were the clergymen Jean de Léry and André Thevet. Their descriptions of the experiences of explorers and colo-

---

[13] Juan Friede and Benjamin Keen, *Bartolomé de Las Casas in History: Toward an Understanding of the Man and His Work* (DeKalb, Ill., 1971), 204–5.

[14] Olive P. Dickason, *The Myth of the Savage and the Beginnings of French Colonialism in the Americas* (Edmonton, 1984), 181–202.

nists in Brazil had a strong impact upon stay-at-home writers and philosophers, such as Michel de Montaigne, as well as upon poets, like Pierre de Ronsard, and the satirist François Rabelais.

Not that the picture was totally idyllic. Brazilian Indians were also described (with apparent accuracy) torturing prisoners to death and indulging in cannibalism. Hans Staden, a German in the employ of the Portuguese, in a book written after his captivity among the Natives, gave ample proof of habits that offended the Europeans, as well as of those characteristics that delighted them.

The international character of the discoveries is well illustrated by the account of the Italian Antonio Pigafetta, who sailed with the Portuguese Ferdinand Magellan on his famous Spanish voyage around the world in 1519–22. Portuguese priests played roles similar to their Spanish brethren in both denouncing and celebrating the Indians.

The inhabitants of the northern hemisphere, despite the climatic differences, impressed European explorers, priests, and traders in similar ways. Thus French accounts of the Native inhabitants of eastern Canada encountered by Jacques Cartier reflected the latter's deep-seated mistrust of Native people and his desire to avoid them as much as possible in situations where he was unable to dominate them. In the case of the colonizing activities of Jean Ribault and René de Goulaine de Laudonnière in *La Floride,* distrust of the Indians was never far below the surface. Yet both of these men were sufficiently dependent on Indians for food and military cooperation against the Spanish that they were prepared to join their Indian allies in wars against other Native groups. Later Dominique de Gourgues actively sought an Indian alliance in order to attack the Spanish. While every Frenchman no doubt believed himself superior to any Indian, active cooperation with Native groups was accepted as essential for the success of French enterprises so close to areas of Spanish power. This policy of *douceur,* which became the cornerstone for the colonization of New France in the seventeenth and eighteenth centuries, encouraged a realistic assessment of the character of Native groups and individuals and of their potential for promoting or thwarting the goals of French entrepreneurs and colonists that is evident in such individuals' accounts of French activities in the New World.

English contact with the Natives of North America was comparatively slight throughout much of the sixteenth century, despite the voyages of John and Sebastian Cabot, John Rut, and others in that period. With English concentration upon the search for a Northwest passage to Asia through the frozen north, of which the three voyages of Martin Frobisher in 1576–8 were the most significant in that century, greater contact with the Native inhabitants was established, but of a largely "now you see them, now you don't" character. Frobisher lost men to the Inuit (Eskimos) and he was able at times to seize or trade with them. Yet contact was always spasmodic and brief, and was carried out in the context of hostility or suspicion. The degree to which the English were still subject to outmoded fears is illustrated by the incident in which Frobisher's sailors brought an Eskimo woman aboard and took off her sealskin clothes to see if she had cloven hoofs!

More extensive contact was established by the expeditions that Sir Walter Raleigh sent to what he called "Virginia" – in honor of the Virgin Queen Elizabeth – in the period 1584–8. These expeditions faced twin perils: the known hostility of the Spanish and the feared hostility of the Native inhabitants of the country in which his men settled. The English were greeted with friendship by the Indians of the Cape Hatteras area, but cultural differences soon led to a parting of the ways. The Indian proclivity for pilfering anything that was left lying about – objects of curiosity to them – met with a harsh response by the English, often resulting in the death of uninvolved and bewildered Indians. Peaceful relations soon turned to hostility, which eventually led to the destruction of England's first colony.

The John White drawings are perhaps the most remarkable legacy of the failed Raleigh attempts at settlement. They are not only the earliest but also the best pictorial evidence of North American Natives that we have. Later expeditions of the seventeenth and eighteenth centuries rarely included observers able to record with skill and care Native appearances and customs. Just as Raleigh sent a skilled artist to the New World, so he also sent a skilled mathematician, Thomas Hariot. Later accounts of the Natives encountered by the English rarely matched Hariot's *A briefe and true report of the new found land* (1588). As J. H. Parry put it: "No travellers' tales or improbable marvels here, but a detailed, accurate and orderly account of the land, its flora and fauna, and its people, as observed by a good scientific mind."[15]

SEVENTEENTH- AND EIGHTEENTH-CENTURY REPORTS AND INTERPRETATIONS OF NATIVE AMERICANS

A great variety of different views were expressed about Native people in seventeenth-century French writings about North America. While many

---

[15] John H. Parry, *The Age of Reconnaissance* (Cleveland, 1963), 213.

explanations were offered about why Indians behaved as they did, few authors failed to express admiration for at least some aspects of Native life. In his *Histoire de la Nouvelle France* (1609), the liberally minded lawyer Marc Lescarbot, who was influenced by Michel de Montaigne's incipient cultural relativism as well as by descriptions of the primitive peoples of northern Europe by the classical authors Strabo and Tacitus, portrayed the Micmacs (Mi'kmaqs) whom he encountered in Nova Scotia as noble savages whose simple way of life was free from many of the vices that afflicted European civilization. On the other hand, Samuel de Champlain, who also knew the Native people of eastern Canada at first hand, described them as rude, undisciplined, and lacking any religious beliefs. The Recollet lay brother Gabriel Sagard, whose works owed much to those of Lescarbot, took a middle position; he admired the Indians' courage, generosity, and affection for other members of their communities, but condemned their religious ignorance and immoral conduct and stressed the need for them to learn to live like Frenchmen.

The Jesuit writings reveal individual variations that reflect their different personalities and views about how mission work could best be accomplished, as well as the often contradictory influences of their religious zeal and extensive secular learning. On the one hand they viewed the Huron country as a remote stronghold where Satan sought to torment an entire people and keep them in ignorance of Christian teaching. Yet they also noted that the Hurons were more generous and less quarrelsome than were most Europeans and sought to isolate them from what they saw as the corrupting influences of French traders and settlers. Many Jesuits were prepared to adopt a relativistic view of customs that did not relate to religion, noting, for example, that standards of physical beauty varied immensely from one culture to another and doubting that there was any one standard by which such preferences could be evaluated.[16] Their opinions of the Hurons varied from admiration for their intelligence and generosity to lurid accounts that stressed the folly and depravity of their religious practices. In both cases, the Jesuits sought to elicit their readers' sympathy and support for their mission's policies.

The accounts of Native people by early French fur traders, such as Pierre Boucher, Pierre-Esprit Radisson, Nicolas Denys, Nicolas Perrot, and Claude Bacqueville de La Potherie, were less dominated by literary stereo-

---

[16] For Paul Le Jeune's summary of this view, see Reuben G. Thwaites (ed.), *The Jesuit Relations and Allied Documents* (73 vols., Cleveland, 1896–1901), 5:107.

types than were the works of their learned clerical contemporaries. A remarkable exception is the memoirs of the soldier Louis-Armand Lom d'Arce, baron de Lahontan, which were published in 1703. His dialogues with a Huron named Adario, which was apparently the pseudonym that he gave to the great Huron chief Kondiaronk, who had died in 1701, were used to ridicule the religious dogmas and social injustices of French society, of which Lahontan saw himself the victim. The message of these dialogues was that Indians were truly free while Frenchmen were slaves. Adario is the direct prototype of the noble savage as conceptualized by Jean-Jacques Rousseau. Yet it is clear that Lahontan's understanding was based on his extensive personal experience of Native life, and the authenticity of the views that he ascribes to Native people is attested by Lafitau (see below) and the earlier Jesuit authors, who confirm Lahontan on matters of fact, although their attitudes toward Native conduct were radically different from his. At least one modern Native scholar argues that Lahontan had a deeper and more accurate understanding of Native culture than did any other European who came to Canada in the seventeenth century.[17] All of this indicates that the so-called myth of the Noble Savage was not simply a product of the salons of Paris, as is often claimed, but a concept that many individuals who had experienced Native life at first hand helped to develop.

By contrast, in his *Moeurs des sauvages amériquains comparées aux moeurs des premiers temps* (1724) Joseph-François Lafitau, a Jesuit who had served as a missionary at Caughnawaga from 1712 to 1717, argued that the more refined customs shared by the ancient Greeks, Romans, and Hebrews and by the Native North Americans were derived from the divinely ordered life of the Patriarchal period, and he attributed cultural differences to peoples having lost sight of God's revelation as they wandered away from the cradle of humanity in the Middle East. Although often lauded as the father of comparative ethnology, Lafitau was in fact the most influential exponent in the eighteenth century of the medieval doctrine of cultural degeneration.

A major step forward in the writing of Canadian history was Pierre Charlevoix's *Histoire et description générale de la Nouvelle France*, published in 1744. A Jesuit priest, Charlevoix had taught at the seminary at Quebec from 1705 to 1709 and later traveled on a fact-finding mission from Quebec to New Orleans by way of Michilimackinac and the Mississippi Valley. Charlevoix provided a systematic account of French colonization,

---

[17] Georges Sioui, *For an Amerindian Autohistory: An Essay on the Foundations of a Social Ethic,* trans. Sheila Fischman (Montreal, 1992), 61–81.

mission work, and conflict with the English, in which the Indians played a major role. His careful evaluation of sources and provision of bibliographies and footnotes marked a significant advance in historiographic techniques as these were applied to the study of North America.

Charlevoix believed that nations, like individuals, had specific characters or temperaments. The features that he attributed to different Native groups were usually based on the stereotypes that the French had assigned to them in the course of their relations. Thus the Hurons (Wendats) were industrious and politically astute; the Ottawas (Odawas) unintelligent; the Illinois cowardly and lustful, but faithful; and the Cayugas gentler than the other Iroquois because they inhabited an area of richer agricultural land, which improved their temperament. He did not restrict negative characteristics to Native people; arguing that French traders and officials were presumptuous and perfidious to the point that it impeded their relations with Native groups.

Like some other French Jesuits of the eighteenth century, Charlevoix subscribed to certain views about human behavior that later were to characterize the thinking of the Enlightenment. Like most Enlightenment scholars, he viewed Native people as being as inherently rational as Europeans. He also believed that the conduct of all human beings was determined by the same calculations of honor and self-interest. The main difference between French and Indians was the extent of their knowledge, the Indians' relative lack of education making them more superstitious and prone to violence. Yet he believed that even the most savage peoples could be improved, intellectually and morally, by associating with culturally more advanced nations. He also believed that among uncultivated people naturally gifted individuals would spontaneously rise above their fellows. As a result, he maintained that some Indian leaders were equal in ability to the most carefully educated Europeans and were naturally entitled to the latter's respect. Because of this talent, even Indian groups that had become politically or economically dependent on Europeans were repeatedly able to outwit them, and this was never easier than when they were dealing with Europeans who regarded Native people as stupid. These insights led Charlevoix to observe that the Iroquois had always ceased attacking the French at the point where they might have done them the most harm. He reasoned that they did this because they wished to protect their independence by continuing to play French and English traders and settlers off against one another.

Charlevoix influenced in content and viewpoint the earliest histories of

Canada that were published in English by George Heriot in 1804 and William Smith in 1815. He also influenced Michel Bibaud's *Histoire du Canada,* published in Montreal in 1837. These writers relied heavily on Charlevoix for their information, paid much attention to Native people, and presented relatively rationalistic interpretations of their behavior. Their views of Native people were also influenced by an appreciation of the role that Indians continued to play as allies of the British against the Americans; a role that declined rapidly in importance after the War of 1812. Meanwhile, French Canadian folklore nourished darker memories of Iroquois attacks against missionaries and French settlers during the seventeenth century.

English settlement in the New World differed from that of the other European nations in the extent to which they attempted to re-create their life in the New World in the same form in which that life existed in the Old World. While all European nations engaged in trade with the Native peoples, fought wars with them, and tried to impose their will upon them, the English were more concerned with establishing English settlements on the land than with exploiting Native labor, interbreeding or intermarrying with the Native inhabitants, mining or plundering Native mineral wealth, or engaging in trade with the Natives to the exclusion of other activities. As a result, the English interpretation of the North American Native was sharply conditioned by the fact that land – its ownership and use – formed a principal concern of both parties in their dealings with the other. Different perspectives upon that issue were, not unexpectedly, held by those English who, with their families, sought to establish farms and plantations, those who sought to preach to and convert Indians, and those who sought to govern the English colonies in a way that maximized their safety and prosperity, to say nothing of those who sought to escape the restrictions of English life and live with the Indians.

The number of English in the latter category, who sometimes voluntarily fled the restrictions of European society in order to enjoy what struck them as the freedom and pleasures of Indian life, were more numerous than is generally realized. The iron-willed governors of the Jamestown colony prescribed the death penalty for running off to live with the Indians, clearly an indication that the attractions of Indian life were great. Those attractions were frequently discussed by colonial writers such as Robert Lawson, Robert Beverley, William Byrd, Thomas Morton, James Adair, and Thomas Jefferson. However distorted when seen through the lens of English economic, religious, and social norms, those attractions seem to have centered on two elements: sexual freedom and freedom from strict hierarchical control by political and social superiors. Additional evidence of the attractiveness of Native American life is provided by the carefully studied literary evidence concerning European captives taken by Indians. James Axtell, Alden Vaughan, Richard Slotkin, and others have pointed out the startling extent to which European captives came to enjoy and even prefer the Indian life into which they had been thrust involuntarily. This literary and especially autobiographical productivity among English settlers contrasts with the far larger number of French *coureurs de bois* and Scottish traders who lived and intermarried with Natives in western Canada and whose descendants constitute the Métis Nation, yet who produced little literary record of their activities.

The "white Indians of colonial America," to use Axtell's phrase, provided a continuing puzzle and threat to the pride and self-assurance of well-behaved English settlers. However confused the argument might have been between the reality of the "noble savage" and of its counterimage, the "brute beast," between the disadvantages of the savage life and the advantages of civilization, the apparent fact that thousands of Europeans had sought voluntarily to take up the Indian way of life was, as Jean-Jacques Rousseau asserted in his *Discourse on Inequality* (1755), proof that happiness is "less the business of reason than of feeling."[18] The impact of the belief (which did not necessarily correspond with reality) that "thousands of Europeans are Indians, and we have no examples of even one of these Aborigines having from choice become European!" as Hector St. John de Crevecoeur put it in his *Letters from an American Farmer* (1782),[19] reinforced earlier statements of a similar nature by Cadwallader Colden and Benjamin Franklin. Twentieth-century scholars Alden Vaughan and Daniel Richter, on the other hand, alluding to the significant number of Christian Indian towns established by the New England authorities, assert that "the evidence suggests a far less one-sided exchange than Colden, Franklin, and Crevecoeur presented; in fact New England colonists were probably more successful than Indians in attracting social and religious converts." Nevertheless, they concede that "ironically, Indian culture incorporated strangers far more thoroughly and enthusiastically than did Puritan New England."[20]

The concerns of English husbandmen and their political leaders were

---

[18] Quoted in William Brandon, *New Worlds for Old: Reports from the New World and Their Effect on the Development of Social Thought in Europe, 1500–1800* (Athens, Ohio, 1986), 111.

[19] Quoted in Alden Vaughan and Daniel K. Richter, "Crossing the Cultural Divide: Indians and New Englanders, 1605–1763," American Antiquarian Society, *Proceedings* 90 (1980), 23.

[20] Ibid., 25.

generally such that their writings deny the attractiveness of Indian life and repudiate its positive character. It was, of course, in the interest of those who sought to acquire and utilize what had been the property of an alien people to deny the relevance (sometimes even the existence) of that people and of its claims to the land. Hence the American land was long depicted, in one way or another, as vacant or virgin, to use the phrase of Henry Nash Smith's *Virgin Land: The American West as Symbol and Myth* (1950, reissued 1970). In the 1960s, 1970s, and 1980s, this view of the American continent as awaiting the bridegroom (a frequent metaphor in the seventeenth-century sermon literature of New England and England) was angrily attacked, and more concern with what Francis Jennings called a "widowed land" — a European America made vacant by the killing off of the Native inhabitants by disease and warfare — was expressed.

English religious figures sometimes found themselves on opposite sides of the debate concerning the legal and moral justifications of the English appropriation of the lands formerly inhabited by the Indians. Thus the Reverend Robert Gray, in a 1609 sermon, asserted that it was a sin in man *not* to take the land "out of the hands of beasts and brutish savages"[21] and Samuel Purchas, the English divine who succeeded Richard Hakluyt as the compiler of exploration and discovery narratives, outdid all his fellow clerics in trashing the New World Natives. In his "Virginias Verger: Or a Discourse shewing the benefits which may grow to this Kingdome from American English Plantations, and specifically those of Virginia and Summer Islands" (1625), Purchas set forth the picture of

So good a Countrey, so bad people, having little of Humanitie but shape, ignorant of Civilitie, of Arts, of Religion; more brutish than the beasts they hunt, more wild and unmanly then that unmanned wild Countrey, which they range rather than inhabite; captivated also to Satans tyranny in foolish pieties, mad impieties, wicked idlenesse, busie and bloudy wickednesse: hence have wee fit objects of zeale and pitie, to deliver from the power of darknesse.[22]

The English colonizer Ferdinando Gorges interpreted epidemics of European diseases as divine interventions intended to encourage European settlement.

On the other hand, Roger Williams, before being banished to Rhode Island, vigorously denied the validity of the patent to New England from a

---

[21] Quoted in Brandon, *New Worlds,* 70.
[22] Samuel Purchas, *Hakluytus Posthumus or Purchas His Pilgrimes: Containing a History of the World in Sea Voyages and Lande Travells by Englishmen and Others* (20 vols., Glasgow, 1905–7), 19:231.

king he felt had no right to grant it. Williams continued to play a role in the lives of New England's original inhabitants and of its later arrivals. While never "going native," he was able to deal with Indians and English alike with respect for the character of both groups. Yet some other ministers in New England were as zealous as those who remained home in England in justifying the appropriation of a country from so "bad" a people.

While Puritan settlers in seventeenth-century New England observed their own legal forms in securing land from its Native owners, their theologians religiously justified the seizure of Indian lands. In addition to arguing that Native peoples had earned or reflected God's displeasure with them but failing to use His gifts, they saw themselves as a New Israel and the Indians as Canaanites, whom they had a God-given right to dispossess and enslave. As late as 1783, Ezra Stiles, the president of Yale University, was to argue that the Indians were probably literally the descendants of Canaanites, who had fled to America at the time of Joshua's conquest.

Cotton Mather, the distinguished New England religious figure and author of *Decennium Luctuosum: An History of Remarkable Occurrences in the Long War, which New-England hath had with the Indian Salvages, from the year 1688, to the year 1698* (1699) and chronicler of the massive *Magnalia Christi Americana; or, The Ecclesiastical History of New-England* (1702) and numerous other historical accounts of the first century of English settlement in New England, excoriated the New England Indians as little better than the scum of the earth: treacherous, filthy, stubborn – in a word, unworthy of sharing the New England earth with the visible saints of the church. His vehement abhorrence of the Native American can be explained in part by his recognition of the very attractiveness of the Indian way of life to pious and obedient settlers living under the guidance of the Puritan religious leaders. Defection, either voluntary or involuntary (as in the case of the captivity of Mrs. Mary Rowlandson, author of the most famous Indian captivity narrative),[23] was a threat to the stability of the New England way and a cause for suspicion and correction. Indian cultures, in which the individual was believed to indulge his natural impulses and exercise a virtually unlimited power of choice, were at odds with Puritan culture, which emphasized the repression of those impulses and the subordination of the individual to constituted authority. It may be

[23] Mary White Rowlandson, *The Soveraignty and Goodness of God . . . Being a Narrative of the Captivity and Restauration of Mrs. Mary Rowlandson . . .* (Boston, 1682).

debated whether the violent and uncompromising Puritan response to the challenge posed by Indian culture – the policy of "regeneration through violence" postulated by Richard Slotkin as a way of resolving this "fatal opposition, the hostility between two worlds, two races, two realms of thought and feeling" – explains Puritan actions.[24] Yet the contrast between the two cultures, and their claims to the same soil, clearly colored the descriptions that each made of the other.

In any event, the existence of Native Americans and their different lifestyles were at the very least elements of confusion to missionaries, soldiers, politicians, and others attempting to describe them, their history, and their character. As Gilbert Chinard noted in his discussion of the continuing contradiction between the brute-beast and noble-savage schools of thought, " 'nearly all the missionaries' of both Canada and the Caribbean assert that the Indians are the most barbarous and inhuman of peoples, and then show us in their accounts just the opposite, what 'commences as an indictment finishes with a dithyramb.' "[25]

Later French writers, who had little, if any, contact with Native people, mainly used Charlevoix as a source of data but altered his interpretations to serve their own purposes. In his widely read *Histoire philosophique* (1770), Guillaume-Thomas Raynal, a popularizer of Enlightenment thought, portrayed North American Indians as noble savages. Like Rousseau and Voltaire, he saw them as exemplifying the essential goodness of human nature when uncorrupted by the evils of civilization. He described Indians as hardy, brave, stoical, and magnanimous. Men were intrepid hunters but gentle in everyday life. They loved their families, were loyal to their friends, and their lives were not ruined by monetary greed or the pursuit of honors and titles. Sexual obsessions were curbed by the need to work hard to stay alive, and even their torturing of prisoners was exonerated as a natural extension of their martial valor. Their principal failing was identified as their lack of scientific knowledge, which allowed them to be tormented by superstitious fears and made them vengeful. The more religiously orthodox François-René de Chateaubriand, who also used Charlevoix as a source, similarly praised Indian life and morals while condemning their ignorance of Christianity.

The *Beautés de l'histoire du Canada*, published in 1821 under the pseudonym D. Dainville, probably the French businessman Adolphe Bos-

[24] Richard Slotkin, *Regeneration through Violence: The Mythology of the American Frontier, 1600–1860* (Middletown, Conn., 1973), 47.
[25] Quoted in Brandon, *New Worlds*, 68.

sange, provides the first indication of the impact of the romantic style on the writing of Canadian history. The main theme of this book was stated to be the conflict between savagery and civilization. Although based largely on Charlevoix, Dainville's book emphasized the Indians' fiery passions, lack of self-control, and love of warfare and vengeance. While he denounced Europeans for stealing Indian land, spreading diseases, corrupting Indian life, and teaching Native people to scorn their ancient traditions, he delighted in gory, detailed descriptions of tortures and massacres committed by both sides, but especially by the Indians. He implied that cruelty and violence were fundamental aspects of human nature, which, if not curbed by the power of the state, would corrupt even the most civilized societies. This view reflected the growing pessimism about human nature that had undermined the French middle class's faith in reason as a guide to human conduct after the excesses of the French revolution. Dainville also stressed that contemporary Indians had not changed, despite the altered circumstances in which they found themselves. This too reflected the tendency of the romantic movement to regard human behavior as largely innate and unalterable, rather than as responsive to historical circumstances.

In attempting to sort through the distortions of reality caused by self-interest and ignorance, as well as by religious, cultural, and legal preconceptions in the seventeenth and eighteenth centuries, can we discover "racism" as the twentieth century knows that term? The answer must be a qualified one. Certainly the Native Americans were seen as different, but that difference was not of the character generally associated with racism in the twentieth century. As Alden Vaughan has shown, the distinction later created by the term "red men" was not to be found in the colonial period of American history.[26] Skin color was not considered a particularly significant feature, in particular because it was considered that underneath the strange appearance of the Indian was a human being capable of abandoning his primitive or debased way of life and becoming a European. Indeed, writers such as Robert Beverley and Thomas Jefferson, in their historical comments on the American Indians, regretted that there had not been more intermarriage between the two groups. Both thought that many of the conflicts between Indian and Anglo-American that did arise would

---

[26] Alden Vaughan, "From White Man to Redskin: Changing Anglo-American Perceptions of the American Indian," *American Historical Review* 87 (1982), 917–29. Dinesh D'Souza, *The End of Racism: Principles of a Multiracial Society* (New York, 1995) discusses the origins of racism in this controversial study.

have been avoided had this desired amalgamation taken place.[27] Later disillusionment over the possibility of making over the Indian led some to harsher judgments, but only gradually did the concept of racial contempt seep into the words and actions of those who knew the Natives best. Physical differences among peoples were generally attributed to environmental factors and not regarded as immutable or irreversible prior to the nineteenth century. Many eighteenth-century European scholars, such as the Comte de Buffon, argued, to the annoyance of Anglo-American settlers, that the climate of the New World was conducive to the degeneration of plant, animal, and human life. Moreover, no clear distinction was drawn between variations in physical, moral, and behavioral characteristics. The colonial attitude toward another category of non-Europeans — Africans — differed radically from that toward Indians. This difference is the subject of a long-continuing debate among American historians.

As disputes over land rights poisoned relations between English settlers and Native people during the seventeenth century, it became increasingly fashionable for European colonists to describe Indians as bloodthirsty monsters who were human only in the shape of their bodies. The Indians' continuing resistance to Euro-American encroachment on their lands throughout the eighteenth century encouraged the view that they were vicious brutes who were innately incapable of being civilized. After the American Revolution, during which period most Indian groups took the side of British, it was widely stated that all Native Americans were savages who should be wiped from the face of the earth. They were increasingly referred to as tawny pagans, swarthy Philistines, copper-colored vermin, and, by the end of the eighteenth century, redskins. The notion that darker color implied inferiority had a long history in European thinking and had been reinforced during the seventeenth and eighteenth centuries as a result of conscious and unconscious efforts to justify the African slave trade by dehumanizing its victims.

Beginning late in the eighteenth century, there was a growing preference for biologically based explanations of human behavior. Differences that had previously been interpreted as reversible adaptations to specific climatic conditions now came to be viewed as immutable racial characteristics. In Europe this change had its roots in the widespread rejection of the

---

[27] Robert Beverley, *The History and Present State of Virginia* (London, 1705), book 1, section 26; also, edited with an introduction by Louis B. Wright (Charlottesville, Va., 1947 and 1968), 38–39; Bernard W. Sheehan, *Seeds of Extinction: Jeffersonian Philanthropy and the American Indian* (Chapel Hill, N.C., 1973), 174.

rationalism of the Enlightenment and in the growing romanticism that accompanied nationalistic reactions to the Napoleonic domination of Europe. In America racist attitudes reinforced the view that Indians were inherently savage and could no more be civilized than an animal's nature could be fundamentally changed. Even those who advocated assimilation now regarded it as a process that would require centuries of effort to bring to fruition. Hence nature itself decreed that Indians must give way to a superior order of human beings, and Americans of European descent believed themselves biologically justified in their efforts to subjugate and replace Native groups.

These ideas were first provided with a "scientific" basis by polygenism: the belief that American Indians, Africans, Europeans, and East Asians were separately created and immutable species, each endowed with its own innate behavioral patterns. Indians were viewed as mentally inferior to Europeans, but as having too independent a nature to make it feasible to enslave large numbers of them. Polygenism did not, however, enjoy a broad following, because it was perceived as contradicting the biblical account of human creation. Ironically, Darwinian evolutionism, which did not deny a common origin for all human beings, provided a more broadly acceptable rationale for racist interpretations of human behavior. According to this doctrine, Euro-Americans could not be blamed for the tragic failure of natural selection, acting over many millennia, to produce Native people who were biologically able to accommodate to the spread of Western civilization. Many Euro-Americans anticipated that the total extinction of the American Indian would soon occur and sentimentally interpreted their replacement by European settlers as a tragic but minor episode in a drama of worldwide technological, moral, and intellectual progress.

NINETEENTH-CENTURY REPORTS AND INTERPRETATIONS OF NATIVE AMERICANS

The early nineteenth century is not celebrated for the development of history as an academic discipline in the United States, but the period is notable for the activities of historical societies and editors to collect the raw materials that later historians would put to good use. Nevertheless there were histories produced that are worthy of note. Thus John Marshall of Virginia, while Chief Justice of the United States (1801–35), wrote a five-volume *Life of George Washington* (1804–07), the first volume of which was titled A *Compendious View of the Colonies Planted by the English on the*

Continent of North America, from their Settlement to the Commencement of that War which Terminated in their Independence. While necessarily a hasty summary, Marshall's book revealed the keen mind that was later to summarize brilliantly the character of the evolving Indian–Euro-American relationship in his decisions in the Cherokee cases, most notably in *Worcester* v. *Georgia* (1832).

This was also a period when important polemical literature about the Indians was written, much of which had a historical cast. The growing negativism toward the possibility of assimilating the Indians spurred proposals in the early nineteenth century to remove them from their traditional homelands in the east to the territories extending beyond the Appalachian chain to the Mississippi River that had been acquired by the Treaty of Paris in 1783, as well as to the vast territories beyond the Mississippi acquired by the United States from France in the Louisiana Purchase of 1803.[28] The issue came to a head in the mid-1820s. Secretary of War James Barbour, and the head of his Indian Office, Thomas L. McKenney, believed that the Indians would eventually be assimilated into the larger American society through education and missionization. Until that time, the integrity of their lands and autonomy was to be respected. McKenney, who had served as Superintendent of Indian Trade under the earlier factory system, and as head of the Indian Office in the War Department from 1824 to 1830, was known for his sympathy for the Indians. One of his extraordinary achievements had been to assemble for the War Department a collection of Indian portraits. As a historian he also produced a sympathetic portrayal of the Native Americans in his *On the Origin, History, Character, and the Wrongs and Rights of the Indians* (1846). Lewis Cass, who was to become Andrew Jackson's Secretary of War, in an 1826 *North American Review* article opposed removal and urged support for existing Indian policy.

Yet all such views were soon to change, and often in the minds of those who previously had supported the policy of assimilation. In 1826 Barbour abandoned his previous rejection of removal and began to support individual (as opposed to tribal) removal, provided this was voluntary and not coerced. Thomas McKenney, similarly, in 1828 concluded that removal was a necessity in order to save the Indians from destruction, although he sought to make the movement voluntary and not forced. Removal, in one

---

[28] Brian W. Dippie, *The Vanishing American: White Attitudes and U.S. Indian Policy* (Middletown, Conn., 1982), 63.

form or another, was now urged as a way of preserving and protecting the Indians' physical and legal existence. Lewis Cass, as Secretary of War under Jackson, submitted a proremoval essay to the *North American Review* in 1829, which reversed the views of his 1826 essay in the same journal. The historian Jared Sparks, editor of the *Review*, was persuaded by Cass's argument, but noted that "After all, this project only defers the fate of the Indians. In half a century their condition beyond the Mississippi will be just what it now is on this side. Their extinction is inevitable."[29] An acid commentary on American Indian policy in this period appears in Alexis de Tocqueville's *De la démocratie en Amérique* (1835), who noted that "It is impossible to destroy men with more respect for the laws of humanity."[30]

The nineteenth century saw the development in the United States of "professional" history and "professional" anthropology, as well as the growth of a literary tradition, all of which provided an enlarged and more sophisticated view of the Native American. But these developments were largely the product of the second half of the nineteenth century rather than the first. Prior to that time the literary figure Washington Irving, capitalizing on his years as United States Ambassador to Spain, produced *The Life and Voyages of Christopher Columbus* (1828), and later wrote accounts of the American Western movement in *A Tour of the Prairie* (1835), *Astoria* (1836), and the *Adventures of Captain Bonneville, U.S.A.* (1851). But Irving's "velvety narrative" reflected, in the words of Stanley T. Williams, "the born romancer exploiting materials which belonged to the historian."[31]

America, in the early years of the nineteenth century, had reached a "state of self-consciousness which made its past seem exciting."[32] Scholars like Peter Force played a vital role in collecting, editing, and publishing the scattered documents of the American past. Force's multivolume *Tracts and Other Papers Relating Principally to the Origin, Settlement, and Progress of the Colonies in North America, from the Discovery of the Country to the year 1776* (1836–46), as well as his *American Archives* (1837–53), collected the documents relating to Indian-settler relations in the American colonies, and provided the documentary base for later historians concerned with the American Indian. Others, like Jared Sparks, produced extraordinary numbers of biographies and narratives, though these were marred by what later

---

[29] Quoted in ibid., 70.
[30] Quoted in ibid., 70.
[31] Stanley T. Williams, chapter on "Washington Irving," in Robert E. Spiller, Willard Thorp, Thomas H. Johnson, and Henry Seidel Canby (eds.), *Literary History of the United States* (3 vols., New York, 1948), 1:250–1.
[32] Eric F. Goldman, chapter on "The Historians," in Spiller et al., *Literary History*, 1:526.

historians were to consider an excessive concern for protecting the reputations of American heroes. Needless to say, the American Indian provided little more than a romantic background to the exploits of Euro-American heroes in the works of such men.

Nor were those more formal historians like George Bancroft able to free themselves from an overly patriotic and naive celebration of American democracy, in which the American Indian – characteristically a "savage" in Bancroft's prose – was an outsider or obstruction, if he played a role at all. Typical of Bancroft's treatment of the Indian was his praise of Andrew Jackson: as "witness to the ruthlessness of savage life, he planned the removal of the Indian tribes beyond the limits of the organized States; and it is the result of his determined policy that the region east of the Mississippi has been transferred to the exclusive possession of cultivated man."[33]

Bancroft's twelve-volume *History of the United States* (1834–82) was celebrated in its time, but its romantic excesses elicited reactions in the work of Richard Hildreth, whose *History of the United States* (1849–52) is seen by some as anticipating the "scientific history" of a later period.[34] Hildreth discussed with accuracy, but with virtually no emotion, such incidents as the murder of the Mingo chief Logan's family during Lord Dunmore's War in 1774 and the massacre of unoffending Christian Delaware Indians on the Muskingum River in 1782 by American forces.[35] Like most good New Englanders, he was appalled by the existence of slavery and learnedly discussed it and other ethical questions in his *Theory of Morals: An Inquiry Concerning the Law of Moral Distinctions and the Variations and Contradictions of Ethical Codes* (1844), *Despotism in America: Or, An Inquiry into the Nature and Results of the Slave-holding System in the United States* (1840), and *Theory of Politics: An Inquiry into the Foundations of Governments and the Causes and Progress of Political Revolutions* (1854). Yet Hildreth's attention to morals did not suffuse his historical writings, and the Indian tended to remain outside the circle of his historical and moral concerns.

The patrician Boston historians Francis Parkman and William Hickling Prescott chose topics for research in which the Native Americans played central roles. Parkman attempted to tell the story of the "American for-

---

[33] *Memoirs of General Andrew Jackson . . . containing a full account of his Indian campaigns, defence of New Orleans . . . To which is added the Eulogy of Hon. Geo. Bancroft* [247–270] (Auburn, N.Y., 1845), 260.

[34] Goldman, "Historians," in Spiller et al., *Literary History,* 1:528.

[35] Richard Hildreth, *The History of the United States of America from the Discovery of the Continent to the Organization of Government under the Federal Constitution, 1497–1789* (3 vols., 1849; rev. ed. New York, 1854), 3:50, 422–3.

est," in which two great European powers, France and Great Britain, struggled for dominance. Powerful Indian nations played vital roles in this story, though always, in Parkman's organization of the story, in support of dominant European interests. Indians were more often treacherous than noble in Parkman's interpretation, as the title of his *History of the Conspiracy of Pontiac and the War of the North American Tribes* (1851) suggests. Although praised by Samuel Eliot Morison as the finest historian of his day, he has been the subject of broadside attacks by Francis Jennings and others for his insensitivity to the Indian side of the story he told. Parkman prided himself on his personal acquaintance with the locales and the subjects of those he wrote about, but his effort to understand "the Indian" was limited by the fact that few Indians remained, and with little power, in the areas where the Great War for Empire between Great Britain and France had been fought. So Parkman, in the summer of 1846, set out for the West, hoping that rubbing shoulders with nineteenth-century Western Plains Indians would give him some appreciation of eighteenth-century Eastern Woodlands Indians. The Indians in Parkman's *The California and Oregon Trail* (1849) reflected the rather supercilious contempt for the "savage" that he likely carried with him from his Beacon Hill library, reinforced by the unfavorable impressions that he gained from three weeks that he spent roughing it with the Oglala Sioux.

Parkman's vision of Native North Americans was conveyed in the most colorful and derogatory terms. Indian women were "dusky mistresses" and "shrivelled hags" who bore "mongrel offspring" to Euro-American traders. Native people lived in "swarms" rather than communities, had "barbaric appellatives" instead of personal names, and their venerable chiefs were described as "greasy potentates." All of these literary devices reinforced Parkman's contemptuous portrayal of Native people. While he described the Iroquois hyperbolically as the boldest, fiercest, most politically astute, and most ambitious of North American Indians, he maintained that they nevertheless remained "thorough savages," and were unlikely ever to have evolved a civilized way of life on their own initiative. Ignoring the importance of agricultural economies to many Native groups, he maintained that the basic mental and physical characteristics of all Indians had been shaped by their common experience as hunting peoples (see also Chapter 8). As "tenants of the wilderness," they lacked the persistence, reason, and foresight of settled nations. While their hunting-based way of life encouraged a spirit of pride, independence, and fortitude, it also made them mentally lethargic and content with a squalid and rude style of life. He also argued that a Euro-American man could quickly learn to be a better hunter or bush-fighter than any Indian and was inclined to believe that Indians were naturally less sensitive to pain and less endowed with refined feelings than were the "higher races."

In the early nineteenth century, some educated Americans admired the achievements of the Native peoples of Mesoamerica, whom they believed to be different from and more intelligent than North American Indians. Even though the polygenist Samuel Morton could find no significant anatomical differences between the skulls of the two groups, he divided them on the basis of cultural criteria into Barbarians and Toltecs. More elaborate traits in the archaeological record of North America were as often attributed to the former presence of Mesoamericans in the area in pre-Columbian times as to the intrusion of Hindu, Welsh, or Scandinavian settlers. John L. Stephens's lavishly illustrated accounts of his discoveries of the ruins of Mayan cities in the jungles of Central America were welcomed as evidence that the allegedly insalubrious climate of the New World had not precluded the indigenous development of at least a rudimentary form of civilization. These attitudes ensured that, while Prescott wrote nothing about the Indians of North America, what he had to say about those in Mexico and Peru was important for the way in which North American Indians were perceived.

Prescott's canvas in his *Conquest of Mexico* (1843) was dramatically centered on the contest between civilized Europe and aboriginal America, each represented by a human figure of heroic proportions: Cortés on the Spanish side and Montezuma on the Aztec side. Prescott's Indians, through dramatic necessity, are arrayed to represent the splendor and might of the Aztec Empire; yet their defeat is inevitable. The structure of Prescott's book is designed, in David Levin's words, "to support a fundamental simple theme: the inevitable ruin of a rich but barbarous empire through its inherent moral faults; the triumph of 'civilization' over 'semi-civilization,' of Christianity (however imperfectly represented) over cannibalism; the triumph of Cortes' 'genius,' 'constancy,' and resourceful leadership over Montezuma's 'pusillanimity' and 'vacillation.'[36]

Prescott's preference for the European side of the story is clear in his literary memoranda. As he noted in 1838, when contemplating the work, "I confess I do not relish the annals or the conquests of barbarians, so much as those of civilized people; nor do I think they will bear expatiating on to any great length. But the overturning of their old empires by a handful of

---

[36] Quoted in Benjamin Keen, *The Aztec Image in Western Thought* (New Brunswick, N.J., 1971), 354–5.

warriors is a brilliant subject, full of important results, and connected with our own history."[37] Prescott conceived of the work as "an *epic in prose, a romance of chivalry.*"[38]

Although Prescott's work was far from a glorification of Mesoamerican achievements, it, nevertheless, triggered a fierce debate on the subject of the character of the Native Americans. Lewis H. Morgan, on reading Prescott's history in the 1850s, was annoyed to find that Prescott's account of Aztec society seemed "utterly contrary to the Iroquois model" of social organization that he had worked out and published in his *The League of the Ho-dé-no-sau-nee, or Iroquois* (1851). "Morgan concluded that the popular Prescott was a major obstacle to establishing American ethnology on a truly scientific basis."[39]

In a paper read before the eleventh meeting of the American Association for the Advancement of Science in Montreal in 1857, Morgan launched his counterattack. Montezuma, he asserted, was merely one of a number of sachems among the Aztecs. If one could break through what he regarded as the "overlapping mass of fable and exaggeration" one would find, he thought, that the Aztec government was a "hereditary oligarchy, very similar to that of the Iroquois."[40] Morgan's paper, published in the *Proceedings* of the American Association for the Advancement of Science, was cited by his fellow resident of Rochester, New York, Robert A. Wilson, in the latter's *New History of the Conquest of Mexico* (1859). Wilson declared the Spanish accounts of the magnificence of the Aztec Empire to be fabulous romances or outright lies.[41]

The debate over the nature of the Native American escalated with the entry of Adolph F. Bandelier — somewhat hesitantly — on the side of Morgan, and of Hubert Howe Bancroft of California in support of Prescott. Bancroft, in 1875–6, brought out his five-volume *History of the Native Races of the Pacific Coast,* the second volume of which was devoted to the Aztecs and Mayas. Bancroft supported the claims of the Spanish chroniclers, accepted the "monarchical and nearly absolute" character of the Aztec government and the splendid character of its court, but at the same time questioned any evolutionary scheme of human development of the sort that Morgan was about to present in an address to the American

---

[37] C. Harvey Gardiner, ed., *The Literary Memoranda of William Hickling Prescott* (2 vols., Norman, Okla., 1961), 1:229.
[38] C. Harvey Gardiner, *William Hickling Prescott: A Biography* (Austin, Tex., 1969), 158.
[39] Quoted in Keen, *Aztec Image,* 382.
[40] Quoted in ibid., 383.
[41] Quoted in ibid., 384.

Association for the Advancement of Science in Detroit in 1875. This address, in which Morgan outlined his theory of three major "ethnical periods" (savagery, barbarism, and civilization), was to become the first chapter of his *Ancient Society* (1877).

Morgan responded to Bancroft's entry into the controversy with an explosive forty-page review (entitled "Montezuma's Dinner") of his second volume in the *North American Review* for April 1876. In the review he asserted that Bancroft had compounded the errors of Prescott in his celebration of "the Aztec monarchy and the Aztec romance" and that his book, and the praise it was receiving, were "nothing less than a crime against ethnological science."[42] Morgan ridiculed the accounts of the sumptuous banquet given by the emperor Montezuma in his palace, as described by the Spanish chroniclers. While one might believe the Spanish histories, Morgan asserted, when they spoke about the acts of the Spaniards, when they spoke of Indian society and government they were totally worthless. The famous dinner, he asserted, was a simple daily meal of the residents of a joint-tenement house, united in a communal household, prepared in a common kitchen, and distributed from a kettle from which each person ate from a clay bowl. Morgan ridiculed the description of Montezuma sitting in a low chair at a table covered with a white cloth. As a result of the increasing pervasiveness of intellectualized racism, many Euro-Americans, who saw little to admire in the Native inhabitants of the United States, were now happy to accept Morgan's view that no indigenous people anywhere in the Western hemisphere had evolved their own civilization.

A curious echo of the "Montezuma's Dinner" controversy is reflected in John Gorham Palfrey's three-volume *History of New England during the Stuart Dynasty* (1858–64). Palfrey, who dedicated his work to Jared Sparks, his classmate at Phillips Exeter Academy and at Harvard, felt it necessary to interpret the Indian King Philip, whose "conspiracy" set back New England's development in 1675–76, as "a mythical character." While conceding a certain determination and skill to Philip, Palfrey concluded that

The title of *King,* which it has been customary to attach to his name, disguises and transfigures to the view the form of a squalid savage, whose palace was a sty; whose royal robe was a bearskin or a coarse blanket, alive with vermin; who hardly knew the luxury of an ablution; who was often glad to appease appetite with food

[42] Quoted in ibid., 391, 393.

such as men who are not starving loathe; and whose nature possessed just the capacity for reflection and the degree of refinement, which might be expected to be developed from the mental constitution of his race by such a condition and such habits of life.[43]

A greater sympathy toward the Indians was shown by the young John William De Forest, whose *History of the Indians of Connecticut from the Earliest Known Period to 1850* was published in 1851 while he was still in his twenties. Beginning at the age of twenty-one with printed materials in the Yale College Library, De Forest spent several years scouring the manuscript volumes of colonial and state records in the state archives in Hartford. His approach to the Native Americans was one of sympathy and understanding. While deploring their "barbarism," he denied the English claim of superior virtue. He was appalled by the "indiscriminate butchery" of the Pequots – men, women, and children – by colonial forces in 1637, wondering how American historians would have characterized an equivalent extermination of the inhabitants of New London by English soldiers during the American Revolution. In dealing with King Philip's War, De Forest's interpretation is more in keeping with recent scholarship than with the conclusions of historians of his own time. He asserted flatly that "Philip formed no general league, no great conspiracy against the English; but he was smarting from humiliations inflicted upon himself and his brother; and, like most of his race, he looked with anger and dismay upon the steady progress of the foreigners in spreading over and occupying the country." Indeed, he characterized the struggle from the Indian point of view as "a war for freedom and existence, and when those were no longer possible, it became a war for revenge."[44]

A U.S. historian of the late nineteenth century who is now almost totally in eclipse is Justin Winsor (1831–97).[45] His best known work is his eight-volume *Narrative and Critical History of America* (1884–9), written by himself and other contributors, but he was also the author of *The Westward Movement: The Colonies and the Republic West of the Alleghenies, 1763–1798* (1897), *Christopher Columbus and How He Received and Imparted the Spirit of Discovery* (1891), *Cartier to Frontenac: Geographical Discovery in the Interior of*

[43] John Gorham Palfrey, *History of New England during the Stuart Dynasty* (3 vols., Boston, 1858–1864), 3:223.

[44] John William De Forest, *History of the Indians of Connecticut from the Earliest Known Period to 1850* (Hartford, 1851; reprint ed. with introduction by Wilcomb E. Washburn, Hamden, Conn., 1964), 279.

[45] William A. Koelsch, "A Proud though Special Erudition: Justin Winsor as Historian of Discovery," American Antiquarian Society, *Proceedings* 93, part 1 (1983), 56, 92.

North America, 1534–1700 (1894), and *The Mississippi Basin: The Struggle Between England and France, 1697–1763* (1895), as well as other studies of local history. How could a man who had, as Frederick J. Turner put it in his review of Winsor's *Westward Movement,* "established his ability in so wide a range of fields, requiring such stores of knowledge, and such a diversity of historical equipment" that he "cannot but be granted a position among the first of American historians"[46] have become so nearly forgotten by his successors at Harvard that he is scarcely mentioned in the 1974 edition of the *Harvard Guide to American History?* In part Winsor's eclipse is due to the fact that he ignored narrative in favor of what he considered a "critical" accumulation of carefully tested data. In addition, he considered geography to be the vital context of historical action, to the point of environmental determinism. Finally, he believed the origins of American history to emerge from the entire experience of European discovery and exploration, not merely from the belated English colonial settlements.

While Winsor's critical essays on the sources, particularly with regard to the cartographic record of early American history, are still models of careful scholarship and continue to be useful, and while his innovative methods as librarian and teacher at Harvard are still deserving of praise, he was burdened with unrecognized biases – racial, religious, and environmental – common to the "serenely confident Unitarian mind" of many nineteenth-century New Englanders.[47] Thus, in his writings, the Indians are invariably "savages," while 3,000 constitute a "horde." When Winsor recounts the arrival of the Jesuit Paul Le Jeune in 1632 at Tadoussac, we are told that "Le Jeune saw for the first time, as they came on board the ship, some of the uncouth and filthy creatures whose interests, as he understood them, were to fill so large a part of his devoted life."[48] Yet Winsor was also willing to express a severe moral judgment about a European figure like Columbus. "He might, like Las Casas," he noted, "have rebuked the fiendishness of his contemporaries; he set them an example of perverted belief." As the New World's discoverer he "might have been its father; he proved to be its despoiler." Can we excuse Columbus because of the standards of the period? "The degradation of the times ceases to be an excuse when the man to be judged stands on the pinnacle of the ages."[49]

[46] Quoted in ibid., 94.
[47] Ibid., 92.
[48] Justin Winsor, *Cartier to Frontenac* (Boston, 1894), 139.
[49] Justin Winsor, *Christopher Columbus and How He Received and Imparted the Spirit of Discovery* (Boston, 1892), 500, 512.

The nineteenth century witnessed the development in both English and French Canada of dynamic but largely avocational historiographic traditions that reflected the influences of nationalism, romanticism, and the fact that Native peoples had ceased to be a living presence in the lives of most Euro-Canadians. French Canadian historians sought to glorify the struggle of their people to survive and maintain their cultural integrity in the face of British expansion. Because of this, Native people were accorded a more restricted and negative role than they had been previously.

François-Xavier Garneau's *Histoire du Canada* (1845–8) was written as a response to Lord Durham's observation that French Canadians were a people with neither a history nor a literature. Like the French Canadian folklore of earlier days, Garneau sought to glorify the achievements of French settlers by stressing the extent to which their lives had been threatened by the Indians. Unlike Charlevoix, he had little personal contact with Native people; hence nothing inhibited him from contrasting the moral virtues and physical courage of the French with the cruelty of the Iroquois and the moral degradation of other Native groups. Scalping, torture, and massacres were given greater emphasis than in previous works. Indians were described as sexually promiscuous, enslaving their women, and mistreating their children. He also implied that prior to the coming of the French, all Indians had subsisted by hunting.

Garneau set the style that was followed by later French Canadian historians, such as Jean-Baptiste Ferland, Etienne-Michel Faillon, and Henri-Raymond Casgrain. As priests, they tended to emphasize the role of the Roman Catholic church in implanting French civilization in North America to a greater extent than Garneau had done. In their efforts to demonstrate the benefits of conversion, they further emphasized what they saw as the negative aspects of traditional Indian cultures. Toward the end of the nineteenth and in the early twentieth centuries, Benjamin Sulte and Lionel Groulx stressed the biological inferiority of Indians in a way that had not been done before. Although French Canadian historians often resented Parkman's portrayal of their ancestors as a backward people by comparison with the New Englanders, they were powerfully attracted by his romantic approach to historiography and spiritedly reproduced his negative stereotypes of Native people, which reinforced views that were already engrained in their own thinking. It was probably also mainly through Parkman that intellectual racism was introduced into French Canadian historiography.

Early English Canadian historians sought to encourage settlement and economic development, later ones to forge a sense of Canadian identity.[50] In general, Native people were accorded even less attention than they were in French Canadian histories. While heroic figures who had been allies of the British, such as Joseph Brant and Tecumseh, were portrayed as Canadian patriots, Indians in general were stigmatized, in a style often colored by Parkman, as a wild and primeval race that was incapable of becoming civilized and hence was doomed to perish as a consequence of the spread of European civilization. The easy subjugation and rapid decline in numbers of Native people were interpreted as inevitable results of evolutionary processes rather than as the consequences of European political and economic policies.

Yet there was considerable ambivalence in the way that English-Canadian historians portrayed Native people at this time. They frequently blamed American historians for exaggerating the cruelty and treacherousness of Indians and relished comparing the "brutal" treatment of Native peoples by the Americans with the "generous" treatment they received in Canada. Historians proudly informed their readers that in Canada Indians had never suffered from racial antagonisms, treaty breaking, removal from reserves, abuse by greedy settlers, or failure to secure justice. J. C. Hopkins affirmed that there was no more splendid page in Canadian history than its treatment of its "native wards."[51] Yet the same historian expressed gratitude that Providence had sent epidemics to sweep away the Native inhabitants of southern Ontario and Quebec, thus leaving the region to be occupied by French and English settlers, who, unlike the Americans, had no wrongs against Natives for which to atone. On the whole, these historians displayed less charity toward Native people than a desire to feel morally superior to their Euro-American neighbors to the south.

Anthropology began as an amateur study in North America in the late eighteenth century, its development greatly encouraged by Thomas Jefferson and the American Philosophical Society. Yet it only acquired professional status, first in museums and later also in universities, during the

---

50 M. Brook Taylor, *Promoters, Patriots, and Partisans: Historiography in Nineteenth-Century English Canada* (Toronto, 1989).

51 J. C. Hopkins, *The Story of the Dominion: Four Hundred Years in the Annals of Half a Continent* (Toronto, 1901), 65.

latter half of the nineteenth century. It also had in the beginning no systematic database. Hence it is scarcely surprising that throughout most of the nineteenth century the interpretation of anthropological findings tended to mirror and reinforce the social prejudices of the period.

Anthropology developed in Western societies out of a romantic curiosity about human diversity as Europeans encountered societies that had simpler technologies than their own and that they judged to be more primitive socially and intellectually as well. This interest was further piqued as antiquarians slowly realized that equally "primitive" cultures had existed in Europe in prehistoric times. Under the influence of Enlightenment philosophy, these two perspectives were combined during the eighteenth century in an evolutionary synthesis that viewed all human societies as evolving from simple to complex. The twin goals of anthropologists were to understand the small-scale societies that European colonists were coming to dominate around the world and to discover more about how Europeans had lived prior to their earliest written records.

In the United States, anthropology was at first identified largely with the study of the American Indian. Its four branches were ethnology, which sought to record the rapidly disappearing traditional cultures of the Indians; anthropological linguistics, which studied their languages; physical anthropology, which defined their physical types; and prehistoric archaeology, which examined the artifactual record of their past prior to European contact. These four branches began to constitute a coherent discipline in the 1840s, when an interest in classifying information about Native languages and cultures became linked to a growing concern with the rich archaeological record of the past and a physical anthropology that sought to account for human behavior in biological terms.

In its early stages North American anthropology was not dominated by any one theoretical position. Most early anthropologists, such as Albert Gallatin, subscribed to the doctrine of cultural evolutionism as it had been formulated by Enlightenment philosophers and popularized by works such as the Scottish historian William Robertson's *The History of America* (1777). They viewed European civilization as the product of progressive cultural elaboration that promoted not only technological but also intellectual and moral progress. Yet they rejected the racist claim that a more evolved culture implied superior intellectual capacity and saw in the achievements of Native people evidence of noble feelings, political acumen, and artistic sensibilities that long antedated any European influence. Daniel Wilson and Horatio Hale were among the few anthropologists who carried this view into the second half of the nineteenth century. Other avocational anthropologists, such as McGill University's John William Dawson, continued to champion the degenerationist view of human history and were in that respect the intellectual heirs of Lafitau.

In the middle decades of the nineteenth century, most anthropologists adopted an evolutionary perspective that interpreted cultural and biological evolution as being interdependent. Beginning in the 1860s, the idea of natural selection, as applied to human beings by the English polymath John Lubbock (Lord Avebury), offered a congenial explanation for the primitive condition of American Indians and their seemingly stubborn refusal to accept the benefits of civilization. This view was championed by the anthropologists at the Smithsonian Institution, who saw it as providing the intellectual underpinnings for a unified approach to their discipline. From an anthropological perspective, the ethnographic study of largely static American Indian cultures was regarded as being scientifically less interesting in its own right than for the information it could provide concerning the early stages in the development of European cultures.[52]

It was generally believed that Native people had lived in the New World for only a few thousand years and had experienced little cultural development prior to the arrival of the Europeans. Hence it was assumed that "prehistoric" cultures would be little different from historical ones. While the archaeological remains along the eastern seaboard did little to challenge this view, the large ancient mounds and more elaborate artifacts found in the Ohio and Mississippi Valleys as European colonization spread westward suggested that a more advanced civilization had existed in that area than was present in early historical times. This gave rise to the Moundbuilder controversy, which persisted throughout the nineteenth century and acquired a religious dimension in the revelations of Joseph Smith, which constitute the basis of the Mormon Church. While some people, particularly degenerationists, viewed the Moundbuilders as ancestors of the American Indians, the most popular explanations linked them to a civilized race that had either retreated south into Mexico or been exterminated by the North American Indians in the period before the arrival of the Europeans. The more extreme versions characterized the Indians as irredeemable enemies of civilization rather than as simply primi-

[52] Curtis M. Hinsley, Jr., *Savages and Scientists: The Smithsonian Institution and the Development of American Anthropology, 1846–1910* (Washington, D.C., 1981); D. J. Meltzer, "The Antiquity of Man and the Development of American Archaeology," in M. B. Schiffer (ed.), *Advances in Archaeological Method and Theory* (New York, 1983), 6:1–51.

tive and justified European expansion westward as retribution for what the Indians had done to the Moundbuilders.

Even when the archaeologist Cyrus Thomas succeeded in 1894 in demolishing the idea that the Moundbuilders were not Indians, he did this by refuting valid as well as exaggerated claims concerning their advanced cultural status and trying to demonstrate that the Moundbuilders were little different from the disrupted Native peoples whom Europeans had encountered in the Midwest in the eighteenth century.[53] What all of these interpretations had in common was the assumption that Indian cultures had not changed significantly prior to encountering Europeans. Joseph Henry, the celebrated physicist who was Secretary of the Smithsonian Institution, used his influence to try to persuade archaeologists to avoid speculation until a sufficient body of data had been collected. Yet the interest in the past and especially in the cultural status of Indians precluded any such objectivity, and Henry's successors at the Smithsonian committed themselves to a cultural evolutionary perspective that was colored by social Darwinism.

Anthropologists, especially those who had personal contact with Native people, tended to view Indian life in a more rounded and objective way than did the average Euro-American. Yet their opinions about the primitive state and inevitable extinction of Native cultures closely agreed with popular Euro-American views on these subjects and helped to reinforce them. The negative views of Parkman and other North American historians cannot be understood independently of those held by the nineteenth-century anthropologists, any more than the latter can be evaluated without taking account of the broader opinions of Euro-American society. Most of these historians were aware of the anthropological work of their era and their views of Indians were shaped by it; indeed, since historians often had little direct contact with Native people they tended to rely increasingly on the opinions of anthropologists. Parkman, in particular, used his extraordinary literary talents to express contemporary scientific as well as popular views. Thus his works became the most enduring expression of Euro-American views about Native peoples in the middle and late nineteenth century.

Although it occurred too late to affect nineteenth-century historiography, American anthropology was transformed in the last decade of the

---

[53] Robert S. Silverberg, *Mound Builders of Ancient America: The Archaeology of a Myth* (Greenwich, N.Y., 1968).

century by the work of Franz Boas, a German who carried out ethnographic research in the Arctic and British Columbia before settling in the United States in 1888. Boas was strongly influenced by German neo-Kantian idealism and by romanticism. He viewed the diversity of cultures as a direct refutation of the fundamental idea of evolutionary anthropology that was then popular in the United States and encouraged his students to study the ways of life of specific Indian peoples, rather than items of culture in isolation from the total cultures of which they were a part. He also opposed explaining differences in human behavior in terms of innate biological factors. He sought to demonstrate that all human races shared an equal biological capacity for change and development and that differences in human behavior were the result of historical rather than biological factors.

Boas rejected the distinction that evolutionary anthropologists had drawn between civilized and primitive cultures as being unacceptably ethnocentric. He denied that there was an absolute scale of values that was applicable to all societies or by which they could be judged in relation to one another. Boasian cultural relativism denied that people of European origin could objectively judge the morality or religious beliefs of peoples living elsewhere in the world by comparing them with their own. Boas's work was also directed against the view that technologically less-developed societies were socially and morally inferior to Western ones.

Boasian anthropology had its share of shortcomings. In particular, it was more interested in reconstructing what Native cultures had been like prior to European contact than in studying the consequences of that contact. Changes that had come about as a result of European presence tended to be regarded as an obstacle that had to be overcome in order to reconstruct the pristine condition of Native cultures. In their opposition to evolutionism, many Boasian anthropologists also continued to underestimate the extent to which Native cultures had changed in the precontact period. Yet, by opposing racism, stressing a holistic view of individual cultures, and denying that one culture could be used as a standard for evaluating the rest, they emphasized as anthropologists had never done before the dignity of Native peoples and of the ways of life they had evolved before the arrival of Europeans.

While it cannot be denied that the mixture of evolutionism and romanticism that succeeded the Enlightenment distorted the lens through which Europeans and Euro-Americans looked at Native Americans, a more serious impediment to understanding was the continuing ethnocentric biases – conscious and unconscious – which influenced the ways in which

non-Native Americans perceived Native peoples. While these biases continued to influence the way in which Native people were portrayed in historical
writing, such biases would find themselves under assault by the more
scientifically minded observers of the twentieth century.

TWENTIETH-CENTURY REPORTS AND
INTERPRETATIONS OF NATIVE AMERICANS

In the late nineteenth and early twentieth centuries, the attention that
historians paid to Native peoples in both the United States and Canada
declined still further, as historians devoted ever more attention to the
lengthening chronicle of the achievements of European settlers. Native
people, who were thought to have no history of their own, were increasingly regarded as the exclusive concern of anthropologists. Indians were
assigned an ever smaller role even in general histories, where they were
normally confined to introductory chapters describing the natural environment and early European settlement. To the extent that they were
mentioned at all, their negative image as a primitive people that was
doomed to disappear persisted, even if this image was expressed in more
neutral language than it had been previously. The growing remoteness of
Native people from the daily lives of most Euro-Americans and their loss
of political power made it easier for historians to ignore the important
role they had played from the seventeenth to near the end of the nineteenth century.

The increasingly peripheral character of the Indian is seen even in the
work of Frederick Jackson Turner, whose famous essay "The Significance of
the Frontier in American History" (1893) reshaped the North American
historical profession and continues to exert a powerful influence on that
profession. Although Turner turned his attention directly to the frontier
between Indian and Euro-American, it was a frontier not of historical
actors of equal significance, but "the meeting point between savagery and
civilization."[54] Just as modern roads and cities owed their locations first to
geological conditions, secondly to the animals who tramped out paths to
water holes and salt licks, thirdly to the Indians who followed the animals
and enlarged the trails, and next to the traders, "the pathfinder[s] of
civilization," and so on sequentially up the ladder of civilization, the

[54] Frederick Jackson Turner, "The Significance of the Frontier in American History" (1893), in
Turner, *The Frontier in American History* (New York, 1920, 1947), 1, 3, 11.

Indian served at best as a part of the natural environment or a lower order of humanity that it was the destiny of Euro-Americans to conquer and reshape into "civilization." Turner assumed that American democracy was a product of the interaction of Euro-Americans with the vast cornucopia of "free" and "vacant" land. He never adequately faced the consequences of determining how the end of the unbroken frontier, announced in the Census of 1890, and the anticipated drying up of "an area of free land" available to Euro-Americans would affect this democracy. Needless to say, Turner did not paint Native Americans in the forefront of his canvas. They served, with nature, as the backdrop.

When Henry Nash Smith published his *Virgin Land: The American West as Symbol and Myth* (1950), he discussed Turner's work in a chapter entitled "The Myth of the Garden and Turner's Frontier Hypothesis." He appropriately treated Turner in terms of myth and symbol rather than historical fact. In what he called the Garden of the World or Garden of the West, the Indian was merely a shadowy threat or a distant memory. Other historians have similarly shaped and defined America's westward movement in terms that virtually exclude the American Indian. Thus, Arthur Schlesinger, Jr., for example, could celebrate Andrew Jackson as the embodiment of the American democratic spirit in his *The Age of Jackson* (1945) without discussing Jackson's dealings with the American Indians.

A renewed interest in the historical study of Native people accompanied the development of economic history during the 1920s. In his pioneering book *The Fur Trade in Canada* (1930), the Canadian economist Harold Innis, partly inspired by Charles McIlwain's study of Indian participation in the colonial fur trade,[55] stressed the important role that Native peoples had played as suppliers of a major staple across the northern half of the continent. Innis assumed that Indians quickly became dependent upon European metal wares and were locked into trading relations that were increasingly controlled by Europeans. As an economic formalist, he elaborated his arguments in terms of purely economic considerations and without trying to understand the fur trade from a Native point of view. Yet, in his writings, for the first time since the 1840s, Native people were assigned a significant and prolonged role in the history of Canada following European discovery. Innis also inspired the American economist George T. Hunt's *The Wars of the Iroquois* (1940), in which Hunt argued that the

---

[55] Charles H. McIlwain (ed.), *An Abridgement of the Indian Affairs . . . Transacted in the Colony of New York, from the Year 1678 to the Year 1751*, by Peter Wraxall (Cambridge, Mass., 1915).

economic implications of the fur trade quickly rendered traditional relations among Native peoples obsolete and created new patterns of alliances and warfare.

Nineteenth-century American anthropology, both in its evolutionist and Boasian formulations, made no provision for studying cultural changes among Native peoples after European contact, although there was abundant historical documentation of this process. Such changes were viewed mainly as a manifestation of cultural disintegration that was best ignored when trying to reconstruct traditional cultures, as Boas did when he deleted sewing machines, but not Hudson's Bay Company blankets, from his descriptions of potlatches. Anthropologists tended not to notice that such changes transformed whole societies instead of being merely the loss or addition of specific cultural traits. The most important exception was James Mooney, who detailed the trauma of cultural change and loss of power in his study of the Ghost Dance, an indigenous religious movement that late in the nineteenth century sought to restore the morale of the Plains Indians.[56] Curtis Hinsley has suggested that Mooney's Irish background helped him to realize that Native responses to Euro-American pressure should not automatically be interpreted as evidence of cultural disintegration.[57]

Beginning in the late 1920s, Boasian relativism and the expansion of history beyond its traditional concerns with politics and biography laid the groundwork for the development of ethnohistory. One of the earliest substantial efforts in this direction was W. C. MacLeod's *The American Indian Frontier* (1928), which attempted to survey the history of Indian–Euro-American relations throughout the New World. While this book was an interesting exercise in social history, MacLeod only succeeded in this goal of viewing frontier history from "the Indian side" in two short chapters dealing with prophetic movements.

The Canadian historian Alfred G. Bailey's *The Conflict of European and Eastern Algonkian Cultures* (1937) was the first major study of Indian history published in North America. Although he was strongly influenced by Innis, Bailey employed a cultural relativist approach in an attempt to understand the changing responses of Native people to European encroachment in eastern Canada. His work is remarkable for its explicit awareness of many cultural as well as economic factors that influenced relations

[56] James Mooney, *The Ghost-Dance Religion and the Sioux Outbreak of 1890* (Washington, D.C., 1896).
[57] Hinsley, *Savages and Scientists*, 207–8.

between Native people and Europeans. In this fashion, Bailey sought to understand the introduction of European technology not simply in economic terms, as Innis had done, but also in relation to the entirety of Native cultural patterns. He also tried to ascertain how exposure to European societies and religious beliefs altered or did not alter Native customs. Bailey's work thus contrasted with and complemented that of Innis. Soon after, the New Zealand anthropologist Felix Keesing published a study of 300 years of cultural change among the Menominis of Wisconsin.[58] Like Bailey, Keesing suggested that many features of Native American cultures that anthropologists had assumed to be aboriginal were in fact the products of interaction with European societies. At the time they were published, however, neither of these studies attracted the attention that in retrospect both seem to have deserved. This illustrates how alien the concept of history still was to American anthropologists.

Nevertheless, beginning in the 1930s, at the same time that it became evident that Native people were not going to die out or easily assimilate, other American anthropologists started to become interested in how the ways of life of Native peoples had changed in response to European domination. They believed that, if anthropologists could discover more about how Native peoples had adapted to the presence of Europeans, they would be able to advise government agencies how to deal more effectively and humanely with them. Those early studies of "acculturation," which aimed to formulate useful generalizations about cultural change, gradually resulted in a growing appreciation of the complexity and diversity of what had happened to different Native groups since European contact. This development was hastened as a result of anthropologists in the United States becoming more familiar with documentary sources as a result of their involvement as researchers in postwar land-claims cases. In this fashion, the study of acculturation slowly evolved into ethnohistory, the birth of which was marked by the publication of Edward Spicer's *Cycles of Conquest* (1962), a monumental study of what had happened to the diverse Native peoples of the Southwest under successive Spanish, Mexican, and American administrations. By that time anthropologists had ceased to study only factors bringing about acculturation and had begun to investigate the ways in which Native groups had resisted acculturation and struggled to preserve their traditional cultures and identities over the centuries. It took longer for

[58] Felix M. Keesing, *The Menomini Indians of Wisconsin: A Study of Three Centuries of Cultural Contact and Change* (Philadelphia, 1939).

ethnohistorians to appreciate the diversity of reactions within Native groups and to realize that European nationalities and Native groups had rarely confronted one another in a monolithic fashion.[59] North American ethnohistorians were slower than their Australian and New Zealand counterparts to utilize archaeological data to understand better the processes that were at work in Native cultures at the time of European contact and to supplement written sources concerning change in early historical times.

Although ethnohistory was pioneered by anthropologists, and more specifically by ethnologists, it soon attracted scholars who had been trained in other disciplines. A few of these were geographers and economists, but most were historians. Each group brought new skills and fresh theoretical perspectives to the study of Native American history, thereby helping to produce works of greater diversity and perceptiveness. Historians also helped to ensure greater rigor in the analysis of written documents, and especially archival materials. This diversity created problems of integration and definition for ethnohistorical research. It is now generally agreed that ethnohistory is not a discipline but a corpus of analytical techniques that scholars from different disciplines can use to study the history of nonliterate peoples.

The last two decades have seen profound changes in the study of Native Americans. Anthropology has been reshaping the way in which American Indian history is written; history on the other hand, has been influencing the character of anthropological writing about Native Americans. An even more important change has been the internal developments within both history and anthropology. Historians have increasingly shifted from an emphasis on the activities of elites to a consideration of communities and individuals, particularly in their social and economic character. The traditional study of North American political and military history has given way to a centrifugal social and cultural history that is focused on specific classes, genders, and racial and ethnic groups. Studies of North American Indian history have been assigned a place alongside that of immigrants, workers, African-Americans, and women. At the same time history has been acquiring a more explicitly cultural and relativistic orientation. There is also an increasingly ideological character to much of this history, which has tended to adopt a perspective critical of the dominant preten-

---

59 Bruce G. Trigger, *The Children of Aataentsic: A History of the Huron People to 1660* (Montreal, 1976). On other developments in the study of Native history around this time, see James A. Clifton, "The Tribal History—An Obsolete Paradigm," *American Indian Culture and Research Journal* 3 (4) (1979), 81–100.

sions of Western culture, as well as an increasing fascination with the epistemological problems inherent in studying "the Other" through the veil of cultural differences and self-interest.

The same trends have influenced anthropology, although anthropologists have outstripped historians in their willingness to engage in ideological and epistemological debates. Anthropology has acquired a historical dimension, as history is increasingly recognized as providing depth to ethnographic analyses and correctives to hastily conceived theoretical formulations.

Influential in driving both history and anthropology toward a new conception of the role of both disciplines was the French *Annales* school of historians, which emphasized collective mentalities, economic and social trends, and unconscious structures. This new emphasis in history reinforced the growing role of structural models in anthropology, of which Claude Lévi-Strauss, also of France, was the leading exponent. Anthropologists, such as Marshall Sahlins, readily adapted the new approach in such essays as "Other Times, Other Customs: The Anthropology of History."[60] Sahlins's work emphasized the manner in which a sophisticated understanding of the latest trends in both disciplines could be used to illuminate the past: for example, in explaining mass religious conversions or sudden military defeat. One of his most famous essays deals with the mystical and political significance of a pole above the New Zealand town of Kororareka (now Russell) as a cause of the Maori revolt of 1844–46. The pole, with its symbolic significance to both sides as an expression of the concept of sovereignty and possession of the earth, was the focus of several years of fighting and negotiating, which, without the cultural understanding that Sahlins brought to the subject, might easily have remained inexplicable.[61]

Sahlins's work with those peoples who verge on "historylessness" is representative of other anthropological studies that deal with "people without history," to borrow the phrase that Eric Wolf used in the title of his study of the incorporation of non-Western societies into a worldwide economy.[62] Some of these studies, such as Wolf's, are governed by theoretical and ideological assumptions drawn more from liberal Western culture than from the actual peoples they study, but others, such as Sahlins's,

---

[60] Marshall Sahlins, "Other Times, Other Customs: The Anthropology of History," in *Islands of History* (Chicago, 1985), 32–72.
[61] Sahlins, *Islands of History*, 54–72.
[62] Eric R. Wolf, *Europe and the People without History* (Berkeley, Calif., 1982).

deliberately reject dependence upon Western theoretical formulations as a way of explaining non-Western behavior. Sahlins asserts that we have gone beyond "the theoretical differences that are supposed to divide anthropology and history" and that "paradoxically, anthropologists are as often diachronic in outlook as historians nowadays are synchronic." We have at last, he asserts, achieved a "structural, historical anthropology."[63] Unfortunately for the student of North America, the leading anthropological theorists, such as Sahlins, Wolf, and Clifford Geertz, have dealt principally with non-Western cultures located outside of North America. Nevertheless, their insights are being applied to the study of Native North Americans by both historians and anthropologists. A growing respect for Native viewpoints and taking account of oral traditions has set new standards in ethnohistorical studies of Native North Americans, as exemplified by Loretta Fowler's *Arapahoe Politics, 1851–1978* (1982).

Yet despite its fruitfulness, the interplay between anthropology and history remains complex and confusing. Paul Rabinow has noted that "the moment when the historical profession is discovering cultural anthropology in the [unrepresentative] person of Clifford Geertz is just the moment when Geertz is being questioned in anthropology."[64] The confusion caused in anthropology by the extraordinary conjunction of the two disciplines has been wittingly parodied by the English anthropologist Edmund Leach, who writes "Why should anthropologists take it for granted that history never repeats itself but persuade themselves that, if left alone, ethnographic cultures never do anything else?"[65]

The study of ethnohistory has also been overtaken by a wave of subjectivism that has called into question the ability of any social science to produce an objective understanding of human behavior. Under the influence of hermeneutics, semiotics, deconstruction, and phenomenology, many anthropologists and historians no longer believe that they are able to consider data independently of their own beliefs and values. As an extension of this, ethnohistorians also no longer feel justified in studying the impact that the presence of Europeans had on Native cultures without first emphasizing the biases of their sources. There is growing consideration not only of the technological and economic contributions that Native peoples made to European colonization but also (as this chapter

---

[63] Sahlins, *Islands of History*, 72.
[64] Quoted, with brackets in quote, in Edmund Leach, review of *Works and Lives: The Anthropologist as Author* (1988) by Clifford Geertz, in *American Ethnologist* 16 (1989), 137.
[65] Leach's review, 140.

illustrates) on how Europeans perceived Native people and on the intellectual impact that the encounter with Native peoples had on European thinking. This development is progressively blurring the distinction between ethnohistory on the one hand and the study of Western intellectual history on the other. Ethnohistorians recognize that European reports of their contacts with Native peoples were greatly influenced by the preconceptions that Europeans brought with them to these experiences. Because it is now seen as impossible to determine what the records left by Europeans tell us about Native behavior unless the preoccupations of their authors are understood and allowed for, European intellectual history has been acknowledged as an essential prerequisite for the study of ethnohistory.

Subjectivism has also increased an awareness of the arbitrary nature and the irresolvability of the theoretical biases that influence the interpretation of Native American history. The most heated controversies take the form of a confrontation between rationalist-materialist and idealist-cultural relativist interpretations of human behavior. No ethnohistorian ignores the importance of cultural traditions in influencing human behavior. Yet rationalists argue that much of what human beings do can be understood in terms of a universal rationality, which seeks to minimize effort or risk in the achieving of basic goals, such as providing food and shelter. The rationalist-materialist school continues to argue that, however Native people initially perceived Europeans, they soon appreciated the utilitarian value of European metalware and quickly became dependent on it. Their efforts to obtain more of these goods led them to ignore traditional supernatural sanctions that limited the taking of game, and eventually brought them into increasingly destructive conflicts with neighboring Native groups over the control of trade routes and hunting territories. Growing reliance on metal goods and decreasing supplies of furs increased dependence on Europeans, which in turn undermined Native self-confidence and their adherence to traditional belief systems.[66] Other historians have stressed rational calculation of the political situation as playing a major role in the struggles of Indian groups to maintain their independence and control of lands.[67]

Under the influence of Sahlins and other cultural anthropologists, a

---

[66] A. W. Trelease, *Indian Affairs in Colonial New York: The Seventeenth Century* (Ithaca, N.Y., 1960); Trigger, *The Children of Aataentsic.*

[67] Francis Jennings, *The Invasion of America* (Chapel Hill, N.C., 1975), *The Ambiguous Iroquois Empire* (New York, 1984), *Empire of Fortune* (New York, 1988).

growing number of ethnohistorians have assigned traditional beliefs a more important role as determinants of human behavior. George Hamell has argued that Native groups initially valued European goods, not for their utilitarian properties, but for the religious significance that they assigned to them in terms of their traditional religious concepts. He further maintains that these traditional evaluations explain relations between Indians and Europeans throughout the two centuries that followed the European discovery of North America.[68] Others have claimed that Native groups were little influenced by European technology or economic considerations and that therefore until at least 1760 most Native groups in the Midwest were able to determine their own destinies in the midst of European colonial rivalries.[69] They also maintain that Indian warfare during the early historical period was mainly a continuation of long-standing conflicts, the scale of which was perhaps exacerbated by the acquisition of European firearms and by a traditional desire to replace unparalleled losses resulting from European diseases by incorporating increasing numbers of prisoners into their societies.[70]

The most extreme subjectivist views maintain that a historical consciousness is totally alien to North American Indians, who have always conceived of their relationship to the cosmos very differently from the anthropocentric one that dominates Western thinking. Calvin Martin denies that ethnohistorians can legitimately write about societies that were not "conceived in history" and did not willingly launch themselves into a historical trajectory.[71] Yet, even if such broad generalizations about the many hundreds of Native cultures that have existed in North America were correct, it is contrary to historiographical experience to suggest that ethnohistorians cannot acquire some understanding of the history of an alien culture or that histories cannot be written about peoples who were themselves not interested in history. Moreover, while every historian recognizes the importance of understanding how events appeared to those who participated in them, this is for the most part a means to historical understanding rather than its end.

[68] George R. Hamell, "Strawberries, Floating Islands, and Rabbit Captains: Mythical Realities and European Contact in the Northeast during the Sixteenth and Seventeenth Centuries," *Journal of Canadian Studies* 21 (1987), 74.
[69] William Eccles, "Review of *Natives and Newcomers*," *William and Mary Quarterly* 43 (1986), 480–3; C. E. Heidenreich, "Review of *Natives and Newcomers*," *Native Studies Review* 2 (1986), 140–7.
[70] D. K. Richter, "War and Culture: The Iroquois Experience," *William and Mary Quarterly* 40 (1983), 528–9.
[71] Calvin Martin (ed.), *The American Indian and the Problem of History* (Oxford, 1987).

Many Native and Euro-American scholars argue that there is a traditional pattern to Native cultures that is irreconcilably different from that of Europeans and that a basic core of Native beliefs and values has survived unaltered despite often massive changes in their ways of life, including conversion to Christianity, over the past 500 years.[72] There is no doubt some truth to this claim. Many Native people have continued to share a common belief in the interdependence of all things and in the need for human beings to interconnect intellectually and emotionally with the cosmos in order to ensure abundance, quality of life, and peace for all. It is also arguably true that such beliefs are more conducive to self-restraint, contentment, and the conservation of nature than are the traditional evolutionary and biblically inspired views of Euro-Americans, which maintain that human beings have an unrestricted right to use other living things for their own purposes. On these grounds, Native people can claim that in many crucial respects their value systems are superior to, and more viable than, those of Euro-Americans.

Yet there is much disagreement about the specific nature of this core of beliefs,[73] and it is far from clear to what extent they are a specifically Native American heritage from some ancestral culture or alternatively a survival of the sort of values that are common to all small-scale, egalitarian societies around the world. Both factors may be involved. There has also been little systematic historical study of how these beliefs may or may not have changed over the centuries. Finally, if a static view is carried too far, it can lead to the conclusion that every aspect of human behavior is determined by the pattern of culture into which an individual is born. Such views deemphasize the role of reason, calculation, and choice and are counterfactual to observations, frequently made in our own lives and in the historical record, that even the most cherished beliefs have been discarded when people cease to believe that they promote their best interests. At one level, modern idealism is far removed from the evolutionary and racist views that inspired Parkman's calumnies about Native peoples, and its adherents sincerely believe that they are honoring and enhancing the traditional values of Native people. Yet they risk sharing with Parkman a minimization of rationality that, upon reflection, Native people may find denigrating and which distorts our understanding of human behavior. Ethnohistorians must strive to find an acceptable middle ground between

---

[72] Ibid.; Sioui, *For an Amerindian Autohistory.*
[73] S. D. Gill, *Mother Earth: An American Story* (Chicago, 1987).

extreme rationalism and extreme idealism. In doing so, they can draw inspiration from the work of Alfred Bailey who identified this problem over fifty years ago.

Along with relativism, the role of ideology in the interpretation of Indian history has increased in significance in recent decades. This increase has been, to a large degree, linked to the rise of Native voices. Many professional anthropologists and historians working closely with North American Natives felt compelled to identify with the interests and aspirations of the peoples they studied, mainly because of genuine sympathy for the Native position. This has led ethnohistorians to address new problems and look at old ones in a less ethnocentric manner. In recent years, sound research has been carried out that has revealed the injustices, coercion, and hypocrisy that have pervaded relations between Native peoples and Europeans as well as the unsuspected resourcefulness with which many Native groups have conducted their relations with Europeans. It has been argued that the major accomplishment of ethnohistory so far is not what has been learned about how Native people have perceived their experiences over the years but what it is revealing about Euro-American attitudes toward Native people.[74]

This ideological commitment was reinforced by the gradual emergence of a growing number of Indian anthropologists and historians, largely in the post–World War II period, who amplified the voices of Indian writers, lawyers, novelists, artists, ministers, and others who increasingly began to represent the Native American world directly. A marriage between liberal, non-Indian scholars, who saw the problems of the twentieth-century world in terms of imperialism, capitalism, racism, and oppression of third world peoples, and the increasingly vocal Native spokespeople seemed logical. But because of the suspicion of many Native Americans that anthropology was a discipline theoretically and historically linked to colonialism, such a marriage was not easy to consummate. Vine Deloria, Jr.'s *Custer Died for Your Sins* (1969), particularly the chapter on "anthros" that first appeared separately in *Playboy* magazine, forced anthropologists to take extraordinary steps to explain or justify themselves. Their response was not difficult to make in the 1960s, when a radical spirit pervaded North American campuses and the Vietnam War created strong anti-establishment feelings on the part of much of the academic establishment. Anthropologists sought to "reinvent" anthropology[75] by making it more useful in a practical sense to

[74] Bruce Trigger, "Alfred G. Bailey – Ethnohistorian," *Acadiensis* 18(2) (1989), 20.
[75] Dell Hymes (ed.), *Reinventing Anthropology* (New York, 1969).

Native Americans, often in the guise of "action anthropology" or "applied anthropology." These same anthropologists also played a prominent role in questioning the epistemological assumptions underlying earlier anthropology, in particular the assumption of the possibility of achieving objectivity and the ability to define and find "truth."[76] Perhaps the most common result of the anthropological revolution was to politicize and radicalize the discipline and to force anthropologists, even while they decried the possibility of certainty in their scholarly judgments, to insist upon the absolute validity of their political judgments.

The lasting impact of Vine Deloria's manifesto was illustrated by the invited day-long session at the Eighty-eighth Annual Meeting of the American Anthropological Association in 1989 on the subject of *"Custer Died for Your Sins:* A Twenty-Year Retrospective on Relations between Anthropologists and American Indians." While continuing to decry what they regarded as Deloria's exaggerations, anthropologists expressed their serious and respectful concern with his criticisms. In response, Deloria launched a follow-up attack on anthropological resistance to the campaign to repatriate and rebury Indian skeletal remains collected by past archaeological expeditions.

The extent to which bias, whether based on sympathy or ideology, has affected the study of Native American history, could be illustrated by many examples. The case of the Hopi Indians is a good one. The Hopis, perhaps the least assimilated of all the Indian peoples in the United States, were, nevertheless, divided by religious and political differences, although the distinction between the two is less than in Western societies. The adoption of a constitution under the Indian Reorganization Act of 1934 exacerbated some of these factional differences. Variously defined "traditional" and "progressive" factions have jockeyed for position within the Hopi community, rejecting, allying themselves with, or ignoring anthropologists and historians who have sought to write their history. Their sensitivity has been particularly stimulated by the Hopi-Navajo relocation dispute, which has sought to resolve the conflict over certain lands claimed or occupied by members of both peoples. Anthropologists have involved themselves in this dispute, largely in support of the Navajos for reasons that are related to their self-interest and antipathy to the federal government's proposed relocation solution. In the process, the interests

---

[76] E.g., Clifford Geertz, "Distinguished Lecture: Anti Anti-Relativism," *American Anthropologist* 86 (1984), 263–278. For a historian's approach to the subject see Peter Novick, *That Noble Dream: The "Objectivity Question" and the American Historical Profession* (New York, 1988).

and arguments of the tribes themselves, on the one hand, and of abstract justice on the other, have been largely ignored.[77]

A more specific instance of how the ideological element can shape historical research on an Indian people is provided by the Danish scholar Armin W. Geertz, who noted that despite his attempt to avoid commitment, "the Hopis told me outright, after allowing me to see how they could frustrate the first three months of my field work, that if I wanted to get any serious research done, then I would have to choose sides." Geertz noted that the choice "did not entail too great a cost," because the traditionalist faction, whose interpretation of Hopi prophecy Geertz showed no signs of believing, "was already suspicious of me anyway and had told me to come back when the apocalypse was over." Another scholar working among the Hopis, Richard Clemmer, chose the opposite path, continuing his long-term involvement with the traditionalists and thereby earning the hostility and opposition of the nontraditionalists.[78] Geertz's comments illustrate the coercive way in which students of Indian history and culture are now compelled or encouraged to conform to Native requirements. Such restrictions must be carefully considered in assessing the validity of work emerging from such a context. Because the Indian Reorganization Act established the basis for the present Hopi tribal government, which is opposed in various ways by the traditional faction, anyone commenting on the current state of the Hopis is inevitably drawn into a hot controversy about the representative character of the Hopi tribal government. Similar, if often less serious, problems in coping with factionalism are encountered in studying many other Native groups.

Some Native people go so far as to deny that non-Natives have either the understanding or moral right to study Native history. Only Native people, they assert, possess the knowledge of their own cultures that is necessary to understand their past. They also argue that, if non-Native historians write about Native history, they should be required to obtain Native permission and agree to share royalties with the people they are writing about before their work is published.[79]

It is easy to understand how history and anthropology have managed to

[77] Wilcomb E. Washburn, "Anthropological Advocacy in the Hopi-Navajo Land Dispute," *American Anthropologist* 91 (1989), 738–43.

[78] A. W. Geertz, "A Container of Ashes: Hopi Prophecy in History," *European Review of Native American Studies* 3(1) (1989), 6; Richard O. Clemmer, "The Hopi Traditionalist Movement," *American Indian Culture and Research Journal* 18(3) (1994), 125–66.

[79] Martin, *The American Indian and the Problem of History*.

repel rather than attract Native people. In this essay we have drawn attention to the different and often negative representations of Native people in successive phases of historiography, which have influenced the textbooks of each period and which, it can be argued, helped to justify policies that served selfish Euro-American interests. These representations clearly relate far more tangentially to how Native people actually behaved than to how European and Euro-American intellectuals have been predisposed to imagine they behaved. With the best will in the world, there is no assurance that modern historians are necessarily more objective in their treatments of Native people than earlier ones were.

Yet this same argument implies that no one but a Japanese historian should write about Japanese history, or a German historian about German history, or even – more extremely – that a Japanese not trained in historiography is more capable of writing about his country's history than is a Western historian who speaks Japanese and has intensively studied Japanese history and culture. It also ignores the fact that the history of North America over the past 500 years has been largely intercultural, in the sense that it deals either with the interaction of Native peoples and Europeans or with Native peoples who have been affected by such interaction. This makes it impossible for any single historian to have an "insider's" view of the total picture. Moreover, while Native people command a rich store of oral traditions that non-Native historians have only begun to record and analyze, European documentation of Native behavior can only be clearly understood once the biases of that documentation have been taken into account. This too is a task that requires a thorough understanding of both Native and Euro-American cultures for the period when the documentation was produced and hence cannot be considered the exclusive preserve of either Euro-American or Native specialists in intellectual history. Finally it can be questioned whether it is markedly easier for modern Native people to understand the mind-sets of their seventeenth-, eighteenth-, or nineteenth-century ancestors than it is for Euro-American historians to understand theirs. In any case, it is counterproductive to try to prevent Euro-American historians from acquiring better knowledge about Native history and culture, since even a limited and imperfect comprehension of Native beliefs and behavior results in a more informed understanding of how generations of Euro-Americans treated Native people. As the problems involved in writing Native history are better understood, it becomes clear that there is a need for growing cooperation between Native people and Euro-American historians and for the recruitment of more Native people into the study and teaching of North American history. It is in the interests of both Native and non-Native people that such research becomes more ecumenical rather than more balkanized in the years ahead.

Over the years, the increasing efforts of historians to deal with Native history and incorporate Native people into their broader understanding of North American history have created major problems of interpretation. The traditional Euro-American conception of Indian history was often "Indian-White" relations, rather than Indian history as such. Governmental relations, acts of Congress or Parliament, and exploits of U.S. Army officers or Hudson's Bay Company officials were frequently the major subject matter of this "Indian history." The unfamiliarity of many historians with the anthropological literature added to its one-sided character. It was also too easy for some Native people and anthropologists to insist that any admixture of Euro-American history with Indian history was somehow invalid. Yet the influence of Euro-Americans upon Indians and of Indians upon Euro-Americans was of overwhelming significance from the earliest times. One has only to look at the character of the deliberations of colonial assemblies to recognize that Indian matters were more often than not the most important concern of the settlers.

Looked at another way: what would the European colonization of America have been like had there been no Indians in the hemisphere? James Axtell has pointed out that America as we know it is almost impossible to conceive without considering the role played by Native Americans. He argues that "without the steady impress of Indian culture, the colonists would probably not have been ready for revolution in 1776, because they would not have been or felt sufficiently Americanized to stand before the world as an independent nation." "The Indian presence," he concludes, "precipitated the formation of an American identity."[80] On the other hand, Indian forms of government, religion, and economic and social organization were profoundly affected by the presence of Euro-Americans. Confederations of Indian peoples, and the consolidation of autonomous villages and groups, as they are known today, were more often than not caused by the need to create a better defense against Euro-American encroachment. Searching for a "pure" Indian postcontact history was, and remains, a fantasy.

As historians turned toward the Indian, they found the field littered with stereotypes, false generalizations, and antiquated historiography. For one

---

[80] James Axtell, "Colonial America without the Indians" (1987), in Axtell, *After Columbus: Essays in the Ethnohistory of Colonial North America* (New York, 1988), 222–43.

thing, most work on the American Indian has dealt with the period when the Indian nations were vigorously resisting the advance of Euro-American settlement. Little attention has been directed toward recent Indian history, despite the fact that the Indian population began its upturn (after the catastrophic decline in numbers in the period of early European contact) early in the twentieth century and has continued to grow ever since.

Another problem prevalent in Indian history was its habitual association with Western history and fur-trade history. In the United States, college undergraduates were apt to call a course in the history of the West "Cowboys and Indians." Until recently, neither Western nor fur-trade history was treated with the same seriousness as other aspects of North American history. Increasingly, however, mainline historians have devoted more attention to "frontier history," challenging or revising the insights of Frederick Jackson Turner and Harold Innis. Revisionist studies such as Patricia Nelson Limerick's *The Legacy of Conquest: The Unbroken Past of the American West* (1987), Richard White's *"It's Your Misfortune and None of My Own": A History of the American West* (1991), and Gerald Friesen's *The Canadian Prairies: A History* (1984) have placed more emphasis on Indian history and on the record of Indian–Euro-American conflict and exploitation. As a result, Western and fur-trade history, seen from a multicultural perspective, has come to experience some of the epistemological debates racking the anthropological profession in its moves toward a "reflexive" and "critical" anthropology. North American history was seen increasingly in terms of a colonial invasion and exploitation of a third world society forced to become a fourth world dependency. Anyone failing to experience the moral outrage that filled the practitioners of this history risked being attacked as insensitive if not benighted.

While the attention focused upon Indian history in recent decades has attracted many scholars into the field, very little progress was at first made toward removing stereotypes and compiling accurate historical evidence for the new hypotheses. Yet Indian orations and statements, which had moved to the historian's pages through the reports of soldiers, missionaries, and traders, were increasingly found to be suspect. A European scholar, for example, showed in detail how the famous oration of Chief Seattle had been created with the aid of sympathetic Euro-Americans.[81] The number of Indians who died in the Cherokee removal, while in reality

---

[81] Rudolph Kaiser, "Chief Seattle's Speech(es): American Origins and European Reception," in Brian Swann and Arnold Krupat (eds.), *Recovering the Word: Essays on Native American Literature* (Berkeley, Calif., 1987), 497–536.

high, was consistently exaggerated by historians unaware of, or unfamiliar with, the primary sources for that event.[82] Similarly, the number of Indians and soldiers killed during the Indian wars has been shown to have been subject to extraordinarily varying interpretations. The evidence suggesting that the Indians achieved a higher "kill ratio" against the American soldiers than the U.S. Army did against them was a shock to those who saw Indian–Euro-American relations in terms of a one-sided massacre of the innocents.[83]

It was not surprising that twentieth-century historians, intensely affected by their upbringing and the traumatic events of the twentieth century, should react with horror to the retrograde views of statesmen like Thomas Jefferson, Andrew Jackson, and Sir John A. MacDonald. Each came on the receiving end of criticism from historians who carried twentieth-century standards of racial justice to their interpretation of eighteenth- and nineteenth-century actions.

Extreme overreaction produced myths that could easily be refuted by reference to the available evidence. Thus the ideas that scalping was a European invention foisted upon the Indians, and that the American Constitution was consciously patterned on the government of the Iroquois Confederacy, found their champions among a Euro-American audience (which included historians) until their fragile supports were undermined by other historians and anthropologists.[84]

More formidable disputes occurred between historians who saw the Indian–Euro-American past in different moral terms. Thus Francis Jennings, in a series of books, railed against the hypocrisy and perfidy of the Puritans in their dealings with the Indians, unswayed by the more respectful approach of Alden J. Vaughan. Jennings introduced moral conviction into his appropriately titled *The Invasion of America: Indians, Colonialism and*

[82] Francis Paul Prucha, "Doing Indian History," in Jane F. Smith and Robert M. Kvasnicka (eds.), *Indian-White Relations: A Persistent Paradox* (Washington, D.C., 1976), 1–10.

[83] Don Russell, "How Many Indians Were Killed? White Man versus Red Man: The Facts and the Legend," *The American West* 10 (1973), 42–7, 61–3.

[84] The controversy has its origins in Donald A. Grinde, Jr., *The Iroquois and the Founding of the American Nation* (San Francisco, 1977), and in Bruce E. Johansen, *Forgotten Founders* (Ipswich, Mass., 1982). Their arguments, plus the work of others, such as Oren Lyons, are conveniently assembled in a Special Constitution Bicentennial Edition of *Northeast Indian Quarterly* (Ithaca, N.Y.) entitled *Indian Roots of American Democracy* (1988). Negative reactions, most significantly that of Elizabeth Tooker, appeared in her "The United States Constitution and the Iroquois League," *Ethnohistory* 35 (1988), 305–36. Johansen and Tooker appear under the same covers in "Commentary on the Iroquois and the U.S. Constitution," *Ethnohistory* 37 (1990), 279–97. On the scalping controversy, see James Axtell and William C. Sturtevant, "The Unkindest Cut, or Who Invented Scalping?" *William and Mary Quarterly* 37 (1985), 451–72.

the Cant of Conquest (1976), as well as into other powerful works, such as *The Ambiguous Iroquois Empire: The Covenant Chain Confederation of Indian Tribes with English Colonies from Its Beginnings to the Lancaster Treaty of 1744* (1984). Contempt for what he saw as the hypocritical Puritans of the seventeenth century and the equally mendacious and self-righteous nineteenth-century historian of Indian–Euro-American relations Francis Parkman encouraged Jennings to lash out at their treatment of the Indians. Jennings went so far as to convince himself that, when he failed to find certain documents in the colonial archives, their very nonexistence was a sign that the wily Puritans had undoubtedly destroyed them to cover up their misdeeds. Alden Vaughan's approach to the same material differed markedly from that of Jennings. In his *New England Frontier: Puritans and Indians, 1620–1675* (1965, 2d ed. 1979), his "assessment of early Puritan attitudes and actions was on the whole favorable," as he noted in the introduction to the second edition. He pointed out that he had argued that "until 1675 the New Englanders generally respected the Indians (though not Indian culture) and tried sincerely to win them to English ways and beliefs." While maintaining his generally favorable interpretation of the New England colonies' actions, Vaughan conceded that, were he to rewrite the book in its entirety, he would draw "more attention to the Puritans' failures, less to their fleeting virtues, and would temper its exculpatory tone."[85]

The fact that a sense of moral concern underlay these historical disputes was brought out in a series of articles by one of the leading practitioners of the history of Indian–Euro-American relations, James Axtell. He emphasized, as Wilcomb Washburn had earlier done, that historical actors are moral beings as well as economic, religious, military, and political ones, and that the historian of Indian–Euro-American relations can deal with the morals and values of the actors without necessarily being moralistic or judgmental. For those historians, such as Bernard Sheehan, who saw the play of Indian–Euro-American interaction as a "process" in which personality was submerged in the sweep of "inexorable," "inevitable," and impersonal social and cultural forces which determined the historical outcome, a focus on the individual as both a historical actor and a moral one was unnecessary, if not improper.[86] Bruce Trigger, in *The Children of Aataentsic: A History of the*

---

[85] Alden Vaughan, *New England Frontier: Puritans and Indians, 1620–1675* (Boston, 1965; rev. ed. New York, 1979), v, xi.

[86] James Axtell, "A Moral History of Indian-White Relations Revisited," (1983), Axtell, *After Columbus*, 171–2.

Huron People to 1660 (1976), chose the "interest group" rather than the individual or a whole people as his unit of analysis but insisted that ethnohistory, as a mirror in which North American society can learn how it has treated Native people, has an important role to play in resolving some of the key moral and political issues that continue to confront contemporary society.[87]

Axtell also asserts that the language of analysis is itself inevitably "loaded" and reflects the observer's biases – however much the observer seeks a value-free objectivity – an argument that challenges the presumed neutrality and efficacy of any ethnographic or historical technique designed to capture reality. Whatever unit one regards as critical to an understanding of interaction between two peoples, one is faced with the problem of accurately describing what happened, how it happened, and why it happened. Because historians must generalize, the manner in which they interpret the scattered data is critical. Is Jennings' use of the term "invasion" to describe the arrival of Europeans in North America accurate? Vaughan reminds us that "the European presence in America *was* an invasion, but it was also partly an invited settlement, partly a commercial interchange, and partly a folk migration."[88]

The work of Jennings, Gary Nash – *Red, White, and Black: The Peoples of Early America* (1974; 3rd ed., 1992, subtitled *The Peoples of Early North America*) – and several others has elicited strong negative reactions for seeming to carry a personal and present-day ideological point of view into the past. Thus Oscar Handlin, in his *Truth in History* (1979), attributes the popularity of their work, and of others such as Dee Brown – *Bury My Heart at Wounded Knee* (1970) – to the baneful effects of the 1960s and the celebration of all groups who could claim "victim" status. The high praise for Jennings's *Invasion of America* he attributes not to the worth of the book but to the "masochistic impulses of its reviewers." Handlin is even more severe on Nash for seeing Indians as "California countercultural rebels, defenders of women's rights, and communist egalitarians – to say nothing of their anticipations of Freudianism."[89]

Words like "invasion," "colonization," or "civilization" now carry pejorative or ironic connotations and have become increasingly objectionable to those unwilling to regard the interaction between Indians and Euro-

---

[87] Trigger, "Alfred G. Bailey," 20.
[88] Review of Jennings in *Western Historical Quarterly* 7 (1976), 422, quoted in Axtell, "Invading America: Puritans and Jesuits," *Journal of Interdisciplinary History* 14 (1984), 645.
[89] Oscar Handlin, *Truth in History* (Cambridge, Mass., 1979), 397–8.

Americans as having had a beneficial effect or constituting a neutral process. Similarly the activities of Christian missionaries have elicited hostile reactions from historians no longer committed, and sometimes antipathetic, to the Christian values of their forefathers, and who may wish the Native Americans had retained fully their traditional religions. As William H. McNeill has put it in writing about the varied perspectives of historians, "what seems true to one historian will seem false to another, so one historian's truth becomes another's myth, even at the moment of utterance."[90]

Yet there is perhaps reason for more optimism. In her book *Lost Harvests: Prairie Indian Reserve Farmers and Government Policy* (1990) Sarah Carter has been able to document the erroneousness of the widely accepted belief that the Plains Indians of Canada were unwilling to take up farming following the disappearance of the bison. Through a careful examination of archival sources she has irrefutably demonstrated that, on the contrary, these Indians hoped to become independent of government regulation by becoming successful farmers. Their failure, after a very promising beginning, was mainly the result of government policies which made farming on reserves unrewarding. Canadian government officials sought to deny responsibility for this failure by attributing it to the Indians' character and traditions, an explanation long accepted by Euro-Canadians, including most historians and anthropologists, and initially by Carter herself. This case admirably demonstrates the extent to which historians and anthropologists have had their views of the past colored by Euro-American prejudice and propaganda. But it also shows that it is possible for non-Native historians to dispel the myths that continue to distort the understanding of Euro-American–Indian relations. In the United States a similar reexamination of Indian agriculture following the General Allotment Act has been undertaken by Leonard A. Carlson, *Indians, Bureaucrats, and the Land: The Dawes Act and the Decline of Indian Farming* (1981), and more recently by Terry L. Anderson and his associates at the Political Economy Research Center, Bozeman, Montana, in various books and articles.

However unique their individual perceptions of the past, the most important task of each historian is to recount the story of the historical process and to try to judge the success or failure of any event or activity (such as agriculture or missionization) not in terms of the historian's twentieth-century values but in light of the options available to the Indians at the time

---

[90] William H. McNeill, "Mythistory, or Truth, Myth, History, and Historians," (1985), in McNeill, *Mythistory and Other Essays* (Chicago, 1986), 3.

and the success of their choice of a particular option in terms of ethnic survival and growth. Whatever the role of history is seen to be, there is little danger now of overlooking the Indian. As McNeill has noted, just as we are "unlikely to leave out Blacks and women from any future mythistory of the United States, . . . we are unlikely to exclude Asians, Africans, and Amerindians from any future mythistory of the world."[91]

BIBLIOGRAPHIC ESSAY

There is now a vast and rapidly growing literature concerning European attitudes and policies toward Native peoples. Among the more important general works are H. N. Fairchild, *The Noble Savage: A Study in Romantic Naturalism* (New York, 1928); H. M. Jones, *0 Strange New World: American Culture – The Formative Years* (New York, 1964); R. H. Pearce, *Savagism and Civilization: A Study of the Indian and the American Mind* (Baltimore, 1965); Hugh Honour, *The New Golden Land: European Images of America from the Discoveries to the Present Time* (New York, 1975); Fredi Chiappelli (ed.), *First Images of America: The Impact of the New World on the Old* (Berkeley, 1976); and R. F. Berkhofer, Jr., *The White Man's Indian: Images of the American Indian from Columbus to the Present* (New York, 1978).

Spanish attitudes are discussed by J. H. Elliott, *The Old World and the New, 1492–1650* (Cambridge, 1970), Lewis Hanke, *Aristotle and the American Indians* (Chicago, 1959); Benjamin Keen, *The Aztec Image in Western Thought* (New Brunswick, N.J., 1971); Anthony Pagden, *The Fall of Natural Man* (Cambridge, Mass., 1982); Tzvetan Todorov, *The Conquest of America: The Question of the Other* (New York, 1984); and Paul E. Hoffman, *A New Andalucia and a Way to the Orient: The American Southeast during the Sixteenth Century* (Baton Rouge, La., 1990). Portuguese attitudes are incorporated in a lavishly illustrated catalog for an exhibition at the New York Public Library, June 2–September 1, 1990, entitled *Portugal-Brazil: The Age of Atlantic Discoveries,* Essays by Luis de Albuquerque, Charles R. Boxer, Francisco Leite de Faria, Max Justo Guedes, Francis M. Rogers, and Wilcomb E. Washburn (Lisbon, 1990).

The beliefs and policies of English settlers and later Euro-Americans are surveyed in F. P. Prucha, *American Indian Policy in the Formative Years: The Indian Trade and Intercourse Acts, 1790–1834* (Cambridge, Mass., 1962), Reginald Horsman, *Expansion and American Indian Policy, 1783–1812*

---

[91] Ibid., 21.

(East Lansing, Mich., 1967); B. W. Sheehan, *Seeds of Extinction: Jeffersonian Philanthropy and the American Indian* (Chapel Hill, N.C., 1973); Sheehan, *Savagism and Civility: Indians and Englishmen in Colonial Virginia* (New York, 1980); Francis Jennings, *The Invasion of America: Indians, Colonialism, and the Cant of Conquest* (Chapel Hill, N.C., 1975); H. C. Porter, *The Inconstant Savage: England and the North American Indian, 1500–1660* (London, 1979); A. T. Vaughan, *New England Frontier: Puritans and Indians, 1620–1675* (2nd ed., New York, 1979); Richard Drinnon, *Facing West: The Metaphysics of Indian-hating and Empire Building* (Minneapolis, 1980); K. O. Kupperman, *Settling with the Indians: The Meeting of English and Indian Cultures in America, 1580–1640* (Totowa, N.J., 1980); and James Axtell, *The European and the Indian: Essays in Ethnohistory of Colonial North America* (Oxford, 1981). Parallels between sixteenth-century English policy toward the Irish and the Indians are discussed in D. B. Quinn, *The Elizabethans and the Irish* (Ithaca, N.Y., 1966).

Policies and attitudes toward Native people in New France are examined by J. H. Kennedy, *Jesuit and Savage in New France* (New Haven, Conn., 1950); F. M. Gagnon, *La Conversion par l'image* (Montreal, 1975) and *Ces hommes dits sauvages* (Montreal, 1984); Cornelius Jaenen, *Friend and Foe: Aspects of French-Amerindian Cultural Contact in the Sixteenth and Seventeenth Centuries* (Toronto, 1976); B. G. Trigger, *The Children of Aataentsic: A History of the Huron People to 1660* (Montreal, 1976); and O. P. Dickason, *The Myth of the Savage and the Beginnings of French Colonialism in the Americas* (Edmonton, 1984).

For biographical information about Francis Parkman and evaluations of his work, see Mason Wade, *Francis Parkman: Heroic Historian* (New York, 1942); David Levin, *History as Romantic Art: Bancroft, Prescott, Motley, and Parkman* (Stanford, Calif., 1959); Howard Doughty, *Francis Parkman* (New York, 1962); Francis Jennings, "A Vanishing Indian: Francis Parkman versus His Sources," *Pennsylvania Magazine of History and Biography* 87 (1963), 306–23; and Robert Shulman, "Parkman's Indians and American Violence," *Massachusetts Review* 12 (1971), 221–39.

In the twentieth century a new scientific methodology emerged and along with it a more careful recognition (not always sympathetic) of the role played by Indians in American History. The new "professional" and "scientific" history that emerged in the twentieth century was exemplified in the work of Herbert Levi Osgood, *American Colonies in the Seventeenth Century,* 3 vols. (New York, 1904–7), in Edward Channing, *History of the United States,* 3 vols. (New York, 1905–12), and in Charles McLean

Andrews, *The Colonial Period of American History: The Settlements,* 3 vols. (New Haven, Conn., 1934–7). A. S. Eisenstadt's *Charles McLean Andrews: A Study in American Historical Writing* (New York, 1956) has discussed Andrews's work in relation to that of his contemporaries. W. Stull Holt, *Historical Scholarship in the United States and other Essays* (Seattle, 1967) discusses the origin of "scientific" history in America.

Andrews's student at Yale, Lawrence Henry Gipson, while not renouncing biography (which Andrews urged his students to eschew), outdid his master in the meticulous documentation of the institutional and imperial context of American colonial history. Gipson, beginning his own scholarly work in 1920, virtually redid the work of Parkman in what eventually became, after revisions, his massive fourteen-volume *British Empire before the American Revolution* (New York, 1967–70), which demonstrated full control of the institutional framework of British rule in America, while not ignoring the character of the individuals who carried out their institutional responsibilities under that rule. Richard B. Morris has given a perceptive appreciation of Gipson in his "The Spacious Empire of Lawrence Henry Gipson," in *Perspectives on Early American History: Essays in Honor of Richard B. Morris,* ed. Alden T. Vaughan and George Athan Billias (New York, 1973), a book which is valuable for its many additional essays on the early historians of Virginia and New England, as well as on Osgood and Carl Becker.

Frederick Jackson Turner has been the subject of innumerable studies. Notable is a study by Ray Allen Billington, who inherited Turner's mantle (some say snatched it away from Frederick Merk), entitled *Frederick Jackson Turner: Historian, Scholar, Teacher* (New York, 1973). See also *The Historical World of Frederick Jackson Turner, with Selections from his Correspondence,* narrative by Wilbur R. Jacobs (New Haven, Conn., 1968). A more critical approach is Richard Hofstadter, *The Progressive Historians: Turner, Beard, Parrington* (New York, 1968). More recently Turner has been attacked and even derided by the "new Western historians" for his insensitivity to the Indian side of the frontier. Patricia N. Limerick, *The Legacy of Conquest: The Unbroken Past of the American West* (New York, 1988), and Richard White, *"It's Your Misfortune and None of My Own": A History of the American West* (Norman, Okla., 1991), are the leading exponents of this school.

Assessments of American historical writing in the twentieth century have tended to ignore specialized works dealing with the American Indian as being outside the mainstream. Thus John Higham's *Writing American*

History: Essays on Modern Scholarship (Bloomington, Ind., 1970) sees the evolution of American history in terms that tend to exclude the perspective of the Indian and the approach of the anthropologist. Similarly Gene Wise, in his *American Historical Explanations: A Strategy of Grounded Inquiry* (2nd ed., Minneapolis, 1980) is more concerned with paradigms or "explanation-forms" used by historians than with the specific manner in which the Indian is dealt with in American historical writing. In *The Past Before Us: Contemporary Historical Writing in the United States,* edited for the American Historical Association by Michael Kammen (Ithaca, N.Y, 1980), a book intended to coincide with the fifteenth meeting of the International Congress of Historical Sciences, held at Bucharest, Romania, there is a similar lack of concern for ethnohistorical work. Eight of the essays deal with "rapidly developing fields in which significant breakthroughs have occurred during the 1970s." Among those subjects are the "new" social and political history, black history, and women's history. But Indian history, or the history of Indian–Euro-American relations, was not one of the essays, even though the decade saw an impressive outpouring of work in the field that was informed by a new understanding of the cultural complexity of the subject. Indian history remained on the periphery of accepted subjects in the profession.

While historians of Indian–Euro-American relations tended to be overlooked by those occupying the mainstream of the historical profession, they formed a closer alliance with anthropologists venturing into the field of history through the common ground of "ethnohistory." Both sides were fulsome in their praise of the other's discipline. Historians devoured anthropological literature, while not always accepting anthropological theories. Anthropologists opened the pages of the histories they had formerly ignored and found the product useful, as Eric Wolf noted in the preface to his *Europe and the People without History* (Berkeley, Calif., 1982). A recognition of that increasing mutual respect appears in a series of essays under the heading "Anthropology and History in the 1980s" by Bernard S. Cohn, John W. Adams, Natalie Z. Davis, and Carlo Ginzburg in *The New History: The 1980s and Beyond: Studies in Interdisciplinary History,* ed. Theodore K. Rabb and Robert I. Rotberg (Princeton, N.J., 1982). European scholars have contributed significantly, often in the pages of the *European Review of Native American Studies,* begun in 1987 and edited by Christian F. Feest.

Stereotypes of Indians in American literature have been discussed by Albert Keiser, *The Indian in American Literature* (New York, 1933) and their treatment in motion pictures by J. A. Price, "The Stereotyping of North American Indians in Motion Pictures," *Ethnohistory* 20 (1973), 153–71. Michael T. Marsden and Jack G. Nachbar have also discussed "The Indian in the Movies" in the section on "Conceptual Relations" in the *Handbook of North American Indians,* vol. 4, *History of Indian-White Relations,* ed. Wilcomb E. Washburn (Washington, D.C., 1988), 607–16. Other essays in the section deal with "The Indians in Popular American Culture" by Rayna D. Green, "Indians and the Counterculture, 1960s–1970s" by Stewart Brand, as well as essays on the Indian hobbyist movement in North America and Europe, and the Indian in literature in English and non-English literature. All deal with the various stereotypes by which the Indian is perceived. A general essay by Robert K. Berkhofer, based on his *White Man's Indian* (New York, 1978), rounds out the section.

General works dealing with Canadian history include Serge Gagnon, *Quebec and Its Historians, 1840 to 1920* (Montreal, 1982); Carl Berger, *The Writing of Canadian History: Aspects of English-Canadian Historical Writing since 1900* (2nd ed., Toronto, 1986); and M. B. Taylor, *Promoters, Patriots, and Partisans: Historiography in Nineteenth-Century English Canada* (Toronto, 1989). Berger's book includes, on pp. 258–320, an insightful survey of current trends in Canadian historiography, including the treatment of Native people. Specific studies that evaluate the treatment of Indians in Canadian historiography include J. W. S. Walker, "The Indian in Canadian Historical Writing," *Canadian Historical Association, Historical Papers* (1971), 21–47; "The Indian in Canadian Historical Writing, 1972–1982," in *As Long as the Sun Shines and Water Flows: A Reader in Canadian Native Studies,* ed. I. A. L. Getty and A. S. Lusier (Vancouver, 1983), 340–57; D. A. Muise, ed., *Approaches to Native History in Canada: Papers of a Conference Held at the National Museum of Man, October, 1975* (Ottawa, 1977); D. B. Smith, *Le Sauvage: The Native People in Quebec Historical Writing on the Heroic Period (1534–1663) of New France* (Ottawa, 1974); and B. G. Trigger, *Natives and Newcomers: Canada's "Heroic Age" Reconsidered* (Montreal, 1985), 3–49 and "The Historians' Indian: Native Americans in Canadian Historical Writing from Charlevoix to the Present," *Canadian Historical Review* 67 (1986), 315–42.

For studies of the treatment of Native people in Canadian popular literature, see John Maclean, *Canadian Savage Folk: The Native Tribes of Canada* (Toronto, 1896), 456–540; Margaret Atwood, *Survival: A Thematic Guide to Canadian Literature* (Toronto, 1972); Leslie Monkman, *A Native Heritage: Images of the Indian in English-Canadian Literature* (Toronto,

1981); and Terry Goldie, *Fear and Temptation: The Image of the Indigene in Canadian, Australian and New Zealand Literatures* (Montreal, 1989).

The development of physical anthropology in America and of racial views concerning North American Indians (and others) has been studied by H. B. Glass, O. Temkin, and W. L. Straus, Jr., eds., *Forerunners of Darwin, 1745–1859* (Baltimore, 1959); C. J. Glacken, *Traces on the Rhodian Shore: Nature and Culture in Western Thought from Ancient Times to the End of the Eighteenth Century* (Berkeley, Calif., 1967); W. D. Jordan, *White over Black: American Attitudes toward the Negro, 1550–1812* (Chapel Hill, N.C., 1968); Reginald Horsman, "Scientific Racism and the American Indian in the Mid-Nineteenth Century," *American Quarterly* 27 (1975), 152–68 and *Race and Manifest Destiny: The Origins of American Racial Anglo-Saxonism* (Cambridge, Mass., 1981); Steven J. Gould, *The Mismeasure of Man* (New York, 1981); and A. T. Vaughan, "From White Man to Red Skin: Changing Anglo-American Perceptions of the American Indian," *American Historical Review* 87 (1982), 917–53, "The Origins Debate: Slavery and Racism in Seventeenth-Century Virginia," *Virginia Magazine of History and Biography* 97 (1989), 311–54, and "Caliban in the 'Third World': Shakespeare's Savage as Sociopolitical Symbol," *Massachusetts Review* 29 (1988), 289–313. Also relevant is William Stanton, *The Leopard's Spots: Scientific Attitudes toward Race in America, 1815–59* (Chicago, 1960).

The most comprehensive history of anthropology is Marvin Harris, *The Rise of Anthropological Theory: A History of Theories of Culture* (New York, 1968); it is written from the point of view of cultural materialism. Alternative treatments include F. W. Voget, *A History of Ethnology* (New York, 1975) and J. J. Honigmann, *The Development of Anthropological Ideas* (Homewood, Ill., 1976). Of special importance for understanding nineteenth-century scientific views of the American Indian is R. E. Bieder, *Science Encounters the Indian, 1820–1880: The Early Years of American Ethnology* (Norman, Okla., 1986). The development of anthropology at the Smithsonian Institution is studied by C. M. Hinsley, Jr., *Savages and Scientists: The Smithsonian Institution and the Development of American Anthropology, 1846–1910* (Washington, D.C., 1981, reissued, with a new foreword, 1994, under the title *The Smithsonian and the American Indian: Making a Moral Anthropology in Victorian America*). George Stocking has edited a "History of Anthropology" series published by the University of Wisconsin Press. One volume of papers, grouped around a specific theme, has appeared every year or two since 1983. Most volumes contain at least a few papers relating to the study of Native North Americans. Representative of the increasing interest in museum history is Douglas Cole, *Captured Heritage: The Scramble for Northwest Coast Artifacts* (Seattle, Wash., 1985). The problems of studying "the other" are outlined in James Clifford, *The Predicament of Culture: Twentieth-Century Ethnography, Literature, and Art* (Cambridge, Mass., 1988).

For a general history of archaeology, see B. G. Trigger, *A History of Archaeological Thought* (Cambridge, 1989). The history of American archaeology is examined by Robert Silverberg, *Mound Builders of Ancient America: The Archaeology of a Myth* (Greenwich, Conn., 1968), and G. R. Willey and J. Sabloff, *A History of American Archaeology* (3rd ed., San Francisco, 1993). A brief history of the beginnings of Canadian anthropology is provided by Douglas Cole, "The Origins of Canadian Anthropology, 1850–1910," *Journal of Canadian Studies* 8 (1973), 33–45, while the history of Canadian archaeology is discussed in W. C. Noble, "One Hundred and Twenty-five Years of Archaeology in the Canadian Provinces," *Bulletin of the Canadian Archaeological Association* 4 (1972), 1–78.

The life and anthropological thought of Lewis Henry Morgan are discussed by Carl Resek, *Lewis Henry Morgan: American Scholar* (Chicago, 1960) and Thomas R. Trautmann, *Lewis Henry Morgan and the Invention of Kinship* (Berkeley, Calif., 1987). For Franz Boas, see A. L. Kroeber et al., eds., *Franz Boas, 1858–1942* (Washington, D.C., 1943); M. J. Herskovits, *Franz Boas: The Science of Man in the Making* (New York, 1953); Walter Goldschmidt, ed., *The Anthropology of Franz Boas: Essays on the Centennial of His Birth* (Menasha, Wis., 1959); and G. W. Stocking, Jr., *A Franz Boas Reader: The Shaping of American Anthropology, 1883–1911* (New York, 1974). Columbia University Press has published a "Leaders of Modern Anthropology" series under General Editor Charles Wagley. Individual volumes include Robert F. Murphy, *Robert H. Lowie* (1972); Julian H. Steward, *Alfred Kroeber* (1973); Richard B. Woodbury, *Alfred V. Kidder* (1973); and Margaret Mead, *Ruth Benedict* (1974). See also June Helm, ed., *Pioneers of American Anthropology* (Seattle, Wash., 1966).

There is as yet no extensive treatment of the history of ethnohistory; for briefer treatments see W. E. Washburn, "The Writing of American Indian History: A Status Report," *Pacific Historical Review* 40 (1971), 261–81 and "Ethnohistory: History 'in the Round,' " *Ethnohistory* 8 (1961), 31–48; and B. G. Trigger, "Ethnohistory: Problems and Prospects," *Ethnohistory* 29 (1982), 1–19. Recent discussions and exemplifications of ethnohistorical methodology can be found in Trigger, *Natives and Newcom-*

ers (Montreal, 1985) and James Axtell, *After Columbus: Essays in the Ethnohistory of Colonial North America* (Oxford, 1988). A bibliography of brief works relating to the aims, techniques, and role of ethnohistory can be found in *Natives and Newcomers,* p. 352.

Recapturing the Indian past through the study of oral traditions is a difficult enterprise. Brian Swann and Arnold Krupat, eds., *Recovering the Word: Essays on Native American Literature* (Berkeley, Calif., 1987) contains an important section entitled "Interpreting the Material: Oral and Written." Perhaps the best North American example of how oral history can throw insights on the distant past is William S. Simmons, *Spirit of the New England Tribes: Indian History and Folklore, 1620–1984* (Hanover, N.H., 1986).

Archaeological methods are surveyed in Frank Hole and R. F. Heizer, *An Introduction to Prehistoric Archaeology* (3rd ed., New York, 1973). More recent discussions and exemplifications of multidisciplinary approaches to studying the past, especially periods prior to adequate written records, include D. F. McCall, *Africa in Time-Perspective: A Discussion of Historical Reconstruction from Unwritten Sources* (Boston, 1964); Claude Tardits, ed., *Contribution de la recherche ethnologique à l'histoire des civilisations du Cameroun* (Paris, 1981); and J. Ki-Zerbo, ed., *General History of Africa,* vol. 1, *Methodology and African Prehistory* (Berkeley, Calif., 1981).

The Garland Library of Narratives of North American Indian Captivities, 311 titles in 111 volumes, selected and arranged by Wilcomb E. Washburn (New York, 1977), assembles in a single collection the many scattered captivity narratives. In a separate volume, *Narratives of North American Indian Captivity: A Selective Bibliography* (New York, 1983), there is a bibliographical listing of the captivity narratives and of modern studies of captivity narratives by Alden T. Vaughan and an introduction to the collection of captivity narratives by Wilcomb E. Washburn, xi–lviii.

3

THE FIRST AMERICANS AND THE DIFFERENTIATION OF HUNTER-GATHERER CULTURES

DEAN R. SNOW

This chapter examines the evidence for the arrival of human beings in the Americas and the subsequent development of American Indian and Inuit hunter-gatherer societies in North America. Coverage ends with the rise of horticultural societies where that occurred, but continues to first contact with Europeans for much of North America. The chapter also explains how archaeologists build chronologies for periods prior to written records, and how colleagues in other disciplines reconstruct the environmental contexts of ancient societies.

APPROACHES TO THE PAST

Like human beings everywhere, all American Indians descend from people who were once full-time hunter-gatherers. Even those who eventually adopted more intensive subsistence strategies often retained hunting and gathering practices as regular supplements and insurance against occasional shortages. After European contact, many North American horticulturalists reverted to full-time hunting and gathering, as firearms and the reintroduced horse made the vast bison herds of the Great Plains more easily accessible. Thus hunting and gathering pervades the history of American Indian societies, providing the context for their initial expansion and subsequent differentiation. However, to carry an understanding of those processes beyond the simplistic stereotypes of popular history, some reassessment of basic concepts and review of archaeological theory is necessary.

Human population movement prior to written records is popularly conceived as migration. Migration, in turn, seems often to imply a model of movement derived from the large-scale, freewheeling rampages of historically recorded pastoralists. Yet this is only one kind of population movement, and probably an uncommon one at that. Another form of migration involves the steady expansion of a population over a broad front, either into vacant land or by displacing some other group. Still another involves the channeled movement of one part of a donor population to colonies in regions already occupied by other populations. Examples of the latter pattern can be found in the recent histories of the United States and the Soviet Union. Still another form of migration involves little more than temporary residence by individuals or small families followed by return migration to their place of origin. In short, human movement over space occurs at several scales, over varying periods of time, and with several possible dynamics.

It is also the case that large-scale movement is rare enough that we cannot simply presume that it occurred without careful substantiation. Rouse has proposed that archaeologists must accept the burden of proof by (1) identifying the migrants as intrusive in a new region, and (2) identifying them with a plausible source. Further, they must (3) establish that archaeological occurrences of the migrating culture were all contemporaneous, (4) show that there is some reasonable hypothesis to explain why movement occurred, and (5) demonstrate that some other hypothesis does not explain the case more easily.[1] These are tough standards, but they reflect the rigor of contemporary archaeology, which has rejected the hypothesized wholesale migrations that were once widely used as explanations of change in the archaeological record.

A concept that probably has greater utility for understanding human history than migration does is that of adaptive radiation. This idea comes from the theory of biological evolution and ecology. Simply put, it is that human cultures occasionally experience the convergence of fortuitous environmental conditions and technological capability. The specifics are as numerous as the cases, and might involve nothing more than the chance mutation of a semidomesticated plant, the eruption of a volcano, the acquisition of the bow and arrow, or the invention of a new means to remove undesirable substances from a starchy food. Whatever the specifics, populations can and do occasionally experience circumstances that allow or induce them to expand rapidly, either into regions not previously inhabited (as sophisticated boats carried the Polynesians into the islands of the Pacific) or at the expense of established populations (as Europeans

---

[1] Rouse codified "The Inference of Migrations from Anthropological Evidence" in *Migration in New World Culture History*, ed. Raymond H. Thompson, 63–8. The collection of articles was published as University of Arizona Social Science Bulletin 27 (1958).

expanded across America). Such expansions are typically limited by environmental factors, such that a culturally uniform population usually expands rapidly to the limits of the environment to which it is adapted, then settles in and begins slow internal differentiation. The process of cultural differentiation occurs at a scale determined by minor ecological variations, the optimum population density of the overall population, and the optimum size of each community. Examples of each of these processes are noted later in this chapter.

It is not unusual for a particular location to witness several such adaptive expansions over the course of thousands of years. At the local level, the archaeological record of these events often looks like a series of very abrupt cultural replacements, interspersed by periods of stability. Unfortunately, archaeologists have not always been successful in distinguishing the arrival of a set of adopted innovations from the arrival of a whole new population. Ambiguous cases have repeatedly reminded us of the importance of Rouse's criteria.

The adaptive expansion of a population typically involves a single language, which after settling into a much broader distribution begins to break up into separate speech communities. This process accompanies the cultural differentiation mentioned above. The last expansion of Eskimos across the Arctic left just such a pattern, and there is still relatively little linguistic variation from northern Alaska to Greenland. Older expansions can be a detected in the distributions of languages in families elsewhere in North America. There are at least twenty-one such language families known for Native North America, and thirty-two more poorly known languages that might have belonged either to one of these or to some otherwise undetected family.[2] As we shall see, the Iroquoian family appears to have expanded northeastward and southward in the Appalachian province from an earlier homeland on the Allegheny Plateau. Eastern Algonquians apparently expanded southward along the East Coast long before European contact. Uto-Aztecans spread north and east through the Desert West, and Siouans westward onto the Great Plains soon after Europeans arrived in the Americas. These are only a few examples of the processes that produced the complex pattern of a language map of Native North America.

---

[2] These numbers reflect the conservative but generally accepted counts used in the multivolume *Handbook of North American Indians* (Washington, D.C., 1978–) and the *Atlas of Ancient America* (New York, 1986). Ancient connections that would unite certain families into larger ones are likely but not yet completely established.

Unfortunately, all or nearly all of the known cases occurred within the last 4,000 years. Archaeologists have developed a continental chronology that is at least three times that long. This means that historical linguistics helps us to understand only the last third of our sequence. Archaeologically well-known populations that predate the last 4,000 years may never be assigned clear linguistic identities, apart from the assumption that they derived from Asian stocks and were in some instances ancestral to known families. There were at least 375 separate languages spoken in North America in 1492. The total North American population 4,000 years ago might have been only a fifth of its 1492 level, but even if speech communities were as large as they were in 1492, there would have been at least seventy-five separate languages in 2000 B.C. Only a couple dozen of these became the founding languages of the families we know from recent centuries. In other words, many ancient American Indian cultures can be known through both archaeology and historical linguistics. But many more became extinct, leaving no clear descendants, or flourished so long ago as to be beyond the reach of modern linguistics, and these can be known only though archaeology.

Even if the specifics for earlier millennia continue to elude us, linguists can assist in understanding the events of the last 4,000 years or so, and in doing so help to elucidate some of the processes that characterized all of human history. Protolanguages can be reconstructed on the basis of the contents of surviving descendant languages. Linguists can, for example, determine whether or not a word for maize was part of the proto-Iroquoian vocabulary (apparently it was not). The presence or absence of such key words help us match speech communities, like proto-Iroquoian, to specific environments and specific archaeological complexes.

The dating of linguistic splits through analysis of vocabulary changes, "glottochronology,"[3] was once quite popular, but has fallen into disfavor in recent years. It turns out that the rate of language change is too variable for the technique to work precisely in a convincing way. Nevertheless, internal linguistic evidence can be used to establish the order of language subdivision, and, when combined with archaeological dating, even very general age estimates can be useful.

A final caution has to do with recent efforts to generalize about the common origins of all American Indian languages. Linguists generally

---

[3] Glottochronology measures the age of the divergence of two or more related languages by assessing the replacement of specific key words in the parent language by newer ones in the daughter languages. Unfortunately, the standard word sample is small and rates of change vary.

agree that the Eskimo-Aleut family appeared only recently in archaeological time in North America, and there are clear linguistic relatives remaining in Asia. Siberian Eskimo speech is related to Chukchi-Kamchatkan languages. Further, it is generally agreed that speakers of Na-Dene, or Athapaskan, languages, which are found in western Canada and the Southwest, represent the second to last movement of people into North America from Asia. There are also probable linguistic relatives for Na-Dene in Asia in the Sino-Tibetan languages. The difficulty is with establishing connections between the remaining families of the Americas and linking them to languages in Asia. Grand syntheses have been tried in the past, but have fallen apart under close scrutiny. For example, the large number and variety of Indian languages along the West Coast has led some researchers to suggest that this would have been the first region of the continent to be occupied. However, others have argued persuasively that there are other more plausible explanations for the large number of languages in the region. The region is a mosaic of many environmental niches, unlike most other regions of the continent, which are broadly uniform. The variety of contrasting niches probably encouraged the fragmentation of West Coast populations into many different local adaptations, a fragmentation that would have encouraged distinct languages to develop locally rather than regionally. In any case, the pattern is probably the consequence of processes that took place over only the last few thousand years. It is unlikely that the traces of movements made 12,000 years ago would be preserved in any detectable form in recent language distributions.

Joseph Greenberg has been responsible for the most recent comprehensive effort, arguing that all American Indian language families, apart from Eskimo-Aleut and Na-Dene, are related and descend from a common ancestor. The problem is that, given the very ancient presence of American Indians and archaeological evidence for an Asiatic origin, the claim is simultaneously acceptable as a given and impossible to prove on the basis of present evidence. The Iroquoian, Caddoan, and Siouan languages might be related at the level of a language phylum. Algonquian-Ritwan might be related to Muskogean at the phylum level (but probably not), and Penutian, spoken in western North America, might or might not be related to Oregon Penutian. However, these and other connections between language families are still being debated by linguists, and the ways in which phyla may be linked still cannot be estimated to the satisfaction of even a majority of them. Thus the approach here is to take the ultimate interconnection of most North American Indian languages for granted, but with no assumptions about precisely how the known families might turn out to have been connected.

THE EXPANSION OF HUMAN POPULATIONS INTO NORTH AMERICA

There can no longer be any doubt that North America was initially populated by hunter-gatherers expanding eastward into what is now Alaska and its portion of the submerged continental shelf. Prior to the end of the Pleistocene, glacial ice locked up so much of the earth's water that sea levels were generally much lower, exposing vast areas of continental shelf. These areas were covered by vegetation and inhabited by game animals. The modern Bering Strait was high and dry, and Asia was linked to North America by a broad isthmus, 1,000 kilometers wide. To Ice Age hunters it would not have been a land bridge at all, but a continuation of the rich hunting grounds of northeastern Asia. Even at the height of continental glaciation, there was no ice to block their expansion into what is now central Alaska, although further expansion to the east and south was temporarily blocked.

All human remains ever found in the Americas are attributable to biologically modern human beings. None of the thousands of known fragments of Neanderthal or older fossil human remains has ever turned up in the Americas. Therefore, we can assume that America was not populated by humans until after people had become biologically modern, and had developed the technology necessary to allow them to survive on and exploit the tundra of northeastern Asia.

These necessary prior conditions were achieved sometime after 40,000 years ago. To focus the picture more clearly, we must turn to the archaeological evidence from Eurasia. The long Lower and Middle Paleolithic sequences gave way to the advanced Upper Paleolithic industries of biologically modern people. With their new stone blade technology, tailored clothing, spear throwers, and fire-making capabilities, these people were able to expand beyond earlier environmental limits into the Subarctic and Arctic. Upper Paleolithic sites from the Kamchatka Peninsula contain evidence of double-walled, wigwam-shaped houses.[4] Artifacts from the sites include bifacial, leaf-shaped projectile points that are very similar to a North American Paleo-Indian type dating to around 11,000 B.C. Radiocarbon dates from the Kamchatka sites put them in a period between 12,300

---

[4] Nikolai N. Dikov, "On the Road to America," *Natural History* 97, 1 (1988).

Figure 3.1. Paleo-Indians and physical geography of North America.

and 11,600 B.C., although the Russian archaeologist Nikolai Dikov uses a supplementary dating technique to argue that the dates should be as much as 2,000 years older. The Dyuktai sites of the Lena River Valley have produced similar points dating to no more than 13,000 B.C.

Dikov also cites a series of sites on the Chukchi Peninsula of northeasternmost Siberia. Here there are archaeological complexes very similar to Paleo-Indian, which he judges are evidence of the dispersal of people into Alaska around 11,000 B.C. Although older evidence of human presence in the Bering region might turn up, nothing found thus far challenges the view that significant human population movements through the area occurred only after the peak of the last glaciation, 16,000 years B.C.

Christy Turner has examined over 200,000 human teeth from America dating from prior to European contact, and has concluded that the occurrences of tiny discrete variations enable us to distinguish ancient populations. For example, American Indians often have ridges on their incisors, a trait known as shoveling. Further, there are diagnostic variations in the numbers of cusps and roots. In terms of these details, all American Indians resemble northeast Asians. The known rates of change indicate that they split from their Asian relatives not much before 13,000 B.C., and there is no evidence for genetic mixture with Europeans or anyone else until after 1492. Statistically, Eskimo-Aleut and Na-Dene populations appear slightly different from other American Indians, differences that are consistent with what we know about the linguistic origins of these populations.

To understand the relationships of these three great groups more fully, we must add evidence from blood groups. Inuits and Aleuts have the B variant of the ABO blood system, but the large Na-Dene nations of western Canada and the Northwest Coast do not. Neither do the great bulk of American Indian nations elsewhere. Other blood group differences distinguish the western Canadian nations from the majority of American Indians. Both blood group and dental studies suggest that the ancestors of most American Indians expanded through and beyond Alaska between 18,000 and 10,000 B.C. This was probably followed by the ancestors of Na-Dene speakers after 10,000 B.C. but before 6500 B.C. The ancestors of the Inuits and Aleuts might have been a separate movement in the same period or slightly later.

The available evidence is consistent with a scenario that would bring ancestral Paleo-Indians into Alaska after 12,000 B.C., reaching the Plains by 10,000 B.C. There might have been earlier failed migrations, but these left few if any undisputable archaeological, biological, or linguistic traces.

Differentiation between interior and coastal adaptations might have occurred very early. Some of the remains found on the Chukchi Peninsula resemble materials from the Gallagher Flint Station, which is located in the Brooks Range of Alaska. These remains, which have been dated to 8500 B.C. and occur at some other Alaskan sites as well, are generally referred to as the American Paleo-Arctic tradition. The assemblages contain cores, blades, and microblades, and are associated with modern fauna as well as with bison and possibly horse and elk remains. This tradition in turn resembles evidence from Anangula in the Aleutian Islands, where the adaptation may already have been decidedly maritime. The fundamental similarities of all of these finds have led some archaeologists to lump them into an inclusive "Beringian" tradition.

A fundamental problem with the detection of first arrivals is that in any plausible scenario they were not numerous. Further, much of the landscape they occupied was inundated by the sea in later millennia. What few archaeological remains the first Paleo-Indians left behind were probably in many cases destroyed or at least submerged in undetectable marine deposits. Fortunately for modern archaeology, human beings require fairly extensive social networks for their long-term survival, so we can safely assume that tiny scattered bands did not simply rush off alone into a continent otherwise vacant of human population. The claims for very early human remains in North and South America are doubted not only because their traces are both rare and ambiguous, but also because small and very isolated finds are inconsistent with what we know about the minimum social requirements of human hunting bands. This point is explained further in the section on Paleo-Indians.

We are also disadvantaged by technical problems in radiocarbon dating for remains that predate 8000 B.C. Analysis of ancient but still living bristlecone pine trees has allowed the detection of variation in atmospheric radiocarbon dating for most of the post-Pleistocene, but not earlier. Further, the half-life of the radioactive isotope of carbon that is essential to the dating technique is only about 5,730 years, so that standard error becomes a serious problem for samples of Upper Paleolithic age. Finally, different organic materials use carbon in different ways. Dates on wood, bone, antler, ivory, and blubber of the same age might produce somewhat different dates in the laboratory, and bone has also created its own problems as specialists have struggled to learn how best to extract residual carbon. In short, radiocarbon dates for the period during which Indians were first reaching the Americas must be examined with considerable skepticism, particularly as technical errors have tended to increase rather than decrease age determinations.

THE ARCHAEOLOGICAL EVIDENCE FOR PALEO-INDIANS

Previous paragraphs have presented a conservative view of American Indian origins. But there are claims to the contrary, and these also deserve some discussion. Well-dated sites prove that Paleo-Indians were widespread in America by 10,000 B.C., but all evidence for an earlier presence is controversial. A warming climate and retreating glaciers set the stage for Paleo-Indians by 12,000 B.C., and rising water created the Bering Strait by 10,000 B.C., an optimal window of opportunity. Yet the possibility of earlier evidence remains. We cannot be certain that the Bering Strait was really a significant barrier to human movement before or after the existence of the land bridge. Clearly early Eskimos had little difficulty crossing it, and early Australians managed to overcome a similar sea barrier. Once again, we must look to archaeology and judge all evidence on its own merits.

Perhaps the most widely accepted evidence of very early human remains came, in the 1960s, from the Old Crow site in the Yukon. Bone tools from the site, most notably a caribou bone flesher, produced dates ranging in age from 20,000 to 41,000 B.C. A date determination run on the flesher itself produced an age of 25,000 B.C., and this was widely accepted by archaeologists (including this author). It seemed possible that the date related to the first peopling of North America, although the possibility remained that Paleo-Indians were not able to expand southward from Alaska and the Yukon until much later. However, new understandings of bone and laboratory techniques to deal with problems in dating bone have led to revised dates for the Old Crow specimens. They now appear to be less than 2,000 years old.

Paleo-Indian artifacts, including points having the type name "El Jobo," have been found in partial association with mastodon bones at the sites of Taima-taima and Muaco in Venezuela. Radiocarbon dating has put the age of the bones at about 11,000 B.C. Unfortunately, the association could have resulted from natural redeposition anytime up to about 8000 B.C. Remains almost as old have been found in the vicinity of Bogota, Colombia, but these lack the distinctive Paleo-Indian spear point. Even though these particular dates seem not to support this interpretation, many Latin American archaeologists have inferred that an earlier generalized foraging culture was widespread in South America, and that El Jobo points were an innovation made in the context of this earlier adaptation.

The possibility of a very early "Lower Lithic" culture has been raised before, especially in Latin America. Richard MacNeish's work at Pikimachay in Ayacucho, Peru, produced dates ranging from 12,500 to 18,000 years B.C. But the specter of Old Crow forces us to question the reliability of dates in this range. Even if accurate, many of the dates are not associated with remains of indisputably human origin.

Elsewhere in Latin America, archaeologists have found a sequence at the site of Pedra Furada, Brazil, where the oldest radiocarbon dates range from 15,000 to 30,000 B.C. The dated deposits include fragments of fallen rock art. Simple house foundations, butchered mastodon bones, and stone artifacts have been reported for the Monte Verde site in Chile. Although the principal deposit is estimated to date to 11,000 B.C., presumed hearths from lower levels produced a radiocarbon date of 32,000 B.C.

One surviving candidate for Lower Lithic status in North America is the Meadowcroft site in Pennsylvania. Samples from which two radiocarbon dates were taken could conceivably have been contaminated by nearby coal deposits, producing erroneous dates in excess of 15,000 B.C. despite the efforts of one of the best radiocarbon laboratories in existence. Just as bothersome is that the dates are associated with what may or may not be a hearth. Associated artifacts include a fragment of cut, barklike material and some stone tools that could, on stylistic grounds, date to much later periods.

In the West, Wilson Butte Cave in Idaho presents similar possibilities and similar problems. No one questions the authenticity of the artifacts found in the lowest levels of the site, but radiocarbon dates indicating ages of 12,500 and 13,000 B.C. were run on animal bone samples that were not in clear association with other artifacts.

Redating has led to the collapse of many claims for pre-Clovis "Lower Lithic" remains in the Americas. Sites such as Lewisville (Texas), Old Crow (Yukon), Calico and Laguna Beach (California), Pikimachay (Peru), Sandia Cave (New Mexico), Tule Springs (Nevada), Koch (Missouri), Taber (Alberta), and several less famous cases have all been discarded or at least thrown into serious question. What is left is a very small number of sites that are disturbingly similar to those that have already failed one test or another. Skeptics have not been without their own scientific failings in this controversy, but for the moment, at least, it appears that all of the really convincing evidence for early Indians is less than 14,000 years old (12,000 B.C.). The oldest convincing dates from Meadowcroft (disregarding the two earlier dates mentioned above) range from 8900 to 12,275 B.C. Analogs from Wilson Butte Cave range from 12,500 to 13,000 B.C. Even if these turn out to be accurate, we are still far from the much earlier dates that were widely accepted only a few years ago. It is just as likely that the evidence from these and other sites will turn out to be consistent with evidence noted above, which suggests that the earliest Indians pressed into North America after 14,000 B.C. Frederick West, C. Vance Haynes, and Paul S. Martin, who have argued in favor of this view for years, may well turn out to have been right all along.

Clovis is the oldest generally accepted Paleo-Indian complex, its hallmark being the Clovis point. Dates for Clovis come from many sites and

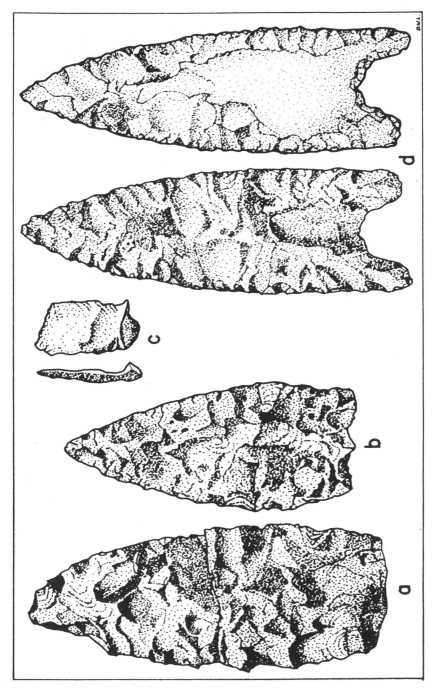

Figure 3.2. Fluted points from the Debert site, Nova Scotia, showing stages of manufacture from preform (a), base preparation (b), removal of the channel flake (c), to finished point (d). (From MacDonald 1968:74.)

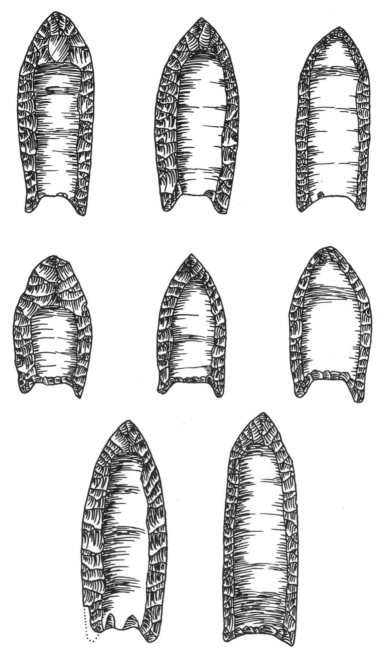

Figure 3.3. Folsom points. Many archaeologists regard specimens of this type to represent the zenith of the flint knapper's art. All points actual size. (From Bell 1958:27.)

consistently range between 10,000 and 9000 B.C. The Clovis point is the most widespread of Paleo-Indian points bearing long thinning flake scars called "flutes." Fluted points can be found nearly everywhere in North America south of the limit of Pleistocene glaciation. The Folsom point is a later, derivative fluted-point style, with a more limited distribution on the Great Plains. Unfluted, leaf-shaped Paleo-Indian points are found in the Rocky Mountain region, and along the spine of the Americas all the way to Argentina. Fish-tailed types are also found in South America.

For a millennium Paleo-Indian hunters exploited both the game species found today in the Americas, and species that became extinct at the end of the Pleistocene. The latter included horses, mammoths, mastodons, camels, and a now extinct species of bison (*Bison antiquus*). The Paleo-Indian tool kit was simple and light, designed for maximum portability. The fluted point, usually made of high-grade chert, probably served as both spear point and knife blade. There were also leaf-shaped or ovate bifacial knives. Chert end scrapers were also made, often with graving spurs, making them multiple-purpose tools for working bone and leather. Tools called *pièces esquilleés,* a term borrowed from the European Upper Paleolithic, are found on some sites. These are bipolar flakes that were apparently used as wedges to split bone, wood, antler, and ivory. Various twist drills and awls were also made of chipped stone, as were specialized gravers and spokeshaves. Nonlithic tools must usually be inferred due to poor preservation, but even with an inventory of such tools, the total kit remained a light one.

HUMAN ECOLOGY IN ICE-AGE AMERICA

The prime movers of the North American Pleistocene were two vast glaciers centered in northeastern Canada and on the Rocky Mountain spine. There were many smaller mountain glaciers and occasional offshoots from the main ice masses, but the glacial history of the later Pleistocene can be described mainly in terms of the advances and retreats of these two large masses.

By 18,000 B.C. the last advance of the Laurentide Ice Sheet pressed as far south as New Jersey in the East. The front stood in Illinois and Iowa in the Midwest, and to the Missouri Valley in the Dakotas. From there the front extended westward to the Pacific, roughly along what is now the U.S. border with Canada. The western (Cordilleran) and eastern (Laurentide) sheets were in collision at this time, so there was solid ice from the

Atlantic to the Pacific. At earlier and later times there was a gap between the sheets, but even then large proglacial lakes would have made human transit difficult or impossible for long periods.

When it eventually retreated, the glacial ice left behind moraine deposits and till that became the foundation for new soil development. Glacial features, such as kettles, kames, and eskers, were left behind as well. The kettles became ponds, and in some cases these eventually changed into bogs. The mounds (kames) and ridges (eskers) of gravel were abrupt features that in some cases later became the foci of Indian burial ceremonialism.

Glacial ice weighed so heavily on the landscape that whole regions were depressed many meters below modern levels. When glacial ice melted, the depressed areas were often filled by temporary glacial lakes that lasted until the land completed its slow rebound.

At the height of the glaciation so much water was locked up in the form of glacial ice that sea levels were many meters below modern levels, with the consequence that the coastline was frequently several to many kilometers seaward from its present location. As the ice melted, sea levels rose more rapidly than the depressed landscape, inundating some coastal areas and occasionally forming inland seas that would later become freshwater lakes. For example, most of the coastal region of Maine was underwater around 10,500 B.C., and the lowlands of modern Lake Champlain and the St. Lawrence Valley were filled by a lobe of the Gulf of St. Lawrence called the Champlain Sea.

Pleistocene geology has done much to clarify the physiography of Paleo-Indian America, helping archaeologists to understand the very different physical settings Paleo-Indian sites had from those that are apparent today. A site that might now have a fine view of the ocean was many kilometers from the sea when it was occupied. Another site seemingly located at random in a patch of undifferentiated forest once had an excellent strategic view across open tundra.

Palynology, the study of pollen, provides one of the best means to reconstruct extinct local and regional environments. Pollen grains are remarkably durable, and, when dispersed by plants each year, they often become incorporated in the sediments at the bottoms of still ponds. Sediments build up over time, forming long records of local pollen rain. After controlling for differential pollen production by different species, the compaction of older (deeper) pond sediments, and other variables, palynologists can provide rough estimates of the relative frequencies of various plants over time. The pollen spectra of ancient forests can be compared to those of modern forests around the continent as one means of reconstructing the extinct environments. With sufficient data, the frequencies of particular plant genera can be plotted in time and space. These approaches have gradually revealed the world of Paleo-Indians to be unlike anything surviving today. Ice sheets over much of the North had compressed vegetational zones to narrow bands across the southern half of the continent. Some tree species that are now relatively widespread may have been confined to small refuge areas. Tundra dominated much of the area around the margin of the glacial ice. However, this was a middle- rather than high-latitude tundra, and the more intense and seasonally more even incidence of sunlight made it a richer environment than modern northern tundras. The tundra, and the now-extinct forests that lay south of it, provided an ideal environment for both the game species that still survive in North America and those that were soon to become extinct. The former included most notably deer, elk (wapiti), pronghorn antelope, moose, caribou, musk ox, and bison. The doomed species included mammoths, mastodons, horses, and various close relatives of modern bison, antelope, and elk.

The environment was unstable, particularly after the glacial ice began to retreat. The retreat occurred as the forward advance of the sheets fell behind the rate of melting at their margins. By the end of the Paleo-Indian period, around 8000 B.C., spruce, pine, and fir were beginning to establish themselves as new forests, where there had previously been only ice or tundra. Birch and alder followed soon after. The changes in the vegetational environment had profound ecological implications for animal species adapted to it, as well as for the human populations that depended upon both for subsistence.

In very general terms, Paleo-Indian sites known to archaeologists can be described in terms of three broad types. First, some sites contain the full range of the limited Paleo-Indian tool kit. These sites were probably occupied by complete bands, small communities made up of both sexes and all ages. Other sites contain projectile points, spokeshaves, knives, and other tools that might have been associated with male subsistence activities; these are usually interpreted as hunting camps. The second type is, in any case, apparently a special- rather than a general-purpose site. Both of these site types tend to be small, often situated on elevated locations that would have afforded good views of game under tundra conditions, or in sheltered areas such as shallow caves. Special-purpose sites also occur as fishing stations and as kill sites.

The third Paleo-Indian site type is the large multiband encampment. Here it is often technically difficult for archaeologists to distinguish large single occupations from successions of smaller occupations by single bands. However, there are enough cases to argue that at least some of them were the sites of temporary congregations of bands, probably for sharing a transitory abundance of food, arranging marriages, exchanging gifts, and engaging in the kind of socializing carried on by all human beings.

Hunter-gatherers typically buffer temporary shortages and variable success in food acquisition by sharing. The risk of spoilage and patterns of unscheduled band movement discourage food storage. Widespread and overlapping networks of friendship also discourage food storage, for anyone doing this for his own future use would be regarded by others as selfish and treated accordingly. Thus, it is no surprise that we find little evidence of food storage in Paleo-Indian sites. A rare exception might be the stone slab cist found at the Vail site in Maine, which could have served as a temporary meat locker.

Given the persisting instability of the environment and the temporary and unscheduled nature of Paleo-Indian movements, little evidence of midden accumulation on and around their sites is to be expected. Further, there was little incentive to modify the environment in even minor ways as a means to increase resource productivity.

The Paleo-Indians of North America were initially free wandering hunters and foragers. Their settlement patterns indicate that they were highly mobile and lived in nonpermanent habitations. It is now generally accepted that Paleo-Indian bands shifted to restricted wandering in large defined territories after their initial expansion allowed them to spread across the habitable portions of the continent.

Surviving hunter-gatherer bands in Australia, southern Africa, and the Arctic show us that individual bands are frequently composed of no more than two dozen people. It has been demonstrated that a group this size will almost certainly become extinct in the long run if left in isolation.[5] Small bands are simply too vulnerable to random catastrophe, and sooner or later they will succumb to it. It does not matter that such a catastrophe may be extremely rare, for it need occur only once. Consequently, bands typically maintain close relations with neighboring bands. By extending

[5] Martin Wobst, "The Demography of Finite Populations and the Origins of the Incest Taboo," in Alan C. Swedlund (ed.), *Population Studies in Archaeology and Biological Anthropology: A Symposium,* Society for American Archaeology Memoir 30 (1975).

the incest taboo and seeking marriage mates outside the immediate band, each band reinforces relations with those surrounding it, pushing the number of face-to-face interactions toward five hundred, the threshold number that mathematical modeling suggests is necessary for long-term survival of the society. Interestingly, this is also about the maximum number of face-to-face interactions most of us are individually able to maintain. It would appear that evolution has selected for this ability to remember several hundred names and faces, a skill that all of us share to a greater or lesser degree.

For Paleo-Indians, the threshold number must have been approached by the development and maintenance of networks of interaction with members of contiguous bands. The archaeological evidence does not allow us to infer larger permanent societies, and theory will not allow us to assume that small ones would have survived in isolation. The archaeological evidence also indicates that the members of such networks sometimes gathered at times and places where food resources would allow it. However, networks were overlapping, and temporary gatherings were not the expression of higher-order societal units. Compared to later hunter-gatherers, the Paleo-Indians were highly mobile and apparently, in the absence of much evidence to the contrary, used only the lightest nonpermanent shelters.

The sizes and distributions of known Paleo-Indian sites suggest that they lived at low regional population densities and in bands having large ranges. The densities of living hunter-gatherers suggest that the density of Paleo-Indians was under 1 per 100 square kilometers. The habitable portion of North America was probably only about 10 million square kilometers at that time, an area that would have supported no more than 100,000 Paleo-Indians. A band of twenty-five would have used a territory of 2,500 square kilometers, and a network of bands totaling 500 would have spread over an area 50,000 square kilometers in size. These are areas almost as large as Rhode Island and West Virginia respectively.

Their primary adaptation was to the exploitation of big game, although there is clear evidence that they exploited less obvious resources such as fish and tubers when the opportunities arose. This focused exploitation amounted to maximization through specialization rather than diversification. This is a successful strategy, especially in the short term, but by deferring short-term risk, such strategies often increase risk in the longer term. It may be that the youth and instability of the environment left the Paleo-Indians with little choice, but by the end of the period major readaptation was inevitable. By 8000 B.C., many of the game animals the Paleo-Indians exploited became extinct as the Pleistocene ended.

An important inference about Paleo-Indian society is that it was characterized by egalitarian organization. This is consistent with other known features of Paleo-Indian culture as well as with norms in living bands of hunter-gatherers. Leadership was ephemeral and based on the personal qualities of strong individuals, There is no convincing archaeological evidence of ranking and no reason to suspect that we should find it. People interacted as equals; the only innate bases for behavior to the contrary were probably differences in age and gender.

The archaeological evidence for the system of overlapping networks can be found in the nature of Paleo-Indian trade and exchange. The fluted point appears to have been an important symbol of Paleo-Indians not only to us but to the Paleo-Indians themselves. Not only were the points skillfully made of exotic materials, finished specimens are often found far from their quarry sources. While other tools might be made from common materials and used only by their makers, fluted points were apparently traded or given as gifts.

The practice of sharing food and other resources could be extended to the mutual benefit of contiguous bands, if ties of gift giving and intermarriage were maintained. Further, hunters from several bands often must have found it convenient to form large hunting parties when the game animals being hunted were particularly large or numerous.

Under these conditions, a prized gift might have traveled hundreds of kilometers, as it passed from one proud owner to another. Each time the gift changed hands it created a new bond of friendship and obligation, or strengthened an old one. However, the system would not have required the face-to-face interaction of the maker and the last owner, nor would it have required anyone to either create or overcome a major social boundary. In the absence of any but the vaguest boundaries, there would not have been a strong sense of ethnicity, and linguistic variation would have been gradual over space, as it has been across the sparsely populated Canadian arctic and subarctic regions in recent times.

Whether or not the Paleo-Indians contributed to the extinction of the large game animals of the Pleistocene is still a matter of debate. On the one hand, it is difficult to credit 100,000 people armed with spears and spear throwers with the extermination of whole species of megafauna. Some specialists have pointed out that the extinctions extended to tiny animals, such as songbirds, that would not have been targets of Paleo-

Indian hunters. These scholars argue that the evidence for a direct Paleo-Indian role is only circumstantial, and that the extinctions were the consequence of rapid and broad environmental changes. In this scenario the Paleo-Indians may have been part of the ecological equation, but were not the prime movers.

In opposition, it has been argued that humans could have had a dramatic effect on animal populations, particularly if they selectively hunted young ones. The passenger pigeon was quickly driven to extinction by Euro-Americans in the nineteenth century by the cutting of nesting trees and the harvesting of flightless squabs, a technique that exterminated the species by repeatedly removing the youngest generation. The argument gains credibility when it is remembered that until near the end of the Pleistocene the game animals of America had never experienced human predation. Many might have had defenses suitable only for protection from nonhuman predation. The musk ox, which apparently escaped extinction only by retreating into regions uninhabitable by early Indians and later Eskimos, is a rare surviving example. Finally, the argument that non-game species, such as small birds, also became extinct has been challenged by some researchers on more general ecological grounds. Where large herd animals have recently disappeared in Africa, the vegetation cover has changed dramatically, extinguishing old niches and creating new ones. Had the large herbivores of Africa not acquired appropriate defense mechanisms through long association with humans, they too might have become extinct, and might have taken minor species with them as vegetation adjusted to their absence.

The question of the role of Paleo-Indians in Pleistocene extinctions remains open for the time being. A simple answer seems unlikely, and resolution of the debate may well await the development of appropriately complex computer models.

HUMAN ADAPTATION FOLLOWING THE ICE AGE

Glacial ice had been retreating for thousands of years, and by 8000 B.C. it was nearly gone. Vegetational zones that had been compressed southward expanded north toward their present locations. The largest of the game animals found their lives disrupted by conditions to which they could not quickly adapt. Some would be extinct soon; others would hang on in refuge areas for a few more centuries. Mammoths and four-horned antelopes disappeared quickly. Horses, ground sloths, and camels soon followed. Mastodons and some species of mountain goat and bison managed to hang on a bit longer. Many smaller species became extinct as well, either because of general environmental changes or because the disappearance of larger species changed the ecological equation.

What had been vast, cool grasslands warmed and dried as part of the general environmental shift. Large lakes disappeared, and species adapted to the previous conditions found their ranges severely restricted. Forests of spruce, fir, and pine moved into regions that had previously been tundra. As the tundra shifted north, it moved into newly deglaciated regions having high-latitude sunlight, and its ability to support grazing animals dropped steadily.

Rising sea levels inundated low-lying coastal zones, creating new beaches and destroying any evidence of earlier human coastal adaptation. Shellfish advanced northward along both coasts as new beds were established. Rivers filled with the meltwater of retreating glaciers cut deep trenches. Then, with the completion of glacial retreat, the valleys silted in and the rivers began to cut sluggish meanders. Gradually the streams cleared of choking sediments and migratory fish began establishing themselves in northern rivers once again. Young soil supported pioneer plants which in turn provided new environments for herbivores and their animal predators.

Paleo-Indians necessarily adapted to the rapidly changing environment, and in doing so became something new in the eyes of modern archaeologists. Generally, the changes involved diversification of food-getting activities, and the development of specialized techniques for exploiting whatever one happened to find locally. Many of the game species that did not become extinct nevertheless disappeared from the local scene. Musk ox herds retreated to the far north, and caribou remained available only to the northernmost bands of hunters. But revival of forest environments brought a broader range of plant foods to replace disappearing game, and the reviving runs of migratory fish provided another attractive new resource. Unlike herds of mobile game, the emerging resources were generally either fixed in their locations or, as in the case of migratory fish, harvestable only as they passed fixed locations. This altered the strategy of Indian hunter-gatherers from one focused on the specialized exploitation of large mobile resources to one focused on the broader exploitation of smaller and often immobile ones.

Like many chronological categories used by American archaeologists, "Archaic" is a term that is somewhat confused by inconsistent usage. It sometimes appears as a period name, usually with an adjective such as

"Middle" or "Terminal," as well as with specific time boundaries. At other times it appears as a culture type, as in "Maritime Archaic," a usage that implies but does not necessarily define time boundaries. These usages did not become separate ones until after the advent of independent dating techniques, particularly radiocarbon. Prior to that time, culture types were used to define chronological relationships in a broad way, so "Archaic" could define both things simultaneously. Finally, although the term was first employed to describe phenomena in the Eastern Woodlands, its use has spread to western North America as well. As used here, "Archaic" refers mainly to a culture type. Periods will be defined by their time boundaries, but we may sometimes also characterize them as Archaic periods in order that the cultural contents of the chronological units do not become lost.

MAJOR TRENDS OF THE EASTERN ARCHAIC

The Archaic cultures of eastern North America are defined by the adaptations they initially made to an environment that had changed dramatically from Ice Age conditions, as well as by subsequent trends over several thousand years. The long-term trends were accompanied by, and to some degree shaped by, the slowing evolution of the environment toward modern conditions. Thus Archaic cultures were those of hunter-gatherers adapting to post-Pleistocene environments. They accomplished this through specialization and increasing technological complexity. As a culture type, Archaic cultures persisted until the third millennium B.C. in some parts of the Eastern Woodlands, much later in others. Plant cultivation and pottery provide archaeological markers for the end of the Archaic in local sequences, but these signals are no longer as clear as was once thought, and the transition from Archaic to more advanced adaptations appears to have been both gradual and variable over time and space. In many other parts of North America, particularly the West and the North, Archaic adaptations were not given up until the nineteenth century. Relatively recent innovations, such as the bow and arrow, replaced older Archaic forms, but the refined hunter-gatherer adaptation remained Archaic in type.

For many years the Eastern Archaic has been discussed mainly in terms of the distributions of key artifact types in time and space. The key artifacts are mainly stone projectile points in distinctive styles, which archaeologists have traditionally assumed to have occupied clearly defin-

Figure 3.4. Map of Eastern Archaic sites.

able periods and geographic ranges. This chronological model is so strongly entrenched in archaeological thinking that associated radiocarbon dates that fall outside the period for which a point type is thought to be diagnostic are often dismissed as erroneous. Similarly, specimens found outside their expected geographic ranges are often explained as strays. It seems increasingly clear, however, that point types could have had long lives, and that they did not necessarily come and go over time in the neat way archaeologists might prefer for chronological purposes. With this caution as a backdrop, the sequence of Archaic point styles that archaeologists depend upon will be briefly described.

By around 8500 B.C., the Clovis points and related styles of fluted Paleo-Indian points were beginning to be replaced by later forms. West and north of the Eastern Woodlands unfluted lanceolate points predominated. These types, which are generally referred to as the Plano tradition, had overall shapes similar to the earlier fluted points, and were often very finely made. Plano points are widespread in sites east of the Rocky Mountains and northward into the Subarctic region of Canada. The western bands were probably primarily bison hunters, the northern bands caribou hunters. Eastern bands worked northeastward across recently deglaciated land north of the Great Lakes, and moved into the St. Lawrence Valley as the Champlain Sea contracted. Some of these eventually reached the Maritime Provinces and Maine, where they might have survived to as late as 6000 B.C.

However, most of the Eastern Woodlands were dominated by bands that evolved locally from earlier Paleo-Indian bands. Plano point types never predominated in most of the region during the Early Archaic period (8000–6000 B.C.). Instead a series of stemmed and notched point types replaced the older fluted points. The new types were often barbed, the notches or stems serving as aids in hafting the points to spear shafts. Unlike the earlier lanceolate points, the newer types were designed to penetrate and remain in a wounded animal, a sign that the Early Archaic bands of the Eastern Woodlands were more heavily equipped. This, in turn, is one of the lines of evidence that archaeologists have used to infer that Archaic bands were less nomadic than their Paleo-Indian predecessors.

Most of the cultural complexes of the 8000 to 6000 B.C. period take their names from projectile point types that are considered diagnostic of them. In the South the names Dalton, Quad, and Hardaway are frequently heard. The Hardaway point, first described for its type site in North Carolina, has side notches, but basal thinning points to its fluted-point ancestry. Dalton points, first defined in Missouri, and Quad points from the Tennessee Valley are both lanceolate with pronounced thinning that shows their fluted-point ancestry even more clearly. Kirk points, also first named in North Carolina, are stemmed and barbed, making them much less similar to earlier lanceolate forms. Farther north, stemmed point types, first observed in Tennessee and West Virginia, bear distinctive notches in the bases of their stems, a feature that has led archaeologists to refer to them collectively as bifurcate base points. For a while, these hallmarks of the Early Archaic period were not widely recognized in the northern portions of the Eastern Woodlands, and some archaeologists thought that the region had been generally abandoned for perhaps two millennia. However, local expressions of the Early Archaic are being increasingly recognized south and east of the marginal areas in which Plano points dominated.

The Middle Archaic period, which lasted from 6000 to 4000 B.C. in the Eastern Woodlands, is marked by the appearance of a new series of diagnostic projectile points. These are often stemmed point types with specific names, such as Stanley, Neville, Stark, and Merrimack. With the advent of the Late Archaic period after 4000 B.C., diagnostic broad, side-notched point types appear. One of these, the Otter Creek type, is particularly associated with the Laurentian Archaic, a regional variant that flourished in the basins of rivers that feed the lower Great Lakes and the St. Lawrence River. Laurentian was related to the Maritime Archaic culture that developed at about the same time around the Gulf of St. Lawrence.

The Eastern Archaic as a culture type is difficult to comprehend if discussed only in terms of a myriad of regional projectile point types. It can even be a misleading exercise given the general failure of the point types to conform consistently well to our temporal and cultural categories. It is more likely that the hunter-gatherers of the Eastern Woodlands can be understood best through an examination of the developmental trends of all these Archaic cultures over time. Indeed, the same general trends characterized post-Pleistocene cultural evolution everywhere in North America. The adaptive strategies of Archaic cultures collectively reveal the character of this culture type. For 5,000 years following 8000 B.C., North America was a vast laboratory in which hunter-gatherer cultures conducted careful experiments in adaptation. Progress was very slow, for there is wisdom in conservatism when the consequences of failed innovation are severe. Overall, the trends were toward the reduction of risk, and an exploitation of resources that was both intensive and diverse. The process of settling-in

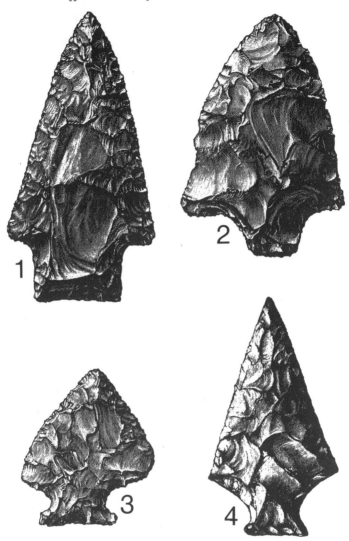

Figure 3.5A. Some Terminal Archaic point types: Genesee (1), Snook Kill (2), Perkiomen (3), and Susquehanna Broad (4). (From Ritchie 1971. Courtesy of the New York State Museum.)

encouraged hunter-gatherer communities to focus on resources that were locally abundant, eventually making them specialists who differed strikingly from Paleo-Indian generalists. But this was specialization only from a continental perspective, because at the local level the trend was toward

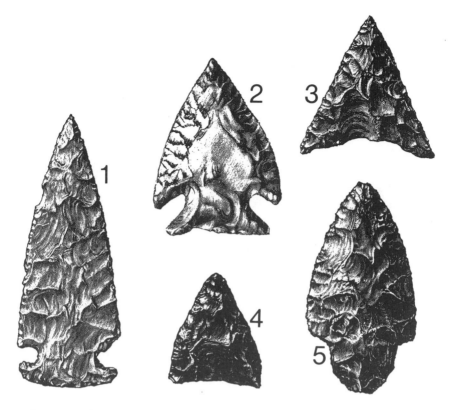

Figure 3.5B. Some New York point types from the Woodland Period: Meadowood (1), Jack's Reef Corner-Notched (2), Levanna (3), Jack's Reef Pentagonal (4), and Adena (5). (From Ritchie 1971. Courtesy of the New York State Museum.)

diversification. The slow process of Archaic development can be summarized as eleven trends,[6] the first of which involved growing care in the scheduling of seasonal movements.

1. Seasonal scheduling, sedentism, and midden accumulation

Archaeological evidence from the centuries following 8000 B.C. generally reflects unspecialized adaptations consistent with the still unstabilized environment. In the face of uncertainty, hunter-gatherer bands probably

[6] Brian Hayden, "Technological Transitions among Hunter-gatherers," *Current Anthropology* 22 (1981).

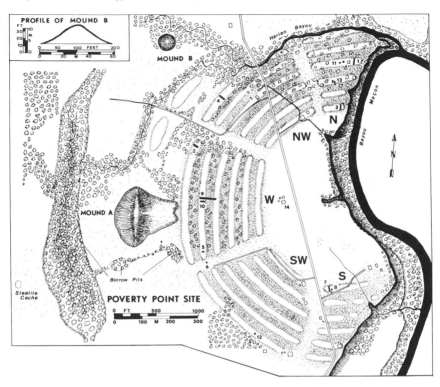

remained mobile, able to take advantage of resources as they presented themselves or were discovered in the course of searching that had to be more random than planned. As environmental change slowed, resources became more predictable, and Indian bands could plan their movements longer in advance. Resource stability also allowed a broadening of the resource base, as the Indians learned how best to exploit specific species. This reinforced patterns of seasonal scheduling in which specific subsistence activities were worked into increasingly complex seasonal rounds. Free-wandering bands might have settled into patterns of restricted wandering within large defined territories even in the Paleo-Indian period. Certainly most bands were exploiting resources within defined territories after 8000 B.C., and many had probably begun using central base camps.

The increasing use of central bases and the scheduling of seasonal movements to special-purpose camps produced archaeological sites that were quite different from those seen for earlier millennia. Base camps are filled with the debris of long occupation. Cache pits reveal that the people

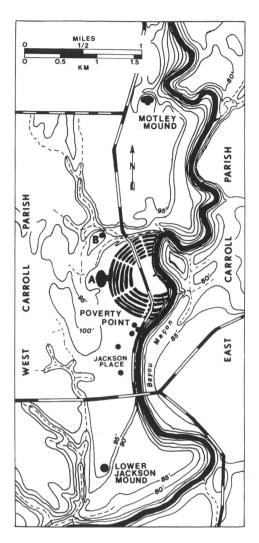

Figure 3.6 (opposite page and left). Poverty Point, plan and regional setting. (Adapted from Webb 1982.)

stored tools, supplies, and perhaps food between seasonal occupations. Middens accumulated around the sites as waste from repeated occupations built up. While these were hardly the permanent villages of some later farming communities, they reveal a kind of sedentism that persisted until European colonization in parts of North America.

Archaic sedentism reached an impressive scale between 1500 and 700 B.C. at Poverty Point, Louisiana. Houses of wood, bark, and mud were erected on long, low ridges arranged around a central plaza. The ridges were in concentric rows, six deep, so that from above the whole village looks like an amphitheater of six nested partial octagons. The outermost octagon has a diameter of about 1,300 meters, Nearly half of what would have been a complete octagonal pattern was apparently never built, for the east side of the plaza has its back to a river. Away from the river, on the other side of the village, stands a large, artificial earthen mound, 20 meters high and 200 meters long on its east-west axis. The extra length was needed to accommodate a long earthen ramp leading from the outermost ridge of the village to the top of the mound. From the top of the mound, the sun appears to rise directly over the center of the village plaza on the mornings of the vernal and autumnal equinoxes.

Other mounds and village sites related to Poverty Point have been found nearby. Before radiocardon dating, some archaeologists suspected that Poverty Point was later, and related to the Adena and Hopewell developments of the Ohio Valley. It is possible that the distant Olmec and other contemporaneous developments in Mexico had some long-range influence in this southwestern corner of the Eastern Woodlands. However, such connections are unnecessary to explain the development of Poverty Point. It can just as easily be interpreted as a local outgrowth of long-term Archaic trends in the Eastern Woodlands.

2. *Evolution of complex technology*

Permanent base camps allowed the expansion of the basic tool kit. Time and effort could now be invested in the production of a more diversified inventory of tools, and the tools could be heavier and less portable. Finished ground stone tools make their first strong appearance in Eastern Archaic cultures. Adzes, celts, and gouges, all heavy woodworking tools, could be left behind in caches when necessary, or moved to new base camps when rare circumstances made the effort worthwhile.

Archaic Indians in northern Michigan discovered sources of copper nuggets on the Keweenaw Peninsula. They further found that these could be beaten into adzes, celts, gouges, and spear points, a technology very different from the subtractive processes used in working stone. Beaten copper becomes brittle after a time, but the copper workers learned to anneal the metal, restoring its malleability, by heating it and plunging it into cold water. The tools they made led early archaeologists to refer to this as the Old Copper culture, but, apart from its unique copper tools, this Archaic culture is quite similar to the Lake Forest Archaic of the interior Northeast. Both were broadly similar to the coastal Maritime Archaic.

Fishing equipment increased in amount and complexity. Stone net sinkers, fiber nets, bone hooks, and traps of various materials were made in forms increasingly specialized to available species. In coastal settings, Archaic cultures learned to harvest marine resources, not least of which were annual migratory fish runs. These drew Indian bands each year to campsites overlooking falls and other points at which the runs could be harvested efficiently.

Food preparation techniques had to advance to make the broadening range of resources edible. Seeds needed to be reduced by grinding, but some (like the acorn) also required leaching or other preparation to make them palatable. Skunk cabbage is an edible vegetable long before most other greens appear in the spring, but is must be repeatedly boiled and drained before being eaten. Food boiling is apparent in Archaic sites, more often from the presence of boiling stones than from preserved containers. Most containers were probably skin bags, folded birchbark, or water-proofed baskets. Boiling was accomplished by heating walnut-sized pebbles in a fire, then dropping them into liquid-filled containers. Little, if any, evidence of this kind of food preparation is found on Paleo-Indian sites, where roasting probably prevailed. At Poverty Point, where the alluvial soils of the Mississippi Valley provided few pebbles, archaeologists have found thousands of fired clay balls, which were apparently used to boil food.

Fiber-tempered pottery, once thought to signal the arrival of agriculture and settled life, first appeared among the Archaic cultures of the Southeast in the third millennium B.C. Placing such vessels directly over fires offered another means to cook food, and would have been an improvement over stone boiling, especially where pebbles were in short supply. A very different, grit-tempered pottery industry was established in the Northeast by 1000 B.C.

The domesticated dog appeared in America sometime during the Archaic. The dog developed from wild ancestors in the Eastern Hemisphere, perhaps domesticating itself as much as it was domesticated by humans. It whimpers like a human baby and in this and other ways elicits a sympathetic reaction from people. In exchange for scraps that humans find inedible, the dog can assist in hunting and even transportation. A small amount of control of its reproduction will select for behavioral traits that make the dog welcome in hunter-gatherer communities. The animal was widespread in the Americas by the time Europeans arrived.

The principal weapon of Archaic cultures was the spear thrower, which had been inherited from Paleo-Indian ancestors. In the Eastern Woodlands, Archaic hunters learned to make advanced spear throwers with flexible shafts, probably of green ironwood. By loading energy in the bent shaft during the course of the throw, the hunter gained velocity. Both the speed and the impact of the spear were increased. By the end of the Archaic in the Eastern Woodlands, the efficiency of flexible spear throwers was being further enhanced by stone weights, often beautifully ground stone objects. The principle exploited by modern golfers and pole vaulters was thus in use long before the invention of fiberglass, and the notion of a flexible shaft made the eventual adoption of the bow and arrow that much easier.

3. Specialization and the pursuit of smaller game

The extinction of the big game species of the Ice Age forced Indian cultures to focus attention on medium-sized species that for the most part still survive. Even without the pressure to shift, it is generally true that there is more meat available per unit of area in the form of rodents than in the form of ungulates. The problem, of course, is that one deer is easier to hunt than are dozens of squirrels. Nevertheless, Archaic hunters gradually shifted from a limited resource base of medium to large game (K-selected species) to the diversified exploitation of more and smaller animals (r-selected species).[7] This trend went beyond the degree of change forced by post-Pleistocene extinctions. Further, it was facilitated by seasonal scheduling within defined territories. While desert bands learned to exploit cyclical peaks in rabbit populations, and northern hunters learned to use hares to buffer fluctuations in the meat supply, Woodland bands learned to regulate the harvest of beavers for the long-term provision of both meat and pelts. Although the deer and its relatives remained critically important for hides as well as meat in areas where they were available, Archaic hunter-gatherers moved well

---

[7] These terms are used by ecologists to distinguish between large animals that invest heavily in producing and caring for one or a few offspring at a time, and smaller animals that produce large litters but suffer from high offspring mortality.

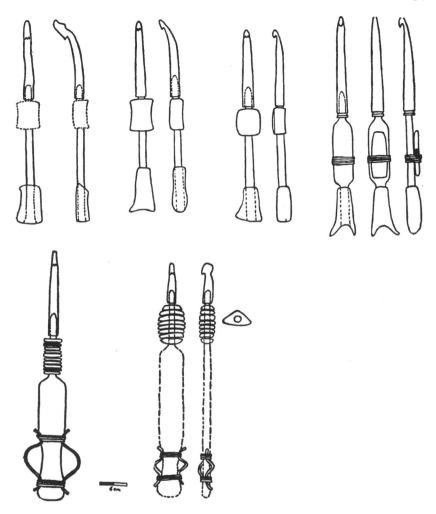

Figure 3.7. Spear throwers, sometimes called "atlatls," as reconstructed from Indian Knoll, Kentucky. Six specimens are shown in alternate views. Grips are at the bottom in each case and hooks are to the top. Various means were used to attach weights to the shafts near the hooks. (From Webb 1974:323.)

down the food chain. Clams and other shellfish became important additions to the diet in coastal areas, especially when other resources were scarce. Similarly, freshwater mussels began to appear in the middens of interior camps.

4. Increasing population density

From the implications of the trends mentioned above, as well as from the increasing density of archaeological sites over time, we can infer that human population density was increasing throughout the Archaic periods. The Paleo-Indians probably lived at a density of fewer that one person per 100 square kilometers. This is consistent with the densities of the Arctic and Subarctic regions in modern times. Archaic bands probably expanded slowly to bring the density into the 1 to 100 per 100 square kilometer range. The surviving hunter-gatherers of southern Canada and the northern United States had population densities within this range. Archaic cultures eventually exceeded one person per square kilometer along the resource-rich West Coast, but elsewhere farming was a prerequisite to regional densities at or above that level.

5. The restriction of band ranges

The steady packing of increasing numbers of people into a given area, which was not necessarily accompanied by increasing sizes of individual bands, seems to have led to a restriction of band ranges. This would have been facilitated by their increasing abilities to maximize the exploitation of a wide range of local resources, which allowed individual bands to live within smaller territories than earlier adaptations would have permitted. While twenty-five individuals might still have comprised a conveniently sized band, a network of 500 individuals remained optimal for Archaic society. However, management of 500 people or more in a single permanent community requires higher-level social organization that was probably still lacking in most of these Archaic communities.

6. Occupation of marginal environments

The marginal habitats that had been left generally unpopulated in earlier millennia were now becoming populated by the expansion of new bands hiving off from older established ones. Their increasing skills for extracting food from the environment allowed productive penetration of all but the most hostile habitats.

7. Environmental modification

Archaic hunter-gatherers were increasingly able to cope with marginal habitats. They were also probably beginning to modify their environment, either deliberately or as a by-product of subsistence activities. Many game animals, notably deer, prefer the edge environments provided by interspersed patches of meadow and forest. Such a patchy environment would have promoted higher deer populations, and Archaic hunters needed only to create and maintain meadows through periodic burning to increase the deer population. Meadows also served as yards in which the deer congregated in easily harvested herds during the late winter months.

Much is often made of the supposed natural environmental responsibility of Native Americans. There is some truth to this when the behavior of, say, some Indian fur trappers is compared to that of nineteenth-century Euro-Americans. However, Paleo-Indians might have been partially responsible for some late Pleistocene extinctions, and Plains Indians are known to have contributed to the near extinction of bison in the nineteenth century. For their part, Archaic hunter-gatherers appear to have modified the environment as did their contemporaries in Europe and elsewhere. However, people having Archaic adaptations still probably lived at densities around ten per 100 square kilometers. The habitable portions of North America were not likely to have exceeded ten million square kilometers during the Archaic periods, suggesting that in very rough terms the total population of the continent probably was not greater than a million people. This is an extremely rough estimate, but sufficient to make the point that even with environmental modification, Archaic hunter-gatherers were not numerous enough or technologically powerful enough to have produced more than just traces of permanent change to their environment.

8. Mortuary ceremonialism

Anthropological theory predicts that the increasing importance of social boundaries will produce symbols to define and reinforce them.[8] Archaeologically we appear to have the evidence for this in the rise of mortuary ceremonialism in the Late Archaic period in the Northeast. Burial mound

---

[8] This process is not necessarily a conscious one, but it appears to be universal. B. J. Williams, *A Model of Band Society*, Society for American Archaeology Memoir 29 (1974).

construction appears as early as 7,500 years ago at L'Anse Amour, Labrador. This Middle Archaic site presaged the development of the Maritime Archaic burial complex later found from this area southward to Maine. There was an emphasis on the use of red ocher pigment in the burials of this complex, a trait that has led to the use of the name "Red Paint" to describe it. Curiously, similar burial complexes are found in maritime contexts in Europe around the same time. But this was more likely an example of parallel cultural evolution than evidence of contact. Developments related to the Maritime Archaic can be found in the Great Lakes basin. Two examples are the Glacial Kame burial complex and that of the Old Copper culture. The former involved use of natural glacial features as mounds for burials. The latter focused on the burial of native copper spearheads, gouges, and other tools with the dead. To varying degrees, all of these Archaic cultures appear to have at least implicitly used burial ceremonialism to define themselves and their territories.

9. *Emergence of competition and social ranking*

Consistent with all of the above is the gradual emergence of social ranking. Archaeologically we see a gradual increase in the differential treatment of the dead, treatment that appears to reflect social differences that went beyond differences in age and sex. Some adult men were accorded lavish burials, others were not. The patterns of interment sometimes suggest that these differences went beyond what one might expect to emerge through the efforts of otherwise equal individuals. We can infer that the egalitarian system of the Paleo-Indian period was gradually replaced by an Archaic one in which social ranking became increasingly important. If analogous historically recorded societies are a guide, high-ranking individuals often represented the larger community or kin group to the outside world, another trait of social boundary maintenance. As we shall see, this had widespread ramifications in subsequent centuries.

10. *Development of food storage*

Large-scale food storage is not characteristic of simple hunter-gatherers, and was probably not strongly developed among Paleo-Indians. Local or short-term shortages are buffered by sharing rather than by storing, for the socially unbounded world of the Paleo-Indians obliged everyone to share food with anyone. The emergence of boundaries and ethnic contrasts during the Archaic periods made it possible for communities to store food for their own future use without having to risk losing their stockpiles to people by now defined as outsiders. The technology and knowledge of how to store food may have been available for many centuries, but it should be no surprise that we see increasing evidence for food storage in Archaic sites.

11. *Cultural introspection*

As an ever-growing number of bands came to inhabit ever-smaller territories, the critical minimum of 500 face-to-face contacts came within increasingly easy reach. No longer were the overlapping social networks of the thinly dispersed Paleo-Indian bands necessary. Increasing population densities made cultural boundaries possible, and local specialization made them inevitable. We see the evidence of this in the archaeological record in a shift toward the exclusive use of local lithic resources. This is further archaeological evidence that band ranges were shrinking, and that growing population was resulting in more rather than larger local bands. The linguistic implications of these processes are that sets of allied bands were becoming regional speech communities having decreasing contact with outsiders. The broadly distributed languages or language complexes of the Paleo-Indian period were probably replaced by mutually unintelligible languages during Archaic times, as socio-linguistic boundaries came to be consciously maintained. These, then, became the protolanguages from which recent North American Indian language families descend. At least twenty-one protolanguages survived as families of daughter languages, and many of the thirty-two language isolates of Native North America may be the sole survivors of other Archaic protolanguages. We can only guess at the number of Archaic protolanguages that eventually expired without modern descendants, but it might have been large, perhaps 50 to a hundred. Many protolanguages, such as proto-Algonquian and proto-Iroquoian, have been partially reconstructed and their ages estimated on the basis of known rates of linguistic change. Most of these dates are no older than the Late Archaic, younger than around 4000 B.C. That leaves many Late Archaic and all Middle and Early Archaic archaeological complexes unaccounted for in linguistic terms. Computer simulation of the processes described here might eventually help us determine how many independent Archaic cultures must have developed and then disappeared, leaving only archaeological traces.

HUNTER-GATHERERS AND THE RISE
OF PLANT CULTIVATION

Intimate familiarity with local food resources eventually led to a symbiotic relationship between Indian and some plant populations. The Canada onion (*Allium canadense*) occurs in isolated patches around Late Archaic period sites in the Northeast.[9] The flowers of this plant do not produce seeds, and it must reproduce from bulbs. It could not have spread easily north of Pennsylvania, so its sporadic appearance as far north as Ontario probably involved the establishment of beds by Archaic hunter-gatherers. Whether or not the creation of such beds was a conscious act, Archaic bands could later exploit them for food on scheduled visits to these sites. Elsewhere, the occasional tending of oak groves might have promoted acorn production, and periodic burning might have enhanced the productivity of patches of seed-bearing plants. Such activity is not farming, but neither is it the mere random exploitation of natural foods.

By the third millennium B.C., Indian cultures in several parts of North America had moved from intensive foraging to the actual cultivation of some indigenous plants. These plants by no means constituted the importance true domesticates have for agriculturalists, and their manipulation may not have even looked much like modern cultivation. Nonetheless, the importance of sunflower, goosefoot, pigweed, knotweed, maygrass, and marsh elder was increasing, and the beginnings of horticulture were being practiced alongside traditional intensive hunting and gathering. Sunflower and sumpweed produced oily seeds, but not all of the plants tended at this time were exploited for their seeds. Goosefoot, knotweed, and maygrass provided starchy flour. Sunflowers included at least one species cultivated for its tubers, a species later named rather inappropriately the "Jerusalem artichoke."

Cucurbits (gourds and squash) native to the Eastern Woodlands were used for their flesh as well as their seeds. Some species later came to North America from Mexico, but it is now known that the first cucurbits to be domesticated in North America were derived from wild ancestors in the central part of the Eastern Woodlands. The resulting new subsistence pattern has been called the "cultivating ecosystem type" by some archaeologists, "early horticulture" by others.[10]

[9] Russell J. Barber, "Disjunct Plant Distributions and Archaeological Interpretations," *Man in the Northeast* 13 (1977).
[10] James B. Stoltman and David A. Baerreis, "The Evolution of Human Ecosystems in the Eastern United States," in H. E. Wright (ed.), *Late Quaternary Environments of the United States,* vol. 2,

Beginning around 2500 B.C. in a few places in the Mississippi drainage, and lasting to at least A.D. 400 in some places, Indians exerted much more control over the propagation and production of these plants than earlier foragers could have imagined, if somewhat less than what true horticulturalists can achieve (see Chapter 4). The low yield of the early cultigens relative to later domesticates suggests that they served mainly to buffer temporary shortages in hunted and gathered wild foods. They were less than true staples, but they were storable, and made a critical difference for people threatened mainly by rare but lethal episodes of starvation.

Social boundaries and societal insulation had made storage practical to Archaic communities. The beginnings of food production probably intensified that strategy, further reducing long-term risk and reinforcing the social and political mechanisms that food storage and distribution entail. Those mechanisms were probably based primarily on kin units, extended family groups led by senior people. It is likely that women were increasingly among those leaders. Societies that rely heavily upon hunting for subsistence are typically dominated by men. However, gathering is often the responsibility of women, and the increasing importance of plant manipulation and plant food storage might have steadily enhanced the role of women.

HUNTERS OF THE GREAT PLAINS

The Rocky Mountains rise abruptly above the High Plains, forming a natural barrier all the way from the Canadian Yukon to west Texas. In fact, the eastern Mexican range, known as the Sierra Madre Oriental, continues the barrier all the way to the Isthmus of Tehuantepec. Streams that originate on the eastern slopes of the Rockies north of Mexico flow generally eastward, often crossing 1,000 kilometers of grasslands before joining the main channel of the Mississippi. The largest of these is the Missouri, which runs along a channel separating glaciated from unglaciated land in the Dakotas. There are many others, including the Platte, the Republican, the Arkansas, the Cimarron, the Washita, and the Red Rivers, all of them tributaries of the Mississippi.

The High Plains support short grasses and sagebrush, whereas the lower elevations of the prairie to the east support taller grasses and occasional stands of trees. Long fingers of woodlands penetrate up the main river valleys westward from the Mississippi as far as they can.

The Holocene (Minneapolis, 1983); Dean R. Snow, *The Archaeology of New England* (New York, 1980), 261; B. D. Smith, "Origins of Agriculture in Eastern North America," *Science* 246 (1989), 1566–71.

Figure 3.8. Plains Archaic sites.

A prairie peninsula extends eastward across southern Wisconsin and northern Illinois and into Indiana. Farther south the vague boundary between the Eastern Woodlands and the Great Plains lies more to the west. The easternmost portions of Texas and Oklahoma really belong to the Eastern Woodlands.

The Plains were more moist and their vegetation more lush during the close of the Ice Age. This was prime habitat for mammoths, horses, and other large game that dwindled to extinction when the climate turned drier and warmer. Many species survived, however, and the Plains of only a century ago were still home to bison, mule deer, elk, black bear, and grizzly bear. Large tracts of the Great Plains were, and still are, best suited to hunters and pastoralists. Even today farmers avoid the unglaciated soils that lie west of the Missouri River.

The big-game-hunting adaptation of the Paleo-Indians persisted longer on the Great Plains than it did in most other regions. Clovis points, which were widespread on the continent, were replaced on the Plains by the even finer fluted points of the Folsom type after 9000 B.C. Fluted points were phased out and replaced by the unfluted lanceolate types of the Plano tradition after 8000 B.C. However, this seems like more an evolution in specific styles than a radical change in adaptation. A big-game-hunting lifestyle persisted through the centuries following 8000 B.C., evolving slowly as average temperatures gradually rose, rainfall gradually decreased, and the largest game animals declined to extinction. By 5000 B.C., the region was mostly treeless except along ravines, and Indian bands had developed subsistence strategies that we call the Plains Archaic.

The American Indian populations of the Plains and the Desert West went through the same process of post-Pleistocene adaptation already discussed for eastern North America. The same Archaic cultural trends have been documented by archaeologists working in the West, although the details are quite different. One reason for the difference is the general dryness of the region. Another is that general post-Pleistocene climatic trends went temporarily beyond modern levels in this region. Relatively moist and cool conditions appear to have prevailed there from 7000 to 5000 B.C., a long period referred to as the "Anathermal." However, an "Altithermal" period, extending from 5000 to 2500 B.C., saw average levels of heat and aridity exceed modern levels. This trend was at its peak around 4400 B.C. Conditions began to return toward modern levels after that, producing "Medithermal" conditions after 2500 B.C. The Altithermal maximum apparently stressed Archaic cultural adaptation in the region, but left Indian populations relatively well positioned to take advantage of Medithermal conditions.

Archaeological sites are very unevenly distributed across all of the Great Plains for the 5,000 years beginning at 5000 B.C. There appear to be significantly fewer sites for the first half of this long period than later, probably because it coincides with the Altithermal period. It is unlikely that the Plains were abandoned during this period, but conditions probably would have led to lower overall population density, and a tendency for Indian bands to concentrate in areas having adequate water. Just as important, the bison herds would have done the same thing, perhaps abandoning large short-grass areas for ranges where grass and water were still adequate to sustain them. It is no coincidence that modern bison, which are smaller than their ancestors, probably evolved to their current average size between 4500 and 2500 B.C. The severe biological stresses of the Altithermal environment would have selected against large body sizes.

The number of known Archaic sites increased dramatically in the Medithermal conditions that followed 2500 B.C. During this period the Great Plains took on their modern character. Plant and animal species that flourished from then on were essentially those of the era when the Europeans first arrived. Modern bison, pronghorn antelope, mule deer, white-tailed deer, black bear, grizzly bear, and elk were the principal surviving game animals. Archaic bands depended upon these as well as on a variety of wild plant foods.

The native horse had died out at the end of the Pleistocene, so mounted nomadism on the Great Plains had to wait until horses were reintroduced by Spanish colonists. The post-Pleistocene Plains produced a variety of seeds, fruits, and tubers for Archaic gatherers, but the bison herds and other surviving large game were difficult for unmounted nomads to exploit. There are buffalo jumps, where teams of Archaic hunters periodically drove herds over cliffs, but despite this clever and occasionally productive hunting technique, the Archaic populations remained thin and scattered. The hunter-gatherers of the Plains gave little resistance to the first wave of Eastern Woodlands migrants who pressed westward into the Plains along the wooded river valleys around 100 B.C. A second major wave of eastern farmers pressed westward along the same routes after A.D. 900 (Chapter 4). In both cases, however, they lived in scattered communities, most of which had to retreat back eastward when occasional extended droughts turned their marginal farming enterprises into failed ones. In central Texas and northward through the High Plains to Alberta, the dominant adaptation remained an Archaic lifestyle through all of post-Pleistocene prehistory.

HUNTER-GATHERERS OF THE INTERIOR WEST

The Coastal Mountains of British Columbia diverge from the Rockies near the West Coast. This chain is continued south by the Coast Range, Cascades, and Sierra Nevada through Washington, Oregon, and California. There is a break in southern California, south of which the Sierra Madre Occidental continues through western Mexico until it converges with the Oriental Range. Between this series of coastal ranges and the Rocky Mountains to the east, and extending from British Columbia to Mexico, is a vast natural province referred to as the Intermontain West or Desert West.

The Desert West is generally dry, more so to the south than to the north. The Mexican and southwestern portions are drained by the Rio Grande and the Colorado River. The region defined by most of Nevada, Utah, and portions of surrounding states is not drained at all, and is consequently known as the Great Basin. Streams here flow inward to end in dry playas or brackish lakes, the largest of which is Great Salt Lake. North of the Great Basin is the Plateau, the intermontain portions of Oregon, Washington, and British Columbia. This last region of the Desert West is drained by two major river systems, the Columbia in the south and the Fraser in the north.

The vegetation of the Desert West varies by latitude and altitude. The species of the Sonoran Desert of Mexico and the Southwest include various saguaro, cholla, ocotillo, and barrel cacti. Valleys have enough moisture to support small trees and shrubs, such as the mesquite, ironwood, and creosote. There is little rain, but it comes twice a year, as gentle showers in the winter and heavy localized storms in the summer. It can freeze here during winter nights, but daytime thaws allow the large cacti to survive in the long term, producing fruit dependably year after year.

The colder Mohave Desert of the southern Great Basin and the northern Southwest is also higher and drier. Winter freezes last long enough to kill the saguaro cacti that might otherwise grow there. Barrel, prickly pear, and cholla cacti, Joshua tree, and Mojave yucca predominate, and there is

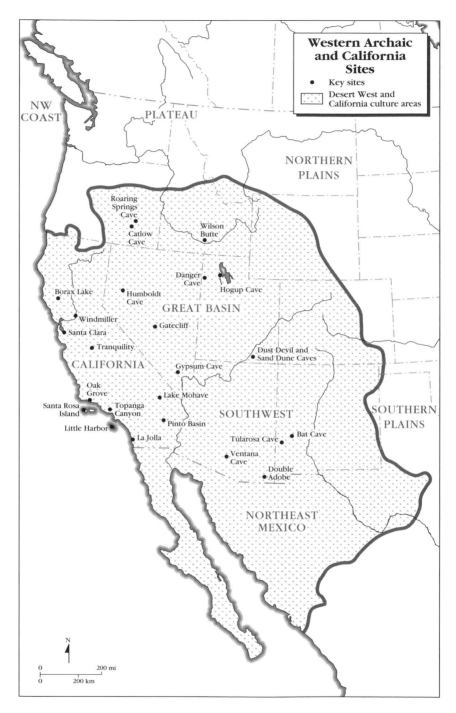

Figure 3.9. Map of Western Archaic and California sites.

generally less food than in the Sonoran desert. To the north lie the Cold Desert of the northern Great Basin and the temperate grasslands and coniferous forests of the Plateau.

Local variations in the Desert West occur largely as the consequence of changes in elevation. Hunter-gatherers were able to seek different food resources by moving up or down the hills and mountains of the region, for even the Mexican desert and the Great Basin are broken up by small scattered mountain ranges. The juniper and piñon forests of the mountain ridges harbored bighorn sheep and vegetable food. Thus environmental variability brought about by rugged terrain makes up to some degree for the Desert West's generally low natural food productivity.

Survivors of the Great Basin

Danger Cave, Utah, is the type site for the Desert Archaic. The site lies thirty-four meters above Great Salt Lake. In the early periods of the cave's occupation, the lake was both higher and larger in area. Cultural remains began to accumulate in the cave by 9000 B.C., and the deposit eventually reached a depth of four meters. Because of the dry environment, materials such as fiber, bone, wood, and leather, which otherwise would have disappeared from the record, were preserved in large numbers. Thousands of artifacts of these materials, along with stone and other more durable remains, document five major stratigraphic zones at Danger Cave.

Long prehistoric sequences have also been established by careful excavation at other cave and rock shelter sites, such as Hogup Cave, Sudden Shelter, and several other places in Utah. In Nevada, key sites have been Gatecliff Shelter, Leonard Rockshelter, and Lovelock Cave, although many others have also contributed significantly to overall understanding.[11] The sites have yielded not only durable artifacts, such as chipped stone tools, milling stones, and bone tools, but also feathers, nets, coiled and twined basketry, mats, and other fiber artifacts. Diets have been reconstructed from seeds, husks, and other remains of edible foods, as well as directly from the contents of human coprolites (archaeologically preserved feces).

Taken together, the evidence indicates that big game hunting remained important during the early part of the Archaic adaptation, but was less specialized and accompanied by seed grinding. People lived in small

---

[11] Details on these sites can be found in the prehistory chapters of volume 11 of the *Handbook of North American Indians* (Washington, D.C., 1986).

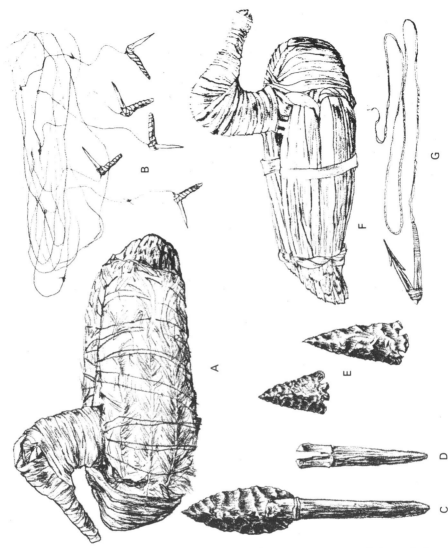

Figure 3.10. Desert Archaic artifacts. Decoys of tule and duck feathers shown at much reduced scale (A & F). Other objects include a bone and wood fishhook on a line (G), five hooks on a setline (B), projectile points (E), a hafted knife or atlatl dart foreshaft (C), and an untipped handle or foreshaft (D). (After Jennings 1974:168.)

mobile groups, and exploited game remaining around the dwindling lakes and marshes of the region. Bison, antelope, sheep, and deer were present, but declining in numbers compared to small rodents, hares, and rabbits. These trends continued after the start of the Middle Archaic period, which began after the Altithermal peak, around 2000 B.C. Rabbit bones and grinding stones are abundant in deposits of this age, and it is clear that the Archaic tendency toward maximization of small game in large numbers had progressed further in the Great Basin than in most regions by the beginning of European contact. Waterfowl and shore birds were taken in earlier millennia, but these are not common in deposits after 1200 B.C., evidence that the marshlands were continuing to dry up. By this time, people were exploiting seasonal variability by maximizing harvests and storing food for future use. In some areas this included intensive winter-time use of piñon nuts. Nineteenth–century documents indicate that Native inhabitants of the Great Basin often migrated annually between stream–bank camps on the valley floor and winter lodges near piñon groves on the mountain slopes.

Large seed-grinding implements are often found in base camps in the western deserts. The stone analogues of mortars and pestles are more familiar to modern eyes, but the flat stone "metate" and its "mano" are more common in these sites. As in the Eastern Woodlands, the establishment of regular seasonal rounds allowed heavy tools to be left in caches for use on future visits to the same sites.

The Late Archaic begins here around A.D. 500, at a time when horticulture was beginning to supplant Archaic culture in the East and in the Southwest. The bow and arrow was introduced to the Great Basin, eventually replacing the spear thrower, and there was a temporary (900 year) intrusion of horticultural Fremont culture villages from the south, but the most successful adaptation remained an Archaic hunter-gatherer one.

We cannot be sure of the linguistic identities of most inhabitants of the Great Basin prior to the arrival of Europeans. Many might have been speakers of Hokan languages, a family that includes numerous California groups and the Yumans of the Southwest. Some, particularly those in the part of the Great Basin that lies in modern California, were Uto-Aztecan speakers. The Late Archaic period undoubtedly saw the arrival of Na-Dene speakers from Canada, and these people may well have been responsible for the introduction of the bow and arrow. The speech and the fate of the Fremont villagers remain unknown.

Late in precontact times, much of the Great Basin was taken over by ancestral Shoshones, Utes, Paiutes, and speakers of other languages belonging to the Numic branch of the Uto-Aztecan family. They apparently expanded northeastward out of a core area in the desert of southeastern California and southern Nevada. After the introduction of the horse, some of them became major carriers of the new tradition of mounted nomadism on the Great Plains.

The Numic expansion is an intriguing problem, because in ecological terms, they were less advanced than the communities they replaced. In one area they replaced Fremont horticulturalists, in another semisedentary ancestors of the Klamaths. It is possible that environmental stress forced out otherwise more advanced adaptations while creating harsher conditions to which ancestral Numic peoples were already particularly well adapted. The Numic expansion may be a rare case of an adaptive radiation filling in behind the ecological collapse of sedentary communities.

Archaic cultures of the Southwest

The hot Sonoran Desert environment of the Southwest is actually an extension of the desert of northern Mexico. In a very general way, the early Archaic cultures of this region were variants of the Desert Culture described for the Great Basin. However, there were differences in detail that cause some archaeologists to avoid inclusion of cultures outside the Great Basin under that covering term. Once again, much of our evidence comes from cave and rock shelter sites. Some of the most familiar names are Gypsum Cave, Ventana Cave, and Bat Cave. In western Arizona and adjacent parts of California, the 8000 B.C. San Dieguito complex gave way to a sequence of phases known as Lake Mohave, Silver Lake, Pinto Basin, and Rose Springs. The first (Sulphur Springs) phase of the Cochise tradition was established in southern Arizona and New Mexico, as well as in northern Mexico, by around the same time. The later Chiricahua and San Pedro phases are well-known precursors to settled life in this part of the Southwest. Paleo-Indians hung on longer in the north, replaced there by an Archaic tradition known as "Oshara" sometime after 7000 B.C. The San Jose and later phases of this tradition were part of the base upon which the village cultures of the northern Plateau were later built. All of these differed from each other and from the Desert Culture in style and in the specifics of their adaptations. But despite variations in detail, the basic theme was the same until the last millennium B.C.

Several later domesticates, most notably maize, were developed early on, at least in part in desert Archaic contexts. Archaic hunter-gatherers were tending maize, gourds, chiles, and avocados in the Tehuacan Valley of southern Mexico by 5000 B.C. These were followed by amaranth, tepary beans, and squash; true cultivation was being practiced by 3500 B.C. Just when some or all of these plants began to spread northward into the Southwest is still not a resolved issue in archaeology. Ambiguous radiocarbon dating at Bat Cave might indicate that maize was in the Southwest by 3500 B.C. However, a more conservative date of 1500 B.C. is more consistent with evidence from other sites and for other early domesticates, particularly beans (see also Chapter 4). Some archaeologists even prefer a date of only 750 B.C. for the introduction of maize. The hunter-gatherers of the Southwest slowly learned to exploit what little moisture was available to them, building the foundations of horticulture and settled life on a Desert Culture base.

The horticultural Hohokam tradition might have been established in southern Arizona as early as 300 B.C. Some archaeologists prefer a later date of A.D. 500. The horticultural Mogollon tradition was established to the east of the Hohokam by A.D. 700, although some archaeologists would put its beginning four centuries earlier. Small pit-house villages were established on the northern plateau of the region as the basis for the Anasazi tradition by 185 B.C. By A.D. 500, the Anasazi tradition was functioning and the Yuman speakers of the Colorado Valley had established their own farming Patayan tradition.

Over the course of three thousand years, the Archaic hunter-gatherers of the Southwest first transformed themselves into the settled Pueblo Indians of the Southwest, then embarked on cultural developments taking them beyond the scope of this chapter. For much of this time, the Southwest apparently had few, if any, surviving hunter-gatherers. However, this changed in the last centuries preceding the arrival of Europeans as droughts forced the contraction of Pueblo societies and much of the region opened up to a new wave of hunter-gatherers from the north.

Na-Dene invaders

We cannot yet be certain when bands of Na-Dene speakers began moving southward out of western Canada, or why they did so. Their descendants are the modern Navajos and Apaches, who were hunter-gatherers at the time of their first contacts with the Spanish. Subsequent adoption of weaving from the Pueblo Indians and both sheep-herding and metallurgy from the Spanish transformed the Navajos in ways that obscure these origins. Adoption of the horse further modified both Navajo and Apache culture. Some Apaches took up horticulture, but most remained hunter-gatherers, while the Navajos made a transition to pastoralism.

One hypothesis is that these bands arrived as early as A.D. 500, but this is based on their presumed association with the Fremont culture, a hypothesis that is not generally accepted. There is little strong evidence for Navajo and Apache bands in the Southwest until around 1500, not long before the first Spanish arrived. Certainly the scene was set for them by the disastrous drought that occurred 200 years earlier; the Pueblos had retreated to a few refuge areas and the region was once again better suited for hunting and gathering. Further research will undoubtedly clarify the timing and circumstances of their incursion.

The Northwest Plateau

The adaptation of hunter-gatherers to the Plateau differed from that of the Great Basin. This was in large part because of cooler temperatures, more rainfall, and major river systems to carry it to the sea. Vegetation in the Plateau region is a mosaic of grasslands and coniferous forest. The Columbian and Fraser systems provide tributaries that serve as spawning grounds for large runs of Pacific salmon. Salmon and other riverine resources provided early Plateau cultures with food supplies that went well beyond those of the Great Basin. Many Plateau bands had settled into semipermanent villages of semisubterranean earth lodges by the first millennium B.C. These were substantial houses that were not possible for the more nomadic bands of the Great Basin. Evidence from Nightfire Island, near the California-Oregon border, indicates that earth lodges were in use there by at least 2100 B.C. and continued until modern times. The nineteenth-century Klamaths lived in such houses, which they abandoned and partially dismantled every summer, living in brush shelters while the earth lodges aired and dried out.

Cultural sequences on the Plateau paralleled those of the Great Basin in some ways. Tool inventories, for example, were generally similar. Much of our evidence comes from caves and rock shelters, notably Marmes Rock on the Snake River in eastern Washington, Wilson Butte Cave in Idaho, and Fort Rock Cave in Oregon. A key sequence is also known for the Five-Mile Rapids sites at the Dalles of the Columbia River. The region was thinly populated: not as thinly as the Great Basin, but certainly much less

Figure 3.11. Western semisubterranean earth lodge. This pit house is from the Plateau region Harder phase, but it resembles early pit houses from many parts of the West. Excavation and the banking of earth on outer walls conserved heat. Side entrance not shown. (After Jennings 1974:185.)

densely than the adjacent Northwest Coast. Plateau societies were not constrained by either topography or each other. Like Great Basin bands, they tended to be far-ranging, occasionally massing without conflict at points of temporary abundance, such as salmon fisheries or piñon groves.

Moose and other large game remained important on the northern Plateau; migratory fish dominated other food sources in the western Plateau; moose, elk, and deer were important in the eastern part of the region, while various plant foods were important everywhere. Camas (a wild hyacinth) provided many Plateau people with a root that was the most important of all available plant foods.

In the nineteenth century, Salishan speakers occupied the northern part of the Plateau. Sahaptin speakers lived along the middle and upper course of the Columbia. The southern Plateau was dominated by Uto-Aztecan Northern Paiutes, Northern Shoshones, and Bannocks. The Klamath-Modocs lived in a western extension of the Plateau between California, the Great Basin, and the Northwest Coast.

Salmon might once have been less important on the Columbia than on the Fraser river system. A steep drop where the Columbia passes through the Cascade Mountains could have stopped migrating salmon for long periods, forcing early Sahaptin-speaking societies to use foraging techniques more like those of the Great Basin than those of the Fraser drainage. Meanwhile the Salishan-speakers of the Fraser apparently maintained a strong riverine orientation and relatively close contacts with their relatives on the Northwest Coast. The Cascade Landslide, which occurred around A.D. 1265, appears to have restored the salmon runs to the upper Columbia tributaries. Thereafter the Sahaptin speakers of the upper Columbia readapted to the exploitation of migratory fish.[12]

THE CALIFORNIA CULTURAL MOSAIC

The 1492 population density of aboriginal California was relatively high, probably over one person per square kilometer. This number produces a total population of over 400,000. Older and generally more conservative estimates are still in the high range of from 300,000 to 350,000. Yet all of these societies were still technically hunter-gatherers. One reason for this situation was the extraordinary richness of the environment, perhaps cou-

---

[12] David Sanger, "Prehistory of the Pacific Northwest Plateau as Seen from the Interior of British Columbia," *American Antiquity* 32 (1967).

pled with the inappropriateness of available plant domesticates under regional conditions. The cultural pattern was a complex mosaic of small territories. These cells, which were particularly small in northern California, were filled by about five hundred culturally diverse independent communities speaking nearly fifty languages belonging to at least six families. This has long been ascribed to a "fish trap theory," which contends that small migrating groups found their way through the mountains to California and never left.[13]

But there must be more to the ecological equation than the tendency of the geography to trap small bands. Part of the answer lies in the complicated pattern of mountains, rainfall (or lack of it), and temperature. The environment is not merely rich, its richness is varied through a large number of small microenvironments. These have encouraged the evolution of dense but very specialized local populations. Further, local populations tended to husband their resources and maintain their territories against incursions by others. Circumstances encouraged the local storage and regulated redistribution of resources through established trade arrangements. We do not find evidence in late sites for the congregation of far-ranging bands at points of temporary abundance as we do in the Great Basin. Nor do we see the pattern of informal sharing to buffer temporary shortages that appears to have characterized the eastern Archaic societies. But the small-scale territoriality of California societies probably developed out of earlier societies that once had these characteristics. How that evolution took place is an important subject for California archaeology.

We can set aside sites such as Texas Street, Calico, and Santa Rosa Island, which were once thought to contain evidence of pre–Paleo-Indian cultures. We can also discount human bone remains such as the skulls from Laguna Beach and Los Angeles, which have turned out to be much younger than once thought. That leaves us with Borax Lake and a few other sites where Clovis points and other typically Paleo-Indian remains have turned up. In at least central and southern California, this is followed by the San Dieguito complex, which is also found in the Desert West. The complex, regarded by many as late Paleo-Indian rather than Early Archaic, might have persisted to as late as 6000 B.C.

A shift to Archaic adaptations is clear by 5500 B.C. The Encinitas tradition of southern California contains milling stones (manos and metates) and

---

[13] This idea has long been attributed to Alfred Kroeber, one of the founders of modern American anthropology.

shellfish remains. The remains of mammals and fish are rarer. When combined with a drop in the frequency of projectile points, these trends imply a shift toward broad exploitation of a variety of resources.

The distribution of languages belonging to the Hokan family is widespread but fragmented in California. This has led several anthropologists to suggest that Hokan is the oldest of the surviving language families of California, and that speakers of its languages were displaced and fragmented by later arrivals. This might be true, but it probably cannot account for all the complexity of the very long prehistoric sequence in California. The Encinitas tradition lasted until A.D. 1000 or later in southernmost California, after which it gave rise to the Cuyamaca phase. This phase in turn led to the Yuman-speaking peoples of historical southern California, a branch of the Hokan family.

Other Hokan survivors are the Pomos of coastal California and several societies such as the Shastas and Yanas of the northern Sierras. Archaeological evidence indicates a greater emphasis on seeds other than acorns in the Sierras. There are also indications that Penutian speakers displaced some Hokan communities here.

The other phases replacing the Encinitas tradition in southern California were the Luis Rey I and II phases. These appear to have been intrusive from the east, and led to the recent Shoshonean-speaking (Uto-Aztecan) groups of the region.

The Chumash language might relate to one of the known language families of California, or it might be a family unto itself. The Chumash people appear to derive from the Campbell tradition, which displaced the Encinitas tradition along the Santa Barbara coast as early as 3000 B.C. Sites of the Campbell tradition contain distinctive hopper mortars and stone bowl mortars, which were specialized seed-grinding implements. However, other artifacts and bone remains indicate a heavy dependence upon hunting, both on land and at sea. This tradition eventually leads to the Canaliño phase, dating to the period of earliest European contact, which is clearly associated with Chumash culture. This was a rich maritime culture that was broadly adapted to sea mammal hunting, fishing, land mammal hunting, and gathering. In addition to artifacts already mentioned, their tool inventory included plank boats, shell fishhooks, abalone shell dishes, and many beads, effigies, and ornaments.

In central California, developments move through the Windmiller, Cosumnes, and Hotchkiss cultures, ending with the historically attested

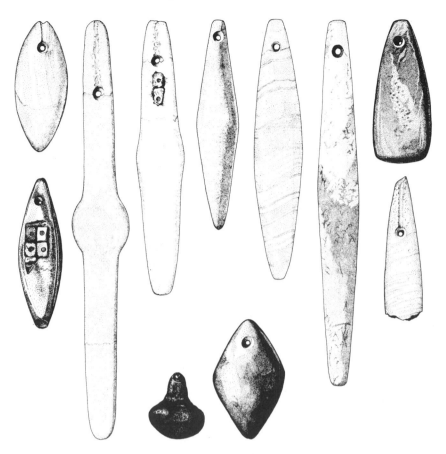

Figure 3.12. Windmiller culture charmstones, central California. Enigmatic objects made from several different stone materials typify the complexity of West Coast archaeology. (From Wallace 1978:33.)

Penutian-speaking communities of the great central valley. These included the Yokuts, Miwoks, Wintus, and related societies. Once again, the adaptation is Archaic in type, but focused on a mix of hunting, fishing, and seed gathering that emphasized acorns. The elaborate "charmstones" for which California archaeology is known are frequently found in the cemetery sites of this tradition.

Yukian is a small family of languages that were spoken by people living in coastal California north of San Francisco Bay. Recent work has indicated that the central coastal area is archaeologically distinguishable from the central interior, especially in the second millennium B.C. But there is no general agreement on how the Yukian societies developed in the context of the complex sequence.

The northern coastal part of California was the homeland of small groups speaking languages of Algonquian-Ritwan and Na-Dene derivation. These societies apparently hived off from the primary areas of their respective language families and kept their linguistic identities after reaching California. The phenomenon of small groups breaking away from large blocks may well have been common in North America, but it is possible that only the insulating adaptive forces at work in California allowed the long-term survival of small, ethnically distinct societies.

The archaeology of northern coastal California still documents this process in only a general way. Cultures such as the Wiyot and Yurok (Algonquian-Ritwan), Karok (Hokan), and the Tolowa and Hupa (Na-Dene) apparently shared a single technological tradition, while maintaining their linguistic distinctiveness. All show similarities with the cultures of the Northwest Coast in their focus on maritime resources, the construction of plank houses, and an emphasis on material wealth.

Although it has been traditional to describe California societies as fragmented "tribelets," recent research has begun to show that there were many formal social and political mechanisms to both maintain and transcend ethnic boundaries. Certain individuals had power that extended beyond their local groups. Systems of ceremonies promoted the status of their local organizers and structured the travel and interactions of participants. Networks of alliance and exchange appear to have been extensive in California, and these would have promoted the redistribution of goods produced in unique local environments. Although the specifics and the antiquity of the phenomena are still unclear, it appears that Archaic societies in California developed large-scale mechanisms of trade and exchange that were similar to those of Adena-Hopewell in the Eastern Woodlands.

THE NORTHWEST COAST

Northwest Coast cultures were distributed along the Pacific Coast from the California-Oregon border through the panhandle of Alaska. They were technically hunter-gatherer cultures despite their spectacular achievements in art and architecture soon after European contact. Languages of at least six families were spoken here aboriginally, and the circumstances of their development may have been as complex as the California case.

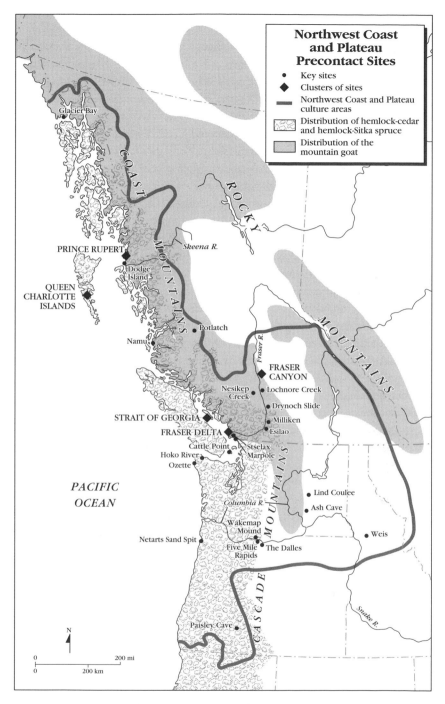

Figure 3.13. Map of Northwest Coast and Plateau precontact sites.

Like California, the Northwest Coast is extraordinarily rich in natural resources. What sets it apart, however, is the region's temperate rain forest. Annual rainfall exceeds 3.5 meters in some places on the Olympic Peninsula, most of it falling during mild winters. The resulting dense forest is an almost impenetrable tangle of large trees and underbrush, the most important of which are hemlock, cedar, and Sitka spruce. In fact the distributions of these species map the culture area very closely. Both the major Fraser and Columbia Rivers and smaller coastal rivers support large runs of Pacific salmon. Five salmon species run upstream on their own schedules. Three other species, herring, smelt, and eulachon (candlefish), also spawn in huge numbers. Shellfish and sea mammals were abundant along the coast; mountain goats and other large mammals were available in the interior.

This paradise for hunter-gatherers was not easy to penetrate. Rising sea levels, rugged mountains, and remnant glaciers might have kept Paleo-Indians out of the area. Alternatively, it might be that early sites exist but are now largely submerged, and invisible to archaeology. In any case, Archaic cultures were in place by at least 7700 B.C. These early populations appear to have come from two sources. First, Paleoarctic hunters brought a microblade technology to the region. Second, side-notched projectile points appear to have come from the interior Plateau. These merged into general Northwest Coast cultural development after 3500 B.C. Large shell middens were accumulating, and people were beginning to produce the bone and ground stone implements associated with later Northwest Coast cultures.

We cannot yet be sure of the direction of population movements. It has been argued that all three of the principal language families (Na-Dene, Salishan, and Wakashan) might derive from post-Pleistocene migrations from Asia.[14] To date, linguistic evidence has indicated such a recent origin only for Na-Dene (see earlier sections of this chapter). Northwest Coast speakers of Na-Dene include the Tlingits and Eyaks, who appear to have moved there from the northern interior. However, Salishan (Strait of Georgia and the Fraser drainage) and Wakashan (coastal British Columbia) both remain unconnected to other North American language families, and their origins await further research. The Haida language of the Queen Charlotte Islands is a linguistic isolate that might be distantly related to

[14] Don E. Dumond, "Alaska and the Northwest Coast," in Jesse D. Jennings (ed.), *Ancient Native Americans* (San Francisco, 1978), 89.

Na-Dene. Perhaps significantly, the earliest known occupation of the Queen Charlotte Islands is by microblade makers having northern connections, around 5000 B.C. The Tsimshians of British Columbia might be an offshoot of Penutians who moved north at an early date.

Apart from the Salishan languages, the speech communities of the Washington and Oregon coasts resemble those of California in their fragmentation. A half dozen Oregon Penutian languages may or may not be related to the Penutian languages of California. Intermixed with them are several Athapaskan languages, and two (Alsea and Siuslaw) that defy classification. The small Chinookan family is found on the lower Columbia, and the even smaller Chimakuan family occurs amongst the Salishan and Wakashan communities of the Olympic Peninsula. Even the larger families, particularly Salishan, are broken into several languages, each spoken in a small territory. It may well be that the processes of boundary maintenance, economic specialization, and cultural insulation that probably led to the fragmentation of aboriginal California were at work here too. In the case of the Northwest Coast, however, the environment probably contributed more to the process. Overland travel is difficult, and local communities have long clustered along streams and estuaries.

Stone labrets (lip plugs), stone clubs, and ground-slate points were common in Northwest Coast assemblages by A.D. 1. Earlier and simpler tools were later replaced by composite ones that incorporated greater use of shell and bone. The array of rich natural resources allowed at least part-time sedentism very early on. Wedges and mauls in archaeological assemblages indicate that large cedar trees were felled and split into straight-grained planks. These were in turn used to build large plank houses and build up the sides of large dugout war canoes.

By A.D. 500, there was a strong regional tendency toward social stratification and the use of material wealth to mark it. Unlike California, the abundant natural wealth of the Northwest Coast was generally uniform throughout the region, and there was relatively little pressure to establish exchange networks. Cultural insulation was maintained more by geography than by local economic specialization. The exception was the tendency for upstream settlements to trade with downstream relatives, but even here the importance of trade was not great enough to lead to the emergence of politically centralized chiefdoms.

Most well-known sites are late. Sites at Ozette and on the Hoko River of the Olympic Peninsula contain well-preserved evidence of the rich material culture of sixteenth-to-eighteenth-century Northwest Coast societies.

SUBARCTIC HUNTERS

The Subarctic is a vast area of boreal forests that extends across Canada north of the Great Lakes and the Great Plains all the way to central Alaska. The Rocky Mountains and the temperate rain forests of the Northwest Coast prevent the Subarctic forests from touching the Pacific Ocean except in southern Alaska. Arctic tundra separates the Subarctic from the Arctic Ocean everywhere but along the southern edge of Hudson Bay. Today the southern portions of the Subarctic are predominantly composed of spruce, pine, fir, birch, and poplar in a variety of combinations. To the north, closer to Arctic tundra, alder replaces poplar, and only the hardiest tree species survive.

Virtually all of the Subarctic, except for central Alaska and the Yukon (Beringia), was heavily glaciated prior to 10,000 B.C. By 8000 B.C., the two great North American ice sheets had shrunk, the Cordilleran sheet a series of remnant ice caps in the Rocky Mountains. The Laurentide sheet of eastern Canada lasted longer, covering all of Hudson Bay and vast tracts around it until after 7000 B.C. Even where the ice had melted away, huge glacial lakes remained. Lake Agassiz covered much of what is now western Ontario and southern Manitoba. Glacial Lake Barlow-Ojibway covered interior portions of modern Quebec and Ontario that were not still burdened by ice. However, by 5000 B.C. the Laurentide ice had shrunk to two caps in Quebec and on Baffin Island, and the glacial lakes had largely disappeared. The depressed Hudson basin was filled by the Tyrrell Sea, much larger than modern Hudson Bay. By 3000 B.C., the rebounding landscape had lifted the innundated lowlands around Hudson Bay back above sea level, As these events unfolded, the tundra around the ice and glacial lakes gradually gave way to pioneer species of Subarctic trees. The bands of distinctive forest environments gradually broadened and shifted northward to their present positions. Game animals, such as caribou, moose, elk, and bear, moved with them, and so did early Indian hunters.

Hunting bands carrying Plano tradition points pressed into the southern fringes of the region between 8500 and 6000 B.C. Some moved close to remnant ice in the Northwest Territories, and several archaeologists believe that Plano bands contributed to the Paleo-Arctic tradition, which was emerging in Alaska and the Yukon at the same time.[15]

[15] Douglas D. Anderson, "Prehistory of North Alaska," in David Damas (ed.), *Handbook of North American Indians,* vol. 5 (Arctic) (Washington, D.C., 1984).

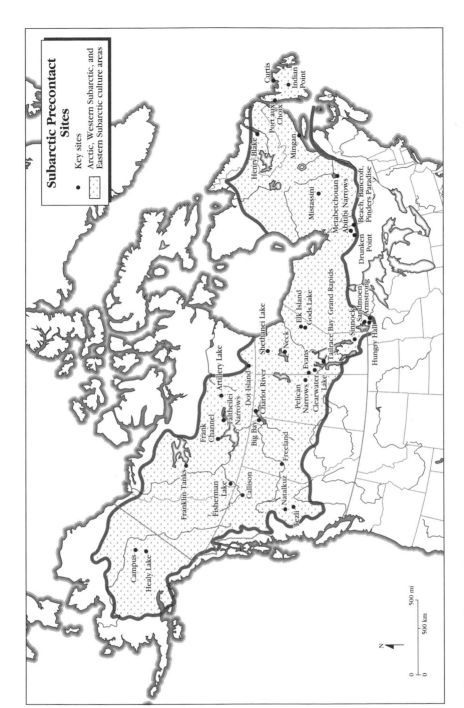

Figure 3.14. Map of subarctic precontact sites.

After 5500 B.C., bands of hunters coming from Plano origins to the south and west took up residence in the new Subarctic forests north of the Great Lakes and around the emerging southern and western shores of Hudson Bay. This adaptation, known as the Shield Archaic, lasted until around A.D. 500. Farther east, Early and Middle Archaic period bands moved northward out of the Eastern Woodlands into the coastal Subarctic areas of the Atlantic Provinces and northern New England. This development, known as the Maritime Archaic, lasted from 4000 to 1500 B.C. Maritime Archaic hunters exploited a rich mix of marine and terrestrial species, and like the people of the Northwest Coast were able to enjoy a lifestyle not within the means of most interior hunters. They were ocean-going hunters of whales and seals, who made heavy stone adzes and gouges that in turn were used to construct large dugout canoes. Fine artifacts of bone and slate turn up in burials that display a complexity of funerary ritual that would not emerge in the Eastern Woodlands until centuries later.

The archaeological picture in the northwestern Subarctic is less clear. Microblade technology spread into Alaska and northwestern Canada from Asia, possibly as early as the Paleo-Indian period. This is called the Northern Interior Microblade tradition by some archaeologists, the Paleo-Arctic tradition by others. It is still unclear how much of it grew out of older Paleo-Indian roots and how much of it was the consequence of new waves of technological influence or migrants from Asia. This thin and widely scattered culture persisted until 1000 B.C.

By 2500 B.C., a new culture known as Northern Archaic was beginning to appear in the Yukon. Again, origins are obscure, but the culture gradually replaced the earlier tradition of the region and continued until A.D. 500. Evidence from interior sites both on the tundra and in forest environments suggests a variable adaptation to interior resources. However, the interior adaptations are consistent enough to justify definition of a single Northern Archaic tradition. It is possible that the people of the Northern Archaic tradition were early Na-Dene speakers, but archaeological dates may put the development too early in time to be accounted for by proto-Na-Dene. Indeed, it is difficult to account for this and earlier developments in terms of any known American Indian language family.

After 500 B.C., hunting bands associated with the Taltheilei tradition contended with expanding Eskimos for the Subarctic forests west of Hudson Bay. Like the Northern Archaic tradition, this one lasted until A.D. 500. Neither of them necessarily ceased at that time, but by then we can be sure that we are dealing with the ancestors of modern Athapaskan peoples.

Similarly, to the east the Shield Archaic became the source of Algonquian-speaking nations after A.D. 500. The pottery-making Laurel culture bridged the thousand years of continuity between the Shield Archaic and the Algonquians north of the upper Great Lakes, while a derivative Shield Archaic persisted in Quebec and Labrador. Like the Athapaskans to the northwest, these ancestral Algonquians were pressed back from northern and eastern coastal areas by expanding Inuit bands after 500 B.C. They survived as interior hunters into modern times, in many ways similar to the ancient Paleo-Indian hunters from whom most Native Americans descend.

LATE ARRIVALS IN THE ARCTIC

The earliest indisputable evidence of humans from the Arctic comes in the form of several stone-tool assemblages dating 9000 to 6000 B.C., which are usually referred to as the Paleo-Arctic tradition. The assemblages contain cores, blades, and microblades, and are associated with modern faunal species, along with some specimens of horse, bison, and elk. The related Anangula tradition, which was mentioned earlier, may already have been adapted to maritime resources. While most American Paleo-Arctic sites contain bifacial tools, the Anangula assemblage is dominated by unifacial tools.

Although hunting and foraging could never be replaced by more advanced food production in the Arctic, regional variations in resource availability led to early differences in tool kits. Certainly beginning around 5000 B.C. the evidence from the Aleutians is that coastal hunters were adapted to marine resources not available to interior hunters.

Arctic prehistory probably became an Eskimo phenomenon after 2500 B.C. Modern Eskimo languages are distantly but clearly related to Aleut. The separation appears to have begun at least this early, because from this time on the Aleutian tradition developed in isolation from the later stages of Arctic archaeology. Nevertheless, although the Arctic Small Tool tradition developed in northern Alaska at this time, not all archaeologists agree that its bearers necessarily spoke proto-Eskimo.

This early (probably) Eskimo tradition expanded rapidly through the maritime Arctic zone extending from the Alaskan Peninsula to Greenland. The Aleuts did not participate in the Arctic Small Tool tradition, and it might even have developed in eastern Siberia before expanding eastward

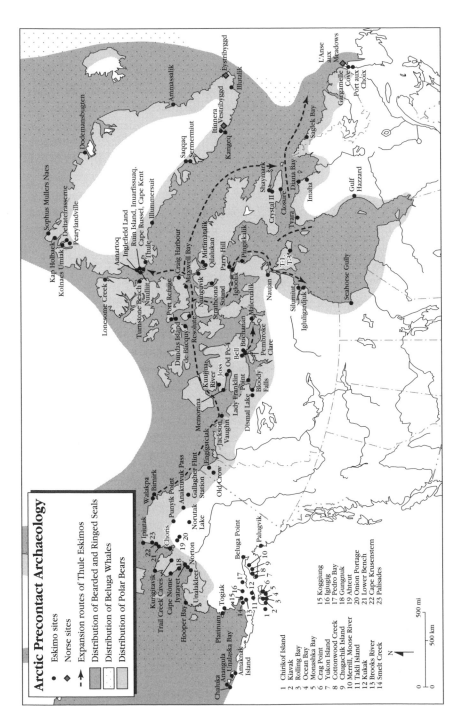

Figure 3.15. Arctic precontact archaeology.

across Alaska and Canada. The adaptation lacked the stone lamps in which later Eskimo cultures burned sea mammal oil for both heat and light. The tradition was consequently dependent upon wood for light and heat, and its bearers could not live far from the tree line.

The Arctic Small Tool tradition people exploited both marine and terrestrial game, and lived in substantial semisubterranean houses. Their tool kit included very small microblades, which were made to be cutting edges for larger composite tools made of bone, ivory, and wood. For this reason, their technology is sometimes characterized as Mesolithic, as compared to the essentially Upper Paleolithic industry of the Paleo-Indians.

The Arctic Small Tool tradition underwent diversification during and after its spread eastward. By 1600 B.C., its adaptation was shifting increasingly toward the exploitation of marine resources, especially sea mammals, in some areas. The shift began earliest in northern Alaska, where it evolved through a succession of phases called Choris, Norton, and Ipiutak. An additional culture, known as Old Whaling, appeared abruptly and then disappeared a century later at Cape Krusenstern during this period. There was less complexity south of Bering Strait, where only the Norton culture appeared. The Aleutian Islands continued in isolation, and the separate Kachemak tradition developed on Kodiak Island.

By 500 B.C., the early Eskimo populations, sometimes known collectively as Pre-Dorset, were spread across virtually all the Canadian and Alaskan Arctic. The northern limit of trees defines their southern limit almost perfectly. They extended their range to northern Greenland too and colonized the east and west coasts of southern Greenland as well. Dorset culture emerged from this base in Canada and Greenland between 500 and 1 B.C. Dorset bands pressed southeastward during this Early Dorset period, taking over the coasts of Labrador and Newfoundland. Climatic change and resulting shifts in wildlife caused the Dorset Eskimos to retreat from Newfoundland and all but northwestern Greenland during the Late Dorset period, A.D. 1 to 1000.

Harpoons, coastal sites, and faunal remains all point to Dorset dependence upon marine mammals, especially seals and walrus. The bow and arrow and small stone lamps are also occasionally found in Dorset sites. But the crude pottery that is found in Norton sites in Alaska is missing from Dorset sites. Snow knives (for igloo construction), ice creepers, and small sled runners, all classic Inuit gadgets, make their first appearance in the Dorset culture. However, dogs, bows and arrows, and drills mysteriously dropped out of many late Dorset inventories. Stone lamps increased in importance at the

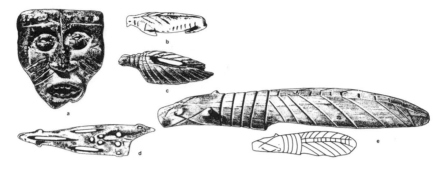

Figure 3.16. Dorset Eskimo art. Objects that were probably connected with shamanism include a soapstone maskette (A), as well as a walrus (B), a falcon (C), two stylized bears (D & E), all of walrus ivory. (From Maxwell 1984:367.)

same time, possibly indicating a move toward a more predominant adaptation to sea mammal hunting. Archaeological evidence indicates that their kayaks, important in marine hunting, were technically as advanced as much later ones. The late Dorset Eskimos lived only as far south as the Arctic Circle on the northwestern coast of Greenland between A.D. 700 and 900.

By around A.D. 900, western Eskimo adaptations were shifting once again. This was probably in response to the Medieval Maximum, the same extended warm period that drew the Norse westward across the Atlantic to Greenland. Birnirk culture developed out of Norton culture in northern Alaska, and this in turn evolved into Thule culture. Thule Eskimo culture was gradually adopted by the other Eskimo communities of Alaska. More dramatic, however, was the culture's rapid adaptive radiation eastward across treeless territory already occupied by Dorset Eskimos. Dominant Thule culture submerged Dorset, through processes still not fully understood. There may have been local annihilations of Dorsets. On the other hand, a few modern Inuit communities strike some anthropologists as possible Dorset survivors, albeit heavily modified by Thule influence. For the most part, Thule bands probably absorbed and acculturated most Dorset remnants. The Thule expansion was fueled by technology that included both kayaks and larger boats called umiaks, the bow and arrow, built-up dog sleds, advanced harpoons, and dozens of other specialized gadgets. The climate was a bit warmer, and ice on great stretches of the Arctic Ocean around Greenland and the islands of northern Canada broke up annually. Beluga whales, bearded seals, ringed seals, and other sea mammals were probably more numerous and widespread than before.

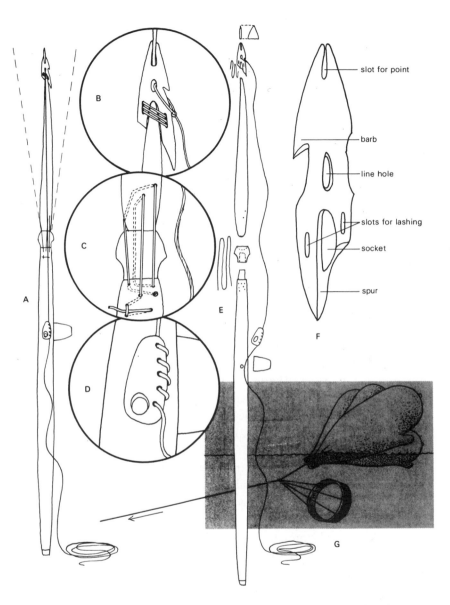

Figure 3.17. Eskimo harpoon. (A) Dashed lines show the degree of flexibility of an assembled harpoon. (B) Harpoon head. (C) Flexible joint showing shaft head separating the shaft from the foreshaft. (D) Line retainer secured to shaft by knob. (E) Exploded view of harpoon showing component parts. (G) Sealskin floats and drag attached to end of line. (From Jennings 1974:341.)

The Thule Eskimos, with their specialized boats and weapons, were well adapted to exploit the whales as well as the smaller sea mammals. They spread eastward, north of Baffin Island, to northwestern Greenland. Bands of them hived off and established themselves on other large islands along the way. Secondary expansions took other Thule Eskimos along both sides of Baffin Island. Some entered Hudson Bay, while others advanced down the coast of Labrador. Favored whale and seal species occurred only as far south as southern Labrador and the southern tip of Greenland, so the advancing Thule Eskimos stopped there as well.

The Thule people were adapted to hunting on and around the sea ice. Norse settlers lived far up the fjords of Greenland, where they could raise sheep and cattle around permanent houses. The opportunity for contact (and conflict) was probably greatest in the summer, when both the Norse and the Thule Eskimos hunted seals around the mouths of fjords.

Cooler conditions returned with the onset of the Little Ice Age after A.D. 1340, drawing the Thule Eskimos farther south on expanding sea ice, and making the hunting of caribou on land more attractive at the same time. By the end of the fourteenth century, the Norse were abandoning their footholds in North America, and the Thule hunters were the sole inhabitants of the Arctic seas.

The Little Ice Age caused the pack ice of the central Arctic to thicken after around A.D. 1600. The Inuit, direct descendants of the Thule Eskimos, had to shift from living in more permanent villages to a pattern of fishing and caribou hunting in the summer, sealing through the sea ice in the winter. The Inuit snow igloo, now symbolic of all Eskimos, is largely a dwelling of the Little Ice Age. The older Thule way of life continued only in the eastern Arctic and in Labrador, where whaling and more permanent villages remained possible.

By the time of their first contact with Europeans, Eskimo speech was composed of dialects of a single language that stretched from Greenland to northern Alaska. The presumed earlier Dorset language(s) had been completely replaced. In 1492 there was also considerable cultural uniformity from Greenland to Alaska, largely as a legacy of the rapid radiation of Thule. There was and still is more cultural diversity among the Alaskan Eskimos. There are at least eight ethnic variants of Alaskan and Siberian Eskimos, speaking five separate languages. While some of these are very similar to Canadian and Greenland Inuit in their hunter-gatherer adaptations, those of southern Alaska show the effects of proximity to the Northwest Coast. Semipermanent houses and even matrilineal clans can be found in some of these communities. Their subsistence strategies take advantage of migratory fish, fowl, and plant resources not generally available farther north.

THE IMPACT OF EUROPEAN COLONIZATION

The Spanish were enduringly established in the Southwest by 1598, and the horse began its reintroduction to North America. Only a century earlier, hunter-gatherer ancestors of the modern Navajos and Apaches had worked their way south along the eastern slopes of the Rockies to take up residence around and among the shrinking Pueblo villages of the Southwest. These Athapaskan-speaking bands, whose closest relatives remained in western Canada, quickly adapted to an environment that had been turning against horticulturalists for many decades. Some, particularly the Navajos, became pastoralists, adopting horses and sheep from the Spanish colonists.

The Shoshones adopted Spanish horses quickly, taking them north and east, introducing them to the Indian societies of the Great Plains. Algonquians such as the Blackfeet, Gros Ventres, and Arapahos, as well as some Crees and Ojibwas, abandoned forest hunting and gathering to become mounted nomadic hunters on the Great Plains. A northern Athapaskan (Na-Dene) group, the Sarsis, also adopted horse nomadism. The Uto-Aztecan Shoshones and Comanches moved on to the Plains from the west for the same reason, in some cases bringing horses with them. Later the horticultural Cheyennes (Algonquians) entered the Plains as well, quickly becoming the quintessential American Indian nation in the eyes of many.

Siouan and Caddoan horticulturalists who had established themselves in earthlodge villages along the streams of the eastern Great Plains sometimes also switched to horse nomadism. The Caddoan-speaking Pawnees took up hunting in the face of pressure from the east and the attraction of the horse. Some Hidatsas on the upper Missouri who could not resist the attraction of mounted nomadism split off and became the Crows. They later maintained close ties and economic exchange with the sedentary Hidatsas.

Siouan-speaking nations that had been part of the Mississippian tradition of the Eastern Woodlands also gave up horticulture and sedentary life, at least for part of each year. They shifted westward, taking advantage of the horse and abandoning the bottomlands of the Ohio and Mississippi Rivers. They were probably the nations that spoke languages of the

Dhegiha branch of the Siouan language family. To the north, the Chiwere branch of Siouan abandoned the woodlands for the prairies when the horse and opportunity presented themselves. The horse reached both branches in the decades around A.D. 1700. Still farther north and west the Dakotas (Sioux) also abandoned farming for horse nomadism. They were accompanied by the Assiniboines, the northernmost Siouans. In most of these cases, people were not just responding to the attraction of nomadic hunting. There were by this time also strong direct and indirect pressures from the east, brought on by European settlement and expansion.

Many Europeans once tended to think of all American Indians as primarily hunters. Many modern Americans still do. This attitude contributed to the notion that removal of eastern nations to Midwestern reservations would solve problems of conflict between expanding Euro-American populations and the Indians' loss of hunting lands. In the end, the opportunity of mounted nomadism and the pressure of displacement by Euro-Americans did bring many Indian nations back to hunting and gathering as full-time subsistence strategies. Probably because there was not enough time for it to occur, the shift did not involve the development of the kind of pastoralism seen earlier in central Asia. Had European expansion been less rapid, and had lethal epidemics not swept the landscape clear of Indian resistance as effectively as they did, the dynamics of historic cultural adaptation and the course of history on this continent would have been very different.

BIBLIOGRAPHIC ESSAY

This chapter has attempted to summarize the broad themes that characterized the cultures of the first Americans and hunter-gatherers that descended from them. I have tried to avoid discussing them in terms of the dry details of specific site excavations. Because this must be a general summary I have also tried to avoid discussing the subject as a series of disconnected regional sequences, although some subdivision by region became unavoidable as the chapter developed.

Michael Coe, Dean Snow, and Elizabeth Benson wrote the heavily illustrated *Atlas of Ancient America* for readers seeking more detailed maps (New York, 1986). The volume covers both continents. Many Canadian scholars have contributed to volume 1 of the *Historical Atlas of Canada,* ed. R. C. Harris (Toronto, 1987), which also provides very detailed maps. Compilation of the sections covering Canadian archaeology (Plates 1–18) was led by J. V. Wright, with contributions from several other archaeologists and geographers.

There are many volumes dedicated to the prehistories of specific states and provinces, too many to list them all individually here. I have included a few of these in cases where the volumes have been particularly influential and have set standards for larger regions.

Detailed and heavily referenced regional treatments of North American archaeology are available in various volumes of the Smithsonian Institution's *Handbook of North American Indians* (Washington, D.C., 1978–) produced under the general editorship of William C. Sturtevant. About half of what will eventually be a twenty-volume series has been published. Many authors have contributed to the regional volumes covering the Arctic, Subarctic, Northwest Coast, California, Southwest (2 volumes), Great Basin, and Northeast. These and future volumes will continue to serve as the best starting points for all but the most recently developed information on regional prehistories. *Ancient Native Americans,* ed. Jesse D. Jennings (San Francisco, 1978) contains a dozen summary chapters by regional specialists. Academic Press has produced a series on the New World Archaeological Record under the editorship of James B. Griffin. Each volume contains a regional treatment of prehorticultural societies. Specific chapters, articles, and volumes from these series are mentioned below.

Paleo-Indians are discussed in many books and articles. A good recent summary can be found in *Early Man in the New World,* ed. Richard Shutler, Jr. (Beverly Hills, Calif., 1983). Skeletal (including dental) evidence of Paleo-Indian migrations is discussed in *Out of Asia: Peopling the Americas and the Pacific,* ed. Robert Kirk and Emoke Szathmary (Canberra, *Journal of Pacific History,* 1985). Evidence for very early migrations to North America, much of which is disputed or rejected by many scholars, is critically evaluated in *New Evidence for the Pleistocene Peopling of the Americas,* ed. Alan L. Bryan (Orono, Me., 1986). A counterargument is presented by Roger Owen's article "The Americas: The Case against an Ice-Age Human Population," in *The Origins of Modern Humans: A World Survey of the Fossil Evidence,* ed. Fred Smith and Frank Spencer (New York, 1984). Clearly the earliest evidence of the first Americans remains the most controversial. A series of fourteen articles written by leading archaeologists for *Natural History* appeared in issues of the magazine from November 1986 to February 1988. These cover many of the most interesting controversies relating to Paleo-Indians in a very readable format.

The subject of Pleistocene extinctions and the possible role of Paleo-Indians is discussed in *Quaternary Extinctions: A Prehistoric Revolution,* a volume of 38 papers ed. Paul S. Martin and Richard G. Klein (Tucson, Ariz., 1984). All of this is synthesized by Brian Fagan in his *The Great Journey: The Peopling of Ancient America* (New York, 1987).

The best starting point for a look at the linguistic evidence is *The Languages of Native America,* ed. Lyle Campbell and Marianne Mithun (Austin, Tex., 1979). Their conservative classification was followed in the *Atlas of Ancient America.* Joseph Greenberg's *Language in the Americas* (Stanford, Calif., 1987) should be used with the understanding that it is controversial. His definition of a few very early language families from which roughly 2,000 historically known American Indian languages are supposed to have descended is not generally accepted by linguists. Nevertheless, Greenberg's linguistic model has been linked to dental and genetic evidence developed by Christy Turner and Stephen Zegura in an article entitled "The Settlement of the Americas: A Comparison of the Linguistic, Dental, and Genetic Evidence" (*Current Anthropology* 27, 1986, 477–97).

Reconstruction of the nonmaterial aspects of early hunting bands depends upon theory and empirical studies drawn from cultural anthropology. B. J. Williams's *A Model of Band Society* (Washington, D.C., 1974) is an excellent source. Inferences about the evolution of band societies and their technologies after the Paleo-Indian period are detailed by Brian Hayden in his "Research and Development in the Stone Age: Technological Transitions among Hunter-gatherers" (*Current Anthropology* 22, 1981, 519–48). The article is accompanied by extensive and informative comments by other scholars. Bruce Smith's *Rivers of Change: Essays on Early Agriculture in Eastern North America* (Washington, D.C., 1992) expands on an earlier article (*Science* 246, 1989, 1566–71). Both trace the independent rise of early plant cultivation in the context of later hunter-gatherer societies in the Eastern Woodlands.

An article by James Stoltman in *Current Anthropology* (19, 1978, 703–46) discusses the various ways in which archaeologists have blocked out, named, and used periods of archaeology in eastern North America. Although his proposed new scheme has not been widely adopted, his summary of existing schemes is a good introduction to archaeological sequences in the Eastern Woodlands.

The regional sequence in the Eastern Woodlands is covered in part by volume 15 (*Northeast*) of the *Handbook of North American Indians* (Washington, D.C., 1978). Robert Funk's chapter entitled "Post-Pleistocene Adaptations" and James Tuck's "Regional Cultural Development, 3000 to 300 B.C." cover the development of archaeological sequences following the Paleo-Indians in the northern part of the Eastern Woodlands. The Southeast volume of the *Handbook of North American Indians* remains incomplete and unpublished.

There are several useful volumes in the Academic Press series on regional archaeology that include chapters relevant to the prehorticultural hunter-gatherers of the Eastern Woodlands. These include *Great Lakes Archaeology* by Ronald Mason (New York, 1981), *The Archaeology of New England* by Dean Snow (New York, 1980), *Archaeology of the Lower Ohio Valley* by Jon Muller (Orlando, Fla., 1986), *Archaic Hunters and Gatherers in the American Midwest* by James Phillips and James Brown (Orlando, Fla., 1983), and *Archaeology of the Central Mississippi Valley* by Dan Morse and Phyllis Morse (Orlando, Fla., 1987).

William Ritchie's *The Archaeology of New York State* (Garden City, N.Y., 1969; reprinted 1980) should be consulted as a basic reference for that state. However, it has also been very influential in regional chronology, setting the tone for archaeology in New England, the other northeastern states, Ontario, Quebec, and the Maritime Provinces. Similarly, Carl Chapman's *The Archaeology of Missouri* (Columbia, Mo., 1975) is a good starting point for that part of the region. *Florida Archaeology* by Jerald Milanich and Charles Fairbanks (New York, 1980) is an excellent point of departure for the southeast corner of the Eastern Woodlands.

Jennings's *Ancient Native Americans* contains a chapter on "The Midlands and northeastern United States" by James Griffin and another on "The Southeast" by Jon Muller, Although both focus principally upon later developments, they summarize earlier developments and will lead the reader to older works on specific sites and subregions. Richard Ford's "Northeastern Archaeology: Past and Future Directions" provides one scholar's view of a future that is already here (Palo Alto, *Annual Review of Anthropology,* 1974, 385–413).

A good basic introduction to Plains archaeology is still Waldo Wedel's chapter, "The Prehistoric Plains," in *Ancient Native Americans.* This will lead the reader to classic works on Plains archaeology. George Frison's *Prehistoric Hunters of the High Plains* (New York, 1978) treats Plains archaeology from the perspective of Wyoming. Robert Bell's *Prehistory of Oklahoma* (New York, 1983) and Lawrence Aten's *Indians of the Upper Texas Coast* (New York, 1983) deal with Plains hunter-gatherers from a more southern perspective.

The Interior West is discussed by Melvin Aikens as part of his chapter on "The Far West" in *Ancient Native Americans*. His bibliography will lead readers with special interests to specific sources such as Jennings's classic work on Danger Cave. Volume 11 (*Great Basin*) of the *Handbook of North American Indians* (Washington D.C., 1986) contains eight chapters on regional archaeology, each dealing with a specific subregion and all authored by established archaeologists. Coverage extends to the edge of the Plateau region, which will be treated in a volume yet to be published. Jesse Jennings provides an introduction and overview to the others in his lead chapter. There are also four chapters dealing with four classes of archaeological remains from the region: rock art, ceramics, basketry, and portable art objects.

The Southwest is a portion of the Interior West that came to be dominated by horticulturalists within the last two millennia of archaeology. However, hunter-gatherers settled the region first and survived through time in certain marginal areas. New waves of hunter-gatherers entered the Southwest late in precolonial times. William Lipe's chapter on "The Southwest" in *Ancient Native Americans* summarizes these developments, although the chapter deals mainly with the well-known horticultural traditions of the region. The complex archaeology of the region can also be accessed easily through Linda Cordell's *Prehistory of the Southwest* (New York, 1984). Regional hunter-gatherer archaeology is introduced by Woodbury's chapter in volume 9 (*Southwest*) of the *Handbook of North American Indians* (Washington, D.C., 1979). Cynthia Irwin-Williams discusses "Post-Pleistocene Archaeology, 7000–2000 B.C.," and James Gunnerson covers "Southern Athapaskan Archeology" in the same volume.

The Plateau is also covered in Aikens's chapter on "The Far West" in *Ancient Native Americans*. There are many scholarly works available for this region, but few syntheses beyond that of Aikens to serve as points of departure for the general reader. The situation is similar for the Northwest Coast. Volume 7 (*Northwest Coast*) of the *Handbook of North American Indians* (Washington, D.C., 1990) has but one chapter on "Cultural Antecedents" by Roy Carlson. Don Dumond synthesizes Northwest Coast archaeology from the point of view of Alaska in his chapter in *Ancient Native Americans*. *Exploring Washington Archaeology* (Seattle, 1978) by Ruth Kirk and Richard Daugherty provides a general introduction to the region.

California archaeology has so many facets that it is difficult to synthesize. Melvin Aikens does so briefly as part of his chapter on "The Far West" in *Ancient Native Americans*. Michael Moratto's book on *California*

Archaeology (New York, 1984) treats the subject at much greater length. Volume 8 (*California*) of the *Handbook of North American Indians* (Washington, D.C., 1978) contains two relevant chapters, one on "Post-Pleistocene Archeology, 9000 to 2000 B.C." by William Wallace and another on the "Development of Regional Prehistoric Cultures" by Albert Elsasser.

The Subarctic is synthesized in magnificent visual detail by volume 1 of the *Historical Atlas of Canada* (Toronto, Plates 5–10, 1987). Volume 6 (*Subarctic*) of the *Handbook of North American Indians* (Washington, D.C., 1981) provides a "Prehistory of the Canadian Shield" by James Wright, a "Prehistory of the Great Slave Lake and Great Bear Lake Region" by William Noble, and a "Prehistory of the Western Subarctic" by Donald Clark.

Arctic archaeology covers an enormous area, and it is made more complex by three national research traditions. Don Dumond attempts to synthesize it all in his "Prehistory: Summary" in volume 5 (*Arctic*) of the *Handbook of North American Indians* (Washington, D.C., 1984). His framework cross-references differing terms for the same phenomena and rectifies conflicting age estimates by providing generally accepted ranges. The Arctic volume provides nine more chapters on subregional prehistories stretching from the Bering Strait to Greenland. Moreau Maxwell's book on the *Prehistory of the Eastern Arctic* (Orlando, Fla., 1985) provides a useful overview of that half of the Arctic. Frederick West's *The Archaeology of Beringia* (New York, 1981) attempts a synthesis of the northwestern Arctic with special attention focused on the earliest arrivals. Volume 1 of the *Historical Atlas of Canada* (Toronto, Plate 11, 1987) provides the best cartographic overview of Arctic archaeology, and its relatively brief descriptive texts will help the reader bridge to the more detailed literature.

4

INDIGENOUS FARMERS

LINDA S. CORDELL AND BRUCE D. SMITH

Throughout much of continental North America that today is included
in the eastern and southwestern United States, Native Americans developed mixed economies based on farming New World domesticates combined with important wild foods obtained by hunting and gathering.
At the time of contact with Europeans, the Native peoples in these two
regions were cultivating many of the same crops. Although there were
no real barriers to travel between what is now the western and eastern
United States, these areas are markedly different in climate and vegetation. The peoples of these two vast regions followed very different paths
in their development of farming economies and in their settlement
systems, subsistence strategies, political institutions, and religious beliefs. This chapter explores the similarities and differences between these
areas with respect to farming and a settled way of life. Chapter 5
examines the development of ranked agricultural societies characterized
by a chiefdom level of socio-political organization in the eastern United
States.

In the western region, indigenous farming peoples inhabited the Southwest culture area which forms part of modern Arizona and New Mexico,
extending into southeastern Utah and southwestern Colorado.[1] Aridity is
the primary climatic feature uniting landscapes of topographic diversity,
including rugged mountains, mesas, and broad valleys. The region encompasses the low basins stretching north from the Sonoran and Chihuahuan
deserts, the higher and often wooded Colorado Plateaus, and the still
higher wooded and forested mountain masses of central Arizona and New
Mexico. Prior to and shortly after European contact, Native farming

---

[1] The Southwest culture area extends, without interruption, into the Mexican states of Chihuahua,
Sonora, and Sinaloa. The organization of this volume and series necessitated limiting boundaries to
conform to the modern southern political border of the United States.

societies extended their settlements onto the undulating short grass plains of Oklahoma and Texas.

When the Spaniards first explored this area, beginning in 1539, the diverse peoples of the Southwest were united primarily through ties of trade and some shared religious beliefs. They were not united in a single political system or by language. Most of the vast land area of northwestern Mexico and the adjacent regions of southern Arizona is the traditional homeland of peoples who speak languages of the Uto-Aztecan family, including the Pimas (Upper Pimas or Pimas Altas) and Papagos (Tohono O'Odham). These designations are useful in reference to modern maps of tribal territories and reservations but they are not always meaningful to the people themselves. For example, the terms *Pima* and *Papago* historically have been used by Euro-Americans to refer to people who recognize no such distinction but view themselves as one people, whom they call O'Odham.

Peoples speaking Yuman languages occupied the lower Colorado River Valley, the lower Gila River Valley, and adjacent uplands in California, Arizona, and southernmost Nevada. The family of Yuman languages belongs to the Hokan language stock. Groups include the Cocopas of the Colorado River delta, then moving north along the river, the Halykwamais, Kahwans, and Quechans at the confluence of the Gila and Colorado Rivers, and the Halchidhomas, Mohaves, and Havasupais of the Grand Canyon. Northwest of the Cocopas, along the Colorado River in California, were the Diegueños, Kamais, and Paipais. The Walapais and Yavapais occupied the uplands in the vicinity of the Grand Canyon (Pai means "people" in Yuman; refering to all Yuman-speaking peoples). The Cocomaricopas and the Opas lived along the lower Gila. Since European contact, the Halykwamais, Kahwans, Halchidhomas, Opas, and Cocomaricopas have merged to form what today is the Maricopa tribe.

The Pueblo Indians occupy twelve villages on the southern edge of Black Mesa, Arizona, and twenty-seven villages in New Mexico. The term "pueblo" is Spanish for village, and Pueblo Indians share a number of important cultural characteristics in addition to their basic farming and settlement pattern. These characteristics include aspects of religious beliefs, ceremonialism, and symbolism. Despite the common features of the lifestyle, however, the Pueblo Indians speak six different languages. The Hopis of Arizona speak Hopi, which is within the Uto-Aztecan language family. The New Mexico Pueblo of Zuni speaks the Zuni language, which is thought to be related to California Penutian. The Keresan language, which does not seem to be closely related to any other North American Indian languages, is spoken by the New Mexico Pueblos of Acoma, Laguna, Zia, Santa Ana, San Felipe, Santo Domingo, and Cochiti. Tiwa is spoken in the villages of Taos, Picuris, Isleta, and Sandia. Tewa is spoken at San Juan, Santa Clara, San Ildefonso, Pajoaque, Nambé, and Tesuque in New Mexico and at Hano or Tewa Village on the first Hopi Mesa in Arizona. Today, Jemez Pueblo in New Mexico is the only village at which Towa is spoken, but Towa was also the language of Pecos Pueblo prior to its abandonment in the nineteenth century. Tiwa, Tewa, and Towa, although separate languages and not dialects of a single tongue, form a closely related language group referred to as Tanoan. Tanoan is part of the Kiowa-Tanoan language family. At the time of initial contact with Europeans, a number of Pueblo Indian villages were located east of the Sandia Mountains on the margins of the Plains and along the Rio Grande Valley south of Isleta. These villages were abandoned as a result of events related to European conquest. Although descendants of the residents of these villages live among some of the modern Pueblos, their languages, Piro and Tompiro, are no longer spoken.

All of the groups mentioned above seem to have had a very long history in the Southwest and share ancient traditions relating to horticulture and farming. Peoples speaking southern Athapaskan languages (Navajo and Apache) entered the Southwest much later, probably in the late fifteenth or sixteenth century. Since they were first observed by Europeans, Navajos and Apaches have practiced some cultivation, which they learned from neighboring peoples. Their most distinctive economic pattern, however, relates to livestock herding, which they adopted as a result of interaction with European peoples.

The Southwest differs from other North American regions in being sparsely inhabited by Euro-Americans even today. The aridity, the lack of navigable rivers and seacoasts, and the lack of abundant mineral resources have discouraged dense settlement in modern times. Largely for this reason, it is also one of the few areas of the United States that retains relatively large populations of Native Americans. Most of the archaeological remains in the Southwest relate directly to the precontact development of these Native populations. For that reason, it has been common for archaeologists to interpret the archaeological remains by reference to direct analogy with the ethnographic record of these societies. The nearly exclusive use of local ethnographic analogy to provide most archaeological inference is the subject of recent scholarly debate. A number of scholars argue that archaeologists working in the Southwest failed to appreciate the scale and the scope of change wrought on the indigenous Americans by the presence of Hispanos and Euro-Americans. For example, today's Pueblo communities are socially strongly egalitarian, and each village is politically and economically independent of other villages. It is commonly assumed that those characteristics are of great antiquity and were ubiquitous among ancient Pueblos. A few researchers suggest that formal systems of political and economic alliances existed among some Pueblos and may have involved managerial elites.[2] The events surrounding European conquest of the region, such as massive population loss that resulted from the introduction of European diseases, and the disruption of trade systems are thought to have destroyed the alliance networks and irrevocably altered the Pueblo world.

The natural and historical landscape of the Eastern Woodlands of North America contrasts sharply with that of the arid Southwest in many respects. Bounded on the west by grasslands, on the east and south by water, and with a northern length-of-growing-season dividing line between farming and entirely hunter-gatherer adaptations, the East was a vast expanse of forest, broken only by a complex system of large rivers and their major and minor tributaries. The Mississippi River and its tributaries dominate the interior heartland of the East. The Missouri, Arkansas, and Red Rivers reach into the grasslands of the west, while the Ohio, Cumberland, and Tennessee extend eastward to the Appalachian wall. East of the mountains and along the Atlantic and Gulf coastal plains, other river systems, large and small, flow into the Atlantic Ocean and Gulf of Mexico. Often providing main routes of movement for early European explorers, traders, and settlers, these river and stream valleys were the settings of Native American farming societies that had cultivated rich floodplain soils for more than a thousand years before the first arrival of Europeans. While these river valley corridors offered a common set of challenges and opportunities to Native American farming societies, the East had witnessed a complex regional mosaic of cultural development prior to first European contact.

The complexity of this developmental mosaic in the Eastern Woodlands is reflected in the diversity of languages, cultural traditions, and types of socio-political organization that were encountered by early Europeans.

---

[2] This view is expressed by Steadman Upham in *Polities and Power: An Economic and Political History of the Western Pueblo* (New York, 1982).

From an original homeland probably located in what is now New York State and central-northwestern Pennsylvania, Iroquoian languages (e.g., Seneca, Huron, Neutral, Tuscarora, Cherokee) had expanded over a broader area of the East by the time of European contact. Algonquian languages (e.g., Cree, Fox, Delaware, Shawnee) were spoken over vast interior and northern areas of the East, and along the northern Atlantic coast, while the Muskogean family (including Choctaw-Chickasaw, Apalachee, Muskogee-Seminole) was the most important language family across the Southeast, being spoken in what is now Louisiana, Mississippi, Alabama, Georgia, and adjacent areas. Siouan and Caddoan speakers along the western edge of the Eastern Woodlands added to the linguistic diversity, a diversity that is mirrored in the complex distribution of almost 100 Native groups identified at European contact.

While early European descriptions of indigenous groups often provide solid, if general, frameworks of analogy for analysis and interpretation of precontact Native American societies, the East differs markedly from the Southwest, in terms of both witnessing the early and large-scale westward displacement of Native American populations, and experiencing a high density of present-day Euro-American inhabitants. In addition, evidence of considerable late precontact change among indigenous societies, combined with the recognized early impact of European diseases and other influences on Native American groups, has necessitated a cautious use of postcontact analogies for interpretation of precontact societies in the East.

FARMERS OF THE SOUTHWEST

The southwest encompasses those portions of the western United States in which the Native peoples depended upon a combination of farming, gathering, and hunting from about 1500 B.C. (Fig. 4.1). Both domesticated and wild plants were important sources of calories and nutrients (Table 4.1). The crops that were farmed included corn (*Zea mays*), squashes (*Cucurbita pepo*), and beans (*Phaseolus vulgaris, P. acutofolius, Canavalia ensiformes*), all of which had a long history of cultivation in Mexico prior to their acceptance in the Southwest. Somewhat later, cotton (*Gossypium* sp.), sieva beans (*P. lunatus*), and pigweed (*Amaranthus hypochondriacus*) were imported, also from Mexico, and cultivated in lower elevation areas of the Southwest. Cotton was used as a source of fiber for textiles, but it is also possible that the seeds were used as food. Other cultivated plants included agave (*Agave parii*), little barley grass (*Hordeum pusillum*), and tobacco

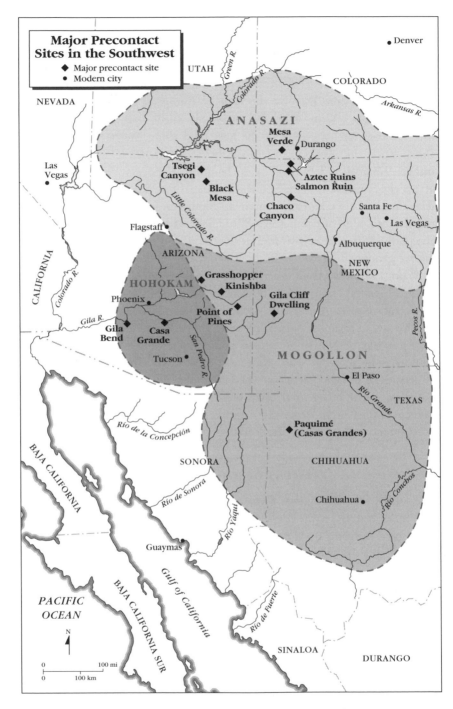

Figure 4.1. Map of the Southwest with major precontact sites.

(*Nicotiana* sp.). Although they are not considered fully domesticated species in the Southwest, several indigenous, nutritious, southwestern plants were encouraged or cultivated. These included sunflower (*Helianthus* sp.), cholla (*Opuntia bigelovii* Engelm.), dropseed (*Sporobollus* sp.), lamb's quarter (*Chenopodium berlandieri*), panic grass (*Panicum* sp.), and Devil's claw cactus (*Proboscidae parviflora*). The last was used to make basketry rather than as a food crop. The native tobacco was used in ceremonies and medicinally.

Turkeys (*Meleagris gallopavo*) were domesticated in the northern Southwest, probably from populations of Merriam's wild turkey. Throughout much of the region, turkeys were kept for food as well as for their feathers, although in some communities they seem to have been kept only for their feathers.

The Southwest is characterized by varied terrain of low basins, rugged mesas, canyons, mountains, and plains. Some of the basin country is only thirty meters above sea level. While they constitute no serious barrier to travel, mountain peaks in the Southwest reach elevations of more than 4,000 meters above sea level. The entire region has a semiarid to arid climate, and there is considerable variation in precipitation from one locality to another and from one year to the next. In general, higher elevation settings receive more precipitation than do lower elevations.

Annual precipitation of less than twenty centimeters characterizes some of the low deserts. Producing crops in these areas requires irrigation. Annual precipitation of thirty-five to forty centimeters is common in the mountains and the higher mesas; however, precipitation is not reliable from one year to the next. For example, Sante Fe, New Mexico, receives an average of 35.9 centimeters of precipitation annually, but actual amounts have ranged from 16.9 to 51.2 centimeters over the past forty years. In addition to variability in abundance from year to year, the timing of precipitation during the year has important consequences for successful farming. Throughout the Southwest, May and June, the months during which most domestic crops germinate, are virtually rainless. Where winter rain and snows have replenished groundwater and soil moisture, seeds will germinate. Otherwise, hand watering may be necessary. The length of the frost-free period also varies throughout the region and over time. In the low deserts, frosts are rare and the length of the growing season is adequate for crops. Elsewhere, particularly in the mountains and in narrow canyons, the frost-free period may not be sufficient to grow corn reliably each year.

Table 4.1 *Nutritional aspects of domesticates and wild foods of the Southwest*[a]

	Calories (per 100 g)[b]	Protein (per 100 g)[b]	Carbohydrates (per 100 g)[c]
Crop			
Beans, common (raw)	340	22.5	61.9
Corn	348	8.9	72.2
Squash, summer	19	1.1	4.2
Squash, winter	50	1.4	12.4
Pumpkins	26	1.0	6.5
Wild Food			
Seeds			
Amaranth	36	3.5	6.5
Lamb's quarter	43	4.2	7.3
Saguaro	609	16.3	540.0
Tansy mustard	554	23.4	71.0
Pigweed	360	–	–
Fruits			
Cholla	393	12.2	79.0
Prickly pear	42	0.5	10.9
Prickly pear (dry)	280	1.7	62.0
Saguaro (dry)	499	10.3	70.0
Nuts			
Black walnuts	628	20.5	14.8
Piñon	635	–	–
Other			
Cholla stems	–	1.6	–
Mesquite beans	419	14.9	73.0
Purslane	20	–	–

[a]Adapted from Richard I. Ford, "An Ecological Analysis involving the Population of San Juan Pueblo, New Mexico," Ph.D. dissertation, University of Michigan (Ann Arbor, Mich., 1968).
[b]Edible portion only.
[c]Includes fiber.

The dual southwestern problems of aridity and short growing seasons are so important that scholars frequently invoke climatic factors as explanations for cultural changes observed in the archaeological record. While it is probably true that at times settlements, localities, and even regions were abandoned because of widespread droughts or shortening of the growing season, southwestern farmers used many ingenious techniques to mitigate the effects of the harsh climate on crop production. In recognition of these Jeffrey S. Dean and other anthropologists have developed a model of behavioral adaptation for a portion of the Southwest (the Colorado Plateaus) which describes interaction among environmental, demographic, and behavioral variables. It also takes account of the complexity of the environmental factors involved.

The model distinguishes two kinds of environmental processes. Low-frequency processes (LFP) involve changes that have periodicities that last longer than a human generation (twenty-five years), whereas high-frequency processes (HFP) have shorter periodicities. LFPs underlie episodes of arroyo cutting and deposition and the raising and lowering of water table levels. HFPs are responsible for annual variation in precipitation and the length of the growing season. Although some HFPs do interact with local topographic features to initiate LFPs, the relations among processes are so complex that identical conditions rarely recur. Human adaptive responses to LFP and HFP changes differ. Changes due to LFPs are perceived and understood as stability. The most basic economic and social adaptations must be made to LFP conditions and need to be flexible enough to allow for shorter term variations. For example, mobile hunters and gatherers living in small groups would constitute one kind of adaptation to LFP conditions.

HFP fluctuations would be explicitly recognized and dealt with through buffering strategies, such as modifying the amounts of game hunted as opposed to quantities of plants collected by hunter-gatherers. Among farmers, increasing the amount of foods stored, extending water-control devices, and gathering additional wild foods are behavioral responses to HFP fluctuations. According to Dean, a key factor conditioning how human populations react to HFPs is how close the human population is to carrying capacity. Thus, "as population levels approach the long-term carrying capacity of the local habitat, HFP environmental fluctuations become more critical to survival."[3] Some options may be constrained and others rendered impossible by the presence of increased numbers of people in the region.

Given the climatic risks to crop production, gathering wild plant foods and hunting remained important for subsistence into modern times. Considerable energy was devoted to storing crops, when possible, and a variety of planting and cropping strategies were developed to minimize crop loss. Some of these strategies required coordination of labor and substantial investment of labor, at least seasonally or on occasion. Some strategies were successful for long periods of time. However, when events triggered

---

[3] Jeffrey S. Dean, "A Model of Anasazi Behavioral Adaptation," in George J. Gumerman, ed., *The Anasazi in a Changing Environment* (Cambridge, 1988), 30–31.

by LFPs reduced the productive capacity of the environment and these were coincident with HFP factors causing a diminution of resources, major changes in adaptation, including regional abandonments, occurred. To some extent, the histories of the regional cultures of the Southwest can be understood as diverse experiments with farming ways of life in a difficult and variable environment.

THE ACCEPTANCE OF FOOD PRODUCTION
IN THE SOUTHWEST

The period between about 1500 B.C. and A.D. 200, which archaeologists refer to as the Late Archaic, began with the introduction of corn, beans, and squash throughout most of the Southwest. Archaeologists use the appearance of painted ceramics to mark the end of this period. Both a lowland route, west of the Sierra Madre Occidental, and a highland route, along the Sierra Madre Occidental, were paths along which corn and other crops were transmitted. Low Sonoran Desert basins, the mountains, and the plateau settings evidence horticulture at about the same time.

Corn is a plant adapted to the humid tropics; neither the low, dry regions of the Southwest nor the higher, moister, but cooler locales are especially well suited to its growth. Raymond H. Thompson suggests that two, slightly different, varieties of maize may have been transmitted north, one type within the low deserts and the other into the mountainous highlands.[4] On the other hand, Wirt H. Wills argues that the period when corn was accepted was one during which the Southwest was somewhat wetter and cooler than it was before and after.[5] For this reason, he proposes that corn was accepted first in the low-elevation areas, and in the more mountainous areas somewhat later. In either case, in order for crops to survive, some investment in their cultivation had to be made. Further, it appears that at least a rudimentary technology of water management was part of the cultural background of groups in northern and northwest Mexico and the deserts of the United States Southwest prior to or coincident with the acceptance of cultigens. Archaeologists agree that the extra effort involved in crop production was most likely undertaken as a buffering strategy to reduce the chances of an inadequate supply of wild food

[4] Raymond H. Thompson, "Early Settlement in Western North America: The Southwest," Plenary Session Paper presented at the Eleventh International Congress of Pre- and Protohistoric Sciences (Mainz, 1987).
[5] Wirt H. Wills, *Early Prehistoric Agriculture in the American Southwest* (Santa Fe, N.M., 1988), 148.

plants and game occasioned by the variable and risky environment. The Native farming peoples of the Southwest developed varieties of corn capable of withstanding a diversity of adverse conditions. Botanical data suggest that the genetic variability present in southwestern maize by 300 B.C. was adequate to account for all the varieties of the crop that were eventually grown in the region.

In addition to corn and other crops, Late Archaic sites of the Southwest share other traits including large, notched projectile points, clay cloud-blower pipes, and basin-shaped grinding stones (referred to as metates and used with small, hand-held grinding stones, called manos). There is a predominance of flexed burials, but extended burials and cremations are known from some sites and areas. Shallow caves and rock shelters were used to process plant foods, to store foods and other goods, and sometimes as places to bury the dead.

Outside of rock shelters, oval to circular pithouses are found. The depth of the floors of these structures may be no more than ten to fifteen centimeters in the Sonoran Desert of Arizona, but in some mountainous areas, floors were dug to nearly a meter below ground surface. In low desert and basin settings, Late Archaic sites with houses were most often located near the upper end of small tributary drainages or near wet meadows, suggesting that crops were planted where they could be watered by relatively slow-moving floodwaters. In mountainous areas, and on the plateaus, Late Archaic sites with houses were more often situated on raised benches or small mesas overlooking agricultural land.

Although some sites, such as Site 33 near El Paso, Texas, and numerous ones on Black Mesa in Arizona, contain several pithouse structures, there is no indication that these houses were occupied simultaneously. In the larger and later sites, such as Shabik'eschee Village, above Chaco Wash in New Mexico, which has eighteen pithouses, earlier structures were dismantled to provide materials for later houses. Characterizing these sites as small hamlets or household compounds, rather than villages, is appropriate.

The presence of the house structures themselves, as well as of extramural, bell-shaped storage or cache pits (some quite large), refuse areas, and burials, provides good evidence that these tiny settlements were reoccupied time and again. Wills provides a useful categorization of the settlement pattern reflected in these sites when he notes: "The implication . . . is that the adoption of maize requires a seasonally repetitive pattern of movement around a particular locality on an annual basis. This may not be sedentism as defined by the extended occupation of a single settlement, but it suggests a very different organization from the wide-ranging hunter-gatherer tactic that . . . is the preferred forager option."[6]

In addition to relatively small, oval pithouses, many early settlements have a single large structure that has been identified as a community lodge or protokiva. Kivas are the semi-subterranean religious structures used in modern Pueblo Indian villages. By analogy the term is used to refer to ceremonial rooms prior to European contact as well. In the southern desert regions of the Southwest, a few early settlement plans consist of separate houses facing plazas or three or four houses facing a courtyard. Throughout most of the Southwest, however, and especially in the northern areas, a segmented settlement plan with separate structures loosely grouped around open plazas, sometimes with discrete refuse areas, is the common pattern.

Some classes of artifacts are common throughout the Southwest. These include clay human figurines, shell jewelry, some turquoise jewelry, cloud-blower pipes, twinned netting and baskets, leather and basketry bags, and triangular, side-notched projectile points. In the southern Arizona desert carved stone bowls, simple stone palettes, and three-quarter grooved stone axes are known from quite early times. To some scholars, the clay figurines have suggested new religious concepts possibly associated with fertility and agriculture. In the northern Southwest, burials in which heads and long bones have been removed from corpses after burial, apparent attempts to protect the heads of corpses from vandalism, and the frequent association of fires and burned human bones in burial caves have suggested belief in witchcraft.

By about the first century A.D., groups in the southern portions of the Southwest were making a polished red or brown ware pottery. By around A.D. 300, brown ware and gray ware were being made in the mountains and plateaus of the northern Southwest. While painted pottery, which varies temporally and geographically, is a hallmark of southwestern archaeology, allowing scholars to recognize different periods and cultural traditions, it is important to remember that this pottery served utilitarian functions for those who made and used it. Pottery, which is both heavy and friable, is most useful as a storage container among groups that are sedentary enough not to have to move from one camping place to the next every few days. Pottery, unlike baskets, can also be set directly over coals

---

[6] Wirt H. Wills, "Early Agriculture and Sedentism in the American Southwest: Evidence and Interpretations," *Journal of World Prehistory*, 2 (1988), 445–88.

or a fire, so that stews or gruels can cook relatively unattended. This may be an advantage when considerable labor must be spent in fields or in processing foods, such as grinding corn. Finally, pottery can be used to cook liquids. One of the ways in which dry, stored corn is made palatable is to cook it with water to make a gruel or porridge. In any case, pottery had become ubiquitous throughout the Southwest by about A.D. 300.

PATTERNS OF REGIONAL EXPANSION
IN THE SOUTHWEST

The period between about A.D. 600 to 700 and 900 is one during which agriculture, small permanent or semipermanent hamlets, and pottery making spread throughout the Southwest. Most groups continued to consume a considerable amount of wild plant food and game, and there is debate among archaeologists about the degree of sedentarism reflected in the settlement pattern. The archaeological literature reflects the view that by the middle or end of this period there was enough local adaptation and differentiation from one region to another for scholars to talk about separate cultural traditions.

We follow Wobst and others in suggesting that visually distinctive styles may function as social boundary mechanisms that can become important in situations of increased regional population densities and competition for resources.[7] Readily identifiable styles in these situations signal social affiliations, identifying those with whom resources are and are not shared and to whom access to territory is given or denied. The lack of such marked boundaries in the early centuries A.D. may imply that population densities were generally low or reflect the necessity for maintaining open social systems, as people adjusted to environmental risks. Although archaeologists define cultures on the basis of similarities in artifact styles, house types, and settlement patterns, it is not known whether the people participating in these cultural traditions spoke the same language or shared a common identity.

Three well-defined cultural traditions, and some less well-marked minor ones, are generally described as having emerged in the Southwest by 700 to 900 (Fig. 4.1). Only the major traditions are examined here. These are Hohokam, Mogollon, and Anasazi. Geographically more peripheral

[7] Martin H. Wobst, "Stylistic Behavior and Information Exchange," in Charles L. Cleland, ed., *For the Director: Research Essays in Honor of James B. Griffin,* University of Michigan, Museum of Anthropology Papers in Anthropology, No. 61 (Ann Arbor, Mich., 1977), 317–47.

and less well-documented traditions include the Patayan of the Lower Colorado River area; the Sinagua around Flagstaff, Arizona; the Freemont of south-central Utah; and the Salado of southeastern Arizona.

The term Hohokam is applied to the pre-European tradition of the desert areas of southern Arizona, particularly the Tonto Basin, and the Gila and Salt Valleys. In this region, water control devices, which eventually included long and elaborate systems of irrigation canals, diverted water from the Gila and Salt Rivers to fields. Villages were located parallel to the courses of the rivers but away from the danger of being destroyed by flood. The earliest ceramics are the polished red and brown wares noted above, while the earliest painted pottery is a buff color with geometric designs in red paint. Throughout the Hohokam area, there are generally fewer painted than unpainted ceramics, but beginning about A.D. 750 to 800, the frequency of painted pottery increases, at least in the areas near the rivers. At about this time painted pottery decoration includes small life forms and geometric elements repeated in bands over the decorated surface of the vessel.

Between about 500 and 1100, there is continuity in settlement configuration in the Hohokam area in general and in the occupation of some sites. Small courtyards or outdoor work areas unite groups of three or four pithouses, and there is rebuilding of houses and house groups. The size of sites, and presumably their population, increase throughout this period, as does the extent of Hohokam settlement. Not surprisingly, the irrigation canals that were an integral feature of Hohokam agriculture also increase in size and in number. In settings away from the rivers, Hohokam settlements also grow more numerous, correlating with the application of diverse agricultural technologies, such as diverting runoff from summer rain showers to the outwash fans of ephemeral streams, where fields were planted.

The increase in the complexity and elaboration of Hohokam culture before A.D. 1000 outstrips that of most other regions of the Southwest. Public architecture at Hohokam sites includes ball courts and platform mounds. Hohokam ball courts are elongated, slightly oval, structures that were excavated into the soil. Some are very large, up to sixty-five meters in length, with more or less parallel sides and expanded, bulbous end fields. Others are smaller and more oval in shape. Ball courts were unroofed and generally have stone end and center markers. Hohokam courts lack certain features of Mesoamerican ball courts, such as stone side walls and and rings. Two rubber balls have been found at Hohokam sites, though not physically associated with a ball court. It is possible that Hohokam ball courts may have served functions that differed from their Mesoamerican counterparts. Some ball court sites contain only one court; others multiple ones. Hohokam platform mounds seem to occur early in the sequence, but do not reach their greatest number or elaboration until after 1000. These mounds at first consist of rubbish and sandy earth piled into mounds, sometimes with flattened tops and capped with caliche. Early Hohokam mounds are generally oval in shape and have a single, insubstantial structure and sometimes smaller features, such as hearths, on top of them.

By about 750 to 800, Hohokam clay figurines were somewhat more realistically made than previously. Stone palettes, stone bowls, and censers are elaborately decorated (Fig. 4.2). The more elaborate items occur most often with cremations. The Hohokam are distinguished from other southwestern groups by the presence of ball courts, platform mounds, and elaborate irrigation systems. The ball courts, platform mounds, irrigation, stone palettes, and mosaic plaques or mirrors are often viewed as being of Mesoamerican or northern Mexican origin. Some scholars deemphasize this Mexican influence. Although they do not deny cultural connections between Mexico and the Hohokam area, they emphasize the fact that the Hohokam economy was able to support this more structured and specialized organization. It has also been pointed out that irrigation, the basis of Hohokam farming, was not a feature of early complex societies in the Valley of Mexico, the hearth of Mesoamerican civilization.

The name of Mogollon is applied to the ancient inhabitants of the rugged mountainous area immediately east of the Hohokam region and encompassing mountains and low-lying basins extending north to central Arizona and New Mexico and south into Chihuahua (Fig. 4.1). Mogollon archaeological remains dated prior to 700 strongly resemble those of the Hohokam. They include simple palettes, clay human figurines, simply carved stone bowls, plain brown and red ware pottery, and red-on-brown painted ceramics. It has been suggested that the Mogollon may have taken up farming somewhat later than the Hohokam, or at least that they depended on hunting and gathering longer. As with the Hohokam, early Mogollon burials may be either secondary cremations, or flexed or extended inhumations. However, inhumations are relatively more common, whereas cremations are relatively more abundant among the Hohokam.

By about 700, the Mogollon pattern is more differentiated from the Hohokam, but, because of its relatively great geographic extent, it is also

Figure 4.2. Diagnostic artifacts of each of the three major southwestern cultural traditions. The Hohokam are known for carved stone bowls, censers, palettes and for shell and etched shell ornaments. (A) Hohokam stone palette with lizard pattern in bas-relief on border. Excavated from the site of Snaketown, ca. A.D. 800 Most Mogollon crafts are not distinctive, however the Mimbres branch is known for spectacular painted bowls produced about A.D. 1000; (B) ceramic cylinder jar, a form possibly unique to Chaco Canyon, is one of 114 excavated from Pueblo Bonito, by the Hyde Expedition of 1896–1899. (C) reconstruction of a turquoise-encrusted cylinder, from Pueblo Bonito by the Hyde Expedition of 1896–1899; (D) Fragment of a painted wooden ritual object from a large cache excavated at Chetro Ketl, Chaco Canyon, New Mexico. (E) Hohokam stone censer with relief carving of a snake from the site of Snaketown, Pinal County, Arizona dates to ca. A.D. 750 or 800. (F) are Classic Mimbres black-on-white bowls from the Swarts Ruin, New Mexico; often such bowls have had a piece punched out of the center, as part of funerary ritual, the sherd is generally found with the burial. The rabbit is probably a lunar symbol. Anasazi artifacts from Chaco Canyon illustrate the height of Anasazi craftsmanship. (Courtesy, Smithsonian Institution; Academic Press; and Noble, *New Light on Chaco Canyon*.)

more internally variable. After initial settlement on ridges and other landform eminences, most Mogollon sites were located near streams, at lower elevations, in closer proximity to arable land. Despite increased dependence on crops, hunting and gathering remained significant aspects of Mogollon economy. From about A.D. 700 to 1000, the Mogollon occupied pithouses. These were generally quite deep, with sloping ramp entry ways. The Mogollon did not build platform mounds or ball courts, but some villages had a very large, communal pit structure referred to as a great kiva, or such structures might be outside any one village in a location that could have been used by several nearby communities. After about 1000 to 1150, Mogollon settlements were more typically single-story, contiguous-roomed, stone pueblos with plaza areas.

Mogollon ceramics after about 600 were polished red wares or polished red-on-brown. After approximately 900, a white slip was applied as background color, providing a greater contrast to the design. After about 1000, Mogollon painted ceramics were black-on-white. Some of the regional styles of this black-on-white pottery are among the most aesthetically appealing ceramics produced in the Southwest, from our point of view. These include the exceptionally well-executed geometric and life forms of Mimbres black-on-white pottery, much of which has been recovered from burials (Fig. 4.2). Although marine shell was traded into the Mogollon area, neither trade items nor crafts among the Mogollon reached the level of abundance or excellence that they had among the Hohokam until near the time of European contact, with the flourishing of Paquimé at Casas Grandes, Chihuahua (discussed below).

Anasazi is the designation given to southwestern peoples living prior to European discovery on the Colorado Plateaus and Southern Rocky Mountains and at times extending their settlements slightly eastward onto the western margins of the Great Plains (Fig. 4.1). Anasazi settlements reached from the Grand Canyon of the Colorado River to the Upper Pecos and extended north into what today is southern Utah and Colorado. As with the Mogollon, the geographic extent of the Anasazi tradition assured considerable regional diversity. As a whole, Anasazi populations, with some increments from the Mogollon, are seen as ancestral to the modern Pueblo Indians of New Mexico and Arizona.

The basic Anasazi subsistence pattern was the same as the Mogollon. In general, Anasazi may have begun producing pottery and constructing pithouses slightly later than Hohokam and Mogollon, but because most Anasazi building was eventually in stone, which preserves extremely well, these sites give the appearance of representing the most highly developed culture in the Southwest. At first, like other southwestern groups, the Anasazi constructed pithouses. In most areas by 750 to 800, these were accompanied by a row of above-ground contiguous rooms made of *jacal* (a Spanish term applied to the local post and adobe construction) or of a combination of stone and jacal. The above ground rooms at first lack fire hearths and domestic debris and seem to have been used as storage facilities. At about the same time, the Anasazi were producing pottery with black painted designs on a gray background. Trade in lithic raw materials, shell, and ceramics is an early and continuing feature of the Anasazi tradition.

Between about 750 and 900, along the Upper San Juan drainage and in adjacent areas of southeastern Utah and southwestern Colorado, Anasazi villages commonly consisted of long, arcing rows of surface dwelling and storage rooms flanking the north and west sides of rows of deep pithouses. In this region, the pithouses were subrectangular and some had their interior space divided by jacal or adobe wing-walls. Some above-ground rooms had slab-lined interiors and jacal walls, although late in the period, in some localities, undressed stone masonry was used for walls.

Communities consisting of about twelve units, each of which contains a line or arc of surface rooms and a pithouse, are fairly common in parts of southern Colorado and Utah, but much smaller settlements, composed of one or two such units, are not at all unusual. In fact, throughout the northern Anasazi area, a type of settlement first described by T. Mitchell Prudden in 1903 and sometimes named after him, developed and prevailed until about the end of the ninth century. Prudden-unit pueblos consist of a regular arrangement of five or six masonry rooms, a kiva, and a trash mound, usually oriented along a north-south axis. Although the term kiva is used for the round, semisubterranean structure in front of the rectangular rooms, Stephen H. Lekson suggests that there is little empirical support for the presence of analogs to modern Pueblo kivas prior to 1300.[8] Lekson contends that the earlier pit structures served as dwellings for some part of the year or for some segment of the local group. Single large structures, which can be interpreted as great kivas, are reported for some locations in the northern San Juan drainage, but no farther south and west. Anasazi ceramics of this period consist of unpainted, gray ware

[8] Stephen H. Lekson, "The Idea of the Kiva in Anasazi Archaeology," *The Kiva* 53 (1988), 218–34.

cooking vessels that have a series of coiled bands at their necks, and black-on-gray painted serving vessels. Pottery, shell, and lithic raw material were traded throughout the Anasazi region.

By 900 horticulture and a pattern of small village settlement had spread throughout the Southwest. Throughout most of the region, settlements were small and may not have been occupied for very long periods of time, perhaps on the order of seven to ten years or less. In mountainous areas and on the plateaus, increased food storage, and perhaps the maintenance of exchange networks, seem to have been the most common strategies for dealing with the unpredictable environment. In the lower desert regions, systems of irrigation canals and apparently complex foci of ritual and community activity, reflected in the ball courts and platform mounds, were important to the success of a farming way of life. In each southwestern region, in the period between 900 and 1500, systems of regionally organized communities developed, flourished for a time, and then collapsed. Descriptions of these systems and current understanding of the ways in which they may have functioned are presented next.

THE REGIONALLY ORGANIZED SYSTEMS

In the region of Hohokam settlement, the period between about 1000 and 1150 did not witness any major changes or innovations. Rather, it was a time when existing patterns seemed to reach their culmination. The sizes of sites that had been occupied during previous periods reached their maximum extent. Coupled with the increase in site size, although the basic irrigation systems were already in place, was a great increase in the amount of irrigated land. In those locations away from the rivers, a variety of agricultural technologies was practiced.

Ritual objects and other craft items, such as stone palettes, bowls and censers, were increasingly elaborately decorated and carefully executed until about A.D. 1000, when this trend was reversed. The craft items and finely made, serrated, stone projectile points are thought to have been produced by specialists. Shell ornaments were carved and etched. The amount of trade in both raw materials and finished items, including shell and stone, between Hohokam and outlying groups is a marked feature of this period. Within the Hohokam core area of the Salt-Gila Basin, regular spacing of communities with ball courts has been demonstrated. David R. Wilcox estimates that most of the 206 Hohokam ball courts known from

165 sites were constructed and in use between about 975 and 1150.[9] Platform mounds increased in number after 1050. Not all sites with platform mounds also had ball courts. Of the thirty-five known platform mound sites along the Gila and Salt rivers, twenty-five also had ball courts. At these sites, the ball court was consistently located north or northeast of the platform mound. Also at these sites, the ball court, platform mound (or mounds), and larger domestic units were loosely arranged around an open plaza. The distributions of ball court and platform mound sites suggest site hierarchies. Sites with platform mounds and sites with ball courts are evenly spaced along canals and rivers and are interspersed by small sites which lack these features.

The geographical extent of Hohokam culture was greater in the eleventh century than at any other time, extending from the lower Gila drainage to drainages north of Phoenix. Sites exhibiting some Hohokam elements have been found as far north as the Verde Valley and the Flagstaff area. Although sometimes interpreted as evidence of Hohokam migrations, more recent explanations emphasize the variable nature of the Hohokam presence in these outlying regions and suggest that differing intensities in Hohokam interaction and trade are more likely reflected.

One of the most impressive sites of this period is the Gatlin site, near Gila Bend, excavated by William W. Wasley and Alfred E. Johnson.[10] The Gatlin site consisted of an elaborate, artificially constructed platform mound that had been modified and repaired through six stages of construction and that eventually measured about twenty-nine by twenty-one meters and stood 3.7 meters high. In addition, the site contained two oval ball courts, two crematoria, twenty-two trash mounds, and an irrigation canal. Despite extensive testing, the remains of only two pithouses were located, suggesting that the site may have served primarily ceremonial rather than habitation functions.

A number of investigators have addressed the nature of the Hohokam regional system, the causes of apparent socio-political complexity, and its functions. The basic tasks of coordinating the labor involved in building and maintaining irrigation systems and, importantly, the need to adjudicate potential disputes over water rights among communities sharing a single canal system have been cited as requiring decision-making, adminis-

9 David R. Wilcox, "The Mesoamerican Ballgame in the American Southwest," in Vernon L. Scarborough and David R. Wilcox, eds., *The Mesoamerican Ballgame* (Tucson, Ariz., 1991), 101–28.
10 William W. Wasley and Alfred E. Johnson, *Salvage Archaeology in Painted Rocks Reservoir Western Arizona,* Anthropological Papers of the University of Arizona (Tucson, Ariz., 1965), 18–25.

trative hierarchies. As noted, site-size hierarchies and the occurrence of public architectural features at the largest sites within an irrigation community have been interpreted as reflecting the existence of these administrative hierarchies.

Other interpretations of the Hohokam regional systems focus on possible interactions with external middlemen and traders from pre-Columbian states in northern and northwestern Mesoamerica, the manipulation of goods in redistributive systems, and the control of elaborate religious or ceremonial systems. These causal factors are virtually identical to those offered for the Mogollon and Anasazi regional systems, discussed below. All of them depend on general ideas about the nature of hierarchy and very specific data regarding the chronology and role of particular sites in Chihuahua and elsewhere in Mexico. Discussion is deferred to the end of this section.

A final point about the Hohokam regional system, however, is that most of the elaboration discussed above did not last beyond about 1400. After 1200, the first in a series of rapid changes in Hohokam settlement configuration took place. Small, dispersed sites were abandoned, and the population aggregated at fewer and larger settlements. At the same time, plaster-capped platform mounds were built within massive adobe retaining walls. These rectangular mounds were surrounded by a compound wall constructed in the same manner as the mound retaining wall and defining a large, rectangular space. Rooms associated with the mounds, within the compound walls, served as residences for a small portion of the population. The spatial separation of a small segment of each community is considered the clearest evidence for social differentiation among Hohokam residential groups. Slightly later the platform mounds were walled off and interstitial areas were filled in. Public architecture changed from previously abundant platform mounds to adobe, multistory great houses, as at Casa Grande, Arizona (Fig. 4.3). Above-ground, multiroom, single-story, walled compounds replaced the pithouse group of domestic architecture. These changes have been attributed to the presence of outsiders (Anasazi or Salado) among the Hohokam or interpreted as indigenous developments. Nevertheless, even these cease sometime after 1400. There is a truncation of the Hohokam presence prior to the appearance of the first European explorers in the area.

The best documented southwestern regional system among the Anasazi had its inception in the tenth century in Chaco Canyon, in the San Juan Basin of New Mexico. Although at first localized along less than thirty

Figure 4.3. Casa Grande, Pinal County, Arizona, is a Hohokam Great House dating to the 14th century. The massive adobe-walled structure was surrounded by a compound wall that also enclosed small, single-story dwelling units. (Courtesy, Smithsonian Institution.)

linear kilometers of Chaco Wash, the system eventually expanded to include about 53,000 square kilometers of the basin and adjacent uplands. The Chacoan system is best known for its large, carefully planned pueblo structures, referred to as towns. The famous sites of Pueblo Bonito, Chetro Ketl, Pueblo del Arroyo, and Pueblo Alto are among them. Chacoan town sites are generally large by Anasazi standards; Pueblo Bonito, the largest, contains more than 600 rooms (Fig. 4.4). The massive walls of the structures taper toward their upper reaches and consist of veneered masonry in which a stone core of overlapped sandstone blocks set in abundant mortar provides most of the structural support, but is faced on both sides with thin, sandstone ashlar veneer. The town sites are also formal, planned structures. They are multistoried and built in D, E, F, or L-shapes, around plazas that are generally enclosed by a low block of rooms or a high wall. Individual Chacoan town-site rooms are larger than those at other Anasazi sites, and have high ceilings. Within every town there are many small kivas, about one for every thirty rooms. Tower kivas, which are circular stone kivas of two or more stories, were sometimes built in the plaza area. Each town also had one or more Great Kivas in the plaza. Great Kivas are structures, measuring more than twenty meters in diameter. Each Great

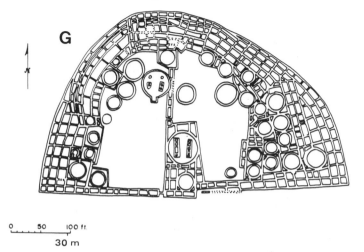

Figure 4.4. Pueblo Bonito is the best known of the eleventh-century Great Houses of Chaco Canyon, New Mexico. With more than 300 ground floor rooms, 30 kivas and 2 Great Kivas, up to five stories of masonry with an estimate of more than 650 rooms, and a highly formal ground plan, it was the model for the most important Chacoan town sites that were central to the Chacoan regional system. (Courtesy, Smithsonian Institution.)

Kiva has a standard arrangement of unusual features: antechamber rooms, some with recessed stairways leading into the kivas; a central raised, stone firebox flanked by a pair of rectangular stone vaults; and a high bench and series of niches along the interior wall. Although when excavated, most of the wall niches were found to be empty, the sealed niches at the Chetro Ketl Great Kiva contained pendants and strings of stone and shell beads.

The massive roofs of the Great Kivas were constructed of wood. One of these was made of more than 350 timbers, a tremendous resource investment in an area where there were few trees. Furthermore, the timbers had come from Ponderosa pine forests many tens of kilometers from Chaco Canyon.

In additional to the timbers, which from the Anasazi perspective may have been the most precious items, the town sites have also yielded other "luxury" or exotic materials, including cylindrical vessels, pottery incense burners, copper tinkler bells, *Strombus* and *Murex* shell trumpets, painted wooden objects, macaw skeletons, and shell, wood, and basketry items inlaid with selenite, mica, and turquoise (Fig. 4.2).

The Chacoan town sites are only one component of the Anasazi regional system of the time. Within Chaco Canyon and the San Juan Basin, small, single-story, village sites with an average of about sixteen rooms are abundant and were contemporary with the town sites. Rooms in these village sites were smaller than those in the town sites, and the village sites themselves do not appear to have been planned, rooms having been added on as needed. Village site kivas were small and lacked specialized features.

The coexistence of town and village sites was not limited to the canyon. By about 1150, this pattern was repeated in some 150 outlying communities spread throughout at least 150,000 square kilometers of the San Juan Basin and beyond (Fig. 4.5). The community clusters, referred to as Chacoan Outliers, consisted of a town site built in Chacoan style with its ashlar veneer, Great Kiva, tower kiva, or both, an enclosed plaza, and usually an associated group of contemporaneous small village sites. Suggestions that the Chacoan sites represent a regional system are based not only on the contemporaneity and architectural similarity of the town sites, but also on the observation that many of the Chacoan Outliers were connected to Chaco Canyon by a system of ancient roads.

The function of the road system remains obscure. The roads themselves are generally straight and change direction by abrupt turns. They do not form a network of connections among sites; rather they radiate from the canyon, or specific sites in the canyon, to outliers and outlying areas in a fashion likened to spokes on a wheel. The roads vary from being up to nine meters in width in and near the canyon to only two or three meters wide away from it. Nevertheless, the width of the roads and the effort entailed in constructing them are difficult to explain in the context of peoples who lacked wheeled vehicles and pack animals. The Chacoans used systems of ditches and diversion dams to channel rainwater runoff to gardens along

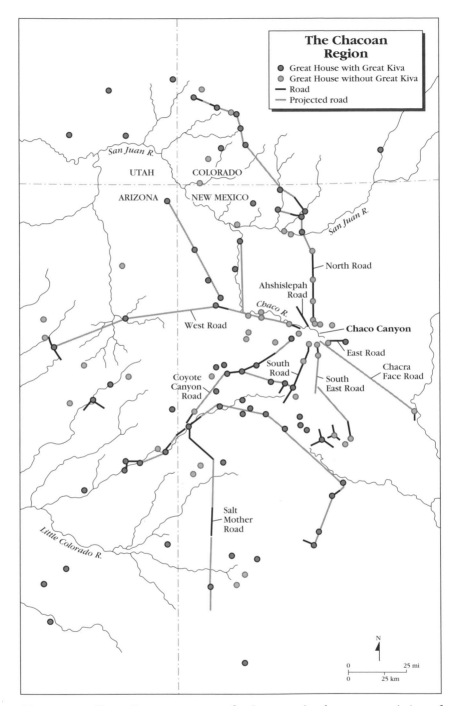

Figure 4.5. Chaco Canyon was part of a larger regional system consisting of Chacoan Great House outliers and associated communities, linked by ancient, formal, roadways. The extent of the system is thought to have included 150 outlying communities over 150,000 square kilometers.

Chaco Wash. Chaco Canyon and the San Juan Basin are relatively barren today and are likely to have been so in the eleventh and twelfth centuries. Therefore, it has been suggested that the roads facilitated the transport of surplus food and building material to the town sites, where they would have been stored until needed by those communities suffering crop short-falls as a result of scant rainfall. Recently, this view has been challenged by some and even questioned by those who initially proposed it.

Paleoenvironmental reconstructions have shown that, while it was cer-tainly not lush in the eleventh and twelfth centuries, the basin received more rainfall more predictably than it had at most other times. Also the known size of the system and road network is greater than would be ex-pected if surplus food were being brought to a central storage area. Finally, there are instances in which two and possibly four roadways run very close together along parallel courses for more than thirty kilometers, a situation that would not be required by any estimates of foot traffic at that time. Given these observations, it is not surprising that the most recent discus-sions emphasize possible symbolic or ritual functions for the roads.[11] De-spite scholarly debate about the functioning of the Chacoan system and the level of organization it represented, there is agreement that the organization of the system is not closely mirrored in modern Pueblo Indian villages, whose residents undoubtedly include descendants of the Chacoan Anasazi.

The Chacoan system seems to have failed and the San Juan Basin was itself largely abandoned by Pueblo peoples long before Europeans entered the Southwest. After 1150, no new Chacoan buildings were constructed in the canyon. Some canyon sites and outliers were modified architecturally. Those who remained in the area seemed to have interacted with the peoples living farther north along the northern San Juan tributaries in southwestern Colorado. In this region, from Mesa Verde north to the Dolores River, very large pueblos were built and maintained throughout the thirteenth century. These northern San Juan Anasazi sites do not manifest the same level of integrated planning as did those of the Chaco system.

The more northern Anasazi successfully farmed the mesa tops and some of the side-canyons of their portion of the Colorado Plateaus. Along intermittent streams, they built systems of check dams and terraces that served to retard erosion and divert runoff to field areas. They also built

---

[11] Recent discussions of the Chacoan road system are given in Stephen H. Lekson, Thomas C. Windes, John F. Stein, and W. James Judge, "The Chaco Canyon Community," *Scientific American* 256 (1988), 100–9, and by R. Gwinn Vivian in "Kluckhohn Reappraised: The Chacoan System as an Egalitarian Enterprise," *Journal of Anthropological Research* 45 (1989), 101–14.

reservoirs to provide household water for communities. Like the Chacoans, those of the Mesa Verde-Cortez and Yellow Jacket Canyon areas
built kivas and multistoried pueblos. But the elaborate Great Kivas,
tower kivas, ashlar masonry veneer, roads, and an abundance of luxury
items were not features common to the northern region. Nevertheless, it
was the pattern of these northern settlements that persisted. Chacoans
eventually made pottery in the style of their northern neighbors, and
later Chaco Canyon sites were built to resemble more closely those of the
north by either the indigenous Chaco population or by that group and
actual migrants from the northern San Juan. Some well-known Chacoan
outliers, such as Salmon Ruin and Aztec, provide evidence of successive
building episodes, with the Chaco occupation preceding a Mesa Verde–
style one.

Eventually, by 1300, even the northern Anasazi area was abandoned by
farming peoples, who moved south to the Upper Chama and Rio Grande
Valleys, the Central Mountains of Arizona, the Zuni Mountains, and the
Hopi Mesas. It was within some of these locations that aspects of the final
episode of regional integration prior to European contact can be seen,
although a key element in the final episode seems to be related in some
way to events much farther south, near the modern town of Neuvas Casas
Grandes in Chihuahua.

Throughout most of its history, the Casas Grandes region had generally
resembled the rest of the Mogollon area in artifact styles and settlement
pattern. However, in the fourteenth century, much of the population was
organized into one very large site which its excavator called the City of
Paquimé. Paquimé consisted of planned, multistoried, adobe-walled great
houses; ball courts; animal effigy-shaped and stone-faced platform mounds;
open plazas with a macaw breeding area; wells; a drainage system; and
workshop areas for the production of copper ornaments, axe heads, and
bells, as well as for marine shell items and turquoise jewelry. Recent reeval-
uation and analysis of the dating of Paquimé, the agricultural system,
burials, and ceramic and other craft manufacture and distribution suggest
that it was indeed an important regional center, though its influence differs
considerably from that originally described for it.

It now appears that much of the craft production and parrot breeding at
Paquimé was either for local consumption or for populations farther to the
south. Yet, either in opposition to the presence of Paquimé, or perhaps in
response to Paquimé's having disrupted access to state-level societies and
markets in northern and western Mesoamerica, very large communities

and alliance systems developed to the north in central Arizona and New Mexico. Although the nature of these alliances is debated, particularly whether or not they involved political and economic hierarchies, craft specialists, and elites, there is agreement that from 1270 to 1350, and occasionally as late as 1400, very large sites evidencing considerable trade in painted ceramics were distributed from the area around Flagstaff, Arizona, to the central Rio Grande Valley in New Mexico. Among the distinctive ceramics that were traded were White Mountain red wares and Jeddito yellow ware. Obsidians, turquoise, and shell may also have circulated among the sites.

After 1425, the cultural map of the Southwest closely resembled what was observed by the first European visitors. The large aggregated communities of the Classic Period Hohokam were abandoned. Later remains in Arizona's Sonoran Desert are more clearly Pima and Papago. There is scholarly debate about whether, or how much, continuity exists between the Hohokam culture and the modern Pima and Papago Indians of Arizona. Most investigators see some continuities, but these are not marked.

Paquimé was burned and abandoned sometime in the late 1400s. Many of the large Late Mogollon sites, such as Grasshopper Pueblo, Kinishba, Pinedale Ruin, and the Gila Cliff dwellings, were also abandoned at this time. However, very large aggregated pueblos were built in the vicinity of modern Zuni Pueblo and along the Rio Grande south of Belen. The sites near Zuni are interpreted as indicating historical connections between the late Mogollon and Zuni Pueblo. The Rio Grande sites, which were villages of the Piro-speaking Pueblos of the sixteenth and seventeenth centuries, also suggest continuity between some Mogollon villages and the Piros.

By far the most secure link between southwestern societies before and after European contact is that between the Anasazi and the Pueblo Indians of Arizona and New Mexico. Even Zuni and those Rio Grande villages, such as Isleta, which received increments of their population from the Piro Pueblos, are thought to be primarily descendants of the Anasazi. Despite unquestionable similarities between ancestral and modern Pueblo populations, there are unsolved questions of two sorts. First, as noted at the outset, Pueblo peoples differ in language and to some extent in social organization. Most archaeologists would agree with the Hopis that the Tsegi Canyon cliff dwellings of Betatakin and Keet Seel and those of Canyon de Chelly are ancestral Hopi villages. There is no consensus among archaeologists, however, regarding the specific homelands of the

Tanoan- as opposed to the Keresan-speaking groups. Although several scholars link the Keresan-speaking villages to Chaco Canyon in a general sense, there is less agreement about which, if any, of the Tanoan languages represents a Mesa Verde element.

The second kind of problem involves the origin of particular aspects of Pueblo culture, such as the virtually pan-Pueblo katcina rituals, which some scholars view as having a strong Mesoamerican appearance. Katcinas are supernatural beings associated with ancestors, rain, and general bless-ing. They join the villagers at certain times of the year and are impersonated by initiates in elaborately costumed, masked performances. The most elabo-rate katcina rituals are today performed among the Western Pueblos – the Hopi villages and Zuni. Yet, excavations in some late precontact Hopi sites (those of Tsegi Canyon) have yielded no symbols or paraphernalia that might be ascribed to katcina ritual. Some scholars derive the katcina rituals from Mexico via the Rio Grande area, noting resemblances between katcinas and rock art depictions. Others argue temporal priority for the appearance of katcinas among the Western Pueblos, citing kiva murals and ceramic elements dating shortly prior to European contact as evidence. A key issue is that, while all acknowledge very close ancestral ties between the Anasazi and the modern Pueblos, there is an appreciation of the disruptions caused to Pueblo culture by the past 400 years of interaction with Europeans and perhaps 500 years of interaction with the Athapaskan-speaking Navajos and Apaches as well.

DYNAMICS OF SOUTHWESTERN SOCIETIES PRIOR TO EUROPEAN CONTACT

Among the salient aspects of southwestern society prior to the arrival of the Spanish are the discontinuities in growth. Apparently complex, inte-grated systems developed and disintegrated; localities and regions were densely inhabited and then abandoned. There is acknowledged continuity between modern Pueblos and the Anasazi and Mogollon, but the roads, Great Kivas, and architecture of Chaco Canyon have no counterparts today. There are resemblances between some Hohokam artifacts and those of the Pimas and Papagos, yet the Pimas and Papagos do not use ball courts or build platform mounds.

Discontinuities in cultural patterns reflected in changes in artifact styles and architectural forms, in the past, have most often been attributed to migrations. For example, the changes from Chaco-style ceramic designs and masonry to those resembling Mesa Verde were viewed as evidence of migrants from Mesa Verde taking over Chaco Canyon. Similarly, the elaboration of Hohokam culture manifest after about A.D. 900 has been viewed as the result of Mesoamerican migrants bringing complex patterns to the Arizona deserts. The disappearance of these patterns and the subsequent hiatus between the Hohokam and the modern Pimas and Papagos were then attributed to the return of those supposed migrants to their ancestral area, leaving the original desert population to become the Pimas and Papagos. While there undoubtedly are instances of migration reflected in the southwestern archaeological record, they are very difficult to demonstrate. Those migration models that invoke Mesoamericans are particularly problematic in that they rarely identify a particular source of the intrusive populations. There is also the difficulty of attributing everything of any complexity to "outside" forces rather than acknowledging the creative abilities of Native southwestern people.

Recently, with some success, archaeologists have reexamined periods of growth and discontinuities in light of the refined paleoenvironmental data available and Dean's differentiation of LFP and HFP climatic events. One result has been the correlation of the inception of successive broad regional patterns with climatic changes (Fig. 4.6). These are recognized in a scheme that differentiates these regional patterns as follows:[12]

Date A.D.	Descriptive Title
1275/1300 to 1540	Aggregation
1130/1150 to 1275/1300	Reorganization
1000/1050 to 1130/1150	Differentiation
770/800 to 1000/1050	Expansion
200/500 to 750/800	Initiation

Briefly, during the Initiation period, the basic southwestern pattern was established. During the period of Expansion, the main, regionally differentiated patterns of the Southwest (Hohokam, Mogollon, and Anasazi) became recognizable. Differentiation, in the scheme, refers to the time when there was extreme stylistic parochialism in some areas, coincident with the formation of apparently more complex, regionally based systems. Reorganization refers to the instability and changes in

[12] This scheme is presented and described in detail by Linda S. Cordell and George J. Gumerman in "Cultural Interaction in the Prehistoric Southwest," in Linda S. Cordell and George J. Gumerman, eds., *Dynamics of Southwest Prehistory* (Washington, D.C., 1989), 6–15.

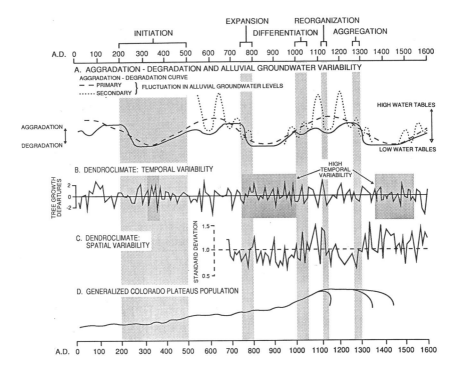

Figure 4.6 Periods of culture change in relation to environmental and demographic variables on the southern Colorado Plateaus, from *Dynamics of Southwest Prehistory,* edited by Linda Cordell and George Gumerman. It has been argued that periods of culture change were initiated rapidly and often synchronously with changes in climatic regimes. (Courtesy, Smithsonian Institution.)

the previously strong, large, regionally based systems. The term Aggregation refers to both the abandonment of large sites and regions and the formation of new large settlements, some of which continued into the period of Spanish settlement and later. The correlation of this scheme with the paleoenvironmental information suggests that discontinuities, including local and regional abandonments, probably did occur when instances of HFP events coincided with long-term, largely unobservable LFP situations that could not be mitigated through behavioral strategies.

Recently, various models have been proposed to explain the in situ development of complex institutions and regional systems of alliances in the Southwest. As explained above, many of these invoke redistributive exchange patterns that would work to even out environmentally induced agricultural shortfalls, but paleoenvironmental reconstructions have failed to document some of the necessary periods of climatic and environmental instability. Another approach suggests that the climatic instability that was being compensated for involved geographical rather than temporal variability. It is argued that the Chaco system and the system of fourteenth-century alliances coincided with periods during which there was the greatest spatial variation in rainfall in the Southwest – not with periods of either unusually high or low rainfall or short intervals of rainfall variability. Pooling of resources would be encouraged when neighboring areas had very different and changing patterns of precipitation.

There are also questions about the degree of complexity attained by any of the prehispanic southwestern societies. No one would maintain that state-level organizations occurred in the Southwest, or that hierarchically organized regional systems were at all stable. Nonetheless, some describe alliances as indicating strong organizational entities with central places and varying degrees of trade, social stratification, and agricultural intensification. Others are more inclined to see precontact societies as more egalitarian and modular, along the lines of the sequential hierarchies described by Gregory A. Johnson.[13] Sequential hierarchies arise to resolve particular problems, after which the group returns to its egalitarian state.

There were no systems in the Southwest that were able to sustain continued growth toward social and political complexity as societies did in the eastern United States and, of course, in Mesoamerica. The natural environments of the Southwest were never as productive as those of many other areas. In sum, the Southwest provides a variety of case studies of ingenious adaptations to harsh, unstable, and changing environmental conditions. The options people used seem to have included modifying the mix of hunting and gathering, as opposed to horticulture, formalizing and disrupting trading systems, perhaps developing redistributive systems on occasion, and resorting to population movements when necessary. It was only with the entry into the Southwest of Europeans and European livestock that many of these behavioral responses became impossible and the "cultural map" of the Southwest achieved its modern form.

[13] See note 2, and Gregory A. Johnson, "Dynamics of Southwestern Prehistory, Far Outside-looking in," in Linda S Cordell and George G. Gumerman, eds., *Dynamics of Southwest Prehistory,* (Washington, D.C., 1989), 378–81.

Table 4.2 *The nutritive profile of pre-maize crop plants, compared to maize and quinoa (percent dry basis)*

Species	Protein	Fat	Carbohydrates	Fiber	Ash
Starchy seeded					
Chenopodium	19.12	1.82	47.55	28.01	3.50
Maygrass	23.7	6.4	54.3	3.0	2.14
Erect knotweed	16.88	2.41	65.24	13.33	2.34
Oily seeded					
Marsh elder	32.25	44.47	10.96	1.46	5.80
Sunflower	24.0	47.30	16.10	3.80	4.00
Cucurbita	29.0	46.7	13.10	1.9	4.9
Maize	8.9	3.9	70.20	2.0	1.2
C. quinoa	12.5	6.0	72.5	5.6	3.4

FARMERS OF THE EASTERN WOODLANDS

Within the deciduous forest region of eastern North America the transition by Native peoples from an exclusive reliance on wild species of plants and animals to farming economies centered on crop plants was neither abrupt nor uniform (see also Chapter 3). In contrast to the Southwest, this transition was not based initially on tropical cultigens introduced from Mesoamerica. The East was an independent center of plant domestication.[14] Based on documented changes in seed morphology, at least four indigenous North American seed plants had been brought under domestication by 2000 to 1500 B.C. (lamb's quarter, marsh elder, squash, sunflower). A total of seven local crop plants was being cultivated prior to the initial introduction of maize into the region around A.D. 200 (Table 4.2). These oily and starchy seed crop plants were high in nutritive value and harvest potential, and were certainly contributing to the diet of some eastern groups by 2000 B.C., perhaps playing a significant role as a storable food supply for the cold season. Judging from their relative repre-

---

[14] Until recently, rind fragments assignable to the genus *Cucurbita* recovered from archaeological contexts in the East (Illinois, Kentucky, Missouri) and dating to 5000 to 3000 B.C. had been identified as evidence of domesticated squash. It was concluded that the squash (and the concept of agriculture) had arrived from Mexico in advance of domestication of indigenous seed crops. It now appears more likely that this early material represents a wild gourdlike squash (cf. *C. texana* indigenous to the East) that was brought under domestication in the East along with three other North American seed plants by 2000 to 1500 B.C. Bruce D. Smith, *Science* 246 (1989), 1566, provides a summary of the evidence supporting the East as an independent center of plant domestication.

sentation in assemblages of seeds from archaeological sites, it was not until between 200 B.C. and the beginning of the Christian era, or perhaps somewhat earlier, that they became major dietary items for groups over a broad interior riverine area of the East (Fig. 4.7). It is this relatively rapid and broad-scale increase in the importance of this set of indigenous crops just prior to the beginning of the Christian era that marks the initial development of a strong horticultural component in the subsistence economies of Native peoples of the Eastern Woodlands.[15]

Judging from information currently available, farming economies appear to have remained largely restricted to this broad interior riverine area of the East until about A.D. 800 to 900; squash (*Cucurbita pepo*) was the only crop plant occurring outside of this area with any frequency. Introduced about A.D. 200, most likely from the Southwest, maize was added to existing horticultural systems, and, based on stable carbon isotope analysis of human skeletal series (Fig. 4.8), it remained a relatively minor crop for another six to seven centuries. During the three-century span from A.D. 800 to 1100, however, maize gained center stage, with much of the East witnessing a dramatic shift to maize-centered field agriculture. Subsequent to this transition, corn agriculture continued to play a major role in the economic base of Native peoples of the East up to and beyond the arrival of Europeans (see Chapter 5).

Over much of the interior riverine area outlined in Figure 4.7, and across the South Atlantic and Gulf Coastal plains, the shift to maize agriculture was accompanied by the development of socially ranked societies with fortified civic ceremonial centers. These centers had central plazas bordered by mounds supporting structures used by corporate groups as well as by the residences of high-ranking lineage members. Often lumped together under the general label of "Mississippian," these socially ranked, agricultural societies are accorded separate attention in the following chapter of this volume. The Woodland period (100 B.C. to A.D. 800) farming societies that preceded the Mississippian emergence will be considered in this chapter, along with a northern tier of maize-based societies dating after A.D. 800 that were non-Mississippian in character and spanned the Northeast and Great Lakes.

[15] Ibid. Active debate continues regarding the relative economic-dietary importance of these pre-maize crops prior to the A.D. 800 to 1100 shift to maize-centered agriculture. Characterizations of the Native peoples of 200 B.C. to A.D. 800 have ranged from affluent hunter-foragers who relied little on food crops, through small-scale garden plot cultivators, to farming societies with considerable reliance on food production.

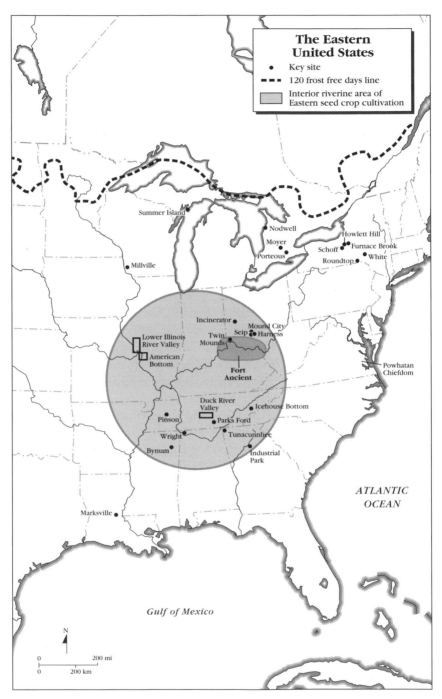

Figure 4.7. Map of the Eastern United States, showing the location of selected archaeological sites and research regions which are discussed in the text. Also shown is the 120 day frost-free line, which provides one measure of the northern limits of agriculture in eastern North America.

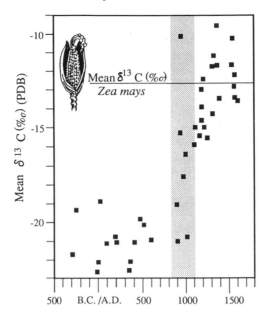

Figure 4.8. The shift to maize-centered agriculture in eastern North America, as reflected by changing mean delta (δ^{13}) C values of human bone collagen samples from sites in the region, from Smith 1989.

In association with the initial increase in the economic importance of premaize seed crops, the interior riverine area of the East witnessed, between about 200 B.C. and A.D. 400, the development and elaboration of a network of Hopewellian societies.[16] For well over a century Hopewellian ceremonial centers have been a focus of archaeological research and excavation, resulting in considerable information regarding their elaborate mortuary ceremonialism, long-distance acquisition and exchange of raw materials and exquisitely finished artifacts, and large-scale construction of geometrical earthworks and mounds.[17]

Survey and excavation of the river and stream valley landscapes surrounding Hopewellian ceremonial centers over the past two decades have provided comparable information regarding the domestic sphere of Hope-

[16] Derived from an archaeological site in south-central Ohio, the term "Hopewell" also serves as the general label for a group of related societies of this time period from the Ohio area, while the more inclusive term "Hopewellian" refers to a much larger and more widely dispersed set of societies sharing some aspects of material culture as the result of participation, to varying degrees, in long distance networks of exchange.

[17] William N. Morgan provides an excellent summary of the earthworks and mound construction of eastern North America in *Prehistoric Architecture in the Eastern United States* (Cambridge, 1980).

wellian societies, at least for some areas. Hopewellian farming societies
were not organized in terms of village settlements. Instead, household
units composed of nuclear or extended families were distributed along
stream and river valley corridors in series of small settlements, each consisting of one to perhaps three households. These small farmsteads are reflected archaeologically by a number of distinctive elements, including
small (5 to 80 square meters) circular to oval structures, "C"-shaped
windbreaks, shallow middens, and clusters of food storage and processing
pits (e.g., large storage pits, earth ovens, hearths, shallow pits, and
basins).[18]

The upper Duck River Valley in Tennessee (Fig. 4.9) exhibits a linear
pattern of small dispersed household settlements that is likely typical for
Hopewellian societies situated in smaller river valleys. In the higher order
drainage system of the Lower Illinois River Valley (Figs. 4.7, 4.10), the
tributary streams entering the valley from the east had a linear pattern of
small settlements similar to the upper Duck River, but the resource-rich
main valley possessed a much more complex pattern of settlements and
ceremonial centers. In addition to small (less than 2 hectares) settlements,
nine larger (more than 2 hectares) "village" settlements have been identified in the main valley of the Lower Illinois River. These formed "complexes" consisting of at least four, and perhaps more, spatially distinct
concentrations of mortuary mounds and permanent villages, all of which
were located on the floodplain (Fig. 4.10). Spaced fifteen to twenty kilometers apart, and associated with tributary streams entering the main
valley from the east, these spatially separated complexes may represent
culturally distinct social groupings within Hopewellian societies in the
region. Known largely through surface collections and often disturbed and
obscured by subsequent occupations, main valley "villages" may in fact
turn out to be settlements of more than three households that had
achieved a greater degree of social and spatial integration than had the
small farmsteads documented for other Hopewellian societies. Alternatively, these villages may represent the accumulated evidence of a large
number of small, short-term occupations that utilized the same location
over a period of several hundred years. The spatial compression of the
settlement pattern observed along smaller streams may have been facili-

---

[18] The Holding Site, located close to St. Louis, is the best described Hopewellian habitation site yet
excavated. Andrew C. Fortier, *The Holding Site: A Hopewell Community in the American Bottom*
(Urbana, Ill., 1989).

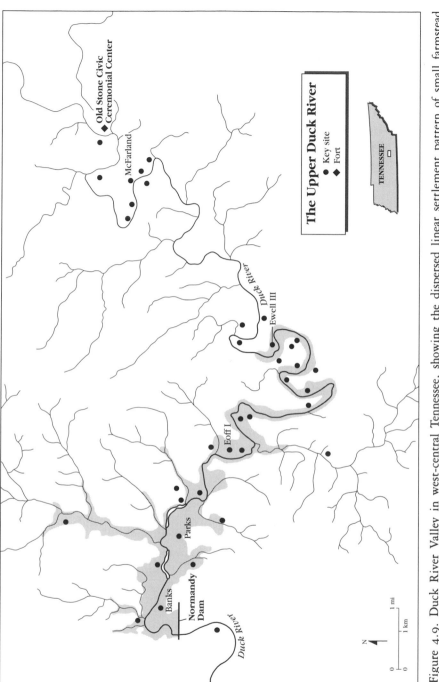

Figure 4.9. Duck River Valley in west-central Tennessee, showing the dispersed linear settlement pattern of small farmstead settlements typical of Hopewellian societies situated in smaller river valleys. (Bruce D. Smith, *Rivers of Change*, Smithsonian Institution Press, 1992, p. 218.)

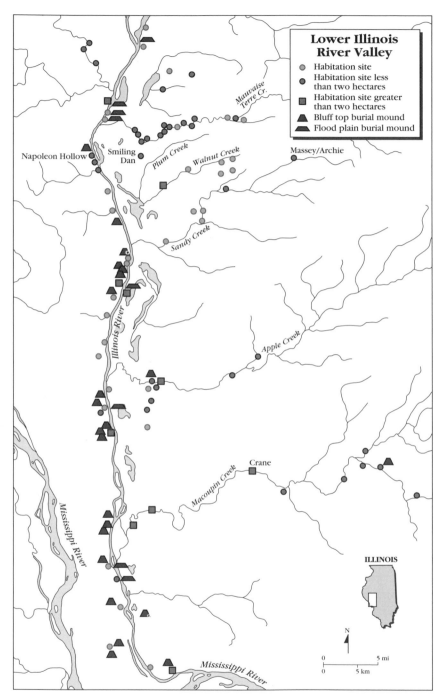

Figure 4.10. The map shows a linear pattern of small settlements in tributary stream valleys and larger habitation sites in the main corridor, with mortuary mound centers in four spatial clusters of culturally distinct social groupings. (Bruce D. Smith, *Rivers of Change*, Smithsonian Institution Press, 1992, p. 228.)

tated by rich, localized resource zones, especially by protein-rich flood-plain lakes and marshes.[19]

Hopewellian populations of different areas of the East were similar in the domestic sphere. For example, they had economies based on small seed crops and a wide range of seasonally abundant wild species of plants and animals, and similar patterns of household settlements. Yet Hopewellian populations exhibited considerable variation in the social and political sphere. Corporate group activities carried out by Hopewellian societies at locations spatially separated from habitation settlements centered in large part on mortuary activities – the rituals of processing, display, and interment of the dead, and the manufacturing of a rich variety of status objects for use in life and as grave goods. These corporate group mortuary programs are manifested in a variety of different ways, and reflect different levels of complexity in different areas of the East.

In the Lower Illinois Valley, for example (Fig. 4.10), the bluffs along the western edge of the valley are dotted with small earthen mounds that exhibit the relatively simple mortuary programs of nearby communities. These mounds cover central burial crypts containing important personages and their grave goods, as well as related individuals buried in close proximity to the crypts. Small mortuary camps near to these crypt-mound complexes served as staging areas for mortuary rituals. The larger, valley floor, loaf-shaped mounds appear to have involved similar, but more elaborate, mortuary activities of the area's Hopewellian societies.

In contrast to the Lower Illinois Valley, the mortuary programs of Hopewell societies in southern Ohio centered on large, conjoined charnel house structures, where the dead and their burial goods were processed, displayed, and interred. Like the bluff-top crypts of the Lower Illinois Valley, the charnel houses of Ohio Hopewell groups were covered by earthen mounds at the end of their use cycle. In addition to serving as charnel houses, these structures likely also played a broader role as "Big Houses," or centers of civic, ceremonial, and religious activities, in Hopewell societies. The considerable corporate labor investment reflected in such "Big House" mortuary structures carried over into the large, geometric earthworks that define ceremonial precincts surrounding many Ohio Hopewell charnel-house mortuary mounds. Organized on grid net-

---

[19] For a summary of Hopewellian farming economies and habitation settlements, see Bruce D. Smith, *Rivers of Change* (Washington, D.C., 1992).

Figure 4.11. Hopewellian earthwork and artifacts. a. The Turner Earthworks of south-central Ohio; b. Peregrine falcon embossed on copper; c. Cutout copper plate designs; d. Copper earspools; e. Sheet copper over cane "panpipe;" f. Engraved stone tablet; g. Engraving on human femur and unrolled design; h. Painted ceramic male figurine; i–k, Platform pipes: plain, roseate spoonbill, and hawk designs; l–n, Hopewell ceramics; o. Obsidian ceremonial spear; p. Conch shell cup; q. Mica cutout of raptor claw. Scale 5cm. (From *The Handbook of North American Indians*, volume 15, Smithsonian Institution Press, 1978.)

works, employing standard units of measurement, and taking a variety of forms, including circles, octagons, squares, and parallel banks, both alone and in combinations, the massive geometric earthworks of the Hopewell area of south-central Ohio embodied considerable engineering and organizational skills in their planning and construction. The locations, orientations, and forms of the massive earthen walls of these often conjoined geometric earthworks demarcated, in both a literal and symbolic fashion, the sacred central precincts of Hopewell societies from the dispersed, small settlement reality of everyday life. These constructions also reflected religious beliefs that we can only poorly understand. In marking the separation between the sacred and the secular, between the corporate ceremonial spheres and the domestic sphere, between death and life, these earthworks also seem to enclose, both symbolically and literally, the manufacture, display, and disposal of artifacts that for over a century have convincingly established the high reputation of Hopewellian artisans.[20]

Working in a wide range of mediums, including textiles, metals, shell, wood, ceramics, and stone, with raw materials often acquired from vast distances, Hopewellian artisans created objects of great beauty (Fig. 4.11). Obsidian was obtained from Yellowstone Park in Wyoming, meteoric iron from Kansas, mica from North Carolina, whelk shell from the Gulf of Mexico, native copper from around the Upper Great Lakes, and silver from northeastern Ontario. The exquisite objects manufactured from such nonlocal materials include copper ear spools, breast plates, and pan pipes; mica mirrors and figurative cutouts; stone platform pipes, discs, and tablets; distinctive ceramic vessels and figurines. These, with a few exceptions, have been found in charnel house, crypt, and burial contexts. They are only rarely recovered from habitation areas. Similarly, there is growing evidence that these objects were manufactured in workshops within or adjacent to ceremonial precincts. If such objects and their visual symbolic messages were created and eventually buried within ceremonial precincts, it may be that the overt manifestation of rich symbolism reflected in elaborately structured, abstract, and representational Hopewellian design motifs, including human hands, raptorial birds, and other animals, was restricted to the corporate ceremonial sphere.

The movement of raw materials and finished artifacts across the cultural landscape of the East shows that there was clear, if sporadic,

---

[20] James A. Brown, "Charnel Houses and Mortuary Crypts," in David Brose and N'omi Greber, eds., *Hopewell Archaeology* (Kent, 1979).

communication and contact over a broad area among societies of the Hopewellian time period. Hopewellian materials have been recovered from burial contexts as far south as Louisiana, southern Mississippi, Georgia, and Florida. Although this wide geographical distribution of distinctive Hopewellian artifact types and design motifs among societies that shared a similar emphasis upon elaboration of mortuary programs within ceremonial centers implies some generally shared elements of mythology and world view, Hopewellian period societies of different areas also exhibited considerable variation in artifact assemblages and mortuary programs.

The 160 hectare Pinson Mounds site, situated in west Tennessee, was the largest Middle Woodland period mound center in eastern North America. Its twelve mounds and geometrical earthworks contained more than 100,000 cubic meters of fill. The Pinson Mounds site shares the geometrical earthworks, crypt interment, crematory basins, and specialized workshops of Ohio and Illinois Hopewellian mortuary centers, but its material culture is quite distinctive, and other ceremonial elements have parallels to the south.[21] Like the McRae Mound in southern Mississippi, which yielded an Ohio-Hopewell—style copper pan pipe, one burial mound at Pinson exhibited layers of colored sand. Flat-topped mounds of unknown function have been documented both at Pinson and other contemporary sites in northern Mississippi. Pinson, along with Copena, Marksville, and many other societies between 200 B.C. and A.D. 400, participated to varying degrees in an interregional exchange of objects and ideas that covered much of eastern North America. Yet it also developed rich and distinctive local manifestations of corporate group integration in terms of its ceremonial centers, group labor projects, and elaborate mortuary programs.

The economic base of many of the southern tier of societies of the Hopewellian period, including Pinson, the Copena groups of the Tennessee Valley, Tunnacunnee, and those of the Gulf coastal plain, such as Marksville, has yet to be adequately documented. It is certainly possible that they will turn out not to have relied strongly, if at all, on indigenous seed crops. If this proves to be the case, eastern North America will provide an interesting example of chronologically contemporary societies, located in different areas and with considerable variation in their reliance

---

[21] Robert C. Mainfort, Jr., *Pinson Mounds,* Tennessee Department of Conservation, Division of Archaeology Research, Series no. 7 (1986).

on food production, following generally similar developmental lines toward stronger corporate group integration.

A variety of Plains Woodland occupations is recognized for the period between about 100 B.C. to A.D. 900 and extending from Oklahoma to Colorado and Texas. Plains Woodland sites are seen as having developed in response, either direct or indirect, to Woodland groups of the East and Midwest. Plains Woodland sites are generally characterized by the presence of cord-marked, grit-tempered pottery in elongated forms with conical bases, corner-notched dart or arrow points, shell disk beads, and burial in mounds or ossuaries. In the Kansas City area, centering around the junction of the Kansas and Missouri Rivers, sites of three to four hectares with storage pits and concentrated refuse deposits occur, with nearby stone chambered, earth-covered burial mounds. These sites have yielded rocker-marked and zone-decorated pottery, and objects of native copper and obsidian, suggesting trade and cultural interactions with Hopewellian communities to the east. Although grinding stones and other tools that may be associated with agricultural activities, such as stone hoes, are also found in Plains Woodland sites, there is no direct indication that the Plains Woodland groups relied on agriculture. Woodland influences in the eastern Plains did not extend to the northwestern Plains, where economies based on gathering, hunting, and communal bison driving continued (see Chapter 3).

LATE WOODLAND FARMERS OF THE EAST, A.D. 400–800

In the Midwest the term "Late Woodland" is often applied to the period from A.D. 400 to 800 that links the preceding Hopewellian societies and the subsequent (A.D. 800–1100) emergence of maize-centered agricultural societies in the East. While an understanding of this four-hundred-year period is of considerable importance, because it constituted a developmental prelude to the subsequent shift to maize-based societies, it is also important in its own right, since it encompassed dramatic changes on the cultural landscape. Because Late Woodland societies are much less visible archaeologically than those that came before or after, the importance of this critical period has long been overlooked, and scholars are only beginning to develop appropriate perspectives for illuminating it. To a considerable degree, this relative loss of visibility during the Late Woodland is due to a reduced presence of archaeological evidence associated with group ceremonial activities and a rather uniform blandness in the domestic life of these societies.

By about A.D. 400, the high level of corporate group integration characteristic of the Hopewellian period had largely disappeared across the East. While small-scale mortuary programs, as evidenced by burial mounds, continued to serve as vehicles of societal interaction and integration during the Late Woodland period, the size and apparent influence of the corporate-ceremonial sphere of societies was significantly reduced. Mortuary activities became more simplified and were dispersed more widely on the landscape. Large-scale, corporate labor efforts in the construction and maintenance of earthworks and mortuary structures almost ceased. Long-distance trade in rare raw materials was substantially reduced. This loss of visibility of the corporate aspects of society and the reduction in the role of ceremonial centers on the cultural landscape marked a significant shift in cultural organization.[22] The Hopewellian pattern of societies, strongly centered on mortuary rituals and their associated symbol systems, was replaced by a more unbounded kinship network of interaction between household units. Populations were still broadly dispersed in individual households or household clusters along the river and stream valleys, but cultural boundaries became more blurred and the concept of distinct "societies" less applicable.

This more uniform, less centered, and less partitioned interaction within the domestic sphere, accompanied by the fading of discrete societal centers and boundaries, was reflected in material culture assemblages that largely lacked decoration and exhibited a sameness over broad areas and several centuries. The bland uniformity of material culture and the loss of elaborate mortuary programs during the Late Woodland make these societies rather uninteresting from an aesthetic perspective. But the shift toward broad and balanced networks of more stable, multiple, interlocking social relationships in the domestic sphere also involved a number of significant social, technological, and economic readjustments. The bow and arrow was introduced into the East, making it easier to hunt deer and other large wild animals. Thinner-walled, better-tempered, more thermally efficient cooking vessels of globular form were developed in concert with a growing reliance on seed crops. The size of territories over which resources were obtained

---

[22] David Braun, "The Social and Technological Roots of "Late Woodland," in Richard Yerkes, ed., *Interpretations of Cultural Change in the Eastern Woodland during the Late Woodland Period*, Occasional Papers in Anthropology 3, Department of Anthropology, Ohio State University (1988).

was reduced, at least in some resource-rich areas, and settlements and locales were occupied for longer periods of time. Increases in the number of known settlements suggest population growth and the filling up of the landscape, perhaps as a result of increased fecundity resulting from shorter birth intervals.

The size of settlements of these farming societies also apparently increased somewhat across large areas of the East during this four-century span;[23] typical settlements were clusters of up to four households that rarely exhibit much internal organization. Larger, more organized farming villages did exist in some areas. Bluff-edge settlements, surrounded by ditches and containing ten or more households, have been recorded in central Ohio (the Waterplant site) and along the middle Ohio Valley by A.D. 600.[24]

NORTHERN AND PLAINS MAIZE FARMERS, A.D. 800–1500

Although the tropical cultigen maize had been introduced into the East by A.D. 200, it was not until after A.D. 800 that it began to dominate food production in the region. Eventually it became established in a broad area stretching from southern Ontario to northern Florida. The adoption of maize-based agriculture was particularly dramatic across a northern latitude zone encompassing the northeastern United States and Great Lakes regions, and extending south into the Fort Ancient area of the Middle Ohio River Valley (Fig. 4.7). Although societies along the southern margin of this northern zone had farming economies based on eastern seed crops prior to A.D. 800, it was the appearance, before A.D. 900, of a variety of maize that required only a short growing season that opened up the Northeast and Great Lakes areas to food-producing economies and fueled a rich and diverse mosaic of cultural development lasting seven centuries.

Usually called northern flint or eastern eight-row, this new, likely locally evolved, race of corn was apparently frost and drought resistant. It was also well adapted to the short summer nights and short growing season of the northern latitudes. While corn spread rapidly and widely

---

[23] Bruce D. Smith, "From Dalton to DeSoto," in Fred Wendorf and Angela Close, eds., *Advances in World Archaeology* 5 (1986).

[24] William S. Dancey, "Village Origins in Central Ohio," in Mark Seeman, ed., *Cultural Variability in Context* (Kent, 1991).

northward over the next several centuries toward the 120-day growing season limit of maize cultivation (Fig. 4.7), other North American and tropical food crops, including sunflower, squash, and beans, were included more slowly and varied more in their relative importance among northern maize farmers.

This rapid shift to maize-centered farming may have been facilitated by two different forms of economic preadaptation. In areas where premaize food-producing economies were already established, such as the Middle Ohio River Valley, maize simply took over the carbohydrate dietary role, replacing the indigenous starchy seed crop mainstays (maygrass and chenopodium), which disappeared after A.D. 1000. Farther north, where farming preadaptations were less well, or not at all, established, preadaptation based on a seasonal scheduling cycle existed in many regions. Spring-summer macroband fishing camps were often located in proximity to good agricultural lands throughout the growing season.

This transition to maize was neither uniform nor universal across the northern latitudes. Different regions witnessed distinctive developmental trends as maize farming was adopted in different ways and to varying degrees between A.D. 1000 and 1500. There was considerable local variation in both economic and socio-political organization. In the western Great Lakes region, for example, the term "Oneota" is used as a general label for societies of this five-century span that exhibited a considerable range of variation in social structure, social complexity, level of reliance on agriculture, and the nature of the habitat zones they occupied. Those Oneota societies having a clear reliance on agricultural crops were distributed in several distinct habitat areas across what is now southern Wisconsin and Minnesota, and parts of Illinois and Iowa. Sometimes fortified, agricultural Oneota villages were perhaps occupied by as many as seventy to ninety people. Judging from the extent and depth of their midden deposits, these villages were larger and occupied over longer periods of time than were their pre–A.D. 1000 antecedents. These permanent agricultural villages were clustered along lake shores, major waterways, and associated wetlands – habitat settings that combined abundant wild species of plants and animals with productive agricultural soils. The specific locations of Oneota villages and of their associated fields may have been selected because of micro-climatic considerations, such as the reduced occurrence of frost on the borders of wetland. Other strategies for dealing with the climatic challenges of growing corn in northern climates, such as preparing ridged fields and mounding the soil, are abundantly evident in Oneota areas.

In particularly ideal environmental settings, such as the Center Creek and Willow Creek localities along the Blue Earth River in southern Minnesota, high densities of Oneota settlements have been recorded, some of which were occupied by from 50 to perhaps as many as two hundred individuals. Excavation of the Vosburg site,[25] one of the forty Oneota sites of the Center Creek locality that was occupied on a number of occasions between A.D. 1000 and 1500, provided evidence of strong reliance on the hunting of large ungulates (bison, elk, and deer) as well as of smaller wetland species (raccoon, muskrat, and beaver). In addition, scapula hoes, numerous bell-shaped storage pits, and the remains of corn, beans, and sunflowers attest to the importance of agriculture in the economy.

Against a background of clear developmental continuity with preceding cultures in the region, the emergence of Oneota and the shift to settled farming villages and maize agriculture was accompanied by changes in material culture that reflected contact and interaction with Mississippian societies to the south (see Chapter 5). Archaeologists actively continue to debate the nature and extent of the influence that Mississippian societies had on cultural development in the Oneota area.

The term Plains Village refers to a series of related cultural manifestations, dating from A.D. 900 to 1850, that are represented by sedentary settlements reflecting a more stable agricultural economy than that of the early Plains Woodland groups. Plains Village sites, scattered along permanent streams of the Central Plains from the Dakotas to Texas, share a number of general features. These include multifamily lodge dwellings, pottery which varies regionally, bone hoes often made from a bison scapula, and small, triangular arrow points. Although the process by which corn was transmitted across the Plains is not known, a productive, eight-rowed variety appears in Plains Village sites along with sunflower, bottle gourd, and beans that are probably of eastern origin.

The Central Plains tradition of the Plains Village pattern is represented by the Upper Republican, Loup River, St. Helena, and Nebraska phases. These are considered generally ancestral to the Pawnees. A Dismal River culture variant to the west has been interpreted as being ancestral to the Plains Apaches. Central Plains tradition villages are small and consist of houses that

[25] Clark A. Dobbs and O. C. Shane III, "Oneota Settlement Patterns in the Blue Earth River Valley," in G. E. Gibbon, ed., *Oneota Studies,* University of Minnesota, Publications in Anthropology, no. 1 (1982).

are square or rectangular with rounded corners. Pottery is cord-roughened or plain-surfaced, and some of it is shell-tempered. In the Dakotas, the Middle Missouri tradition, which incorporates a number of temporal phases, developed into the Mandan, Hidatsa, and Arikara peoples. Middle Missouri settlements tend to be larger than those of the Central Plains tradition. Houses were semi-subterranean, rectangular, and large; some cover more than ninety square meters. Pottery was universally grit-tempered.

On the southern Plains, the Wichitas can be traced back from the Great Bend and Norteño complexes to the Panhandle, Custer, and Washita River phases. House forms for all these were rectangular, and pottery was both cord-roughened and plain, with more varied forms of pottery occurring later in time. Bison scapula hoes, digging sticks with bone tips, and hoes made of bison horn cores increase in frequency through time, suggesting greater reliance on agriculture.

In the Fort Ancient area of the Middle Ohio River Valley, the A.D. 1000 transition to maize farming was accompanied by a variety of changes in material culture and social organization. Many of the changes in material culture and technology were clearly influenced by the Mississippian societies of the Lower Ohio River Valley and beyond (see Chapter 5). Large jar-form ceramic vessels were tempered with shell, and often carried curvilinear, incised design motifs showing downstream influences. Triangular arrow points, stone discoidals used in the game of "chunky," and weeping eye motifs appear, as do other distinctive elements of Mississippian culture. Distributed along the terraces of the Ohio River and its tributaries, Fort Ancient agricultural villages are numerous between A.D. 1000 and 1200. Larger in size than preceding Late Woodland villages (such as the Waterplant site), early Fort Ancient villages also exhibited more complex internal organization. As is the case in Iroquoian areas to the north and east, such villages provide valuable insights regarding the organization of their respective societies. The Fort Ancient communities were often surrounded by a stockade wall, and had shallow, irregular storage-trash pits, burials, and rectangular, single-family house structures arranged around central open areas or plazas. Burial mounds were often associated with these fortified farming villages. Both village and mound burials contained few grave goods, and burial populations exhibited little evidence of status differentiation.[26]

---

[26] C. Wesley Cowan, *First Farmers of the Middle Ohio River Valley*, Cincinnati Museum of Natural History (1987).

Large-scale excavation at the Incinerator site, a small eleventh-century Fort Ancient village occupied for perhaps only twenty-five years, offered a rare opportunity to analyze the internal community organization and integration of individual household units in Fort Ancient society. Dominated by a centrally located post complex, the large plaza of the village was in turn bounded by concentric rings of burials, storage and trash pits, wattle and daub houses with thatch roofs, and surrounding stockade lines. Fourteen structures were exposed during the excavation of approximately half the habitation zone, suggesting a village of perhaps twenty to thirty households and 150 to 200 people. Discrete clusters of structures, each consisting of three to four households (perhaps representing lineage segments), were identified. The distribution and disposal of distinctive ceramics within each cluster suggest that these were matrilocal residential areas. Based on their size, differentiation, material culture contents, and placement within a "sacred area" defined by the arcs of solstice alignment with the plaza's central post, two structures on the west side of the plaza were identified as community structures, probably used for assemblies and councils and as repositories for ritual paraphernalia.[27]

If these interpretations of the Incinerator site are correct, some, and perhaps many, stockaded Fort Ancient farming communities were comprised of individual households, organized in matrilineage segment clusters that were distributed around plazas with central posts, and integrated through community-level ceremonies and structures situated within a solstice arc area. That such ceremonies of community integration were in turn centered on the growing season, maize, and perhaps the green corn ceremony, still practiced in recent times, is suggested by the placement of an internal post and hearth in one of the ceremonial structures at the Incinerator site. These two features were in sunrise alignment with the plaza's central post on two days each year – April 24, the current date of earliest safe frost-free planting, and August 20, when corn that took 120 days to come to maturity would be "green."

The characteristic central-plaza community pattern of fortified Fort Ancient settlements continued into the fifteenth century, but progressively fewer villages are documented after A.D. 1200. This may reflect

---

[27] James M. Heilman, Malinda C. Lileas, and Christopher A. Turnbow, *A History of 17 Years of Excavation and Reconstruction – A Chronicle of 12th Century Human Values and the Built Environment*, The Dayton Museum of Natural History (1988); and James A. Robertson, "Chipped Stone and Functional Interpretations: A Fort Ancient Example," *Midwest Journal of Archaeology* 9 (1984).

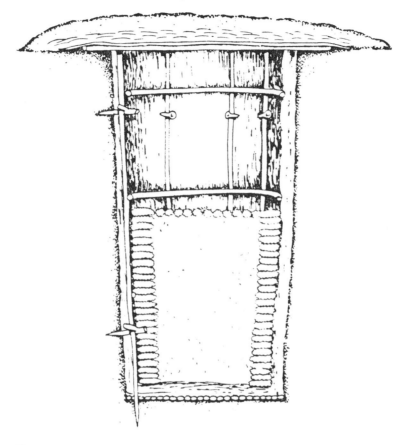

Figure 4.12. Cross-section diagram of a Fort Ancient storage pit. Capable of holding 30 to 40 bushels of shelled and stacked corn, these below-ground silos were lined with grass and animal skins. (From *First Farmers of the Middle Ohio Valley,* by C. Wesley Cowan, Cincinnati Museum of Natural History, 1987.)

either a population decline in the area, or an amalgamation of smaller, dispersed settlements to form larger villages. Associated with this apparent reduction in the number of villages was the development, after A.D. 1200, of a very efficient and distinctive below-ground storage system for maize. Large grass-lined and capped cylindrical silos measuring one meter in diameter and one to two meters in depth were constructed within villages, and were capable of holding 1 to 1.5 cubic meters of maize kernels or stacked cobs (Fig. 4.12). By A.D. 1450, the community plan of earlier times is lacking in the few remaining large Fort Ancient villages so far identified along the middle Ohio River. Plazas with central posts are absent, and lineage segment clusters of single-family dwellings were replaced by large, multiple-family structures exhibiting no overall village organization. It is not yet clear if there was in fact a population decline through the fourteenth and fifteenth centuries, which would have paralleled the "empty quarter" demographic decline along the Lower Ohio and adjacent portions of the Mississippi Valley (see Chapter 5). On the other hand, the documented trends toward fewer, possibly larger, villages, the loss of internal community organization, and the transition to a longhouse dwelling pattern, exhibit strong developmental parallels with the Iroquoian region of the Northeast.

In the seventeenth and eighteenth centuries, the Iroquois confederacy of the Mohawk, Oneida, Onondaga, Cayuga, and Seneca peoples in what is now New York State played a dominant role in the history of the northeastern Woodlands (see Chapter 7). It is appropriate that the integrative metaphor of the longhouse was adopted to describe this linearly arranged league, with the Senecas and the Mohawks serving as the respective "keepers" of the western and eastern doors. The distinctive extended-family structure has a deep time depth and long historical continuity among the inhabitants of this region. The social organization of the longhouse strongly influenced political developments leading to the formation of the northern Iroquoian confederacies during the fifteenth and sixteenth centuries. In clear contrast to the Mississippi Valley and its tributaries, where small, single-family structures reflect the role of nuclear families as the basic economic units of society, multifamily socio-economic groups formed the communal basis of society among the northern Iroquoians and their Algonquian neighbors even prior to the addition of maize horticulture to existing hunting, fishing, and foraging economies. An oval structure with two hearths at the Summer Island site (A.D. 200), a seven by twelve meter "incipient long house" at the Porteous site (A.D. 825), and "oblong communal houses" at the White site (A.D. 800 to 1000) and the Roundtop site (A.D. 1070) all attest to the existence of a widespread and basic pattern of multiple-family, communal socio-economic units in this region prior to A.D. 1000. By A.D. 1100, distinctive longhouse structures were present across the northern Iroquoian area. At the stockaded Miller site (A.D. 1100), six longhouses ranging in size from fifteen to twenty meters were recorded, each having five hearths arranged down the middle of the structure (Fig. 4.13). Although excavations at numerous sites dating between A.D. 1200 and 1400

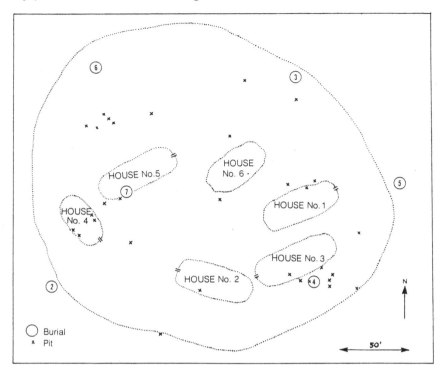

HOUSE No.5

HOUSE
No. 6 ·

HOUSE No. 1

HOUSE
No. 4

HOUSE No. 3

HOUSE No. 2

N

○ Burial
× Pit

50'

Figure 4.13. Settlement plan for the Miller site, showing the surrounding palisade wall and the outlines of houses, which are 15 to 20 meters long, the largest of which had five hearths down the center. (From Walter A. Kenyon, 1968, Royal Ontario Museum.)

document an apparent increase in maximum longhouse size (Nodwell 49 m, Furnace Brook 70 m, Moyer 102 m, Howlett Hill 111 m, Schoff 133 m) that reached a peak in the early fifteenth century before declining, the inherent structural and social form of longhouses remained constant, embodying the important principles of corporate group cooperation and longhouse kin group solidarity.[28] Iroquoian settlements were relocated at intervals of ten to thirty years as nearby soils and sources of firewood became exhausted. The new settlement was usually only a few kilometers from the old one.

The long-term (A.D. 1000 to 1500) continuity in the importance of extended-families and matrilineal clan segments as the basic building

[28] James A. Tuck, "Northern Iroquoian Prehistory," in Bruce Trigger, ed., *Handbook of North American Indians,* vol. 15, *Northeast* (Washington, D.C., 1978).

blocks of northern Iroquoian societies is paralleled by a similar long-term stability in the subsistence economies of the region. The mixed horticulture, hunting, fishing, and foraging of northern Iroquoian societies described at European contact has a developmental history that can be traced back to, and in some respects before, the initial introduction of maize into the region. As was the case throughout much of the East, the initial adoption of maize by societies in the northeastern Woodlands, while having profound effects on subsequent culture history, was largely an additive process. As across the East, maize farming was easily accommodated into preexisting hunting, fishing, foraging, and, in some areas, gardening economies. Long-established annual patterns of broad-based hunting and fishing continued to focus, up to European contact, on seasonally abundant and relatively low-cost, well-packaged species (combining high yield and seasonal abundance) as the major sources of protein to balance increasing dependence on maize diets. Across most of the East, the white-tailed deer (*Odocoileus virginianus*) was the most important single game animal and also the major source of skins for clothing. The fall to mid-winter individual stalking and group driving of this species by Iroquoian horticulturalists, so well documented historically, continued a seasonal hunting pattern that had existed for thousands of years. Similarly, warm season spearing, netting, and trapping of Great Lakes and riverine fish populations and the utilization of other seasonally abundant species, such as migratory waterfowl, represent long-established, if regionally variable, economic patterns.

Paradoxically, the archaeologically documented long-term dual continuity of kin solidarity and cooperation at the multifamily longhouse level, and of the annual economic cycle of farming, fishing, and hunting, seemingly both framed and fostered the major developmental trends of northern Iroquoian history over the five-century span between A.D. 1000 and 1500. As indicated archaeologically by a progressive increase in village size and numbers through time, this half-millennium period witnessed major demographic growth, likely fueled by the addition of significant maize farming after A.D. 1000 to preexisting economies. Correlated with the transition to maize farming and the expanding role of women as food producers was the shift, by A.D. 1100 to 1200, of village locations away from riverine and lake-edge settings to higher, more defensible positions. The pattern of intervillage alliance building, warfare, blood revenge, and prisoner sacrifice so well described by Europeans in the seventeenth century appears to have become well established in many areas by A.D. 1200 to 1300. This was associated with a dramatic increase in population and resource competition between dispersed villages. There was a related dramatic expansion of warm season warfare as an avenue for status building among Iroquoian warrior-hunters.

In a balancing response to escalating levels of intervillage hostility and blood revenge, a broad-scale pattern of village consolidation began, with defensive alliances drawing dispersed smaller villages together into larger, fortified settlements, some of which came to have over 1,500 inhabitants. As the clan segments of earlier villages consolidated within stockade walls, longhouses grew longer and an intravillage pattern of disparity in longhouse length developed between locally dominant and minor clans. The parallel trends of increasing village and longhouse size appear to reflect the expanding application of the structural principles of long house integration to form increasingly larger social units. While effectively reducing the threat of conflict and cycles of revenge within the ever lengthening "walls of the longhouse," this expansion of social boundaries carried with it an increased risk of small-scale conflicts escalating into higher level hostility among the larger social groups being formed. Helping to reduce this risk after A.D. 1300 to 1400, however, was an expansion of forested buffer zones between the merging larger societal groups, as allied villages coalesced into a series of distinct, spatially separated population clusters. At the close of the fifteenth century a series of distinct northern Iroquoian population clusters were well established around the Lower Great Lakes, setting the stage for the final development of the longhouse as the integrating concept that resulted in the Iroquois, Huron, and Neutral confederacies.

East and south of the Iroquoian area, along the Atlantic Coastal plain and piedmont regions, maize agriculture supplemented hunting, fishing, and gathering economies to varying degrees after A.D. 1000. As far south as southern Delaware, maize agriculture was apparently of only limited importance. More permanent houses and larger storage pits were built, but societies maintained seasonal patterns of movement between coastal and interior settlements.[29] Along the coastal plain of Maryland and Virginia, maize farming was more important, with permanent, sometimes fortified villages consisting of up to several dozen extended family dwellings appearing along major rivers after A.D. 1000 to 1100.[30] At

---

[29] Jay Custer, *Delaware Prehistoric Archaeology* (London, 1984).
[30] Dean Snow, "Late Prehistory of the East Coast," in Bruce Trigger, ed., *Handbook of North American Indians*, vol. 15, *Northeast* (Washington, D.C., 1978).

about the same time in the Virginia piedmont, settlements increased in size and shifted to large river systems, in proximity to high-yield agricultural soils, as groups paralleled downstream societies in adding maize farming to their economic base. Throughout this broad coastal plain and piedmont region, agricultural villages appear to have been relocated every ten to twenty years. They apparently were organized in small polities showing little evidence of strong social ranking or complex socio-political organization. Against this backdrop of relatively stable and small-scale political organization, the emergence of the Powhatan chiefdom was a very late development, quite likely largely occurring within the context of European contact.[31]

COMPARISONS AND DISCUSSION

Within both the eastern and western United States, Native peoples independently developed farming economies that supported complex and varied social systems. Neither the timing of developments nor their forms were much the same in the two areas, reflecting disparate origins and adaptations to markedly different environments. There were no impenetrable barriers to travel between the wooded river valleys of the East and the highlands and semideserts of the Southwest. The exchange and transfer of some items, such as the bow and arrow and, perhaps, maize, suggest that at least some form of indirect communication did occur between the two areas. Yet, the opportunity afforded by knowledge of what was available in other regions was not sufficient to cause either increased interaction or parallel trends of development.

In both the East and Southwest, the initial experimentation with crops occurred at about the same time, around 1500 B.C. The establishment and spread of a farming way of life, however, had primacy in the East. There farming was an independent development and not based on introduced crops. In the East, the early seed crops were marsh elder, lamb's quarter, sunflowers, and squash. The eastern crops seem to have become major dietary components by about the start of the Christian era. In the Southwest, the introduced tropical crops, corn, squash, and later beans, augmented a diet based on gathering wild plant foods and hunting. Although not enough human bone chemistry measurements are available for the Southwest, most investigators would suggest that a commitment to farm-

[31] Jeffrey Hantman, "Between Powhattan and Quirank," *American Anthropologist* 92 (1990).

ing comparable to that in the East occurred somewhat later, by about A.D. 500 to 700.

The similarity in timing of the initial domestication or adoption of agricultural crops suggests similarity in the underlying causes of the move to farming. These are likely to be found in post-Pleistocene, postglacial, climatic and vegetation changes that resulted in the stabilization of floodplain environments in the East and the expansion of deserts and woodlands that reduced grasslands and foraging areas for large game in the Southwest. At the same time, there had been successful filling-in of the landscape with human populations skilled at collecting and hunting locally available foods. It has been suggested that initial steps in agriculture may have slightly increased the amount of food available to store for use in winter and early spring, when supplies may have been low and no new crops were yet available.

The initial crops and the general farming strategies differed greatly between the two regions. In both regions, plant foods provided good sources of calories and dietary nutrients (compare Tables 4.1 and 4.2). In the East, these were derived from domestic plants. In the Southwest, in contrast, the most nutritious foods were from wild plants, whose growth was tolerated or encouraged in fields and around settlements. In the East, the domestication of native plants was itself a major technological innovation, but other innovations associated directly with farming were generally not necessary. The arid and unpredictable climate of the Southwest required additional technological innovations if agriculture were to become reliable. Irrigation may have been necessary and present in the lower deserts by the start of the Christian era. Irrigation canals in the Hohokam area were certainly in place by A.D. 200 to 300. Throughout the Southwest, wherever farming communities spread and local conditions required them, modifications were made to fields. Irrigation canals, diversion ditches, mulched gardens, terraced gardens, check dams, and reservoirs were not restricted to particular subcultural areas, but were constructed as appropriate to the landscape.

Throughout both the East and Southwest, the earliest farming settlements are better described as household or farmstead settlements, or hamlets, rather than villages. Those of the Hopewellian societies of the East supported a degree of labor investment in ceremonial centers far greater than anything manifested at a comparable period in the Southwest. Despite local variability in scale, the investment in earthworks, mounds, charnal houses, and in the production of elaborate goods, implies a degree of social differentiation that was attained in the Southwest only much later and more fleetingly.

We have noted that the Woodland period in the East and the Initiation period in the Southwest manifested considerable stylistic homogeneity over great distances. Yet the character of the stylistic homogeneity and its context were quite different. In the East, the distinctive Hopewellian artifact types and design motifs suggest, at some level, a shared iconography, shared values, and participation in a shared belief system. The distribution of exotic, finished items of trade reinforces this interpretation. The stylistic homogeneity and similarities in artifacts among the Initiation period settlements in the Southwest occur in connection with utilitarian, generally household, items. These similarities in style reflect a lack of social boundaries rather than participation in the same system of values and religious beliefs. There is also a lack of social differentiation of individuals reflected in the mortuary customs of the early southwestern farmers. Finally, in the Southwest of that time, there is nothing comparable to the scale of the Pinson Mounds site.

Whatever instigated the decline in the Hopewellian pattern and the change to a sameness and uniformity in material culture in the East, it occurred at a time (between A.D. 400 and 800) when the Southwest farming communities manifested subregional stylistic differences. These subregional styles perhaps indicate social or political boundaries for the first time. Not only are the decorative elements on ceramics distinctive within the various southwestern subregions, but items such as ball courts, cremation burials, and censers are restricted to the Hohokam area, suggesting that there was no belief system common throughout the Southwest. Only within the Hohokam tradition at this time is the elaboration of craft items at its height. There is a commonality between the East and Southwest at this time only in that in both areas, population seems to have increased, as did the size of individual settlements.

The period between about A.D. 1000 and 1200 is distinctive in both the East and Southwest, but there are some features of development which may be common to both regions. At a basic level, the beginning of this period in the East is marked by the transition to maize agriculture. The East and Southwest henceforth shared economic reliance on corn, beans, squash, and a diversity of wild plant foods and game. The ability of eastern flint corn to withstand short growing seasons was crucial to its adoption by an increasing number of societies, particularly those to the north of the old Hopewellian systems. In the East, then, farming experienced its greatest geographic expansion. In the Southwest, this was also the period during which farming was practiced over the broadest geographic area. The expanded southwestern distribution of maize at this time has been attributed to generally favorable climatic conditions for farming and the development and implementation, locally, of a variety of soil and water conservation practices.

The spread of maize farming in the East encouraged the formation of increased numbers of villages and increased internal organization in these villages. The fortified, stockaded Fort Ancient villages of Ohio contained both areas for sacred activities, such as solstice alignments and repositories for ritual paraphernalia, and areas for the daily domestic activities of households. This is in contrast to the previous Hopewellian pattern of large, sacred sites with mounds, earthworks, and charnal houses spatially separated from the dispersed domestic households.

In the Southwest at this time of differentiation and regional systems, sites were not overtly fortified. The regional systems of the Hohokam and the Chaco Anasazi incorporated public architecture within residential sites. Hohokam ball court communities were also centers of habitation. The town sites in Chaco Canyon were largely residential and were also located within an area densely populated with small villages. Many of the Chacoan outliers not only had a resident population but were associated with small villages or hamlets. Shared beliefs within the Hohokam region are evidenced by the ball courts themselves. The configuration of Chacoan town sites with their plazas, Great Kivas, and tower kivas is also an iconography of architectural forms indicating shared values and participation in a common belief system. Despite the impressive scale of both regional systems, which seems to compare favorably in extent with regional systems of the East, neither approached the size of some of the more complex Hopewellian networks. If one compares the longevity of regionally organized systems, Hopewell's four hundred years is twice that of the Hohokam or Chacoan systems at their height. On the other hand, Hopewell does not seem to have been as tightly integrated as either of the two southwestern systems. Furthermore, the southwestern systems, although not always as integrated as they were in the eleventh and twelfth centuries, in their entirety lasted far longer than did Hopewell.

Within the area of the East dominated by the Fort Ancient pattern, there was a decline, over time, in the number of villages that may have been due either to population loss or to the gradual aggregation of population into fewer but larger villages. Farther south, along the Lower Ohio, regional population decline is more apparent (see Chapter 5). In the Southwest, the changes in both the Hohokam and Chacoan areas that occurred at about A.D. 1200 suggest that mechanisms that had integrated the ball court and Chacoan outlier communities no longer operated, but neither area seems to have suffered immediate population decline. There were shifts in the distribution of population in both areas, and these seem to have been accompanied by aggregation into larger settlements. Regional abandonments did occur in the Southwest by A.D. 1300, but these are correlated with the formation of very large, aggregated settlements in adjacent locations.

The fourteenth and fifteenth centuries, before contact with European cultures, witnessed complex chiefdoms in the Mississippian East (see Chapter 5), the regionally organized system around Paquimé in Chihuahua, and some form of alliance network among the large villages of the ancient Pueblo homeland (Anasazi and Mogollon). By this time, patterns that would be identifiable as distinctively Iroquoian in the seventeenth and eighteenth centuries had developed in the Northeast. Within these systems there were elements that would become familiar to Europeans as indicative of particular ethnic or cultural groups. Thus, the "longhouse" as a structure has considerable time-depth in the Iroquoian area. Similarly, kivas are unambiguously identifiable features of late Anasazi Pueblo sites. Specific elements within each of these societies – iconographic motifs – are identifiable, and often continue to be meaningful to modern Native Americans. Yet, by the fourteenth and fifteenth centuries, some very large patterns were either disappearing or had already been lost. The particular belief system and settlement configuration that related to the Hohokam ball court, platform mound, and great house sites did not continue into the modern period. Similarly, the mounds and workshops of Paquimé itself, and its surrounding settlements, were part of a system that was truncated before Europeans entered the area.

Not only was there a lack of continuity in occupation in some areas between the period prior to the arrival of the Europeans and that which followed, but the integrative mechanisms that continued to be in operation at the time Europeans entered America were largely disrupted by the events of the contact period. The alliance structure that included katcina rituals and trade, which linked together the large, aggregated fourteenth-century pueblos, was not observed by Europeans. Similarly the rich complexity of Mississippian chiefdoms (see Chapter 5) also went unrecorded. The early European accounts of groups such as the Natchez people provide only a pale and partial reflection of the richly complex Mississippian societies that flourished prior to contact. Archaeology is a vital tool in providing knowledge about these systems today.

BIBLIOGRAPHIC ESSAY

General overviews of the archaeology of the Southwest and introductions to the extensive literature of primary and secondary sources relating to that area may be found in *Prehistory of the Southwest* by Linda S. Cordell (Orlando, Fla., 1984); the *Handbook of North American Indians,* vols. 9 and 10, *Southwest* (Washington, D.C., 1979, 1983) ed. Alfonso A. Ortiz; William D. Lipe's chapter, "The Southwest," in *Ancient Native Americans,* ed. Jesse D. Jennings (San Francisco, 1978); and *Dynamics of Southwest Prehistory,* ed. Linda S. Cordell and George J. Gumerman (Washington, D.C., 1989). Somewhat older, but still useful, is *Southwestern Archaeology* by John C. McGregor (Urbana, Ill., 1965) and volume 1 of *An Introduction to American Archaeology* by Gordon R. Willey (Englewood Cliffs, N.J., 1966). *An Introduction to the Study of Southwestern Archaeology* by Alfred V. Kidder (New Haven, Conn., 1924) was the first comprehensive summary of the archaeology of the Southwest and still provides an insightful perspective; the 1963 Yale University Press edition, with an introduction by Irving Rouse, is particularly useful.

In addition to these sources, good overviews of the Native peoples, languages, ethnic distributions, and the period immediately preceding contact with Europeans may be obtained from several chapters in *Columbian Consequences,* vol. 1, *Archaeological and Historical Perspectives on the Spanish Borderlands West,* ed. David Hurst Thomas (Washington, D.C., 1989); *The Frontier People: The Greater Southwest in the Protohistoric Period,* by Carroll L. Riley (Albuquerque, N.M., 1987); *American Indians of the Southwest,* by Bertha P. Dutton (Albuquerque, N.M., 1983); and *The Protohistoric Period in the North American Southwest, A.D. 1450–1700,* ed. David R. Wilcox and W. Bruce Massey (Arizona State University Anthropological Research Papers, No. 24, Tempe, Ariz., 1981). Excellent discussions of Southwest environments, climatic change, cultural adaptations, the adoption of agriculture, and farming strategies are given in *The Anasazi in a Changing Environment,* ed. George J. Gumerman (Cambridge, 1988); *Prehistoric Agricultural Strategies in the Southwest,* ed. Suzanne K.

Fish and Paul R. Fish (Arizona State University Anthropological Research Papers, No. 33, Tempe, Ariz., 1984); "Early Agriculture and Sedentism in the American Southwest: Evidence and Interpretations," by Wirt H. Wills in the *Journal of World Prehistory* 2 (1988); and, also by Wills, *Early Prehistoric Agriculture in the American Southwest* (Sante Fe, N.M., 1988).

Works that examine the minor or geographically peripheral cultural traditions of the Southwest are James H. Gunnerson's *The Fremont Culture: A Study in Culture Dynamics on the Northern Anasazi Frontier (including the Report of the Clafin-Emerson Expedition of the Peabody Museum)* (Papers of the Peabody Museum, Vol. 59, No. 2, Peabody Museum of Archaeology and Ethnology, Harvard University, Cambridge, Mass., 1969); Randall H. McGuire and Michael B. Schiffer, eds., *Hohokam and Patayan: Prehistory of Southwestern Arizona* (New York, 1982); and Harold S. Colton's *The Sinagua: A Summary of the Archaeology of the Region of Flagstaff, Arizona* (Museum of Northern Arizona, Bulletin 22, Flagstaff, Ariz., 1946).

Current discussions of the major regional traditions and regionally organized systems of the Southwest are provided for the Hohokam by Patricia L. Crown in "The Hohokam of the American Southwest," *Journal of World Prehistory* 4 (1990); McGuire and Schiffer's edited volume on the Hohokam and Patayan, listed above; David E. Doyel, ed., *The Hohokam Village: Site Structure and Organization* (Glenwood Springs, Colo., 1987); and Emil W. Haury in *The Hohokam, Desert Farmers and Craftsmen: Excavations at Snaketown, 1964–1965* (Tucson, Ariz., 1976). A concise introduction to the archaeology of Chaco Canyon and the San Juan Basin is given in "The Chaco Canyon Community," by Stephen H. Lekson, Thomas C. Windes, John R. Stein, and W. James Judge, which was published in *Scientific American* 256 (1988). More detailed examination of Chaco Canyon is given in *Chaco Canyon: Archaeology and Archaeologists,* by Robert H. Lister and Florence C. Lister (Albuquerque, N.M., 1981) and *The Chacoan Prehistory of the San Juan Basin,* by R. Gwinn Vivian (San Diego, Calif., 1990). The Northern San Juan, Mesa Verde Anasazi sites are described by Arthur H. Rohn in *Cultural Change and Continuity on Chapin Mesa* (Lawrence, Kan., 1977) and by Frederick W. Lange, Nancy Mahaney, Joe Ben Wheat, and Mark L. Chenault in *Yellow Jacket: A Four Corners Anasazi Ceremonial Center* (Boulder, Colo., 1986). The Mimbres branch of the Mogollon tradition is described by J. J. Brody in *Mimbres Painted Pottery* (Albuquerque, N.M., 1977) and Steven A. LeBlanc in *The Mimbres People: Ancient Pueblo Painters of the American Southwest* (London, 1983). The regionally organized system that developed around Casas Grandes is described in

Casas Grandes: A Fallen Trading Center of the Gran Chichimeca, vols. 1–3, by Charles C. Di Peso (Dragon, Arizona Amerind Foundation Series 9, 1974).

Important discussions of how the complex institutions and regional systems of alliances of the Southwest may have developed are found in *Ripples in the Chichimec Sea: New Considerations of Southwestern-Mesoamerican Interactions,* ed. Frances Joan Mathien and Randall H. McGuire (Carbondale, Ill., 1986); Steven Plog, *Stylistic Variation in Prehistoric Ceramics: Design Analysis in the American Southwest* (Cambridge, 1980); and *The Sociopolitical Structure of Prehistoric Southwestern Societies,* ed. Steadman Upham, Kent G. Lightfoot, and Roberta A. Jewett (Boulder, Colo., 1989), as well as in chapters in the Cordell and Gumerman edited volume and in Vivian's book on Chaco.

A number of general archaeological summary volumes of North America provide coverage of the Eastern Woodlands, including Jesse D. Jennings's *Prehistory of North America* (3rd ed., Mountain View, Calif., 1989), and Jennings's, ed., *Ancient Native Americans* (San Francisco, 1978), as well as *An Introduction to American Archaeology* (Englewood Cliffs, N.J., 1966), by Gordon R. Willey. In addition, a number of excellent recent summaries have been produced that encompass portions of the East: Bruce D. Smith, "The Archaeology of the Southeastern United States: From Dalton to DeSoto," in Fred Wendorf and Angela Close, eds., *Advances in World Archaeology,* vol. 5, (Orlando, Fla., 1986); Dean Snow, *The Archaeology of New England* (New York, 1982); Jon Muller, *Archaeology of the Lower Ohio River Valley,* (Orlando, Fla., 1986); John A. Walthall, *Prehistoric Indians of the Southeast* (Tuscaloosa, Ala., 1980); Dan F. Morse and Phyllis A. Morse, *Archaeology of the Central Mississippi Valley* (New York, 1983); Robert W. Neuman, *An Introduction to Louisiana Archaeology* (Baton Rouge, La., 1984); Robert E. Fitting, *The Archaeology of Michigan* (New York, 1980); William Green, James B. Stoltman, and Alice Kehoe, eds., *Introduction to Wisconsin Archaeology,* Wisconsin Archaeologist 67 (3–4) (1986); Carl H. Chapman, *The Archaeology of Missouri* (Columbia, Mo., 1975); Mark Mathis and Jeffrey Crow, *The Prehistory of North Carolina* (Raleigh, N.C., 1983); Jay Custer, *Delaware Prehistoric Archaeology* (Newark, N.J., 1984); William A. Ritchie, *The Archaeology of New York State* (Garden City, N.Y., 1965); William A. Haviland and Marjory W. Power, *The Original Vermonters: Native Inhabitants, Past and Present* (Hanover, N.H., 1981); and Ronald J. Mason, *Great Lakes Archaeology* (New York, 1981). In addition, Bruce G. Trigger, ed., *Handbook of North American*

Indians, vol. 15, *Northeast* (Washington, D.C., 1978) contains several good chapters on the archaeology of the region.

A number of recent edited volumes and summary articles provide descriptions of farming economies in the East, including William Keegan, *Emergent Horticultural Economies of the Eastern Woodlands* (Carbondale, Ill., 1987); Gayle Fritz, "Multiple Pathways to Farming in Precontact Eastern North America," in Fred Wendorf and Angela Close, eds., *Journal of World Prehistory* 5 (1991); James B. Stoltman and David Baerreis, "The Evolution of Human Ecosystems in the Eastern United States," in H. E. Wright, Jr., ed., *Late-Quaternary Environments of the United States,* vol. 2 (Minneapolis, 1983); Patty Jo Watson, "Early Plant Cultivation in the Eastern Woodlands of North America," in David Harris and Gordon Hillman, eds., *Foraging and Farming* (London, 1989); and Bruce D. Smith, "The Origins of Agriculture in Eastern North America," *Science* 246 (1989), 1566–71.

The best single source of Hopewellian societies remains *Hopewell Archaeology* (Kent, 1979), ed. David S. Brose and N'omi Greber. *The Hopewell Site* (Boulder, Colo., 1989) by N'omi Greber and Katherine C. Ruhl is a recent reanalysis of the Hopewell site, an important Hopewell corporate ceremonial center. In his report *The Holding Site* (Urbana, Ill., 1989), Andrew Fortier provides a detailed analysis of a small Hopewellian habitation settlement. For Hopewellian subsistence and settlement patterns, see Bruce D. Smith, *Rivers of Change* (Washington, D.C., 1992).

The Plains Village traditions were defined by Donald J. Lehmer in "The Sedentary Horizon of the Northern Plains," *Journal of Southwestern Anthropology* 10 (1954). An excellent recent discussion of the economy of these traditions is given in John O'Shea, "The Role of Wild Resources in Small-scale Agricultural Systems: Tales from the Lakes and Plains," in *Bad Year Economics, Cultural Responses to Risk and Uncertainty,* ed. Paul Halstead and John O'Shea (Cambridge, 1989). Richard I. Ford discusses the history of crops and agriculture on the Plains in two chapters, "The Processes of Plant Food Production in Prehistoric North America," and "Patterns of Food Production in North America," in *Prehistoric Food Production in North America,* ed. Richard I. Ford (Anthropological Papers of the Museum of Anthropology, University of Michigan, No. 75, Ann Arbor, 1985).

For information on the Plains Woodland, see Alfred E. Johnson and Ann S. Johnson, "K-Means and Temporal Variability in Kansas City Hopewell Ceramics," *American Antiquity* 40 (1975); J. M. Shippee "Archaeological Remains in the Area of Kansas City: The Woodland Period,

Early, Middle, and Late," *Missouri Archaeological Society, Research Series* 5 (1967); L. J. Roedl and J. H. Howard, "Archaeological Investigations at the Renner Site," *Missouri Archaeologist* 19 (1957); Waldo R. Wedel, "The Prehistoric Plains," in *Ancient Native Americans,* ed. Jesse D. Jennings (San Francisco, 1978); and Susan C. Vehik, "The Woodland Occupations," in *Prehistory of Oklahoma,* ed. Robert E. Bell (New York, 1984).

With the exception of the short booklet by C. W. Cowan, *First Farmers of the Middle Ohio River Valley* (Cincinnati, Ohio, 1987), no overview of Fort Ancient societies has been published since the classic *Fort Ancient Aspect* (Ann Arbor, Mich., 1943), by James B. Griffin. Several good descriptions of Fort Ancient settlements are available, however, including David Brose "The Archaeological Investigation of a Fort Ancient Community near Ohio Brush Creek, Adams County, Ohio," *Kirtlandia* 34 (1982), and James M. Heilman, Malinda C. Lileas, and Christopher A. Turnbow, *A History of 17 Years of Excavation and Reconstruction – A Chronicle of 12th Century Human Values and the Built Environment* (Dayton [Ohio] Museum of Natural History, 1988). The economic basis of Fort Ancient populations is detailed in Gail Wagner, "The Corn and Cultivated Beans of the Fort Ancient Indians," *Missouri Archaeologist* 47 (1986).

Oneota societies are discussed by James Stoltman in "Ancient People of the Upper Mississippi Valley,' in *Historic Lifestyles in the Upper Mississippi River Valley,* ed. J. Wozniak (New York, 1983), and in two edited volumes: G. E. Gibbon, ed., *Oneota Studies* (Minneapolis, 1982), and Gibbon, "The Mississippian Tradition: Oneota Culture," in *Introduction to Wisconsin Archaeology, Wisconsin Archaeologist* 67 (1986).

Discussion of Iroquoian prehistory can be found in James V. Wright, *The Ontario Iroquois Tradition* (Ottawa, 1966); William A. Ritchie and R. E. Funk, *Aboriginal Settlement Patterns in the Northeast* (Albany, N.Y. 1973); Christine F. Dodd, *Ontario Iroquois Tradition Longhouses* (Ottawa, 1984); Gary Warrick, *Reconstructing Ontario Iroquoian Village Organization* (Ottawa, 1984); James A. Tuck, *Onondaga Iroquois Prehistory: A Study in Settlement Archaeology* (Syracuse, N.Y., 1971); William D. Finlayson, *The 1975 and 1978 Rescue Excavations at the Draper Site: Introduction and Settlement Patterns* (Ottawa, 1985); and Dean Snow, *The Iroquois* (Oxford, 1994). Snow argues that the Iroquoians migrated north from Pennsylvania at the end of the Middle Woodland period.

5

AGRICULTURAL CHIEFDOMS OF THE EASTERN WOODLANDS

Bruce D. Smith

The long and complex history of the eastern United States prior to European contact has often been viewed as being largely peripheral to, and derivative from, cultural developments in Mesoamerica. This tendency to look south of the border has been particularly pronounced in attempts to account for the agricultural chiefdoms that emerged around A.D. 1000, and flourished across much of the eastern United States right up to the arrival of Europeans. These were the largest and most hierarchical indigenous societies to develop north of Mexico. At first glance, a proposed derivation of the principal features of these agricultural chiefdoms from Mesoamerica does not seem unreasonable. There are obvious, if only general, parallels in public architecture, iconography, socio-political organization, and economy.

The Mississippian chiefdoms of the East constructed flat-topped, rectangular mounds, sometimes of considerable size, arranged around open plazas. Such mound-plaza areas were the central focus of fortified civic-ceremonial centers that often had a sizable resident population. In addition, Mississippian societies were markedly hierarchical. Their constituent kin units or clans were ranked, with political and religious power and authority maintained, through inheritance, in the highest ranking clans. Elaborate iconographic systems developed in Mississippian chiefdoms, reflecting and supporting both their hierarchical structure and their larger worldview. Some of the elements of these iconographic systems (e.g., snakes, raptorial birds, costumed dancers, trophy heads) have vaguely Mesoamerican parallels encouraging a search for connections south of the border. The important role of two Mesoamerican crop plants – maize (*Zea mays*) and beans (*Phaseolus vulgaris*) – in the agricultural economy of Mississippian societies also suggests Mesoamerican connections, with the shift to maize-centered agriculture in eastern North America between A.D. 800 and 1000 corresponding to the initial emergence of Mississippian chiefdoms.

With the exception of maize-centered agriculture, which formed the economic base of societies over much of eastern as well as southwestern North America after A.D. 1000 (see Chapter 4), the characteristics of Mississippian societies briefly outlined above (monumental architecture, hierarchical socio-political structure, complex icongraphy) serve to distinguish these groups from other Native societies of North America. But, while Mississippian chiefdoms are distinctively different from other maize-centered agricultural societies of North America, and in ways that encourage comparisons with Mesoamerica, their initial emergence and subsequent florescence were entirely independent of any influence from south of the border. The rapid episode of social transformation that marked the initial development of Mississippian societies over a broad area of the East between A.D. 800 and 1000 is not yet fully documented, but it is well enough understood to confirm its indigenous nature. There are numerous clear continuities with earlier cultures in the region. Maize certainly played an important role in the initial appearance and subsequent history of Mississippian chiefdoms, in that it offered a new vehicle for social and political change. As a highly productive and storable crop, maize permitted the accumulation of an agricultural surplus that could be manipulated and used in social transactions, providing a potential lever for establishing and maintaining social inequality. Maize was not a prime mover or cause of the development of Mississippian culture, in and of itself, but rather was a new and powerful element of change in the hands of Mississippian societies. Alterations in lithic and ceramic tool assemblages, particularly in connection with maize farming and the processing, storage, and cooking of maize, also occurred during the initial development of Mississippian societies. Probably the most interesting and important aspect of the Mississippian emergence was the reorganization of society, as reflected in dramatic changes in the internal structure and location of communities in relation to the social and geographical landscape. Prior to around A.D. 700, settlements over much of the eastern United States were relatively small and undifferentiated, with little evidence of any coherent community plan. Small burial mound sites served as the regional foci of social and political integration. After A.D. 800, emerging Mississippian societies began to become more firmly anchored to particular segments of river-valley agricultural land. Communities became larger in size and exhibited a clear central focus in their organization. Houses were distributed around a central courtyard or plaza, a common space often having a central post or other feature. Large nondomestic structures were frequently located adjacent to the central plaza.

Mound construction for other than mortuary purposes had also begun in some areas on a modest scale by A.D. 800, and by two centuries later, the reorganization and refocusing of communities and societies inward around a central plaza and mound complex was evident over a broad expanse of the eastern United States. Although occurring over a relatively brief span of perhaps 300 years, the emergence of Mississippian chiefdoms in the East thus shows clear and obvious lines of regional developmental continuity and coherence. Rather than representing the simple introduction of crops, people, or innovative ideas from Mesoamerica, the initial development of Mississippian societies was a complex in situ process of socio-political transformation.

AN OVERVIEW OF MISSISSIPPIAN SOCIETIES

Early in this century William H. Holmes identified a series of "ceramic provinces" for eastern North America. Based on a rich variety of shell- or limestone-tempered vessel forms, Holmes's "Middle Mississippi" province encompassed the central Mississippi Valley and surrounding areas. Initially used by Holmes to designate a particular geographical area yielding shell-tempered ceramics, the term "Mississippian" subsequently became a general label for the societies that manufactured these pottery vessels over a broad area of eastern North America from around A.D. 800 up to European contact (Fig. 5.1).

In addition to sharing the manufacture of shell-tempered ceramics, Mississippian societies appear generally similar in the archaeological record in a number of other respects. The range and general shapes of ceramic vessel forms are fairly comparable over broad areas, with storage and cooking jars, water bottles, large flat "pans," and food-serving bowls accounting for the majority of Mississippian ceramic assemblages. A range of other objects of Mississippian material culture, from small, triangular arrow points to deer ulna awls, were also generally similar across the East. Mississippian groups constructed and lived in rectangular, either wall-trench or single wall-post structures, with thatch roofs and cane wattle walls, sometimes covered with clay. Judging from the small size of these houses, nuclear or extended families of perhaps five to ten individuals formed the basic social and economic unit of Mississippian societies.

Figure 5.1. Map of eastern North America, showing the extent of the
Vacant Quarter and the river-valley locations of selected Mississippian sites.

These societies were also similar in terms of their general subsistence adaptation. Mississippian groups were river-valley maize farmers. They also grew a variety of other crops of lesser importance, and continued long-established patterns of floodplain foraging for wild species of plants and animals. While these maize-farming populations were often in large measure distributed across river-valley landscapes in small, single-family farmsteads, larger settlements were also integral to their socio-political organization. Situated at the cultural and geographical center of Mississippian polities were large, often fortified, settlements with flat-topped, earthen mounds bordering on a central plaza or public space.

Fortified ceremonial centers with mounds, along with shell- or limestone-tempered ceramics and maize farming head the list of general archaeological attributes of the Mississippian societies of the river valleys of eastern North America. Stretching across more than seven centuries and considerable river-valley real estate, however, the "Mississippian" label encompasses considerable cultural and developmental diversity. Beneath the general similarities in material culture, mound centers, and maize agriculture, there are clear patterns of variation from region to region and river valley to river valley. The river-valley landscapes inhabited by Mississippian groups were not uniform across the East in terms of their size and floodplain topography. The quality and distribution of arable soils also varied within and between regions, as did the relative abundance of wild species of plants and animals. As a result, subsistence economy and landscape demography varied, as did the relative health of Mississippian populations.

Beneath the surface similarities exhibited by these archaeologically documented river-valley maize-farming societies, there was also considerable cultural diversity. If the distribution map of languages across eastern North America drawn after the arrival of Europeans can be projected back in time, Mississippian societies communicated in a variety of different languages. Muskogean languages were spoken across the Gulf Coastal Plain and Lower Mississippi Valley, and Iroquoian languages in the Piedmont and southern Appalachian areas, while Caddoan languages were spoken along the southwestern fringe of Mississippian cultures. Belief systems and worldview also varied from region to region. Similarly, different regions and river valleys witnessed distinct and largely independent developmental histories over more than seven centuries of cultural change. Polities of quite different sizes and complexity developed and flourished in different areas for varying periods of time.

Given the rich mosaic of cultural diversity described by Europeans from the sixteenth to the eighteenth centuries, no less socio-political variation can be reasonably ascribed to the preceding Mississippian period. Even though many aspects of these regional patterns of cultural diversity are not preserved in the archaeological record, research conducted over the past half century has served to illuminate many regionally distinct manifestations of Mississippian culture. As the complex cultural-developmental mosaic labeled "Mississippian" slowly comes into better focus, it becomes more difficult and less worthwhile to construct general, all-encompassing characterizations of Mississippian culture. Alternatively, and in an attempt to provide a description of Mississippian societies that takes full advantage of emerging evidence of heterogeneity, this chapter will emphasize regional variations on general aspects of Mississippian culture, organized under a number of topical headings. Following this general discussion of Mississippian society, the developmental histories and socio-political organization of three of the better documented Mississippian polities at different levels of complexity will be considered.

THE RIVER-VALLEY ENVIRONMENTS OF MISSISSIPPIAN SOCIETIES

If all the known Mississippian settlements were plotted on a map of the Eastern Woodlands, the resulting pattern would closely follow the river systems of the region. With a few exceptions, Mississippian societies occupied river-valley floodplain corridors. These river-valley landscapes were shaped into characteristic, if ever changing, patterns by the force of seasonal floodwater. During floods, the velocity of swiftly flowing floodwater suddenly drops as the waters rise and overflow the river bed, and large amounts of suspended silt, sand, and nutrients are deposited. Lighter clay particles are carried greater distances away from the river toward the valley edge before they settle to the bottom. This deposition of large amounts of soil along the edges of the river bed forms natural levees – low ridges that parallel the river and confine it during the long, seasonal intervals between floods. Periodically, rivers break through these naturally formed low levees of sand and silt, abandoning some channel segments as they cut new ones. Over time, as a result of this continual, meandering process of channel formation, a river becomes flanked by a wide zone of "oxbow lake" segments and their associated natural levees which are formed by superimposed and coalesced abandoned channels.

This meander belt, with its undulating hill-and-swale topography of oxbow lakes, cane breaks, and low sand ridges, is in turn bordered on either side by lower elevation back swamps. In these areas, the floodwaters of spring become the shallow, stagnant, and slowly shrinking backswamp ponds of summer and early fall.

This floodplain landscape of swamps, oxbow lakes, and low, natural levee sand ridges is present in greatest complexity within the lower alluvial valley of the Mississippi River, which extends southward from the confluence of the Ohio and Mississippi Rivers to the Gulf of Mexico. Reaching a width of 160 kilometers by the latitude of Memphis, Tennessee, the Lower Mississippi Valley was a complex environment of vast cypress swamps crosscut by the low sand-ridge topography of active and relict meander belt systems of the Mississippi River and its tributaries. Such complex environments of coalesced levee ridges, lakes, and swamps were rich in both arable land and wild floral and faunal resources. One of the most important attributes of these floodplain meander belts was their levee soils. Sandy, well drained, and easily tilled with simple hoe technology, these soils were well suited to the cultivation of corn and other field crops. In addition, levee ridges received new soil and nutrients deposited by seasonal floodwater.

The spring floods also carried nutrients of another sort. Many main channel and oxbow lake species of fish, including catfish, bullheads, and suckers, followed the floodwater to feed and spawn in shallow, seasonally inundated areas. As floodwater receded, many of these fish were subsequently trapped in the ever smaller and shallower pools of summer and fall, providing an easily accessible and abundant supply of fish protein.

Forming a north-south migration corridor with abundant lakes and aquatic vegetation food sources, the Mississippi Valley was and is a major spring and fall flyway for tens of millions of ducks, geese, and other migrating aquatic species of birds.

The edge-area zones between terrestrial and aquatic habitats also supported a number of plant and animal species of economic importance to Mississippian populations. Raccoons, opossums, and swamp and cottontail rabbits foraged along the edge areas of swamps, lakes, and rivers, as did the white-tailed deer. The sandy banks of the main channels of rivers and streams also provided colonization opportunities for stands of a number of seed-bearing plant species, including wild beans (*Strophostyles*), marsh elder (*Iva annua*), and chenopod (*Chenopodium berlandieri*). Brought under domestication several thousand years earlier and grown in Mississippian agricultural fields, marsh elder, chenopod, and other seed plant species were also abundantly available as wild plants in sand-bank and edge-area settings. Similarly, the stands of oak-hickory forest along natural levee ridge systems provided an annual crop of acorns and hickory nuts, as well as berries and fruits, for Mississippian groups to harvest.

While established in greatest areal extent and complexity in the lower Mississippi Valley, the general floodplain landscape of swamps, oxbow lakes, levee-ridge farmland, and plant and animal resources described above was also present to a lesser degree along the major tributary rivers of the Mississippi, as well as other rivers that flowed toward the south Atlantic coast and Gulf of Mexico. Moving outward from the Mississippi Valley and upstream into the Appalachians to the east and Ozarks to the west, river valleys support scaled-down, natural levee-ridge and backswamp zones, while valley terrace systems become more evident. Backswamp and oxbow lake fish resources were less abundant in smaller river-valley settings, and migratory waterfowl would have been similarly less available outside the Mississippi flyway. Thus, while offering the same general set of environmental opportunities, the broadly dispersed river-valley corridors inhabited by Mississippian societies also differed considerably in terms of the availability and accessibility of aquatic protein resources. This variability in aquatic resources is mirrored, not surprisingly, in regionally different patterns of Mississippian subsistence.

MISSISSIPPIAN SUBSISTENCE ECONOMIES

Within the valley of the Mississippi River and the lower reaches of its tributaries, migratory waterfowl and slackwater species of fish often contributed more than half of the animal protein consumed by Mississippian populations. Analysis of seasonal growth rings on fish scales from several Mississippi Valley sites indicates that fish were obtained primarily during the spring and early summer, when they could have been seined and speared during the spring spawning run and then easily "corralled" as the waters of temporary floodplain ponds receded. Along the Mississippi flyway, migrating ducks and geese also represented an easily accessible and virtually inexhaustible seasonal food source, with a great volume and variety of species crowding the corridor during the fall (October to November) and spring (March to April) migration peaks. While harvesting in the northern section of the flyway was limited to the spring and fall migration peaks, exploitation in the southern, waterfowl overwinter-

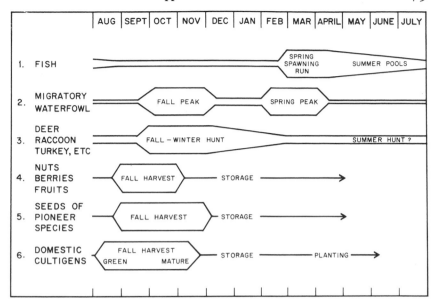

Figure 5.2. The use of principal wild and domesticated food sources by Mississippian societies at different seasons of the year. (From *Alabama and the Borderlands,* ed. Reid Badger and Lawrence Clayton, 1985, University of Alabama Press, p. 73.)

ing, section of the flyway would have been possible throughout the winter. Outside this central corridor and in nonaggrading floodplain situations, Mississippian populations focused more on shoal area fishing and on terrestrial species of animals as sources of dietary protein. The white-tailed deer (*Odocoileus virginianus*) was the single most important animal species in Mississippian economies. Analysis of deer mandibles indicates a fall-winter period of hunting. Next in importance among terrestrial species were the raccoon (*Procyon lotor*) and turkey (*Meleagris gallopavo*). These two species, along with less important animals, like the opossum (*Didelphis marsupialis*), rabbits (*Sylvilagus* sp.), and squirrels (*Sciurus* sp.), were likely also exploited primarily during the fall and winter months (Fig. 5.2).

Reflecting the continuation of a long-standing pattern of hunting and foraging, the wild species of plants and animals of primary importance to Mississippian economies shared a number of important attributes. They occurred in high density in known locales at known seasons of the year, were relatively invulnerable to overutilization, and could be harvested easily, with relatively little energy expenditure, in comparison to the other species available in the environment.

Added to, or layered onto, this continuity in the focused and selective utilization of certain wild species of plants and animals was river-valley farming centered on maize, a crop plant introduced into eastern North America by around A.D. 200. Maize did not abruptly transform eastern economies upon initial introduction, but rather remained a minor crop within premaize indigenous seed-crop farming systems until about A.D. 900 to 1000. Stable carbon isotope analysis of human bone samples has documented the rapid increase in the dietary importance of maize across much of the Eastern Woodlands at this time. Correlated with the initial emergence of Mississippian societies across the East, this transition to maize agriculture did not result in the complete replacement of premaize farming systems. Many of the earlier food crops, including squash (*Cucurbita pepo*), chenopod, knotweed (*Polygonum erectum*), and marsh elder, continued to be grown in Mississippian field plots even after maize came to dominate the agricultural economy. Unlike the northern latitudes, where a single, eight-rowed type of maize was grown, a variety of different races of corn were grown farther south. Present in the East by A.D. 1000, the common bean became an important crop in some, but not all, areas by A.D. 1200. Pollen records indicate increased land clearance after A.D. 1000, and large, use-polished stone hoes recovered from Mississippian sites reflect the simple hoe technology employed in farming the sandy, natural levee soils of river floodplains.

The transition to an increased reliance on maize as a food crop is also documented by changes in the skeletal biology of Mississippian populations. Adult females in some populations show signs of strenuous long-term use of upper arm muscles, probably associated with long hours spent pounding corn in wooden mortars. Dental caries and related degenerative conditions associated with the consumption of starchy corn pulp also increase dramatically after A.D. 1000. In broader terms, however, the overall health of Mississippian populations does not generally decline, as might be predicted under recently popular theories regarding the impact of agricultural economies. Some Mississippian populations along the central Illinois and Cumberland Rivers exhibit the very low levels of general health associated with chronic population/resource imbalance and the risks of poor harvests. At the same time, many other Mississippian populations at relatively high demographic levels were generally in good health. A number of studies have failed to find much difference in the health of high-status as opposed to low-status individuals within several of the larger Mississippian polities that had marked differentiation in social ranking. Like the patterns of regional diversity in river-valley environments and subsistence economy opportunities outlined above, this marked variability in the general health status of Mississippian societies underscores the largely independent, if locally impinging, historical trajectories of individual Mississippian polities.

LANDSCAPE DEMOGRAPHY

Ranging in size from considerably less than a thousand to thousands of people, individual Mississippian polities each occupied and controlled specific segments of river-valley landscapes and adjacent upland areas. Surrounding each polity's river-valley "homeland," which encompassed backswamps, oxbow lakes, active channel, and natural levee farmlands, were sometimes extensive upland hunting areas. These often largely unoccupied hunting zones would have frequently formed substantial buffers between neighboring Mississippian societies.

Within these homeland areas of different Mississippian polities, the individual single-family household units that formed the basic economic units of Mississippian society were likely self-sufficient. The small, dispersed farmstead settlements of individual households are a common component in the landscape of most Mississippian polities. A substantial number of such farmsteads have now been excavated, and they share a number of common elements. Apparently occupied for less than five to ten years before being relocated, Mississippian farmstead settlements contain one, and often two, house structures, with the dual structure pattern conforming to the hot season–cold season house pairings that would later be described by Europeans. Usually, the smaller of the two structures, the cold-season house, is more substantially constructed, with internal hearths and storage pits. Larger and not as well insulated, warm-season houses were likely the primary household structure during all but the coldest weather. Characteristically arrayed around the single or paired houses of Mississippian farmstead settlements is a series of different activity areas, with artifact distributions, storage and cooking pits, and hearths reflecting a wide range of domestic activities, including tool manufacture, butchering, processing of plant foods, and cooking. Much of Mississippian life took place at the household level in such small settlements dispersed along

the natural levees of river valleys of the East (Fig. 5.3). This pattern of widespread distribution of small, single-family household settlements along the natural levee farmlands of Mississippian societies was efficient in economic terms; providing a relatively uniform and balanced access by a group's basic economic units to wild plant and animal resources and to the well-drained arable soils of levee ridges.

Overlaying and frequently overriding these considerations of optimum resource accessibility, however, were social factors that structured Mississippian societies and the distribution of family units on the cultural landscape. Balancing the outer boundary of Mississippian societies, the hunting-territory buffer zone that surrounded a polity's river-valley segment "homeland," was a strong center, a focus of social identity and interaction. These central settlements of Mississippian polities (Fig. 5.4) are easily visible on the archaeological landscape due to their most dominant feature – flat-topped, rectangular mounds constructed entirely of basketloads of earth. Although the largest such structure (Monks Mound at the Cahokia site) covers 6.5 hectares and is thirty meters high, most Mississippian mounds have more modest dimensions. Often containing a layer-cake history of sequential enlargement and renewal, the mounds of Mississippian central settlements were arranged around a central plaza or plaza – open public spaces. Habitation areas were distributed around central mound and plaza precincts, sometimes occupying considerable areas. Exhibiting considerable variation in size, from less than four hectares to more than 100, the central settlements of Mississippian societies were also often bounded by a surrounding fortification wall and ditch.

These central settlements mirrored, at a reduced scale, the larger social and spatial organization of Mississippian societies, with palisade walls, like hunting buffer zones, forming a distinct and defended outer boundary around the houses of individual family units, and the mound and plaza precincts forming a central focus of corporate identity and interaction (Fig. 5.5).

Often occupied for a century of more, these Mississippian mound centers present a wide range of difficult problems of excavation and interpretation. The area enclosed by defensive walls may have changed over the duration of

---

Figure 5.3 (opposite page). A reconstruction of the Gypsy Joint site, a small single-family farmstead of the Powers Phase. This painting by John Douglass shows the cold and warm weather houses, hearth, and outdoor activity areas documented during excavation of this site, as well as Powers Fort, the mound ceremonial center of the Powers Phase chiefdom, in the background. Courtesy, Smithsonian Institution Press.

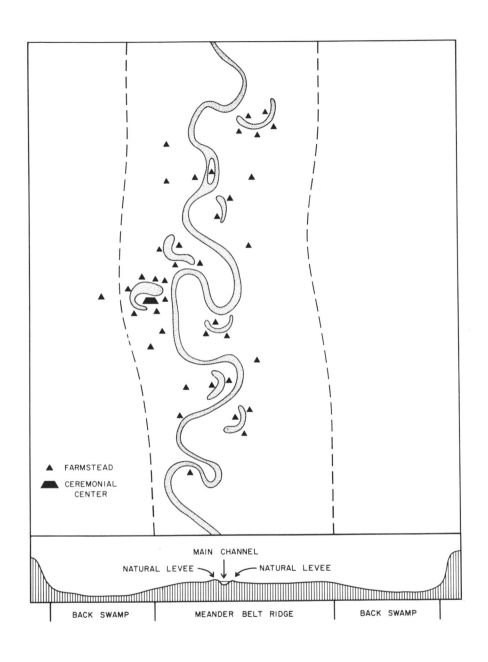

▲ FARMSTEAD

◣ CEREMONIAL
CENTER

MAIN CHANNEL

NATURAL LEVEE → ↓ ← NATURAL LEVEE

BACK SWAMP   MEANDER BELT RIDGE   BACK SWAMP

occupation of such settlements, as palisade walls and bastions were rebuilt and relocated. In the habitation areas of such settlements, thick midden deposits, sometimes a meter or more in depth, are often present. These middens contain a complex and often confusing record of the rebuilding of houses and other structures, repeated digging of storage and cooking pits, and considerable reworking of cultural deposits. The size of habitation areas within such mound centers also varied considerably through time, as outlying family units were drawn into the central settlement over the short or long term for reasons of common defense and social interaction, such as seasonal ceremonies and the burial of high-ranking individuals.

MISSISSIPPIAN POLITICS AND SOCIO-POLITICAL ORGANIZATION

Many aspects of Mississippian society, such as language, belief systems, kinship and social organization, and political structure are not reflected in much detail in the archaeological record of eastern North America. In contrast to the subsistence economy of Mississippian polities, for example, which can often be described in detail, based on abundant plant and animal remains recovered from Mississippian settlements, belief systems and social structure leave relatively little hard evidence in the archaeological record. Fortunately, however, there is a rich abundance of early accounts and descriptions of Native American groups in the Southeast, which provide a strong basis for analogy and general interpretive speculation regarding less well-represented aspects of Mississippian societies.

Mound centers were the seat of socio-political power in Mississippian polities. The political history of these mound and plaza precincts of Mississippian central settlements is often archaeologically complex and difficult to interpret in detail. Except for large central posts and occasional associated pit complexes, which are sometimes present, central plazas are usually devoid of archaeological features. Such extensive, open public areas were certainly the location of feasts and ceremonies of social integration, likely keyed to specific points in the annual seasonal cycle. The flat-topped

---

Figure 5.4 (opposite page). The idealized placement of Mississippian settlements along the meanderbelt ridge landscape of a river-valley floodplain. (From *Alabama and the Borderlands,* ed. Reid Badger and Lawrence Clayton, 1985, University of Alabama Press, p. 76 drawing by G. Robert Lewis.)

mound or mounds, situated adjacent to the central plazas of Mississippian centers, supported structures that facilitated corporate integration and social control in a variety of different ways. While the archaeological remains of these mound summit structures are often difficult to interpret in terms of specific functions, it is sometimes possible to identify mortuary structures where the remains of important personages were displayed and retained, along with their personal objects of status and office. The number and nature of such offices and roles of authority and power within Mississippian societies certainly varied across space and time. In the abstract, and based on southeastern historical analogs and general descriptions of chiefdoms, these different roles or offices can be sorted out into three overlapping areas of responsibility, with an initial division into secular and religious life, and the secular sphere then split into internal management and control and external relations and defense.

Offices or roles of authority relating to belief systems and spiritual matters would have been concerned with mediation between a society and the major forces at work in the cosmos in order to maintain the spiritual stability and correctness of a polity within the larger universe. Such offices of spiritual and cosmic mediation would have involved participation in ceremonies of corporate recognition marking significant events, both seasonal and episodic, in the history of Mississippian societies. Such personages of cosmic mediation were extremely important to Mississippian groups. Even though the cosmos was in large part ordered and predictable, there were anomalies and dangers, periods of vulnerability and threat. Maize harvests were subject to failure. Neighboring societies could turn hostile. The inevitable death of important individuals could precipitate periods of uncertain transition. Mississippian "priests," to use the term loosely, shepherded Mississippian societies through such periods of danger and uncertainty by ensuring that the proper seasonal round of ceremonies was carried out and that the society's rites of passage were correctly accomplished. They ensured proper care and respect of the dead, the departed ancestors, and that harmony with the larger forces of the world was maintained. Many of the

Figure 5.5 (opposite page). A reconstruction of Powers Fort, the civic-ceremonial center of the Powers Phase. This painting by John Douglass shows the fortification wall, central plaza, habitation areas, and the four earthen mounds of this central settlement of the Powers Phase. The three smaller mounds likely were the location of the dwellings of high status personages, while the large mound supported the "temple" or meeting house of the chiefdom. Courtesy, Smithsonian Institution Press.

activities associated with such priestly responsibilities would have been carried out within mound summit mortuaries and other types of ceremonial structures, and "priests" may well have lived in structures elevated on mounds above the general populace.

Within the secular sphere of some Mississippian societies, considerable authority and power were apparently placed in the hands of a single individual – a chief. These powerful individuals also often may have resided on mound summits, elevated both figuratively and literally above the general population. From these elevated positions of authority, Mississippian chiefs occupied the apex of highly structured social systems, in which clans were ranked relative to one another in terms of political power and religious authority.

Individuals filling priestly and chiefly roles in Mississippian society were drawn from the highest ranking clans, and were concerned with ensuring both the continued existence of the chiefdom and their own elevated and central positions of status and authority in the natural and cosmically ordained scheme of things. At the center of each individual Mississippian society, on the plaza and its surrounding mounds, chiefs and priests would reaffirm their central authority and position in the world through ceremonies and feasts of integration, and would orchestrate corporate labor projects, such as the construction of fortification walls and the enlargement of mounds.

This periodic enlargement of mounds both added to the physical and social elevation of high-ranking members of the chiefly clans, and symbolically and literally built upon the past – adding to the history of chiefly authority, the line of descent of chiefs running from generation to generation, back through time to the point when the ceremonial center was first established. The record of chiefly descent, the history of authority being passed from generation to generation, is recorded in these mounds, which are layer cakes of sequential addition, of ritually sanctified rebuilding of chiefly houses, the repository of ancestors, and other community structures. Peeling back these mounds, layer by layer, down through earlier generations of chiefly authority, the beginning is eventually reached; the point in time when the founding chief or chiefly couple first established the central settlement and laid claim to a particular parcel of floodplain landscape. It was essential for the paramount clan, the chief and kinsmen, constantly to reaffirm their ties to this founding event and personage. This kinship tie of descent, down through a line of authority, constituted the core of justification, of legitimacy, of their central and elevated position. It constituted their claim of authority over the land and the populace. This legitimacy was reaffirmed in numerous ways: the distinctive dress and ritual surrounding important personages, their central roles in seasonal ceremonies of harvest and renewal, and of course, the actual occupation of the mounds themselves, which not only contained the record of earlier chiefly occupation, but often the earlier chiefs and priests themselves, buried with all their symbols, their visual markers of authority. These objects of authority also carried sacred designs, invoking symbolic concepts, reaffirming and reminding the general populace that the rulers belonged at the center and deserved an elevated position, and affirming that the order and structure of society blended into the overall order of the cosmos.

A wide range of different kinds of materials were employed in the manufacture of objects that distinguished the elite, by serving as visual markers of their authority and status and of the cosmically sanctioned nature of their positions in society. Likely under strict social control in terms of possession, display, and use, such objects were also controlled in terms of who was allowed initial access to them. Access was limited in two important respects. The raw materials used in the manufacture of such objects were often not locally available. The skilled artisans able to transform raw materials into finished objects of beauty and symbolic power were also rare, and their products were made only for certain individuals and certain sanctioned uses. Copper from the upper Great Lakes and southern Appalachian regions was exchanged across eastern North America and crafted into remarkable ritual garments and ritual objects for the notables: large headplates depicting the peregrine falcon, or humans dressed as falcons (Fig. 5.6); large, cutout heads of human and feline form; copper feathers, maces, arrows, earl spools, and hair ornaments. Similarly, mica from North Carolina and galena (lead sulfide producing a white paint) from Illinois and Missouri were widely exchanged in eastern North America during the Mississippian period.

Human and animal figurines made from an easily worked, red bauxite clay, resembling catlinite and obtained from an as yet undetermined location, were also exchanged across the East, and have been recovered from a number of major Mississippian centers, including Shiloh in Tennessee, Spiro in eastern Oklahoma, and Cahokia in Illinois, as well as from other locations in Arkansas, Illinois, Louisiana, and Mississippi (Fig. 5.7). Sometimes found broken and discarded in a ceremonial context, other times recovered unbroken in mound summit deposits, these figurines were employed in elite-controlled rituals of social integration and cosmic media-

Figure 5.6. Mississippian elite individuals wearing the costume of a peregrine falcon, as depicted in large copper plates recovered from the Etowah site in north Georgia. (Philip [sic] Phillips and James Brown, *Pre-Columbian Shell Engravings from the Craig Mound at Spiro, Oklahoma*, p. 126.)

tion, often seemingly centered on themes of agriculture and fertility. Sometimes engraved with elaborate symbolic motifs, large cups crafted from conch shells obtained along the south Atlantic and Gulf coasts were also used in Mississippian ceremonial contexts, and were exchanged across the East. In addition, elaborately engraved gorgets depicting a range of symbols and subjects were painstakingly crafted from the difficult-to-work conch shell, as were shell maskettes and the drilled conch shell beads that are so commonly recovered from Mississippian contexts in the region. Unlike many of the "prestige" goods described above, shell beads were not so narrowly restricted in manufacture or use, but rather appear to have been a common medium of exchange for establishing and fulfilling a wide range of mutual obligations, including patronage-fealty relationships. Requiring a distinctive microlithic tool kit and considerable investment of time and energy, shell beads were manufactured in both mound centers and smaller outlying settlements and were apparently a common currency for both high-level, large-scale and local, low-level, day-to-day transactions. They also flowed both inward toward the Mississippian chiefs, reaffirming roles of fealty and obligations, and outward again, as patterns of patronage and reward were either renewed or refashioned.

While other objects of material culture, and perhaps agricultural products, also certainly contributed to the complex Mississippian webs of constantly renegotiated intrapolity social obligation and reciprocity, there is no significant evidence to suggest the longer distance interpolity movement of foodstuffs or of other categories of goods that were expensive to transport. With the exception of agricultural hoes made of Mill Creek (Illinois) chert or other high-quality materials, there is little evidence of large-volume exchange of utilitarian items among Mississippian polities. Mill Creek chert hoes have been recovered as far as 700 kilometers from the southern Illinois quarry area, but the vast majority have come from sites within a radius of 200 kilometers of the source area. The long-distance movements of goods between Mississippian societies appear to have involved almost exclusively "prestige" items made of exotic materials and destined for use, display, and control by important personages. Just as the intrasocietal manipulation and control of these objects and the power of the symbols they embodied helped to reaffirm the position of the Mississippian elite, so too the exchange of such objects between Mississippian polities served as a medium for establishing and redefining interpolity relationships of equal and unequal interaction – reflecting the relative status, position, and power of neighboring elites and the polities they represented. Relations of equality and political alliance between polities, as well as inequality and tribute obligation were commonplace on the Mississippian landscape, and always subject to change.

This sphere of interpolity interaction constitutes the third area of different roles or offices of authority in Mississippian societies. At the same time that priests mediated relations with the surrounding cosmos, and both priests and chiefs struggled to maintain internal social order and their own preeminence through control of the material world, central spaces, the past, and the cycles of time, there was also a constant necessity to deal with the challenge of neighboring, potentially hostile Mississippian polities. Within this larger context of interpolity interaction there would have been ongoing mutual measuring by neighboring groups as they assessed the military strength, resources, and social cohesion of their potential floodplain competitors. The relative strength of different Mississippian polities could have been measured in terms of a number of criteria, including population size, agricultural success, and stored reserves; level of internal social cohesion and the success of the leaders in maintaining authority and control over their respective populations; the movement of luxury goods; and the number, prowess, and fierceness of their warriors.

As might be expected, skill and success in warfare was of central importance for interpolity interaction, with leadership in warfare comprising the third general category of responsibility and role of authority in Mississippian groups. There was in all likelihood considerable variation in the scale, frequency, and intensity of warfare across the East during the Mississippian period, and there is still frequent debate regarding the size, strategy, and goals of Mississippian warrior groups. For individual warriors, battle provided one of the few avenues to higher social position and standing within often rigidly ranked Mississippian polities. Leadership in battle, fierceness, and success against the enemy were rewarded with honors and privileges, badges of office, recognition as an important personage, perhaps even alliance through marriage with elite personages. The top positions of authority and leadership in battle may have been drawn from the higher-ranking clans, providing probably the clearest arena within Mississippian groups for the ever present tension between privilege through birth as opposed to individual ability, the struggle of ascribed against achieved status.

Fault lines of social inequality and differential privilege pervaded Mississippian societies, providing constant internal challenges for the elite. How to maintain control and power over the lower-ranking clans? How to minimize the budding off of such lesser privileged segments of society under aspiring leaders frozen out of power by their position at birth? Such internal challenges of socio-political dynamics also extended onto the regional landscape of intersocietal interaction, where the basic goal of any Mississippian polity and its ruling elite was to neutralize, at the very least, its neighbors through political alliance and military standoff, and preferably, to attain the upper hand by forcing them into a dominated tributary relationship. Mississippian warfare often consisted of chronic, small-scale border raids and skirmishes, which were usually designed to reaffirm a polity's ability to defend its autonomy, rather than representing an attempt to extend its dominance over neighboring groups. Like warfare, tributary relationships varied considerably over time and space, ranging from token tribute situations, through more substantial seasonal demands for agricultural products and other goods, to wholesale incorporation of neighboring polities as a second level within "complex" or "regional" chiefdom political structures.

While both the archaeological and historical records provide numerous

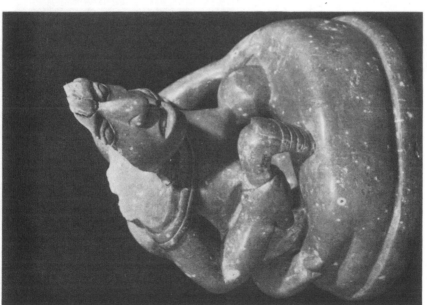

Figure 5.7. The Birger Figurine, from the BBB Motor site, in the American Bottom. (From Tom Emerson, et al., *The BBB Motor Site*, American Bottom Archaeology, FAI-270 Site Reports, University of Illinois, p. 255.)

examples of Mississippian chiefdoms and their descendant polities during the sixteenth century exerting influence and extending control over other nearby, and sometimes rather distant, societies, it is difficult to establish with any accuracy the nature and degree of control that actually existed. Historical accounts in the Southeast of powerful chiefs dominating vast areas are not uncommon, but rarely are details provided regarding the level of local autonomy that remained within such larger spheres of chiefly influence. The various societies allied with a more powerful chiefdom in a regional socio-political network could very well have been arrayed along the full range of possible intersocietal interactions. The economy and socio-political systems of relatively weak nearby groups might have been directly controlled, while stronger, more distant groups more likely would have been dominated indirectly, through sizable tribute obligations of warriors, prestige goods, and harvest surplus. More distant or more powerful groups that were only tenuously allied might grudgingly acknowledge their domination through a small tribute offering each year. Such regional-scale networks of alliance provided stability for smaller societies under the protective umbrella of stronger chiefdoms, while at the same time requiring some loss of autonomy on their part.

The archaeological record provides less information regarding regional-scale socio-political interaction and alliances than do early historical accounts. Regional scale or "complex" chiefdoms that dominated and integrated other polities to varying degrees can sometimes be recognized archaeologically by the larger size of their mound centers. The centers of such regional chiefdoms often have a greater number of mounds and plazas, and larger ones, comprising the central ceremonial precinct, as well as expanded habitation areas and palisade walls. The Moundville site, located just south of Tuscaloosa, Alabama, is one of the best preserved regional centers. A small single-level center established about A.D. 1000, Moundville extended its authority over a number of neighboring polities by about A.D. 1200, and grew in size to over 100 hectares, as twenty mounds were constructed around a plaza of thirty-two hectares in a relatively short period of time. Regional centers such as Moundville also often yield an increased variety and quality of prestige goods accompanying elite burials, and evidence exists of more complex mortuary programs and corporate ceremonies. While such prestige goods in many cases likely represent the material record of tribute and alliance formation, the nature and importance of such transactions are often difficult to discern. It is similarly difficult to document the movement of foodstuffs as tribute in the archaeological record. As a result, while it is obvious that individual Mississippian chiefdoms did not exist in isolation, but rather were participants in complex and often unstable regional networks of socio-political alliance and influence, it is rarely possible to recognize more than the barest outline of such interaction in the archaeological record.

To complicate further the interpretation of the archaeological record, Mississippian socio-political patterns of regional interaction were far from stable and unchanging over a span of more than 700 years. The Mississippian period witnessed complex historical cycles of domination and decline, with the political alliances and fortunes of individual chiefdoms sometimes shifting rapidly and repeatedly, while other chiefdoms apparently remained relatively stable over long periods of time. Some chiefdoms, such as Cahokia, grew rapidly in complexity and size for several hundred years, before beginning an almost as rapid period of decline. Other Mississippian chiefdoms seemingly experienced slower, longer-term trajectories of growth, and their mound centers appear to have been continually occupied over hundreds of years. Other chiefdoms apparently occupied the same river-valley landscapes over several centuries, while periodically moving their mound center between different locations.

While the description of Mississippian chiefdoms provided to this point is accurate enough in terms of general characterization, it is essential to offer a set of more specific case studies to underscore the numerous historical variations on this general theme that were acted out in different river-valley and regional contexts across the Eastern Woodlands of North America. Different river-valley settings and larger regional interaction spheres each witnessed distinctive historical sequences of development involving chiefdoms that varied considerably in size and complexity, stability and internal organization, and means of integrating and controlling the constituent units of society. In order to present a better picture of Mississippian variability, brief descriptions of specific developmental and organizational aspects of three quite different Mississippian societies will be presented in the following sections of this chapter. These brief descriptions of (1) the Powers Phase, (2) Cahokia and the American Bottom, and (3) Spiro provide specific examples of many of the topics covered above, and offer clear illustrations of the differences and similarities that existed in the scale, complexity, and organizations of Mississippian groups.

Distributed across an area of less than twenty-five square kilometers in southeastern Missouri, the mound center (Powers Fort), villages, and farmsteads of the Powers Phase clearly fall toward the lower end of the size scale for Mississippian societies. Powers Phase settlements other than Powers Fort were occupied for only a short span of time, less than ten to twenty years, prior to being abandoned, offering an unequaled opportunity for a "slice in time" view of the social and spatial organization and distribution of a Mississippian society.

Dwarfing Powers Phase in size and complexity, the Cahokia site and the outlying mound centers, villages, and other settlements of the American Bottom, east of St. Louis, Missouri, represent the largest concentration of mound construction activity north of Mexico. The developmental cycle of Cahokia and the American Bottom involved rapid growth to unequaled scale and complexity, followed by an equally steep socio-political decline.

Located in eastern Oklahoma, near the western boundary of Mississippian societies, the Spiro site is on the surface quite unremarkable in comparison to other Mississippian mound centers, consisting of only a few mounds and a small associated habitation area. But one of the mounds at Spiro, the Craig Mound, was looted in the 1930s and found to contain a large assemblage of unusually well-preserved and aesthetically impressive textiles and objects manufactured of shell, wood, copper, and bone. In addition to underscoring the complexity of the socio-political system that was centered on the Spiro site, the artifact assemblage removed from the Craig Mound offers an unrivaled opportunity to consider the rich iconographic complexity of a Mississippian polity.

THE POWERS PHASE

Situated along the Ozark escarpment in southeastern Missouri, at the western edge of the lower Mississippi Valley (Fig. 5.1), the small area occupied by the Powers Phase around A.D. 1300 is bounded on the west by the Ozark uplands and on the east by local swamps and low ground. Thus surrounded by uplands and swamps, the well-defined territory of the Powers Phase polity consists of a group of six, low, well-drained, interfluve sand-ridge "islands" separated from each other by low swampy areas (Fig. 5.8). For much of the year the low-lying areas between these ridges would have been inundated. As a result, the ridges can be viewed as comprising an archipelago in the swamp – a group of low, sandy islands in a sea of what would have been stagnant, standing water during all of the year, except for periods of seasonal flooding. These still waters provided a rich abundance of fish and migratory waterfowl for Powers Phase populations, while the oak-hickory forests of the ridges and Ozark uplands supported deer, turkey, raccoon, squirrel, and rabbit, all of which were important food animals. The sandy, well-drained soil of these ridges was easily tilled and well suited to the slash-and-burn, digging stick, and hoe agriculture of the Powers Phase. Maize was the primary field crop, but beans were also grown, along with a number of indigenous crop plants, including sunflower, marsh elder, chenopod, and erect knotweed. While this small area of adjacent sand-ridge "islands" is clearly isolated in many ways, it is also situated where the Little Black River enters the Mississippi Valley from the Ozarks. The valley of the Little Black and other streams provided easy access into the Ozarks, and to a major Mississippian-period route for the movement of information and materials along the northeast-to-southwest-oriented escarpment. The similar escarpment-edge placement of other Mississippian polities where rivers exit the Ozarks, along with the presence of trade items such as Mill Creek chert hoes and galena, attests to the role of this escarpment-edge trail in the movement of goods from areas to the north. It is thus no accident that Powers Fort, the civic-ceremonial mound center of the Powers Phase, is located close to the Little Black River entrance to the uplands.

Named after the landowner at the time, Powers Fort was first excavated and described in the 1880s. Fronting on a cypress swamp to the east, the five hectare civic-ceremonial mound center of the Powers Phase was enclosed on its other three sides by a fortification wall and ditch (Fig. 5.5). Within these protective walls, the corporate ceremonial precinct consisted of a central plaza, or public space, with a large rectangular earthen mound situated on its north edge and a row of three smaller mounds aligned along its western border. The large mound and adjacent plaza were likely the focus of a variety of polity-wide activities and ceremonies. Excavation of this large mound in the 1880s uncovered evidence of a structure, and exotic painted, polished, and engraved ceramics have been recovered on the mound's northwest periphery. The smaller west-side mounds could have been the location of less inclusive social subgroup activities and could have also supported the houses of prominent personages in the secular and religious life of the chiefdom.

Materials collected from the ground surface suggest the presence of residential areas to the northwest, west, and south of the row of three smaller mounds (perhaps more extensive than indicated in the artist's reconstruction of Powers Fort shown in Fig. 5.5). A small block excavation in one of these areas exposed a vertical sequence of three superimposed residential structures, indicating episodes of rebuilding in the same location.

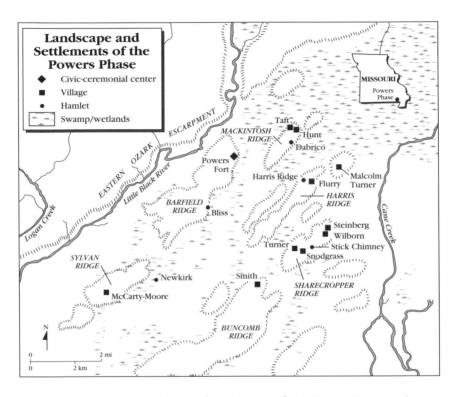

Figure 5.8. The distribution of settlements of the Powers Phase on low sand ridges along the Ozark Escarpment of southeast Missouri. (Adapted from Bruce D. Smith, ed., *Mississippian Settlement Patterns,* Academic Press, 1978, p. 215.)

It was not until the 1960s that any evidence of other Powers Phase settlements came to light, when James E. Price located what appeared to be a number of large villages situated on the six sand ridges of the Powers Phase area. On the ground surface, these village settlements consisted of numerous small areas of dark soil and associated high-artifact densities. Systematic collecting and mapping, along with aerial reconnaissance, showed these dark soil stains and high-artifact densities to be arranged in rows. The subsequent, almost total, excavation of two adjacent village settlements (the Turner and Snodgrass sites) confirmed these soil stains as being the location of burned house structures situated just beneath the ground surface. To date, ten Powers Phase villages (all burned) have been identified. None of these villages is located on the "island" ridge that

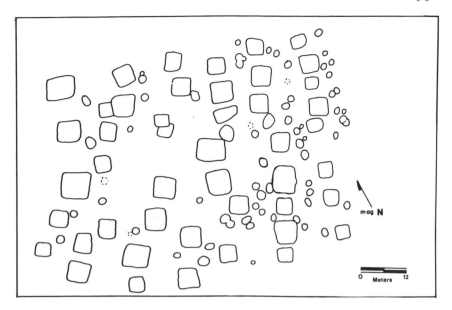

Figure 5.9. The community plan of the Turner village settlement of the Powers Phase, showing the arrangement of house structures and refuse pits around a central courtyard. (From Bruce D. Smith, ed., *Mississippian Settlement Patterns*, Academic Press, 1978, p. 218.)

supports Powers Fort, while the other five adjacent "islands" have from one to four villages each (Fig. 5.8). The villages appear to vary considerably in size, from perhaps forty structures to more than ninety. Six of these villages appear to represent three pairs, each comprised of one large and one small village, of which the extensively excavated Turner and Snodgrass villages are the only well-documented example. Located only 150 meters apart, the Turner and Snodgrass sites are quite different from each other in some respects, while at the same time displaying a number of shared organizational principles.

Covering about 0.6 hectares, and enclosed by a fortification ditch and palisade, the Turner site contained forty-four rectangular structures organized around a small open area or plaza on the west side of the village (Fig. 5.9). The forty-four structures were arranged in six roughly parallel rows, oriented northeast to southwest, of from five to eight houses each. This pattern is repeated in the orderly rows of burials in the Turner cemetery, which was located beneath the small plaza of the village.

While most of the structures in the Turner village are nuclear family

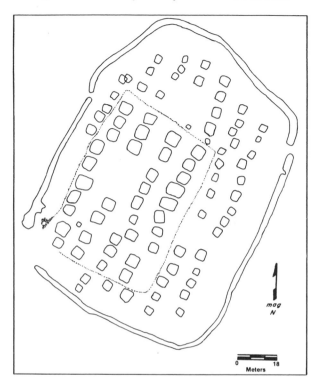

Figure 5.10. The community plan of the Snodgrass village, showing the surrounding palisade ditch, internal white wall, central courtyard, and habitation structures of this Powers Phase settlement. (From Bruce D. Smith, ed., *Mississippian Settlement Patterns,* Academic Press, 1978, p. 219.)

dwellings, several structures adjacent to the plaza, on its north and west sides, appear to have had corporate functions. There is a clear parallel here to the spatial organization of the corporate-ceremonial sector plaza and mounds at Powers Fort. A granary structure containing stacked cobs of maize and stores of other food crops was situated on the north edge of the plaza at Turner, while larger structures with nondomestic artifact assemblages were situated along its west side. It is difficult as yet to discern any distinct social subgrouping within the village, in terms of either structural or material culture clusters.

With ninety-four structures arranged in seven rows of from five to fourteen structures each, the nearby 1.0 hectare Snodgrass site is also centered on a plaza close to its western edge (Fig. 5.10). Like Turner, it is surrounded by a fortification wall and ditch. Two, and perhaps three, gate areas have been identified. As at Turner, large corporate structures are located along the western edge of the plaza at Snodgrass. In contrast to Turner, the Snodgrass village has no cemetery; only a small number of burials are scattered across the site.

While sharing a similar focus on a west side plaza and adjacent corporate buildings, the Snodgrass site contains twice as many structures as Turner and exhibits a more complex community plan. A white clay stain, apparently the remains of an internal clay wall of unknown height, separates thirty-seven "inner" structures at Snodgrass from a group of more than fifty smaller structures located outside the white clay wall. The smaller "outer" structures contained relatively small artifact assemblages in comparison to those located inside the white wall. As is the case at Turner, analysis to date of the Snodgrass site provides little evidence of obvious internal social subdivisions in the form of spatial groupings of structures, other than perhaps the duality suggested by the white clay wall. It is interesting to note that the Turner site is very comparable in terms of size, number of structures, and general community plan, to that portion of the Snodgrass site bounded by the white clay wall.

In contrast to Powers Fort, there is very little evidence of any rebuilding of structures at either Turner or Snodgrass, or at Flurry and Wilborn, two other Powers Phase villages that have been partially excavated (Fig. 5.8). Since it is estimated that the lifespan of Powers Phase wooden structures would have been perhaps ten years, this lack of rebuilding, along with limited refuse deposits, suggests that these village settlements were occupied for a decade at most, and perhaps for less than five years before being burned and abandoned. While this short time span of village occupation provides a rich variety of opportunities to study the internal organization and dynamics of a Mississippian polity, it also makes it difficult to establish which village settlements were occupied at any one time. Were, for example, the Turner and Snodgrass villages, located only 150 meters apart, occupied at the same time, or sequentially? One of many possibilities, for example, is that the village sites of each of the different ridge "islands" of the Powers Phase area represent the sequential habitation episodes of a single community. Further complicating a detailed reconstruction of the landscape demography of the Powers Phase is the existence of more than 100 small, farmstead settlements that are scattered across the sand-ridge islands of the region.

One of these settlements (the Gypsy Joint site) has been completely excavated, and provides an example of what likely lies beneath the numerous, small, surface stains and artifact concentrations identified as farmsteads during surveys (Fig. 5.3). Situated on the highest elevation of a low knoll, the Gypsy Joint site consisted of two burned house structures and a surrounding arc of pits and associated activity areas. Rather than representing different family units, the two house structures at the Gypsy Joint site appear to have been occupied by a single-family group during different seasons of the year, conforming to the hot season–cold season pattern described in different parts of the Southeast after the arrival of Europeans. The central structural element at Gypsy Joint was a warm-weather structure of single wall-post construction that lacked internal storage pits and hearth areas. In contrast, the cold-weather structure, situated in alignment with the arc of pits and activity areas at the site periphery, was smaller, had more substantial wall-trench construction, and contained both a hearth and storage pits. It was likely utilized during the winter season. The arc of cooking pits and activity areas was the location of a wide range of tool-manufacturing and food-processing and preparation activities. Based on the size of houses at Gypsy Joint and the range of activities that were carried out, the site was likely occupied by an extended-family group of seven to ten individuals for a span of perhaps one to three years.

The numerous other farmstead settlements identified through surface surveys were likely occupied by family groups of similar size and composition for comparable lengths of time. Once again, it is difficult to establish which of these farmstead settlements were occupied at the same point in time and which were contemporaneous with the various village settlements on different ridges.

Even given these difficulties of establishing exact patterns of landscape demography for the Powers Phase, a series of general speculations regarding levels of socio-political organization can be offered that seem warranted, given what is known of the region. Based on the scale and bounded nature of the six sand-ridge "islands" occupied by the Powers Phase, it is likely that each supported separate and discrete social segments of the society. The absence of any clear divisions within villages argues against the presence of portions of many or all of the clans or other subsections of the Powers Phase chiefdom in each village community, and lends support to the proposition that the location of such internal socio-political divisions within the Powers Phase followed and conformed to the landscape of ridges in a swampy setting. Within each of the ridge-based subsections of the Powers Phase polity, the plaza and associated corporate structures of one or more village settlements would have served as a focal point for social integration. The size of the cemetery at the Turner site, for example, indicates that it served a larger group than occupied the village itself, suggesting its role of integration for a group that extended beyond the village to include outlying farmsteads and perhaps other villages as well. Similarly, the smaller house structures outside the white wall at Snodgrass might represent "town houses" that were occupied only seasonally, or during collective ceremonies, by family units that spent much of each year in outlying farmsteads.

In much the same way that focal village settlements and the activities centered on their plazas and corporate structures served in various ways to integrate the inhabitants of a specific ridge, the central plaza and mounds of Powers Fort were the setting for full polity activities and personages that integrated the societal groups of the various ridges. The smaller mounds at Powers Fort may have supported the (seasonal?) habitation structures of high-ranking individuals from the different ridge-system societal subgroups.

The planning and corporate labor expended in the mounds and fortification walls at Powers Fort, as well as the degree of organization and control evident in the community plans of the Turner and Snodgrass sites, argue for a relatively tightly organized polity. But as yet, the only artifactual evidence of differential status ranking within the Powers Phase consists of some high-quality, possibly "elite," ceramics found at Powers Fort. High-status burials have yet to be discovered at the civic-ceremonial mound center. Similarly, no high-status individuals have yet been identified in the burial populations of excavated village settlements, where grave goods and grave placement reflect a low level of status differentiation based on gender and age, with no indications of ascribed status. In addition, while differential social ranking might be indicated by some aspects of internal village planning, such as variation in structure size and placement in relation to the plaza, and differences in constituent artifact assemblages, such variation appears to have been limited and clinal in nature.

Paralleling the absence of much evidence at the village level for status differences within the ridge-system societal subgroups, there are only a few, if obvious, indications of differential status separating the populations of different ridge systems. Given the placement of Powers Fort on the largest of these ridges, and its apparently central role in integrating not only the polity as a whole but the population of its ridge as well, it is likely that the inhabitants of the Powers Fort ridge enjoyed a paramount social position within the Powers Phase and the ceremonial center itself. Further research may delineate additional aspects of social ranking within and among the constituent units of Powers Phase society. With the exception of the actual placement of Powers Fort, however, the village settlements (and populations) of different ridges appear relatively equal in social standing and political power.

In terms of polity size and complexity, the Powers Phase certainly falls toward the lower end of the range of Mississippian societies that occupied the river valleys of eastern North America. At the same time, however, it is generally comparable in scale to many of these maize-farming groups, with polities the size of the Powers Phase accounting for a sizable majority of the Mississippian world.

At the other end of this range of size and complexity in Mississippian polities, standing alone and in stark contrast to the Power Phase and the numerous other societies of similar small scale, is Cahokia, the largest and most complex Native American polity to develop north of Mesoamerica.

CAHOKIA AND THE AMERICAN BOTTOM

Just across the river from St. Louis, Missouri, the relatively narrow valley of the Mississippi River bulges briefly eastward, forming a broad floodplain area known as the American Bottom. Encompassing about 350 square kilometers of coalesced, natural levee ridges, oxbow lakes, and marshes, the American Bottom contains an archetypal combination of fertile and easily worked, floodplain, agricultural soils, and abundant habitats for the fish and waterfowl so favored by Mississippian societies (Fig. 5.11). Over a span of five centuries, from around A.D. 900 to 1400, this area witnessed a remarkable cycle of cultural growth and decline, as the most complex pre-Columbian polity north of Mexico emerged, flourished for a time, and then receded below the level of archaeological visibility.

Throughout this developmental cycle, the Cahokia site occupied a central position in the American Bottom (Fig. 5.12). This impressive mound center has captured the imagination of a number of prehistorians eager to cast Cahokia as a great city – the urban capital of a powerful state-level society of large population size and having political control over vast territories of eastern North America. While these claims of vast size, complexity, and socio-political reach are often greatly overdrawn, the Cahokia site is indeed impressive. Estimated as covering an area of perhaps

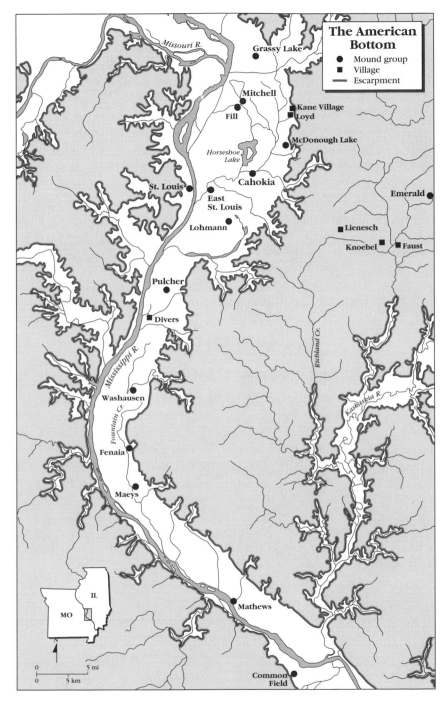

Figure 5.11. Map of the American Bottom region east of St. Louis, Missouri, showing the location of selected Mississippian settlements.

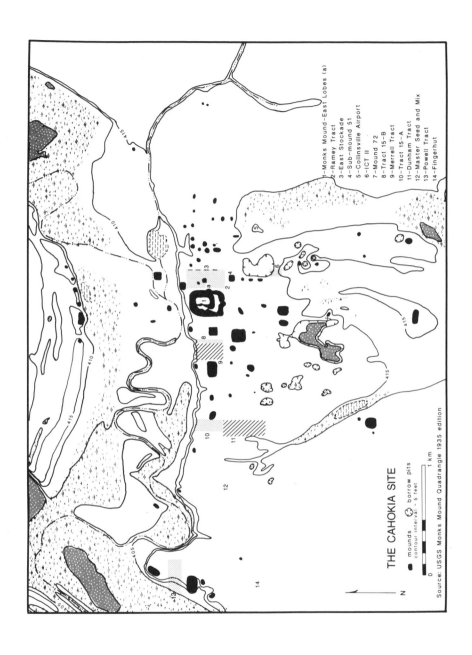

THE CAHOKIA SITE

■ mounds. ⊗ borrow pits
contour interval - 5 feet

0 _____ 1 km

N

Source: USGS Monks Mound Quadrangle 1935 edition

1-Monks Mound-East Lobes (a)
2-Ramey Tract
3-East Stockade
4-Sub-mound 51
5-Collinsville Airport
6-ICT II
7-Mound 72
8-Tract 15-B
9-Merrell Tract
10-Tract 15-A
11-Dunham Tract
12-Master Seed and Mix
13-Powell Tract
14-Fingerhut

thirteen square kilometers, the site includes approximately 100 earthen mounds that were used for burial purposes or as platforms for buildings. Mound clusters and associated plazas distributed across the site apparently served as the civic-ceremonial focus of different specific subcommunities and their residential areas.

The central area of Cahokia is dominated by Monks Mound, the largest prehistoric mound north of Mexico. Construction on the mound was begun about A.D. 900, completed by A.D. 1150, and it was still being used as late as A.D. 1300. Built entirely of earth, basketload by basketload, it measures 316 meters by 240 meters at its base, reaches thirty meters in height, and has four different levels or platforms. Monks Mound is larger in areas at its base than the whole of Powers Fort, the civic-ceremonial center of the Powers Phase.

A large palisade wall enclosed an eighty-three hectare central precinct at Cahokia. Included within this fortified central core was Monks Mound, a number of other mounds, including Mound 72, and several residential areas and open plazas. At least five circles of posts were located in or near this central precinct at Cahokia, measuring up to 130 meters in diameter. It is thought that they likely functioned to track the location of sunrises and sunsets along the horizon.

A portion of a densely occupied residential area adjacent to this central precinct that was exposed through large block excavation is the source of many of the higher population estimates for Cahokia at its peak, which occurred around A.D. 1050–1150. House structures uncovered in this block excavation were all assumed to have been occupied at the same time, and a population estimate for this one specific dense habitation area was then multiplied to cover the entire estimated area of the Cahokia site. Population estimates for Cahokia resulting from this projection ranged from 26,000 to 43,000, depending on which of various assumptions about how many people lived in each house was used. As a result, population ranges of 30,000 to 40,000 for the site can commonly be found in the literature. Much of the Cahokia site, however, had a considerably lower population density than the "downtown" residential area employed as the

Figure 5.12 (opposite page). Map of the Cahokia mound center, the largest pre-Columbian settlement north of Mexico, showing the location of mounds and excavation areas. (Reprinted from *The Mississippian Emergence* {Washington, D.C.: Smithsonian Institution Press}, p. 122, by permission of the publisher. Copyright 1990.)

basis of projections; hence these higher-end population estimates are likely four to five times greater than the actual population of Cahokia at its peak. Even at lower, more reasonable population estimates, in the thousands rather than tens of thousands, Cahokia was still the largest population concentration north of Mexico prior to the arrival of Europeans.

Considerably smaller in scale and population when compared to Cahokia, a number of other town and mound-plaza centers were distributed across the American Bottom during the Mississippian period, including the East St. Louis, Mitchell, Lohmann, Grass Lake, Lunsford-Pulcher, and Mathews sites. The northernmost of these was twenty kilometers north of Cahokia, the southernmost sixty-five kilometers to the south. As documented primarily through analysis of surface-collected materials and limited excavations, these mound centers appear to have had quite diverse occupational histories. Their spans of occupation were of unequal duration and intensity, and they each attained local prominence for only portions of their history.

Rather than living in downtown Cahokia or at any of the smaller mound centers, many of the inhabitants of the American Bottom lived in small outlying settlements, within a low-density landscape of scattered farmsteads. Occupied for only a few years, these small, farmstead settlements, like those of the Powers Phase, consisted of a small number of rectangular house structures, along with associated pit features and hearths. Across the floodplain landscape of the American Bottom, some favorable and topographically distinct locations for farmstead settlements exhibit evidence of extended habitation or superimposed occupational episodes. These locations often served to integrate surrounding communities dispersed in small farmsteads, as indicated by the presence of specialized corporate structures. Small, circular sweatlodges and large, rectangular dual-hearth structures occur alongside typical Mississippian houses, and likely were a focus of activities and attention for families living in small outlying settlements. In terms of integrating a low-density, dispersed community, these specialized structures are perhaps comparable to the plaza-edge structures of the Turner and Snodgrass sites, with mound centers, such as Powers Fort and those of the American Bottom, in turn serving to organize societal groups on a larger scale. As was apparently the case in the Powers Phase region, community boundaries in the American Bottom were likely strongly influenced by topography, with habitable levee ridges often separated by sizable areas of marsh and open water (Fig. 5.11).

The socio-political landscape of the American Bottom during the Mississippian period thus likely contained a number of generally equivalent societal groups, each centered on a mound-plaza complex, with lower-level nodes of integration scattered across the islands of habitable land. Rather than forming a rigid, centralized, and highly organized system, these different groups, with Cahokia at the center, were probably politically independent to varying degrees, as mound centers and their resident elite held sway over territories and outlying dispersed communities of different sizes for differing periods of time. Lower-order, local-level elite likely occupied those favorably situated outlying settlements with specialized structures, where they carried out administrative and control directions for the mound-centered elite. Paralleling their political quasi-independence, the different mound-centered societies of the American Bottom were likely self-sufficient economically. Each of the mound centers appears to have had a distinct history of florescence and decline within what were undoubtedly complex, interlocking cycles of developmental interaction among mutually impinging societies.

Throughout these cycles of cultural growth and decline in the American Bottom, Cahokia was at the center of this web of socio-political interaction. Cahokia leaders directly controlled a wide expanse of floodplain adjacent to the site, while at the same time maintaining varying degrees of indirect administrative and tributary oversight of other mound-centered communities throughout the American Bottom. While generally similar to that of other mound-centered societies of the region, Cahokia's structure of direct administration and community integration was clearly more elaborate, as evidenced by the BBB Motor and Sponeman sites. Situated within a few miles of Cahokia, both of these small, lower-level nodal sites of the Cahokia system contained elaborate mortuary features, as well as remarkable fertility theme figurines crafted from a nonlocal bauxitic clay resembling catlinite.

This paramount position of Cahokia and its elite is reflected in its ability to draw tribute labor from surrounding societies for such large corporate-labor projects as the construction of Monks Mound, the large fortification walls of the central precinct, and the woodhenges and other public structures of downtown Cahokia. The preeminent position of the Cahokia elite within the socio-political fabric of the American Bottom can also be seen in the elaborate mortuary rites carried out at Cahokia, with burials uncovered during excavation of Mound 72, located just south of Monks Mound, providing an excellent case in point. Constructed over a portion of a woodhenge solar observatory no longer in use, this mound played a role in the mortuary ritual for central-precinct elite at Cahokia that involved a sequence of related burial episodes. The personage of paramount importance within the burial population of the mound was distinguished both by location and by associated burial furniture. He was also accompanied in death by a number of other elite personages of lower status, as well as by a group of young female retainers who were sacrificed and interred in a mass grave placed over a post pit of the woodhenge.

While certainly less elaborate than Mound 72, the burial context of lower-order elite in the Cahokia system also indicates the role of mortuary programs in affirming the distinct and separate status of higher-ranking segments of society. The communal mortuary facility of the Wilson Mound, west of Cahokia, for example, contained numerous bundle burials accompanied by marine whelks and shell beads. Nonelite burials through-out the Cahokia system can be clearly differentiated from Wilson Mound and other elite mortuary facilities in terms of both their location and the degree of elaboration of burial goods and burial programs.

The development of Cahokia and the American bottom into the most complex socio-cultural system in eastern North America prior to European arrival is not known in detail, but can be sketched in general outline. Cahokia evolved at about A.D. 950 to 1000 into paramount position in the American Bottom from a group of mound-centered societies of generally equal scale and complexity. Large-scale construction of Monks Mound began about this time, as did the building of other mounds at Cahokia. By A.D. 1100, woodhenges and central precinct palisade lines had been built. All of these corporate-labor projects reflect the establishment of Cahokia's ability to command large labor forces from other polities with'n the region. It is also at this time that the growing power and authority of the Cahokia elite are reflected in dramatically more elaborate mortuary programs, such as that evidenced in Mound 72.

Cahokia's achievement of preeminence by A.D. 1000 and its degree of control over relations among other American Bottom polities is also reflected in a broad shift in landscape demography – the dispersal of household units formally clustered in large, village settlements to form scattered networks of single-family farmsteads. This change in the distribution of population reflects the expansion of Cahokia's central authority and the normalization of relations, at least for the short term, among American Bottom polities. The actual social and political mechanisms by which Cahokia integrated these other mound-centered societies into a single, large system are not known, but judging from descriptions of other midrange, "chiefdom" level groups, it most likely involved the extension of existing and overlapping networks of status and obligation both through the acknowledgement and acceptance of lower-order elite into Cahokia's social fabric, and the insertion of Cahokia functionaries into local-level positions of authority.

Kinship-based socio-political structure defined both the outward limits of Cahokia's expansion of influence and authority, and its essential vulnerability, with each of the various mound-centered societies that together comprised the larger regional system harboring both the latent desire and inherent ability to escape the central control of Cahokia. Such regional-scale or complex chiefdoms are quite unstable, and the Cahokia florescence had largely fragmented by A.D. 1150 to 1200, as indicated by the beginning of a large-scale depopulation of the American Bottom. Rising ground-water levels and a resultant reduction in farmland, along with depletion of firewood, have both been suggested as factors contributing to the collapse of the Cahokia system. Whatever the mix of social, economic, and environmental factors that were involved in the decline of the complex chiefdom at Cahokia, it was dramatic. Rather than simply involving a scaling back to the preexisting regional pattern of a set of generally equal polities, the post–A.D. 1200 to 1300 aftermath of Cahokia witnessed the large-scale abandonment of the river floodplain and the appearance of smaller-scale polities in upland stream-valley settings.

Distinctive Cahokia design motifs and artifact forms of the A.D. 1000 to 1200 period of florescence that have been recovered from Mississippian mound centers across the eastern United States attest to contact and interaction over broad geographical areas. Some efforts have been made to construct from these scattered objects and elements of style a far-flung empire of political domination and economic extraction. Inherent in many of the scenarios that have the American Bottom drawing tribute and trade in the form of deer skins and agricultural surplus from societies as far away as western New York are the far too large population estimates for Cahokia that carry with them the necessity of substantial nonlocal provision. Given existing knowledge regarding the size and nature of the greater Cahokia political and economic systems, neither the capacity to exert control over long distances nor the need for a bulk agricultural surplus would appear to have been present. There is no question that communication and the exchange of lightweight, high-status objects took place between the elite of the Cahokia chiefdom and of other Mississippian polities across the river valleys of eastern North America.

While the full social and political import of this exchange of objects between polities is not clear, it is extremely doubtful that any direct control was involved or that anything other than perhaps token tribute relationships existed, particularly as the distances separating polities increased. Cahokia's role in causing the initial development of "Mississippian" level societies in different regions of the East has also often been overplayed, as complex local developmental processes are explained in terms of "influence" from Cahokia (as indicated by a few American Bottom artifact forms).

Cahokia was neither the core of a broad empire nor the prime mover in the development of Mississippian societies in other areas of the East. Its sphere of influence and control rarely extended much beyond the American Bottom. While Cahokia and the American Bottom was certainly the largest and most complex society to develop in the region, it was in most aspects of basic organization and structure quite comparable to the much smaller and far more abundant Mississippian societies, such as the Powers Phase, that occupied river-valley settings across the East well into the sixteenth century.

SPIRO AND THE GREAT MORTUARY

Extending from the Mississippi River up into the southern Plains, the Arkansas River is a major, natural, east-west avenue of travel. The Spiro site is located along the valley of the Arkansas River in eastern Oklahoma, on the border between two major environmental zones, the Eastern Woodlands and the Prairie Grasslands. Spiro was the mound center for a Mississippian society that was largely dispersed in small, farmstead settlements along the Arkansas and several of its tributaries. Maize and local seed crops were grown in river-valley fields, and deer, raccoon, and turkey were hunted, along with other animals, in the floodplain forests.

Occupied from around A.D. 800 to about A.D. 1350, the Spiro site conforms in many respects to the community plans of other Mississippian civic-ceremonial centers, with two flat-topped platform mounds (Brown Mound and Copple Mound) and four smaller, dome-shaped mounds, encircling a vacant oval area roughly 200 by 300 meters in size. The center of this plaza area appears to have been marked by a large post. Situated on a low, dissected upland at the edge of the river valley, the plaza and surrounding mounds lack an encircling fortification wall. Evidence of habitation extends onto the adjacent, lower-elevation terrace, where three additional mounds are located along the terrace edge. Two of these terrace-edge mounds were small, with the third, the Craig Mound, measuring about 100 meters long by 30 meters wide. Rather than resulting from a single construction episode, the Craig Mound was composed of four, linearly conjoined, conical mounds, with the northernmost of these being twice as large as the other three. Following a pattern observed at similar ceremonial mound centers upstream from Spiro, the Craig Mound was the location of a mortuary precinct consisting of a large charnel house, used for the preparation and display of deceased notables prior to their interment in adjacent accretional burial mounds. Built up of layers of scattered mats, bark, burials, grave goods, and earth fill, the three smaller cones of the Craig Mound were such accretional burial mounds, while the larger mound was the location of a series of charnel structures. While the periodic closing and dismantling of these charnel houses and the interment of their (often broken) contents in adjacent burial mounds was the norm at Spiro, one mortuary structure and its contents was left intact, and simply covered over with a clay mound, thus preserving them in a remarkable state until they were unearthed by looters in the 1930s. After this interment, the sequence of charnel house construction, use, and dismantling had been resumed on the summit of the clay mound. The largely intact mortuary structure measured about eighteen by twelve meters in size, and dated to the A.D. 1200 to 1350 period of political expansion and increasing complexity at the site. The objects commercially mined from this charnel house, often termed "the great mortuary," and now dispersed among many museums and private owners, include items more varied, rare, and numerous than the contents of any other single mortuary so far found in eastern North America. This remarkable collection of grave goods places Spiro apart from all other Mississippian sites, and provides a unique window on the artistic abilities, rich symbolism, and complex worldview of a Mississippian society.

Throughout the Mississippian period occupation of the Spiro site (A.D. 800 to 1350), the Craig Mound locality served the purpose of housing the ritually and socially significant dead of the community. While most individuals were interred in the cemeteries of outlying villages and farmsteads, it was here that prestigious ancestors were honored and watched over. The habitation areas at Spiro appear largely to predate A.D. 1200; after this point in time, as the Spiro polity grew in complexity and influence, the site became a specialized mortuary-temple town.

Within the great mortuary itself, three general categories of prestigious burials of the honored elite can be identified. The most spectacular and highest ranking of these were the cedar-pole litter burials. Resting on an extensive split-cane floor, these litters ranged in size from sixty by sixty centimeters to two by two meters, and contained a few skeletal elements of a single honored individual, surrounded by rich deposits of engraved marine shell cups and gorgets, shell and pearl beads, fabric robes, and a variety of other objects of wood, metal, and stone. Innumerable caches of artifacts were also placed on the floor of the great mortuary among the litters, as were partially disarticulated extended burials surrounded by a few artifacts. A third category of burial consisted of disarticulated human remains in basketry chests, also accompanied by burial goods, including copper plates. These three categories of burials appear to represent three different top levels or categories of Spiro society, distinguished spatially and in terms of mortuary treatment from both the lower ranking regional elite of outlying centers and the general populace interred in scattered cemeteries. The diverse array of artifacts found in the great mortuary include very few utilitarian objects, but are almost exclusively items reflecting high social standing as well as ritual and military responsibilities. Marine shell beads in a variety of shapes and sizes are present in abundance, along with masses of arrowheads representing large clusters of arrows. Headdresses and ornaments for the hair, ears, and neck are common, including earspools, copper plumes, copper headdress plates, and gorgets. Exaggerated in form and manufactured from nonfunctional materials, weapons and weapon-derived objects are also common, including mace- and knife-form warclubs and monolithic- and celt-form axes. Ritual or ceremonial objects include human figurines, large effigy pipes, bird staffs, face masks, and the famous engraved, marine-shell cups recovered in large numbers from litter-burial containers. These were quite likely restricted in use to ceremonial settings, perhaps for the consumption of the caffeine-rich purgative "black drink" made from *Ilex vomitoria*.

Remarkably intact textiles were also recovered from the great mortuary, including polychrome mantles and kilts and other items of clothing incorporating feathers and fur. These were for the most part items of costume, no doubt worn by individuals during the elaborate ritual impersonation of mythical beings, and the adoption, the invocation, and often the combination of numerous visual markers of such creatures.

These ritual performances, the costumes involved, and the creatures in question, both real and mythical, are all depicted in the rich corpus of engraved designs present on over 500 marine-shell cups that were deposited, both intact and as scattered fragments, in the great mortuary. While much of the detailed meaning inherent in these designs is beyond reach, and may well not have been known to most of Spiro society apart from the personages buried in the Craig Mound, their significance can be more generally explained when viewed in the context of the historically documented belief systems of southeastern peoples, and the interpretive framework offered earlier regarding the three overlapping areas of responsibility of Mississippian elite: (1) mediation between society and the larger forces at work in the cosmos, (2) maintaining and legitimizing the internal social order, and (3) defending the society from external threat through military prowess.

Central to the worldview of many southeastern peoples, as described historically, was the concept of an ordered universe, often having a tripartite division into the sky or upper world, earth or this world, and a dark and cold underworld, often reached through streams and other bodies of water. In the upper world, often represented by raptorial birds, there was a structure and stability, things existed in a purer and grander form, order and predictability reigned, and beings of the upper world could do remarkable things. The upper world was also the realm of the sun, a central deity of southeastern peoples. Being the source of all warmth, light, and life, the sun was linked in this world to the sacred fire, a symbol of purity and the sun's earthly representative and ally. In contrast, the underworld was a place of disorder and change, where creatures, such as snakes, lizards, and frogs, dwelled. It was the realm of madness and monsters who came out of rivers, lakes, and mountain caves. A distinctive attribute of these monsters, reflecting their embodiment of disorder and anomaly, was that they combined features of creatures from more than one, and often all three, worlds. The Uktena monster of the Cherokees, for example, had the scaly body of a large serpent, the antlers of a deer, and a bird's wings.

Various forms of a monster very similar to the Uktena, that combined a bird's wings, deer antlers, and a snake's body, are depicted on the shell cups recovered from the great mortuary at Spiro, as well as on artifacts from other Mississippian sites across the Southeast (Fig. 5.13). Other monsters of the underworld also abound on the Spiro shell cups, such as the Piasa or underwater panther, that combined the body and head of a mountain lion with the tail of a snake and the feet, and sometimes the wings, of a raptorial bird (Fig. 5.13). Like the Uktena, such water cougars had a controlling influence on underworld creatures, and stood in opposition to beings of the upper world. Uktena and Piasa-like monsters depicted on the Spiro cups, also often incorporated human elements, suggesting the ritual

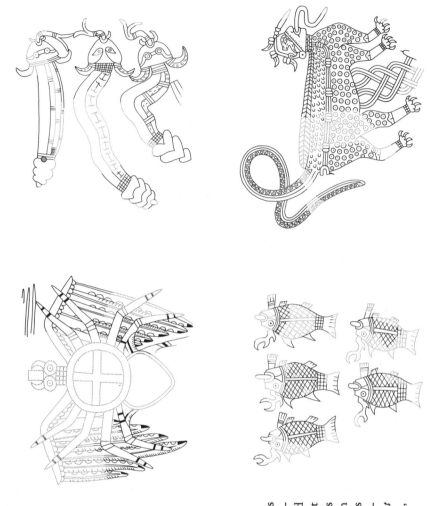

Figure 5.13. Selected monsters depicted in Spiro shell art, including winged spiders, horned snakes, antlered fish, and a cat with feathers, scales, a snake's tail, and a human head. (From Philip Phillips and James Brown, *Pre-Columbian Shell Engravings from the Craig Mound at Spiro, Oklahoma,* pp. 222, 233, 239, and 247.)

Figure 5.14. A Mississippian elite individual wearing the costume of a peregrine falcon, depicted in a carved conch shell cup from the Craig Mound, Spiro, Oklahoma. p. 245 from *Pre-Columbian Shell Engravings from the Craig Mound at Spiro, Oklahoma,* by Philip Phillips and James Brown, 1978, Peabody Museum Press, Harvard University.

impersonation of these creatures by Spiro individuals responsible for mediation with the cosmos.

Religious practitioners at Spiro and across the Southeast did not, however, limit their ritual representations to anomalous monsters of the underworld. Humans taking the role of a raptorial bird, frequently the peregrine falcon, are a dominant theme in the shell art at Spiro and across the Mississippian symbolic landscape (Fig. 5.14). These falcon dancers were impersonating a creature of the upper world, generally analogous to "Tlanuwa," the great mythic hawk of the Cherokees and the mortal enemy of the Uktena.

Like the historically described peoples of the Southeast, Mississippian polities lived between two worlds that were neither entirely friendly nor hostile toward them, but which were locked in cosmic opposition with each other. Caught between these powerful and opposing forces of the overworld and underworld, Mississippian polities and their religious practitioners were constantly under pressure to maintain a delicate balance of order through appropriate ceremonial and ritual mediation.

The Spiro shell cups thus not only illustrate these opposing forces of the universe and record the efforts at ritual mediation by various elite personages, but were also active means for ensuring the success of such rituals. Almost all of the shell art from Spiro that depicts and was involved in cosmic mediation, as indicated through representation of monsters of the underworld, ritual impersonation of creatures of both the overworld and underworld, and other depictions of cosmically directed ritual activities (scenes centered on a vertical pole, panel, or sun–sacred fire design), fall into one of the two general categories of shellwork identified at Spiro, the Craig school.

In contrast, the subject matter of Braden, the other major "school" of shell art represented at Spiro, is largely the intertwined themes of warfare and death (Fig. 5.15). Warriors armed with arrows and warclubs dance across the shell cups of the Braden school. Symbols of warfare also abound. Arrows and maces occur as isolated design elements, as do skulls, scalps, corpses, broken bones, body parts, and severed trophy heads. The arrow sacrifice of enemies is also depicted on a number of cups. Snakes, often shown with arrow heads and representing the underworld (and death?), are also common on Braden-school cups. Double-headed snakes intertwined in a complex knot are a frequently recurrent theme. Perhaps these are the "tie-snakes" of southeastern belief systems that lurk in the no-man's-land between polities to seize the unwary and carry them to the underworld.

The subject matter and ceremonial focus of the Braden school thus parallel and balance those of the Craig school. It is concerned not with maintaining the correct order and stability of a polity caught in the middle of an endless struggle and conflict between the upper and lower worlds, but rather with ensuring with the help of allies the polity's survival through force of arms against an outside world of potential enemies.

The similarities in these two spheres of ceremonial concern are obvious — both deal with the complexities of self-preservation and of maintaining order, stability, and security in a turbulent world of powerful outside forces and ever-changing contexts of power and alliance. It is

Figure 5.15. Braden design motifs of warfare and death, depicted on a carved conch shell cup from the Craig Mound, Spiro site, Oklahoma, showing heads, skull, and broken bones. (From Philip Phillips and James Brown, *Pre-Columbian Shell Engravings from the Craig Mound at Spiro, Oklahoma*, plate 57.)

obvious as well that these two spheres of ceremonial concern are not mutually exclusive, but overlap and interconnect extensively, in that maintaining balance and alliance in the cosmos would have been an essential aspect of any Mississippian society's efforts to chart a safe course in dealing with neighboring polities. Both the potent forces of the upper world and the monsters of the underworld would be powerful allies indeed.

The rituals and ceremonies reflected in the Spiro cups and other such items recovered from Mississippian sites thus played an important role in preserving and protecting Mississippian polities. In addition, they had a deeper inherent purpose in maintaining the socio-political status quo and the privileged position of higher-ranking kinship units and individuals. Hidden in the shell art of Spiro, and in other ritual objects and art of all Mississippian societies, and embedded in their worldview, was the constant struggle of the ascribed status elite to maintain their power, position, and privileges.

THE DECLINE OF MISSISSIPPIAN SOCIETIES

This struggle for social position and political power was played out in different ways in innumerable Mississippian societies over a span of more than 800 years, as the history of individual polities followed distinct, often cyclical, pathways of rise and decline within regional socio-political settings. Into this vibrant and heterogeneous cultural landscape of greater and lesser chiefdoms, small-scale regional politics, and falling and rising fortunes, the European arrival and encroachment of the sixteenth century introduced a dominant and generally uniform trend of rapid socio-political decline. As discussed in the following chapter, European diseases, and to a lesser extent cultural domination, had a devastating effect on Native American societies in eastern North America, causing the rapid and nearly universal disappearance of chiefdom-level socio-political organizations.

Yet, in an unusual historical twist, the central Mississippi Valley, situated deep in the interior and therefore relatively immune from early European impact, witnessed, for reasons as yet unknown, a dramatic and fairly widespread episode of decline and abandonment well prior to the arrival of European explorers or introduced diseases. After about A.D. 1400, this "vacant quarter" stretched north from the confluence of the Ohio and Mississippi Rivers as far as the American Bottom and Cahokia and south almost to the Arkansas-Missouri state line, as well as upstream for considerable distance along the Tennessee and Cumberland Rivers (Fig. 5.1). The Native American groups present in this vacant quarter after 1400 appear to have been small in size and complexity and did not live in large villages or construct mound centers.

In contrast, Late Mississippian polities to the south of the vacant quarter flourished well into the sixteenth century, with the Nodena Phase (1450 to 1650) (Fig. 5.1) identified as the powerful chiefdom of "Pacaha" encountered by the Hernando de Soto *entrada* in 1541. With four mounds and extending over two kilometers along Bradley Ridge, just north of

Memphis, Tennessee, the Bradley site was likely the capital of Pacaha. Over sixty other Nodena phase sites have been identified, organized into southern, middle, and northern clusters, with the Bradley site dominating the southern cluster. These clusters consisted of village sites and secondary mound centers, such as the Upper Nodena and Middle Nodena sites of the middle cluster of sites. Relatively few smaller, outlying sites have been identified, suggesting a Late Mississippian consolidation of population into larger, often fortified settlements. Reflecting the regional political situation at the time, this change in population distribution rendered the Nodena phase and other neighboring polities all the more vulnerable to the epidemic diseases that arrived with de Soto. The two-century-long archaeological record of the Nodena phase and neighboring groups documents the decline of the Pacaha chiefdom after its month-long encounter with de Soto and his men in 1541. One of the secondary mound centers of the middle cluster of the chiefdom, the Upper Nodena site, was 6.2 hectares in size and contained a central plaza bordered by two mounds, with residential sectors and small cemeteries at the site periphery. This settlement was apparently abandoned at about the time of de Soto's arrival, and was likely replaced by the much smaller nearby Middle Nodena site. This suggestion of substantial reduction in the size of this secondary center, reflecting population relocation and diminution due to both disease and warfare with the Spanish, continued in the middle cluster area of the Nodena phase, which appears to have been abandoned by 1600.

The southern cluster of Nodena phase sites, centering on the capital at Bradley, appears to have grown in population at about the same time, with the Bradley site in particular yielding abundant European trade goods. Several sites in the Nodena northern cluster also continued into the seventeenth century, but by 1673, when Louis Jolliet and Jacques Marquette came down the Mississippi by canoe, the region inhabited by the Pacaha chiefdom was largely abandoned, only isolated house structures being recorded. It is possible that the remnants of this chiefdom relocated 160 kilometers to the south during the first half of the seventeenth century, to the mouth of the Arkansas River, reemerging in historical accounts under the general label Quapaw. Of the other Late Mississippian polities that bordered the Nodena phase (Pacaha) at the time of de Soto's crossing of the Mississippi, two had recently been brought under its control (the Walls phase – "Quizquiz", – and the Belle Meade phase – "Aquixo"), and a third (the Parkin phase – "Casqui") was coming under increasing pressure. While the Nodena phase cycle of expansionist growth was interrupted by de Soto, their neighbors shared a far worse fate than simple political subjugation – they too were to disappear from the landscape in the next century, as disease reduced populations and their homelands were abandoned.

Farther south along the Mississippi, a Late Mississippian chiefdom in the vicinity of the present-day city of Natchez, Mississippi, survived through the seventeenth century and well into the eighteenth century, to be described in some detail by Antoine Simon Le Page du Pratz as the "Natchez." Considerable archaeological information is now available regarding the Grand Village of the Natchez (the Fatherland Site) and a number of outlying dispersed "villages." While this archaeological information in many respects complements written accounts about the Natchez and provides valuable insights regarding many aspects of Natchez life, it also serves to underscore the difficulties involved in attempting very detailed archaeological inference of periods of considerable social transformation.

Moving east from the Mississippi Valley, the Tellico Dam project on the Little Tennessee River involved extensive archaeological research on settlements in east Tennessee dating to the period 1400 to 1700, and provided another rich record of the changes that occurred in late Mississippian society as a result of contact with European explorers. One of the most extensively excavated Late Mississippian centers in the Tellico area was the Toqua site, which by 1400 covered a little over two hectares and had a population of about 250 to 300 people (Fig. 5.16). Surrounded by a palisade wall, the village centered on an open plaza and an adjacent earthen mound, which contained evidence of at least sixteen phases of construction over a period of 250 to 300 years, and the burials of a number of the chiefdom's elite.

The Mississippian societies and mound centers of the Little Tennessee River Valley, such as Toqua, Bussell Island, and Citico, flourished up into the sixteenth century, until de Soto's forces entered the area in early June 1540. While certainly not as eloquent as written accounts regarding the brutality of the Spanish toward the Native inhabitants of the region, the archaeological record reflects the devastating impact of the first encounter. Hereafter the palisade wall at Toqua was markedly reduced in size, cutting

Figure 5.16 (opposite page). Artist's reconstruction of the late Mississippian town of Toqua, in eastern Tennessee, at around A.D. 1500, showing the palisade wall, adjacent fields, habitation areas, mounds, and central plaza. (Courtesy, Frank H. McClung Museum, The University of Tennessee, Knoxville, artist Thomas R. Whyte.)

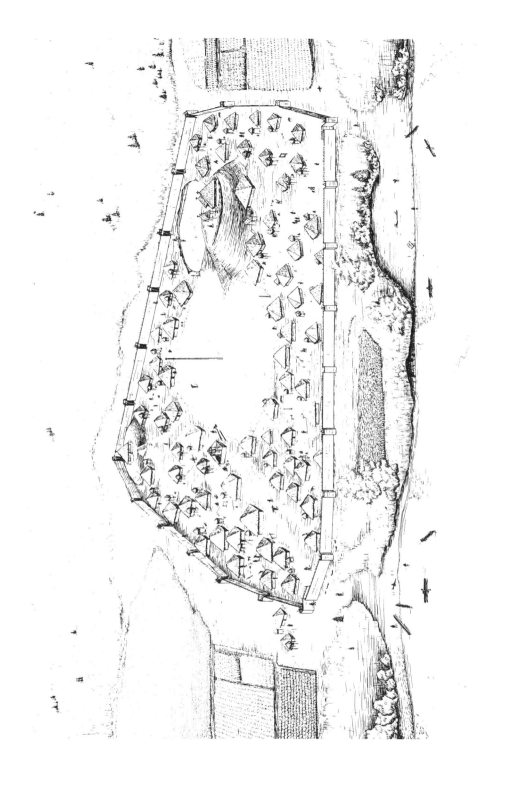

across the plaza and making the site more defensible. This decrease in the size of the settlement, along with the presence of numerous multiple burials, attest to the impact of introduced diseases. By 1600, the Mississippian centers in the valley were greatly reduced in importance, and in 1673, when English traders entered the region, they encountered the Overhill Cherokees. These Overhill Cherokee groups may have been recent arrivals, expanding westward into the area as remnant Mississippian populations relocated south to join Creek polities.

To the south, across the broad Piedmont and Gulf Coastal Plain regions of eastern North America, the archaeological record reflects an overall trend similar to that described above for the Memphis, Tennessee, and Tellico areas. Early Spanish accounts provide vivid descriptions of powerful Late Mississippian chiefdoms, many of which can now be fairly confidently associated with specific sites and river drainages. In the brief span of a century or less after this initial contact, the basic fabric of Mississippian socio-political organization rapidly unraveled. Populations declined due to disease, major mound centers were abandoned, and the large-scale and complex patterns of cultural consolidation and relocation had begun.

BIBLIOGRAPHIC ESSAY

James B. Griffin provides a concise overview of the ways in which perceptions and definitions of Mississippian agricultural chiefdoms have changed over the past century in "Changing Concepts of Mississippian Cultures," in *Alabama and the Borderlands: From Prehistory to Statehood,* ed. R. Reid Badger and Lawrence A. Clayton (University, Ala., 1985), 40–63. Griffin concludes his essay with a general set of boundary conditions for "Mississippian." Following Griffin's essay in the same volume (64–79), Bruce D. Smith provides a complementary brief overview of Mississippian societies, defining a basic Mississippian adaptive niche within the river-valley environments of eastern North America. Christopher Peebles and Susan Kus also provide a definition of Mississippian in "Some Archaeological Correlates of Ranked Societies," in *American Antiquity* 42 (1977), 421–48.

There are numerous summaries of the Mississippian societies that existed in different areas of the region. Bruce D. Smith includes an overview in "The Archaeology of the Southeastern United States: From Dalton to De Soto, 10,500–500 B.P.," in *Advances in World Archaeology*. vol. 5, ed. Fred Wendorf and Angela Close (New York, 1986), 1–92. In *Prehistoric Southern Ozark Marginality: A Myth Exposed* (Columbia, Mo., 1984), James A.

Brown discusses Mississippian societies in the Ozarks. Considerable useful information regarding Mississippian settlements and ceramic assemblages in the Lower Mississippi Valley area can be found in *Archaeological Survey in the Lower Mississippi Alluvial Valley* (Cambridge, 1951), ed. Philip Phillips, James A. Ford, and James B. Griffin, as well as in *Archaeological Survey in the Lower Yazoo Basin, Mississippi* (Cambridge, 1970) by Philip Phillips. Robert W. Neuman discusses Mississippian societies in Louisiana in *An Introduction to Louisiana Archaeology* (Baton Rouge, La., 1984), and John Walthall provides coverage of Alabama in *Prehistoric Indians of the Southeast* (University, Ala., 1980). David Hally describes the Mississippian period in Georgia in "The Mississippian Period," in *Early Georgia* 3 (1) (1975), 37–53, and Hally and James L. Rudolph provide an additional summary in *Mississippi Period Archaeology of the Georgia Piedmont* (Athens, Ga., 1986). David Brose summarizes what is known of North Florida in "Mississippian Period Cultures in Northwestern Florida," in *Perspectives on Gulf Prehistory* ed. Dave D. Davis (Gainesville, Fla., 1984), 165–97. Another fine state summary is provided by David G. Anderson in "The Mississippians in South Carolina," in *Studies in South Carolina Archaeology,* ed. Albert C. Goodyear III and Glen T. Hanson (Columbia, Mo., 1989), 101–32. Dan and Phyllis Morse describe Mississippian settlements and cultural development in the Central Mississippi Valley in *Archaeology of the Central Mississippi Valley* (New York, 1983). Jon Muller summarizes Mississippian groups along the lower Ohio River in *Archaeology of the Lower Ohio River Valley* (New York, 1986). The Mississippian polities in Missouri are discussed by Carl H. Chapman in *The Archaeology of Missouri* (Columbia, Mo., 1975). Jefferson Chapman provides an overview of the Mississippian groups of eastern Tennessee in *Tellico Archaeology* (Knoxville, Tenn., 1985). At a smaller scale, the chapters of *Mississippian Settlement Patterns,* ed. Bruce D. Smith (New York, 1978), provide descriptions of the nature and distribution of the settlements of Mississippian polities in different areas of eastern North America.

A number of publications deal with the Powers Phase, including *The Snodgrass Site of the Powers Phase of Southeast Missouri,* by James E. Price and James B. Griffin; Price's chapter in *Mississippian Settlement Patterns,* 201–32; and *Prehistoric Patterns of Human Behavior* (an analysis of the Gypsy Joint site), by Bruce D. Smith (New York, 1978). Smith's study *Middle Mississippi Exploitation of Animal Populations* (Ann Arbor, Mich., 1973) discusses the subsistence economy of the Powers Phase and other nearby polities.

George Milner's recent article on the American Bottom was the primary reference for my coverage of that area – "The Late Prehistoric Cahokia Cultural System of the Mississippi River Valley: Foundations, Florescence, and Fragmentation," in *Journal of World Prehistory* 4(1) (1990), 1–43. Melvin Fowler provides a valuable summary of the maps and mounds of the Cahokia site in *The Cahokia Atlas* (Springfield, Ill., 1989). The recent FAI-270 project in the American Bottom has produced a remarkable twenty-volume set of reports on the region, in addition to a summary volume, *American Bottom Archaeology,* ed. Charles J. Bareis and James W. Porter (Urbana, Ill., 1984). In this summary volume, an overview of the Emergent Mississippian period (128–58) is provided by John Kelly et al., and the Mississippian period (158–86) is discussed by George Milner et al. A number of important Mississippian period sites are reported on in the FAI-270 series, including *The BBB Motor Site,* by Thomas E. Emerson and Douglas K. Jackson (Urbana, Ill., 1984); *The East St. Louis Stone Quarry Site Cemetery,* by George R. Milner (Urbana, Ill., 1983), and the remarkable Range site, which contained a series of more than twenty settlements that spanned the Mississippian emergence in the region – *The Range Site 2: The Emergent Mississippian Dohack and Range Phase Occupations,* by John E. Kelly et al. (Urbana, Ill., 1990). Further discussion of the Range site and the Mississippian emergence in the American Bottom region can be found in "Range Site Community Patterns and the Mississippian Emergence" (67–112) and "The Emergence of Mississippian Culture in the American Bottom Region" (113–52), by John E. Kelly, in *The Mississippian Emergence,* ed. Bruce D. Smith (Washington, D.C., 1990). The latter volume includes summary chapters on the initial development of Mississippian societies in different areas of the East. A consideration of early mound construction can be found in the chapter by Martha Rolingson (27–51), and the role of trade in the development of Mississippian cultures is discussed in the chapter by James A. Brown et al. (251–75).

The Spiro site is described in a four-volume report entitled *Spiro Studies* (Norman, Okla.); volumes 1 and 2 appeared in 1966, volume 3 in 1971, and volume 4 in 1976. In a landmark publication, Philip Phillips and James Brown provide a detailed and exhaustive description of the motifs present in the shell art of Spiro in *Pre-Columbian Shell Engravings from the Craig Mound at Spiro, Oklahoma* (Cambridge, 1984). Brown provides additional insights into Mississippian symbolism in "On Style Divisions of the Southeastern Ceremonial Complex: A Revisionist Perspective" in *The Southeastern Ceremonial Complex,* ed. Patricia Galloway (Lincoln, Nebr., 1989), 183–204. The volume contains a variety of other excellent papers on Mississippian symbolism, including "Water, Serpents, and the Underworld: An Exploration into Cahokian Symbolism," by Thomas Emerson (45–93) and "Some Speculations on Mississippian Monsters" by Vernon J. Knight, Jr. (205–11). Knight also provides interesting and provocative perspectives on Mississippian social organization in "Social Organization and the Evolution of Hierarchy in Southeastern Chiefdoms" in *Journal of Anthropological Research* 46 (1990), 1–23, and "The Institutional Organization of Mississippian Religion" in *American Antiquity* 51 (1986), 675–87.

The Vacant Quarter is discussed by Stephen Williams in "The Vacant Quarter and Other Late Events in the Lower Valley," in *Towns and Temples along the Mississippi,* ed. David Dye and Cheryl Cox (University, Ala., 1990), 170–80. This edited volume also contains excellent discussions of a number of other aspects of the late-Mississippian and early post-Columbian periods in the area of Memphis, Tennessee. Phyllis A. Morse discusses the late Mississippian Parkin Phase in "The Parkin Site and the Parkin Phase" (118–34), while Dan Morse considers the contemporary Nodena phase in "The Nodena Phase" (69–97). Charles Hudson et al. cover the latter part of the de Soto *entrada* in "The Hernando De Soto Expedition: From Mabila to the Mississippi River" (181–208). Christopher Peebles offers an interesting discussion of the decline of the Moundville chiefdom in "Paradise Lost, Strayed, and Stolen: Prehistoric Social Devolution in the Southeast," in *The Burden of Being Civilized,* ed. M. Richardson and M. Webb (Athens, Ga., 1986), 24–40.

6

ENTERTAINING STRANGERS: NORTH AMERICA IN THE SIXTEENTH CENTURY

BRUCE G. TRIGGER AND WILLIAM R. SWAGERTY

Until the 1960s, anthropologists and ethnohistorians paid little attention to North America in the sixteenth century. Although aware of European exploration at that time, they generally assumed that Native cultures had remained static until Europeans established direct and lasting contact with them, often in the seventeenth century or later. Most anthropologists believed that descriptions of Native cultures dating from the seventeenth century recorded ways of life that had persisted essentially unchanged from much earlier times. As a result, little was done to discover and explain the significance of what had happened to Native people in the century following the Columbian discovery of the Western hemisphere. Even in the southeastern United States, where it has long been recognized that European *entradas* and diseases might have had a major impact on indigenous cultures at that time, there was little systematic investigation of the nature and extent of these changes. Today it is generally acknowledged that the sixteenth century was a time of major changes over large areas of North America. Yet it is far from agreed how geographically extensive or far-reaching were the transformations brought about by European contact.

The sixteenth century is a difficult period to study from the point of view of Native history. Much of the written documentation takes the form of maps or lists of place names, accompanied by a few notes containing material of historical and ethnographic interest. Only a small corpus of written documents furnishes detailed eyewitness accounts of contacts between Native North Americans and Europeans at that time. Many of these are official or semiofficial accounts of European exploration and settlement which illuminate individual regions for only brief periods. Whole classes of encounters that must have been very common, such as those between European whalers and fishermen along the east coast of Canada, went unchronicled, although their large scale is attested in commercial records preserved in the archives of European coastal cities.[1]

Even the most detailed accounts of European activities supply few data from which Native perceptions and motives can be reliably inferred; there is nothing comparable to the many detailed records of the conquests of Mexico and Peru that were produced not only by Spanish participants but also by Native witnesses and their mestizo descendants. The records that are available also present and interpret data in stereotyped ways that scholars must understand before they can be used effectively as historical documents. Finally, written records note only what was happening along the eastern and southern fringes of North America. Vast areas that might have been influenced indirectly by European encounters are undocumented in this manner.

Until recently, the archaeological record for the sixteenth century was little studied because previous generations of archaeologists had been led to believe that little would be discovered that was significantly different from what was described in the earliest written accounts. This situation has only begun to change since the 1970s. Growing attention is now being paid to what many archaeologists call the "protohistorical period," which extends from the earliest evidence of European goods or diseases in a region to the start of detailed and continuous written records.[2] Archaeological research on this and the subsequent early period of sustained contact with Europeans is now greatly increasing what is known about what happened to Native cultures during the sixteenth century.

Yet, while future studies may elucidate significant changes in population size, settlement patterns, economic behavior, and even religious rituals at this time, archaeology alone seems unlikely to reveal much about Native American perceptions and feelings. Finally, Native oral traditions that purport or have been thought to refer to the sixteenth century are few in number and frequently show clear evidence of reworking, if not invention, at a later date. Because of the lack of precise information about so many topics, the few solid facts that are available must necessarily be linked together with material of more doubtful authenticity and often

---

[1] Laurier Turgeon, "Pour redécouvrir notre 16e siècle: les pêches à Terre-Neuve d'après les archives notariales de Bourdeaux," *Revue d'histoire de l'Amérique française* 39 (1986), 523–49.

[2] The chronology for the protohistoric period varies across North America. It begins in the fifteenth century for those regions in the Caribbean and North America first contacted by European explorers and fishermen. Elsewhere, especially in such interior regions as the Plains, Plateau, and Great Basin, it begins some 200 or more years later. A sixteenth-century protohistoric dateline applies to the Northeast, Southeast, Southwest, and California, as well as the whole of Mexico.

with pure speculation. The paucity of reliable data has made discussion of what happened to Native people in the sixteenth century highly vulnerable to fads and short-lived enthusiasms.

NORTH AMERICA IN 1492

At the time of the Columbian voyages North America was a continent in flux, a landmass filled with diverse peoples whose social, political, and economic relations with each other were complex. Contrary to what used to be believed, from the Caribbean to Hudson Bay more cultural change probably was occurring then than at any previous time. Some of these transitions had been centuries in the making; others were recent developments, but uninfluenced by the European reconnaissance and eventual invasion of America.

Like their ancestors, the Native North Americans of this period spent most of their time with their own kin, seldom traveling beyond the prescribed geographical boundaries of a locality or region. Life revolved around subsistence cycles and attendant ceremonialism that celebrated long-term ecological adaptations to lands ranging from patchy hunting and gathering territories, such as the Great Basin and the Arctic, to lusher regions, such as the Southeast, where horticulture and sometimes marine resources alone supported large, sedentary populations. The majority of Native North Americans were semisedentary town and village dwellers who had extensive hunting territories and precise geographical knowledge about their respective regions.

Yet, by the sixteenth century, the lives of many North Americans were determined by increasingly complex political, social, and economic systems. For example, the period after A.D. 1300 had seen increasing reliance on corn agriculture and a rapid expansion of population among the Iroquoian-speaking peoples who lived around the Lower Great Lakes. Some of their settlements now contained up to 2,000 people, while communities had united to form small nations, and "leagues" or "confederacies" may already have started to develop in the course of the fifteenth century.

Although parts of the Southeast were becoming politically and residentially decentralized as Late Mississippian ceremonial centers were abandoned in the period preceding European contact (see Chapter 5), evidence has also been found of chiefdom formation and persistence. Some groups, such as the Coosas of Georgia and the Powhatans of Virginia, appear to have been consolidating at this time.[3] It is not clear, however, whether these developments were wholly uninfluenced by European intrusion or reflect, in whole or part, responses to outsiders.

Scholars agree that in the period immediately preceding European contact the Southwest witnessed the redistribution of populations aggregated into large communities within regions formerly scarcely inhabited and a florescence in ceremonialism and art, reflected in the spread of the Katcina cult, the increasing manufacture and trade of elegant ceramic wares, and colorful kiva murals. Sites that would become important contact points with the first waves of Spanish explorers and colonists, such as Hawikuh at Zuni and Pecos Pueblo, expanded during this period, and the Rio Grande Valley became dotted with individual communities, while many abandonments occurred in the Western Anasazi sector.

At the dawn of the sixteenth century, the various peoples of North America were linked in different ways with neighboring, and in some cases, distant cultures. Economic exchanges and warfare both resulted in a sharing of goods and ideas. In some areas contact with outsiders was increasing around 1492, while in others there was contraction in multicultural interaction and exchanges of material culture.

Interregional trade between the Southwest and neighboring regions continued to be important in the economies and ceremonial lives of its peoples in the period immediately before contact.[4] Major "trade centers" included the pueblos of Zuni and Pecos. Trade networks emanating from the Puebloan heartland connected it to the Plains, Great Basin, and California, as well as northern Mexico. Although foodstuffs, storage containers, clothing, and hides constituted the largest volume of interregional exchange, exotic goods flowed into the Southwest from all directions. After the Athapaskan intrusions of the late fifteenth and early sixteenth centuries, the Pueblos received more goods from the east. Middlemen traders, such as the Jumanos and the Antelope Creek and Panhandler Aspect peoples, crossed the Plains and Texas, and were joined in later times by Comanches and various Apaches. In turn, these groups traded with the Caddos, Wichitas, and Pawnees. Utes, Paiutes, and later Shoshones carried on exchanges between the Southwest and the Great Basin.

---

[3] For the Coosas, see Charles Hudson, Marvin Smith, David Hally, Richard Polhemus, and Chester DePratter, "Coosa: A Chiefdom in the Sixteenth-century United States," *American Antiquity* 50 (1985), 723–37.

[4] Carroll L. Riley and Basil C. Hedrick, eds., *Across the Chichimec Sea: Papers in Honor of J. Charles Kelley* (Carbondale, Ill., 1978); Frances J. Mathien and Randall F. McGuire, eds., *Ripples in the Chichimec Sea: New Considerations of Southwestern-Mesoamerican Interactions* (Carbondale, Ill., 1986).

In California, major "trade centers" did not develop because of the relatively equal distribution of resources along the coast and the abundant game and acorn supplies in the immediate interior. Smaller trading "hubs" or "nodes" linked the numerous linguistic and cultural groups of that region. Several import-export centers, notably villages of the Pomos and Shastas in the north and the Owens Valley Paiutes and the Washoes in the Great Basin, stand out as special hubs linking several cultures and probably processing the largest volume of trade goods. "Trade feasts," such as those known for the Pomos and Chumashes, also afforded a mechanism for exchanging surplus goods with neighbors. Shells from central and southern California were traded into the Great Basin, as well as to the Southwest and beyond.

Many northern California peoples traded with the Indians of Oregon. These goods were transported by Klamath, Molalan, Kalapuyan, and Modoc middlemen-traders. Their ultimate destination was the Dalles on the Columbia River, the largest trade center in the Northwest and possibly all of North America. There each summer thousands of resident Wasco-Wishrams and their neighbors at Celilo Falls harvested and processed millions of kilograms of salmon, and exchanged it for a wide variety of goods from the Plains, Plateau, Northwest Coast, and California. Southern goods were exchanged for northern ones, and interior for coastal. This basic pattern continued well after the beginning of the European maritime trade and was also typical of parts of the Arctic, where seasonally traders exchanged goods and products of the coast for those of the interior.

Eastern North America was likewise crisscrossed by exchange networks, many of which were of considerable antiquity. Trade across ecological boundaries sometimes involved staples, such as the surplus corn that the Hurons traded with the Nipissings, and possibly with other Northern Algonquian peoples, in return for pelts and dried fish. Most trade however, was in luxury items, including marine shells, copper, and fancy furs. Exotic cherts continued to be passed from one band to another throughout the boreal forests. Native copper from the Lake Superior region was carried east to the St. Lawrence River and south into what is now the United States. Marine shells were traded north and west from the Gulf of Mexico and from areas along the east coast such as Chesapeake Bay and Long Island. Incised Gulf conch was distributed throughout the Mississippian region. Pipestone (catlinite), mica, lead (galena), flint, and buffalo hides made their way eastward from the Plains. While exotic goods continued to

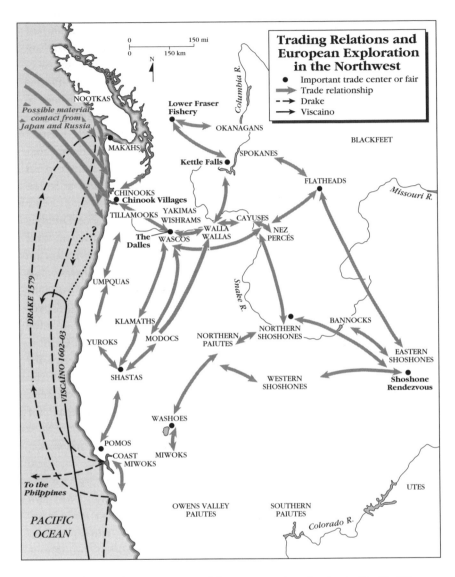

Figure 6.1. Trading relations and European exploration in the Pacific West in the earliest contact period.

play an important role in gift exchange among the rulers of southeastern chiefdoms, farther north such trade appears to have remained limited compared to what it had been prior to A.D. 400. Among the northern Iroquoian-speaking peoples exotic goods of any kind were rarely included in burials until after the appearance of the first European goods. In some cases this restriction of trade correlated with persistent intergroup warfare. Conflicts between the Neutral Iroquoians of southwestern Ontario and their Central Algonquian–speaking neighbors continued into the seventeenth century. Warfare between the St. Lawrence Iroquoians and their Huron and Petun neighbors to the west seems to have lasted into the sixteenth century.

A long-standing debate exists about the degree to which Indians of the Southeast, especially Florida, interacted with Caribbean groups, particularly the Guanahatabeys of western Cuba and the Tainos of the Greater Antilles, including Cuba. The latter groups were superb navigators and skilled oarsmen. For the early hispanic period there are references to trade and traffic between Cuba and southwestern Florida, and at least one colony, an Arawak village, was reported as a permanent settlement among the Calusas by a Spanish sailor shipwrecked in the 1550s. Despite some isolated cultural similarities, the negative archaeological evidence and ethnobotanical dissimilarities, especially the lack of manioc (cassava) in the Southeast, support the view that there was little, if any, significant contact between Florida and the Caribbean in pre-Columbian times. Thereafter, Europeans witnessed contact by Native fishermen and traders across what once had been a very real cultural and geographical barrier, the Gulf Stream.[5]

NATURE OF EUROPEAN CONTACT

Columbus's "discovery" of the New World was one consequence of a search by the centralizing monarchs of Western Europe for new sources of wealth to help pay for their growing armies and civil administrations and to cope with a growing trade deficit with the East that was continuously draining their supplies of precious metals. Beginning in the fifteenth century,

[5] On this debate, see John W. Griffin, ed., *The Florida Indian and His Neighbors* (Winter Park, Fla., 1949); William C. Sturtevant, "The Significance of Ethnological Similarities between Southwestern North America and the Antilles," *Yale University Publications in Anthropology* 64 (1964); Ripley P. Bullen, "Were There Pre-Columbian Cultural Contacts between Florida and the West Indies: The Archaeological Evidence," *Florida Anthropologist* 27/4 (1974), 149–60.

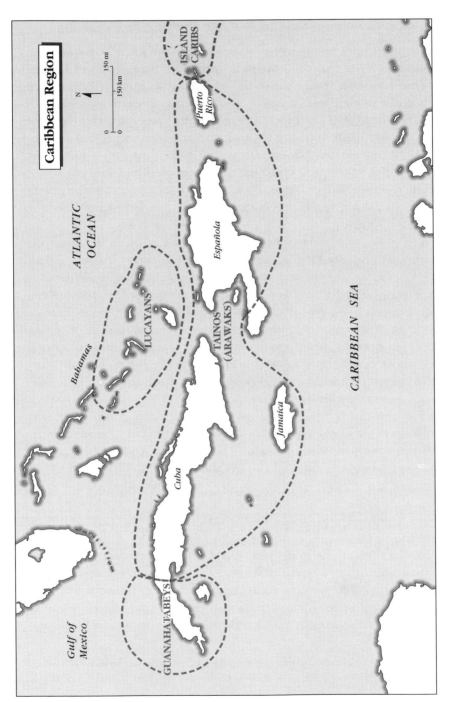

Figure 6.2. The Caribbean region.

Portugal and Spain began to encourage long-distance sea voyages in search of overseas sources of gold, silk, spices, and slaves and to settle islands off the coast of Africa where sugar could be grown. In due course, they also began to search for sea routes that would give them direct access to the riches of the Orient. The Spanish voyages of discovery were supported financially and technically by merchants in Italian cities such as Genoa and Florence, whose prosperity was being threatened by growing Turkish control of the eastern Mediterranean and by Portugal's increasing domination of the trans-Saharan gold trade.

In 1492 Columbus thought that he had reached the Orient when he landed in the Bahamas. Five years later Giovanni Caboto was sailing English ships across the North Atlantic looking for a still shorter sea route to the East. By 1522, however, it was evident, as a result of coastal explorations and Vasco Nuñez de Balboa's overland discovery of the Pacific Ocean in 1513, that these explorers had not reached Asia and that no sea passage joined the Atlantic and Pacific Oceans between Florida and the stormy southern tip of South America. This was followed by a spate of voyages aimed at locating open water somewhere between Florida and Labrador. Between 1524 and 1527, French, Spanish, and English expeditions charted the eastern seaboard of North America without discovering a sea passage to the Orient. Hopes of finding such a sea route south of the Arctic Circle were finally extinguished in 1535, when Jacques Cartier discovered that the Gulf of St. Lawrence was merely the estuary of a vast river. Yet throughout the sixteenth century Europeans, such as Giovanni da Verrazzano and Pedro Menéndez de Avilés, continued to hope that some part of North America would turn out to be a narrow isthmus, while in the seventeenth century explorers, such as Samuel de Champlain, Henry Hudson, and René-Robert Cavelier de La Salle, were still seeking for rivers flowing into the Atlantic that had their headwaters near the Pacific Ocean and that, like the roads the Spanish had built across Mexico, might serve as profitable trade routes between the Orient and Europe.

Within a decade after the conquest of Mexico, Spaniards began to explore the shores of the Pacific. Several attempts by Hernán Cortés to establish beachhead colonies in Baja California in the 1530s failed because of Indian alienation and internal problems among the colonists sent from Mexico. In 1540 Hernando de Alarcón reached the Colorado River delta, while the Indians of Alta (Upper) California met Spaniards for the first time in 1542, when the ships of Juan Rodríguez Cabrillo skirted the west coast as far north as Monterrey and spent the following winter among the Island Chumashes at San Miguel Island. In 1579 Francis Drake reached northern California on his voyage around the world.

Throughout the sixteenth century, European ships generally sailed either directly westward to Newfoundland or by way of the Canary Islands and the Caribbean to Florida; Spanish ships returned home by following the Gulf Stream. Apart from Florida, the east coast of what is now the United States was visited only by explorers, privateers, and fur traders traveling between Newfoundland and the Caribbean. Because of this, throughout most of the century Native people living between Maine and North Carolina had much less regular contact with Europeans than did those who lived either in Florida or in Atlantic Canada. The most prolonged and regular contact occurred in the vicinity of Spanish settlements in the southeastern United States and in conjunction with the summer visits of fishermen to the Northeast coast.

In the sixteenth century relations between Europeans and Native Americans were based on encounters that varied greatly in their intensity, regularity, and duration. Except in the far south, adjacent to areas of Spanish settlement in Mexico and the West Indies, these contacts were restricted to coastal areas, including the St. Lawrence Valley. For the Native peoples who lived in these areas, such encounters involved opportunities as well as dangers. The rest of this section will examine the nature of these contacts, while the following sections will assess their biological consequences and Native responses to them.

Prior to Columbus's reaching the West Indies, Portuguese explorers had encountered many indigenous societies along the west coast of Africa. To win their goodwill and initiate trade, they gave these peoples presents of European goods, which varied in amount and value according to the estimated importance of the leaders with whom they had dealings. The ubiquitous glass bead was first doled out by Columbus upon landfall in 1492 and became a standard item in most encounters during the century that followed. Beads and metal bells, along with hatchets, knives, rattles, feathers, and cloth, constituted a "gift kit" carried by early explorers, including Columbus, Hernán Cortés, Panfilo de Narváez, Francisco de Coronado, Tristán de Luna, and many other sixteenth-century expeditions.

Already in 1501, somewhere along the northeast coast of North America, Gaspar Corte-Real encountered Indians who possessed what he identified as a broken gilt sword and two silver rings of Venetian origin. In 1524 Verrazzano distributed blue beads together with small bells and other trinkets made of copper among the Narragansetts. It is not known if the copper ornaments that the Narragansetts already had were of European origin or made from native copper. While the St. Lawrence Iroquoian fishing party that Cartier encountered at Gaspé in 1534 were initially reluctant to have any dealings with the French, Iroquoian men began to row out to the French ships after they realized that the French would give them knives, glass beads, combs, and other small trinkets. Even the women emerged from their hiding places in the woods to receive a comb and a tin bell and ring each. At the same time, the Iroquoians carried off any goods that the French left lying about unattended. Cartier also distributed knives, hatchets, beads, and tin trinkets to the Indians of Hochelaga when he visited their settlement on the Island of Montreal the following year. These goodwill presents constituted an important source of European goods in the early years of contact. By offering reciprocity, they also made it safer for European ships to take on the supplies of firewood and fresh water required for their return voyage, and in some areas provided the basis for the development of various kinds of trading relations.

The shores of Drake's Bay and nearby Coast Miwok villages in northern California have yielded an assemblage of over 800 sixteenth-century exotic items, mostly Chinese porcelain sherds. These have been attributed to two events: Drake's brief visit in 1579 and the shipwreck of the Spanish Manila galleon, the *San Agustín,* in 1595. Drake must have given some of these dishes (which were booty from a Spanish vessel) to his hosts, who converted them into scrapers, pendants, and other ornaments after they were broken. Other sherds, with edges rounded by the abrasion of sand and sea, are thought to have been recovered by the Coast Miwoks after they were washed ashore from the wreck of the *San Agustín.*[6]

Indian fishermen and coastal residents became adept at salvaging cargoes from numerous ships that were wrecked on shoals and reefs, especially off the coasts of Florida. Very early in the century, the Calusas of southern Florida gained a reputation for recovering goods and live "Christians" (who were sometimes killed but usually adopted and later ransomed) whenever a ship hit one of the keys – "Los Mártires." Spanish items, including coins, were traded into the interior or exchanged for other goods with the Spanish after 1565. At Mound Key, a 32-hectare shell midden in the middle of Estero Bay which has been identified as

[6] Edward P. von der Porten, "Drake and Cermeño in California: Sixteenth Century Chinese Ceramics," *Historical Archaeology* 6 (1972), 1–22.

Calos, the central town of the Calusa chiefdom, many examples of sixteenth-century Spanish pottery have been found. Calos was a special entrepôt and distribution point in southwestern Florida.[7]

The Calusas were not alone in diving for underwater treasure and distributing it through exchange networks. For the Ais, Jeaga, and Tequesta peoples on the southeast Florida coast, the 1550s through the 1570s were especially good years in the business of salvage and the enslavement and ransoming of shipwreck victims, as French, Spanish, and English corsairs competed for wealth and sovereignty in North American waters.

Whenever possible, Europeans tried to salvage their own shipwrecks and keep precious bullion and hardware out of Indian hands. In 1554 the carrack *Santa Maria del Camino* was lost on the coast of Florida, but her cargo was salvaged by Spaniards. That same year, another salvage operation, complete with Native divers from Mexico and primitive diving bells, succeeded in retrieving about half of the 1.5 million pesos that went down with three Havana-bound ships off Padre Island, Texas. Although the local Indians did not recover a share of this wreck, they stalked and killed all but a few of the 250 or so survivors who were attempting to walk back to Mexico.[8]

Most of the early documented contacts between Europeans and Native peoples took place as a result of European efforts to determine the geographical extent of North America and the nature of the waters along its coastlines. The voyages of Diego Miruelo (1516), Francisco Hernández de Córdoba (1517), Juan de Gijalva (1518), Alonzo Alvarez de Piñeda (1519), and Estevão Gomes (1524) helped to fill in geographical holes and gave Europeans a better idea of the ethnographic diversity of North America. None appears to have improved relations between Indians and Europeans.

A common practice was to abduct one or more Native people as trophies of a voyage. In 1502 three Indians whom Sebastian Cabot had brought from the "Newfound Island" to England were presented at the court of Henry VII dressed in Native costumes; at least two of them were still living in London two years later. In 1577 Martin Frobisher transported an Inuit and his kayak to England. In 1509 Thomas Aubert of Rouen seems to have carried off seven Indians from North America to Normandy,

---

[7] Clarence B. Moore, "Certain Antiquities of the Florida West Coast," *Journal of the Academy of Natural Sciences of Philadelphia* 11 (1900), 349–94; Randolph J. Widmer, *The Evolution of the Calusa: A Nonagricultural Chiefdom on the Southwest Florida Coast* (Tuscaloosa, Ala., 1988).

[8] J. Barto Arnold III and Robert S. Weddle, *The Nautical Archaeology of Padre Island: The Spanish Shipwrecks of 1554* (New York, 1978).

although elsewhere it was claimed that these Indians had been rescued from a canoe drifting on the Atlantic Ocean. Along the eastern seaboard of the United States, Verrazzano kidnapped a small boy and tried unsuccessfully to carry off a good-looking young woman. Many of these captives were exhibited as curiosities, the men giving public displays of their skills as canoeists or archers and the women showing how they made clothes. There is no evidence that most of them were ever returned home.

Other Native people, usually young men, were carried off in the hope that they might learn to speak a European language and be able to serve as informants about their homelands and as interpreters on future voyages. One of the Indians that Lucas Vázquez de Ayllón's expedition abducted from the coast of South Carolina in 1521 was baptized Francisco de Chicora. He lived comfortably among his captors for five years, enjoyed favorable attention at the Spanish court, and won the trust of Ayllón. Another Indian from Chesapeake Bay whom the Spanish had taken prisoner in 1561 was baptized Don Luis de Velasco. He was carefully educated by the Spanish and became the confidant of Pedro Menéndez de Avilés, the Spanish commander in Florida. In 1534 Cartier treacherously seized two teenage sons or nephews of the St. Lawrence Iroquoian chief, Donnacona, and kept them at his hometown of St. Malo over the winter, where they learned to speak some French. Cartier's plan was to have them guide him to their homeland, which was located west of where he had been on the Gaspé Peninsula in 1534, and to use them as translators. The utilitarian nature of the kidnapping is indicated by the fact that no attempt appears to have been made to baptize these boys, despite the pious claims that were later to be made for Cartier's explorations. In 1536 Cartier entrapped and carried off Donnacona and his two sons so that the old man could tell the king and other French officials tales of a land rich in precious metals that lay to the west. Before an expedition to conquer this land could be launched, Donnacona and all but one of the ten Iroquoians that Cartier had kidnapped in 1536 were dead. As late as 1605 George Weymouth seized five Indians from coastal New England as potential informants and interpreters. While these kidnappings occurred relatively infrequently and often far apart from each other, news of them must have spread widely along the eastern seaboard.

By the end of the century French kidnappings had given way to fur traders taking young Indians on goodwill visits to France. About 1584 a number of Indians spent the winter in St. Malo as guests of Jacques Noël, Cartier's nephew. In 1602 the fur trader François Gravé Du Pont presented two Montagnais from Tadoussac at the court of Henri IV. They returned home to confirm to their elders that the French king supported the fur traders' promises to help them fight the Iroquois. The following winter the son of a Montagnais chief died at the French court, where he was living in the household of the Dauphin. The aim of these visits was to promote trust and goodwill between the French and their Indian trading partners. Like many Indians who visited France throughout the seventeenth century, most of these young men were probably sons of chiefs who had long been on good terms with French traders and hence were confident that the boys would be returned home. The traders from St. Malo no doubt hoped that these Indians would learn to speak French. After they returned to Canada, they might serve as interpreters and later, as chiefs, would be able to understand what was being said to them well enough to enter into more complex relations with the French. On the whole, fewer Indians came to France in the sixteenth century, either as prisoners or guests, from North America than from Brazil. In 1550 fifty Brazilian natives participated in an elaborate tableau illustrating life in South America that was staged when King Henri II visited Rouen.

The initial stages of the Spanish penetration of the New World have been described as a period of overt, state-supported plundering that was quickly followed by the imposition of tribute on Native populations. Early successes in tapping precious metals and human slaves on Española soon prompted many Spaniards and other Europeans to scan the coastlines of North America for similar resources. On the return from his second voyage Columbus brought thirty American Indian prisoners from Española. They were sold as slaves in Seville, and for the next few years several hundred Indians were sold in Seville or Cadiz every year. In 1501 the Portuguese explorer Corte-Real kidnapped a large number of North American Indians, who were offered for sale in Portugal. Gomes also abducted many natives, probably near the mouth of the Penobscot River, in 1525. Fifty-eight of them were still alive when he arrived with them in Spain.

By 1509, as placer deposits and native Arawaks both declined rapidly in Española, slave raids began in earnest. The Lucayans of the Bahamas bore the brunt of the first large-scale enslavements, which left that island chain virtually depopulated by 1514. With Indian slaves fetching 150 pesos each after 1509, compared with only five pesos in 1508, the Lesser Antilles were largely emptied of their Native inhabitants by 1520 for work in the mines and on the plantations of Española, Puerto Rico (after 1508), Jamaica (after 1509), and Cuba (after 1511). In a quarter of a century, the

Native population of the Spanish main had become a "sorry shell" of its former self.

The arc of Spanish activities had been expanding north since 1513, when Juan Ponce de Léon, a veteran of the Columbian voyages and the conqueror of Puerto Rico, briefly set foot on the Florida peninsula looking for slaves and any other readily transportable loot. His intentions must have been surmised by the resident Ais and Calusas, who resisted and forced the Spaniards back into the sea.

Ponce de Léon would try a second time to penetrate the world of the Calusas in 1521. Again forced to retreat, this time with a mortal wound, he left behind several slain crewmen and more than twice as many fatally wounded Indians. Meanwhile, several contacts between Caribbean-based Spaniards and Indians of the Southeast, particularly Florida, occurred. Some, such as the voyage of Pedro de Salazar (1514–16), succeeded in capturing boatloads of Indians for labor gangs. Somewhere along the Carolina coast, hospitable Indians who traded with the Lucayans opened talks with Salazar and his crew. Five hundred landed on Española in chains.[9] In 1550 an ordinance was issued forbidding bringing any captive American Indians to Spain. The high mortality rate among Indian slaves, probably even more than the Spanish government's opposition to their illegal capture, helped to curb these mass kidnappings. There is no evidence of such piratical raids along the east coasts of North America after the 1520s.

By the early sixteenth century English and French voyages of exploration in the northwestern Atlantic had begun to attract European fishermen, who had long exploited the marine resources of the eastern Atlantic, to fish off the Grand Banks. Although the activities of these fishermen are poorly documented, what appears to be the earliest record of a cargo of Newfoundland fish arriving in England dates from 1502, while, by 1506, Portugal was levying customs duties on codfish brought from North America. Norman fishermen were active by 1504, and, by 1511, the Bretons were regarded as experienced pilots in Newfoundland waters. The French Basques joined the fisheries after 1512, and the first fishing fleet set out from Bordeaux in 1517. Despite an early interest, the English did not return to Newfoundland until 1522. The codfish that these fishermen brought back to Western Europe were a welcome addition to the diet of a

---

[9] Paul E. Hoffman, "A New Voyage of North American Discovery: Pedro de Salazar's Visit to the 'Island of Giants'," *Florida Historical Quarterly* 58 (1980), 514–26.

rapidly increasing and protein-hungry population. To ensure that large numbers of experienced sailors were available to defend the realm in wartime, the government of Elizabethan England promoted the fisheries by increasing the number of days on which fish but not meat could be eaten.

Fishing remained a seasonal activity, with few, if any Europeans remaining over the winter. Each summer, ships crossed the Atlantic and their crews fished close to shore in small boats. They preserved the codfish on shore by eviscerating, lightly salting, washing, and drying them on racks. At the end of the season, the ships returned to Europe, where most of the catch was sold in southern ports. After the middle of the century, some ships sailed to the offshore banks, where the cod were heavily salted in the hold without touching shore. This was the wet, or green, fishery, which, unlike the dry one, did not involve significant contact with Native people.

The Portuguese and Spanish Basques fished mainly off the south and east coasts of Newfoundland, while the Bretons first fished along the Strait of Belle Isle and off Cape Breton and the nearby coasts of Nova Scotia. Around 1540 Spanish and French Basques, sailing in ships of up to 600 tons, gained control of the Strait of Belle Isle and for forty years hunted whales along the south coast of Labrador, where they established seasonal stations for rendering train oil from whale blubber. Whaling required larger crews and more specialized equipment than did cod fishing. As many as 1,000 Basques were engaged in whaling at that time. Portuguese and Spanish activity declined toward the end of the century as a result of piracy and royal exactions of men and capital for military adventures, most notably the Spanish Armada of 1588. Beginning in the 1570s English fishermen won control of most of the eastern Avalon Peninsula of Newfoundland, while French and Spanish Basque fishermen operated in the Gulf of St. Lawrence and around much of the rest of Newfoundland. By the late sixteenth century more ships and men were crossing the North Atlantic each year to fish and hunt whales than were sailing between Spain and its colonies in the New World. In 1578 Anthony Parkhurst estimated that between 350 and 380 vessels were involved in the Newfoundland fishery.[10]

The dry fisheries and whaling were labor-intensive industries that each summer landed thousands of Europeans on the northeastern shores of

[10] R. Cole Harris, ed., *Historical Atlas of Canada,* vol. 1, *From the Beginning to 1800* (Toronto, 1987), 47; Turgeon, "Pour rédecouvrir notre 16e siècle," 529–30.

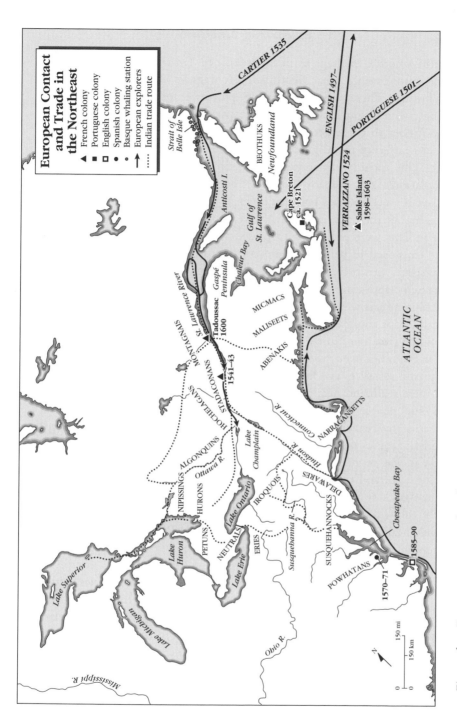

Figure 6.3. European contact and trade in northeastern North America in the sixteenth century.

North America, perhaps as many as 20,000 by 1580. These fishermen came into contact with Beothuks, Montagnais (Innu), and Micmacs (Mi'kmaq). There was considerable potential for conflict with these groups, who might have resented Europeans poaching their fish and cutting timber to construct drying flakes. Europeans were annoyed by the Indians pilfering metal goods left at fishing sites from one season to the next. This included their extracting iron nails and planks from fishing installations. Yet, in many instances, intimate and friendly relations seem to have been established between fishermen or whalers who returned to the same harbor each year and the Native people who inhabited the region. The Indians were pacified with presents, and occasionally some of them were employed in helping to process the catch. The main link in many areas seems, however, to have been, almost from the beginning, a growing but often clandestine trade in animal skins. Relations between the Basques and Montagnais were so good, apart from one skirmish reported for 1574, that shallops could be left in Labrador over the winter without fear they would be stolen or burned to retrieve the iron nails.

On the other hand, the Beothuks, who may have been more dependent on coastal resources and have had fewer furs to trade with Europeans than did their mainland neighbors, were described as early as 1540 as a rude and cruel people with whom Europeans could neither deal nor converse. Later in the century Europeans had to arm their fishing boats against Beothuk attacks and to guard the gear they left on shore against theft. By 1583 it was reported that the Beothuks had abandoned their southern fishing sites and retreated northward as European fishermen established themselves along the coast.

By the 1580s some Micmac bands also had a reputation for being "subtle" and "cruel," which suggests that relations between them and European fishermen did not always proceed smoothly. These disputes may have arisen partly as a result of competition among Native groups for access to European fishermen or alternatively as a result of rivalries among the European fishermen themselves. While these fishermen sometimes may have ventured as far south as the coast of New England and Iberians occasionally may have landed along the east coast of the United States on their way to the northern fisheries, there is no evidence that regular fishing extended farther south than Nova Scotia during the sixteenth century. Annual contacts between fishermen and Native people were restricted to Newfoundland, Nova Scotia, Labrador, and the Gulf of St. Lawrence.

In addition to continued face-to-face meetings with European fishing expeditions along the Atlantic seaboard, there were at least six other main types of direct contact between Native North Americans and Europeans between 1526 and the first successful European colonization in the 1560s. The first was a continuation of meetings along coastlines involving European exploratory parties, itinerant traders, and ships putting in for provisions or to avoid storms: Verrazzano (1524), Cartier (1534), Melchior Diaz (1539), and Cabrillo (1542–3) are examples.

A second type of experience was new. It involved direct meetings between interior peoples and European explorers and would-be colonists. These Europeans wintered among Native peoples and had formal charters or instructions to establish permanent colonies, although they invariably failed to do so. In the Spanish sphere the most important were the Narváez expedition (1528–33), best remembered for the peregrinations of the four survivors across Texas and the account written by the expedition secretary, Alvar Núñez Cabeza de Vaca (1542); the de Soto expedition (1539–43) into the Mississippi heartland and Texas; the Coronado (1540–2) expedition into the Southwest; and the Luna expedition to the Southeast (1559–61).

In the Spanish zone of exploration in the Southwest, archaeologists have unearthed several pieces of chain mail and some brass hardware believed to be crossbow bolts, but none of these items can be directly attributed to a specific pre-1598 expedition. This dearth of material evidence is perplexing in that Coronado led a force of some 300 Spaniards and hundreds of Native servants through the Pueblo country and onto the Plains. His "muster" accounts for 227 cavalry and 62 infantry. Although most of these troops were to return to Mexico, much of their equipment and many of the approximately 1,000 horses and 600 pack animals did not. The documentary record refers to transfers of "barter articles" such as "glassware, pearl beads, and jingle bells, which the Zunis prize very highly as something they have never seen before." No artifacts directly associated with any of the Colorado River, Baja California, or Alta California reconnaissance expeditions have been identified in Indian sites.[11]

In the Southeast, the record of Spanish intrusion is far more abundant and widespread. Pre-1600 European artifacts in the interior Southeast include brass bells, gorgets, animal-effigy pendants, and tinkle cones; iron halberds, daggers, chisels, wedges, and celts; and glass chevron and

---

[11] Bruce T. Ellis, "Crossbow Boltheads from Historic Pueblo Sites," *El Palacio* (Santa Fe, N.M.) 64/7–8 (1957), 209–14; Waldo R. Wedel, "Chain Mail in Plains Archeology," *Plains Anthropologist* 20 (1957), 187–96.

Nueva Cadiz beads. Most have been found in the context of traditional Native burials. At least some of these goods were lost, abandoned, or given away by Spanish explorers traveling through this region. Additional evidence of the scale of transfers can be inferred from musters, inventories, and correlations of what was intended for trade with what was reported to have been returned to home ports. The 300 or so survivors of the original 600 to 700 Hernando de Soto expeditionaries left nearly all of their equipment behind, scattering weapons, tools, and clothes from Florida to Texas.

Landing places, routes, and exact locations of most bivouacs continue to baffle researchers for most of pre-1565 "La Florida," although they have located de Soto's 1539–40 wintering camp in a large Appalachee town near Tallahassee. This site has produced a clearer picture of what a large army on the move left behind after an extended bivouac. Only 10 percent of the artifacts consist of European material, with the Spanish olive jar, the "jerry can" of the Spanish Empire, the major non-Native ceramic. This indicates that de Soto intended to live off the land or be resupplied. Chain mail, which proved useless against Native arrows, has also been found. Dozens of wrought iron nails indicate that the Spanish were constructing substantial shelters and palisades. Trade beads have also been recovered. In due course, this site should permit a chronology of all "probable" de Soto artifacts throughout the Southeast and clarify the route of the expedition led by him, and after his death by Luis de Moscoso. The most recent studies carry his expedition north into what are now North Carolina and Tennessee before turning south and west toward the Mississippi River.[12]

In the French sphere, the Cartier (1535–6) and Cartier-Roberval expeditions (1540–3) impacted Indian lives in the interior. Once Cartier realized that the St. Lawrence Valley was not a sea route to the Orient, he attempted to justify further French exploration by discovering mineral wealth. Stories that chief Donnacona had told about the interior of the continent were interpreted as evidence that there existed to the west of Montreal a "Kingdom of the Saguenay" that was rich in gold and silver and inhabited by light-skinned people who wore woollen clothing. Impressed by Donnacona's stories and hard-pressed for bullion to finance his Italian wars, Francis I decided to challenge Spanish claims to sovereignty over the whole of North America and invested a nobleman, Jean-François

---

[12] On de Soto's route, see the discussion in Jerald T. Milanich and Susan Milbrath, eds., *First Encounters: Spanish Explorations in the Caribbean and the United States, 1492–1570* (Gainesville, Fla., 1989) and in David Hurst Thomas, ed., *Columbian Consequences*, vol. 2 (Washington, D.C., 1990).

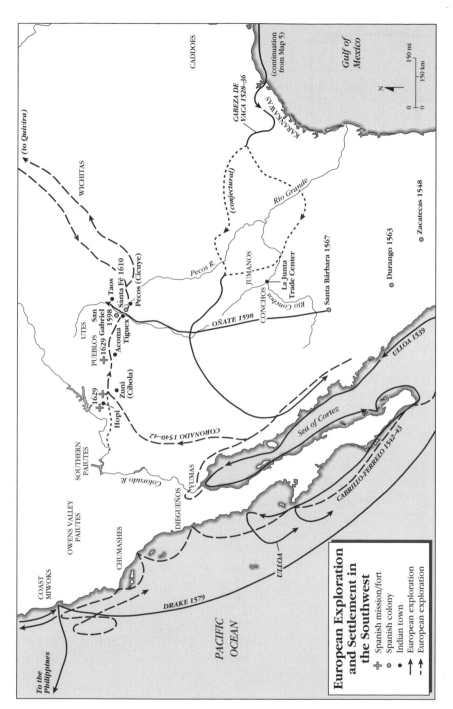

Figure 6.4. European exploration and settlement in southwestern North America in the sixteenth century.

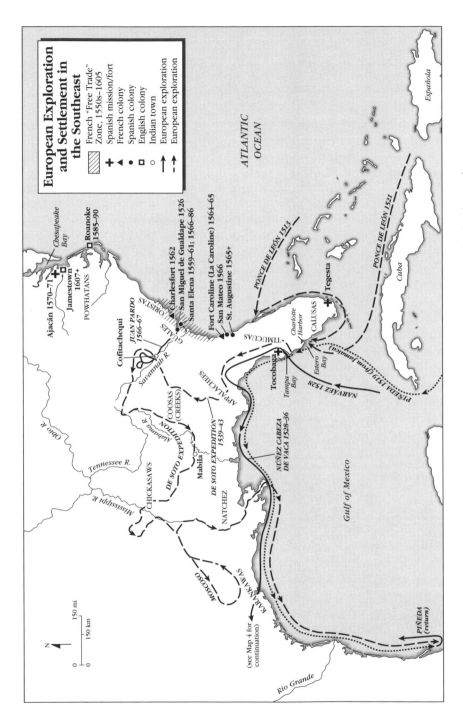

Figure 6.5. European exploration and settlement in southeastern North America in the sixteenth century.

de La Rocque, sieur de Roberval, with vice-regal powers to discover and subdue this kingdom. Two expeditions, the first led by Cartier in 1541 and the second by Roberval in 1542, failed to penetrate west of the Lachine Rapids at Montreal, which Cartier had reached in 1535, and seem to have convinced the French of the mythical status of the Kingdom of the Saguenay. Cartier hoped that he had assured the success of his expedition by discovering gold and diamonds near Quebec, but, when his finds turned out to be valueless, official interest in Canada ceased immediately.

A third type of contact involved the meeting of North American Indians with Mesoamerican and Caribbean Natives who accompanied European expeditions. During *entradas,* such as those of de Soto and Coronado, these Indians served as foot servants who performed a multiplicity of essential tasks, from bearing burdens and cooking to translation and communication by signs. They were often listed as "allies" in official musters and generally acted as such on campaigns. It appears that local Natives did not treat them differently from European soldiers and officers. By midcentury many were undoubtedly mestizos who were hispanic in culture.[13]

A fourth type of contact experience was with missionaries. Priests accompanied several voyages of reconnaissance and overland expeditions. Three Franciscans were with Francisco de Ulloa's Gulf of California expedition of 1539, the same year another Franciscan, Marcos de Niza, was sent north to check rumors of a well-peopled and wealthy province known as Cibola (Zuni). Niza returned to that province in 1540 as one of six priests accompanying Coronado into the Southwest, two of whom decided to remain behind to do mission work. One is believed to have been killed while ministering in Quivira (on the Plains), while a second remained in Cicuye (Pecos) and was never heard of again. The Ayllón and Luna colonies included some Dominicans. Twelve priests served de Soto's expedition; four died during the first year. During the costly battle of Mabila, the largest single confrontation of the trek, the remaining clerics lost all their clothes and sacramental equipment. A few individual Indians were declared to have become "Christians" by the de Soto chroniclers, but no large-scale conversions are reported. Given the rapid pace of the expedition, even Holy Days were violated by the Spaniards. This is not to suggest that all of them took their Catholicism lightly. A "dry mass" was held throughout the expedition according to one source, but the overall

[13] Carroll L. Riley, "Mesoamerican Indians in the Early Southwest," *Ethnohistory* 21 (1974), 25–36; Kathleen A. Deagan, *"Mestizaje* in Colonial St. Augustine," *Ethnohistory* 20 (1973), 55–65.

impression is that proselytization was a low priority throughout this four-year search for treasure.

Nor was mission work a priority for the French under Cartier in the 1530s and 1540s or Ribault in 1562. Two Protestant pastors were with the French colony at Fort Caroline. Their presumed influence on the local Indians was a cause of Spanish concern, as reported by Menéndez after the conquest in 1565.

Roman Catholic missionization of North America began in the Caribbean and fanned out from there and central Mexico in the first quarter of the sixteenth century. Prior to permanent European settlements in the 1560s in the Southeast and 1598 in New Mexico, the major Spanish experiments north of Mexico and the Caribbean were undertaken by Dominicans under Luis de Cáncer in 1549 in Florida and Franciscans led by Father Augustín Rodríguez in New Mexico in 1581. The choice of landing sites in Florida did not match the ideal: to contact Indians who had not been previously antagonized by military force or slave raiders, to live among them without military escort, and to show a different side to the European incursion. Instead, in the Tampa Bay region, four priests, including Cáncer, were killed almost immediately after stepping ashore to begin work among the Timucuans. One de Soto army survivor held captive was freed, but the memory of the aggressive 1539 landing must have influenced the hostile reception that the Indians gave to the unarmed priests. This prototype of martyrdom was to be repeated in the Southeast several times by 1603.

As part of the royal ordinances promulgated in 1573 for the entire Spanish realm, ecclesiastics were to be favored over private citizens in all new discoveries. A maximum of twenty soldiers were to be allowed into unpacified lands to accompany priests willing to extend Spanish sovereignty and the Christian faith. Thus, unlike the Cáncer mission, Rodríguez and two friars set out in 1581 escorted by eight soldiers and nineteen Indian servants. The choice of the commanding officer proved disastrous for the friars and for the possibility of mending ill feelings which had lasted since the incursion of Coronado, who had battled the Zunis and alienated most of the Natives of the Rio Grande Valley. The three priests pursued their mission work without military guards, while the armed escort mapped towns and possible mining areas, often clashing with the local Indians.

News of large "cities" and possible mineral wealth stirred additional *entradas* into New Mexico. In 1582 locating the "lost" missionaries and "new" Indian souls became the object of the priest Bernardino Beltrán,

while the expedition's co-leader, Antonio Espejo, was interested in surveying the land and its potential. This clash in purposes affected Indian
relations, prompting Beltrán to leave the main party without benefit of his
two religious colleagues, who were reported martyred. Favorable reports
to authorities by Espejo led to colonization in 1598, after three additional
secular probes.

There has been much debate in recent years about the volume and
importance of a fifth type of interaction, the fur trade, in the middle and
late sixteenth century. Because much of this trade was carried on as a
sideline by fishermen, privateers, and explorers who were anxious to
avoid taxes and customs duty, little information is available concerning
it. Some have maintained that the fur trade began early in the sixteenth
century and increased steadily in importance. Others have argued that it
was sporadic and of little significance until the 1580s, and that even
then the profits individuals could make from trading for furs were much
less than those to be made from fishing.[14] It is fairly clear that the beaver
trade was important only in the last two decades of the sixteenth century.
There is, however, evidence that trading for fancy furs and animal hides
was of considerable importance prior to that time.

In Europe fancy furs used as elements of clothing had long been valued
as status symbols. Sumptuary laws failed to curtail the growing demand
for these furs as the population and prosperity of Western Europe increased
in the course of the sixteenth century. There was also a growing demand
for leather, which encouraged Spanish settlers in the West Indies to turn
to less labor-intensive cattle raising as the Native population declined. It
did not take long to realize that deer, moose, walrus, and caribou hides
could supplement the skins of domestic cattle. In North America, wild
animal skins were used to make clothing, which, especially in northern
regions, were vital for survival. These were often made from deer, moose,
or caribou hides and from beaver skins, which were worn with the fur left
on. Fancy furs were valued as luxury goods and often traded from one
Native group to another over long distances. For example, in the early
seventeenth century, black squirrel skins from southern Ontario were
traded into Quebec, where Algonquins and Montagnais used them to
make fancy robes, while raccoon skins from south of Lake Erie were traded
into northern Ontario.

[14] John A. Dickinson, "Old Routes and New Wares: The Advent of European Goods in the St.
Lawrence Valley," in Bruce G. Trigger, Toby Morantz, and Louise Dechêne, eds., *Le Castor Fait
Tout: Selected Papers of the Fifth North American Fur Trade Conference, 1985* (Montreal, 1987), 25–41.

The evidence for the exchange of furs and hides with Europeans is extremely limited. In 1524 Verrazzano found that the Indians of coastal Maine already had established a protocol that avoided hand-to-hand contact but permitted trading with passing ships. A year later Gomes's pilot and possibly other members of his crew brought sables and other valuable furs back to Spain. There is evidence that fur trading had begun in the vicinity of Cape Breton Island and the Strait of Belle Isle at least as early as the 1530s. Although the large gathering of Micmacs that Cartier met in Chaleur Bay did not have vast numbers of furs with them, they held up skins on the ends of sticks to indicate that they wanted to trade. While the details of this encounter indicate that trading was perhaps still intermittent this far from the ocean, the knowledgeable way in which these Indians dealt with the French suggests that they may already have been trading with Europeans nearer to Cape Breton Island. The direct course that Cartier followed from island to island across the Gulf of St. Lawrence also indicates that even this area was already familiar to one or more members of his crew. Later that summer on Anticosti Island, Cartier encountered some Montagnais who had come from farther up the St. Lawrence River to trade with European fishermen at the Strait of Belle Isle. They may have been carrying European goods as far inland as the St. Lawrence Iroquoians at Stadacona, who already may have been engaged, either directly or indirectly, in trading furs by this time. While those who oppose the idea of an early fur trade make much of the fact that the Stadaconans are reported to have exchanged food, but not furs, with Cartier over the winter of 1635–6, it is significant that when Donnacona was carried off to France the following year, his followers gave him three bundles of beaver and seal skins, presumably to trade with the French. Still more tenuous evidence are the Indians whom Cartier encountered amassing muskrat skins between Quebec City and Montreal.

In 1537 a quantity of ironware was being taken to the Strait of Belle Isle to exchange for marten and other furs. Four years later Indians were reported to be coming to that area to trade "deer" and "wolf" (*loup marin,* or seal?) skins for iron axes, knives, and similar items; among these Indians appear to have been Iroquoians from the vicinity of Quebec City. These reports suggest that already by the late 1530s, if not earlier, some trading had become routine along the southern coast of Labrador. Although for several decades Spanish Basque whalers completely kept Breton fishermen out of that area, the trading continued.

As yet there is little archaeological evidence bearing on relations between Europeans and Native people in that region. Written records indicate that in the late sixteenth century copper kettles were among the most popular items that the Basques were trading with Native people along the north shore of the Gulf of St. Lawrence. Historical and archaeological evidence also suggests that European goods were being carried to the north and west by the various Native groups that came to that area to trade each year. As these goods wore out, scraps of metal were exchanged from one group to another, dispersing European goods still farther into the interior.[15]

The evidence of early European trading along the Strait of Belle Isle increases the likelihood that furs and skins were being traded for in other areas. One of the most flourishing zones of trade was probably centered on Cape Breton, although our documentation for European activities in that area is poorer than it is for southern Labrador. Yet, in 1569, a French ship is specifically reported trading for furs near Cape Breton, and still earlier, in 1545, the French navigator Jean Alfonse had noted that large quantities of furs were available along the coast of Maine. Such knowledge may have enticed some European fishermen to explore beyond their usual fishing areas in search of furs and hides. This suggests that a Portuguese agent in France may not have been exaggerating when he reported, around 1540, that many thousands of animal skins were being brought to that country each year from the New World. Shipping records indicate that the Norman fishermen from Honfleur and Le Havre who were trading around Cape Breton late in the sixteenth century were supplying fewer copper kettles than were the Basques operating farther north, although they were providing a considerable range of goods.[16]

While fancy furs made up part of this trade, much of it probably consisted of hides. "Deer" skins were reported as an item of trade along the Strait of Belle Isle in the 1540s. These were probably caribou skins, which also seem to be mentioned in the will of a Basque whaler from Orio in 1557.[17] In 1565 Menéndez claimed that 6,000 "buffalo" hides were arriving annually at La Rochelle in France. While there is no reason to believe, as he did, that these hides were being traded into eastern Canada from as

[15] Laurier Turgeon, "Basque-Amerindian Trade in the Saint Lawrence during the Sixteenth Century: New Documents, New Perspectives," *Man in the Northeast* 40 (1990), 81–7, see esp. 84–5.
[16] Ibid., 85; W. R. Fitzgerald, L. Turgeon, R. H. Whitehead, and J. W. Bradley, "Late Sixteenth-century Basque Banded Copper Kettles," *Historical Archaeology* 27 (1993), 44–57.
[17] Selma Barkham, "A Note on the Strait of Belle Isle during the Period of Basque Contact with Indians and Inuit," *Inuit Studies* 4 (1980), 51–8.

far south as Virginia, his report may provide evidence of the scale on which one group of fishermen were able to collect hides in Atlantic Canada. In 1580 an English vessel commanded by Simon Fernandez brought back sample hides, probably of moose, from the New England coast. The same year, the crew of another vessel, commanded by John Walker, raided an Abenaki village along the Penobscot River and carried off 300 hides.

While the exchange of furs and hides between Native people and Europeans does not appear to have been as extensive or regular beyond the area of the northern fisheries, it occurred on a limited scale everywhere where there was contact between the two groups. Survivors of both the de Soto and Coronado expeditions returned to Mexico in Native-made skin clothing and with bedding of furs traded or seized from Native hunters. Later Spanish colonizers, such as Menéndez and Oñate, seized opportunities to extract as tribute Native-tanned skins, which fetched revenues needed for the struggling colonies of Florida and New Mexico.

French privateers appear to have traded with the Indians along the east coast of North America at the same time that they preyed upon Spanish shipping. One French vessel is reported to have bartered knives, fish-hooks, and shirts for 1,000 marten skins in Chesapeake Bay in 1546 and to have obtained an equal number of skins farther south. In 1560 official Spanish documents claimed that French privateers were visiting the Southeast coast almost every year to trade for gold (from wrecks?), pearls, and marten skins. Despite Spanish efforts to exclude them, the French continued to trade in this region throughout the 1590s.[18]

While many different kinds of furs and skins were purchased prior to 1580, there was growing emphasis on beaver pelts during the last two or three decades of the century. This development was connected with an increasing demand for felted beaver hats among the nobility and middle classes of Western Europe. More research is needed to determine whether the felting industry expanded because of new fashions, which increased the demand for beaver pelts, or because of the growing availability of beaver fur. Felting this fur required removing the long guard hairs, leaving only the short, barbed underhair. In the sixteenth century, this necessitated either sending the fur to Russia or buying pelts that had been trapped during the winter and worn by the Indians with the fur next to the body

---

[18] David B. Quinn, ed., *New American World: A Documentary History of North America to 1612*, 5 vols. (New York, 1979), 1:217–18.

for 15 to 18 months, until the guard hairs had been rubbed out. Thus Indians were able to exchange their worn-out clothing for European goods. The growing demand for beaver pelts was also to the advantage of Native hunters, since beaver were more economical to hunt than were other fur-bearing animals. On average, beaver meat yielded seven times the number of calories that had to be expended to trap them. While this was less than the ten- to twenty-five-fold yield from hunting moose or caribou, it was much greater than the 0.7- to 0.1-fold yield from fancy fur-bearing animals such as foxes.[19] Already by 1583, castoreum, or beaver civit, which Europeans used to make perfume and medicine, was being obtained from Native people along the Northeast coast. This specialized exchange provides further evidence that the fur trade was by then already on a regular basis.

The growing demand for beaver pelts encouraged the entry of professional traders into the North American trade. In 1583 the French explorer Etienne Bellenger and his backers attempted to found a fur-trading post and mission on the Bay of Fundy or along the Maine coast. Although conflict with Indians frustrated his plans, Bellenger returned to France with a cargo of hides, marten, otter, and lynx pelts, and enough beaver to make 600 hats. While his cargo was worth less than the average fishing ship had grossed twenty-five years earlier, the launching of this expedition reflected a growing awareness of a new source of profit.

The main geographical focus of the professional fur trade quickly became the St. Lawrence River. Seventeenth-century sources suggest that Europeans had been visiting Tadoussac since 1550, and there is considerable evidence that French Basque whalers were active in that area in the late sixteenth century. At least some of these whalers seem to have engaged in fur trading on a casual basis. It was almost certainly the profits already being derived from the fur trade at Tadoussac that, in 1581, induced a Breton syndicate to send a small ship to the St. Lawrence Valley specifically to trade for furs. The following year, a larger ship was sent which made a fourteen-fold profit. In 1583 three ships were despatched, one of which carried Jacques Noël, a nephew of Jacques Cartier. That year Richard Hakluyt saw in a Paris depot furs from Canada that were estimated to be worth 15,000 livres. In 1584 merchants from St. Malo sent five ships to the St. Lawrence, and the following year they planned to send

[19] Harvey A. Feit, "The Ethno-ecology of the Waswanipi Cree; Or How Hunters Can Manage Their Resources," in Bruce Cox, ed., *Cultural Ecology* (Toronto, 1973), 115–25.

twice as many, while the Norman and French Basques also remained active in the fur trade. This was an uneconomical situation, since, during the busiest years of the seventeenth century, only two ships were needed to transport the entire fur trade of New France. By 1587 rival trading vessels were battling each other on the St Lawrence River. The following year Noël and a partner obtained a monopoly of mines and furs in Canada in return for a commitment to fortify and settle the country at no cost to the royal treasury. The monopoly was abandoned, however, following protests from the parliament of Brittany.

In the early 1580s French fur traders were operating upriver from Tadoussac, especially around Lac St. Pierre and Montreal Island. While the merchants of St. Malo later claimed that they had continued to visit the Montreal area into the early seventeenth century, the large numbers of Algonquins who were coming from the Ottawa Valley to Tadoussac to trade at that time suggest that the upriver commerce was neither as regular nor on as large a scale as the Malouins later implied. By the end of the sixteenth century, Tadoussac was clearly the most important fur-trading center and had replaced the Strait of Belle Isle as the major source from which European goods were reaching Indians living north and west of the St. Lawrence Valley (see also Chapter 13). In return for European goods, the Montagnais who lived there were receiving furs that had been traded from group to group from as far north as James Bay and as far west as Lake Huron. In addition to the Algonquins, Maliseets or Abenakis from Maine were trading at least some of their furs at Tadoussac. This suggests that, despite increasing French and English activity along the coast of New England, even as far north as coastal Maine trading encounters between Native peoples and Europeans were not yet as dependable as they were along the St. Lawrence River or in the Gulf of St. Lawrence.

Raleigh's Roanoke Island colony, as well as the early-seventeenth-century Jamestown settlement, exchanged European wares for both food-stuffs and skins. Yet, despite sixty years of recorded visits by explorers, pirates, and missionaries, in the early 1580s the Indians of coastal Virginia were reported to possess only a few iron tools that they had obtained from a shipwreck twenty years earlier, and as late as 1607 an iron axe was still regarded as a rich present. The situation appears to have been substantially the same as when, after a Spanish official had found European goods in Indian villages north of Florida in 1564, he correctly attributed them to recent visits by French colonists. In 1610 Captain John Smith reported that the Iroquois (whom he called the Massawomeks) got their European goods from the St. Lawrence Valley and that the Susquehannocks, an Iroquoian group living north of Chesapeake Bay, were supplying Algonquian groups who lived between them and the Powhatan realm with iron hatchets and knives, as well as with pieces of iron and brass. This southward movement of European goods suggests the continuing importance of a pattern of exchange centered on the St. Lawrence Valley and the Maritime Provinces, which antedated the appearance of more abundant and reliable supplies of European material along the central coast of the United States. While some European goods may have been carried from Chesapeake Bay northward into the Lower Great Lakes region in the sixteenth century, along with supplies of marine shell, caution is needed in seeing this area as being the major source of European goods for the interior of the continent at this time. In any case, archaeological evidence suggests that European goods were reaching the Lower Great Lakes area only in small quantities and possibly only intermittently prior to the 1580s.[20]

A final type of direct contact was the colonial venture, which, whether it was succesful or not, introduced Native Americans to a wide variety of European material culture and behavior. About 1520 João Fagundes, a native of Viana, Portugal, explored the coast of North America between Maine and Sable Island. Soon after, he established the first European colony in North America since the Norse settlements (see Chapter 14). This Azorean-style community, which combined fishing, soap making, and farming, was probably located on Cape Breton Island, and appears to have lasted for several years – a record for North America until the founding of St. Augustine almost forty-five years later. While little is known about this colony, it has been suggested that Micmac hostility played a role in its abandonment. It is the only example of a European fishing settlement being established in North America in the sixteenth century.

The successive colonies that Cartier and Roberval established were both located at Cap Rouge, just west of Stadacona, in 1541 and 1542. Each lasted only one winter. While occupied by both men and women, they appear to have been regarded mainly as bases for exploration and conquest. From these short-lived settlements the Indians of the St. Lawrence Valley

[20] William R. Fitzgerald, "Chronology to Cultural Process: Lower Great Lakes Archaeology, 1500–1650," Ph.D. dissertation, Department of Anthropology, McGill University, 1990; for a different view, see James W. Bradley, *Evolution of the Onondaga Iroquois: Accommodating Change, 1500–1655* (Syracuse, N.Y., 1987). James Pendergast offers a different view of the identity of the Massawomecks in his *The Massawomeck: Raiders and Traders into the Chesapeake Bay in the Seventeenth Century* (Philadelphia, 1991).

acquired European goods not only in exchange for food but also from the material the French left behind.

Like their counterparts to the north, Indians of the Southeast and Southwest gained new items from the tons of European material carried into their regions by would-be colonizers. Ayllón's original party consisted of about 500 men and "all the supplies and provisions" they required. Many of these supplies were lost when the flagship sank as it approached the Carolina coast, but some items filtered into Indian hands through trade with the colonists at San Miguel de Gualdape, Spain's first municipality north of Mexico, and later through the Indians' scavenging of the abandoned site. Fourteen years later the de Soto expedition found Biscayan axes, a Spanish dagger, and various European beads at the large inland settlement of Cofitachequi, only two days' travel from San Miguel. Although the site of San Miguel has never been located, burial mounds on St. Simon's Island, off the Georgia coast, confirm the early integration of European artifacts into Native mortuary ritual. Nueva Cadiz beads (rarely produced after 1600) and copper coins minted in Seville between 1517 and the early 1630s are time markers for Ayllón's colony, shipwreck debris, or perhaps the trade or spoils of war with coastal slavers.[21]

The inventory of the Juan Pardo expeditions in the Southeast is a poignant example of the importance by midcentury of hardware in trade, diplomacy, and the ability of Europeans to lay more permanent foundations for successful colonies. Operating out of Santa Elena, Pardo and his cavalry built six forts in the Carolina interior between 1566 and 1567. Instructed to pacify with goodwill and not conquer by force, Pardo placated Native headmen with distributions of a large volume of hardware, buttons, cloth, and necklaces. Chisels, wedges, hatchets, and knives were presented as gifts. In addition, the forts were stocked with lead, powder, nails, and many tools for constructing European-style redoubts. All of these became Native possessions when the forts were overrun by Indians within a year or two of their construction.

A similar scattering of French trade goods and tools occurred to the south in Florida during the short-lived occupation of the region from Parris Island to the St. Johns River by French colonists under the command of Jean Ribault and René de Goulaine de Laudonnière. From the late 1550s to the end of the century, the French communicated and traded

---

[21] Charles Pearson, "Evidence of Early Spanish Contact on the Georgia Coast," *Historical Archaeology* 11 (1977), 74–83.

with the Timucuan and Guale polities and were generally well received. After building the thirty-man garrison of Charlesfort among the Guales in 1562 (abandoned within a year) and the larger settlement of Fort Caroline among the Timucuan-speaking Saturiwans in 1564, the French were on the path toward establishing an elaborate trade nexus when they were expelled by the Spanish *adelantado* Menéndez in 1565.

The French became middlemen traders and political brokers in diplomacy among competing confederated Indian polities. Yet it did not always work to their advantage when one Indian polity or community was alienated in the interest of sealing an alliance with another by supplying French *harquebusiers* (gunners) or granting liberal trade standards. Once set in motion, the inertia of a "divide and conquer" policy wrought ill consequences for the enterprise at large and for individual Frenchmen who struck out on their own on private trading ventures. Several did not return, even though they married into Native families, learned Native languages, and became resident traders in the field, a pattern later to become familiar on other frontiers of French North America.[22]

Still, even after the capture of Fort Caroline and the execution of most of its garrison by Menéndez, Frenchmen were given refuge in Guale and Timucuan villages. Their presence up the coast and in the interior (280 were reported to have escaped from shipwrecks and been harbored by the Guales during 1577 alone) and repeated French incursions, especially the retaliatory strike by Dominique de Gourgues which leveled Fort San Mateo on Amelia Island in 1567–8, served to undermine Spanish policy.[23]

Permanent European settlement in the Southeast is associated with Menéndez and early Florida. That occupation dates to 1565 at the garrison town of St. Augustine and 1566 at Santa Elena on Parris Island in South Carolina. Under the strong leadership of Menéndez and the less tenacious grip of his successors, Spain succeeded in holding the province until 1763, but the price paid by resident Indian peoples was high.

Indians who aided other Europeans were dealt with harshly; those who cooperated were given the benefit of clergy and enticed into trading and social alliances. Menéndez personally married the sister of Carlos, the leading Calusa chief, to seal an agreement with that powerful chiefdom in

[22] James W. Covington, "Relations between the Eastern Timucua Indians and the French and Spanish, 1564–1567," in Charles Hudson, ed., *Four Centuries of Southern Indians* (Athens, Ga., 1975), 11–27.

[23] Mary Ross, "French Intrusions and Indian Uprisings in Georgia and South Carolina (1577–1580)," *Georgia Historical Quarterly* 10/3 (1923), 251–81.

1566. The betrothal was clearly an act of expediency, but Menéndez's overall Indian policy was initially based on idealism and genuine faith that Indians and Europeans could coexist in Florida.

To accomplish this Menéndez reasoned that he would have to bring an end to inter-Indian warfare and factionalism. He sought to do this by extracting pledges of peace from Indian leaders and exchanging Native women and boys for Jesuits, who would reside in Native towns. Ultimately, it was believed, the hispanicized Natives would convert the rest of their people to Spanish lifeways and beliefs. For most of the Indians with whom the Spanish were in contact, the program of the Spanish invaders was unattractive, but experiments by Native leaders were sometimes approved by their followers. However, unruly soldiers, discontented colonists, intolerant priests, and often deceitful Spanish officials, acting in Menéndez's frequent absences, alienated most Native polities. Military garrisons were needed to protect mission towns. Sharp rifts between Spanish military, civilian, and religious personnel further reduced tolerance levels between them and Native people. Local skirmishes, assassinations, rebellions, and rejections of priests from Chesapeake Bay (Ajacán) and Santa Elena in the north to the missions and outposts of southern Florida thwarted the original strategy and crippled the colony.

In 1572 the few remaining Jesuits left, soon to be replaced by a handful of Franciscans who ministered mainly to the settlements at Santa Elena and St. Augustine. As religious orders changed, so did Indian policy and the pattern of European settlement. No longer the Indian-rights advocate, Menéndez proposed a war of "blood and fire" and the enslavement of survivors for work on plantations in the Caribbean. A quarter of a century out of line with judicial and ecclesiastical laws defining Indian rights, the request was denied. Encroachments by civilians and their livestock, militance by soldiers, including the assassination of the Calusa leader Carlos in 1573, and a few attempts by missionaries to congregate Native populations around European centers characterized the region up to 1587. Native retaliation included numerous killings of Christians, as well as of their hogs, cattle, and horses; continued threats to aid the French; and apostacy and the rejection of missionaries. These and other internal colonial problems, Francis Drake's sack and plunder of St. Augustine in 1586, and Indian rebellions in Guale forced contraction. Santa Elena was abandoned and all troops were concentrated on the Florida peninsula.

Thirteen Brown Robes arrived in 1587 to assist the two resident priests and were assigned to Indian villages near St. Augustine. Until 1612, after which an extensive chain of missions was built to house several thousand neophytes, priests were few in number and usually did not remain long in Florida. In 1595 five missions between St. Augustine and the Georgia border served Timucuans, and four missions had been built among the Guales on four sea islands, serving a total of 1,500 "Christian" Indians. Two years later the Guales rose in revolt over Franciscan interference in succession to the leadership of their chiefdom, a confrontation centering on the Native practice of multiple marriages. The revolt temporarily purged the region of Spaniards and was the climax of previous rebellions dating back to 1576. Five of the six priests died, and the province was not reassigned until 1603, following a lengthy pastoral visitation, restoration of the destroyed mission complexes, and renewed trust with the Guales.

In the course of the sixteenth century St. Augustine became, through *mestizaje,* North America's first "melting pot." Archaeological evidence indicates that, of all known Spanish sites in Florida and the Caribbean, it was the poorest and its inhabitants were the most dependent on local Native foodstuffs, ceramic wares, and architecture. The average colonist or soldier interacted with the local Timucuans, adopting Native foods and food preparation as well as intermarrying with Native women. Of the 1,200 soldiers in Menéndez's initial force, 100 were married and brought their wives. A request, six years later, for 100 additional men and only six women would have been unusual had considerable marriage with Native women, following Menéndez's own example, not occurred in the meanwhile. Throughout the century the overwhelming majority of recorded marriages were with local women, whether European, mestizo, or Indian. We are not sure of the motives that (insofar as they had a choice) prompted Native women to cross the cultural and biological boundary. It may have been that, as in the rest of Latin America, marrying a Spaniard became a source of prestige and material gain for an Indian woman and her family. Franciscan priests noted that women were the most fervent converts, and they used them as catechists in the conversion of other Indians. By 1600 a *criollo* culture had crystallized in Florida's main Spanish settlement.

The Spanish settlement of the Southwest was an outgrowth of the founding of mining and agricultural towns on Mexico's northern frontier. Discoveries of silver at Zacatecas in Neuva Galicia in 1546 and subsequent strikes at Durango and Santa Bárbara in Nueva Vizcaya in 1563 and 1567 led to the founding of these important towns, which served both as the "outer wall" protecting Spanish civilization to the south and as the "mothers" for provinces to be organized farther north, particularly Nuevo México.

In 1598 under Juan de Oñate, scion of a wealthy mining family, 400 soldiers, colonists, friars, and Mexican Indians marched north with ten times that number of livestock. Six months later they arrived in the Española Valley and occupied one portion of the inhabited pueblo of Yunque, which they renamed San Juan Bautista. They cut windows and doors into the adobe walls of first-floor rooms and introduced new fire-places with cooking shelves inside and round baking ovens outside. They also built a church and laid out a plaza. The Pueblo Indians supplied the settlers with manpower for enlarging traditional irrigation canals. The introduction of thousands of cattle and sheep and the unprecedented cut-ting of trees for fences and fuel greatly altered the ecology of the Puebloan world. Ninety-nine percent of the pottery used by the Spanish settlers was made by the Pueblo Indians, indicating that this was indeed a remote frontier colony inhabited mainly by settlers of modest to poor means. It was replaced by the new capital of Santa Fé in 1610, and finally abandoned in 1617.

Until that happened, the infant Spanish settlement, now centered at San Gabriel del Yungue, was the only "urban" European enclave between the Franciscan province of New Mexico and that administered by the same mendicant order in Florida. The site of the colony seemed appropriate, since the San Juan Tewa were known to be more hospitable than downriver groups, especially the Tiwa, whose food had been taken as tribute as recently as 1581 by Father Rodríguez's nemesis, Francisco Chamuscado, and who had also been attacked by Coronado a generation earlier.

During the nine years Oñate served as leader of the New Mexico colony, he faced many of the same problems as did the Spanish in Florida. Like Menéndez, he sought "pledges" of obedience and allegiance from village leaders and counted on the mission program to aid in pacifying as well as hispanicizing the Pueblos. Seven caciques, said to represent thirty-four pueblos, took oaths. Spanish relations with the Rio Grande Pueblos were never stable, but they were better than those with the more distant Western Pueblos and Plains peoples.

Trouble began in the autumn of 1598, during a search for an overland route to the Gulf of California and the fabled mineral deposits so often spoken of by past expeditions. While visiting Acoma to trade, Juan de Zaldívar, Oñate's nephew and *maesa de campo,* as well as fourteen soldiers were killed by the Keresan-speaking Acomas, under the leadership of Zutacapán. Oñate determined to make an example of Acoma by declaring a war "by blood and fire" against these "rebellious" Natives. After a two-day siege, the mesa top was captured and approximately 600 out of the 6,000 Acomas were killed. Pueblo warriors who surrendered were executed; those who resisted were burned out of their hiding places and kivas (religious chambers). Around 500 survivors were rounded up and marched to distant Santo Domingo Pueblo. Males over twenty-five were to have one foot cut off, before they, together with younger men and women, were bound as personal servants to Spaniards for twenty years. Children were placed in foster homes under Spanish supervision.

Many Acomas escaped and reestablished their community between 1599 and 1620. But the legacy of this episode, compounded by other punitive expeditions against the Jumanos in 1599, exaction of tribute through *encomienda* (tribute labor), and frustrations on the part of the colony's leader as a result of not finding silver or precious stones, poisoned Spanish-Indian relations and planted seeds that were to germinate eighty years later in the Pueblo Revolt.

BIOLOGICAL EFFECTS

It has long been known that the meeting of the two hemispheres in the late fifteenth and early sixteenth centuries ushered in a new biological era for the world at large. Only recently have scholars begun to unravel the long-term implications of what generally are called "the Columbian exchanges" between Europe and the Americas, transfers that impacted forever on the demography and natural history of the planet. Almost from first landfall, unintended swapping of germs resulted in new epidemiological onslaughts on both continents.

Disease was not unknown in ancient North America. One scholar has listed the following ailments: bacillary and amoebic dysentery; viral influenza and pneumonia; arthritis; rickettsial (microorganismic) fevers; viral fevers; American leishmaniasis (protozoan); American trypanosomiasis (parasitic protozoans); roundworms and other endoparasites; syphilis and pinta (both treponemal infections); and a mild form of typhus.[24]

Many illnesses evident in skeletal remains in the eastern United States have been attributed to arthritis, tuberculosis (especially spinal varieties), treponemal infections, Paget's disease (Osteitis Deformans), periostitis, acute osteomyelitis, and myeloma (bone cancer). In addition, dietary defi-

---

[24] Marshall T. Newman, "Aboriginal New World Epidemiology and Medical Care, and the Impact of the Old World Disease Imports," *American Journal of Physical Anthropology* 45 (1976), 667–72.

ciencies associated with overdependence on carbohydrates in a maize-rich economy affected many horticulturalists. There is also evidence of high infant mortality among the precontact Pueblo and Middle and Late Woodland peoples in eastern North America. Anemia appears frequently in the Southwest prior to 1492, while dental problems, especially severe tooth wear primarily caused by grit from grinding stones, affected many of the cultures encountered by Europeans in the sixteenth century, but was more serious among acorn and shellfish harvesters of California than among the carie-prone horticulturalists of the Southwest. Still, relative to Europe, North America lacked a heavy disease pool, especially numerous crowd infections, and was seemingly a healthier place for its inhabitants.

Life expectancy and average age at death for North American Indians varied and cannot be precisely determined. Yet, despite the lower level of infectious diseases, life expectancy does not appear to have been significantly greater in sixteenth-century North America than it was in Europe. Middle Mississippians may have averaged twenty-five years, although the odds of living twice that long increased once the age of fifteen was achieved, if the skeletal material from the Cahokia and St. Louis mounds area is typical. Residents of Pecos Pueblo also had a mean age at death of twenty-five to twenty-seven. Archaeological data indicate that town dwellers may have lived less long than did more dispersed groups because of the same sanitation and attendant microbial problems that troubled sedentary populations in preindustrial Europe. For example, tuberculosis was common in the relatively dense population centers of the Northeast, particularly among the Iroquoians, who lived in smoky, multiple-family longhouses. Along the Texas coast during late pre-Columbian and protohistoric times, the average person could expect to survive to around thirty, a figure comparable to England in the eleventh century. There, as elsewhere on both sides of the Atlantic, a few people lived very long lives, but longevity and mean age at death, bracketed between ages twenty-five and thirty, did not improve much, as a result of high infant and juvenile mortality, especially in large population centers, high fetal and female mortality during childbearing, and losses from warfare.

The number of Indians living around A.D. 1500 in North America is subject to grand speculation. Scholars have abandoned the early low estimates of James Mooney and Alfred Kroeber and now build upon the methodological framework proposed by Woodrow Borah and Sherburne Cook for Central Mexico and the Caribbean. Their calculation of 100 million for the Americas would have more Indians in the New World than the seventy million people estimated to have lived in Europe (excluding Russia) at the beginning of the sixteenth century. Henry Dobyns has proposed even higher estimates ranging from 90 million up to 200 million.

Mooney's original 1,152,950 for America north of the Rio Grande (with contact dates suggested as ranging from A.D. 1600 to 1845) was revised downwards by Kroeber to 900,000. Dobyns has suggested a range of between ten and eighteen million for North America (including the Caribbean), while Douglas Ubelaker has doubled the Mooney/Kroeber estimates to between 1,894,350 and 2,171,125, excluding the Caribbean. Data from the Smithsonian's *Handbook of North American Indians* pose a range of 1,213,475 to 2,638,900 for the same region about A.D. 1500, while Russell Thornton has argued for a total of seven million or more for the area north of Mexico.

Controversies abound in Native American historical epidemiology as well as in historical geography. At issue is the debated presence of malaria, yellow fever, pulmonary tuberculosis, and venereal syphilis before the Columbian encounter. After 1492 there is no doubt that the formerly relatively disease-free environment of the Americas was plagued with frequent "virgin soil" epidemics of diseases against which Native Americans had built up no genetic resistance. Moving in the opposite direction was venereal syphilis, probably from New World sources, which sailors took back to Europe as early as 1493. Merchants, soldiers, and emissaries spread the disease within two decades into every corner of Europe and beyond into Africa and Asia, killing thousands and infecting hundreds of thousands more.

The great killer diseases unintentionally introduced by germ-, spore-, and parasite-bearing Europeans, Africans, and their animals were smallpox, measles, influenza, bubonic plague, diptheria, typhus, cholera, scarlet fever, trachoma, whooping cough, chicken pox, and tropical malaria.

Española suffered the first outbreak of smallpox in 1518, which rapidly killed one-third to one-half of the resident Arawaks and other enslaved Indians. Infection spread rapidly throughout the Greater Antilles and accompanied Spaniards onto the Mesoamerican mainland. During the fateful summer of 1520 the epidemic swept the Aztec capital of Tenochtitlan and so weakened the defenders that many died of hunger and thirst while others were too weak to resist the conquerors. Beginning in 1520 and continuing into the 1530s, a pandemic condition existed whereby Indian, African, and European carriers incubated the disease while traveling and lethally infected populations along traditional trade routes and during European expeditions of reconnaissance, enslavement, and colonization. The southern boundary of this first "disease horizon" may have been the pampa and the Rio de la Plata region of South America. To the north documentary evidence for the Southeast and Texas confirms major trauma, but inferential evidence beyond into California, the Southwest, the northern Plains, and Northeast, as postulated by Dobyns, is plausible but unconfirmed.

The undisputed existence of a major ailment as early as 1526 in the Southeast derives from the documentary records of the Ayllón, Narváez, and de Soto expeditions and is one of the clearest windows available for testing a major demographic collapse in the archaeological record. For example, in the province of Cofitachequi (ruled by a female chieftain in present-day South Carolina), de Soto's army found "large uninhabited towns, choked with vegetation, which looked as though no people had inhabited them for some time." Indian testimonials confirmed that "there had been a plague in that land and they had moved to other towns."[25] Marvin T. Smith's archaeological study of Late Mississippian sites in the interior Southeast corroborates the view that major political changes accompanied biological holocaust (see also Chapter 5). Disease disrupted chiefdoms, forced abandonment of towns, and led to regrouping of refugee-survivor populations into new confederated polities such as those of the Creeks, Cherokees, and Catawbas. These nations and their neighbors in the historical Southeast must be understood in a social context quite unlike that at the beginning of the sixteenth century. With decentralization, cultural traditions did not disappear, and a clear preference for residing in formal towns continued among Creeks, Cherokees, and others. Never, again, however, would southeastern Indians boast of complex chiefdoms with large ceremonial and decision-making centers.[26]

In Texas, some Native groups described in detail by Cabeza de Vaca during his prolonged trek were not recontacted until the late seventeenth or early eighteenth centuries, by which time many had vanished or been amalgamated into new ethnic groups. Cabeza de Vaca reported a fatal stomach ailment among some of his hosts, and noted that it reduced the Karankawa population by one-half. Elsewhere he mentions widespread

---

[25] Fidalgo de Elvas (Anon. Gentleman of Elvas), *True Relation of the Hardships Suffered by Governor Fernando de Soto and Certain Portuguese Gentlemen during the Discovery of the Province of Florida*, ed. James A. Robertson, 2 vols. (Deland, Fla., 1932), 1:93.

[26] Marvin T. Smith, *Archaeology of Aboriginal Culture Change in the Interior Southeast: Depopulation during the Early Historic Period* (Gainesville, Fla., 1987).

blindness among villagers. The pathology of these chronic diseases may be linked to a pandemic or to localized phenomena, such as an outbreak of influenza that spread with Cabeza de Vaca but did not infect the entire region. By the time the party reached the La Junta trade center, the townspeople there were described as "the best formed people we have seen, the liveliest and most capable," suggesting that smallpox had not visited that section of the Rio Grande Valley by 1530.[27]

The western limit of the pandemic may have been somewhere between modern-day Chihuahua and the Valley of Mexico. Although many pueblos are known to have been abandoned during the sixteenth century and later, no direct correlation with disease has been established in the documentary or osteological record. The traditional explanation of Athapaskan pressure and successful raiding of rancherian and Puebloan peoples remains in favor. However, several scholars have challenged this and are not content with negative evidence. They have interpreted the breakdown of regional systems of political and economic interaction as the direct result of catastrophic population loss during the first seventy-five years of Spanish contact, a phenomenon resembling what happened in the Southeast. Steadman Upham, in particular, is convinced, from the analysis of volume and variety of pre- and postcontact ceramic wares, that the Puebloan world suffered a cataclysmic decline in aggregated population beginning around A.D. 1520. What Coronado saw in 1540 may have been a reconfigured human landscape quite different from the fifteenth-century Southwest.[28]

Most discussion over the northern limit of the pandemic has focused on the Iroquoians and the North Atlantic seaboard, where the first major epidemic on record dates to 1616–18. Virginia Miller does not believe that pandemics of southern origin reached as far north as Atlantic Canada or that seasonal contacts between Indians and Europeans triggered widespread infections. She is convinced, however, that the 1616 epidemic, which leveled some of New England's Indian populations and left others nearly intact, had antecedents among the less dense populations of sixteenth-century Atlantic Canada. She agrees with the Jesuit missionary Pierre Biard that localized outbreaks of European diseases, in combination with growing reliance on European dietary items such as alcohol, biscuits,

[27] Alvar Núñez Cabeza de Vaca, *The Journey of Alvar Nuñez Cabeza de Vaca and His Companions from Florida to the Pacific, 1528–1536,* ed. Adolf F. Bandelier, trans. Fanny Bandelier (New York, 1904), 37–8, 132–3, 151–2.
[28] Steadman Upham, *Polities and Power: An Economic and Political History of the Western Pueblo* (New York, 1982); see also Upham, Kent G. Lightfoot, and Roberta A. Jewett, *The Sociopolitical Structure of Prehistoric Southwestern Societies* (Boulder, Colo., 1989).

and dried peas, had severely reduced otherwise healthy populations by the start of the seventeenth century.[29] Her case study of the Micmacs may be supported by the trajectory of the 1616 plague, which seems to have struck Indians who traded with the French, but spared those trading primarily with the Dutch. This localized pattern of germ transmission may have been present in Atlantic Canada since at least 1535, when Cartier and his crew wintered near Stadacona. What is assumed without evidence to have been an outbreak of some European disease led to the death of about 10 percent of the 500 Native inhabitants of that community. Repeated, localized infusions of European diseases into the region may have played a role in the disappearance of the St. Lawrence Iroquoians by the late sixteenth century.

A higher frequency of multiple interments among the Senecas and Eries and osteological indications of a high mortality rate among young people at the Seneca Cameron site have been interpreted as evidence of European epidemics reaching the Iroquois in the late sixteenth century. Dobyns has argued that the frequent relocation of Seneca settlements reflects the impact of repeated epidemics throughout that century, although he notes that "the archaeological record does not indicate the attrition in numbers of settlements one might expect."[30] Periodic relocation was inherent in Iroquoian slash-and-burn agriculture. The largest Onondaga site, which covers about 1.5 hectares, appears to date from late precontact or early protohistoric times, while fragmentary data suggest that its seventeenth-century counterpart was only half that size. On the other hand, Dean Snow's systematic study of the size and number of Mohawk settlements finds no decline in population before the seventeenth century, while Gary Warrick's detailed analysis of all known Iroquoian sites located between Lake Ontario and Georgian Bay indicates a stable population from about A.D. 1400 until the major decline of the 1630s. There is therefore reason to believe that there may not have been any major outbreaks of European diseases in the Lower Great Lakes region prior to the historically recorded ones that began in this region in 1633. These studies also suggest that the population densities in these regions in late precontact times may not have been as high as Dobyns has calculated, even if population declines were

---

[29] Virginia P. Miller, "Aboriginal Micmac Population: A Review of the Evidence," *Ethnohistory* 23 (1976), 117–27; Miller, "The Decline of Nova Scotia Micmac Population, A.D. 1600–1850," *Culture* 2/3 (1982), 107–20.

[30] Henry F. Dobyns, *"Their Number Become Thinned": Native American Population Dynamics in Eastern North America* (Knoxville, Tenn., 1983), 313–27.

almost as precipitous as he believes. The northern Iroquoian peoples may have shrunk from a total of about 110,000 people in the sixteenth and early seventeenth centuries to about 8,000 by 1850. On similar grounds, Snow has estimated a preepidemic Micmac population of about 12,000 people rather than Miller's 50,000, a figure that he believes also provides an ecologically more reasonable aboriginal population density for that region.[31]

Archaeological site counts and estimates of settlement and roofed areas have been interpreted as indicating that the Middle Missouri area, where early Europeans encountered the Mandans, Hidatsas, and Arikaras, suffered a marked population decline not long before the Europeans first reached that area. Yet imprecision in dating leaves it uncertain whether the onset of this decline began in the sixteenth or seventeenth centuries, although archaeological evidence currently favors the later date. Moreover, no evidence has been found to indicate that diseases, rather than ecological or other factors, were primarily responsible for this decline.[32]

Current archaeological evidence does not appear to favor major epidemics in the vicinity of the Lower Great Lakes or the Middle Missouri region in the sixteenth century. While satisfactory archaeological data are available for only a few areas, the Mohawk and Huron-Petun evidence emphasizes the danger of assuming that virtually the whole of North America was swept by a series of pandemics beginning as early as 1520, or even 1600. If the Lower Great Lakes and Middle Missouri regions were not hit by major epidemics in the course of the sixteenth century, it is unlikely that areas farther to the north and west were either. Furthermore, if epidemics were confined mainly to the Southeast and Southwest, Dobyns's overall estimates for the aboriginal population of North America will have to be reduced. It is also likely that the lower density of population outside the Southeast was a major factor limiting the spread of European diseases over the whole continent. The dissemination of pathogens in these latter areas may have been made easier as the development of equestrian nomadism and the fur trade increased the frequency of intergroup contact on the Plains and in the boreal forests.

At least seventeen major epidemics are on record for the New World

[31] Dean R. Snow and William A. Starna, "Sixteenth-century Depopulation: A View from the Mohawk Valley," *American Anthropologist* 91 (1989), 142–9; Gary A. Warrick, "A Population History of the Huron-Petun, A.D. 900–1650," Ph.D. dissertation, Department of Anthropology, McGill University, 1990; Snow, *The Archaeology of New England* (New York, 1980), 35–6.

[32] Ann F. Ramenofsky, *Vectors of Death: The Archaeology of European Contact* (Albuquerque, N.M., 1987), 102–35.

between 1520 and 1600. The magnitude in numbers of deaths in areas infected by virgin soil epidemics has been calculated at percentages ranging from thirty to as high as seventy-five during the initial outbreak. Recurrence of the disease or the appearance of others, especially measles and influenza, could, in the course of three generations, wipe out a Native group. During historical plagues in both the Old and New Worlds, mortality increased due to despondency and lack of life-support services. Many bedridden victims literally starved to death or died of dehydration, while others took their own lives once infected. Cultural as well as biological discontinuities taxed once strong, but now weakened, Native societies. Native medical remedies for many ailments included sweatbaths and plunges into cold water, both of which increased the odds for dying of smallpox. The power of shamans and priests was tested as never before, but magic, ritual, and medicines saved only a fraction of prepandemic populations.

Those who survived the encounter with European pathogens were often scarred for life. Where the epidemics hit hardest, political, social, and economic worlds had to be reconfigured. New rules and restrictions made necessary by the biological reality of the presence of microbes and of people, animals, and plants from other worlds now applied. Some Native groups coped; others did not. Intermarriage and concubinage between Native women and the invading Europeans were common in the still small areas of European contact and settlement. New peoples emerged from this process, with some resistance to New and Old World microbes and with the sociological preconditions for the eventual formation of mentalities neither European nor American.

By the start of the era of sustained colonial enterprises in the seventeenth century, marked by the founding of Jamestown (1607), Quebec (1608), and Santa Fé (1610), the Native people of North America had already endured more than a century of human and nonhuman biological encounters. As Francis Jennings has suggested, the continent that lay before the Spanish, French, and English alike might best be thought of as a "widowed landscape," a veteran of more than a century of unintentional, but highly lethal, germ warfare.[33]

We will never know precisely how many Europeans or how many Indians met each other, slept with each other, or infected each other

---

[33] Francis Jennings, *The Invasion of America: Indians, Colonialism, and the Cant of Conquest* (Chapel Hill, N.C., 1975).

during brief as well as sustained contacts. Recent work on itinerant European fishing expeditions alone has forced a new mental construct for Atlantic North America. The occasional voyage of exploration by the likes of a Columbus, Verrazzano, or Cabot must now be set into the context of the tens of thousands of Europeans who were involved in North Atlantic whaling and fishing expeditions. Add to this the many poorly documented and undocumented privateering expeditions where Europeans preyed upon each other, as well as upon coastal Native Americans, and the weight of numbers shifts from a relatively insignificant handful of Europeans to several hundred thousand spread across four generations.

Even so, the actual record of those who left their ships for a land-based North American expedition or colony renders down to a small number of Europeans, Africans, and Native Americans from other cultural regions of the Americas. Approximately ten thousand Spaniards entered or were born north of the Caribbean and Mexico during the sixteenth century. French and English colonization efforts along the St. Lawrence and the Atlantic coast pale by comparison. Together, would-be colonists of all three European nationalities constitute a demographic profile smaller than many single Native American polities, even after the epidemiological holocaust. Spaniards remained vastly outnumbered by Timucuans in Florida and by Pueblo Indians in New Mexico. The French during their brief period of settlement constituted a very small minority among Iroquoian- and Algonquian-speaking neighbors along the St. Lawrence River. Similarly, Raleigh's Roanoke, the early settlements along the James River, and Plymouth Plantation were mere islands in a sea of Native peoples.

The paradox is the degree to which the balance of biological weights became tilted in the invaders' favor across the course of the seventeenth century, initially because of the sixteenth-century exchange of pathogens, followed by genetic intermixing and cultural accommodation, and ultimately through the advantages afforded by staple commodity extractions and abundant food economies in many parts of North America. It is not surprising that by the mid–seventeenth century, much of Europe envisioned "America" as the cornucopia of the world, allegorically depicted in art as a bare-breasted North American woman welcoming strangers to the produce of her garden in this, the "new golden land."[34]

---

[34] Hugh Honour, *The New Golden Land: European Images of America from the Discoveries to the Present Time* (New York, 1975).

NATIVE RESPONSES TO EUROPEAN CONTACT

How did Native Americans first perceive and respond to the bearded, curiously dressed strangers who arrived on their shores in large ships from an ocean that many Native people believed was a realm of supernatural beings? Overt reactions of Indians, as reported by Europeans, ranged from terror and flight to fascination and reverence, to veiled suspicion, to overt hostility. There is also a compelling body of evidence that early-sixteenth-century Europeans were widely regarded as powerful shamans and possibly as spirits.

The Spanish who explored the Caribbean islands late in the fifteenth century were convinced that Native people regarded them as divine beings. Already in 1492, Columbus concluded that the Lucayan inhabitants of the Bahamas thought that he had come from the sky. While this belief may have been partly a product of European vanity and ethnocentrism, its veracity in at least some instances is suggested by the Spanish experience that such beliefs could be exploited to control Native people.

Folk traditions, mostly recorded generations after the events occurred, suggest that at least some Native North Americans regarded newly arrived Europeans as supernatural spirits or the souls of the dead returning to earth. The Montagnais and Micmacs believed the first ships they saw to be floating islands inhabited by supernatural beings. New England Indians added that they had thought the sails of such ships to be white clouds and the discharge of their guns thunder and lightning. In 1761 elderly Delawares stated that their ancestors had admired the white skins and fancy clothing of the very first Europeans they met, especially the shiny red garments worn by their leader, who gave them presents. They concluded that the ship was a boat belonging to their supreme deity and prepared offerings and entertainment for him. Belief in the divinity of Europeans was still common in the Upper Great Lakes region in the seventeenth century, a period for which more detailed and reliable documentation is available.[35]

There is, however, little in the oral traditions of most Native peoples that permits scholars to distinguish first impressions of Europeans from memories and happenings relating to other periods and even from mythi-

---

[35] Bruce G. Trigger, "Early Native North American Responses to European Contact: Romantic versus Rationalistic Interpretations," *Journal of American History* 77 (1991), 1195–1215; Bruce M. White, "Encounters with Spirits: Ojibwa and Dakota Theories about the French and Their Merchandise," *Ethnohistory* 41 (1994), 369–405.

cal events. Among the Zunis and other Pueblos, the Chákwaina Katcina represents Estevanico, the Moorish guide with the Marcos de Niza party who was killed at the Zuni town of Hawikuh in 1539 for his arrogant behavior and molestation of Indian women. Even today, this Black Katcina is known to all the Pueblos as a horrible ogre. At the other extreme, while the Cherokees have a dim but persistant tradition of a strange White race preceding their migration from the north into their later homeland in the Southeast, it is impossible to determine the historical significance of this tradition. While we know that de Soto contacted several Cherokee towns in present-day Georgia and that they were visited by Pardo during his explorations twenty-six years later, the modern Cherokees have no evident memories of these events, although such memories may be bound up in some of their myths in forms unrecognizable to modern scholars. It may be impossible to distinguish the historical from the mythical when it comes to studying Native memories of sixteenth-century encounters with Europeans.

Most of the evidence that Native people initially attributed supernatural power to Europeans comes from the records of European explorers. When Cartier visited the St. Lawrence Iroquoian town of Hochelaga in 1535, the sick of that community were brought to him to heal. Cabeza de Vaca and some of the other survivors of the Narváez expedition were able to cross Texas in the 1530s because the hunter-gatherer peoples of that region welcomed them as healers, the report having spread that Cabeza de Vaca had successfully extracted an arrowhead long embedded in a man's chest. Later, in the course of de Soto's travels in the southeastern United States, sick Indians were sometimes brought to him to be healed. This suggests that in the early sixteenth century Europeans were widely regarded as powerful shamans or as spirits. It is not known to what extent such beliefs were suggested by knowledge that Europeans came from the ocean, which was associated with supernatural powers, or that they were not subject to many new diseases that were affecting Native people.

The account of Drake's voyage to California in 1579 states that the Coast Miwoks ritually lacerated their faces in the presence of the English and offered sacrifices to them, despite the efforts of the sailors to make them stop. In 1587 English colonists in Virginia reported that, because Indians had fallen ill and died in each Native community they had passed through, while they themselves did not become ill, they were viewed as spirits of the dead returning to the world in order to draw more victims after them. In Florida the Timucuans are recorded as kissing a large stone column carved with the arms of the King of France that Ribault had erected and worshipping it as an idol. Indians are also reported to have worshipped or brought offerings to crosses erected by Coronado in the Southwest. Cabeza de Vaca had adroitly used the cross as a symbol, as a result of which it came to be associated with his powers to cure disease. Later in the course of his travels he advised the Indians of the Lower Pima region to erect crosses in their villages to be safe from Spanish slave raiders operating on the northern frontier of Mexico. Thus it is possible that at least some Native interest in the symbolism of the Christian cross was political rather than religious or supernatural.

Europeans were prepared to try to exploit North American Indian beliefs in their supernatural power. In the course of their penetration into the southeastern United States, de Soto and his followers, drawing upon their experiences in Mexico and Peru, claimed that he was the "Child of the Sun" and in this capacity had a claim upon the obedience of local chiefs. When he died of some viral ailment in 1541, his men quickly buried him in the Mississippi River to prevent the local Indians from learning about his mortality.

Some historians and anthropologists assume that these scattered pieces of evidence provide insights into how all Native North Americans perceived Europeans during the early stages of their encounters. They believe that similar culturally conditioned behavior determined Native responses in other situations, but was either less obvious or failed to be noted by less sensitive or less interested European observers. The documentary evidence that religious beliefs played an important and widespread role in influencing Native behavior is in fact very limited and contradictory evidence is frequently encountered. For example, on at least two occasions, Native rulers pointedly rejected Spanish claims that de Soto possessed supernatural powers, including the statement by Moscoso that de Soto had not died but only gone to the sky for a few days to confer with the gods. The ruler of Guachoya, who mocked this claim, nevertheless volunteered two human sacrifices, which were traditional in that area at the funerals of chiefs. In general, the early chronicles portray Native American relations with Europeans as having been governed from the start by straightforward concerns with exchange, defence, and, in more hierarchical societies, the ability to impress outsiders with internal political and social control.

Whatever particular groups of Indians may have believed Europeans to have been upon first meeting, it did not take long after the development of regular direct contact for all of them to conclude that Europeans were human beings, or at least mortal, like themselves. While the Hochelagans brought Cartier their sick for him to heal, the Stadaconans, who were better informed about Europeans and may even have traded to a limited extent with Breton fishermen along the lower north shore of the St. Lawrence prior to meeting Cartier, did not assign supernatural powers to the French. When Cartier attempted to conceal the number of sick and dead among his crew during the winter of 1535–6, it was not because he believed that the Stadaconans thought the French were immortal, but because he feared they might attack him if they realized how weak his forces had become.

The origins and homelands of the newcomers must have perplexed most sixteenth-century Indians as they pondered the possibilities. Early contacts with shipwrecked Spanish sailors, would-be conquerors, such as Ponce de Léon and Narváez, and colonists, such as Ayllón, provided Native people with numerous opportunities to learn about Europeans. As early as 1513, Ponce de Léon was considered a defeatable menace by the Indians of Florida, and most Spaniards who were shipwrecked on the Atlantic and Gulf coasts thereafter were not credited with supernatural powers. If useful at all, it was as slaves and a source of future ransom payments. Most of the original Narváez shipwreck survivors of 1528 and those of Padre Island in 1554 were hunted down and killed by local Indians. Had the Chumashes succeeded, none of Cabrillo's crew would have returned to report on California in 1543.

Such knowledge was transmitted far inland through the diplomatic exchange networks that linked the adjacent peoples and chiefdoms of the southeastern United States. When de Soto's expedition penetrated deep into the region, his oddly complexioned, malodorous, and strangely clad Europeans and their African, Indian, and mestizo servants were met with physical resistance and defensive posturing rather than with veneration. The Muskogean ruler of Achese and his people were so astonished by armored men astride horses that they plunged into the nearby river. Most Indians, however, had advance warning of the arrival of de Soto's force and prepared for it. Throughout the de Soto narratives, there is strong evidence that, as the expedition penetrated farther inland, many Native leaders provided food, shelter, burden-bearers, and concubines to the Spanish army because they had heard this was the most expedient way to rid their lands of the invaders, although a costly one in terms of women and food stores. Such compliance lasted until Spanish exactions and weakening strength spurred Native leaders to renew both overt and clandestine resistance.

The rulers of the hierarchical societies of the Southeast had no intention of being upstaged by their European counterparts or of yielding to them unless they were compelled to do so. Time and again they and their priests sought to demonstrate their authority, even in the midst of veiled cooperation and slick diplomacy. The Timucuan leaders made a point of demonstrating their custom of sacrificing the first-born son of all married women in honor of their ruler. A similar display of power involved the slashing with a dagger of the Timucuan chief's favorite son upon the return of a war party without enemy scalps "to renew the wounds of their ancestor's death so they would be lamented afresh." For sleeping while on guard and other offenses, commoners were publicly clubbed to death while kneeling before the chief. On both sides of the Atlantic the sixteenth century was a brutish age, especially during times of famine, war, and pestilence. Neither hemisphere had a sharp advantage in placing a high value on human life, and, in hierarchical societies, Native leaders often were quite ruthless, even at the expense of their subjects' lives, when demonstrating their power to Europeans.

Trading contacts between the Indians of northern Mexico and the southwestern United States may have provided the latter with the information necessary to assess in advance what kind of beings the Spanish and their horses were. Echoes of beliefs surrounding the original encounter between the Spanish and the Aztecs in central Mexico at the time of Coronado's expedition may be found in a prophecy attributed to the Pueblos that strangers would come from the south and conquer them.[36] Yet among the Pueblos these beliefs did not stifle resistance.

In every quarter of European-Indian interaction during the sixteenth century Indians had ample opportunity to observe the physical weaknesses of Europeans. Native warriors were quick to learn where their arrows could penetrate European armor, where it could fail. Although Europeans held a decided advantage in technology with their horses, man-killing dogs, and finely wrought iron weapons, a trail of their graves marked every major *entrada* and lined every colonial settlement. Not all were from disease and other natural causes.

Still more detailed knowledge of Europeans was acquired by Indians

---

[36] "Prophecies of Our Grandparents," in Alvina Quam, trans., *The Zunis: Self-Portrayals by the Zuni People* (Albuquerque, N.M., 1972), 3.

who were taken prisoner by them and managed to return to their own people. This was especially the case with Indians who had been carried to Mexico or Europe in the course of their captivity. When Francisco de Chicora returned to South Carolina with Ayllón's settlers, he and the other Indian interpreters managed to elude the colonists and rejoin their own people. In 1535 the two sons of Donnacona, who had been kidnapped and taken to France, advised their people to charge the French more for food, since the goods Cartier was giving them in exchange were worth little in his own country. Don Luis de Velasco played a leading role in murdering the Jesuit priests whom he had accompanied back to his homeland. Familiarity with Europeans and outward adoption of their beliefs and habits did not signal that the loyalty of these captives had been secured.

The first impressions that Native people had of Europeans and the initial strategies they devised for dealing with them often seem to have been strongly influenced by their traditional beliefs. Where contact remained limited or indirect, these interpretations persisted without modification for long periods. Where relations became direct and increasingly intense, it appears that these interpretations were rapidly altered by rational assessments of what Europeans were like and what they had to offer. In at least some areas these assessments spread inland ahead of European exploration. Because communications were more effective, this appears to have happened more quickly in densely settled regions, such as the Southeast, than in more thinly settled ones.

These shifting interpretations also influenced changing attitudes toward European goods. As we have seen, such goods were obtained not only by exchange but as gifts from European explorers, from shipwrecks and abortive settlements, from material abandoned at fishing stations, and by theft from European visitors. Throughout the sixteenth century European goods were secured most regularly in the fishing areas of Atlantic Canada and along the coasts of Florida. Explorers, privateers, and traders frequented the intervening coast of what is now the United States on a more intermittent basis until European colonization began in the Chesapeake Bay area in 1570. European explorers carried goods as far up the St. Lawrence as Montreal and deep into the Southeast and Southwest. With the founding of St. Augustine, there was for the first time an enduring European settlement capable of supplying goods to Native people on a regular basis.

In recent years George Hamell has sought to define the basic religious beliefs of the Algonquian, Iroquoian, and Siouan-speaking peoples of northeastern North America, using ethnographic data recorded from earliest contact to the present day. He concludes that the cosmologies of these peoples associated certain natural substances with physical, spiritual, and social well-being both during life and after death. These substances included marine shells, native copper and silver, rock crystals, and various other colored stones. Such substances, which came from beneath the earth or water, were ascribed to supernatural beings, such as the horned serpent, panther, and dragon, who were the guardian-spirit patrons of medicine societies. While Hamell's interpretations remain controversial, especially in their specific detail, they appear to explain the inclusion of objects made from marine shell, native copper, and rock crystals in burials of the Eastern Woodlands from the Late Archaic period, over 6,000 years ago, until after European contact. Hamell also argues that the Indians equated European copper, brass, and tin with native copper and silver, and glass beads with rocks and crystals. Because the Europeans possessed such large amounts of metalware and glass beads and came from the ocean, where in Native cosmology mythical time and space converged, they were regarded as supernatural beings or the returning spirits of the dead.[37]

Hamell's ideas may account for the historically attested interest of Native peoples in European copper, brass, and tin objects and in glass beads. They would also explain why copper and brass kettles were cut into tiny fragments, which were dispersed by exchange among the peoples of the northeastern Woodlands during the sixteenth century, and why most of these goods are found in burials rather than in living sites. In the centuries prior to the appearance of European goods, burial ritualism utilizing exotic materials had reached one of its periodical low ebbs in this region. It would therefore appear that the arrival of these goods stimulated a revival of burial ceremonialism and the attendant intergroup exchange of luxury goods. The renewed emphasis on securing objects made from ritually important substances and burying them with the dead would also account for the increasing exchange of marine shell during this period.

---

[37] George R. Hamell, "Trading in Metaphors: The Magic of Beads: Another Perspective upon Indian-European Contact in Northeastern North America," in Charles F. Hayes III, ed., *Proceedings of the 1982 Glass Trade Bead Conference* (Rochester, N.Y., 1983), 5–28; Hamell, "Strawberries, Floating Islands, and Rabbit Captains: Mythical Realities and European Contact in the Northeast during the Sixteenth and Seventeenth Centuries," *Journal of Canadian Studies* 21/4 (1987), 72–94; Christopher L. Miller and George R. Hamell, "A New Perspective on Indian-White Contact: Cultural Symbols and Colonial Trade," *Journal of American History* 73 (1986), 311–28.

Although marine shell was a North American product, it was as important as copper or rock crystals in Native religious beliefs, and Europeans never provided a satisfactory substitute for it.

In other parts of North America Native leaders also valued the new European goods they acquired. Funerary evidence from sites throughout the Southeast and in California dating to the first generations of contact often contain a mixture of Native and European grave goods, indicating rapid integration of glass, porcelain, stoneware, copper, brass, and iron into Native social and religious systems.

When Verrazzano visited the relatively isolated Narragansetts of southern New England in 1524, he found them anxious to obtain blue beads as well as bells and other trinkets made of copper. They were not interested in iron items. This suggests that these people were seeking only those objects that had precise counterparts in their traditional belief and exchange systems. The Delawares reported that they hung the first metal axes and hoes they were given on their chests as ornaments and used European stockings as tobacco pouches.

Yet it did not take long for Native people to appreciate the technological value of European goods and to become increasingly reliant on them, once they became available on a regular basis. While iron knives probably performed no better than stone hide scrapers, they cut better and were more durable and easier to keep sharp than were stone tools. Metal tools also performed better as perforators, needles, and projectile points than did the stone and bone tools that the Indians had used hitherto. Verrazzano discovered that the Indians of Maine, who presumably had more contact with European fishermen and their goods than did the Narragansetts, would exchange their furs only for "knives, fish-hooks, and sharp metal," although they were wearing European copper beads in their ears. Likewise, the Micmacs whom Cartier encountered in Chaleur Bay in 1534 not only made it clear that they wished to barter with the French, but also specifically sought hatchets, knives, and ironware, as well as beads, in exchange. While, the following year, the inhabitants of Hochelaga were pleased with any European goods that Cartier gave them, the Stadaconans, like the Micmacs, wanted hatchets, knives, and awls, as well as trinkets.

These data suggest that, while peoples such as the Narragansetts and the Hochelagans, who were remote from European fishermen at Cape Breton and the Strait of Belle Isle, were pleased to secure glass beads and copper and tin trinkets which had symbolic value in their own cultures, already by the 1520s and 1530s groups that lived closer to the trading areas were also anxious to obtain metal cutting tools, which they valued for their utilitarian qualities, and were soon putting these tools at the top of their shopping lists. Although scraps of copper continued to dominate the indirect trade with the interior, by the beginning of the seventeenth century Native groups living as far inland as the Lower Great Lakes were seeking metal cutting tools in preference to all other European goods. While these tools were buried with the dead, they were also used in everyday life and, when they wore out, were cut up and refashioned to make Native-style cutting tools using techniques that Indians hitherto had employed to work native copper. This suggests that, whatever Native people initially believed about Europeans and the goods they brought with them, it did not take long after regular supplies of European goods became available for them to appreciate the practical advantages of iron cutting tools, metal kettles, and to a lesser extent woollen clothing. Few groups were so dependably supplied with European goods during the sixteenth century that they could afford to abandon significant aspects of their traditional technology. Yet, by early in the following century, the Montagnais of Tadoussac were no longer making birch-bark vessels and stone axes, were wearing much French clothing, and buying French long-boats in order to travel more safely on the St. Lawrence River.

Much archaeological work will have to be done before the extent to which European goods were reaching various parts of eastern North America becomes clear. Current research suggests that prior to 1580 only small quantities of European goods were reaching the Iroquoian peoples who lived around the Lower Great Lakes, mainly in the form of scraps of copper and a few iron bar celts. Glass beads were exceedingly rare at this time. A similar situation seems to have prevailed in southern New England. This suggests that coastal groups in eastern Canada who had access to a wide variety of European goods were only passing along worn or more common items to peoples who lived farther from regular supplies of such material. After 1580 many more iron axes, knives, and glass beads, but still apparently no whole copper and brass kettles, identifiable by their iron rim bands, are found on Iroquoian and southern New England sites. This reflects the greater amount of European goods reaching Tadoussac and the Gulf of St. Lawrence at this time.[38]

The archaeological record suggests that European goods were trans-

[38] Fitzgerald, "Chronology to Cultural Process."

ported into the interior in the sixteenth century along well-established trade routes. One of these ran from Tadoussac across the boreal forest of southern Quebec to the upper part of the Ottawa Valley and from there to Lakes Huron and Superior. This was the route along which native copper from the Upper Great Lakes region reached the St. Lawrence. When not blocked by warfare, goods were also carried along the St. Lawrence and then up the Ottawa River. These two routes appear to have supplied the bulk of the European trade goods found around the Lower Great Lakes. Most of the St. Lawrence Iroquoians living west of Montreal seem to have been dispersed prior to the arrival of European goods, which would explain why so few of these goods are found in this part of the St. Lawrence Valley.[39] While, in the mid–sixteenth century, the Algonquins carried some European goods up the St. Lawrence to trade with groups living north and south of Lakes Ontario and Erie, this route was cut by warfare with the Iroquois, which seems to have begun around 1570. European goods were also carried south along the Richelieu River to upper New York State and interior New England, from Tadoussac south to Maine, and from Nova Scotia and Newfoundland south along the coast at least as far as New England. In the last three decades of the sixteenth century, Chesapeake Bay also may have become a source of European goods for the interior, as well as providing most of the marine shell that was traded northward into the Lower Great Lakes region. In the late sixteenth century the increasing availability of European goods emphasized east-west exchange patterns, which grew more important than the north-south ones that had predominated prior to European contact. Furs, and in particular beaver pelts, also became the primary item that was exchanged for European products.

Where trade routes brought European goods in exchange for Native peltry and other prized commodities, and where Europeans established colonies, behaviorally significant exchanges occurred. Without doubt, Indians gave more to Europeans in terms of foodstuffs than they received, at least in the sixteenth century. Nevertheless, the new faunal introductions, especially chickens, pigs, sheep, and horses, and to a lesser degree cows, were the basis of a potential, but in the sixteenth century largely

[39] For the discovery of what appears to be an awl manufactured from an iron nail at the St. Lawrence Iroquoian McKeown site, near Prescott, Ontario, see James V. Wright and Dawn M. Wright, "A News Item from the McKeown Site," *Arch Notes, Newsletter of the Ontario Archaeological Society* 90/5 (1990), 4, 32. This is the first well-documented archaeological find of material likely to be of European origin in a St. Lawrence Iroquoian site west of Montreal.

unrealized, revolution in diet and transportation. While Mesoamerican and southwestern Indians are known to have kept domesticated turkeys and parrots, the European barnyard complex was quite new and did not catch on rapidly. Europeans did not willingly give valuable horses, sheep, and cows to Indian drovers, since the Indians considered them menaces in their cornfields and often killed them. Hogs, perhaps the ancestors of the razorback of the Southeast, were lost on most *entradas,* especially that of de Soto. Some but not all became the prey of Native archers who skirted Spanish camps. During the seventeenth century, hogs and sheep would become important in Native diets in both the Southeast and Southwest, and the horse diffused widely onto the Plains and Plateau, racing ahead of actual European exploration or contact.

Several katcinas reflect the introduction of European animals to the Southwest. Wakás, the Cow; Kanela Katcina, the Sheep; Pichoti Katcina, the Pig; and, Kavayo Katcina, the Horse were fashioned and integrated into Hopi ritual. At Jémez, Acoma, and Santo Domingo, the Dancing Horse Katcina was adopted after colonization to reflect Santiago, the saint of horseriders. Horse races followed by chicken fights still commemorate the arrival of Coronado, which most Pueblos celebrate with a sense of "wry revenge" as a day of mourning as well of important changes, especially in diet, material culture, and religious life.[40]

In general, Native populations that were geographically remote from European centers of colonization did not change much, not even in their culinary preferences or eating patterns, as a result of the introduction of European, African, and Asian cultigens. But they did add many items to their botanical worlds. While wheat, oats, rye, and barley were experimented with, they did poorly in early Florida. In New Mexico, from a mere seven fanegas (400 liters) of wheat planted in 1599, an estimated 1500 fanegas were produced at San Gabriel by 1601. Yet in neither region did wheat replace corn for Indians or Europeans. New varieties of high-yielding corn, beans, and squash from other parts of the Americas came with traditional European garden crops, such as lettuce, cabbage, peas, chickpeas, cumin, carrots, turnips, garlic, onions, artichokes, and cucumbers. Many of these ended up in Indian gardens, although it is difficult to assess how much importance was placed on them relative to traditional Native cultigens.

[40] Frederick J. Dockstader, *The Kachina and the White Man* (Bloomfield Hills, Mich., 1954); Joe S. Sando, *The Pueblo Indians* (San Francisco, 1976).

Several independent sources on early New Mexico mention the success of Pueblo farmers in growing maize, cotton, beans, calabashes, and fine melons, varieties of which are thought to have been incorporated into Pueblo gardens between Coronado's intrusion of the 1540s and the colonization of the 1590s. Until Oñate's time, there is no evidence of any orchards among the Pueblos or any other southwestern Indians. Although many types of fruit were introduced and grown by Spaniards, it appears that there was selective screening by groups living far from Spanish towns, such as the Hopis and nations of the Lower Colorado River. At Walpi, the oldest continuously occupied village site in North America, and one never successfully missioned, by A.D. 1690 Hopis were growing peaches, apricots, plums, cherries, chiles, and onions, in addition to watermelons and canteloupes. Pueblo and Spaniard exchanged varieties of tobacco (*Nicotiana attenuata* for *Nicotiana rustica*), but one does not find a Mediterranean wheat-olive-grape complex anywhere in sixteenth-century America among Native, nonmissionized populations. Once mission complexes were built, diets became very Europeanized, a process visible at early seventeenth-century Abo and Awatobi, where adobe bricks from the Franciscan missions (both built in 1629) contain seeds and pips of wheat, apricots, wine grapes, European plums, coriander (cilantro), and chile peppers. The coriander and chile are especially important as time markers for the earliest use of these now culturally essential crops by Pueblo peoples.

In the Southwest, Spanish blacksmiths hammered out ironware for European and cooperative Pueblo villagers alike. The Pueblo Indians also adopted the Spanish outdoor beehive oven (*horno*), interior corner fireplace (*fogon*), and formal chimney with stacked broken pots for venting smoke; these replaced traditional center-floor hearths. Pueblo Indians also began using frames to make adobe bricks, but they did not increase the size of their buildings to match the raised skyline of European-engineered, Indian-built adobe churches, with their lofty belltowers. Nor did they add hispanic, wrap-around porticos to their buildings. Some Pueblos followed the Spanish example of cutting doors and windows at ground-floor level, and they added small, circular, skylight windows. However, they rarely trimmed out their houses with carved lintels, sills, or corbels.[41]

Alliances with Europeans occurred at diplomatic tables and on the

41 Richard I. Ford, "The New Pueblo Economy," in Herman Agoyo et al., eds., *When Cultures Meet: Remembering San Gabriel del Yunge Oweenge* (Santa Fe, N.M., 1987), 73–91; Florence H. Ellis, "The Long Lost 'City' of San Gabriel del Yungue, Second Oldest European Settlement in the United States," in *When Cultures Meet*, 10–38.

battlefield as well as in kitchens and bedrooms. When the St. Lawrence Iroquoians encountered Cartier in 1534, they were at war with the Micmacs over fishing rights along the Gaspé Peninsula and anxious not to be disadvantaged in their relations with the more powerful Hochelagans. Their leader, Donnacona, believed that closer ties with the French might provide a more regular supply of iron weapons that would permit his people to defend themselves better against the Micmacs and enhance their relations with the Hochelagans. Hence he was hopeful as well as concerned when Cartier carried off his two sons in 1534. When, however, the next year Cartier, failing to understand Native protocol, established a winter camp and proceeded to visit Hochelaga without first concluding an alliance with Donnacona, his actions soured relations between the French and the Stadaconans.

The professional traders from St. Malo who did business in the St. Lawrence Valley at the end of the sixteenth century took greater care than Cartier had done to establish good relations with the Indians. A formal alliance was concluded with the Montagnais of Tadoussac, which involved a yearly presentation of weapons to help the Montagnais fight the Mohawks, who were raiding the St. Lawrence Valley. In 1600 a trading post was established at Tadoussac where sixteen Frenchmen remained over the winter. Most of them died as a result of illness and lack of provisions. Those who survived owed their lives to the Montagnais who fed and cared for them.

Elsewhere similar patterns of economic and political favoritism on the part of Europeans can be found. It was, after all, to their advantage to make friends, or at least gestures toward such, with local peoples. Long-lasting alliances were rare, but short-term pacts with specific goals were fairly common. During de Soto's trek, a number of inter-Indian rivalries were exploited by the Spaniards as a way of combining forces with one Native group to subdue another. During Espejo's reconnaissance of New Mexico in the 1580s, Zunis joined Spanish ranks to fight Hopis. Even better-documented alliances occurred in Florida, where both French and Spanish leaders became involved in inter-Indian rivalries. The French provided their own *harquebusiers* for specific campaigns between two powerful Timucuan rulers in the 1560s, while Menéndez surprised the French garrison at Fort Caroline in 1565 by recruiting guides from a polity not enthralled with the French presence.

Menéndez became entangled in numerous interethnic struggles in

South Florida and gambled on the Calusas to come out the winners. The combination of priests, unruly soldiers, and the determination of Native leaders to retain sovereignty combined to unravel the tenuous pacts of peace and friendship. Ultimately the Calusas and their neighbors were so weakened by assassinations of their leaders and conflicts with colonizers that they lost bargaining power. In the long run this pattern ran true for all those Indians in the Spanish zone of colonization who were motivated to try the diplomatic road on the side of the Europeans. Neither partner in these fragile alliances benefited. Alienation of the Native allies usually followed quickly on the heels of even the most successful campaign.

Although the French stay among the Timucuans was short, their legacy and the relations they established continued to plague the Spaniards after 1565 and may be thought of as the most "successful" alliance within the region. For the rest of the century Spanish officials feared, with good cause, the return of the French to reestablish a colony among their "friends." Many Frenchmen remained after the 1560s as refugees in remote Indian villages to the north of the Spanish garrisons and were accused by Spanish officials of inciting the Indian uprisings of 1577–80. A lucrative trade with coastal Guale and Orista Indians continued along the South Carolina and Georgia coasts throughout this period, as French corsairs anchored offshore and loaded their holds with deerskins, sassafras, and china root in exchange for European manufactured items. An attempt by the French to establish a "free trade" zone with Indians on the Savannah River in 1605 was thwarted by the combined force of missionized Indians from St. Catherine's Island and Spaniards from St. Augustine. Thus ended France's bid for Florida.

It is arguable that any European settlement, however strongly fortified, could not endure in the long run without either totally conquering the local inhabitants or reaching terms of agreement on lasting co-occupation that bore some resemblance to reciprocity. Through various types of accommodation, both Indians and Europeans came to accept each other's presence, although cultural boundaries were generally maintained and relations were strained, even during the best of times.

Examples include the previously mentioned decisions of many southeastern peoples to give de Soto and his roving army what they demanded as they scoured the land for signs of wealth. To the west, many Pueblos reluctantly vacated their homes or opened their doors to Spanish soldiers, beginning with Coronado's campaign. Rather than lose people through resistance, many Pueblo Indians also paid tribute in the form of food, blankets, and other goods during the winter of 1540–1, a pattern that continued with Oñate's exactions of the late 1590s.

The Calusas and neighboring Tocobagas allowed Jesuits and garrisons of soldiers into their country during the 1560s and exhibited a high level of tolerance only to be very disappointed in Spanish behavior and ultimate goals, which brought a rapid end to these once hegemonic south Florida peoples. Far to the north, although the Stadaconans were outraged by Cartier's behavior, they allowed the French to build a fortified winter camp near their settlement in 1535, handed over a number of children as evidence of goodwill without demanding French youths in return, and continued to trade food with the French. They also taught Cartier how to use a drink made from white cedar to cure scurvy. Despite such evidence of goodwill, Cartier continued to fear a Stadaconan attack and treated the Indians with rudeness and even violence. His kidnapping of Donnacona and various other Indians the following spring created lasting hostility between him and the Stadaconans.

While Native people first encountered Europeans with a mixture of fear and curiosity, bad experiences at the hands of Europeans, or reports of such experiences, produced various forms of overt resistance. Pre-1560 Florida may well be described as a battle zone in which competing slavers, privateers, and would-be colonists were trying their luck among Native populations well aware of European intentions and thus prepared to resist. Even had the Narváez expedition not been wrecked by a powerful hurricane, the Appalachees and other Gulf Coast tribes were already predisposed to keep unwanted strangers out of their lands. Later, when de Soto entered their territory with odds in his favor, the Appalachees abandoned their central towns and croplands and carried on a protracted guerilla war that involved will-timed and well-concealed ambushes.

While, in 1524, Verrazzano was welcomed by the Narragansetts and Native groups living farther south along the east coast of North America, those Indians he encountered farther north were less courteous and more wary in their dealings with him. They avoided the French when they landed and insisted on carrying on trade by lowering a basket from a rocky ledge to Verrazzano's crew in their boats below. These contrasting attitudes seem to reflect the varying frequencies with which the Indians were encountering Europeans at this time. Likewise, in 1527, John Rut's Italian pilot was slain when he went ashore, a very different treatment from the friendly reception accorded to one of Verrazzano's men who had fallen into the hands of Native people along the Hatteras shore only three years before. Unpleasant encounters with Europeans, including attempted kidnappings, probably account for these differences.

When Cartier returned to Canada in 1541, he outraged the Stadaconans by not bringing back any of their people whom he had kidnapped in 1536 and by establishing a fortified settlement a short distance west of Stadacona, once again without asking permission. That winter, his settlement was besieged by all the Indians in the Quebec City region and more than thirty-five colonists were killed. In the intervening years the Iroquoians had established a dependable trading relationship with the European fishermen and whalers who frequented the Strait of Belle Isle. While the Stadaconans were less hostile to Roberval, they did not tell his colonists how to cure scurvy, which ravaged his settlement. It is also possible that in the spring of 1543 Roberval attempted to feed his hard-pressed colony by plundering rather than purchasing corn from the Hochelagans. If so, conflict between the French and the Iroquoians may have spread throughout the St. Lawrence Valley.

In 1571, Don Luis de Velasco, an Indian boy who had been captured by the Spanish near Chesapeake Bay in 1561, persuaded his people to murder the Jesuit priests who had established the Ajacán mission in his homeland in 1570. His action clearly built on a growing resentment of Spanish efforts to control the Natives of this region, but must have been influenced, in part, by what he had experienced elsewhere during his enforced travels to Mexico and the Spanish Caribbean.

Europeans often labeled resistance as "revolts" even before a colonial presence had been established. There are numerous examples of Indians merely defending their homes and evidence that the fear of disruption of ceremonial calendars or unwillingness to yield sacred ground brought on warfare. Coronado's poor relations with Pueblos began at Zuni when he entered that complex during the summer solstice ceremonies of 1540. The timing could not have been worse. Although his helmet saved him from death, the rock that a Zuni threw from his housetop was meant to kill a stranger who had profaned a sacred ritual.

Elsewhere during that same expedition, to make room for the Spanish during the winter months, the people of one large settlement in the Puebloan province of Tiguex were forced to vacate their homes, taking with them "nothing but themselves and the clothes they had on." After living with linguistic neighbors beyond the boundaries of their own sacred space, they rallied and resisted. Casualties were high for both sides. Fifty

Spaniards and their Mexican allies were wounded or killed. Six hundred Tiguan males are reported to have perished, many by execution after surrender, and their wives and children were enslaved in this the largest battle in the sixteenth-century Southwest. The Tiguans never recovered, and the Rio Grande Pueblos did not forget this affair, but were wary from that time forward of all Spanish incursions.

The southeastern counterpart to the great battle at Tiguex took place in October 1540 at Mabila, in present-day Alabama. Pretending friendship, a powerful ruler named Tuscaluza honored the Spanish with social dances, gifts of marten skins, and food. Meanwhile, an estimated 5,000 Mobilian, Choctaw, and other warriors assembled in a multigroup effort to eradicate the intruders. In a battle that lasted over seven hours, they failed and suffered an estimated 2,500 to 3,000 casualties, including women and children. But, as with the Tiguans, stories of their bravery and willingness to resist were carried along Native trails and waterways, and the deep scars inflicted on the Spanish column remained. In hindsight, this resistance constituted the critical turning point of de Soto's campaign and signaled Spanish weakness to other groups who were now willing to fight.

There was resistance to friars and civilians on the east coast, where Timucuans quickly rejected the Spanish program of colonization and fought Menéndez's troops for a decade beginning in 1566. While building and reinforcing the central towns of St. Augustine and Santa Elena, block-houses were constructed at strategic points throughout Florida for control of Indians as well as defense against European rivals. When Gourgues returned for a retaliatory strike in 1568, Timucuans, especially Saturi-wans, eagerly helped the French to storm and burn three Spanish block-houses. Other revolts, uninspired by the French, swept Native lands where blockhouses had been built. In southern Florida the entire garrison at Tocobaga were killed during the winter of 1567–8, and the outpost at Tegesta was abandoned after four soldiers were slain. In the general war-fare that ensued, surviving Indian populations moved away from Spanish zones of occupation. The failure of the Jesuit mission at Ajacán was the final blow for that order, which left Florida in 1572. The Franciscan missionary program attracted some Native groups; others continued to live in swamp lands and among other peoples to the north.

As the century closed the last of a series of revolts against missionaries occurred along the Georgia and South Carolina coasts in the territory known as Guale. Sporadic rebellions, brought on by epidemics followed by apostasy and attempted revitalization movements, broke out in 1576 and lasted until 1582. A second mission field was established on the coast in 1595 with seven priests in residence. All but one perished in the second major Guale Revolt of 1597. A third group of priests began ministering to the rapidly declining coastal groups in 1605. By 1609 most surviving missionaries had moved onto the barrier islands into convents and mission settlements.

There are many other examples of resistance to European authority and colonization. The above case studies illustrate the varied responses and mixed record of success experienced by Native groups who chose the path of armed resistance before, during, and after European programs of acculturation and domination had been instituted.

The European presence also brought about political changes and relocations in the course of the sixteenth century among Native groups living far from areas reached by European explorers. Many of these were related to efforts to obtain more European goods. The Micmacs appear to have used their command of metal weapons to expand their hunting territories. As early as the 1530s they were at war with the Stadaconans for control of the Gaspé Peninsula. In the early seventeenth century, as the Micmacs expanded their hunting territories westward, some Maliseets were forced to seek refuge among their Montagnais trading partners in the Saguenay Valley. In the second half of the sixteenth century, the remaining St. Lawrence Iroquoians were dispersed, and, by about 1570, the Mohawks and Oneidas were at war with the Montagnais and Algonquin bands who lived north of the St. Lawrence. These conflicts may have been caused by Iroquois efforts to gain more direct access to sources of European goods along the St. Lawrence River.

While it has not proved possible to demonstrate archaeologically when Iroquoian confederacies first developed, there is no reason to doubt later Huron and Iroquois claims that such units had started to form in the context of increasing intergroup competition prior to the arrival of the Europeans. The Iroquois confederacy may, however, have been strengthened by the need for these inland groups to cooperate to secure a share of European goods in competition with Native groups to the north and east who were already armed with wooden-armor-piercing iron axes and metal arrowheads. The coming together of all the groups that made up the Huron confederacy in a small area at the southern extremity of Georgian Bay by the end of the sixteenth century seems to have been motivated at least in part by a desire to be located as close as possible to secure trade routes leading by way of Lake Nipissing to the St. Lawrence Valley. What appears in the archaeological record as a few scraps of metal may have been a sufficient catalyst to bring about major economic and socio-political changes. The Hurons thus provide further evidence of the importance among Native groups living this far inland of religious and ceremonial behavior.[42]

It has been proposed that the southward relocation of the Susquehannocks in the late sixteenth century was to be closer to European traders on Chesapeake Bay and to monopolize the northward movement of marine shell from that region. Alternatively, John Smith's observations suggest that they may have moved south to avoid the Iroquois, with whom they were at war and who may have been better armed with European weapons than they were at that time.[43]

Closer to areas of European activity, in the Southwest, there was much shifting for survival and better access to resources long before the arrival of the Europeans; much of it seemingly in response to changes in climate. Many settlements also were abandoned soon after Spanish contact. Possible explanations of these movements include a continuation of droughts, especially toward the end of the sixteenth century; direct responses to European incursions, especially where epidemics might have hit; internal political, economic, or social pressures and factionalism; and external pressures from Indian immigrants to the region, especially after the arrival of Athapaskans from the north, beginning after A.D. 1500.

In parts of the Southeast, by 1540, some Late Mississippian chiefdoms were in the process of fragmenting, possibly as a result of massive losses to European diseases as well as other poorly understood environmental or political factors. Opinions remain divided on the extent to which the Powhatan chiefdom, Tsenacommacah, which exerted control over approximately thirty territorial units and 16,000 square kilometers of the Virginia coastal plain, was or was not a response to European contact. Some have argued that this chiefdom originated before the middle to late sixteenth century as a result of local environmental stresses related to an increasing population. Archaeological data have not, however, resolved the question of whether the population of this region was expanding or had already begun to decline as a result of European diseases by this time. Others argue that the Powhatan chiefdom developed as a political response by Algonquian groups who found themselves caught between Siouan- and Iroquoian-speaking

[42] Bruce G. Trigger, "The Historic Location of the Hurons," *Ontario History* 54 (1962), 137–48.
[43] John Witthoft, "Ancestry of the Susquehannocks," in John Witthoft and W. F. Kinsey III, eds., *Susquehannock Miscellany* (Harrisburg, Penn., 1959), 19–60.

enemies to the west and Spanish and English intruders to the east. Frederick Fausz proposes that Powhatan's subjugation and absorption of the independent Algonquian groups lying closest to Chesapeake Bay reveals "a strategic necessity to control the estuary and its major tributaries which had already served as 'highways' for hostile trans-Atlantic invaders." Powhatan is also reported to have been motivated by prophecies that he would be conquered by a nation coming from the east.[44]

A final important question for understanding the history of sixteenth-century North America is the degree to which those Native societies most exposed to European incursions lost or gave up political sovereignty in the midst of the onslaught of pressures outlined in this essay. We have presented various cases of Indian societies consolidating to oppose European colonization or to defeat specific European tactics or strategies. The outstanding examples of interethnic, intervillage cooperation against a common foe include the actions of the Appalachees from 1528 to 1561, the Mobile-Choctaw alliance during the Battle of Mabila in 1540, and the actions of the Chickasaws and Coosas (historic Creeks), both of whom show signs of confederated political systems in the archaeological and documentary records.

Resistance to Coronado by the cluster of six Zuni settlements in 1540 and at the battle of Tiguex which followed also indicates strategies extending beyond village boundaries, but one does not find at this time pan-Pueblo or pan-Indian organization in the Southwest comparable to the highly orchestrated revolts of the seventeenth century, such as the Great Pueblo Revolt of 1680.

CONCLUSION

More than any other, the sixteenth remains the unknown century of North American history. This results from the assumption by previous generations of historians and anthropologists that little significant change took place in Native cultures at this time, a belief that long inhibited archaeological research on this period. Today it is generally admitted that this

---

[44] Christian F. Feest, "Virginia Algonquians," in Bruce G. Trigger, vol. ed., *Handbook of North American Indians,* vol. 15, *Northeast* (Washington, D.C., 1978), 253–70; J. Frederick Fausz, "Patterns of Anglo-Indian Aggression and Accommodation along the Mid-Atlantic Coast, 1584–1634," in William W. Fitzhugh, ed., *Cultures in Contact: The Impact of European Contacts on Native American Cultural Institutions, A.D. 1000–1800* (Washington, D.C., 1985), 225–68; E. Randolph Turner, "Socio-political Organization within the Powhatan Chiefdom and the Effects of European Contact, A.D. 1607–1646," in *Cultures in Contact,* 193–224.

assumption was wrong. In the 1980s anthropologists began to understand the importance of this century for determining the relationship between early written accounts of Native life, which date mainly from the seventeenth century and later, and precontact times, which were the principal focus of archaeological research in the past. It is expected that in coming decades "protohistorical" studies will revolutionize our understanding of what happened to specific Native groups in southern and eastern North America during the sixteenth century and that, as a result of these studies, a general picture of changes in Native life at this time will emerge. Until such an archaeologically informed understanding has been achieved, any interpretation of the sixteenth century will remain highly provisional.

Nevertheless, some patterns are emerging. The sixteenth century was clearly a time of major changes over vast areas of North America. Native life, especially in the East and Southwest, was very different at the end of this century from what it had been at the beginning. Yet the widespread resilience of Native cultures during this first wave of European-induced biological, material, and cultural invasion foreshadowed the resiliency that Native peoples would display in succeeding centuries.

The most widespread and important impact of European contact upon Native people was the introduction of European diseases and the dramatic fall in population that these diseases brought about. The clearest impact was in the southeastern United States, where declining population played a major role in the simplification of the hierarchical societies that had evolved in this region and in the craft specialization associated with Mississippian cultures. There is also evidence of a dramatic decline in the Native population of Atlantic Canada and probably also in the Southwest. It is not clear, however, how far European diseases penetrated inland to the north and west. Evidence from the Lower Great Lakes region indicates that in northern areas not exposed to direct contact there may have been few, if any, major epidemics in the sixteenth century. If so, this would suggest that the precontact population of these regions was lower than recent revisionist estimates have claimed, which in turn may account for why disease transmission was less effective than in the Southeast or in later times when, as a result of the development of equestrian nomadism and the fur trade, there were probably more frequent and rapid intergroup contacts in the interior than there had been during the sixteenth century.

The gradually increasing amounts of European goods that became available during the sixteenth century circulated along trade routes far into the interior of the continent. Yet it was not until near the end of the century that sufficient quantities of these goods were reaching the interior to have a significant impact on Native technologies. Throughout most of the century the major item to circulate in the Northeast was small scraps of metal kettles, which appear to have been valued for the religious significance of the material from which they were made.

The arrival of these scraps of metal in the Lower Great Lakes region stimulated a renewed emphasis on burial ceremonialism, which also increased the demand for marine shell and other Native goods that had religious meaning. In the Southeast large quantities of European goods were interred with high-ranking individuals. In some areas this activity stimulated the growth of intergroup trade and led Native groups to relocate so as to be better positioned to obtain such goods. In the Northeast the intensification of trade had, by the end of the sixteenth century, given rise to the fur trade. It appears that Native people quickly appreciated the technological value of European metal tools and clothing and that coastal groups grew reliant on them as soon as they became available on a regular basis.

The efforts of Europeans to conquer and settle in the southeastern and southwestern United States and to a lesser degree in the St. Lawrence Valley posed a different set of challenges for Native peoples. They were at a disadvantage by comparison with Europeans because of their small-scale political units and less complex military technology. Even the larger hierarchical societies of the southeastern United States were rarely sufficiently integrated to pursue a common policy against the invaders. Yet, early in the century, before their numbers were significantly reduced by European diseases, the Indians of Florida had succeeded in expelling successive European invaders by direct confrontations and a scorched earth policy.

Later, Native peoples employed a mixture of resistance and accommodation to deal with Europeans. Some groups sought alliances with Europeans in the hope that the newcomers would help to defend them against more powerful neighbors or to extend their control over weaker ones. Most sixteenth-century intrusions, however, eventually led to conflict with Native groups, as Europeans plundered and enslaved or otherwise sought to control them. The disruption that was caused by such activities must rank second only to European pathogens among the factors that were destabilizing Native life at this time. Yet, except where Europeans learned to be more accommodating, throughout most of the century no European settlement was sufficiently well established to withstand growing Native resistance.

While the sixteenth century was to end with only two small areas of European settlement in North America, many thousands of Europeans had visited the continent as explorers, would-be conquerors, fishermen, fur traders, and missionaries. A few had lived for considerable time as captives, especially among the Indians of coastal Florida, or had made their way from one Native group to another in their efforts to return to areas of European settlement. On the other hand, only a few Indians had visited Europe and returned to tell of their adventures. At first many Native people imagined Europeans to be supernatural beings or the returning spirits of the dead, a view that was reinforced by kidnappings and the spread of new diseases in the wake of some European visits. By the end of the century the impact of European activities along the eastern and southern periphery of the continent had already brought about many changes in Native life, some of which extended far into the interior of the continent. While the negative impacts of European contact were very great, Native people who had established direct contact with Europeans had already settled in their own minds who Europeans were and evolved the pragmatic modes of interacting with them that were to shape their responses to growing European intrusion in the following centuries. Over large areas of the east, European trade appears to have stimulated intergroup exchange and higher levels of ritual activity, not all or even most of which was necessarily a response to European diseases.

BIBLIOGRAPHIC ESSAY

Most published works on sixteenth-century North America written from the late fifteenth century to the present have focused on European images and perceptions of the environment and the Native cultures at "first contact." Those interested in a detailed chronology of these contacts should consult Samuel Eliot Morison, *The European Discovery of America: The Northern Voyages, A.D. 500–1600* (New York, 1971) and sections of *The European Discovery of America: The Southern Voyages, A.D. 1492–1616* (New York, 1974). David Beers Quinn has produced the most useful detailed analysis of these contacts in *North America from Earliest Discovery to First Settlements: The Norse Voyages to 1612* (New York, 1977). This should be compared with Carl O. Sauer, *Sixteenth Century North America: The Land and the People as Seen by the Europeans* (Berkeley, Calif., 1971), a masterful interpretation by a historical geographer.

The literature on "first images" has not grown appreciably since the release of Stefan Lorant, *The New World: The First Pictures of America* (New York, 1946). Notable additions include Hugh Honour, *The New Golden Land: European Images of America from the Discoveries to the Present Time* (New York, 1975) and the published proceedings of an international conference held in 1975, *First Images of America: The Impact of the New World on the Old,* ed. Fredi Chiappelli, 2 vols. (Berkeley, Calif., 1976). Visual images from the French experience are found in Olive Patricia Dickason, *The Myth of the Savage and the Beginnings of French Colonialism in the Americas* (Edmonton, 1984) and François-Marc Gagnon, *Ces hommes dits sauvages* (Montreal, 1984). Watercolors by John White provide unparalleled ethnographic information concerning Native societies of the Atlantic seaboard. *The American Drawings of John White, 1577–1590,* ed. Paul Hulton and David B. Quinn (London, 1964), has been updated and expanded as Paul Hulton, *America: 1585: The Complete Drawings of John White* (Chapel Hill, N.C., 1984). Those interested in Flemish engraver Theodore De Bry, whose printing firm published a multivolume series on "America" in several languages between 1590 and 1634, should consult Bernadette Bucher, *Icon and Conquest: A Structural Analysis of the Illustrations of de Bry's Great Voyages,* trans. Basia Miller Bulati (Chicago, 1981).

Unfortunately, no comparable visual imagery from Spanish North America has been synthesized, although several libraries and museums interpreting the meaning of the Columbian Quincentenary in 1992 have accompanying publications. In addition to exhibition catalogs such as *First Encounters: Spanish Explorations in the Caribbean and the United States, 1492–1570,* ed. Jerald T. Milanich and Susan Milbrath (Gainesville, Fla., 1989), researchers will find *America in 1492,* ed. Alvin Josephy, Jr. (New York, 1992) lavishly illustrated and informative on thematic aspects of Native societies in the Americas on the eve of European invasion. These include language, science and technology, the arts, trade and communication, and social systems. Those seeking in-depth understanding of specific cultures and their histories should consult the appropriate volumes of the Smithsonian Institution's *Handbook of North American Indians,* especially those on *Northeast,* ed. Bruce G. Trigger (Washington, D.C., 1978), *Southwest,* ed. Alfonso Ortiz, 2 vols. (Washington, D.C., 1979, 1983), *Indian-White Relations,* ed. Wilcomb Washburn (Washington, D.C., 1988), and *Southeast,* ed. Raymond D. Fogelson (in progress).

Biological and demographic aspects of early contact are explored in Alfred W. Crosby, Jr., *The Columbian Exchange: Biological and Cultural Consequences of 1492* (Westport, Conn., 1972), in Crosby's more recent

Ecological Imperialism: The Biological Expansion of Europe, 900–1900 (Cambridge, 1986), as well as in *Disease and Demography in the Americas,* ed. John W. Verano and Douglas H. Ubelaker (Washington, D.C., 1992). The global context for microbial transfers is discussed in William H. McNeill, *Plagues and Peoples* (Garden City, N.Y., 1976). Henry F. Dobyns, *"Their Number Become Thinned": Native American Population Dynamics in Eastern North America* (Knoxville, Tenn., 1983) proposes maximum ranges for populations in the Americas at contact, a subject evaluated and critiqued in Russell Thornton, *American Indian Holocaust and Survival: A Population History since 1492* (Norman, Okla., 1987). Those interested in archaeological investigations on earliest epidemics will find useful discussion in *Columbian Consequences,* ed. David Hurst Thomas, 3 vols. (Washington, D.C., 1989–1991), as well as in monographs by Ann Ramenofsky, *Vectors of Death: The Archaeology of European Contact* (Albuquerque, N.M., 1987) and Marvin T. Smith, *Archaeology of Aboriginal Culture Change in the Interior Southeast: Depopulation during the Early Historic Period* (Gainesville, Fla., 1987). The penetration of pandemics into the Lower Great Lakes area during the sixteenth century is discussed by Dean R. Snow and William A. Starna, "Sixteenth-century Depopulation: A View from the Mohawk Valley" *American Anthropologist* 91 (1989), 142–9, and by Gary Warrick, "A Population History of the Huron-Petun, A.D. 900–1650," Ph.D. dissertation, Department of Anthropology, McGill University, 1990. Epidemics introduced by way of Atlantic Canada are discussed by Virginia P. Miller, "Aboriginal Micmac Population: A Review of the Evidence," *Ethnohistory* 23 (1976), 117–27. For possible evidence of major epidemics in the Columbia River basin in the early sixteenth century, see S. K. Campbell, *Post-Columbian Culture History in the Northern Columbia Plateau* (New York, 1990).

On botanical and zoological transfers, the aforementioned studies by Crosby are important. Specialized discussion is contained in Charles B. Heiser, Jr., *Seed to Civilization: The Story of Food,* rev. ed. (Cambridge, Mass., 1990); John C. Super, *Food, Conquest, and Colonization in Sixteenth Century Spanish America* (Albuquerque, N.M., 1988); and *Foraging and Farming: The Evolution of Plant Exploitation,* ed. D. R. Harris and G. C. Hillman (London, 1989).

For the Spanish theater of exploitation and colonization during the sixteenth century, John Francis Bannon, *The Spanish Borderlands Frontier, 1513–1821* (New York, 1970) provides the best one-volume introduction. The three-volume series *Columbian Consequences,* ed. David Hurst Thomas (Washington, D.C., 1989–1991) contains archaeological and ethnohistorical assessments of early contact history. Woodbury Lowery, *The Spanish Settlements within the Present Limits of the United States,* 2 vols. (New York, 1901, 1911) is still essential for early Florida, as are various works by Herbert Eugene Bolton, especially *The Spanish Borderlands: A Chronicle of Old Florida and the Southwest* (New Haven, Conn., 1921). Works by Smithsonian-based ethnologist John Reed Swanton, especially *Final Report of the United States De Soto Commission* (Washington, D.C., 1939), remain basic references for the entire Southeast, as does Edward H. Spicer, *Cycles of Conquest: The Impact of Spain, Mexico, and the United States on the Indians of the Southwest, 1533–1960* (Tucson, Ariz., 1962) for that culture area. An excellent, well-balanced interpretive overview of Spanish activities in both regions is found in David J. Weber, *The Spanish Frontier in North America* (New Haven, Conn., 1992).

Chronicles by European explorers and colonists are available in a variety of formats and are most readily accessible in English in David Beers Quinn, *New American World: A Documentary History of North America to 1612,* 5 vols. (New York, 1979). These translations are generally quite accurate, but researchers will want to consult the authoritative editions in the original languages or as released in English for scholarly use. The following paragraphs include examples of this literature.

For Spanish Florida, additional documents and insights are found in *The Narrative of Alvar Núñez Cabeza de Vaca, translated by Fanny Bandelier . . . with Oviedo's Version of the Lost Joint Report,* translated by Gerald Theisen (Barre, Mass., 1972); *True Relation of the Hardships Suffered by Governor Fernando de Soto and Certain Portuguese Gentlemen during the Discovery of the Province of Florida,* ed. and trans. James Alexander Robertson, 2 vols. (Deland, Fla., 1932); *Narratives of the Career of Hernando de Soto in the Conquest of Florida,* ed. Edward Gaylord Bourne, trans. Buckingham Smith, 2 vols. (New York, 1904); Garcilaso de la Vega, *The Florida of the Inca,* trans. John and Jeanette Varner (Austin, Tex., 1951); *The Luna Papers: Documents Relating to the Expedition of Don Tristán de Luna y Arellano for the Conquest of La Florida in 1559–1561,* trans. and ed. Herbert Ingram Priestley, 2 vols. (Deland, Fla., 1928); Eugenio Ruidíaz y Caravia, *La Florida, Su Conquista y Colonización por Pedro Menéndez de Avilés,* 2 vols. (Madrid, 1893); Pedro Menéndez de Avilés, *Adelantado, Governor, and Captain-General of Florida: Memorial by Gonzalo Solís de Merás,* trans. Jeanette Thurber Connor (Deland, Fla., 1923); *Colonial Records of Spanish Florida: Letters and Reports of Governors and Secular Persons,* trans. Jeanette Thurber Connor, 2 vols. (Deland, Fla., 1925, 1930).

Anthropological and archaeological investigations of early Florida have resulted in a very rich body of literature. Especially important are summaries in *Tacachale: Essays on the Indians of Florida and Southeastern Georgia during the Historic Period,* ed. Jerald Milanich and Samuel Proctor (Gainesville, Fla., 1978); Kathleen A. Deagan, *Spanish St. Augustine: The Archaeology of a Colonial Creole Community* (New York, 1983); Deagan, *Artifacts of the Spanish Colonies of Florida and the Caribbean, 1500–1800, Volume 1: Ceramics, Glassware, and Beads* (Washington, D.C., 1987); and essays in *First Encounters,* ed. Milanich and Milbrath (Gainesville, Fla., 1989).

For Spanish activities in the Southwest, edited works by the team of George P. Hammond and Agapito Rey are standard, especially *Narratives of the Coronado Expedition, 1540–1542* (Albuquerque, N.M., 1940); *The Rediscovery of New Mexico, 1580–1594 . . .* (Albuquerque, N.M., 1966); and *Don Juan de Oñate, Colonizer of New Mexico, 1595–1628,* 2 vols. (Albuquerque, N.M., 1953). Other important source materials include *A Colony on the Move: Caspar Castaño de Sosa's Journal, 1590–1591,* ed. Albert H. Schroeder and Don S. Matson (Salt Lake City, Utah, 1965); Adolf F. A. Bandelier, "Documentary History of the Rio Grande Pueblos," *Papers of the School of American Archaeology 18* (Santa Fe, N.M., 1910); and Fray Alonso de Benavides, *Memorial,* trans. Mrs. Edward E. Ayer (Chicago, 1916). Additional documentary sources are found in the microfilm edition of the *Spanish Archives of New Mexico,* 22 reels (Santa Fe, N.M., 1967) and in *Historical Documents Relating to New Mexico, Nueva Vizcaya and Approaches Thereto, to 1773, Collected by Adolf F. A. Bandelier and Fanny R. Bandelier,* ed. Charles Wilson Hackett, 3 vols. (Washington, D.C., 1923).

Historical archaeology of early New Mexico has not been widely reported. Two short interpretive volumes have recently been released: Herman Agoyo et al., eds., *When Cultures Meet: Remembering San Gabriel del Yunge Oweenge* (Sante Fe, N.M., 1987) and Florence Hawley Ellis, *San Gabriel del Yungue as Seen by an Archaeologist* (Santa Fe, N.M., 1989).

For Spanish activities in California, the cumulative work of Henry R. Wagner is essential, especially his edited collection, *Spanish Voyages to the Northwest Coast of America in the Sixteenth Century* (San Francisco, 1929). Harry Kelsey's excellent study *Juan Rodriguez Cabrillo* (San Marino, Calif., 1986) sheds new light on that important explorer. Archaeological investigations at Drake's Bay are summarized by Edward P. von der Porten,

"Drake and Cermeño in California: Sixteenth Century Chinese Ceramics," *Historical Archaeology* 6 (1972), 1–22.

European activities along the east coast of North America are analyzed in *Cultures in Contact: The Impact of European Contacts on Native American Cultural Institutions, A.D. 1000–1800*, ed. William W. Fitzhugh (Washington, D.C., 1985). The most important written sources relating to early French exploration have been edited by Henry P. Biggar in *The Precursors of Jacques Cartier, 1497–1534* (Ottawa, 1911); *The Voyages of Jacques Cartier: Published from the Originals with Translations, Notes and Appendices* (Ottawa, 1924); *A Collection of Documents Relating to Jacques Cartier and the Sieur de Roberval* (Ottawa, 1930). Early studies dealing with European activities in northeastern North America in the sixteenth century, such as *The Early Trading Companies of New France* by Henry P. Biggar (Toronto, 1901); *Crucial Maps in the Early Cartography and Place-Nomenclature of the Atlantic Coast of Canada*, a collection of papers by W. F. Ganong (Toronto, 1964); *The Conflict of European and Eastern Algonkian Cultures, 1594–1700: A Study in Canadian Civilization* by Alfred G. Bailey (St. John, 1937; reprinted Toronto, 1969); and *The Fur Trade in Canada* (New Haven, Conn., 1930, rev. ed. Toronto, 1956) and *The Cod Fisheries: The History of an International Economy* (New Haven, Conn., 1940) by Harold A. Innis, have been superseded on many specific points by Bernard G. Hoffman, *Cabot to Cartier: Sources for a Historical Ethnography of Northeastern North America, 1497–1550* (Toronto, 1961); Denys Delâge, *Bitter Feast: Amerindians and Europeans in Northeastern North America* (Vancouver, 1993); Bruce G. Trigger, *Natives and Newcomers: Canada's "Heroic Age" Reconsidered* (Toronto, 1985); and Laurier Turgeon, "Basque-Amerindian Trade in the Saint Lawrence during the Sixteenth Century: New Documents, New Perspectives," *Man in the Northeast* 40 (1990), 81–7. For differing syntheses of a voluminous archaeological literature relating to the Lower Great Lakes region, compare James W. Bradley, *Evolution of the Onondaga Iroquois: Accommodating Change, 1500–1655* (Syracuse, N.Y., 1987) and William R. Fitzgerald, "Chronology to Cultural Process: Lower Great Lakes Archaeology, 1500–1650," Ph.D. dissertation, Department of Anthropology, McGill University, 1990. For a review of the varied ways in which European goods reached Indians see James F. Pendergast, "The Introduction of European Goods into the Native Community in the Sixteenth Century," in *Proceedings of the 1992 People to People Conference*, ed. C. F. Hayes III (Rochester, N.Y., 1994), 7–18.

On the brief, but important French colony in Florida see Jean Ribaut, *The Whole & True Discovery of Terra Florida*, ed. Henry P. Biggar (Deland,

Fla., 1927); *Laudonnière and Fort Caroline: History and Documents,* ed. Charles E. Bennett (Gainesville, Fla., 1964); and Bennett's edition of *Three Voyages: René Laudonnière* (Gainesville, Fla., 1975). Additional narratives and images of Indians as portrayed by Jacques Le Moyne are found in *The New World,* ed. Stefan Lorant (New York, 1946). Additional discussion is provided by Paul H. Hulton, *The Work of Jacques le Moyne de Morgues: A Huguenot Artist in France, Florida, and England,* 2 vols. (London, 1977).

English activities during the sixteenth century are best analyzed by David Quinn, especially in his survey *North America . . . to 1612* (New York, 1977) and in his highly interpretive *England and the Discovery of America, 1481–1620* (London, 1974). The context for English expansion is brilliantly analyzed by Kenneth R. Andrews in *Trade, Plunder, and Settlement: Maritime Enterprise and the Genesis of the British Empire, 1480–1630* (Cambridge, 1984).

Documents of English and other European imperial efforts in sixteenth and early-seventeenth-century North America were first systematically collected by Richard Hakluyt in *The Principall Navigations, Voiages and Discoveries of the English Nation* (London, 1589). The Hukluyt Society, based at the British Museum, has published facsimiles of all Hakluyt's works and the important chronicles of trans-Atlantic English colonial probes and earliest settlements. These include Irene A. Wright's *Documents concerning English Voyages to the Spanish Main, 1569–1580* (London, 1932) and her *Further Voyages to Spanish America, 1583–1594* (London, 1951); Quinn's edited collection, *The Roanoke Voyages, 1584–1590,* 2 vols. (London, 1955); and Philip Barbour's collection, *The Jamestown Voyages under the First Charter, 1606–1609,* 2 vols. (London, 1969).

Henry R. Wagner, *Sir Francis Drake's Voyage around the World* (San Francisco, 1926) contains important documents on English contact with the California coast, a subject of continued controversy as summarized by Harry Kelsey, "Did Francis Drake Really Visit California?," *Western Historical Quarterly* 21 (1990), 445–62.

7

NATIVE PEOPLE AND EUROPEAN SETTLERS IN EASTERN NORTH AMERICA, 1600–1783

NEAL SALISBURY

As the seventeenth century opened, the relationship between Native peoples and Europeans in North America east of the Mississippi had an established history but uncertain future.[1] Over the preceding century, the presence of Europeans, their goods, and their microbes had affected many Indians, particularly on the eastern seaboard and in the southeastern interior. Depopulation and migration had caused the disappearance of numerous communities, and European goods had begun to constitute a small but significant portion of many groups' material cultures. These changes, in turn, had brought alterations in subsistence, social and political organization, exchange, and patterns of alliance and rivalry.

Yet for all the transformations they had experienced, eastern North Americans continued to understand themselves, the world they lived in, and even the newcomers, in terms that were essentially rooted in their precontact lifeways and values. Most Indian communities still occupied the familiar, well-defined territories from which they had long drawn their material needs and within which they had constructed their cultural identities and their relations with other groups. And in spite of all their efforts to establish a more substantial presence, Europeans remained outsiders everywhere (except around St. Augustine in Florida) as the sixteenth century drew to a close.

All this would change after 1600. The next two centuries witnessed the explosive and historically unprecedented spread of European societies, economies, and cultures in one form or another throughout the eastern portion of the continent. Colonization would pose serious challenges to Indians' ability to maintain continuity in and control over their ways of life, their homelands, and their cultural identities.

---

[1] The author is grateful for the assistance of Paula Wagoner in preparing the final text and the maps for this chapter.

INDIANS AND THE ESTABLISHMENT OF EUROPEAN
COLONIES, 1600–1660

The turn of the seventeenth century marked the beginning of competition among European nations to colonize North America. Whereas previous expeditions of soldiers, traders, and settlers tended – whether by accident or design – to be on their own, those of the new century had more sustained, substantial, and informed backing from their home countries. Increasingly, their ventures were reinforced or followed up rather than being forgotten or allowed to disintegrate. The reasons that more Europeans were now able and willing to commit the necessary financial, political, and human resources for permanent colonies were due first of all to developments at home, indeed to nothing less than the emergence of capitalism and the mercantile nation-state, and the consequent desire to gain advantages over competitors in the contest for resources and territory outside Europe. England, France, and the Netherlands – each in its own way – were now positioned to challenge Spain and Portugal by establishing their own American empires. Yet it is noteworthy that, even under these new conditions, the earliest colonial enterprises succeeded only by building on earlier patterns of Indian-European exchange and alliance and by taking advantage of dislocations arising from earlier Native interactions with Europeans.

Although Europe's few outposts in eastern North America remained widely scattered through the 1610s, their importance was far greater than the few marks they made on a map might suggest. Each served to facilitate the interaction of microbes, material goods, people, and ideas from both North America and Europe. The consequences of such increased interaction became apparent over the subsequent four decades as epidemics, intensive hunting, heightened exchange, war, and English immigration transformed the demographic and political map of eastern North America. Above all, the period was marked by a concentration of political power in several European colonies plus the Five Nations Iroquois, though each of these entities depended on its ties with other Native groups.

Native exchange and Europe's first outposts, 1600–1620

The impact of earlier contact relations was most readily apparent in the St. Lawrence Valley, where the Mohawks continued their attacks on the

Montagnais (Innu) trading with the French at Tadoussac. In order to increase the flow of thick northern beaver pelts and to secure it against imperial rivals and countrymen acting on their own, the French moved, after the turn of the century, to fortify their presence and influence on the St. Lawrence. The establishment of a permanent French trading post at Quebec in 1608 further enhanced the Montagnais' position among other Indians while providing a measure of insurance against both Mohawk raiders and winter food shortages. In 1609 and again in 1610, the support of Champlain and other armed Frenchmen enabled parties of Montagnais, Algonquins, and Hurons (Wendats) to rout the usually feared Mohawks. In 1615, the French and Hurons sealed an alliance and together attacked an Oneida or Onondaga village. Thereafter, the Hurons were the linchpin of New France's economy, supplying beaver pelts obtained from the Nipissings, Neutrals, Petuns, and Ottawas (Odawas) in exchange for a widening array of metal, glass, and cloth goods and protection from Iroquois aggression.

As the material and political effects of French trade became apparent, other would-be colonizers converged on the Northeast. In 1609, Henry Hudson led a Dutch expedition up the river that soon bore his name, making contact with various Algonquian-speaking groups and stimulating an influx of traders into the region. The center of commercial attraction for these merchants was the area around modern Albany, home of the Algonquian-speaking Mahicans but near Mohawk country as well. (The Mahicans are not to be confused with the Mohegans of southern New England.) The Mohawks found in the Dutch the quantity and quality of European goods that they and the other Iroquois had sought on the St. Lawrence and, in particular, the metal axes, knives, and arrowheads to counter those used against them by their enemies to the north. In 1615, a Dutch attempt to emulate the military role of the French on the St. Lawrence failed when three traders accompanying a Mohawk-Mahican expedition against the Susquehannocks were captured and had to be ransomed. Nevertheless, Dutch traders found ready markets for their wares, expanding their activities to the south coast of New England, Long Island, and the lower Delaware Valley.

To the east, meanwhile, the Micmacs (Mi'kmaqs), like their Montagnais allies, adapted to the era of permanent colonization by building on earlier fur trading ties with the French. They used French shallops to move furs, wampum, and European goods among Basque and Norman traders, Beothuks, Maliseets, Passamaquoddies, and Abenakis. In 1605, a French expedition established Port Royal on the Nova Scotia shore of the Bay of Fundy, giving particular prominence to the local Micmac band and its sagamore, Membertou. Although they experienced devastating European diseases, increased economic dependence on the French, and wholesale nominal conversion to Christianity, Membertou and his allies vigorously sought to maintain control of the flow of goods between eastern Abenakis and Europeans in the face of direct inroads by both French and English. The principal focus of Abenaki resistance to Micmac control of this trade was the Penobscot sagamore, Bashaba, who sought unsuccessfully to trade with both Port Royal and an English expedition to the Kennebec in 1605. Having failed, the Abenakis were no match for the guns and other metal weapons wielded by the Micmacs and their allies in a devastating attack on Chouacoet, at the mouth of the Saco, in 1607. After an English expedition shut down Port Royal in 1613, Micmacs and Abenakis alike were dependent on the annual visits of French traders. The Micmacs' condition was especially precarious because they had come to rely on the French even for food. In spite of this dependence, however, they routed the Abenakis even more decisively in 1615 in a battle that resulted in the death of Bashaba. The Micmacs continued to inspire fear among coastal Natives as far south as Cape Cod until shortly after the Massachusetts Bay colony was established in 1629.

While the French and the Dutch quickly established themselves in northeastern North America by building on Native alliances and rivalries and by observing at least the outward forms of Native reciprocity, would-be English colonizers repeatedly sought to establish footholds along the northeastern coast by intimidating and coercing Indians. This was the pattern in English encounters with Wampanoags at Martha's Vineyard in 1602, 1611, and 1614 and at Cape Cod in 1603 and 1614, and with Kennebec Abenakis in 1605 (as noted above) and 1607. An English colony established on Newfoundland in 1610 was intended to promote trade ties with the Beothuks. But after some fishermen attacked a party of friendly Natives, the already wary Beothuks cut off all ties with the English and withdrew to the interior.

With the exception of a tiny post at Pemaquid on the Maine coast, the English remained shut out of contact with Natives from Newfoundland to Nantucket during the first two decades of the seventeenth century. Into the breach stepped French traders who, visiting annually, monopolized trade with Abenakis, Pawtuckets, Massachusetts, and Wampanoags. But then between 1616 and 1619, epidemics struck these Indians, killing 90 percent and exposing the survivors to the depredations and demands of Europeans, Micmacs, Narragansetts, and Pequots. In the face of this catastrophe, the Pokanoket Wampanoags, led by Massasoit, welcomed the tiny Puritan-dominated colony of Plymouth in 1621. In return for supplying the English with corn and a basis for legitimacy among Europeans, the Indians obtained protection against enemies and a prominent place among Native communities in southeastern New England. However, when Plymouth sought to extend the alliance to the Nausets on Cape Cod and the Massachusetts to the north, the colony met resistance and resorted to coercive tactics.

By 1621, then, the area bounded by the St. Lawrence and Hudson drainages and the Atlantic Ocean had been transformed to a zone of Indian-European interaction and competition, arising from the colonial efforts of French, English, and Dutch. Farther south, a second such zone on Chesapeake Bay constituted a study in contrast to the first. Here, in the absence of European competitors and with substantial financial resources at its disposal, an English colony employed force against Indians and succeeded. Tsenacommacah, or the Powhatan "confederacy," placed some 15,000 to 20,000 Algonquian-speakers under Powhatan, the *werowance,* or leader, on the coastal plain from the south shore of the Potomac to the James. Despite their suspicions of the ill-equipped newcomers who landed on the James River in 1607, the Powhatans saw possibilities of friendship because of the settlers' desperate need for food and the abundance of their metal goods, especially copper, which the Powhatans valued highly. The capture of John Smith and his subsequent "rescue" by Powhatan's daughter, Pocahontas, was probably an adoption ceremony in which the Indians expressed their alliance with the English. But following a ceremonial "coronation" of Powhatan by the English in 1608, the colonists sought to establish their clear superiority to the *werowance* and his followers. When the Natives responded by refusing to supply the English with corn, the result was war. During the winter of 1609–10, the Indians besieged Jamestown, nearly starving out the colony, but the subsequent arrival of reinforcements enabled the English to drive all Natives from the James River by 1611. In 1614, after Pocahantas was captured and converted to Christianity, a bitter Powhatan submitted to a humiliating peace with the colony. Instead of returning to her people, Pocahontas married the wealthy planter John Rolfe and moved to England. Thus the people of Tsenacommacah were already demoralized when the beginnings of commercial tobacco production in 1618, and the consequent surge of English immigration, generated new epidemics and pressures for Indian land.

The new century also saw the revival of Spanish Florida from the ashes of the Guale revolt (1597–1601). By the early 1620s, the Franciscans had resumed most of their missions among the eastern Timucuans and Guales, and established several new ones, especially among the western Timucuans. The missionaries made inroads by presenting the sacraments as efficacious in summoning supernatural power to the aid of worshippers. In addition, the missions supported favored *caciques* and *cacicas,* who oversaw the exchange of Native-grown agricultural produce for European cloth and glass, and traded some of the latter materials with peoples of the interior. However, the thoroughness of many Indians' conversions to Catholicism is doubtful, especially in view of their widespread refusal to observe monogamy in their marriages. The resumption of contact also brought a series of new, destructive epidemics that, between 1613 and 1617, killed half of the 16,000 Indians linked to the mission system.

Wampum and the rise of the Mohawks

During the 1620s, coastal Algonquians from the Hudson to the Merrimack had to adapt to the growing power of English, Dutch, French, and Iroquois in their region. The key element in this expansion was not an imported commodity but the indigenously crafted marine shell beads known as wampum. To northeastern Indians, wampum beads were symbolic "words" communicating messages of peace and condolence as well as recording their histories. And to the Iroquois, wampum was the means whereby the mythical Deganawida assuaged the grief of Hiawatha, paving the way for the formation of the Five Nations Confederacy. Dutch traders discovered the value of wampum to Natives while working the shores of Narragansett Bay and Long Island Sound, where shells for the beads were most abundant. By the mid-1620s, Indians in this area spent their winters in the specialized production of wampum beads; Narragansett and Pequot sachems exchanged the beads with Dutch traders for metal, glass, and cloth goods; and the Dutch in turn added the beads to the range of goods offered to fur-producing Indians in the interior. Previously a material in short supply and handled primarily by shamans, wampum now circulated in large quantities and favored those Indians most adept at dealing with Europeans. The Dutch not only circulated it among their allies on the Hudson but used it to lure New France's allies into trading with them and

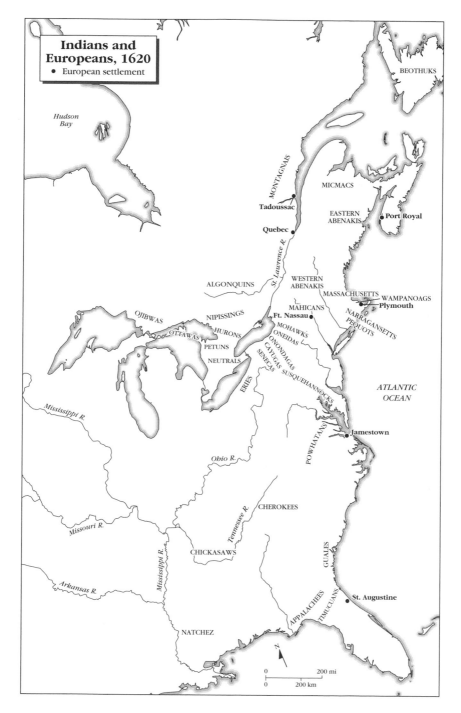

Indians and Europeans, 1620
• European settlement

BEOTHUKS

Hudson Bay

MONTAGNAIS

MICMACS

Tadoussac

EASTERN ABENAKIS

Port Royal

Quebec

WESTERN ABENAKIS

ALGONQUINS

St. Lawrence R.

MASSACHUSETTS

WAMPANOAGS
Plymouth

OJIBWAS

NIPISSINGS

MAHICANS

Ft. Nassau

NARRAGANSETTS

PEQUOTS

OTTAWAS

HURONS

MOHAWKS

PETUNS

ONEIDAS

ONONDAGAS

NEUTRALS

CAYUGAS

SENECAS

SUSQUEHANNOCKS

ERIES

ATLANTIC OCEAN

Mississippi R.

POWHATANS

Jamestown

Ohio R.

Tennessee R.

CHEROKEES

Missouri R.

CHICKASAWS

Mississippi R.

GUALES

Arkansas R.

APPALACHEES

TIMUCUANS

St. Augustine

NATCHEZ

N

| 0 | 200 mi |
| 0 | 200 km |

Figure 7.1. Selected Indian groups and areas of European settlement, 1620.

sold it to Plymouth's traders, who dispensed it among the Abenakis and other coastal Algonquian-speakers north of Cape Cod.

It was the prospect of wampum that drew the Ottawa Valley Algonquin and the Montagnais allies of the French to begin carrying many of their furs to the Mahicans after the Dutch established a new Hudson River post at Fort Orange in 1624. Seeing their old enemies favorably received there and fearing that once again they would be cut off from direct access to European goods, the Mohawks promptly negotiated a treaty with New France, itself concerned at the loss of furs that the Algonquins' shift posed. Soon after, war broke out between the Mahicans and Mohawks, essentially over control of access to Fort Orange. Although the Dutch furnished soldiers and tried to enlist Algonquin participation, the local Mahicans were soundly routed by 1630. Thereafter, the Mohawks enjoyed free and direct access to Dutch traders on the Hudson, and quickly became the source of an ever-growing abundance of European goods, including guns, for the other Iroquois.

The combined impact of the Mohawks' triumph and English immigration transformed Indian life and the wampum trade in southern New England during the 1630s. By 1633, 3,000 European settlers had overwhelmed the 200 Massachusetts and Pawtuckets around Massachusetts Bay, taking land and providing protection against the Micmacs in exchange for corn. A smallpox epidemic that swept through the Northeast in 1633–4 claimed not only most of these Indians but large numbers of Natives to the west, where it undermined the rapidly expanding traffic in furs, wampum, and European goods. Most vulnerable were the Pequots, whose attempts to control all trade on the lower Connecticut River had already earned them the resentment of the Narragansetts, Mohegans, and other Indians, as well as the Dutch. In their isolation, the Pequots made an alliance with the Massachusetts Bay colony, which the latter used as a basis for extracting large amounts of tribute as well as deference and land. By 1636, a new English colony, Connecticut, was established where the Pequots had only recently dominated. When the Pequots balked at paying some of the tribute and accepting blame for the deaths of some Englishmen, the colonies of Massachusetts and Connecticut, aided by the Mohegans and Narragansetts, launched a surprise, predawn attack on their village at Mystic. In all, several hundred villagers of all ages and both sexes were killed. The remaining Pequots were hunted down; those whose lives were spared were put under the supervision of Narragansetts and Mohegans, or enslaved by the English. A few Pequots eluded their pursuers and sought Mohawk support with a gift of wampum. But having already received a larger gift from the Narragansetts, the Mohawks killed these Pequots. As a result, Pequot autonomy was crushed, the English were secure on the Connecticut, and the Narragansetts became a primary source of wampum for the Mohawks.

The Beaver Wars

While coastal Indians confronted the decline of commercial trade, Natives in the interior experienced its advent. In fact, the two phenomena were linked, for as soon as furs had been depleted in one area due to overhunting, Indian and European traders sought new sources. The fact of competition in the trade only further speeded this process. The most rapid expansion of fur trading – and its cultural, political, and military consequences – during the seventeenth century occurred in the vast St. Lawrence–Great Lakes drainage. By midcentury, the region had been the scene of upheavals and dislocations as severe as those experienced by Indians in and near the coastal colonies. Underlying these events was the fierce competition between New France and the Five Nations Iroquois for control of the region's furs, a conflict that would shape much of eastern North American history for the rest of the century and beyond.

Their triumph over the Mahicans and their minor but instrumental role in the Pequot War serve to elevate considerably the position of the Mohawks within the Five Nations Confederacy. For it gave them unrivaled access to the two categories of exotic goods most desired by all the Iroquois–European manufactures and wampum. As they distributed these items to their confederates, they further stimulated the trapping of beavers so that the Iroquois' own hunting territories were soon depleted. At the same time, the Hurons had exhausted the supply of beaver pelts in their own territory and become heavily dependent for pelts on trade with the Nipissings, Ottawas, and other peoples to the north and west. As in precontact times, they delivered corn to these peoples in exchange for meat, though the volume of trade was now much higher. In addition, they provided neighboring peoples with European goods and received tobacco, shell, copper, and other items exchanged long before the arrival of Europeans. While both the Hurons and the Iroquois were depleting their hunting territories of fur-bearing animals, their situations differed in two important respects: on the one hand, the Hurons had Indian allies who provided them with the thick northern pelts most desired on European markets; on the other, the Iroquois had European allies who would soon provide them with guns.

After the brief English occupation of Canada (1629–32), these discrepancies were further magnified when the French insisted that the Hurons accept Jesuit missionaries in their villages as the price of reviving the alliance that had become central to both peoples. The renewal was no sooner consummated than a series of epidemics, culminating in a massive outbreak of smallpox in 1639–40, struck the Hurons with such force that their population of 21,000 was cut in half. As disease and death swept their ranks, the Hurons focused on Jesuit witchcraft as the source of the disaster. But while most Hurons would have liked to rid themselves of the Jesuits and their destructive power, they were restrained by their dependence on the French for trade and protection from the Iroquois. It is noteworthy that no hostile action was directed against French traders and officials during the epidemics; indeed, the volume of Huron-French trade remained about the same through the 1630s despite the steep decline in the Huron population. This indicates that the survivors were becoming relatively more dependent on such trade.

As the epidemics receded, allowing them to repair their reputation among the Hurons, the Jesuits came to terms with the economic realities of New France. Beginning in 1643, Huron traders who became Christians were given special treatment at French posts, including higher prices for their furs and permission to buy guns. Yet while over half the Huron traders converted during the next five years, less than 15 percent of the total population was Christian. The effect was to sow deep divisions in a society that placed high value on consensus in its social, political, and religious life.

Like the Hurons, the Five Nations Iroquois confronted the crises posed by declining furs and depopulation from disease. With the advantage provided by Dutch guns, Mohawk parties attacked Algonquins and Hurons carrying pelts to the French at Montreal, diverting these goods to Fort Orange where they obtained cloth and metal goods, including guns. They also obtained captives, some of whom were tortured to death but most of whom were adopted as replacements for Mohawks who had died from disease or in the escalating cycle of raids and counter-raids. It was in this period that the Mohawks began distributing wampum from southern New England and elsewhere throughout the Five Nations to cement social and political relationships both with the Confederacy and with outside allies. As the other Iroquois nations took up the pattern of raiding, wampum was presented to erstwhile enemies at peace conferences and to console the mourning relatives of Iroquois dead.

The violence generated by Huron-French trade created a ripple effect extending beyond the rivalry with the Iroquois. When the Ottawas sought to trade European goods for furs on Lake Michigan in the late 1620s, they precipitated a conflict with the Siouan-speaking Winnebagos that was still festering when the French tried to intervene in 1634. By the early 1640s, the Iroquoian-speaking Neutrals had expanded their hunting territories by driving the Sauks, Foxes (Mesquakies), Potawatomis, and other Central Algonquians from the Michigan peninsula to the western shore of Lake Michigan. There they came into conflict with the Winnebagos who, after being defeated by the Algonquians and suffering a catastrophic epidemic, were obliged to accept the invading refugees as neighbors. The pan-Algonquian community at Green Bay would subsequently become a major center of pro-French, anti-Iroquois power in the west.

After the Dutch West India Company in 1639 relinquished its monopoly on trade with Indians at Fort Orange, the flow of weapons to the Mohawks and other Iroquois escalated even further. This increased flow, combined with mounting deaths from epidemics and raids, led the Iroquois to escalate their raiding into coordinated, full-scale warfare in quest of captives and pelts, warfare that was directed first against the Hurons.

Thus the Hurons were under intense pressure in the late 1640s from both the Jesuits and the Iroquois. As they began attacking and destroying whole villages in 1648, the Iroquois offered the Hurons peace, trade through them with the Dutch, and the opportunity to be reunited with captured relatives. The effect was to reinforce anti-Jesuit traditionalists among the Hurons who now called for dropping the French alliance for one with the Iroquois. But fear of the Iroquois led many more to look to the Jesuits. Within a year, over half the nation had been drawn into Christian ranks. But far from animating the new believers, these conversions were part of the collective resignation that overtook the Hurons as the Iroquois utterly destroyed them as a political entity in the winter of 1648–9. While some remained with the Jesuits, eventually establishing a Christian community at Lorette, near Quebec City, many voluntarily joined their fellow Hurons living among the Iroquois. Still others fled to the villages of their Petun, Neutral, and Erie allies.

To prevent these allies from reviving an independent Huron nation and to gain control of the furs from the eastern Great Lakes and upper Ohio Valley, the Iroquois dispersed the Petuns, Neutrals, and Eries during the early 1650s. They then drove most remaining Ottawas, Shawnees, and other Algonquian-speakers out of Michigan and the Ohio Valley. Most of these refugees joined the others in Wisconsin, though some Eries and Shawnees went south. But when the Iroquois tried to attack Green Bay in 1653, the refugees there, led by the Potawatomis, repelled them, giving rise to a temporary peace that permitted the resumption of trade between the Algonquians and fur-starved New France. Here was the first suggestion that Iroquois military power and expansionism might have some limits.

Between Iroquoia and Europe: Indians in the colonies

The expansion of Iroquois and European power had a marked effect on Indians residing within the French, English, and Dutch colonies. The history of the Montagnais and Algonquins continued to be shaped by their ties with New France and hostility toward the Iroquois. By the 1640s they were completely dependent on the fur trade, while the French relied heavily on them for military assistance against the Five Nations. In addition, they were, like the Hurons, increasingly subjected to Jesuit proselytizing. In 1637 the Jesuits constructed a village for converts, complete with church and French-style houses, at Sillery, outside Quebec. Their goal was to instill Christian morality and discipline and European culture (including farming by men) among the Montagnais and Algonquins. Although numbering over 100 residents during peak periods, Sillery was limited in its appeal and growth by Jesuit coercion, epidemics, Iroquois raids, fires, intense factionalism, and the lure of hunting and trading.

The Jesuits soon recognized that their mission to the Montagnais, like that to the Hurons, was inextricably linked to the fur trade. During the 1640s, they abandoned the goal of "civilizing" the Indians in parishes for "flying missions" in which they carried their message to hunters in the bush. At the same time, they built additional reserves for refugee Indians, modeled on Sillery, but more flexible in terms of cultural styles and concessions to the fur trade and further sheltered from what the missionaries regarded as the deleterious influence of secular French society.

To the south, the Abenakis sought to maintain their autonomy on the frontier between New England and New France. Plymouth colony traders began trading wampum and maize for pelts among the Kennebec Abenakis in 1625, and, within a few years, English traders were active among all the Eastern Abenakis. These contacts were frequently laden with tension, often resulting in violence, especially as alcohol became more widely dispensed among the Natives. During the 1630s, the Kennebecs sought to introduce their wampum in New France, but were rejected by the suspicious French and Montagnais who feared that it would result in Canadian furs going to the English. Only when some of the Kennebecs joined a Sillery war party against the Iroquois and expressed interest in Christianity, did they begin to find a response on the St. Lawrence. By 1646, some were living at Sillery. The same year the Jesuits sent Father Gabriel Druillettes to their principal village. Druillettes arrived in the midst of a deadly epidemic against which the Kennebecs' shamans were powerless. By selflessly administering to the needs of the sick, declining the gifts usually demanded by shamans, and preaching a message of social and moral rejuvenation compatible with traditional beliefs and rituals, Druillettes succeeded in planting the seeds of a "conversion" that actually represented a new religious syncretism.

When Druillettes returned to Kennebec four years later, he found that his preachings had taken root, but his purpose this time was more explicitly political. After the dispersal of the Hurons, the French sought to forge an anti-Iroquois alliance that would completely surround the Five Nations. Accordingly, Druillettes was dispatched to build on his ties with the Kennebecs to secure the New England region for the French cause. While failing to enlist the Puritan colonies of New England, he gained the support of the Sokokis of the upper Connecticut River, the Pawtuckets at Pennacook, on the lower Merrimack River, and the Mahicans (though violence between these groups and the Iroquois would not erupt for another decade).

Druillettes's inability to enlist New England in his cause was rooted not simply in a Puritan indisposition toward the welfare of French Catholics, but also in the indirect but crucial links between the English colonies and the Mohawk Iroquois. For more than two decades after the Pequot War, a powerful alliance of Narragansetts, Niantics, Pocumtucks, and others supplied wampum to the Mohawks, which the latter dispensed among the Five Nations during the period of their "Beaver Wars." For their part, the New England Natives received furs which they added to dwindling local stocks and traded to colonists for English goods. The latter exchanges were, in turn, part of a larger pattern in which Indian clients – from relatively autonomous groups such as the Narragansetts to "praying Indians" such as the Massachusetts – provided furs, wampum, maize, land, and labor to English patrons – traders, political leaders, ministers. The patrons, in turn, supplied the Indians with manufactured cloth, metal, and glass goods. Each side provided the other with military and diplomatic support, and their commerce enabled each to gain standing in the eyes of other Indians or English. Archaeological evidence has clarified the influence of these exchanges on Native material culture in the mid–seventeenth century. Narragansett and Wampanoag burials are in large cemeteries, reflecting the impact of high, contact-induced mortality, and the corpses are accompanied by large quantities of the goods, especially European items and wampum, that solidified alliances and social relations for Natives.[2] While seeking to limit the land base and political influence of the Narragansetts, the colonies of Massachusetts and Connecticut also depended on these Indians for trade and friendly ties to the Mohawks. As a consequence, the constantly tense relations between the Narragansetts and these English colonies, and the latter's Mohegan allies, never erupted into full-scale violence during the middle decades of the seventeenth century.

In New Netherland, on the other hand, the same decades were marked by fierce warfare as the Munsees and western Long Island Indians found themselves squeezed between Dutch settlers on one side, and the Mahicans and Mohawks on the other. Settler communities had begun to form after the "purchase" of Manhattan Island and the founding of New Amsterdam in 1626. Indians and Dutch welcomed the opportunities to trade with one another, and the number of settlers was initially too small to cause much concern among the Natives. But this harmony was strained in the 1630s as the depletion of local fur-bearing animals from overhunting and the expansion of Dutch farming deprived the Indians of their two most lucrative commodities, pelts and maize. Intercultural tensions flared as the number of immigrants living in close proximity to Natives rose sharply at the end of the 1630s, and were compounded when the colony attempted to tax the Indians and exercise judicial authority over them. At the same time, a decline in fur resources – and, consequently, their ability to trade with the Dutch – led the Mahicans

---

[2] William Scranton Simmons, *Cautantowwit's House: An Indian Burial Ground on the Island of Conanicut* (Providence, R.I., 1970); Susan G. Gibson, ed., *Burr's Hill: A 17th Century Wampanoag Burial Ground in Warren, Rhode Island* (Providence, R.I., 1980); Paul A. Robinson et al., "Preliminary Biocultural Interpretations from a Seventeenth-Century Narragansett Indian Cemetery in Rhode Island," in William W. Fitzhugh, ed., *Cultures in Contact: The Impact of European Contacts on Native American Cultural Institutions, A.D. 1000–1800* (Washington, D.C., 1985), 107–30.

and Mohawks to demand additional tribute in the form of wampum from the Munsees. From 1643 to 1645, the Munsees and their Long Island allies fought both Mahicans and Dutch, and the treaty ending the conflict included Mahicans and Mohawk "mediators" as well as Dutch and local Indians. Tensions did not subside after peace was restored in 1645 because the balance of power between Dutch, Mahicans, and Mohawks on one hand, and local Algonquians on the other, had grown more uneven. Even before new outbreaks of violence during the 1650s (the "Peach" and Esopus wars) ended in defeat for subject Indians, their subordinate status differed little from that already imposed by treaty on the other non-Mahican Algonquians in New Netherland. By the time of the English conquest in 1664, only a few Indian enclaves remained in lower New Netherland; most Munsees lived among the Mahicans to the north or among other Delawares to the west, and most Long Island Indians resided at the eastern end of the island.

To the south of New Netherland and the Iroquois country, the Susquehannocks emerged as a major anti-Iroquois force by midcentury. A power in the upper Chesapeake when encountered by John Smith in 1608, the Susquehannocks were subsequently prevented by the Lenape Delawares and the Powhatans from making contact with New Netherland and Virginia respectively. Only as the European presence in their own area became permanent did the Susquehannocks reestablish themselves. William Claiborne of Virginia found them eager clients when he established a trading post on Kent Island in 1631. But the new colony of Maryland challenged this relationship three years later by allying with the rival Piscataways against the Susquehannocks, in exchange for land and a Jesuit mission, and driving out Claiborne. Although some Delawares had burned a Dutch settlement on the Delaware River in 1632, they and the Susquehannocks, with whom they were now reconciled, welcomed the founding of New Sweden in 1638. Following a rout by Maryland in 1642, the Susquehannocks obtained Swedish arms, enabling them to crush a second Maryland expedition in 1643. They then destroyed the Jesuit mission and reestablished ties with the Piscataways and other allies of Maryland. Besides their trade and diplomatic links with New Sweden, they established, through the Delawares, an uneasy relationship with New Netherland and, through Claiborne, an alliance with Virginia.

By the mid-1640s, the Susquehannocks were actively challenging the Iroquois. In 1647, delegations of Susquehannocks and Hurons visited one another's villages to renew their alliance against the Five Nations. After the Iroquois crushed the Hurons, the Mohawks sought to administer similar treatment to the Susquehannocks in the winter of 1651. Again, Swedish arms enabled the Susquehannocks to prevail and they repulsed the Mohawks. But then, fearing a concerted Five Nations attack and recognizing New Sweden's growing weakness, the Susquehannocks concluded an alliance with Maryland. After New Netherland drove the Swedes off the Delaware in 1655, the Dutch colony became the Susquehannocks' most reliable trade partner; from this position the Dutch persuaded the Susquehannocks to make peace with the Mohawks in 1658, and enlisted their aid in subjugating the Esopuses.

As Indians on the upper Chesapeake reached accommodations with Europeans, the influx of tobacco planters and laborers into Virginia led to war and the erosion of Native life and autonomy. In search of spiritual revitalization, many Indians were initially drawn to the Virginia Company's policy of encouraging them to live among the English and convert to Christianity. In the winter of 1621, the new *werowance,* Opechancanough, endorsed this policy and opened up additional land for English settlement. But other Indians rallied around a charismatic shaman, Nemattanew, known to the English as "Jack of the Feathers" for the elaborate costume he had begun wearing during the war of 1609–14 as a form of countermagic to English armor. In March 1622, an Englishman shot and killed Nemattanew after suspecting him of murdering a colonist. The killing galvanized the hitherto divided Indians against the English. The Powhatans and their allies, led by Opechancanough, arose in a surprise attack on the colony, killing 350, nearly one-third of its population. These events in turn galvanized the English, leading them to wage a war of extermination. By 1634, they had driven all surviving Indians out of the lower James and York drainages, rewarding themselves with some 300,000 acres (121,200 hectares) of land.

Over the next decade, Virginia's tobacco economy passed through its boom period while the English population reached 8,000. In desperation, Opechancanough, now in his nineties, coordinated another surprise attack, resulting in nearly 500 English deaths. The ensuing war lasted from 1644 until 1646, when the English captured Opechancanough, who was then murdered by a guard in defiance of Governor William Berkeley's orders. The resulting treaty deprived Indians of land south to the Blackwater River and sharply restricted their movements within the colony. The Powhatan confederacy was destroyed as a political entity and many of its constituents, as well as other groups, were now subject to attacks and other forms of pressure from an ever growing settler population and economy.

As Virginia's European population continued to rise after midcentury, the planters turned their attention beyond the Tidewater region to the lands of the Piedmont and their occupants. Piedmont Indians found themselves subjected to increasing harassment, sometimes in the form of violent attacks. The colonists generally succeeded in intimidating the Indians with the notable exception of a group of Eries, refugees from the Beaver Wars, who turned back a formidable Virginia effort to expel them from the fall line area of the James River in 1656.

In Florida, meanwhile, the Franciscans concentrated their missionary efforts on the Guales, Timucuans, and, after 1633, Appalachees. References to the middle decades of the seventeenth century as a "golden age" in missionary history overlook the disastrous epidemics that repeatedly swept the Florida Natives in this period. In addition, the influx of soldiers and missionaries created conflicts between these two Spanish groups over treatment and control of the Natives. There is no doubt that the forced labor of Indians on soldier-owned plantations, which the missionaries criticized, was a major cause of an Appalachee rebellion in 1647 and one involving both Appalachees and Timucuans in 1656. But in each case, the Indians destroyed all of the missions in the rebellious areas, indicating dissatisfaction with Christianity as well. Although the missionaries recovered from the first uprising, claiming 26,000 converts in Florida as a whole in 1655, they failed to regain momentum after the second. Meanwhile, the movements of Indian refugees and European goods north to Carolina and west to the interior brought change to Natives in those areas, but without direct contact with Europeans.

ACCOMMODATION, RESISTANCE, AND ANGLO-FRENCH
IMPERIAL ASCENDANCY, 1660–1701

The decade of the 1660s marked a shift in the situation of Indians throughout much of eastern North America. Escalations of European settlement, of Indian-European trade, and of Anglo-French imperial competition led many groups to adopt new diplomatic and military strategies. With the English supplanting the Dutch on the Hudson and France introducing a military force and forging an alliance with Indians in the Ohio Valley and Great Lakes, the Iroquois sought diplomatic accommodations with these

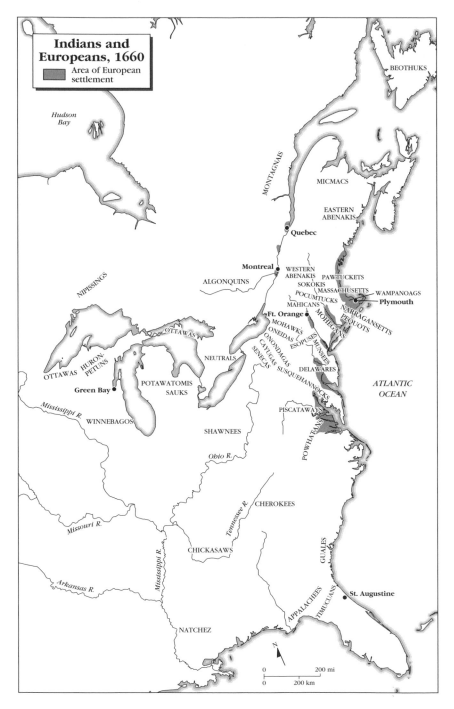

Figure 7.2. Selected Indian groups and areas of European settlement, 1660.

two great powers. In the Southeast, the steady decline of Spanish power was hastened by the establishment of South Carolina and its instigation of a trade in Indian slaves that engulfed most of the region's Natives by the end of the century. At the same time, additional influxes of settlers fueled conflicts between coastal Natives and colonies, often aided by Indian allies, from New England to Carolina.

Iroquois accommodation in the Northeast

The 1660s saw the Iroquois' ascendancy of the preceding quarter century quickly reversed as their enemies on all sides, Indian and European, found new sources of strength and unity while their Dutch allies were conquered by the English. After the Beaver Wars, the Indians of the western Great Lakes and the Illinois region began a remarkable transformation. Sandwiched between hostile Iroquois to the east and Dakotas to the west, interethnic villages of Central Algonquian and northern Iroquoian refugees (along with some Siouan-speaking Winnebagos) emerged during the 1660s and 1670s around the new French trading posts and missions at Chequamegon Bay, Sault Ste. Marie, Green Bay, Michilimackinac, Kaskaskia, and Starved Rock. During the 1660s and 1670s, epidemics and famines inflicted heavy losses on the villages, and older intergroup rivalries plagued efforts to re-create the harmony of earlier village life. These centrifugal tendencies were countered by others that facilitated unity among the many peoples, and trade between them and the French: intermarriage, adoption, and the adaptation and spread of traditional rituals associated with the Hurons' Feast of the Dead, the Ojibwas' Midewiwin, and the Great Plains calumet.

Although French-Indian ties in the Upper Great Lakes were strengthened, the various parties did not immediately forge an alliance that could successfully challenge Iroquois power. A far more immediate threat to the Five Nations in 1660 was the Susquehannocks. Although New Netherland had overseen a Mohawk-Susquehannock truce in 1658, this agreement only fueled the resentment of the four western Iroquois nations at Mohawk and Dutch attempts to shape League diplomacy. In 1660, some Oneidas attacked the Piscataways, challenging the Susquehannocks' claim to be the latter's protectors. The raid alarmed Maryland officials who, fearing loss of the colony's fur trade to the Dutch, rushed military assistance to the Susquehannocks. The payoff came in 1663 when some

800 Senecas, Cayugas, and Onondagas launched a massive attack on the now well-fortified, main Susquehannock village. Aided by a contingent of Delawares, the Susquehannocks beat back the attack, providing a clear demonstration to Indians and Europeans alike that the Iroquois were not invincible.

At the same time, the League's allies to the east were shifting their loyalties toward their fellow Algonquian-speakers in Canada. Although the Mahicans had been party to the anti-Iroquois alliance of northeastern Algonquians fashioned by the Jesuit Druillettes in 1650, there is no record of Iroquois complaint about Mahican-Abenaki contacts for another decade. Thereafter, Mahicans supported Montagnais, Abenakis, and Sokokis in escalating raids and counterraids between these groups and the Iroquois. In 1664, a large Mohawk contingent was repulsed when it tried to capture a Mahican village. Once again, the Iroquois proved less than invincible. By then anti-Iroquois sentiment, and with it the pattern of raiding, had spread to the Connecticut Valley and thence to the Massachusett Christian Indians under the patronage of the Puritan missionary John Eliot. Compounding the Iroquois' difficulties, English troops seized New Netherland in 1664, depriving the Iroquois of the Dutch arms and other goods so vital in their rise to power, and more French settlers arrived in Canada along with troops whose express goal was to end the Iroquois threat to New France.

In the face of these developments, the western Iroquois nations made peace with the French in 1665, while the Mohawks sought to hold back. To bring them around, French expeditions twice raided the Mohawk country in 1666. The ability of the French to penetrate to, and burn, Mohawk villages, and the friendly reception accorded them by nearby Dutch residents, convinced the Mohawks to join the accord in 1667.

Having pacified the Five Nations, the French sought to expand their control of Indian-European trade in the Northeast at the expense of the Dutch and English at Albany. Besides establishing a string of new posts on the Upper Great Lakes in the 1660s and 1670s, they built Fort Frontenac, on the northern shore of Lake Ontario, in 1673 and a post at Niagara, in Seneca country, in 1676. In keeping with the terms of the peace agreement, they also sent Jesuit missionaries to work among the Iroquois. Beginning their work among Christian Huron adoptees, the Jesuits soon began effecting conversions among the larger Iroquois population, including some headmen, of whom the Onondaga Garakontié was the most prominent. The initial reception accorded the missionaries and their new converts by the Iroquois was tolerance, no doubt from a desire to smooth relations with the French and also from the feeling of vulnerability following their recent string of military defeats. But, as among the Hurons three decades earlier, Christianity eventually served to polarize communities that had always relied on consensus and eschewed coercion in the maintenance of social order.

As the traditionalists regained their self-confidence, they increased their hostile pressures on the missionaries and their followers. Beginning in 1673, the Jesuits shifted from trying to convert all Iroquois to the policy they employed toward other Indians: the establishment of communities composed exclusively of neophytes. In response, hundreds of Iroquois moved to Native Christian settlements in Canada or to new ones established for their benefit, of which Caughnawaga (Kahnawake) near Montreal was the most prominent. Ostensibly hostile to one another, the two Iroquois factions actually maintained close ties: hunters from the Five Nations joined their kinsmen in exploiting the lands formerly inhabited by the Hurons, and Christian Mohawks in Caughnawaga established the illicit ties with their traditionalist brethren to the south that gave all Iroquois access to trade with both Montreal and Albany. These ties would persist until the end of the colonial period.

The peace with France enabled the Mohawks to seize a diplomatic advantage over the Algonquian-speakers to the east with whom they were fighting. Raids back and forth between Mohawks on one hand and Mahicans, Sokokis, Pocumtucks, Massachusetts, and others continued through the 1660s. The Mohawks repeatedly sought English aid in bringing about peace with their opponents, something that New York, Connecticut, and Massachusetts officials desired as a means of stabilizing the fur trade and reducing the danger of Indian violence against settlers. But the Algonquians repeatedly demurred, fearing that New York sought to make them tributaries of the Mohawks. With England, France, and the Iroquois all at peace with one another, the Algonquians were isolated from significant sources of outside support, just as tensions with rapidly expanding settler communities were growing. Under these conditions, the Mahicans and other Hudson "River Indians" beseeched New York's protection from the Mohawks in 1675.

Obtaining Mahican submission was one of the first acts of Edmund Andros, who became governor of New York following the brief Dutch reconquest of 1673–4. As the agent of the colony's proprietor, the Duke of York (later King James II), Andros intended to impose a scheme of

imperial order on both Indians and colonies in the Northeast from his base
at Albany. Toward this end he joined forces with the Iroquois, who sought
an advantageous peace with their enemies to the east. With rapidly growing settler societies and economies encroaching from one side, and the
Iroquois-English coalition on the other, coastal Natives from Maine to the
Chesapeake confronted a regional crisis in the mid-1670s that threatened
their continued autonomy.

In southern New England, two consequences of Algonquian-Iroquois
polarization were the end of the region's fur trade and the severing of the
wampum trade between local producers and the Mohawks. These developments deprived many Natives of ties with powerful outsiders, both Indian
and European, just as English demographic and economic growth was
creating pressures for expansion. Taking advantage of this vulnerability,
traders claimed land in lieu of payments on debts, the authorities seized
lands of Indians found guilty of crimes, missionaries sought to reduce
Indians into villages, and speculators and colonial officials intensified
efforts to persuade Natives to sell land. Missionaries, alcohol, and the
encroaching market economy combined with the Indians' eroding land
base to drive Pokanoket Wampanoags, Narragansetts, Nipmucks, and
Pocumtucks – groups that had maintained a degree of autonomy despite
ties with one or another of the colonies – into violent opposition to the
English in what became known as "King Philip's War" (1675–6). Groups
whose ties to outside Indians had been severed earlier, such as the Mohegans, Pequots, and Massachusetts, sided with the English.

During the initial stages of the war, the anti-English Indians held the
advantage with their surprise attacks on settlements and companies of
troops. The turning point came in January 1676 when a New York–armed
force of Mohawks attacked and dispersed a conclave of Algonquians, gathered from New York, New England, and New France, and pursued those
accompanying the Pokanoket leader, Metacom (or "King Philip"), back to
New England. Thereafter, the combination of hunger, disease, the Mohawks, and a revitalized English military effort that made use of friendly
Indians as scouts and troops, led to the uprising's defeat.

In northern New England, the eastern Abenakis had striven for decades
to maintain neutrality between the French to the north and the English
who increasingly populated the Maine coast. But by the early 1670s, they
bitterly resented the abusive practices of English traders and the gratu-
itous violence of some English settlers. When King Philip's War broke
out, the Abenakis initially tried to remain neutral. But fears of Abenaki

ties to the French and to hostile Natives in southern New England led the English to restrict the supply of ammunition needed for hunting. Along with the deliberate drowning of an Indian child by some colonists, this action led all Eastern Abenakis to take up arms against the English by summer 1676. Unlike the conflict in southern New England, the two sides fought to a standoff until establishing a peace in August 1677, formalized in a treaty the following year.

English expansionism and rapprochement with the Iroquois also led to upheavals on Delaware and Chesapeake bays. Seeking to expand toward Delaware Bay, Maryland broke with the Susquehannocks and established an alliance with the Five Nations in 1674. Having isolated the Susquehannocks, the colony then ordered them to evacuate their homeland and move to a vacated Piscataway village on the Potomac.

Their new locale placed the Susquehannocks on a frontier rife with tensions arising from the desires of settlers in the Chesapeake colonies for additional tobacco-growing land. In Virginia these tensions fused with a widespread resentment by colonists toward Governor William Berkeley and his cronies. This small group monopolized a considerable amount of the colony's scarce land while resisting settler aggression against, or expansion onto lands occupied by, Indians with whom they maintained a monopolistic fur trade. In 1675, a dispute between some Virginia settlers and nearby Doeg Indians led to violence. Virginia and Maryland militia units were called out. They attacked Susquehannocks as well as Doegs in defiance of official colony policies. When Berkeley sought to prevent further attacks on Indians friendly to Virginia, a young planter, Nathaniel Bacon, raised a company of volunteers who deliberately and systematically set about attacking the colony's Native tributaries and allies. Berkeley's efforts to stop the attacks led to a destructive civil war that ended after Bacon died the following year.

The results of the various conflicts were disastrous for Natives in the coastal colonies. Regardless of their degree of loyalty to colonial authorities, all coastal Native groups in southern New England and the Chesapeake suffered severe population losses and were reduced to scattered enclaves. These afforded some measure of cultural autonomy but severely restricted Native subsistence choices and political power. In lower New York as well as in these areas, Indians were now less able than ever to resist pressures to sell land, so that the encroachment of colonial society and economy only reinforced their isolation.

By enabling New York's Governor Andros to consummate a new relationship with the Iroquois, the wars had political consequences over an even broader area. As King Philip's War was winding down, New York proclaimed the Mahican village of Schaghticoke, above Albany on the Hudson, a place of refuge for Indians fleeing New England. Then, in an effort to sort out lines of authority and jurisdiction among Iroquois, Mahicans, New York, the New England colonies, southern New England Native groups, and the Schaghticoke refugees, Andros called a conference at Albany in April 1677 that resulted in the first "Covenant Chain" treaty. By this agreement the Mohawks and Mahicans on one hand, and the colonies of Massachusetts and Connecticut on the other, agreed not to deal directly with the other's tributary or subject Indians but to go through a formal conference of all parties at Albany.

Later in the same year, Andros oversaw an agreement encompassing New York, Maryland, Virginia, the Iroquois, and the Delawares over the disposition of the Susquehannock refugees from Bacon's Rebellion. In this treaty, all other Indians were made tributaries of the Iroquois, even the Piscataways and other "subjects" of Maryland. Although building on precedents established by the Iroquois and New Netherland, the new treaties were regarded as the first links of a new "silver" chain of friendship, in contrast to the older "iron" chain. The shift of metaphor was appropriate, for the new chain considerably broadened the role of allied Indians in intercolonial affairs and presaged the role the Iroquois would play in those affairs for much of the next century.

Seeming to have solved their problems to the east, the Iroquois turned their attention once again to the west. In so doing they were prompted not only by the desire to break into the expanding trade between Indians and French on the Upper Great Lakes, but by a massive smallpox epidemic in 1679 that claimed about 10 percent of their population. Replicating the pattern of the "Beaver Wars," the Iroquois launched a series of massive attacks on the Illinois, Miamis, and other Indian groups between 1680 and 1683. In response, the French began fortifying and garrisoning their western posts and transforming their trade networks with the refugee villages into a unified military alliance. For their part, the Iroquois received only token military aid from their Covenant Chain allies at Albany because of the formal peace between England and France.

During the 1690s, the Iroquois suffered a new cycle of defeats, more crushing than any suffered theretofore. On one hand, they were more politically isolated than ever. The political upheavals that followed England's Glorious Revolution in New York, known as Leisler's Rebellion, produced a government that was anti-French but ineffective. Thereafter, New York politics were dominated by men with little interest in the Iroquois. Deep divisions emerged within the Five Nations between pro-French, pro-English, and neutralist factions, with many of the first migrating to the Iroquois towns in Canada, where they joined the military effort against their kinfolk. On the other hand, their enemies were stronger and more unified than ever. While French forces conducted two invasions deep into Iroquois country, well-armed Abenaki, Canadian Iroquois, and Great Lakes Indians attacked from east, west, and north. These Indians drove the Iroquois from their southern Ontario hunting territories, which were subsequently occupied by the Mississaugas, a branch of the Ojibwas (Anishinabes). Although following the strategy of their earlier wars, the Iroquois this time were unable to obtain sufficient quantities of either captives or pelts to realize success. It is estimated that the Iroquois lost 500 of 2,000 fighting men and 1,600 of a total population of 8,600 between 1689 and 1698.[3] By the late 1690s, Indian allies of the French were selling northern and western pelts directly to Albany merchants, bypassing the Iroquois.

Even on their solidly English southern flank, the Iroquois grew more isolated. The establishment of Pennsylvania in 1681 introduced a new source of European trade and alliance for Indians in the Delaware and Susquehanna valleys, outside the hierarchical Covenant Chain in which they were junior partners. William Penn carefully cultivated the Delawares on the Schuylkill, purchasing from them the land for Philadelphia and establishing for them a trade center upriver. On the Susquehanna, Penn overrode New York's claims, based on a spurious submission by the Iroquois who had been erroneously credited with conquering the Susquehannocks there. By the end of the seventeenth century, a number of Susquehannocks, fleeing the destruction in the Iroquois country, had returned to their former homeland along with some Seneca and Shawnee refugees. In 1701, these "Conestogas," as they were now termed, signed a treaty with Pennsylvania in which their lands were protected, trade was guaranteed to both sides, and a refuge was provided to the Conoys of Maryland. Although an Onondaga sachem was present, the proceedings pointedly excluded the Covenant Chain. The Iroquois were now bereft of significant political influence on any outside Indian groups.

[3] Daniel Karl Richter, "The Ordeal of the Longhouse: Change and Persistence on the Iroquois Frontier, 1609–1720" (Ph.D. diss., Columbia University, 1984), 337.

As the century grew to a close, the strength of pro-French and neutralist factions among the Iroquois increased dramatically, leading to peace between the Five Nations and the Mission Iroquois in the winter of 1699–1700. Ever larger numbers of Iroquois favored a peace with France that would be compatible with the English connection, not only in the interests of ending conflict and promoting trade but in order to quell the fiercely divisive factionalism that was further sapping Iroquois strength. In 1700 and 1701, pro-French and neutralist Iroquois conducted negotiations at Montreal while their pro-English counterparts did the same at Albany. The end result was the Grand Settlement of 1701, in which the French opened hunting lands and trading posts as far west as Detroit to the Iroquois in exchange for Iroquois neutrality in future Anglo-French wars. They also persuaded their western allies to make peace with the Five Nations. In their treaty with the English, the Iroquois maintained their customary trading privileges at Albany and agreed to allow Protestant missionaries to work among them. The Covenant Chain was explicitly redefined to exclude Iroquois military activity on behalf of the English. Although closer to and more dependent on Europeans than ever, the Iroquois had found the peace, both internal and external, and the free trade they had long sought.

Indians and the slave trade in the Southeast

Although a significant English presence was established in Carolina only after 1670, the patterns of Indian-European interaction associated with that colony can be glimpsed in the fleeting contacts of the preceding decade. On Albemarle Sound, the Algonquian-speaking Weapemeocs sold their coastal lands to settlers in 1660 and 1662 and moved inland. The early years also saw at least two instances of hostility between colonists and local natives at Cape Fear. Although these early colonial efforts amounted to little, the pattern of Native-settler conflict over land had been established. The second pattern – the exchange of European goods, including guns, for deerskins and Indian slaves – had its roots in the activities of Virginia traders who moved into Carolina to do business with the Erie refugees known as Westos, the various Siouan-speaking piedmont peoples who would soon be called Catawbas, and the Iroquoian-speaking Tuscaroras. After resisting efforts by Virginia to expel them from that colony's frontier in 1656, the Westos within another decade became the principal clients of the Virginia traders. Heavily armed, their quests for deerskins and slaves led them to attack Yuchis, Cherokees, and other interior groups and to force the closing of two Spanish missions among the Guales in Florida.

The influx of English colonists into the Albemarle Sound and Charles Town areas of the Carolinas during the 1670s displaced the Virginians while reinforcing their patterns of interaction with the Natives. The newcomers were also beset by tensions similar to those that rocked the Chesapeake colonies during the same decade. In what later became North Carolina, colonists agreed in 1672 with the powerful Tuscaroras to promote trade and restrict settlement. Opponents of the agreement took control of the government in 1675 but were overthrown shortly thereafter in Culpeper's Rebellion. In South Carolina, the proprietors aligned with the Westos, arming them and encouraging slave raids on Spanish Indian missions. But the proprietary monopoly antagonized private traders, who saw the Westos themselves as potential slaves, while other colonists were alienated by frequent incidents of Westo violence against settlers. Taking Indian policy into their own hands, some colonists known as the "Goose Creek men" joined with a recently arrived band of Shawnee refugees known as Savannahs and waged an all-out war on the Westos, dispersing them by 1684.

The destruction of the proprietary monopoly in South Carolina opened the way for the spread of Indian-English trade throughout the Southeast, and furthered the weakening of Spanish influence among Natives there. By the mid-1680s, most Guales were fleeing south to St. Augustine, west to the interior, or north to Carolina. The Guales in Carolina became known as Yamasees. Since the establishment of Charles Town, small numbers of interior Muskogean-speakers, called "Creeks," occasionally arrived to trade with the English and urge closer ties between the two peoples. During the late 1680s, the English began a massive trade with the Creeks while Spanish troops sought to counter their influence. The newcomers exchanged cloth, guns, and other goods for deerskins, slaves, and horses, the latter two of which the Indians obtained in raids on Spanish-Indian settlements. For the remainder of the century, Yamasees and Creeks raided Appalachee and Timucuan missions. Their task was made easier by Spanish persistence in the policy of not arming Native allies. Instead, the Spanish sought to protect the Indians by reinforcing their military presence, overlooking that their soldiers' treatment of Indians was one of the principal causes of the latter's alienation. Although the Spanish could coerce some Creeks into professing loyalty for a time, most preferred to trade with the English, even moving their villages if necessary to exercise that preference. By the end of the century, most Appalachee and Timucuan missions had been destroyed and Spain's presence beyond the St. Augustine area was limited.

The activities of English traders soon extended to Indians who lived beyond the areas of Spanish influence. By the late 1680s, they traded with Upper Creeks, who raided Cherokees and Choctaws for slaves, and the Chickasaws, who obtained slaves among the Choctaws and the badly weakened Illinois on the Mississippi River. They also traded with the Cherokees, who complained to the Carolinians about Creek slave raids. But the Cherokee trade was definitely a lower priority to the English than the Creek, and the Cherokee complaints went unsatisfied. By the end of the century, English trade and the slave wars had galvanized tendencies toward confederation among both attackers and attacked, most remarkably among the ethnically and linguistically pluralistic Creeks.

THE SEARCH FOR NEUTRALITY, 1700–1744

The first half of the eighteenth century was marked by an extraordinary jockeying for power and influence in which Indian nations, European empires, and English colonies aligned with and against one another in a constantly shifting kaleidoscope of alliances and rivalries. Beneath these seemingly random fluctuations, however, were two distinct tendencies. On the one hand, English and French power was gradually being extended over the eastern half of the continent, and only the most successful Indian groups were able to reconcile their need for European trade ties with their desire to avoid involvement in Europe's conflicts. What made such neutrality possible at all was the relative balance of power between England and France, with a weakened Spain bolstering the latter. On the other hand, the advantages enjoyed by the English over the French, both in supplying higher qualities and quantities of trade goods at lower prices and in populating their colonies in unprecedented numbers, threatened to erode that balance altogether. But the seriousness of this threat was apparent to few until the middle of the century.

Expansion and war, 1700–16

As the French made peace with the Iroquois in 1701, they simultaneously set out to ensure that their hold on trade around the Great Lakes would

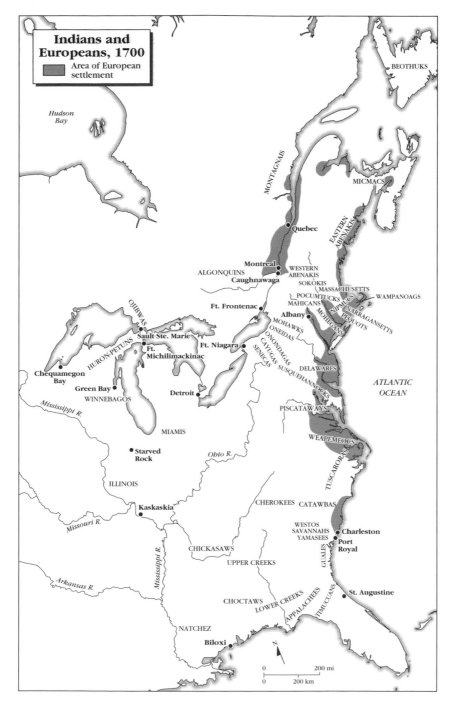

Indians and Europeans, 1700

☐ Area of European settlement

Hudson Bay

BEOTHUKS

MONTAGNAIS

MICMACS

●Quebec

EASTERN ABENAKIS

Montreal●
ALGONQUINS
Caughnawaga

WESTERN ABENAKIS
SOKOKIS
MASSACHUSETTS
POCUMTUCKS NIPMUCS WAMPANOAGS
MAHICANS NARRAGANSETTS

OJIBWAS

Ft. Frontenac●

Albany●
MOHAWKS
ONEIDAS
ONONDAGAS
CAYUGAS
SENECAS
SUSQUEHANNOCKS
MOHEGANS PEQUOTS

Sault Ste. Marie●
HURON-PETUNS
Ft. Michilimackinac●
Ft. Niagara●

DELAWARES

Chequamegon Bay●

Green Bay●
WINNEBAGOS

Detroit●

ATLANTIC OCEAN

PISCATAWAYS

Mississippi R.

MIAMIS

WEAPEMEOCS

●Starved Rock

Ohio R.

TUSCARORAS

ILLINOIS

CHEROKEES CATAWBAS

Kaskaskia●

Missouri R.

WESTOS
SAVANNAHS
YAMASEES
GUALES

●Charleston
Port Royal

CHICKASAWS

Mississippi R.

UPPER CREEKS

Arkansas R.

CHOCTAWS
LOWER CREEKS
APPALACHEES
TIMUCUANS

St. Augustine●

NATCHEZ

Biloxi●

N

| 0 | 200 mi |
| 0 | 200 km |

Figure 7.3. Selected Indian groups and areas of European settlement, 1700.

not again be disrupted. With Antoine Laumet de Lamothe Cadillac as commandant, they built Fort Pontchartrain at Detroit as a new site for allies and refugees from throughout the Great Lakes and Ohio regions to congregate and trade. The fort's presence was expected to discourage the Iroquois from any notions they might entertain about invading the region once again and, along with France's new colony in Louisiana, to provide a barrier to English expansion westward. But instead of enabling the French to control and direct their allies, the new center had just the opposite effect. Having been drawn closer to the Iroquois, with whom they were now at peace, resident Indians such as the Huron-Petuns, Miamis, and Mississaugas began taking their furs to Albany for the better prices offered there, rather than selling them to the French. French efforts to disrupt this trade after 1708 served only to fan resentment against the French and to strengthen pro-English elements among the Iroquois. The result was the participation by many Iroquois in two English invasions of Canada and support for the Foxes in their war against New France and its Detroit allies. Only the bungling of the invasions by the English prevented the Iroquois from returning permanently to the anti-French posture of the preceding century, and only the pleas of the westernmost Senecas prevented over 1,000 other Iroquois from invading Detroit.

At the same time, the French failed to anticipate the conflicts that arose as a result of congregating at one locale so many groups accustomed to unimpeded French trade. When violence erupted in 1706 between Ottawas on one hand and Huron-Petuns and Miamis on the other, the Miamis returned to the Maumee River and the Ottawas moved across the Detroit River while the French stood by. An even more bitter conflict began in 1712 after combined Dakota and western Ojibwa raids in Wisconsin drove more than a thousand Foxes, along with some Mascoutens and Kickapoos, to the Detroit area. Their arrival, and Fox claims to prior ownership of hunting lands around Detroit, aroused the resentment of most Natives already there. At the same time, Fox-Iroquois ties led the French to fear that the Foxes were engaged in a massive conspiracy with the Iroquois and English to destroy Detroit. The French ignored Fox requests for mediation as allied Indians slaughtered or captured most of them and their friends at Detroit in 1712. Thus began the "Fox wars" that disrupted the French alliance in the west for the next quarter century.

Meanwhile, the French were establishing a counterweight in the Southeast to the rapid expansion of the English and the equally precipitous decline of the Spanish. They erected Fort Biloxi in 1699 and Mobile in

1701 from where they made contacts with Choctaws, Chickasaws, Natchez, and other groups. With the outbreak of Queen Anne's War (the North American phase of the War of the Spanish Succession) in 1702, trade and imperial war were intertwined as the Appalachees fought for their long-standing Spanish supporters, the Chickasaws and Creeks for the English, and the Choctaws for the French. During the course of the conflict, Creek-English forces killed and enslaved still more Indian allies of the Spanish in Florida, and destroyed the remaining Guale, Timucuan, and Appalachee missions, driving the Spanish to the confines of St. Augustine and their new fort at Pensacola. With the Chickasaws, they conducted a successful attack on the French at Mobile and stunned the Choctaws with their slave raids. By war's end in 1712, the Creeks had emerged as the most powerful Native force in the Southeast.

While Queen Anne's War served to extend the enterprises of English merchants to Indians throughout the southeastern interior, trader abuses and a mounting influx of settlers created tensions with Natives closer to home. Such tensions led many of the Savannah Shawnees, who had replaced the Westos as clients of South Carolina, to begin moving north to Pennsylvania in 1707. When South Carolina attempted to prevent their departure, some Savannahs conducted raids on English towns. The colony retaliated by arming allied piedmont Indians, who were coming to be known collectively as Catawbas. In turn, the Shawnees enlisted the aid of the Iroquois in attacking the Catawbas. Now that the Five Nations were at peace with the Detroit Indians, the Catawbas became the new object of the "mourning wars" in which Iroquois sought captives for adoption to replace their dead. The Iroquois' ability to attract the participation of Conestogas, Shawnees, and Great Lakes allies of the French also helped restore some of the diplomatic prestige they had lost during the recent wars. At the same time, Catawba retaliatory attacks on Shawnees in Pennsylvania helped to persuade that colony to approve passage for the Iroquois-led raiding parties. Thus began seventy years of intermittent warfare between the Iroquois and Catawbas.

Growing colonial pressures on the once-prosperous Tuscaroras in North Carolina also drew Iroquois attention southward. By the turn of the century, settlers were occupying lands of some Tuscarora allies, and a series of incidents had led to tensions between the Tuscaroras and traders in Virginia. In addition, the Tuscaroras' ties to Virginia had made them the targets of retaliatory raids by Iroquois and Conestogas for that colony's treatment of the Susquehannocks during Bacon's Rebellion. In 1710,

Tuscarora delegates traveled to Pennsylvania to make peace with the Five Nations and Conestogas as hundreds of Swiss and German immigrants arrived to settle in their immediate vicinity. In the following year, the Lower Tuscaroras rose up and attempted to drive out the newcomers with a sudden strike, but they were defeated by the intervention of South Carolina, Virginia, the Yamasees, and the Cherokees on behalf of North Carolina. By 1713, 1,500 to 2,000 Lower Tuscaroras moved north to live among the Iroquois, who incorporated them as the sixth nation in their confederacy in 1722. The Upper Tuscaroras who remained became tributaries of Virginia and North Carolina, but their position grew increasingly untenable as the Euro-American populations of the two colonies increased around them. Well before the century was out, most moved farther into the mountains or joined their Lower Tuscarora kin among the Six Nations, as the Iroquois now became known.

As Queen Anne's War drew to a close, the abuses of Indian allies by South Carolina traders – cheating, enslavement, violence – undermined the formidable alliance that had facilitated the spread of English power over much of the Southeast. Because of such incidents the Creeks made peace on their own with the French and Spanish in 1712. Similar resentments, along with the intrusions of cattle ranchers on their lands, led the Yamasees, now residing near Port Royal, to launch a series of surprise attacks on English trading houses and settlements in 1715. At the same time, the Creeks and Catawbas arose to assassinate the English traders in their villages. The "Yamasee War" was really a pan-Indian uprising, the most extensive one yet in colonial North America, and one that seriously threatened the future of South Carolina. It failed only because the Cherokees, whose support was sought simultaneously by the Creeks and Carolina, elected to avenge past Creek attacks and joined the English. With Cherokee support and that of Virginia, South Carolina crushed the Yamasees and drove the Creeks and Catawbas back from the areas of English settlement. Renewed Iroquois attacks, now actively encouraged by the English, also weakened the Catawbas.

Neutrality and dependence, 1716–20

Having exhausted military solutions to the dilemmas posed by the pervasiveness of European economic power, Native groups returned after the wars of 1702–16 to diplomacy. Certainly the most astute diplomats in this period were the Creeks, under the leadership of the Coweta *mico,* or "emperor," Brims. Having made peace with the French and Spanish, and having fought the English, Brims and the Creeks devised a long-term strategy for dealing with these three powers on their periphery. That strategy became apparent in 1717 when the Creeks simultaneously permitted the French to construct Fort Toulouse on the Alabama River, sent a delegation to Mexico City to solidify their ties with the Spanish, and made peace and restored trade with South Carolina. By exploiting factions favoring each of the European powers and by using his sons as personal emissaries, Brims developed the most sophisticated and successful of all Indian "play-off" systems. Most importantly, the Creeks gave each European nation enough to maintain the alliance but not so much as to jeopardize their own neutrality or autonomy. Thus, while pledging friendship with the Spanish in 1717, they refused them permission to build a fort among the Lower Creeks, allowing them to get no closer than Appalachee. In making peace with the English, they disappointed the French; at the same time, they refused South Carolina's efforts to establish a Creek-Cherokee peace, instead allying with the Iroquois, who had begun attacking the Cherokees. Similarly, they declined to repudiate the Yamasee refugees and Appalachees in Florida who periodically attacked South Carolina settlements and trading parties.

The Creek strategy in the South was paralleled in some respects by that of the Iroquois in the North. Having grown frustrated and resentful at the ways in which both British and French tried to use them during Queen Anne's War, the Iroquois likewise reaffirmed their friendship with each power in 1717, along the lines of the neutrality proclaimed in the Grand Settlement. Like the Creeks, they sought to turn the factionalism within their ranks to their advantage. This new diplomatic policy was strengthened by a traditionalist revival, sparked by a major smallpox epidemic, by resumption of the mourning wars and accompanying rituals, and by a new influx of refugees, both into Iroquois ranks and as allies on the periphery of the Confederacy. As seen above, Iroquois military activity was now directed southward against Catawbas and Cherokees. But while the southern raids yielded some adoptees for the Iroquois, far more newcomers now arrived voluntarily. Upper Tuscaroras from North Carolina, Shawnees from South Carolina, Susquehannocks and others from the Chesapeake frontier served to fuel suspicions of the English and thereby strengthen Iroquois neutrality. The incorporation of the militantly traditionalist Upper Tuscaroras into the League reinforced anti-European tendencies already at work, especially in the rejection of missionaries.

Most Indian groups did not have the resources, the favored locales, or the past histories and reputations of the Creeks and Iroquois. Survival in a world increasingly pervaded by Europeans with their microbes, material goods, and political imperatives required that these Natives have a shrewd understanding of the newcomers and a strong sense of their own cultural identity. The Catawbas, for example, only finally consolidated as a distinct people during the first two decades of the eighteenth century, drawn from a range of Carolina piedmont communities shattered by disease, enslavement, and war with both English and Iroquois. Thereafter, while growing increasingly dependent on Virginia and South Carolina traders, they avoided becoming captive allies of either. Using the guns obtained in such trade, they strengthened their new national identity in the course of retaliating against the Iroquois and raiding such southern allies of the Iroquois as the Upper Tuscaroras, Nottoways, and Meherrins.

Whereas Anglo-French rivalry led Creeks and Iroquois to reconcile internal factions through policies of neutrality, it led in the lower Mississippi Valley to a hardening of the alliances formed during Queen Anne's War. Thus the Choctaws, as principal allies of Louisiana, protected French interests from depredations by Creeks and Chickasaws, and the Chickasaws aligned solidly with the English while maintaining close ties with the Creeks. Although committed to distinct European powers, Choctaws and Chickasaws succeeded, at least for the moment, in maintaining their internal coherence. Such was not the case with the Natchez, who were bitterly split by French construction of Fort Rosalie on their land in 1716. Factions arose, with one group welcoming the new post, the other moving closer to the Chickasaws in bitter opposition.

Lacking more than one European power to whom they could conceivably turn, the Cherokees found themselves isolated in the aftermath of the Yamasee War. They had joined with South Carolina against its Indian enemies at a critical moment during the fighting only to have that colony renew its ties to the Creeks soon after the fighting ceased. In reestablishing trade with the Creeks, the English supplied them with far more guns and ammunition than they sold to the Cherokees, allowing the Creeks to resume their attacks on the Cherokees. At the same time, the Cherokees were under frequent attack by the Iroquois and by the French-allied Choctaws. Moreover, the English – seeking to regulate their trade through a public monopoly – obliged Cherokee traders to travel to specified locations where they charged prices the Cherokees found too high, furnished goods of both inadequate quality and quantity, and were illiberal in extending credit.

Although resumption of small-scale trade with Virginians and an end to the public monopoly in South Carolina eased some of these conditions by the early 1720s, the Cherokees' isolation from an adequate alternative source of goods and diplomatic support left them vulnerable in a way that their rivals were not.

In the far Northeast, Anglo-French rivalry presented both new opportunities and new dangers to the Micmacs and Eastern Abenakis. In the Treaty of Utrecht (1713), France had ceded Acadia to England but the precise boundaries of the cession were left undefined. Nevertheless, the treaty brought an English presence to Micmac country that paralleled the return of English settlers and traders in larger numbers than ever to Abenaki country. Throughout the far Northeast, Indians sought to play the two powers off against each other in order to maximize their autonomy but ended up favoring the French. Familiarity with the French, the sympathetic activities of French missionaries, and French recognition of the importance of gifts as symbols of reciprocity were countered by English land-hunger and insistence that Natives submit to English sovereign authority. In addition, the unregulated private trade in Maine and the train of abuses it entailed, including violence and alcohol, alienated most Abenakis.

French expansion in the Mississippi Valley and Upper Great Lakes, 1720–44

In 1722, the French established the permanent capital of Louisiana at New Orleans, on land acquired earlier from the Chitimachas. From there they hoped to anchor the southern half of their North American empire and, through trade and alliance with Indians in the Mississippi Valley, to deter British expansion from the east and Spanish expansion from the southwest. The principal barrier to their success quickly proved to be the Chickasaws. With their ample supplies of guns and other trade goods from the English in South Carolina, and the security afforded by their firm ties with the powerful Creeks, the Chickasaws alternately attacked and offered peace to the Choctaws, Natchez, Illinois, and other Indian allies of the French. The French preferred a state of war between Choctaws and Chickasaws, fearing that peace between the two groups would favor the English with their cheaper, more abundant goods. Indeed, the possibility of peace with the Chickasaws and trade with the English was alluring to many Choctaws, leading the French to spend lavishly on gifts and scalp bounties that only reinforced the growing factionalism among Choctaws in the 1720s.

Of more immediate concern to the French were the Natchez. The tensions that had been created by the construction of Fort Rosalie on Natchez land in 1716 mounted during the 1720s as French and enslaved African immigrants moved into the area around the fort to establish and work tobacco plantations. The Natchez mounted an uprising against the French in 1729 after the latter demanded that they move their villages to make room for expanded tobacco production. Aided by a rebellion of slaves in New Orleans and by some timely Chickasaw-English overtures to the Choctaws, the Natchez initially drove the French from Fort Rosalie. The French countered with new overtures to the Choctaws, who then played a principal role in suppressing the Natchez in the following year.

Although assisting the French against the Natchez, the Choctaws' own complaints against their European allies were by no means satisfied. A continual shortage of goods and new inroads by the English led the French to increase their gifts to war leaders, thereby undermining the authority and prestige of civil chiefs. The result was two decades of internecine strife fueled primarily, but not exclusively, by a war leader named Shulush Homa, or Red Shoes. This remarkable figure created a political base independent of the civil chiefs while shifting his allegiance back and forth several times between the French on one hand and the English and Chickasaws on the other. Although French-supported Choctaws succeeded in forcing the Chickasaws to sue for peace in 1740, the superior ability of the English, compared to the French, in maintaining their supply lines minimized the effect of this military victory.

To the north of the settled area of Louisiana, the French likewise attempted to expand their presence and were likewise deterred by Native resistance. As in the South, the resistance originated in part with the Chickasaws, whose incessant slave raids of the Illinois people helped undermine this most dependable ally of the French on the upper Mississippi. Expansion was also hampered by splits among France's allies and by opposition to French trade by other groups. The Foxes, Sauks, Mascoutens, and Kickapoos were joined by Dakotas and Winnebagos in attempting to block French trade west of Lake Michigan. But in mounting a united effort against the Foxes and their allies during the 1720s, the French were able to smooth over many of the tensions among their Detroit-centered allies. Then, after winning over the Mascoutens, Kickapoos, and Dakotas, the French enlisted Illinois, Huron-Petuns, Ottawas, Christian Iroquois, and others in a concerted series of assaults on the Foxes and Sauks. By 1736, they had inflicted heavy casualties on these groups and driven most of them across the Mississippi River. Only the pleading of the Illinois and other Indians led the French, in the following year, to allow willing survivors to return to the east side of the river. With the establishment of Fort Marin in 1738, many Foxes and Sauks resumed trading with the French.

In attempting to expand their trade activities westward, the French sought not only to increase profits and solidify alliances but also to prevent the westward expansion of trade activity by Britain's well-financed Hudson's Bay Company. Toward this end, they established several new trading posts and forts on the hunting lands of their Ojibwa allies and of the Assiniboines and Crees, principal clients of the British, during the early 1730s. The eastern Dakotas, previously aligned with the Ojibwas against the Crees and Assiniboines, resented this new connection between the French and their principal rivals. In 1736, they attacked Fort St. Charles on Lake of the Woods and killed twenty French, including the explorer Jean-Baptiste Gaultier de la Vérendrye. Using French arms, the Ojibwas then turned on the Dakotas, driving them away from Lake Superior and establishing a series of new villages near its western end. This assault reinforced the westward movement of Dakotas into the Mississippi Valley and the buffalo-hunting lands to the west, while the ensuing Ojibwa-Dakota war temporarily drove the French from the upper Mississippi.

Refugees in upheaval: Pennsylvania and Ohio, 1720–44

In the eastern Great Lakes, the French made their boldest peacetime move yet against the Iroquois when they fortified their Niagara post in 1721 in order to intercept the furs that their western allies had been taking to Albany for more than a decade. The British countered by building Fort Oswego in 1727, a post that restored their advantage over the French but enabled Indians to trade directly with the English without going through the Iroquois country to Albany. These moves seriously undermined the role of the Iroquois in the Great Lakes fur trade and were one factor in their focusing most of their attention southward for the next half century.

In Pennsylvania, the influx of both refugee Indians and European settlers, plus the movements north and south of Iroquois and Catawba war parties, heightened tensions, particularly over conflicting claims to the Susquehanna Valley and other western lands. Pennsylvania sought to extinguish Iroquois claims to the valley in order to control trade and settlement there, but without alienating the Iroquois with their powerful influence among the local Indians. Meanwhile, Virginia sought to end attacks by Iroquois and their allies on Native clients of that colony. In 1722, New York hosted a treaty conference at Albany in which the governors of Virginia and Pennsylvania met with Iroquois representatives to resolve these issues. Pennsylvania agreed to allow the Iroquois to trade at Philadelphia, while the Five Nations appeared to have dropped their claims to Conestoga lands. Virginia and the Iroquois agreed that Indians from each side of a frontier between them would not cross that line. What was most significant about the two treaties was that they assumed Iroquois hegemony over refugee Tuscaroras, Delawares, Shawnees, and Conestogas – none of whom were represented at the conference. After more than two decades of dormancy, the Covenant Chain was revived as an instrument of joint Anglo-Iroquois interests.

For the Tuscaroras, the Albany treaties were followed by their acceptance as members of the Iroquois Confederacy; for the other refugees, the agreements brought added tensions as the Iroquois cooperated in efforts to open lands for European settlers. Many Shawnees and some Delawares were forced to move west to the Ohio, where they confounded their English and Iroquois overlords by making contact with the French and their Indian allies there. The Delawares of the Delaware Valley, on the other hand, attempted to remain in their homelands in the face of intense pressures to move west. Between 1729 and 1734, Pennsylvania's proprietors bought more then 50,000 acres (20,000 hectares) from Delaware leaders, which they then sold to settlers and speculators. Thereafter, Nutimus, leader of the largest remaining concentration, resisted further cessions. To get his land, the Penn brothers and James Logan concocted both a forged deed and – with the cooperation of the Six Nations – a myth of previous Iroquois conquest of the Delawares to implement the notorious Walking Purchase. The consequences of the fraud were of utmost significance: the Delawares were removed and, for the first time, settlers from the English colonies crossed the Appalachians, thereby impinging on many Native groups as well as on French interests.

With settlers moving into Pennsylvania, the Ohio Valley became the principal magnet for Native refugees from upheavals induced by European expansion. Originally ordered to move west by the Iroquois as a means of opening land for settlement, Shawnee and Delaware migrants rebuffed the efforts of Pennsylvania and the Iroquois to control them. After initially making overtures to the French, they adopted a posture independent of all the powers – French, English, and Iroquois – claiming ownership of the Ohio. In this they were joined by increasing numbers of "Mingos," Iroquois who had earlier begun moving west to hunt with the Indian allies of the French but who, during the 1730s and 1740s, were augmented by others and were growing independent of the Six Nations. Farther west, the French encouraged the Mascoutens and Kickapoos, detached from their alliance with the Foxes in 1735, to resettle among the Miamis on the Wabash River, a tributary of the Ohio. Reinforcing the neutrality of all these groups was the growing presence of English traders with all the commercial advantages they offered. Those advantages, along with past experience and their ties to all three powers, led the multi-ethnic refugees to resist domination by any one group and to display increasingly what the French, with some anxiety, termed "republican" tendencies.

Shifting frontiers in the Southeast

During the 1720s, the Southeast continued in a state of upheaval as Spanish-backed Yamasees and Appalachees raided Carolinian outposts and trading parties while the Creeks and Cherokees remained at war, both of them armed by the English. In keeping with their policy of neutrality, the Creeks initially resisted English pressures to repudiate the Yamasees. But a host of factors combined to undermine the delicate balance presided over by their leader, Brims. The unreliability of Spanish and French supplies of guns and other trade goods strengthened pro-English forces among the Creeks. At the same time, Creek-Cherokee hostilities endangered Carolina traders, leading the colony to seek a peace between the two groups. After an English expedition destroyed Yamasee villages adjacent to St. Augustine in 1728, making plain the weakness of the Spanish, Brims consented to a break with the Yamasees and peace with the Cherokees. The French treatment of the Natchez in 1729 and the death of Brims sometime in the early 1730s further eroded potential resistance to the founding of Georgia in Creek territory south of the Savannah River. James Oglethorpe, the colony's founder, successfully presented himself to the Creeks as a trade partner who would be preferable to the Carolinians. Consequently, he received permission to establish a settlement in exchange for sending traders to Creek towns. Although the English presence was growing, the Creeks, for the moment, balanced the four centers of European power on their periphery against one another, and though divided by the Anglo-

Spanish war that broke out in 1739, most Creeks resisted pressures from all sides to become involved.

The Cherokees, hitherto more dependent than the Creeks on trade with South Carolina, likewise grew more critical of that colony during the 1720s. South Carolina's deregulation of the public monopoly in 1721 alleviated the shortages of goods that had prevailed but brought a return of the abuses that everywhere seemed to characterize private trading by the English. Moreover, the Cherokees were inadequately equipped to defend themselves against raids by Creeks, Iroquois, and Indian allies of the French. In this situation, growing numbers of Cherokees sought alternatives or counterweights to dependence on South Carolina and its insensitive traders. In 1727, for example, the Overhill branch of the Cherokees entertained a delegation of pro-French Miamis from the Ohio Valley. That they also sought a stronger national identity, comparable to what Brims had brought the Creeks, became evident three years later during the visit of an eccentric English nobleman, Sir Alexander Cuming. Stopping at each Cherokee town, Cuming presented himself with much pomp and ceremony as a direct royal emissary, bypassing South Carolina, and led the Indians in a toast to the monarch. He also promoted the naming of Moytoy, a village leader, as "emperor," and took a delegation back to England to sign a treaty with the king himself. Cuming, who hoped to be named viceroy of Cherokee country, later reported that the Cherokees acknowledged English sovereignty in these rituals, which is doubtful. But by appealing to their incipient nationalism, he contributed to both the revitalization of Cherokee life and the revival of English prestige at a critical moment.

In England, on the other hand, the principal effect of Cuming's publicity and the Cherokee delegation's visit was to stimulate commercial interest in the southern frontier. Within three years, Georgia was founded and quickly became for the Cherokees, as it did for the Creeks, an alternative trade partner to South Carolina. But the trade competition between the two colonies had negative effects for many Cherokees and heightened their desire for independence. In 1736, another eccentric outsider, Christian Priber, a German intellectual, awakened in many Cherokees an even keener sense of their own national possibilities than had Cuming. Priber arrived in the Overhill town of Great Tellico in 1736 and immediately became a full member of the community adopting Cherokee dress, marrying a Cherokee woman, and learning the language. He found in the Cherokees a people who, in their values and institutions approximated the

"Kingdom of Paradise" he hoped to establish on earth. As a step toward realizing the kingdom, Priber urged the Cherokees to lessen their dependence on all Europeans, especially the English, while strengthening their ties with other Indians. Although his message was neutralist in intent, South Carolina officials feared he was in league with the French. To co-opt the movement Priber inspired, they recognized the emperorship and, after Moytoy's death in 1741, manipulated the naming of his successor. Then, in 1743, they ordered the arrest of Priber, who died in prison a year later.

Alongside these developments, the Cherokees, like other southeastern Indians, continued to be victimized by armed conflicts among Natives that were rooted in the fur trade and in European imperial and colonial rivalries. Iroquois and Upper Tuscaroras plus Shawnees and other pro-French Natives fought with Cherokees and Catawbas; Cherokees fought with Creeks while both, along with the Chickasaws, fought with the Choctaws. In addition, piedmont groups like the Catawbas and the Upper Tuscaroras were increasingly crowded by settlers as the English colonies quickened the pace of their westward expansion.

The far Northeast

English expansion in Nova Scotia (formerly French Acadia) and upper Massachusetts (now coastal Maine) upset the delicate balance that Micmacs, Maliseets, and Eastern Abenakis had sought to maintain since the Treaty of Utrecht gave Britain a foothold in Maritime Canada. Responding to a growing English presence, Micmacs attacked an English post at Canso in 1720 and the Kennebec Abenakis of Norridgewock did the same to a nearby English settlement in the following year. In 1722, full-scale war broke out all along the coast from the Kennebec to Cape Breton. The Indians were openly supported by the government of New France as well as by the French missionaries, Antoine Gaulin among the Micmacs and Sébastien Rale at Norridgewock. The English introduced troops from lower New England, including Wampanoags, Mohegans, and other Native subjects of the colonies there. While the Micmacs were generally successful in harassing the English in Nova Scotia, the colonists applied severe military pressure in Maine, destroying Norridgewock and killing Rale. In 1725, the Penobscots, Maliseets, and Micmacs agreed to a peace in which they acknowledged British sovereignty and agreed not to disturb English settlers, while Britain agreed not to disturb the

Natives in their subsistence activities or religion. By 1727, the Abenakis south of the Penobscot had followed suit. Thereafter, tensions between Natives and colonists resumed, occasionally erupting into violence.

IMPERIAL DECLINE AND THE END OF INDIAN DIPLOMACY, 1744–1783

In less than four decades after 1744, the political landscape of eastern North America was transformed more profoundly than at any time since the arrival of Europeans. First came the Seven Years' War between Britain and France, in which most Indians sought in vain to maintain the balance of European forces that had prevailed since the beginning of the century. In the end the French were vanquished and the Indians confronted a victorious Britain whose principal rivals were now its own colonies. Despite many misgivings, most Indians supported the British during the ensuing revolutionary struggle, recognizing that the rebels sought not only political independence from the Crown but an independence of all ties, economic and political, with Indians and an end to Indian sovereignty.

Struggle for the Ohio Valley

The outbreak of imperial warfare in 1744, after three decades of formal peace, was felt most immediately in the Ohio Valley. Many of the recently arrived "republican" Indians repudiated the French with their high prices, the scarcity of their goods, and their insistence that the Indians join them in fighting the English. In 1747, a group of Huron-Petuns, or Wyandots, led Mingos, Shawnees, Miamis, and others in attacks on French traders at several locations, making clear their view that the French had overstepped the bounds of reciprocity in asking for more while offering less. They now began dealing instead with the growing numbers of Pennsylvania merchants who frequented the valley; some, most notably Mingos, Shawnees, the Wyandots of Sandusky, and the Miamis of Pickawillany, formally allied with Pennsylvania.

The alliances of Ohio Indians with Pennsylvania represented a blow not only to France but also to the Covenant Chain, rooted as it was in the New York-Iroquois axis. Since 1736, prior to removing the Delawares under terms of the Walking Purchase, Pennsylvania had recognized the Six Nations as supreme among Indians in the colony; now it dealt directly with the Mingos, who had withdrawn from the Confederacy. Republican

Indians and English colonists included the Six Nations in their deliberations only when it was expedient to do so. Iroquois power was also weakened by British efforts to enlist it in the struggle against France. While most Iroquois resisted, a few, mostly Mohawks under the influence of British agent William Johnson, participated in a disastrous attempt to attack Montreal.

After the war, the French countered the unraveling of their western Indian alliance with a show of force. In 1749, Captain Pierre-Joseph Céloron de Blainville led an expedition from Montreal to the Great Lakes and down the Ohio, forcefully reasserting French power and demanding that the Indians expel all English traders. Although this action persuaded the older Great Lakes allies to return to the French cause, it had little impact on the "republicans" of the Ohio. These communities had broken away from political leaders allied with the French and were developing ties with the English. Beginning in 1752, the French struck directly at this new alliance. While Pennsylvania and Virginia negotiated for land with the Ohio Indians at Logstown, a force of French, Ottawas, Ojibwas, and Potawatomis attacked the Miami community at Pickawillany, killing its leader, Memeskia (also known as Old Briton and La Demoiselle) and taking many prisoners. The Logstown conference ended with the Mingos confirming the Virginia-Iroquois Treaty of Lancaster (1744), in which Virginia gained title to all lands south of the Ohio, and agreeing to construction of a British post at the junction of the Monongahela and Allegheny rivers. The Miamis and other Indians now saw the English as more directly threatening their lands, while being unwilling or unable to protect them adequately, and so they abandoned them and renewed their French ties. By 1754, the French had driven all English traders from the Ohio Valley and begun erecting a string of military forts, including Fort Duquesne on the site of Virginia's partially constructed post.

The Greater Southeast

As on the Ohio, the outbreak of war in 1744 restricted the availability of French goods on the lower Mississippi, while solidifying Louisiana's insistence on the loyalty of its Indian allies. This lack of reciprocity was particularly resented among the already divided Choctaws. In 1745, Red Shoes opened new negotiations with the Chickasaws and English; soon, South Carolina traders, like their Pennsylvania counterparts to the north, were peddling their wares in new territory to the west. But the kind of

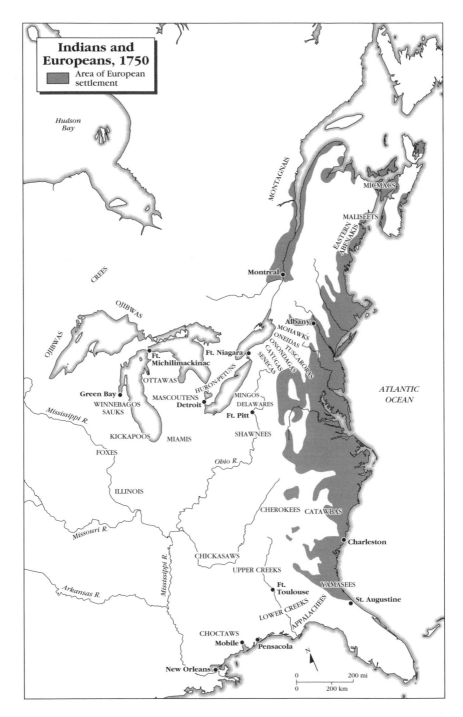

Indians and Europeans, 1750

Area of European settlement

Hudson Bay

CREES

OJIBWAS

OJIBWAS

MONTAGNAIS

MICMACS

MALISEETS

EASTERN ABENAKIS

Montreal

Ft. Michilimackinac

Ft. Niagara

OTTAWAS

Albany

MOHAWKS
ONEIDAS
ONONDAGAS
TUSCARORAS
CAYUGAS
SENECAS

HURON-PETUNS

Green Bay

MASCOUTENS

Detroit

MINGOS

DELAWARES

ATLANTIC OCEAN

WINNEBAGOS
SAUKS

Mississippi R.

Ft. Pitt

KICKAPOOS

MIAMIS

SHAWNEES

FOXES

Ohio R.

ILLINOIS

Missouri R.

CHEROKEES CATAWBAS

Mississippi R.

CHICKASAWS

Charleston

Arkansas R.

UPPER CREEKS

Ft. Toulouse

YAMASEES

St. Augustine

LOWER CREEKS

APPALACHES

CHOCTAWS

Mobile

Pensacola

New Orleans

N

0   200 mi
0   200 km

Figure 7.4. Selected Indian groups and areas of European settlement, 1750.

abuses that had frequently strained South Carolina's relations with the Cherokees provoked an even stronger reaction among many Choctaws. After a pro-French Choctaw assassinated Red Shoes in 1747, the civil war dividing the nation reached its bitterest heights. Following two years of fighting, French soldiers and their Choctaw allies suppressed the surviving followers of Red Shoes. As on the Ohio, decisive military action, along with Native misgivings about English aims, combined to return the advantage to the French.

Meanwhile, the momentary prospect of a Choctaw-English alliance stirred Louisiana's Governor Pierre de Rigaud de Vaudreuil de Cavagnial to make diplomatic initiatives among the Creeks, the greatest potential impediment to such an alliance. In this he was aided by growing Lower Creek discontent with the English, especially in Georgia where the colony was embroiled in a series of running disputes with Mary Bosomworth, the powerful mixed-blood niece of Brims, who was both widow and wife of ambitious English traders. Bosomworth sought to maintain her uneasy role as broker between the Lower Creeks and Georgia, but Georgia refused both to honor her land claims on behalf of the Creeks and to provide her and her husband with what they deemed appropriate compensation for services rendered the colony. At the same time, many Creeks resented South Carolina Governor James Glen's pressuring them to attack the French at Fort Toulouse.

Vaudreuil's efforts were undermined in early 1747 when Cherokee-Iroquois raids forced the Creeks to turn back to the English for arms, ammunition, and diplomatic help in calling off the Cherokees. The resultant peace was short-lived, and the Lower Creeks were soon engaged in a ferocious war with the Lower Cherokees in defiance of South Carolina's wishes. A new peace was finally obtained in 1752 through the delicate efforts of the Bosomworths, who had abandoned Georgia to reside among the Lower Creeks.

The Seven Years' War and the fall of France, 1754–63

Even before the French seized control of the upper Ohio, the effects of Indian alienation from the English cause were apparent. In 1753, Virginia commissioned the young George Washington to lead an expedition that would inform the French that their forts were on British soil. Along the way, he attempted to gather support from Shawnees, Delawares, and other republicans. In the end, he could find only four Mingos to join him, and even these remained with the French instead of returning with him. After France seized the upper Ohio in the following year, Washington returned with an even larger force. His few Mingo supporters again abandoned him, and he blundered into having to surrender to the French at Fort Necessity, reinforcing Native doubts about English military capabilities.

By this time, alienation of Indians by the English had spread beyond the Ohio. The weakening of the Covenant Chain alliance, the declining role of the Six Nations and Albany in Indian-European trade, and the defection of many Iroquois to Ohio and Quebec led those who remained to question the value of maintaining their special tie to the English. Of all the Six Nations it was the Mohawks, traditionally the most staunchly pro-English, who declared the Covenant Chain a dead letter in 1753. With imperial war on the horizon, a shaken Board of Trade in London ordered colonial governors to convene a treaty conference at Albany the next year to restore the alliance. Although the Albany Congress reaffirmed the form of the Covenant Chain, delegates actually exacerbated Native grievances through a series of questionable purchases of Indian land.

War broke out on the Ohio in 1755 when General James Braddock, at the head of 1,300 British troops, set out to recapture Fort Dusquesne. Although many Mingos, Shawnees, and Delawares were still willing to deal with the English, Braddock put them off with his high-handed manner and his candid avowal that they would lose their lands if the English won. Along the way, a small contingent of French and about 1,000 allied Indians, mostly from the St. Lawrence and Great Lakes region, utterly routed Braddock's expedition. Soon Shawnees and Delawares were attacking frontier settlements in Pennsylvania and driving colonists from their homes. The French and their allies, now including many Iroquois, quickly followed the victory over Braddock by seizing the British forts Oswego in 1756 and William Henry in 1757 and massacring many of their occupants. Despite some victories in Canada, the British situation grew ever more desperate through the summer of 1758.

As the French advantage increased, many Iroquois and Ohio Indians saw the need to restore balance between the two European powers by resuming their support of the English. But Delaware and Shawnee antagonisms toward both Iroquois and English constituted major obstacles to this strategy. Teedyuscung, a self-proclaimed "king" of the Delawares, sought (1) to unite the various Delaware bands and to secure a homeland for his own people in the Wyoming Valley of western Pennsylvania, (2) an investigation of the Walking Purchase in order to expose it as a fraud, and

(3) independence from the Iroquois so the Delawares could deal directly with Pennsylvania and other European governments. For their parts, the Shawnees and other Ohio groups feared that an alliance with the British would entail legitimization of Iroquois claims to authority over them and ownership of their lands. Finally, in a treaty conference at Easton, Pennsylvania, in October 1758, the Ohio Indians and Pennsylvania Delawares accepted Iroquois suzerainty as the surest means of ridding their lands of the French and minimizing the expansionist threat posed by the British. As a direct upshot of the Treaty of Easton, most Ohio Indians abandoned Fort Duquesne leaving the French unable to hold it against the British. Other French forts on the Ohio and Great Lakes soon followed. By 1760, British-Indian victories had forced French Governor General Vaudreuil to surrender all of Canada to England.

The fall of France in Canada was followed by a period of profound disillusionment for Indians on the Great Lakes and Ohio. Instead of withdrawing, the British installed large garrisons in the former French posts, from which they sought to dominate the Natives. General Jeffrey Amherst then ordered a cessation of present-giving to the Indians at the posts, an order that included both food and ammunition needed to hunt. He also demanded the return of all British captives held by the Indians, including adoptees who were content in their new homes. In addition, Amherst seized land belonging to the Senecas which he granted to some of his officers. Adding to the tensions was the invasion of the Wyoming Valley by Connecticut settlers in 1762. The New Englanders expelled the Delawares living there and burned Teedyuscung alive in his cabin. Epidemics and dissension among the Indians themselves compounded their discontent, leading many to believe that a French return would restore stability to the region.

In the South, the war between Britain and France meshed with one between the Cherokees and the colonies. Chafing for decades under the restrictions imposed on their trade by both South Carolina and Virginia, the Cherokees after 1750 were increasingly pressured by encroaching English settlers. Both colonies signed new treaties with the Cherokees in 1755, in part to secure their support in the war with France. But trader abuses persisted, and the resentment of many Cherokees over their treatment while supporting English troops on the Ohio led to violence with frontier settlers in Virginia which in turn triggered all-out war in 1759. Divided among pro-British, pro-French, and neutralist factions, the rival Creeks enjoyed the fruits of trade with both sides while avoiding the perils of war. The Cherokees, on the other hand, were dependent on the French and accordingly suffered shortages of food and ammunition due to Britain's successful blockade of French ships. Although initially devastating frontier settlements and seizing an English fort, they were no match for a British contingent of 2,800 troops that swept through their country in 1761, burning homes and crops. In that year, the Cherokees capitulated in treaties with South Carolina.

France's military disintegration was confirmed when the Treaty of Paris, formally ending the Seven Years' War, was signed in January 1763. The treaty awarded French Canada, Spanish Florida, and Louisiana east of the Mississippi to Britain, and gave Louisiana west of the Mississippi to Spain. It thus made official the expulsion of France from mainland North America and of Spain from land east of the Mississippi.

Frontiers in upheaval, 1763–75

The most immediate Native reaction to the expulsion of France came from Ohio and Great Lakes Indians, already desperately alarmed over Amherst's policies. Though many continued to hope for a French return, others turned to a new religious movement, based on the preachings of Neolin, the "Delaware Prophet." Drawing on Native traditions as well as Christian revivalism, Neolin called on Indians to join in a united rejection of all European ties and ways so they could once again enjoy material well-being, political autonomy, and cultural integrity. As Indian resentment against the British grew, many fused these divergent hopes by directing Neolin's anti-Europeanism toward the British. Among the most articulate to do so was the Ottawa war leader Pontiac.

During the spring and summer of 1763, Indians throughout the Great Lakes and upper Ohio attacked the occupied forts, beginning with an assault on Detroit, led by Pontiac. Although hardly the sole instigator implied in the term "Pontiac's Rebellion," the Ottawa leader did help coordinate several other attacks near Detroit and then moved to Illinois from where he sought to enlist Mississippi Valley Indians in the uprising. Most of the assaults were successful, but the Indians failed to take the key British positions at Detroit, Niagara, and Fort Pitt. Fort Pitt was retained after English officers presented smallpox blankets to a Delaware delegation urging its surrender, setting off an epidemic that spread among upper Ohio Indians during the ensuing year. Shortages of food and ammunition, dissension among Natives, and recognition that the French were not going

Figure 7.5. Selected Indian groups and areas of European settlement, 1763.

to return led most Indians to cease fighting by 1765. Pontiac himself submitted to Sir William Johnson in the following year.

Even during the rebellion's earliest phases, British officials endeavored to establish imperial authority by controlling the ever more explosive relations between Natives and colonists. In October 1763, King George III issued a royal proclamation that dealt with several aspects of imperial policy in postwar North America but above all with Indians. Land west of the so-called "Proclamation Line," along the crest of the Appalachians, remained in Native hands and could only be alienated with Crown approval, while sales of Indian land to the east were to be carefully regulated by colonial governments. A system of licensed traders was established and British officials were to keep criminals and fugitives off Indian land. Enforcement of these provisions was to be carried out by the superintendants of Indian affairs in the northern and southern districts, whose positions had been established in 1756. Yet the proclamation had limited effect from the very beginning as provisions regarding both trade and settlement went unenforced, fueling Indian resentment once again.

In the South, the activities of unregulated traders and the incursions of settlers from Virginia to Georgia onto the lands of Cherokees, Creeks, and Catawbas fanned the flames of anti-English sentiment during the early 1760s. In February 1763, Creeks and Cherokees met with Choctaws and French at Fort Toulouse to discuss common grievances and the developing movement to the north. The news of the French and Spanish cessions at Paris strengthened the determination of many to prevent British troops from occupying the French and Spanish forts. In this situation, southern Indian agent John Stuart convened a congress at Augusta in November 1763 that included the governors of the four southern colonies plus Cherokees, Lower Creeks, Choctaws, and Chickasaws. Smaller numbers of Upper Creeks and Catawbas also attended. Most conspicuous by their absence were members of the militantly Nativist Creek faction led by a headman named the Mortar. The Lower Creeks made a substantial cession of land in exchange for forgiveness of some past legal offenses. Elsewhere, the conferees agreed on boundaries between Native and settler lands but, in some cases, these agreements were not formalized.

Although making substantial concessions to each Native group at Augusta, the English realized their overall goal of preventing the spread of pan-Indian war from the North to the South. This was especially critical because the efforts of the British to assert their authority in Florida and Louisiana presented an analogous situation to that on the Great Lakes and

Ohio. In spring 1765, Stuart traveled first to Mobile where he persuaded the Choctaws and Chickasaws to accept English authority and trade and the Choctaws to cede land along the coast and lower Mobile and Tombigbee rivers. The two groups also helped the English establish themselves in the Mississippi Valley so as to counter Pontiac's activities in Illinois. Stuart then went on to Pensacola where, in May 1765, the Mortar and other Upper Creeks agreed not only to peace but to a regulated trade from Pensacola and Mobile and to the cession of a ten-mile wide strip between the two posts.

Despite the short-term successes of imperial officials and troops in pacifying most Indian groups by 1768, other pressures were building that would doom this policy in the long run. The phenomenal economic and demographic growth of the colonies, and the militant republicanism accompanying it, lay at the root of most of the factors undermining imperial policy: the influx of Euro-American settlers, speculators, traders, and hunters on Indian lands; the inability or unwillingness of colonial authorities to prevent violence or punish crimes and treaty violations committed by such interlopers; the inability of the Crown to maintain garrisons at many forts, to furnish gifts to its Native allies, and to finance its Indian superintendents due to colonial resistance to royal prerogative and further taxation. The power of these forces became apparent in 1768 when the Board of Trade returned control of Indian-English trade to the colonial governments and when, in a treaty conference at Fort Stanwix, New York, William Johnson persuaded the Iroquois to cede vast tracts of Shawnee, Delaware, and Cherokee hunting land on the Ohio that the Six Nations had in fact never occupied or controlled.

The Treaty of Fort Stanwix, along with other cessions during the decade after the Seven Years' War, set off a rush of speculators and settlers along the frontiers from Pennsylvania to Georgia, while colonial governments ignored or actively aided Euro-American perpetrators of violence. Farther west, the distribution of presents and other forms of Indian-English exchange dried up as the British evacuated more forts. In response, the Shawnees sought to reestablish the old alliance of Great Lakes and Ohio Indians, along with those of the Southeast, as an entity independent of both English and Iroquois. Their effort was resisted by William Johnson and by pro-English Iroquois who, threatening to attack groups joining the Shawnees as violators of the Covenant Chain, succeeding in splitting the potential alliance. Meanwhile, various efforts by the Shawnees and other Indians to bypass Johnson and negotiate directly with Pennsylvania, the Crown, or the squatters themselves were ignored. Among both Indians and English on much of the frontier, older lines of authority had been discredited or otherwise weakened, leaving little alternative to all-out war.

In spring 1774, rumors of an Indian declaration of war led two parties of Virginians to begin killing as many Indians on the Ohio as they could find, including at least eight friendly Mingos from a village headed by one Logan. Iroquois diplomacy and coercion prevented outraged Delawares, Senecas, and other potential allies – even most Mingos – from taking up arms against the English. But Logan led a band of Shawnees and Mingos in killing a number of settlers equal to the number of Indians recently slain, thereby providing Virginia with a pretext for waging "Dunmore's War" on the diplomatically isolated Shawnees. After losing a battle with the Virginians at Point Pleasant, the humiliated Shawnees agreed to give up their hunting rights in Kentucky in exchange for a pledge that the English would not settle north of the Ohio.

The American Revolution and the fall of Britain, 1775–83

The responses of Indians to the outbreak of war between Great Britain and its mainland colonies south of Canada varied greatly, depending both on recent events and longer-standing ties. Natives everywhere were under pressure from both sides, initially to remain neutral and later to join actively on one side or the other. Those who suffered most heavily from the incursions and depredations of settlers and other interlopers on their land were the quickest to take up arms against the secessionists. Ohio Valley Mingos, still smarting under the attacks that had provoked Dunmore's War, raided settlements in Kentucky in hopes of driving all Europeans from the new territory. They had support from some Shawnees, Delawares, and Wyandots, though most Ohio Indians still recognized the Treaty of Fort Stanwix, establishing the Ohio River as a boundary between Indians and colonists. Similarly, the Cherokees, harassed by settlers on their land and receiving no satisfaction from any of the southern colonies, began attacking frontier colonists from Virginia to Georgia in May 1776.

The ability of the British to maintain supplies of trade goods also stood them in good stead. The reliability in this respect of Fort Michilimackinac and Green Bay won them the initial support of the Foxes, who had fought the French in the western Great Lakes for much of the century, and of their Sauk and Winnebago allies. In addition, they continued to rely heavily on their Chickasaw allies in the middle Mississippi Valley.

The great confederacies of Iroquois and Creeks, meanwhile, were badly divided. While most Iroquois initially sought to remain neutral, the Oneidas, under the influence of the Congregationalist missionary Samuel Kirkland, generally favored the Patriots while most Mohawks followed Joseph Brant (Thayendanagea), the English-educated protégé of William Johnson, in supporting the British. The Creeks, many of whom had strong ties both with British Indian agents and with traders in South Carolina and Georgia, were likewise divided. But above all, they were distracted by their own war with the Choctaws, a conflict which British agent John Stuart struggled unsuccessfully to mediate in order to free those who wanted to support the British and Cherokees.

Aside from the Oneidas, the Americans' most likely Native allies were those who were not threatened by settlers from the new nation and who had long-standing ties with the French, as well as those who were ill-disposed toward Britain. Caughnawagas, Abenakis, Maliseets, and Micmacs in the far Northeast all initially leaned toward the rebels, not only because of their French ties but because of Britain's early military failures in Canada. Yet the support of each was predicated on the Patriots' success both in delivering trade goods and in continuing to win on the battlefield. On the Illinois and Wabash Rivers, Illinois, Kickapoos, Potawatomis, Miamis, and others leaned toward the Americans at the outset, as well as to the Spanish at St. Louis, again out of loyalty to the French and because of Britain's failure to maintain the flow of supplies. In addition, the Americans had the support of eastern groups, such as the Catawbas of South Carolina and the Stockbridge Indians of Massachusetts, that were entirely subjugated to the authority of colonial governments and surrounded by non-Indian settlers.

While Native-settler conflict in Kentucky remained sporadic at the outset, that along the Cherokees' eastern frontier quickly developed into full-scale war. By the summer of 1776, the Cherokees were attacking frontier settlers from Virginia to Georgia. But the colonies recovered from their initial shock and organized retaliatory expeditions that burned most Lower, Valley, and Middle towns. A year later, the Cherokees signed treaties — with South Carolina at DeWitt's Corner and with North Carolina and Virginia at the Long Island of the Holston — in which they ceded virtually all their land in South Carolina and much of that in North Carolina and eastern Tennessee.

As they subdued the Cherokees, the rebels rapidly lost ground among Indians to the north. During the fall of 1776 and winter of 1777, Joseph

Brant traveled throughout Iroquois country, galvanizing support for the British and encountering significant resistance only among the Oneidas and Tuscaroras. During the following summer, nearly a thousand Iroquois participated in the British offensive against the Americans in the Hudson Valley. Although many Iroquois were disillusioned by the series of failures leading to England's defeat at Saratoga, most remained within the British fold. In 1778, Brant led a sweeping campaign against the settlements and grain fields of Wyoming, German Flats, and Cherry Valley in order to deprive the Continental Army of its food supplies.

The example of the Iroquois together with continued tensions on the Ohio led increasing numbers of Wyandots, Shawnees, and Delawares to join Mingo raids on the settlements there. After separate incidents in which peace-seeking Seneca and Shawnee chiefs were murdered by settlers, the Shawnees as a whole undertook to carry out coordinated raids throughout Kentucky. Although the Delawares struck an alliance with the Americans, most were reluctant to join the latter in their proposed campaign against Detroit. The Delawares' reluctance was reinforced by the Americans' failure to supply arms and other supplies and by the death in September 1778 of their pro-American chief, White Eyes, who was murdered (unbeknown to the Delawares) by American soldiers.

Elsewhere, Indians who supported or leaned toward the Americans began moving away from them. Although some Maliseets joined the Patriots in defending the St. John Valley from invading British troops in 1777, the success of the British in consolidating their hold on the far Northeast led most Abenakis, Maliseets, and Micmacs toward a prudent neutrality. Far to the west on the Wabash River, the formerly American-leaning Kickapoos, Miamis, Potawatomis, and others aided British General Henry Hamilton in capturing the French village of Vincennes in December 1778, from a small American contingent. Although the Spanish and Americans made inroads among the southern Indians in 1778, shortages of goods and the successful invasion of Savannah by Britain in December enabled that nation to mobilize most Creeks, Choctaws, and Chickamauga Cherokees along with the ever-loyal Chickasaws.

In 1779, the Americans mounted a series of expeditions designed to reverse this course of events. In February, George Rogers Clark's expedition to Illinois made a surprise capture of Vincennes after the withdrawal of Hamilton's Indian allies left him vulnerable. In April and again in December, Virginia forces raided Chickamauga towns, burning houses and corn stores. In May, John Bowman led a force of Kentuckians in the destruction of most Shawnee villages on the Ohio. In August, Daniel Brodhead moved north from Pittsburgh, burning a dozen Delaware and Seneca villages while troops commanded by John Sullivan and James Clinton destroyed forty additional Six Nations villages, leading more than 5,000 Iroquois to seek refuge in Canada. In the following year, American and Spanish troops destroyed a Sauk-Fox village on the Rock River in Illinois for having participated in a British-Indian assault on St. Louis.

For all the effort expended by the soldiers and all the terror and hardship experienced by the Natives, the expeditions provided the Americans with few concrete gains. The Great Lakes Indians who considered closer ties with the new nation were alienated by the shortage of supplies and by the failure to mount an assault on Detroit despite months of preparation and discussion. Those, like the Shawnees, Iroquois, and Cherokees, whose homes and fields were devastated, fought on with renewed determination. In the deep South, on the other hand, the failure of the British to supply adequately and treat appropriately their Creek and Choctaw allies contributed to the loss of Pensacola, Augusta, and other key posts that these Indians had earlier helped defend.

The news that Britain had conceded defeat and was leaving them to deal with the Americans on their own was met with disbelief and then concern and resentment by Indians everywhere. Though the Cherokees, Chickasaws, and some Creeks made peace with the new nation before the Treaty of Paris was formally signed in November 1783, many others in both North and South discussed the formation of a confederation to resist the seizure of still more land by the republic. Those Creeks who had favored the British were now led by the shrewd Alexander McGillivray, who began negotiating with the Spanish as the last best hope of resisting American expansionism. Although the United States had gained recognition by the countries of Europe, including even its recent colonial master and then enemy Britain, most Natives continued to deny its legitimacy.

These denials were based on considerations that were anything but abstract. Indians recognized that the new nation constituted a political force in which the landholding and commercial aspirations long held by most British colonists had been elevated to national purpose. This self-proclaimed, American-based "empire of liberty" represented a more sinister threat to Native existence than any that had originated in Europe during the preceding three centuries.

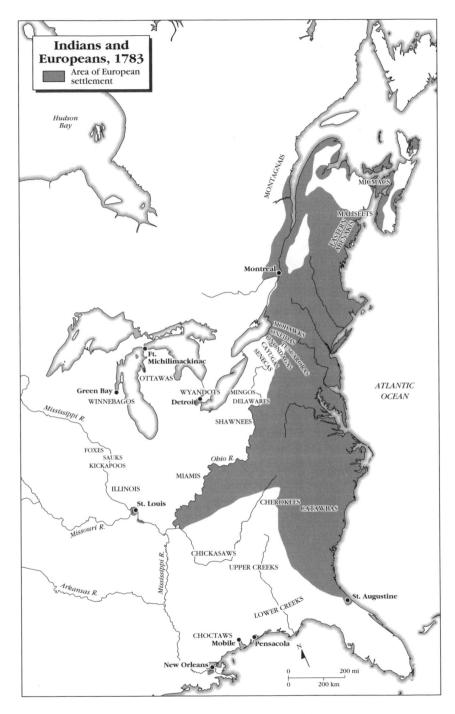

Figure 7.6. Selected Indian groups and areas of European settlement, 1783.

EPILOGUE

The social landscape of eastern North America presented a vastly different face in 1783 than in 1500 or even in 1600. How had Native peoples fared in the face of nearly two centuries of invasion and relentless expansion by Europeans and their colonial progeny? Did the newcomers succeed in destroying them and their cultures or were Native Americans able to minimize the material, cultural, and psychological effects of colonization? The evidence is ambiguous, making clear that there are no simple answers to these questions.

On the one hand, there can be no doubt as to the enormity of the toll exacted on Native Americans during the colonial period. The two most recent estimates of Indian population in 1500 and 1800, respectively, vary so markedly as to render impressionistic any effort actually to measure the demographic impact of European contact. Nevertheless, the decline was clearly drastic, whether we accept Russell Thornton's indication that the population went from just over five million to 600,000 in the present "lower 48" of the United States, or the far more conservative decrease of 1,894,350 to 1,051,688 for all of North America, suggested by Douglas H. Ubelaker. During the same period, the non-Indian population grew from virtually zero to over five million within the new United States alone.[4]

Initially, this catastrophic mortality resulted from "virgin soil epidemics" of smallpox and other Eastern Hemisphere diseases for which Native Americans lacked immunities. Although new diseases continued to strike with devastating force, other consequences of colonization added to the causes of high Indian mortality during the seventeenth and eighteenth centuries. The most important of these were warfare, alcohol, and the dietary changes and malnutrition that arose when trade conditions or loss of land affected Indian subsistence. Declines in fertility occasioned by all of these factors, along with enslavement and voluntary emigration, further reduced the numbers of Indians.

These losses were symptomatic of still others that compounded the demoralization being experienced by many Native Americans. With their numbers and their land base shrinking, most Indians were growing ever

---

[4] Russell Thornton, *American Indian Holocaust and Survival: A Population History since 1492* (Norman, Okla., 1987), 32, 90; Douglas H. Ubelaker, "North American Indian Population Size, A.D. 1500 to 1985," *American Journal of Physical Anthropology* 77 (1988), 291; *Historical Statistics of the United States, Colonial Times to 1970* (Washington, D.C., 1976), 8.

more dependent on cloth and metal goods, which could only be procured from non-Indians. Yet the reciprocal exchanges, embedded in diplomacy, by which they formerly obtained such goods were more often assuming the form of commercial transactions in which the Natives had little to offer. The end of such alliances and, for many Indians, of the ability to play European powers or interest groups off against one another, meant that Natives in much of the East were confined to small tracts of land and subjugated to a variety of economic and legal restrictions – unless they could, and chose to, emigrate. In the face of such powerlessness, the rapid spread of alcoholism, violence, and witchcraft accusations plagued a number of Indian communities after the Revolution.

What was most remarkable, however, was the persistence of Indian community life and cultural identity in the face of such overwhelming odds. Throughout their long presence in North America, Indians had demonstrated their ability and willingness to confront changing ecological and social conditions and even to thrive on such change. This flexibility was particularly evident during the colonial period as Indians interacted with Europeans as allies or rivals in trade, diplomacy, war, religion – even as neighbors and kin – and as they altered their lives, often radically, to accommodate or resist the newcomers' impact. But regardless of their relations with colonists, most Indians recognized that European societies and cultures were, in terms of fundamental values, different from their own. While many, by necessity or choice, joined other Indian communities, few found European or colonial society so alluring that they wished to remain in it permanently. Given the strength of their ties to one another and to their common past, as well as the hostility of most colonists, even the most devout Christian converts and the most loyal colonial subjects remained distinctly and self-consciously Indian. That persistence marked the limits of the Euro-American conquest and provided a measure of continuity to American history from pre-Columbian times through the eighteenth century.

BIBLIOGRAPHIC ESSAY

The scholarly literature on Native peoples and their relations with non-Indians in the colonial East has undergone a remarkable transformation over the last two decades. While historians and anthropologists alike long neglected this period, the rise of an interdisciplinary "ethnohistory" has fostered an outpouring of significant work on every region and from every perspective. The most basic reference works are the relevant volumes in the *Handbook of North American Indians* (gen. ed., William C. Sturtevant), vol. 4, *History of Indian-White Relations,* ed. Wilcomb E. Washburn (Washington, D.C., 1988), and vol. 15, *Northeast,* ed. Bruce G. Trigger (Washington, D.C., 1978). Volume 14, *Southeast,* ed. Raymond Fogelson, is in preparation. Although regional in focus, two historical atlases are also valuable: R. Cole Harris, ed., *Historical Atlas of Canada,* vol. 1, *From the Beginning to 1800* (Toronto, 1987) and Helen Hornbeck Tanner, *Atlas of Great Lakes Indian History* (Norman, Okla., 1987).

Provocative discussions of some of the major issues in colonial Indian history are Francis Jennings, *The Invasion of America: Indians, Colonialism, and the Cant of Conquest* (Chapel Hill, N.C., 1975), part 1, and two essay collections by James Axtell: *The European and the Indian: Essays in the Ethnohistory of Colonial North America* (New York, 1981) and *After Columbus: Essays in the Ethnohistory of Colonial North America* (New York, 1988). Axtell has also written the standard work on the relations of European Christian missionaries with Native peoples: *The Invasion Within: The Contest of Cultures in Colonial North America* (New York, 1985). A controversial discussion of the fur trade is Calvin Martin, *Keepers of the Game: Indian-Animal Relationships and the Fur Trade* (Berkeley, Calif., 1978); a group of responses by specialists representing a variety of geographical perspectives is Shepard Krech III, ed., *Indians, Animals, and the Fur Trade: A Critique of "Keepers of the Game"* (Athens, Ga., 1981). The most careful assessment of the Indian population, both before and after European contact, is Russell Thornton, *American Indian Holocaust and Survival: A Population History since 1492* (Norman, Okla., 1987).

Most of the scholarship on the colonial East can be best approached by region. For upper New England and the Maritime Provinces, several studies are now available that cover the relations of Abenakis, Micmacs, and other groups with the French and English. The most important of these are Kenneth M. Morrison, *The Embattled Northeast: The Elusive Ideal of Alliance in Abenaki-Euramerican Relations* (Berkeley, Calif., 1984); Colin G. Calloway, *The Western Abenakis of Vermont, 1600–1800: War, Migration, and the Survival of an Indian People* (Norman, Okla., 1990); L. F. S. Upton, *Micmacs and Colonists: Indian-White Relations in the Maritimes, 1713–1867* (Vancouver, 1979).

Another solid body of work is that concerned with southern New England. Earlier studies by Douglas Edward Leach, *Flintlock and Tomahawk: New England in King Philip's War* (New York, 1958; repr. New York, 1966), and Alden T. Vaughan, *New England Frontier: Puritans and Indians, 1620–1675* (Boston, 1965; rev. ed., New York, 1979), have been supplemented by Jennings, *Invasion of America;* Neal Salisbury, *Manitou and Providence: Indians, Europeans, and the Beginnings of New England, 1500–1643* (New York, 1982); William Cronon, *Changes in the Land: Indians, Colonists, and the Ecology of New England* (New York, 1983); Yasuhide Kawashima, *Puritan Justice and the Indian: White Man's Law in Massachusetts, 1630–1763* (Middletown, Conn., 1986); and Patrick Frazier, *The Mohicans of Stockbridge* (Lincoln, Nebr., 1992).

The relationships of New France to the Hurons and other eastern Canadian Native groups have likewise been the focus of a number of fruitful studies. The most notable are Bruce G. Trigger, *The Children of Aataentsic: A History of the Huron People to 1660,* 2 vols. (Montreal, 1976) and Conrad E. Heidenreich, *Huronia: A History and Geography of the Huron Indians, 1600–1650* (Toronto, 1971). Two studies that place developments in early New France in a larger regional context are Bruce G. Trigger, *Natives and Newcomers: Canada's "Heroic Age" Reconsidered* (Montreal, 1985) and Denys Delâge, *Bitter Feast: Amerindians and Europeans in Northeastern North America,* trans. Jane Brierley (Vancouver, 1993). More general studies of French attitudes and policies toward, and relations with, Native peoples include W. J. Eccles, *The Canadian Frontier, 1534–1760* (New York, 1969; rev. ed., Albuquerque, N.M., 1983); Eccles, *Essays on New France* (Toronto, 1987); Cornelius J. Jaenen, *Friend and Foe: Aspects of French-Amerindian Cultural Contact in the Sixteenth and Seventeenth Centuries* (New York, 1976); Olive Patricia Dickason, *The Myth of the Savage, and the Beginnings of French Colonialism in the Americas* (Edmonton, 1984).

The Iroquois have likewise been the subject of much of the recent rethinking by scholars. For the seventeenth century, one should consult Daniel Karl Richter, *The Ordeal of the Longhouse: The Peoples of the Iroquois League in the Era of European Colonization* (Chapel Hill, N.C., 1992). Allen W. Trelease, *Indian Affairs in Colonial New York: The Seventeenth Century* (Ithaca, N.Y., 1960), goes beyond the Iroquois to cover developments throughout New Netherland and New York. On Iroquois diplomacy, particularly treaty-making and the Covenant Chain system of alliances, see Francis Jennings, ed., *The History and Culture of Iroquois Diplomacy: An Interdisciplinary Guide to the Treaties of the Six Nations and Their League* (Syracuse, N.Y., 1985); Daniel K. Richter and James H. Merrell, eds., *Beyond the Covenant Chain: The Iroquois and Their Neighbors in Indian North America, 1600–1800* (Syracuse, N.Y., 1987); Richard Aquila, *The Iroquois Restoration: Iroquois Diplomacy on the Colonial Frontier, 1701–1754* (Detroit, 1983); and two volumes by Francis Jennings: *The Ambiguous Iroquois Empire: The Covenant*

Chain Confederation of Indian Tribes with English Colonies from Its Beginnings to the Lancaster Treaty of 1744 (New York, 1984) and *Empire of Fortune: Crown, Colonies, and Tribes in the Seven Years War* (New York, 1988). Also see Stephen Saunders Webb, *1676: The End of American Independence* (New York, 1984). For the revolutionary period, see Barbara Graymont, *The Iroquois in the American Revolution* (Syracuse, N.Y., 1972); Anthony F. C. Wallace, *The Death and Rebirth of the Seneca* (New York, 1969).

West of the Iroquois, Indians endeavored throughout the colonial period to construct a coalition that could offset the power of the Iroquois Confederacy as well as that of the French and British. The definitive study of that effort is Richard White, *The Middle Ground: Indians, Empires, and Republics in the Pays d'en Haut, 1650–1812* (Cambridge, 1991). The history of one group can be traced in James A. Clifton, *Prairie People: Continuity and Change in Potawatomi Indian Culture, 1665–1965* (Lawrence, Kans., 1977). Developments north of the Great Lakes can best be approached through Arthur J. Ray, *Indians in the Fur Trade: Their Role as Hunters, Trappers, and Middlemen in the Lands Southwest of Hudson Bay, 1660–1870* (Toronto, 1974), and those to the west through R. David Edmunds and Joseph L. Peyser, *The Fox Wars: The Mesquakie Challenge to New France* (Norman, Okla., 1993) and Gary Clayton Anderson, *Kinsmen of Another Kind: Dakota-White Relations in the Upper Mississippi Valley, 1650–1862* (Lincoln, Nebr., 1984). For the pivotal developments in the Ohio Valley during the eighteenth century, the older studies by Randolph C. Downes, *Council Fires on the Upper Ohio: A Narrative of Indian Affairs in the Upper Valley until 1795* (Pittsburgh, Penn., 1940); Wilbur R. Jacobs, *Wilderness Politics and Indian Gifts: The Northern Colonial Frontier, 1748–1763* (Stanford, Calif., 1950; repr., Lincoln, Nebr., 1966); and Jack M. Sosin, *Whitehall and the Wilderness: The Middle West in British Colonial Policy, 1760–1775* (Lincoln, Nebr., 1961), remain valuable but should be supplemented by Jennings, *Ambiguous Iroquois Empire,* and White, *Middle Ground* (both already cited), plus Michael McConnell, *A Country Between: The Upper Ohio Valley and Its Peoples, 1724–1774* (Lincoln, Nebr., 1992), and Gregory Evans Dowd, *A Spirited Resistance: The North American Indian Struggle for Unity, 1745–1815* (Baltimore, 1992). On the Delawares, many of whom moved from Pennsylvania to play a critical role on the Ohio, see C. A. Weslager, *The Delaware Indians: A History* (New Brunswick, N.J., 1972); and Anthony F. C. Wallace, *King of the Delawares: Teedyuscung, 1700–1763* (Philadelphia, 1949).

Studies of the Southeast are likewise proliferating. For general introductions, consult J. Leitch Wright, *The Only Land They Knew: The Tragic Story of the American Indians in the Old South* (Knoxville, Tenn., 1983), and the essays in Peter H. Wood et al., eds., *Powhatan's Mantle: Indians in the Colonial Southeast* (Lincoln, Nebr., 1989). A brief account of the revolutionary period is James H. O'Donnell III, *Southern Indians in the American Revolution* (Knoxville, Tenn., 1973). For the Chesapeake, the most important works are Helen Rountree, *The Powhatan Indians of Virginia: Their Traditional Culture* (Norman, Okla., 1989); J. Frederick Fausz, "The Powhatan Uprising of 1622: A Historical Study of Ethnocentrism and Cultural Conflict" (Ph.D. diss., College of William and Mary, 1977); and Wilcomb E. Washburn, *The Governor and the Rebel: A History of Bacon's Rebellion in Virginia* (Chapel Hill, N.C., 1957). For the interior, a group of older studies remain critical: Verner Crane, *The Southern Frontier, 1670–1732* (1928; rev. ed., 1956; repr. New York, 1981); David Corkran, *The Creek Frontier, 1540–1783* (Norman, Okla., 1967); Corkran, *The Cherokee Frontier: Conflict and Survival, 1740–62* (Norman, Okla., 1962); John Richard Alden, *John Stuart and the Southern Colonial Frontier* (Ann Arbor, Mich., 1944). These should be supplemented by the excellent study by James H. Merrell, *The Indians' New World: Catawbas and Their Neighbors from European Contact through the Era of Removal* (Chapel Hill, N.C., 1989); Tom Hatley, *The Dividing Paths: Cherokees and South Carolinians through the Era of Revolution* (New York, 1993); and a very good environmental history, Timothy Silver, *A New Face on the Countryside: Indians, Colonists, and Slaves in the South Atlantic Forests, 1500–1800* (Cambridge, 1990). For Florida, the central works are Jerald T. Milanich and Samuel Proctor, eds., *Tacachale: Essays on the Indians of Florida and Southeastern Georgia during the Historic Period* (Gainesville, Fla., 1978); Robert Allen Matter, "The Spanish Missions of Florida: The Friars versus the Governors in the 'Golden Age,' 1606–1690" (Ph.D. diss., University of Washington, 1972); David Hurst Thomas et al., "The Archaeology of St. Catherine's Island: 1. Natural and Cultural History," *Anthropological Papers of the American Museum of Natural History* 55/2 (1978), 155–248; and John H. Hann, *Apalachee: The Land between the Rivers* (Gainesville, Fla., 1988). Two outstanding studies centering on the lower Mississippi Valley are Daniel H. Usner, Jr., *Indians, Settlers, and Slaves in a Frontier Exchange Economy: The Lower Mississippi Valley before 1783* (Chapel Hill, N.C., 1992) and Richard White, *Roots of Dependency: Subsistence, Environment, and Social Change among the Choctaws, Pawnees, and Navajos* (Lincoln, Nebr., 1983), chaps. 1–5.

8

THE EXPANSION OF EUROPEAN COLONIZATION TO THE MISSISSIPPI VALLEY, 1780–1880

MICHAEL D. GREEN

For Eastern Indians and the United States both, the century from 1780 to 1880 was a period of experimentation, learning, adjusting, and ultimately, struggling for dominance over the land and its resources. During that century, Native Americans experienced steady decline in population and power. While they won important victories through warfare, politics, and judicial action, in the end they lost all but tiny remnants of their lands east of the Mississippi. Required to relocate west of the river in Indian Territory, their numbers continued to decline even as they attempted, often quite successfully, to build new lives and communities in unfamiliar country. But the combined effects of the American Civil War and the economic penetration of corporate America brought a second round of defeats so that by 1880 the nations of Indian Territory, like those scattered groups that had avoided removal and remained in the East, were surrounded and in imminent danger of dispossession and fragmentation.

The Indian policy of the United States government during its first century was not designed to exterminate Native Americans, but it was created to meet the needs and wishes, economic, political, and spiritual, of its citizens. Those needs and wishes rarely coincided with the interests of Native Americans and, when in conflict, Indians, often denigrated as culturally and racially inferior, found themselves overwhelmed by the superior power of federal and state governments. Humanitarian interests in the United States decried the suffering of Native people and struggled to alleviate it, but the methods and goals of the well-meaning required a cultural transformation so complete that most Indians rejected it. Rather, Native people and groups sought to find their own answers to the questions they faced. The range of their solutions reflected a degree of imagination, inventiveness, and adaptation that scholars have only recently begun to understand. But the characteristic that clearly unites this history is the determination of Native groups to preserve their autonomy and control their destiny.

Unintentionally, federal policy in this first century provided Native Americans with the most important tools for achieving those goals. From the earliest times the English government and its colonial representatives in America had conducted business with Native groups through a diplomatic process Englishmen called treaties. Time and repetition had institutionalized the treaty procedure with an atmosphere of legality and propriety that suggested it was the only correct means for conducting such relations. Treaty diplomacy as it was understood in Europe reflected at least partially the political reality of America.

Treaties are the acts of sovereigns. By engaging in treaty relations with Native nations, Europeans recognized the actuality of sovereignty even as they frequently rejected its legality. Autonomy, or self-government free from outside control, is central to the definition of sovereignty. When the United States embraced the treaty system as the mechanism for conducting its relations with Native nations, it learned that it must also extend the recognition of sovereignty that underlay the colonial treaties. Congress's Indian policy in the 1780s, shaped largely by its Revolutionary experience, rejected such recognition and the results were disastrous.

Several assumptions accompanied recognition of sovereignty which partially defined federal Indian policy and influenced, often decisively, the ways that policy was administered. The recognition of sovereignty, indeed, so fully permeated relations between the United States and Native nations that Congress felt constrained formally to deny it in 1871 as a prerequisite to proceeding with the final dismemberment of Native political institutions and the dispossession of Native lands. But until 1871 the assumption that Native nations could be expected to behave as sovereigns influenced federal Indian policy and its administration as well as the ways those nations shaped their histories.

EFFECTS OF THE REVOLUTIONARY WAR

The September 1783 Peace of Paris ended the American Revolution and formalized England's recognition of the independence of the United States. It was a political conclusion to a military confrontation that began in April 1775 in Massachusetts and ended in October 1781 in Virginia. The six and a half years of war left large areas scarred, thousands dead, and affected the lives of millions more. The Indians of eastern North America figured importantly in the conflict, and many groups faced massive problems of postwar recovery and reconstruction.

Few nations suffered more grievously than the Cherokees. Their attacks on the back country settlements during the summer of 1776 produced devastating retaliatory invasions by armies from Virginia and the Carolinas. While many people fell before them, the invaders did most of their damage against the villages, homes, fields, and granaries of the Cherokees. Soldiers burned some fifty towns and tens of thousands of bushels of stored corn and beans; they cut or burned hundreds of acres of fields and orchards, and killed or confiscated several hundred head of livestock. Such destruction drove many thousands of Cherokee people into the forested Appalachians to eke out a subsistence on nuts, wild plants, and game. Repeated, though smaller scale, invasions spread the decimation and made large areas of the eastern Cherokee Nation uninhabitable. The treaties Cherokee leaders reluctantly signed in 1777 to bring an end to the conflict cost them most of the land east of the Blue Ridge, forcing the refugees to build new homes elsewhere.

Some 500 families displaced from the Lower Towns crossed the mountains to the junction of Chickamauga Creek and the Tennessee River (present-day Chattanooga) and established new towns there. Led by Dragging Canoe, this movement was partially motivated by outrage at the cession of their home regions in 1777, and the Chickamauga towns became a center of opposition toward the eastern Cherokee leaders as well as of hostility to the settlers moving into the Tennessee and Cumberland River country. The Chickamauga towns thus became targets for ongoing strikes by settler forces, and peace did not come there until the mid-1790s.

But nearly everywhere in the Cherokee Nation, the picture was the same. Hungry, homeless, dispirited people were seeking enough peace and security to build homes, break land for corn fields, and learn where to find game. With few places to go and little to hope for, Cherokee society in the 1780s was on the brink of disintegration.

North, the nations of the Iroquois faced many of the same challenges. Divided by the Revolution, the once powerful Confederacy was split and dysfunctional. While Oneidas and Tuscaroras allied with the United States, the Mohawks remained attached to the king. Onondagas, Cayugas, and Senecas mostly supported the royal cause as well. With the Mohawk Joseph Brant playing a decisive role, Iroquois warriors in concert with British regulars and Loyalist militias ravaged the New York and Pennsylvania countryside. Clearly enjoying the upper hand, the

Iroquois saw their country seriously invaded only once, during the fall of
1779, but that was enough to destroy all but two of the towns of the
nations allied with England. The Mohawks, living closest to the American settlements, had fled their country in 1777 and were already refugees, some near Montreal, others at Niagara, when General John Sullivan's army swept through. By 1780, the British garrison at Niagara
attempted to feed and house several hundred more refugees. Sullivan, of
course, spared the towns of the allied Oneidas and Tuscaroras, but the
British avenging Sullivan's invasion forced those Natives to seek shelter
at Schenectady. At war's end, only two of the approximately thirty
Iroquois towns remained intact and the overwhelming majority of Iroquois people were displaced persons.

The Oneidas and Tuscaroras returned to their lands after the war and
began to rebuild. The Senecas, westernmost and the least disrupted by
invading armies, reestablished their villages on the Genesee and Allegheny
Rivers. Onondagas and Cayugas were divided. Some returned to their
prewar locations, others remained, with the Mohawks, close to the British.
The Mohawks could never return. Frederick Haldimand, Lieutenant-
Governor of Upper Canada (Ontario), rewarded their loyalty with grants of
two reserves in Canada – one on the Bay of Quinte, the other in the valley of
the Grand River. By 1785 the Mohawks plus groups of Onondagas,
Cayugas, and allied Delawares, Nanticokes, and others had settled permanently in Ontario.

Except for some Senecas, wherever they settled the Iroquois had to
begin anew. If they were Mohawks or Cayugas moving to Grand River in
Canada they had to learn a new land, fell trees, build homes, and break
fields just as immigrants to any new place. If they were returning to the
lands they had fled, their task was perhaps easier but more painful.
Oneida, Tuscarora, and Onondaga families faced burned-out homes, ravaged fields, and a familiar countryside stripped by war.

West of the Appalachian Mountains, the Revolutionary War was fought
mainly as localized raids, the result of which was much depredation and
loss of property but little military confrontation or loss of life. Delawares
and Shawnees living in the Ohio Valley moved northward to be farther
from the Kentucky militias. They confronted the same challenges of
rebuilding in new places that the many Cherokees and Iroquois faced, but
their lands were not wasted and they were generally free from the constant
threat of invasion. Farther north in the Great Lakes country, Ottawas
(Odawas), Chippewas (Anishinabes), Potawatomis, and others experienced

economic hardship caused by the wartime disruption of the trade but were not invaded.

South of the Ohio River, except for the Cherokees, the war did not significantly penetrate Indian country. Creek, Choctaw, and Chickasaw warriors participated in battles, notably in Georgia and West Florida, but no invading armies leveled their towns or drove their people into flight.

The Revolutionary War was significant in the histories of the eastern Indians, but for most the immediate effects were less noticeable than was the long-range impact. Native nations participated or not as their local circumstances, political ties, and economic well-being dictated. But except for the Cherokees and the Iroquois, whose devastated territories imposed real hardships, the Indians could well interpret the war years as simply more of the same pattern of conflict that pitted one group of Europeans against another and provided opportunities or imposed obligations that Indian groups had to address. And even the suffering experienced by the Cherokees and Iroquois had been far from total. Their local institutions still functioned, their people were alive, and their warriors remained powerful.

CONQUERED NATIONS POLICY

In addition to recognizing the independence of the United States, the Peace of Paris also defined its boundaries west of the Appalachian Mountains. The Great Lakes limited the new nation to the north, the Mississippi River on the west, and in the south the United States and Spanish Florida met at the thirty-first parallel. Within that vast expanse of territory U.S. sovereignty held sway by right of conquest. The title England transferred had been acquired by right of conquest from France and by right of discovery, the European international law concept that justified the occupation and acquisition of regions inhabited by "uncivilized" peoples. England and her colonies frequently supplemented the right of discovery with treaties conducted with Native groups that acquired through purchase either their permission to occupy lands or their title to the use of the land. With such a body of precedent, both English and American treaty makers assumed the legality of the transfer of British title in 1783. Despite the history of British-Indian treaty relations and the implied assumption of Native national sovereignty, there was no sense that the Indians should be consulted or included in the negotiations. According to European international law, England's sovereignty in America was unrelated to Indian claims or rights. Victory meant, quite simply, that the United States acquired England's territorial rights in America.

Well before the conclusion of peace, Congress began to organize future relations with the Native American peoples by appointing commissioners to be responsible for each of three regions: northern, central, and southern. At the same time, it included in the Articles of Confederation (drafted in 1777, ratified in 1781) a provision that Congress would have the "sole and exclusive right of . . . managing all affairs with the Indians." Attached to this statement of Congressional authority, however, was a modifying clause, "not members of any of the states," which injected a note of ambiguity that could be clarified only with a precise definition of the boundaries of the states. In the absence of that, Congress and the states with claims to land west of the Appalachians prepared for peacetime dealings with policies that reflected their anxious desire to control and exploit the land and its resources.

The policy devised by Congress argued that, because of their alliances with the defeated Great Britain, the Native peoples had forfeited their rights to any land within the boundaries of the United States. By virtue of the right of conquest, U.S. sovereignty was established and Congress had the legal right to expel the now "landless" Indians to places outside its borders. Perhaps recognizing both the practical impossibility and the pointlessness of such an extreme act, however, Congress also proclaimed its generous forbearance toward the eastern Indians by offering them permission to remain on at least those portions of their former lands that were not immediately needed by the United States. This policy, justified by a very narrow and literal interpretation of international law, reflected a Congressional mentality that was both overconfident after having defeated Great Britain and desperate over the fiscal crisis that years of war had imposed on the new nation. Thus from the beginning Indian policy took shape in a broader context of national and local economic and political concerns. The U.S. government never made Indian policy solely, or even largely, with an eye on the Indians. Rather, Indian policy was designed to serve primarily the interests of the United States and its citizens.

During the mid-1780s, when the Articles of Confederation stood as the frame of government for the United States, Congress devised a western policy capable of accomplishing several things simultaneously. On one hand, lawmakers wished to expand economic opportunity to American citizens. Republican theorists believed that the survival of the United

States depended on the ability of its citizens to retain and preserve their individual independence in a national economy based on agriculture. Republicanism thrived in a society composed of free, independent, propertied farmers. But such a system could work successfully only if adequate amounts of productive land were available. Without land for the growing numbers of American farmers, republican theorists argued, the United States would degenerate into a society of cities inhabited by masses of propertyless, resentful, corruptible people who could be manipulated and controlled by demagogues. American virtue and liberty would be lost and the revolutionary crusade would have been in vain. For those who agreed with this scenario, the survival of American republican institutions depended on the expansion of American farmers into the West.

Land was available. In 1784, Virginia ceded to the United States its claims to the country north and west of the Ohio River. Designated a national domain under the administration of Congress, this region held millions of fertile acres. Congress's second goal was thus to create a procedure to make this land available to the public. In 1785, the lawmakers drafted the Land Ordinance. This bill created a system for surveying the region into square mile parcels which would be sold at public auction at a minimum price of one dollar per acre.

In offering the public domain for sale, Congress revealed its third goal. Under the Articles of Confederation, Congress had neither money nor income and its impoverishment was both an embarrassment and an inhibition to effective government. By defining the West as a national commodity to be sold in the marketplace, Congress expected to reap a profit that could solve its financial problems.

Congress enacted the Northwest Ordinance in 1787 to aid in the fulfilment of these goals. Experience demonstrated that large numbers of Americans were not willing to buy and occupy Congress's western land without, among other things, assurances that the political future of their communities was secure. This act established a system whereby, as population increased and civic institutions were created, the western territories would be organized and ultimately admitted to the union as states fully equal to the original thirteen.

This transparently expansionist policy could not possibly succeed, however, without a supportive Indian policy. It was not enough to claim a right of conquest title to the West. The United States had to inform the Indians of their fate and gain their acceptance of it. To accomplish this, Congress appointed commissioners to negotiate three treaties with the tribes resident in or having claims to the country it planned to sell. The first set of talks were at Fort Stanwix, New York, in 1784 with representatives of the Six Nations Iroquois. The second were held in 1785 at Fort McIntosh on the Ohio River not far downstream from Pittsburgh with Delaware, Wyandot, Chippewa, and Ottawa delegates. And in January 1786, Shawnee representatives met United States commissioners at Fort Finney, near the present site of Cincinnati. More dictated than negotiated, these treaties expressed Congress's interpretation of its right of conquest title, required that the Native peoples acquiesce to the loss of their rights to their land, demanded their immediate surrender of the lands in southeastern Ohio that were about to be surveyed and sold, announced Congress's generous tolerance of their continued but temporary use of the remaining land northwest of the Ohio River, and "gave peace" to the nations formerly allied with the defeated enemy Great Britain.

While Congress's plans for expansion and profit were limited to its national domain, the lawmakers nevertheless also turned their attention to the problem of securing a peace with the Native nations of the South. Congressional authority was in doubt south of the Ohio River because Virginia owned Kentucky, North Carolina held Tennessee, and Georgia claimed most of Alabama and Mississippi. Those states argued that the southwest lay within their boundaries, and Georgia and North Carolina were busily dictating their own right of conquest treaties to delegations of Creeks and Cherokees. Despite its dubious authority, Congress opened talks during the winter of 1785–6 at Hopewell, South Carolina, that resulted in treaties with the Cherokees, Choctaws, and Chickasaws. In the Choctaw and Chickasaw treaties the United States recognized their prewar borders, agreed to open trade, granted peace, and demanded recognition of its sovereignty in place of England's. The Cherokee treaty was much the same except that the United States also recognized the wartime cessions made to the Carolinians and demanded a small additional tract. U.S. guarantees of the boundaries of all these nations, quite opposite to its policy in the North, were interpreted by Georgia and North Carolina as illegal intervention in their domestic affairs and bitterly denounced. New York and Pennsylvania took similar positions, and they too conducted treaties of peace and cession with the Iroquois nations still residing within their boundaries.

By 1786, Congress's policy was in place. North of the Ohio River, it would dictate terms of surrender to the Native peoples that would strip them of their lands and leave them dependent as well as defeated. South of the Ohio, where it had no land claims, Congress hoped only for peace. But the states with western claims had policies as expansionist as any devised by Congress. Justified by a right of conquest doctrine that made sense in Paris, such policies could work west of the Appalachians only if they could be made to make sense there as well. The reaction of Native leaders throughout the region soon demonstrated that in the absence of armed conquest, no such policies would be tolerated.

ALEXANDER MCGILLIVRAY AND THE REACTION OF THE SOUTHERN INDIANS

From north to south, Native leaders greeted the news that a defeated England planned to give them and their lands to the United States with disbelief, shocked amazement, dread, and outrage. English officers in Indian country, in fear of their lives, sometimes denied the stories and fled before their erstwhile Indian allies could learn the truth. In a kind of collective cry of astonishment, leaders and warriors undefeated in battle demanded explanations. How could England have been defeated? What of the promises of friendship and assurances of protection the King's officers had made? And if it was really true, how could the King betray his allies by giving away their land?

Alexander McGillivray, well educated, well read, and politically astute, may not have been surprised by the news of England's defeat, but he was nevertheless astonished by the King's faithlessness and as concerned as any other Indian leader about the effects American independence would have for his people, the Creeks. The son of a wealthy Scottish immigrant trader and a Creek woman of the Wind clan, McGillivray had served during the war as an officer in the British Indian service. But his identity was Creek and the Creeks readily accepted him as such. In a matrilineal society he acquired at birth the clan of his mother and thus his status as a Creek was unquestioned. His bicultural experience made him valuable to the Creeks, and by war's end he had risen in prestige and influence to a position of leadership within the nation that was virtually without precedent.

McGillivray believed that the Creek Nation was a sovereign independent nation with rights to its territory that the Peace of Paris could not legally impair. He explained his position repeatedly in correspondence but nowhere more clearly than in a letter of July 10, 1785 to Arturo O'Neill, Spanish governor of West Florida, which described the views expressed at a recent conference of chiefs of the Creek, Chickasaw, and Cherokee Nations:

We . . . hereby in the most solemn manner protest against any title claim or demand the American Congress may set up for or against our lands, Settlements, and hunting Grounds in Consequence of the Said treaty of peace between the King of Great Brittain and the States of America declaring that as we were not partys, so we are determined to pay no attention to the Manner in which the British Negotiators has drawn out the Lines of the Lands in question Ceded to the States of America — it being a Notorious fact known to the Americans, known to every person who is in any ways conversant in, or acquainted with American affairs, that his Brittannick Majesty was never possessed either by session purchase or by right of Conquest of our Territorys and which the Said treaty gives away. . . . nor did we . . . do any act to forefit our Independence and natural Rights to the Said King of Great Brittain that could invest him with the power of giving our property away.

In arguing that the British grant was illegal and the claims of Congress and the states were spurious, McGillivray was instrumental in forging a Creek policy of reaction and resistance. Always the irreducible minimum was Creek sovereignty — the right of "a free Nation" to protect "that inheritance which belonged to our ancestors and hath descended from them to us Since the beginning of time."[1]

The immediate enemy was Georgia. In November 1783 Georgia commissioners dictated at Augusta to a handful of Creek headmen a right of conquest treaty that demanded three million acres (1,212,000 hectares) of land as compensation for wartime damages done by Creek warriors. The two most prominent of the headmen in question, Hoboithle Miko (Tallassee King) and Eneah Miko (Fat King), had been linked by trade to Georgia and had led a pro-American faction during the Revolution. But the immediate cause of their acceptance of the cession was to open the way for the reestablishment of trade for their towns. Wartime disruptions had brought economic disaster to the Creek Nation, and the most pressing need was to reopen the flow of goods.

McGillivray was disgusted by the sale and the willingness of the two headmen to agree to it. As he saw it, the Treaty of Augusta illustrated three problems: securing the territorial integrity of the Creek Nation, reestablishing a trade in the goods the Creeks had come to depend on, and imposing some degree of political discipline on Hoboithle Miko, Eneah Miko, and any other Creek headman who might decide to pursue independent policies.

Solutions to the first two issues lay in Spanish Florida. As early as

---

[1] Alexander McGillivray to Arturo O'Neill, July 10, 1785, in John W. Caughey, *McGillivray of the Creeks* (Norman, Okla., 1938), 92.

September 1783, McGillivray was in Pensacola trying to make trade arrangements. His plan required Spanish permission for a Loyalist trading company, Panton, Leslie, in exile in St. Augustine, to expand to Pensacola to supply the Creeks and open a market for Creek deerskins. As McGillivray stressed to Governor O'Neill, "Indians will attach themselves to & Serve them best who Supply their Necessities." He preferred not to trade with Georgians, he said, but if Spain refused to cooperate the Creeks would have no choice. Georgia was trying everything it could to cement the Creeks to its interests and if it succeeded, McGillivray warned, Georgia "Will Make the worst use of their Influence & will Cause the Indians from being friendly to Spain to become Very dangerous Neighbours." But if O'Neill would agree to a treaty that permitted trade and guaranteed Creek lands, McGillivray promised to block American expansion and protect Florida. The Treaty of Pensacola, signed June 1, 1784 by O'Neill, McGillivray, and several Creek headmen, effectively responded to McGillivray's demands by promising support and protection of Creek lands and opening the way for trade.[2]

McGillivray's third problem, dealing with Hoboithle Miko and Eneah Miko, proved to be much more difficult. The Creek Nation was a "confederacy," an alliance of many autonomous groups, and it had no central government capable of making national policy or coercing conformity. McGillivray hoped to create such a thing because he believed that political unification and governmental centralization were necessary to make Creek national sovereignty meaningful. Only then could the nation successfully defend its land. But his goals ran head on into a deep and layered history of regionalism, factionalism, town autonomy, and a clan system that protected its members from injury.

Thus shielded, Hoboithle Miko, Eneah Miko, and others signed, in 1785 and 1786, two additional treaties with Georgia. Both confirmed the 1783 cession and added another large parcel to it. Expressing his frustration that "our Customs (unlike those of Civilized people) Wont permit us to treat [them] as traitors by giving them the usual punishment," McGillivray had to be satisfied with the destruction of all of Hoboithle Miko's property, including his house and livestock.[3]

The Creek cessions to Georgia, dictated by an expansionist policy which rivaled that of Congress, presented a crisis that ultimately influ-

[2] McGillivray to O'Neill, Jan. 1, 1784, in Caughey, 65.
[3] McGillivray to Vizente Zespedes, Nov. 15, 1786, in Caughey, 139.

enced a significant change in the history of U.S. Indian policy. As the disputed lands attracted settlers, McGillivray and the Spanish authorities in Florida perfected their agreement. Both wanted the Georgians expelled – McGillivray because the lands rightfully still belonged to the Creeks, the Spanish because American settlements were getting too close. With Spanish arms, in 1786 McGillivray sent Creek warriors to drive off the Georgians. In concert with the Chickamaugas, other Creek warriors attacked the settlements in the Cumberland country of Tennessee. Their successes caused the Spanish to worry about too much Creek power, however, and in 1787 O'Neill stopped the flow of guns and powder and urged McGillivray to make peace with the Americans. McGillivray's dependence on Spanish arms ultimately forced him to comply. But talks with peace commissioners in 1787 and 1788 broke down when Congress required that McGillivray accept the validity of the cessions to Georgia.

But events in Philadelphia were changing things. The Constitution, drafted in 1787 and presented to the states for ratification in 1788, redefined the relationship between the states and the federal government. McGillivray's military successes against Georgia were possible, in part, because under the Articles of Confederation Georgia was isolated. Without money, an army, or unambiguous political authority over Indian affairs within the boundaries of a state, Congress could not intervene. But under the Constitution, Georgia could expect the support of an effective central government with the power, at least in theory, to defend its frontiers and assert its sovereignty. War with the United States would give the Creeks "much to fear . . . , especially since the new government is established on a basis which renders it capable of making war on us in a fashion that would assure them a complete success," wrote McGillivray.[4]

McGillivray understood what had happened. American lawmakers, confronted with the same problems he faced of factionalism, political disagreement, and the particularism of local identities, had beaten him in finding solutions. In uniting the states under a strong central government, the Americans had done exactly what he hoped the Creeks could do. In the process, the Constitution empowered Georgia and threatened an end to McGillivray's dream of safeguarding the territory and sovereignty of the Creek Nation.

At the same time, Congress had been reconsidering its Indian policy.

[4] McGillivray to Carlos Howard, Aug. 11, 1790, in Caughey, 274.

Largely as a result of widespread and overwhelming opposition to the right of conquest treaties, the Northern Native nations had united to reject as fraudulent the land cessions of the mid-1780s and served notice that they would not abide by them. Furthermore, they had launched vigorous and deadly warfare in order to preserve intact the Ohio River boundary between their lands and the territory they recognized as now legitimately the property of the United States. Combined with this was the ongoing war in the South that engaged Creek and Chickamauga warriors against the Cumberland settlements and Georgia which Congress was powerless to stop. The western country that Congress claimed was in flames and the cause of the conflagration was clearly the right of conquest policy that Congress and the states had embraced. Congress set about to reverse itself, beginning in a small way with the Indian Ordinance of 1786 which established a streamlined structure to administer relations with western Indians and provided for the development of a renewed trade with them. Congress went much further in this direction the next year in the Northwest Ordinance. Drafted primarily to establish stable governments in its western territories, Congress took the occasion to pledge that

the utmost good faith shall always be observed towards the Indians, their lands and property shall never be taken from them without their consent; and in their property, rights and liberty, they never shall be invaded or disturbed, unless in just and lawful wars authorised by Congress; but laws founded in justice and humanity shall from time to time be made, for preventing wrongs being done to them, and for preserving peace and friendship with them.

This language was a clear repudiation of the right of conquest policy.

McGillivray had played a significant role in this resistance. He had hosted a delegation of Shawnee, Wyandot, Mohawk, and Oneida chiefs sent by the alliance of northern groups to find support and aid in the South and had opened talks with the southern nations in order to expand into the South the coalition of Native groups united against American westward expansion. At the same time, of course, he continued his own offensive.

But McGillivray had his hands full dealing with Georgia and rebuilding flagging Spanish confidence and support while at the same time advancing his political agenda in the Creek Nation. The establishment of the Constitutional government was thus a threat and a promise which, depending on how he played it, could be the doom or the salvation of the Creek Nation. When, in 1789, President George Washington sent an envoy to McGillivray to invite him to New York to discuss the present and future relations between their two nations, McGillivray was ready to go.

In the spring of 1790, McGillivray led a delegation of Creek headmen to New York. After long days of negotiations with Secretary of War Henry Knox, the administration official most responsible for the reversal of Congress's right of conquest Indian policy, the Creeks, Knox, and President Washington concluded the Treaty of New York. The two nations made peace and the Creeks accepted the "protection" of the United States. The United States accepted McGillivray's argument that the three right of conquest treaties with Georgia were invalid, and McGillivray agreed to a cession of a large part of the disputed lands, explaining later that they were already occupied by Georgians and it would be impossible to oust them. The United States also agreed to guarantee the boundaries of the Creek Nation. This promise, coupled with an article that prohibited the Creeks from conducting treaties with any of the states, changed the nature of Georgia's expansionist threat. Georgia could neither force additional treaties on the Creek Nation through compliant headmen nor expect federal support for encouraging its citizens to encroach on Creek territory. Furthermore, the United States authorized the Creeks to punish American citizens who settled illegally in the nation. A provision kept secret from the Spanish opened trade through the United States. McGillivray wanted this to hedge against the possibility that Spain might interfere with the current trade arrangement with Panton, Leslie for English goods.

The Washington Administration agreed to the Treaty of New York, which was an impressive diplomatic victory for McGillivray, for several reasons. Most importantly, it freed the United States to concentrate its attention on the resistance of the Indians north of the Ohio to its schemes to settle and organize the Ohio country. But also, it enabled the new Constitutional government to take control of Indian affairs in the South. The Constitution contained no ambiguous proviso such as that included in the Articles of Confederation to limit the government's sole and exclusive authority to conduct relations with the Indians. The treaty also clearly indicated the direction Washington's Indian policy was taking, away from the right of conquest policy of the Confederation Congress to a program of peaceful relations achieved through treaty negotiations and an emphasis on Native American culture change and assimilation. Indeed, stipulations for the distribution of agricultural implements, livestock, and other appurtenances of Anglo-American agrarian civilization contained in the Treaty of New York represent the first official commitment of the Washington

Administration to this new policy. Neither Washington nor Knox wanted expansionist states interfering with their plans.

McGillivray was pleased with the result. Under the protection of both the United States and Spain, with the Creek Nation's territory guaranteed against future encroachments by Georgia, and assurances of continued access to the goods and markets necessary for economic recovery, Mc-Gillivray could expect the Treaty of New York to provide the peace and stability he needed to achieve his centralist political goals.

GREENVILLE

Well before the Revolutionary War, Native Americans in the Ohio Valley and Great Lakes region had realized that the presence of Europeans on their continent threatened to alter forever their destinies. Many believed the expected changes might be for the better, and as European manufactured goods came into their lives they were convinced. Others suggested, however, that because the Europeans brought diseases as well as goods and sought land as well as the skins of animals, the price of change might be too high and indeed the changes themselves might be bad. Such opinions intensified and spread, the disagreements they reflected deepened, and by the middle of the eighteenth century the argument had become clearly visible as the shaper of policies and actions. One side of this division, termed Nativist by historians, sought to forge bonds between Indian groups to create a pan-Indian force based on spiritual power and ritual and articulated by prophecy. The other side, called accommodationist, was particularistic. These people intended to cooperate with the Europeans, gain strength from the association, and enhance the power and prestige of their specific nations.

While holding divergent views about how best to deal with the European presence, both groups intended actively to influence the future. They were neither hysterical reactionaries nor mindless pawns. And despite several decades of often bitter struggle between the two factions, the period between 1775 and 1795 was marked by their unification and cooperation. The issues that brought them together emerged in the Revolutionary struggle between the American states and the British Empire and continued until the United States achieved its right of conquest aims in the Ohio country. Never before and never again did the Native people west of the Appalachians achieve such a degree of pan-Indian unity as in this period when the divisive forces of prophetic religion and ethnic particularism were united and transcended by a spirit of pan-Indian defense of territory and autonomy.

For the Northern Indians, English support was critical. The dictated treaties of the mid-1780s and the occupation of the Ohio Valley country under the color of those treaties posed immediate threats to the region that were periodically underscored by raids of looting conducted by Kentucky militia. Guns and powder, along with a number of other goods, could come only from Canada, and the British in Canada were happy to offer support and encouragement. The king's policy of retaining the military and trading posts in the Great Lakes country in defiance of the boundaries agreed to in the Treaty of Paris depended for success on Indian cooperation. Working with and sometimes through Joseph Brant, the Mohawk who had led the movement of many Iroquois to permanent homes on the Grand River, British officials encouraged the solidification of wartime Indian unity, hosted or facilitated a series of councils, and led the Indians of the region to expect substantially more help than the British actually provided. But the trade continued and the flow of weapons was undiminished. Thus the wartime alliance between England and the Indians continued.

The chief feature of the Indian defense of the Ohio country was the formalization of the alliance system whose roots ran back to the period when the French and the northwestern Indian nations politicized and militarized their trade relations and directed them against the British. This ancient system had become the basis of the alliance between the Indians and the British during the Revolutionary period, and after the war, with British encouragement and the active involvement of Joseph Brant and the Iroquois, it gained strength.

The first postwar meeting of the Grand Council of the western alliance occurred at Sandusky in the Wyandot country in the fall of 1783. Located in present north-central Ohio, it was a convenient place where the delegates from more than thirty nations could gather. At the meeting, the delegates both agreed that the boundary between Indian country and the United States should be the Ohio River and pledged that only Council representatives would negotiate with American commissioners. The Ohio River boundary had been established by the Fort Stanwix treaty of 1768, and the Indians believed that only a river boundary could protect their country from the casual encroachment of settlers and their livestock.

But Congress was unwilling to recognize the Grand Council as the sole negotiating authority for the western Indians. Anxious to shatter the alliance, one of the goals of its right of conquest policy had been to isolate vulnerable groups and manipulate compliant leaders. Thus treaties concluded in the mid-1780s with small, unrepresentative gatherings sowed seeds of discord within the alliance.

The response of the Grand Council meeting at Detroit in December 1786 was to denounce these treaties as invalid because they had not been negotiated with its representatives. Individuals or small groups had no authority to agree to any alteration of the Ohio River boundary, the Council announced, and thus any pact they signed with the United States could have no force. Brant presided at the Detroit meeting and set its tone with a report of his recent conference with the British colonial secretary in London, which had left him optimistic about continued British support. He also delivered a keynote address that stressed the need for continued unity and cooperation. The Council concluded with a formal communiqué to Congress outlining its position on the treaties and the Ohio River boundary, calling for a negotiation between the two bodies and asking that in the meantime Congress suspend the survey of southeastern Ohio authorized by the Land Ordinance of 1785.

The negotiation requested by the Grand Council was delayed until January 1789. Conducted at Fort Harmar (present Marietta, Ohio) with Wyandot, Delaware, Ottawa, Chippewa, Potawatomi, Sauk, and Iroquois representatives, the treaty reaffirmed the cessions of the right of conquest treaties and thus violated the Ohio River boundary. But the treaty of Fort Harmar introduced the principle that the United States should pay for any lands ceded by Indian groups. In that sense it rejected the extreme land claims of the right of conquest policy and adhered to the position taken in the Northwest Ordinance.

If this treaty was to settle the trouble in the Ohio country, it failed. The largest delegations at Fort Harmar were Senecas, Wyandots, and Delawares, the three tribes most divided between Nativist and accommodationist factions. Events in 1787 and 1788 had exacerbated those divisions. Elements of the Indian groups living nearest to American settlements and thus most vulnerable to pressures and threats had emerged to argue compromise. Congress had not suspended the survey, had sold lands to two land companies, and had encouraged the establishment of the town of Marietta adjacent to Fort Harmar. All of this, of course, had been assumed by the Northwest Ordinance which established the formal political organization of the country north and west of the Ohio River. Such behavior indicated that American policy to cross the Ohio was unshakable and that to continue to demand the preservation of that boundary must lead to war. Wyandot and Delaware accommodationists were terrified by that prospect.

Farther west in present northwestern Ohio, where the headwaters of the Wabash and Maumee rivers were close, lived many villages of Shawnees, Miamis, Delawares, and other Indians. The Shawnees were refugees from farther south who had fled the frequent invasions of Kentucky militia, the Delawares were refugees from farther east. Gathered together in unprecedented numbers, these villages represented many of the nations of the western alliance and were led by some of the most outspoken architects of the policy of united defense of the Ohio River boundary. During the late 1780s warriors from these villages frequently attacked settlements in Kentucky and on the lower Wabash, causing the United States to build forts at Vincennes and Louisville. Raids continued, however, and often included attacks on commercial traffic on the Ohio River. All these targets were directly or indirectly related to American efforts to occupy the Ohio country and thus represented attempts to execute the policy of the Grand Council to preserve the river boundary. But President George Washington wanted the Wabash and Maumee groups to endorse the recently concluded agreement of Fort Harmar. To that end, in the fall of 1789, he ordered Arthur St. Clair, governor of Northwest Territory, to open talks with the Wabash and Maumee Nations to see if a peaceful solution were possible. The Indians rejected his overtures, however, saying that they would conduct business with the United States only through the Grand Council. Thus rebuffed, St. Clair advised Washington that only armed force could secure Ohio.

The job of chastising the Wabash and Maumee Indians fell to Brigadier General Josiah Harmar, commander at Fort Harmar. After a summer recruiting enthusiastic militiamen from Kentucky and western Pennsylvania, in September 1790 he led his badly equipped and poorly prepared army of nearly 1,500 men from Fort Washington (present Cincinnati) up the Great Miami River. Well aware of the advance, the resident Miamis, Shawnees, and Delawares abandoned their villages. Noncombatants moved down the Maumee River, and warriors positioned themselves to await the enemy. Harmar succeeded in burning five empty villages, but contingents of his force blundered into two ambushes where some 250 of his men were killed. Harmar and the remainder of this force beat a hasty retreat to Fort Washington, where Harmar blamed the catastrophe on militiamen he characterized as untrained, undisciplined, and cowardly.

During the summer of 1791, while the United States was organizing a second invasion of the Wabash and Maumee country, Kentuckians launched two raids of their own. By October the army was ready, under command of Governor St. Clair, and it retraced Harmar's route of the year before. With about 2,000 men, St. Clair marched into an ambush prepared by Little Turtle, Miami war leader, that killed or wounded almost half his army. With 630 dead, St. Clair's defeat was the most costly any United States army ever suffered at the hands of Native warriors.

The Indians of the Wabash and Maumee country returned to their villages overjoyed by the victory of their warriors. For the second time in a year they had mauled and expelled a large American army, a clear indication that the military might of the western alliance was supreme. Nevertheless, many Miamis, Shawnees, Delawares, and others whose towns had been destroyed by Harmar or who feared repeated invasions of their country moved down the Maumee River toward Lake Erie. One of these towns, located where the Auglaize River joins the Maumee, was founded by Captain Johnny's Turtle clan Delawares. The town, known as "The Glaize," became a magnet for other refugee groups and by 1792 was a densely populated settlement of some 2,000 persons. It was a center of militant support for the western alliance and in September 1792 was the location of the first meeting of the Grand Council since 1788. Representing the multinational, pan-Indian character of the alliance in its own refugee population, The Glaize was a fitting place for the Council to reaffirm its unity and assert once more its refusal to compromise on the Ohio River boundary.

While in session, the Council entertained Captain Hendrick Aupaumut, a Stockbridge Indian commissioned by the War Department to convey overtures of peace. Understanding the advantages of negotiating from strength, the Council expressed its willingness to meet American commissioners. But, it warned, talks would be useless unless the United States gave up its attempts to occupy land north and west of the Ohio.

The next summer, three American commissioners journeyed to Detroit to negotiate with the Grand Council. They announced that the United States was willing to return all of the land ceded at Fort Harmar in 1789 except for the grants around Marietta and Cincinnati that had been sold to land companies and were being settled. In addition, the commissioners formally repudiated the right of conquest argument that had justified United States policy in the 1780s. But the commissioners also offered a great deal of money – $50,000 immediately and $10,000 annually – if the Council would reverse itself and accept the whole Fort Harmar cession.

Thus despite the Grand Council's repeated insistence in the Ohio River boundary, the United States persisted in demanding lands north and west of that river.

The Council spokesmen replied with a rejection and a remarkably imaginative solution to the problem of American settlement on the Indian side of the Ohio. "Money, to us, is of no value, and . . . no consideration whatever can induce us to sell our lands." But there was a way to remove the settlers from the area and still achieve peace.

We know that these settlers are poor, or they would never have ventured to live in a country which has been in continual trouble. . . . Divide . . . this large sum of money, which you have offered us, among these people: give to each, also a portion of what you say you would give to us, annually, . . . and we are persuaded they would most readily accept of it, in lieu of the lands you sold them. If you add, also, the great sums you must expend in raising and paying armies, with a view to force us to yield you our country, you will certainly have more than sufficient for the purposes of re-paying these settlers for all their labor and their improvements.[5]

This practical suggestion fell on deaf ears, however, because the United States was neither prepared to give up its plans for the Northwest Territory nor ready to admit defeat at the hands of Indians.

While the peace talks were proceeding, Congress and the executive were also preparing for war. With a large appropriation, Congress authorized a doubling of the U.S. Army, and the president appointed General Anthony Wayne to command it. Authorized to raise, organize, train, and equip his force for a third, hopefully successful, invasion into the Wabash and Maumee heartland of the western alliance, Wayne methodically set about his task. The alliance did no less. When the talks at Detroit broke down, the Grand Council sought assurances from the British, whose agents predicted that war was imminent between England and the United States. Speeches delivered by the governors of Upper and Lower Canada affirmed it. Thus when Wayne marched north in the spring of 1794 the warriors of the western alliance, reassured by the British to expect active help, were waiting. Wayne occupied The Glaize without opposition and from there descended the Maumee toward a place in the forest where a tornado had uprooted the trees. Here, near British Fort Miami, the warriors of the alliance waited. Wayne advanced slowly, perhaps aware that warriors fasted before a battle and would be hungry. On August 20, 1794,

[5] Reply of Representatives of Western Alliance, Aug. 16, 1793, in *American State Papers: Indian Affairs*, 1:356.

when he arrived at Fallen Timbers, more than half the 2,000 man alliance army had left to find food. The battle lasted two hours and few were killed on either side, but the British barred the gates of their fort and refused to support the Indians. After the battle, Wayne's army burned the towns and fields in the area and retired from the field to await events. The defeat, added to British refusal to support the warriors, caused a cracking in the western alliance that led, for the moment at least, to its collapse.

During the winter of 1794–5, while forted up at Greenville, a post he had constructed on his march north, Wayne entertained visiting chiefs and did his best to shatter what remained of their faith in the British. By summer, when he hosted the negotiation that cost the Indians most of the present state of Ohio, the British had released the news of Jay's Treaty which settled relations between England and the United States. The provision most crucial to the western alliance, aside from the affirmation of peace, required the British to evacuate their posts on American soil. Thus the decade of encouragement and promises, aid and supplies, which had been so vital to the strength of the western alliance, came to an end.

The Treaty of Greenville, negotiated between Wayne and representatives of the nations of the western alliance, was signed August 3, 1795. By its terms the Indians ceded all but the northwestern corner of present Ohio plus many sites for military posts throughout the Great Lakes country. In return, the United States recognized the rights of the Indians to the lands unceded, another repudiation of the right of conquest policy, and paid money, goods, and services for the land sold. And of course the treaty established peace.

The long years of war had been terribly difficult for the western tribes. Their trade had been disrupted and their lives thrown into disarray. The treaty extended American trade into the western country and promised that it would be conducted in a fair, honest, and honorable way. And the newly instituted "civilization" policy of the Washington Administration was made available as well. But the hard fact was the Ohio River was no longer a boundary between Indian country and the country of American settlers. The boundary now was a line run by surveyors and marked on a map and of course wholly unable to keep out settlers and their livestock.

INDIAN POLICY, 1789–1812

During the summer of 1787, the Shawnees and Miamis fought Kentuckians, the Creeks and Chickamaugas fought Georgians and Tennesseans,

and delegates to the constitutional convention in Philadelphia debated the
political shape of the United States. No one in Philadelphia was unaware of
the warfare in the West and no one was disinterested in the security implications of the conflicts, but few believed that these problems were central to
the business at hand. Except for the Native people who remained in tiny
surrounded communities in the seaboard states, Indians were not of the
United States. The "wild" and "uncivilized" western peoples were foreigners, their nations were not subject to the laws of the United States, and their
political affairs were of concern to the American government only in matters
of military or diplomatic import. Thus Indians appear in the Constitution
only to be excluded from tax levies and population counts or, along with the
states and foreign countries, to be subject to Congressional regulation in
their commerce with the United States.

In April 1789, following the ratification of the Constitution, George
Washington was inaugurated and took office as president. Washington's
former commander of artillery in the Continental Army, Henry Knox, had
been Secretary of War in the Confederation government since 1786 and
the new president kept him in that post. The War Department was
responsible for administering United States relations with Native Americans. Knox had considerable experience and definite ideas about Indian
affairs, and Washington listened to him. No one was more influential in
shaping Washington's thinking on the subject, and in agreement they put
together an Indian policy that remained in place for decades to come.

As the government official most directly responsible for conducting
U.S. relations with Indian tribes, Knox had been particularly burdened by
the warfare in the West. Given the ambiguous authority granted Congress
by the Articles of Confederation and the absence of both an army and
funds to raise one, there had been little he could do. But he had reached
several firm conclusions. Most of the trouble, he believed, stemmed from
the aggressive expansion into Indian lands by the states and their frontier
citizens. Therefore, no path could lead to peace that did not effectively
control the actions of the states and their citizens. And achieving peace
was his goal. Peace was far less expensive than war but more significantly
peace was far more honorable and just than war. Honor and justice were
important to Knox and he believed that in its dealings with the Native
nations, honor and justice should be the hallmarks of American policy. If
the United States intended to take seriously its role as exemplar of republican values, or if the United States cared about its reputation in the world
and in the books of future historians, then honor and justice must guide

its relations with the Indians. "The United States can get nothing by an Indian war," Knox wrote as he retired in 1794,

but they risk men, money, and reputation. As we are more powerful, and more enlightened then they are, there is a responsibility of national character, that we should treat them with kindness, and even liberality. It is a melancholy reflection, that our modes of population have been more destructive to the Indian nations than the conduct of the conquerors of Mexico and Peru. The evidence of this is the utter extirpation of nearly all the Indians in most populous parts of the Union. A future historian may mark the causes of this destruction of the human race in sable colors.[6]

But war is what the Washington government inherited in 1789. Knox and Washington agreed on the policy of conciliation and negotiation with the Creeks that led to the 1790 Treaty of New York partly because they believed Georgia was the aggressor, partly because they thought war in the South would be even more costly and difficult than it would be in the North, and partly because the United States had no landed interests immediately at stake in the South. But also, and importantly, they did not want to be saddled with two wars at the same time. They preferred to settle the matter of the Ohio settlements peacefully, but the refusal of the western alliance to give up its commitment to the Ohio River boundary left them, they concluded, no choice. War in the Northwest, Knox and Washington believed, was both necessary and just.

Knox's and Washington's pursuit of war in the Northwest dramatized the essential goal of their policy, which was the continued expansion of the United States into the lands of the Indians. But they were absolutely serious in their insistence that their Indian policy also be rooted in honor and justice. Their problem was to accomplish "expansion with honor."

Knox and Washington were certain that expansion with honor was possible. The government should recognize and respect the Indians' right of occupancy in their land and should purchase that right in a free and voluntary arrangement. This, of course, underscored the process already underway of rejecting Congress's right of conquest claims of the mid-1780s. Having purchased the land, the boundary between Indian lands and lands open for settlement should be marked and enforced so that American citizens would be prohibited from encroaching on Indian property. This would minimize conflict by removing its most common cause. As the ceded tract filled with settlers who felled the trees and established

---

[6] Henry Knox, Report, Dec. 29, 1794, in *American State Papers: Indian Affairs*, 1:543.

farms, the wild game would flee and the Indians on their side of the boundary would pull back in pursuit. Their numbers would also decline because "uncivilized" Indians simply could not live adjacent to "civilized" Americans. Thus when the government approached them for another cession, the Indians, fewer in number and withdrawn from the region, would agree to sell. Knox and Washington firmly believed that this scenario of orderly advance, firm boundaries, and Indians receding and willing to sell could be made to happen. It would be a slower process than the states and their citizens preferred, but it would be an honorable and just alternative to aggression, encroachment, and war.

Neither Knox nor Washington believed there was an alternative to expansion. Expansion was as necessary as it was inevitable. But honor and justice demanded that American expansion should not continue to cause the extinction of the Indians. It need not, Knox believed, if the Indians could be "civilized" and incorporated into American society. Native Americans could share the benefits of expansion by gaining the opportunity to exchange their inferior way of life for the presumably superior one of the Americans. Knox and Washington, like most other men of the time who were influenced by Enlightenment thinking, believed that Native Americans were inherently equal to Anglo-Americans in mental ability. Their obvious and undoubted deficiencies were caused by environment and lack of experience, not race, and by changing their circumstances they could become exactly like Americans. Believing that Native people were educable, that their cultures could be changed, their conditions improved, and their elimination averted, Knox concluded that to refuse to extend the opportunity was immoral. "How different," he wrote,

would be the sensation of a philosophic mind to reflect, that, instead of exterminating a part of the human race by our modes of population, we had persevered, through all difficulties, and at least had imparted our knowledge of cultivation and the arts to the aboriginals of the country, by which the source of future life and happiness had been preserved and extended."[7]

As with so much of Knox's and Washington's Indian policy, this element also had its practical side. "Civilized" Indians, by definition plow farmers with economic interests shaped by the market place, would see the value of selling surplus lands for money to invest in their farms.

Congress responded to the policy designed by Knox and Washington with five Trade and Intercourse Acts. First passed in 1790, the series was

---

[7] Henry Knox, Report, July 7, 1789, in *American State Papers: Indian Affairs*, 1:52.

elaborated until 1802 when the policy and its administrative detail was firmly established. The 1802 law served as the basis of Indian policy legislation until a major rewrite, in conjunction with a sharply divergent philosophy of Indian relations, in 1834.

The initial goal of the Trade and Intercourse Acts was to establish a trade with the Indians on a carefully regulated basis that would ensure fairness and minimize discontent. Another element of the package prohibited any purchase of land from Native groups unless it was accomplished through public negotiation with federal authorities. A provision of the 1796 act defined the boundary between Indian country and the United States and elaborated on earlier prohibitions of encroachment and settlement on Indian lands. To reduce further the chances for conflict, the legislation provided for the arrest and punishment of citizens of the United States who committed crimes in Indian country. Also, Congress authorized the president to give gifts of agricultural tools and implements, draft and stock animals, spinning wheels, looms, and other articles of "civilized" life to Native people to aid and encourage their cultural transformation.

While the Trade and Intercourse Acts provided the details of Knox's and Washington's Indian policy, the application of the laws fell on U.S. citizens, not Indians. The acts were drafted to prevent conflict, preserve the peace, and give legislative definition to the administration's goals of conducting honorable and just relations with the Indians by regulating the actions of its citizens. Indians were outside the legislative jurisdiction of the United States. The mechanism for conducting relations with the Indians, the treaty, was therefore drawn from the realm of international diplomacy.

The practice of negotiating treaties with Native nations emerged early in the seventeenth century as English colonies attempted to devise ways to deal peacefully with groups that were usually more powerful than they. By the time of the Revolution, treaties were so firmly imbedded in the pattern of relations between American colonies and Native nations that Congress and the states automatically continued the practice. Knox and Washington institutionalized the system in part because of this precedent, but they also had a particular problem that the treaty system could help them solve. The war in the South in the 1780s began when Georgia dictated its right of conquest treaties to the Creeks. Knox blamed Georgia for the bloodshed and believed that the only way to ensure peace in the future was to restrain the states by denying them a role in Indian affairs. The Constitution addressed this issue when it gave Congress the sole right to regulate commerce with the Indian nations but Knox wanted further authority. He found it in Article I, Section 10 of the Constitution which said "No State shall enter into any Treaty. . . ." If Knox could confirm the treaty as the proper vehicle for conducting Indian relations, he could deny the states whatever pretence to legitimate interference they might cite. Washington agreed and recommended to the Senate that the proper procedure for dealing with Indian groups was through the negotiation of treaties which would then be submitted for its advice and consent. In 1790, the Senate agreed. Thus treaties with Indian nations were handled by the federal government in the same way it would handle a treaty with a European nation.

While the problem and its solution were quite specific, the implications of the treaty system were broad and significant. Treaties rest on a set of assumptions that were widely held, the most important of which is that the parties to a treaty are sovereign. They have to be because treaties can succeed only through the good will and good faith of the participants. Each party must be able to believe that the other has the power as well as the will to fulfill its obligations. If one of the parties lacks that power, the treaty is meaningless. The act of engaging in treaty relations is in itself a recognition of sovereignty. The assumption of sovereignty and its implicit recognition as applied to Indian nations was not accidental, however. Knox argued that "the independent nations and tribes of Indians ought to be considered as foreign nations, not as the subjects of any particular State."[8] It suited his purposes in 1789 to recognize the sovereign nationhood of Indian peoples because doing so elevated them above the level of the states, thus removing the states from Indian affairs. It made relations with Indians a nation-to-nation business. Until 1871, United States relations with Native nations proceeded through the treaty system and the Senate ratified some 400 treaties. This century of intergovernmental relations established a body of legal and judicial precedent that continues to recognize the sovereignty of Indian nations.

An additional element went into the Indian policy created by Knox and Washington. Trade remained vitally important to Native people, being the main source of the manufactured goods they had come to rely on. Conflicts and bloodshed over various abuses and shady practices dotted the history of the trade and governments had made repeated attempts to preserve peace through regulation of the traders and their business. Con-

[8] Ibid., 1:53.

gress enacted the 1790 Trade and Intercourse Act with such regulation as its paramount goal. Washington became convinced, however, that federal efforts to regulate private trade would not achieve all his purposes. For, in addition to providing a fair and honest trade with accurate weights and measures that could ensure peace, he wanted to hold down prices, control the kinds of goods purveyed, and build a loyalty to the United States that could break the economic ties that bound Native peoples to the interests of the Spanish in Florida and the British in Canada. After several years of urging, in 1796 Congress gave Washington a federally financed and managed system of trading posts. Called the factory system (the trading posts were "factories"), this enterprise was organized to accomplish all of Washington's goals. Until 1822, when the political power of private trading companies finally succeeded in destroying this powerful competitor, the factory system worked quite well.

This Indian policy was a complex and multifaceted program designed to make relations between the United States and its citizens and the Indians peaceful, ensure that the continued expansion of the United States occurred in an atmosphere of honor and justice, and present Native people with the opportunity to become "civilized" and enter into American society. To accomplish all of this, Knox and Washington needed a bureaucracy. An administrative apparatus took shape slowly, but by 1793 Congress authorized the appointment of federal agents to reside among the Indians, encourage their "civilization" through the distribution of the president's gifts, train them in their use, and generally represent the government's interests to the Indian peoples. Over time the United States opened relations with more groups, those relations became more complex, the Trade and Intercourse Acts became more comprehensive, and the burgeoning American population put increasing pressure on the lands of the Indians and on the government to acquire them. As all this occurred, the number of agents grew and their tasks became both more difficult and more important. Some agents, such as Benjamin Hawkins who represented the government to the Creeks from 1796 to 1816, came to exercise enormous influence over the Indian peoples with their lessons in "civilization" and their political advice.

When Thomas Jefferson assumed the presidency in 1801, he inherited an Indian policy that he had helped shape as a member of Washington's first cabinet. He was in full agreement with its theoretical foundation and was even more enthusiastic than Knox and Washington about the "civilization" of Native people, but he was also more deeply committed to the continued expansion of the United States into Indian country. He believed that the survival of the American republic depended on its ability to widen the range of economic opportunity for its citizens. No friend of urban industrial development, Jefferson advocated continued economic emphasis on agriculture and trade. As the American population grew from 3.9 million in 1790 to 7.2 million in 1810, space had to be found. Like his predecessors, Jefferson found room in Indian country.

Since the time of the Puritans in early seventeenth-century Massachusetts, Europeans and Anglo-Americans had constructed an argument to justify the taking of Indian land that rested on the idea that commercial agriculture, with its privately owned parcels of land, plows, fences, and livestock and its production of surplus crops, was morally superior to the life ways of Native Americans. Europeans and their American descendants often described the Indians as wandering hunters who refused to subdue and develop their land. They would not credit the agricultural subsistence base of nearly all eastern Native societies because in those societies women were the farmers. Believing that the important work of society was done by men, they defined Indian societies by what men did. Despite all the evidence to the contrary, Euro-American thinkers about Indians never learned to understand, appreciate, and accept gender-based allocations of tasks that differed from their own. Thus the "civilization" policy that Knox and Washington devised and Jefferson embraced described the need to help the Indians advance from the hunter to the agrarian state, but actually meant the reversal of Indian gender roles to conform to those of Anglo-Americans. Such changes were fundamental, intimate, and went to the heart of the ways Indians for generations had organized their lives. They were not simple job changes. But Americans rarely understood that. Instead, they saw "civilization" as a means to acquire more land. Jefferson believed in the "civilization" and assimilation of Indians in American society, but he also believed that the United States must acquire more land from them more quickly than ever before. Thus the period leading to the War of 1812 was marked by the tensions and conflicts that Knox and Washington had hoped they had ended.

THE WEST, 1789–1815

The twenty-six year period 1789–1815 is bounded by the inauguration of Constitutional government and the end of the War of 1812. This is the period when the Knox-Washington-Jefferson Indian policy of "expansion with honor" enjoyed its most complete trial. It represented the effort to conduct relations with Native Americans on a moral basis that would redound to the benefit of all. It succeeded brilliantly in its expansionist goal but failed to bestow the blessings of "civilization," or to meet the needs of Native Americans, and it ended not in peace but in bloody conflict.

The Treaty of Greenville brought a brief period of peace to the Northwest after more than a quarter century of warfare. The western alliance had failed to hold the Ohio River boundary but the line drawn in the treaty seemed so far away from the settlements in the Ohio Valley that the Indians of the region looked forward to a time to recover and reorder their lives. Furthermore, the Treaty of Greenville had formally repudiated the right of conquest doctrine of the decade before, thus apparently ensuring secure ownership of the region west of the line.

This hope for security and stability faded quickly, however. In 1800, Congress carved Ohio Territory out of the Northwest Territory. The residue, Indiana Territory, had virtually no land available for settlement. With a capital established at Vincennes and a governor, William Henry Harrison, who also served as Superintendent of Indian Affairs, there was reason to fear that a push would begin to open land for settlement.

The pressure on Indian country came more quickly and aggressively than anyone could have guessed. In 1802, President Jefferson learned that Napoleonic France had acquired Louisiana from Spain. The prospect of Napoleon becoming a neighbor horrified Jefferson, who immediately set two policies in motion. One, to safeguard use of the Mississippi River as a commercial artery to the outside world, led to the ultimate purchase of the entire French colony in 1803. The other, fed by fears of meddlesome French agents who might stir up the Indians, was to acquire Indian title to as much of the land that fronted on the Mississippi as quickly as possible. To Jefferson, this was a crisis which required emergency measures.

Between 1803 and 1809, United States commissioners negotiated fifteen treaties of cession with the Native owners of lands in the Indiana Territory. Most were conducted by Governor Harrison, who proved to be an especially adept and ruthless bargainer, with chiefs and headmen whom he often intimidated or bribed. But Harrison paid for the tracts with money and goods and the promise of annual payments into the future and he rarely had trouble getting the necessary signatures. By

1809, the United States had acquired Indian title to the lands along the Ohio River to the Mississippi and up the Mississippi to the Wisconsin River.

Remarkably, most of the land Harrison acquired during these extraordinarily busy six years was hundreds of miles from the nearest settlements. Frontiersmen were not squatting on these lands and would not be for, in some cases, decades to come. And by 1805 the French threat had passed with the United States gaining control of Louisiana. But the pressure on Harrison to buy more land continued. In part, the explanation for the frenzy of land purchase long after the emergency was passed can be found in Jefferson's enthusiasm for the "civilization" program. The argument had initially been that Indians, once "civilized," would happily sell their surplus hunting lands for money to develop their farms. But the Indians were not becoming "civilized." To hasten the process, the connection between expansion and "civilization" became reversed. Buy the hunting lands from "uncivilized" Indians, the new argument went, and economic necessity would force them to become "civilized" or starve.

In the South, encroachment by settlers who crossed the boundary lines to squat on unceded Indian land was a continuing problem. The region was more heavily populated by non-Indians than the North and the states of Georgia and North Carolina continued to pursue aggressive policies of land acquisition. Clearly, Knox's attempts to block the interference of those states through the use of the treaty system were not working. The states easily outmaneuvered the system by encouraging their citizens to cross the boundaries, after which these squatters would then clamor for protection and the purchase of the land they had occupied.

The evidence of the success of such a policy became apparent very early. North Carolinians had entered the Cherokee Nation in large numbers in violation of the 1785 Treaty of Hopewell. Their uproar, and the demands of the state, produced the Treaty of Holston in 1791, its purpose being to acquire the lands the squatters illegally occupied. Thus rewarded, North Carolina squatters soon crossed the line again, to be rewarded a second time with the 1798 Treaty of Tellico.

Pressures on Cherokee land came from the west as well. When North Carolina surrendered its western territory to the United States, Congress organized it as the Territory Southwest of the Ohio River. The territory was already home to two settlements, one at Knoxville, the other at Nashville. The intervening country belonged to the Cherokees. In 1796 the territory entered the Union as the state of Tennessee and immediately clamored for the land that separated their settlements. Almost annual negotiations between the United States and the Cherokees from 1797 to 1806 produced four treaties, each representing a reluctant sacrifice of a tract of country that commissioners frequently purchased with bribery.

The Creeks experienced the same kind of pressure. Responding to the demands of Georgia, federal commissioners met Creek headmen in 1796 to buy more land. In the face of the Creek refusal, however, the Treaty of Colerain simply confirmed the boundaries established in 1790. Georgia was outraged and the press of squatters continued, to be rewarded by cessions in 1802 and 1805.

The Choctaws and Chickasaws had generally been isolated from the press of settlement and demands for land, but the French acquisition of Louisiana changed that. Negotiations proceeded with both nations but both refused to sell.

While expansion was always the central theme of Indian policy, "civilization" was vitally important as the means for making "expansion with honor" honorable. Because "civilization" always rested on the assumption that it was the American model that Native people should emulate, the "civilization" policy was generally the same both north and south of the Ohio River. It demanded that Indian men be farmers and their wives spin and weave, make clothes, and keep house. Ideally, this should occur on each family's privately owned parcel of land, but efforts to break down the Indians' notion of communal ownership were sporadic at best. The children of the ideal "civilized" Indian family should attend school, learn to read, write, and speak English, and become Christian. The educational end of the "civilization" policy was generally conducted by missionaries, usually evangelical Protestants, and it was rarely possible to draw a line between their Christian and secular teaching.

Beside the obvious religious conflicts inherent in the "civilization" program, the American model required a reversal of the gender roles of most eastern Native American groups. Much has been made of the supposed humiliation that men suffered when they did women's work, but the real problem was much more serious than embarrassment. The spiritual linkage and ritual knowledge that made agriculture possible and productive belonged to women and was related to plants, except for the growing of sacred tobacco, which in some groups was a male responsibility. Male farming was therefore a defiance of the spiritual universe. Men's ritual knowledge linked them to animals, not plants. It made more sense for men to become stock raisers and horse traders than to become farmers.

But the hunting economy, especially in the South, was fast breaking down. In combination, the evaporation of the deerskin market and the decline of the deer herds undercut the southern Indian economy and jeopardized the continued flow of necessary goods. Southern Indians in the 1790s were stuck in a severe economic depression. Conditions in the North were not so serious, however. The chief export of northern Indians was not deerskins but luxury fur and hatter's pelts, and demand for them remained strong. Furthermore, overhunting had not decimated the fur-bearing animals. Civilizers argued that agriculture was not only God's intended way to live and use the soil, it provided a more stable, predictable, prosperous way of life than hunting. In the South, this was rapidly becoming true.

Some southern Indians took hold of a plow and farmed, but the distinctive southern culture provided many with an alternative. The southern model of civilization included slavery. Slaves of African origin had been a part of the worlds of southern Indians since the mid–eighteenth century and during the Revolution fairly large numbers of them found their way into the Cherokee and Creek nations as captives, escapees, or the property of Loyalist refugees. Cherokee and Creek men discovered that they could escape the collapsing hunting economy and become "civilized" and prosperous by becoming slaveholders. Most became neither farmers nor slaveholders, but a highly visible and increasing few did. They caught the eye of government officials and word of their achievements made its way to Washington where Jefferson was fond of citing them as examples of the success of his policy.

Such was not the case in the North. With no slavery to help men become "civilized" and a hunting economy that continued to supply their needs, few Northern Indians saw "civilization" as a useful or necessary alternative to current practice.

Prior to 1815, on both sides of the Ohio, Native nations retained their autonomy substantially intact and their social organization continued to square with reality. But this was not true of the Iroquois in New York. In a state of military, political, and economic decline since the 1760s, they suffered the final blow in the 1780s and 1790s when they were left with nothing but a collection of scattered reservations which generated social and cultural problems so serious they were threatened with the collapse of their culture.

Iroquois social structure was adapted to a pattern of life in which men were away from their villages for long periods of time on missions of war, trade, and diplomacy. Iroquois women remained in the villages, developed strong relations based on matrilineal kinship, and farmed. A successful system, it was wholly unsuited to reservation life. Men unused to sedentary unemployment often found outlets in fighting, drinking, and competing for one another's wives. Traditional religious rituals were unable to cope with the new situation. Out of this cultural crisis Handsome Lake, a Seneca living on a reservation on the Allegheny River and one of the worst offenders, emerged in 1799 as a prophet and visionary and became one of the most influential religious leaders in Native America.

Handsome Lake's visions told him and all Senecas to give up drinking, combat the witches who were corrupting society, and refrain from sexual promiscuity, wife beating, fighting, and gambling. Persons guilty of these acts must repent and publicly confess. Gradually, additional visions enabled Handsome Lake to develop a coherent religion that blended specific traditional rituals with certain innovations and broadened its purview to include social problems as well as individual actions. Handsome Lake urged the Senecas to live in nuclear families and be faithful in their marriages, he believed Seneca children should attend school and learn how to farm as Americans did, he vigorously opposed the sale of any more land, he favored the adoption of American tools and artifacts, and he recommended that Senecas and Americans should get along together. He also stressed the importance of preserving the institutions of Seneca life that identified them and gave them pride. Handsome Lake taught his message to the Senecas and the other Iroquois nations and many people accepted it. By the time of his death in 1815, Handsome Lake had developed an alternative to the "civilization" program that accomplished many of its economic and social goals while preserving the Indian identity of its followers. He addressed the social problems that threatened to destroy the Senecas and identified and recommended the adaptation necessary for their survival in a radically changed world.

While Handsome Lake was very much a Seneca responding to specific Seneca problems, he was also part of a wider Northern Woodland prophetic tradition that had a deep and vital history. In this sense Handsome Lake was not unique. At the same time he was teaching his message to the Senecas, two Shawnee brothers, Tenskwatawa and Tecumseh, were beginning to offer a militant Nativist message based on prophecy. Like Handsome Lake, they were reacting to the pressures of land loss, settlement, and the "civilization" program. They were also part of the same cultural history.

Defeat at Fallen Timbers and the Treaty of Greenville shattered the cooperation between Nativists and accommodationists that had marked Indian society in the Great Lakes country since the Revolution. To the Nativists, the accommodationist treaty chiefs were betraying their people with their land cessions. Corrupted by Harrison, more interested in money, goods, and flattery than in the welfare of their people, these leaders had permitted the Americans to take their lands. The message of Tecumseh and Tenskwatawa was pan-Indian unity rejuvenated and strengthened with spiritual power.

Tenskwatawa began his prophetic mission in 1805 when, like Handsome Lake, he had visions that urged personal and social repentance and showed the way to healing with ritual and ceremony and the recovery of lost spiritual power. In 1809, Tecumseh joined his brother in the prophetic movement by challenging Harrison over the Fort Wayne treaty. Tecumseh argued that it, along with the other treaties of cession Harrison had negotiated, was invalid because it was concluded with an unrepresentative and unauthorized group of treaty chiefs. God had given the land to all the Indians, Tecumseh explained, and no small group could sell it. In this, Tecumseh took the same pan-Indian stand the western alliance had taken in the 1780s when it tried to hold the Ohio River boundary. Compliant individuals concerned only with their own or their group's particular interests had threatened that boundary and thereby jeopardized the future of all the Indians of the Northwest. Now, twenty years later and the Ohio River boundary long gone, Harrison followed the same tactic to strip the rest of the country from the Indians. The Shawnee brothers set out to stop him by rebuilding the western alliance last seen in the early 1790s.

Harrison understood the danger such a program could have. If the prophets were not stopped they could unite the Indians of the Northwest against the United States and its expansionist policy. Harrison's solution to the problem posed by Tenskwatawa and Tecumseh became clear late in 1811. Increasingly fearful of the growing strength of the rejuvenated alliance, his concern magnified on receipt of reports that Tecumseh was talking with southern Indians about their joining the alliance. On the other hand, Harrison concluded that a strike against Tenskwatawa's village, Prophetstown, would more likely be successful in Tecumseh's absence. Thus, in September, he led an army of some 1,000 men up the Wabash River. Tenskwatawa, who knew of the invasion plan, decided to meet the Americans in combat. Before the battle he performed various rituals designed to make his warriors immortal and invincible while rendering the American troops confused and impotent. Thus fortified, Tenskwatawa's men attacked Harrison's camp on the morning of November 7, the day of his intended attack. In terms of casualties, the battle was roughly a draw. But Tenskwatawa's rituals had failed, Harrison's troops were effective, and Indian warriors were killed. Denouncing Tenskwatawa as a fraud, his followers after the battle packed up their families and abandoned Prophetstown. Harrison's men found it empty and burned it. Discredited, Tenskwatawa never recovered his lost stature.

Tecumseh returned from the South in January 1812 to find the alliance broken and scattered. With the help of British gifts of weapons and food, he set out to rebuild the movement. By spring numbers of Winnebagos, Kickapoos, and Potawatomis rejoined Tecumseh and his Shawnee and Wyandot followers. They reestablished the village at Tippecanoe Creek that Harrison had destroyed, and Tecumseh opened talks with both Harrison and the British. War between the United States and England, brewing for the past year, flared up in the west in mid-1812. Tecumseh and many of the warriors who followed him allied with the British. Hard fighting resulted, by the summer of 1813, in American successes which caused the British, with Tecumseh and the remainder of his dwindling army, to withdraw from the Detroit area. In early October 1813, at a stand on the Thames River in Ontario, an American army led by Harrison attacked and scattered the British and Indian force. In the fighting Tecumseh was killed. His death effectively ended the western alliance. For the Indians who had listened to Tenskwatawa and Tecumseh, who had allied against the frantic pace of land loss at the hands of Harrison, and who had followed Tecumseh into alliance with the British, American military successes demanded that they must now reach a new accommodation with the United States. Militant Nativist pan-Indianism had not worked.

In the South, events led to a similar set of conclusions. The constant pressures of settlers who disregarded the boundaries and encroached on Indian lands, coupled with the aggressive demands of state officials that the Indians must sell and make way for their citizens, led to repeated negotiations between federal agents and Indian leaders for cessions the Indians were increasingly reluctant to make. While bribery and threats sometimes paid dividends, often the Indian groups withstood the pressures. But only at great cost. Factions emerged that disputed the proper steps to take and the Nativist-accommodationist split that divided many northern tribes characterized southern Indian politics as well.

In addition to the widespread political and economic pressures that accompanied the collapse of the hunting economy and the unceasing demands for land from federal and state officials, the Creeks faced problems caused by their location. Occupying fertile lands adjacent to the rapidly filling Georgia cotton settlements, they were the recipients of much of the government's "civilization" efforts. Many eastern or Lower Creeks responded to United States agent Benjamin Hawkins's program while most western or Upper Creeks, farther distant from Hawkins and more insulated from his demands, remained less open to the cultural changes he recommended. The Creek Nation thus developed something of a regional polarization that was tied to the federal policy of "civilization." Although the Nativist-accommodationist factionalism did not conform exactly to regional lines, some degree of concentration did develop in which Nativists were more likely to be Upper Creeks and accommodationists were more likely to be Lower Creeks.

This growing factional division reached an explosive level in the period beginning about 1805, the date of a treaty with the United States that ceded a large block of land and agreed to the construction of a road through the nation to connect Washington with New Orleans. Opponents raised such heated arguments against the road that in 1811, after several years of failed efforts, the United States simply built it over Creek objections.

Tecumseh's 1811 search through the South for allies met with success largely among the Upper Creeks, who at the time of his arrival were angry over the road and the ongoing program of accommodation to Hawkins and the federal policy of "civilization." Welcomed by a group of prophets and spiritual leaders who were forming a Nativist movement, Tecumseh won an interested audience. Many Upper Creeks embraced his message of pan-Indian unity against American expansion, adopted the rituals and ceremonies he taught them, and a few accompanied him north to learn more. In the spring of 1812, on their return to the Creek Nation, some of these new disciples of Tecumseh and the Creek prophets killed several settlers in Tennessee. An outcry arose, the United States demanded punishment, and Hawkins insisted that the Creek National Council arrest the perpetrators. The Council dispatched William McIntosh, a powerful Lower Creek leader, to head the attempt. In the process of tracking down and arresting the killers, McIntosh and his police force killed them. Their friends and relatives claimed that McIntosh and the National Council had murdered their kinsmen to satisfy Hawkins and the federal government and demanded vengeance.

From all sides, Upper Creeks with grievances coalesced behind the prophets. Big Warrior, the leading chief of the Upper Creeks, was the handiest representative of the accommodationist leadership of the nation and an early target of Nativist outrage. Burning and plundering the plantations and livestock herds of "civilized" Creeks, the Nativists marched on Tuckabatchee, Big Warrior's town, and laid a siege that was broken only when the National Council sent McIntosh and a force of warriors to the rescue. The fighting between the accommodationist National Council and its warriors and the prophets and their Nativist followers quickly turned to civil war. After the August 1813 battle at Fort Mims, where Nativist warriors defeated and slaughtered a compound of "civilized" Creeks and their families, the Creek civil war became a general conflagration involving the U.S. army and the militias of Georgia, Tennessee, and Mississippi Territory. Commanded by Tennessean General Andrew Jackson, the combined force of Americans and Choctaw, Cherokee, and Creek accommodationist allies swept through Upper Creek country. Several battles inflicted heavy casualties on both sides, but finally, in March 1814 at the Battle of Horseshoe Bend, Jackson's forces crushed the Nativist opposition. Some 800 warriors in league with the prophets lost their lives in this bloody encounter which ended the Creek War.

In August 1814, Jackson dictated a treaty of peace and surrender to the badly divided and desolated Creek Nation. Forced to give over twenty million acres to the United States as punishment, the Creeks were helpless to resist. The Nativist movement was destroyed, the prophets and their followers were dead, in hiding, or in exile among the Seminoles in Florida, and the military power of the Creeks was shattered beyond repair.

The defeat of the Creeks in the Creek War and the scattering of the western alliance in the western campaigns of the War of 1812 brought an end to an era in U.S. relations with Native Americans. For the first time since English settlements began to cross the Appalachian Mountains in the 1760s, there was no effective Indian military power to resist. The destruction of this power, of course, should never have been necessary. The policy of "expansion with honor" had been designed specifically to avoid the use of force in the occupation of the continent. American expansion was supposed to have been slow, smooth, and harmonious, the behavior of the settlers was to have been controlled to avoid encroachment on Indian lands, and the Indians were to have become "civilized" quickly enough to see the benefit of selling their surplus lands for money to invest in their farms. Thus, Indians and Americans would have settled into a peaceful and neighborly relationship. Indians were to have entered into American society, welcomed by their American fellow citizens, where honor and justice would prevail. These were the expectations of Knox, Washington, Jefferson, and the policy they created was to have made it reality. The bloody warfare in the west that coincided with the War of 1812 revealed in stark and bloody detail that "expansion with honor" was a failed policy.

POST-1815

The year of 1815 is a watershed in American history. The Treaty of Ghent did more than end the War of 1812. To many Americans it confirmed the independence of the United States in a most decisive way. John C. Calhoun called the War of 1812 the "second American Revolution" and in the sense that it demonstrated the ability of the American experiment in republican self-government under the Constitution to remain whole and functioning while directing the defense of the nation, he may even have understated his case. Certainly the ability of such a governmental system to function and survive a time of extreme crisis had remained the great unanswered question. The War of 1812 provided the affirmative answer.

A popular spirit of ebullient nationalism was apparent everywhere, and evidence of all kinds seemed to demonstrate that the future was ripe and beckoning. The value of American goods soared in a world market depressed for years by the Napoleonic wars in Europe. American producers busily expanded their operations, American ships returned to the seas in ever growing numbers, and American citizens looked west to fertile lands that promised to become, in their hands, a garden of opportunity.

Numbers tell the story. Between 1816 and 1819 four new states – Indiana, Mississippi, Illinois, and Alabama – entered the Union. In 1810 their territorial population totaled 77,000. In 1820, the new states contained 305,000 people. Furthermore, the older states with claims to large areas unoccupied by American citizens – Georgia, Tennessee, and Ohio – grew in that decade from 744,000 to 1.3 million people. The magnitude of this growth and movement of people is even more spectacular than it appears because nearly all of it occurred in the last half of the decade.

The great attraction in the South was the Creek cession of 1814. This vast tract of land included much of Alabama's fabled Black Belt, a region of extraordinarily fertile land capable of producing bumper crops of cotton. High cotton prices between 1815 and 1819 promised a level of prosperity that the older cotton states could no longer match. To the north, the Harrison treaties negotiated before 1809 made fertile land available in Indiana and Illinois to grain and livestock farmers. Steamboats appeared on the western rivers in 1811 and by the end of the decade were carrying the produce of these newly acquired lands to market at New Orleans. Such improvements in transportation technology, stimulated by the western explosion of population and production, gave access to markets in distant places that encouraged further growth. Despite the periodic panics and depressions that marked the years between 1815 and 1850, a national market developed that linked the new and booming West to the rest of the country and the world.

The real and imagined prosperity of the West, magnified by the emergent national market, depended, of course, on the continued availability of land. Because the undeveloped blocks of western lands belonged to and were used by Native Americans, nothing could happen without their cooperation. Everything stood on the foundation of Indian relations and the policies that influenced them.

Two sets of diametrically opposed ideas collided in the years after 1815. One set, which gained increasing force in the communities and council houses of Native America, was that they had already sold all the land they could spare. Survival would be impossible if more land was lost. Strengthened by this resolve, Native leaders refused to negotiate with federal commissioners, or if they agreed to talk they refused to sell. Claiming their rights as sovereigns free to pursue their collective interests, they repeatedly rebuffed government requests to purchase their lands.

The second point of view appears in the statements of federal officials which decried the slow pace of the "civilization" of the Indians and challenged the policy of recognizing the sovereignty of their nations. Early in 1817, Andrew Jackson, commanding general of the southern military district, launched a verbal attack on Indian sovereignty as part of a comprehensive plan to protect the South from foreign invasion. Indians should be speedily replaced on the land by American citizens who could be organized to defend it. But the reluctance of Indian peoples to sell the land blocked such a solution. As long as the United States recognized the sovereignty of these nations and accepted their sovereign right to refuse to sell, the South, Jackson argued, would remain uninhabited and vulnerable. Jackson's solution to the problem was to reject the notion of Indian sovereignty, stop fooling with the "absurd" treaty system, and simply legislate national boundaries in ways that best suited the interest of the United States. This was a proper and legal concept, Jackson believed, because the Indians were subjects of the United States, not sovereigns, and could not claim a legal right to sovereignty. Secretary of War Calhoun agreed. Writing to Congress in December 1818, Calhoun asserted that "the time seems to have arrived when our policy towards them should undergo an important change. . . . Our views of their interest, and not their own, ought to govern them."[9] Along with Jackson, Calhoun viewed the idea of Native national sovereignty and the treaty system that flowed from it mainly as impediments to the acquisition of Indian land and the expansion of American settlements. President James Monroe shared these concerns even as he clung to the "expansion with honor" hope of his predecessors. Indian policy should somehow benefit the Indians too, however, and like Knox, Washington, and Jefferson, Monroe saw this best accomplished by exposing Native people to the advantages of American culture. To him, therefore, rejecting the sovereignty of Native groups implied denying them the power to resist "civilization." "To civilize them, and even to prevent their extinction, it seems to be indispensable that their independence as communities should cease, and that the control of the United States over them should be complete and undisputed."[10]

But the idea that Native nations were sovereign and that relations with them should be conducted through the treaty system lay at the foundation of U.S. Indian policy, and before the War of 1812 no one in high federal office had ever significantly challenged the system. In the postwar world, however, things were different. "The neighboring tribes are becoming daily less warlike, and more helpless and dependent on us," Calhoun wrote. "They have, in a great measure, ceased to be an object of terror, and have become that of commiseration."[11] Jackson was more blunt. "The arm of government [is] sufficiently strong," he announced, to force the Indians

---

[9] John C. Calhoun to the House of Representatives, Dec. 5, 1818, in *American State Papers: Indian Affairs*, 2:183.

[10] James Monroe, Second Annual Message, Nov, 16, 1818, in James D. Richardson, comp., *Messages and Papers of the Presidents* (Washington, D.C., 1896), 2:46.

[11] Calhoun to House of Representatives, Dec. 5, 1818, in *American State Papers: Indian Affairs*, 2:183.

to comply with the demands of its Indian policy. Congress was unresponsive to these recommendations, however, and continued to adhere to the concept of Indian sovereignty and the treaty system.

In the absence of policy alternatives, Calhoun made imaginative use of the tools at hand to continue the flow of Indian lands into the hands of Americans. Until legislation in 1822 closed down the factory system, Calhoun found its power over Indian economies useful. By threatening to withhold trade he could manipulate the decisions of Native leaders. He could also counter the influence of private traders who might advise headmen contrary to government wishes. Calhoun also turned to the "civilization" program that had, since the 1790s, characterized Indian policy. It was hard to forge piecemeal appropriations for agricultural implements, livestock, and training into a coherent program, but in 1819 Congress enacted legislation that provided $10,000 per year for "civilization." Calhoun canvassed the Protestant mission boards for proposals for schools and training centers to be located within Indian communities and offered federal money for buildings, salary supplements, and tuition for Native students. Monroe's public statements suggest a sincere interest in "civilizing" Indians, but Calhoun's views were substantially more practical. In return for federal subsidies, he expected the missionaries to support government policies and use their influence to help him achieve his goals.

The period after the War of 1812 was a time of transition for Indian policy. Policymakers like Calhoun and Monroe continued to pay lip service to the expansion with honor goals of previous years, but within the context of the rapidly changing postwar world the element of honor shrank further into the background as the pressure for expansion became ever more compelling. The key to this transition lies clearly in the altered power relations between Indians and Americans. Indian military power was smashed and Indian population decline paralleled dramatic American population increases. Western Indians on both sides of the Ohio River faced a new magnitude of challenges and experimented with new and innovative ways to meet them.

BRITISH NORTH AMERICA

The War of 1812 is no less important in the history of Northern Indians and their relations with Canada. After the American Revolution, British authorities in Canada continued their wartime friendship with Native people. In addition to treaty making with the Ojibwas in order to secure land for Loyalist settlement in Upper Canada (Ontario) and to provide secure reserves on the Grand River and at Tyendinaga for the King's Iroquois allies displaced from New York, Royal officials continued diplomatic and trade contacts with the Indians of the Great Lakes country. Indians on both sides of the border came to depend on the annual ceremonies to renew the alliances, both for the satisfaction of perpetuating friendship with the King and for the value of the gifts the agents distributed in the King's name. During the War of 1812, large numbers of northern Native warriors fought with British forces against the Americans. But after the war the British realized, as did the Americans, that this had been the last of the conflicts. In light of this, Royal officials in Canada reassessed their relations with Native people and concluded, more or less simultaneously with their American counterparts, that in the future the Indians would have little or no role of significance to play in their society. This conclusion was underscored by rapidly increasing competition for land as the settler population of Upper Canada exploded. Meetings and conferences with Indian leaders continued, but their purposes changed. Instead of strengthening the chain of friendship with valued allies, Royal agents demanded land sales. And rather than distribute gifts to perpetuate loyalty, officials offered annuities in payment for lands that were pegged to the size of Indian populations, not to an agreed upon value of the region surrendered, so that the costs to the Crown would decrease over time as the Indians died off.

Two sets of attitudes emerged to influence Royal Indian policy. One reflected the conviction that Native cultures must give way to a new "civilized" pattern of life. Similar to the views of American policymakers of the late eighteenth and early nineteenth centuries, missionaries and government officers in Upper Canada after 1815 believed that Native people should abandon their hunting ways, which were rapidly becoming uneconomic in any case, and become settled farmers. To achieve this transformation, they recommended the establishment of specially managed communities under the direction of missionaries. The Jesuit and Sulpician praying towns founded in seventeenth-century Quebec — Sillery, Lorette, Caughnawaga, Odanak, and others — should provide the models. Formally described in an 1828 report by H. C. Darling, an official of Upper Canada's Indian department, plans were quickly underway for the creation of a series of such villages. One, built on the Credit River for Methodist Mississaugas led by Reverened Peter Jones, a Mississauga minister, became a thriving agricultural settlement.

By the end of the 1830s, however, another interpretation of proper Indian policy emerged. Expressed most vigorously by Francis Bond Head, Lieutenant-Governor of Upper Canada, this view represented official frustration over the slow pace of Indian "civilization." As in the United States, many Canadian Indians believed formal education was an important and necessary tool to be adapted to their own purposes. Officials and missionaries, on the other hand, assumed education should serve the transforming policy of "civilization." Locked in a dispute over uses and purposes, government authorities concluded that the refusal of Indians to conform was in fact their failure to understand and appreciate what was offered. Bond Head, echoing the critiques of United States "civilization" policy of a decade before, believed that the problems lay in easy association between Indians and Canadians. Indians learned the vices of "civilized" life, he complained, but not its virtues. His solution to the problem was segregation. Indians should be isolated away from Canadian society, not put into model communities in the midst of that world. To that end Bond Head negotiated with Ojibwas for the purchase of the rugged and rocky Manitoulin Island in Lake Huron. Here Indians could hunt, fish, and die at their own pace and out of the way. Whichever opinion – "civilization" or segregation – one held, officials agreed on the initial premise that "uncivilized" Native people offered Canada little of value.

In Lower Canada, exempt from the provisions of the Royal Proclamation of 1763 which recognized the treaty rights of Native people, no one attempted to redefine the status of Indians, many of whom lived on church missions. After 1780, when Loyalist settlers began to arrive in the Maritime Provinces, an increasing non-Indian population began to encroach on Indian lands. British governors established reserves for these Indians under a variety of treaty relations, many of which were later reduced in size.

"CIVILIZATION"

North of the Ohio River, the normal subsistence cycle of summer and fall planting and harvesting, winter hunting from scattered camps, and spring maple sugaring became steadily less reliable. Declining animal populations south of the Great Lakes made the winter hunt less productive in both edible meat and marketable furs and hides. Increased reliance on farming and gathering staved off starvation but could not fulfill the needs of the people for necessary hardware, clothing, and other manufactured goods. If survival on the land was not impossible, economic pressures demanded changes that were both hard to avoid and hard to design.

The U.S. government's plan of "civilization" offered one model for survival. Coupled with its ongoing efforts to purchase lands, the United States continually refocused its schemes to transform Indian men from hunters into farmers, Indian women from farmers into housekeepers, and Indian youth from undisciplined waifs into school children. The renewal of this program after the War of 1812 is evident, for example, in the experience of the Potawatomis. A populous nation with villages extending in a large arc around the lower third of Lake Michigan, the Potawatomis had been part of the Euro-American trade network for well over a century. First in association with the French, then the English, and now the Americans, the Potawatomis had long since embraced a fur-trade economy. Its postwar collapse had serious implications.

Government agents at Detroit, Chicago, Green Bay, and Peoria had instructions from Washington to encourage the Indians in "civilized" pursuits and to distribute agricultural implements as gifts. The Civilization Act of 1819 made more money available to purchase such gifts and also encouraged the involvement of church mission groups. Isaac McCoy, a Baptist minister from Kentucky, arrived at Fort Wayne in 1820 to supplement the agent's "civilization" efforts. McCoy opened a school for Potawatomi children, established a model farm to instruct Potawatomi men, and preached the virtue of "civilized" life along with the Baptist gospel. Through most of the 1820s, McCoy and the regional government agents labored to transform the Potawatomis into an American-style agricultural people.

After an initial response of guarded interest, the Potawatomis rejected the American solution to their economic woes. The American yeoman farmer was not the Potawatomis' preferred acculturation model. Long acquainted with French Canadian traders, both as business partners and as intermarried kinsmen, Potawatomi men preferred a life of commerce to one of agriculture. Not only was it a less structured and confining profession, trade conveyed political as well as economic opportunity and influence. Indeed, by the 1820s a new group of leaders emerged in many Potawatomi villages that linked economic and political positions. The biracial and bicultural progeny of generations of French-Potawatomi association, this economic elite turned language and commercial skills into political power and seemed, for a time at any rate, to hold the key to Potawatomi survival.

Between 1816 and 1840, Potawatomi leaders signed twenty-eight treaties of land cession with United States commissioners. Many of the treaties conveyed Potawatomi claims to regions used and claimed jointly with several other groups, which tended to be hunting areas of declining value. Many treaties reserved in Potawatomi ownership specifically described tracts that included villages and fields. Many of the treaties stipulated that while the Potawatomis had sold their title to the lands, they could continue to use them until they were needed for American settlers. And all the treaties provided payments for the surrendered claims. The government paid at the time of the sale and in annual installments for a specified number of years. These yearly payments, called annuities, constituted an income for the Potawatomi signatories and those for whom they were responsible. Two things happened. Federal commissioners sought out bilingual and bicultural Potawatomis on the assumption that they would be easier to deal with, and control over the annuities gave these bicultural Potawatomis political power.

After the War of 1812, as the Potawatomi experience suggests, the annuities became an increasingly important feature of northern Indian life. Paid in both cash and goods, they provided the income lost as the fur trade shrank. Just as the fur trade had created a dependency that threatened the autonomy of the Indian groups involved, so too did the annuities. But the result was even more debilitating because the annuity system gave the federal government direct control over the Indian economies. And as Native leaders in the fur-trade period had attempted to balance economic dependency against political autonomy, so this emergent group of annuity chiefs found it necessary to safeguard their positions and the well-being of their people while avoiding as much as possible the political implications of this new form of economic dependency.

The postwar treaty system encouraged the annuity solution to the economic problems of the Potawatomis because most of the cessions did not require the immediate surrender of land. Thus the chiefs could obtain an income for their people without an apparent cost. Such an arrangement, though shortsighted and dangerous, was easy and attractive. It might be years before the United States demanded the lands be sold. The temptation to mortgage the future to meet present needs was overwhelming, and other Indian peoples in the Great Lakes country followed the same practice.

While this policy coincided nicely with federal desires to acquire Indian land, the emergence of the bicultural Franco-Indian commercial and political elite did not accord with federal "civilization" plans. Indeed, the disinterest of the Potawatomis and other northern Indians in the yeoman farmer model frustrated the agents of American "civilization." Before the 1820s ended, for example, Isaac McCoy had abandoned the Potawatomi mission at Fort Wayne and moved west.

The government's "civilization" policy met with much better success in the South. The slaveowning planter model attracted many southern Native men. And because the Cherokees and Creeks in the East and the Choctaws and Chickasaws in the West constituted two islands of Indians surrounded by a sea of Americans, the market place of southern rural America was never far away. As a result, a range of "civilized" economic opportunities unavailable in the North existed for southern Indian men seeking to replace their collapsed fur-trade economy.

The southern nation widely recognized in the post–War of 1812 period as the most "civilized" was the Cherokee, which numbered about 14,000 in 1826 and 16,542 in 1835. Devastated by invasions during the Revolution, rocked by domestic discord and frontier conflict in the 1780s and 1790s, and debilitated by economic collapse as the deerskin trade evaporated, the Cherokees by the end of the eighteenth century were at a crossroads. Survival and prosperity required radical changes and the Cherokees, by careful selection and imaginative adaptation, cashed in on the "civilization" program.

From federal agents the Cherokees received implements and tools for agriculture and household manufacture, livestock and poultry, and artisans ready to teach their skills as well as to practice their crafts. In 1804, Moravian missionaries established the first school for Cherokee youth. Within the decade Presbyterian missionaries and private tutors founded four more schools and together the five institutions enrolled almost 100 students. The American Board of Commissioners for Foreign Missions entered the Cherokee field in 1817, opened eight more schools, and over the next sixteen years taught 882 students. Added to these were two Baptist and six Methodist schools which operated intermittently. While the Cherokees were never well educated by contemporary American standards, their children had educational opportunities at least equal to the surrounding rural American communities and far superior to those of any other Native nation. By the 1820s the Cherokees had clearly identified an English-language American education as an important element in their cultural transformation.

While training their youth for the future, Cherokee adults adapted a variety of "civilized" practices to their needs. Women expanded their traditional household duties to become spinners of yarn and weavers of cloth. Almost certainly, they also remained the primary agriculturalists, except perhaps in those families (7.4 percent in 1835) that owned slaves. But agriculture became increasingly Americanized through the use of plows and draft animals. By the end of the 1820s, for example, the number of plows and the number of farms were nearly identical. Probably Cherokee men did the plowing. Farms in 1835 averaged fourteen acres (5.6 hectares) in cultivation, however, so further male intrusion into the female world of agriculture was probably minimal.

Male economic activities were more likely to occur away from home, as they always had. Hunting, of course, continued. The collapse of the deerskin market never meant that men stopped hunting – it simply meant that commercial hunting was no longer profitable. Many Cherokee men became livestock raisers. At the end of the 1820s the Cherokees owned 7,600 horses, 22,000 cattle, about 42,000 hogs, and over 2,500 sheep. Cherokee men also built and maintained turnpikes; owned and operated ferries and toll bridges; kept and worked in stores, taverns, and mills; and pursued such skilled occupations as blacksmithing and silver-smithing, carpentry, and various mechanical trades. In 1835 over 1,000 Cherokees could read English – doubtless many times that number could speak it – and 4,000 could read Cherokee.

The evidence of literacy in Cherokee reflects the unique accomplishment of Sequoyah, a silversmith who devised a system for writing his language. Illiterate in English but obviously aware that the ability to read and write gave Americans a tremendous advantage in their dealings with the Cherokees, he set out to equalize their relations. Sequoyah discovered that the Cherokee language was spoken with eighty-five syllables. Assigning a symbol to each syllable, learning to read and write was simply a matter of memorizing the symbols. Sequoyah introduced his system in 1821. In 1828 the nation launched the *Cherokee Phoenix,* a weekly newspaper printed with adjacent columns of English and Cherokee. The organ of the nation, the *Phoenix* published its laws and official announcements along with the news.

As remarkable as the economic and social changes were, Cherokee political innovations made them famous. Like many other Native groups, the Cherokees learned the hard lesson that part of their self-defence depended on their ability to control the actions of their own people. Otherwise, young warriors intent on gaining prestige might attack American settlers and invite retaliation, which rarely punished the perpetrators.

Thus, in the name of national security and the better regulation of foreign policy, the Cherokee Nation evolved a National Council. The process was underway by the mid–eighteenth century and by century's end the Council had become a formally established institution. Councilors soon realized, however, that the centralized administration of foreign policy could not succeed without intruding on domestic affairs. Thus in 1808 the Council enacted legislation to create a mounted national police force to suppress horse stealing, an activity that was sure to provoke outside interference in Cherokee affairs.

The Council's assertion of domestic authority marked the beginning of a remarkable governmental innovation. As it removed political authority from the towns, hitherto autonomous in domestic affairs, the Council claimed an unprecedented role in Cherokee life. The Council followed this precedent in 1810 with the even more revolutionary act of disallowing clan vengeance. No longer could the clans perform the functions of courts and executioners in interpersonal relations. Over the next several years the Council further centralized Cherokee government through the establishment of an Executive Committee that had, as its chief function, sole jurisdiction in the conduct of relations with the United States. In 1820 the Council carved the nation into eight legislative and judicial districts, in order further to undermine local autonomy by making Council delegates responsible to their districts rather than their towns. The next year the Council created a Supreme Court. Finally, in 1827, an elected convention drafted a national constitution. Ratified and in place the next year, the Cherokee Constitution proclaimed the sovereignty of the nation and formally established a republican form of government with a judiciary, a bicameral legislature, and a powerful executive branch headed by an elected Principal Chief.

The constitutional government had a range of tasks to perform. "Civilized" Cherokees, accumulating property, wanted laws, police, and courts to guarantee the security of their possessions. Under increasing pressure from the neighboring states, the Cherokee Nation needed a government more able to represent and defend its interests in its diplomatic relations with the United States. But in addition, the Cherokees were fighting a public relations battle, both in Congress and in the urban Northeast. A formally institutionalized republican government on the American model, many hoped, would go far to convince skeptics of the strides toward "civilization" the nation had taken.

The Creeks tended to be less interested than the Cherokees in the federal "civilization" program. Like the Cherokees, they received plows, spinning wheels, looms, and other implements of "civilized" life, and some Creeks, notably in the Lower Towns of the Chattahoochee Valley, moved toward the kind of plow agriculture that formed the basis of the "civilization" policy. Several Creek families even acquired slaves, planted cotton, and entered the regional market. But the Creeks remained suspicious of American education, permitting the establishment of only two mission schools, and Creek men generally did not enter commercial and mechanical occupations. The Creek National Council did pursue a centralist course, however. It adopted a written code of laws in 1818, established a national police force, undercut clan authority by forbidding clan vengeance, and by the middle of the 1820s was making serious attempts to erode traditional town autonomy in favor of a unified national governmental system. The Creeks did not draft a constitution, however, or copy in other significant ways the political institutions of the United States.

Farther to the west, the Choctaws and Chickasaws faced the same economic collapse as their deerskin trade melted away. With encouragement from U.S. agents and Protestant missionaries, plow agriculture and livestock grazing gradually provided a new economic base. Beginning with the Natchez Trace, both nations were also crisscrossed by an extensive network of roads which provided a host of commercial opportunities for Indian entrepreneurs. Both nations welcomed the establishment of mission schools to provide their youth an English language education and vocational training. They also experimented with various governmental alterations. The Choctaws drafted a constitution in 1826, but unlike that of the Cherokees it did not follow the republican model of the United States. The Chickasaws, like most other southern nations, drafted a written law code and created a national police force.

None of this evidence of "civilization" applied uniformly in any of the nations. Just as the sons and grandsons of intermarried traders had emerged to take useful leadership roles in diplomatic relations with the United States, so they also emerged as an economic elite. Their bilingual and bicultural talents gave them advantages in their dealings with Americans, and their socialization at the hands of trader fathers and grandfathers gave them commercial experience and economic ambitions that tended to set them apart. They were the ones who encouraged schools, and their English-speaking children entered them prepared to succeed in ways their non–English-speaking friends found difficult. They were the ones most likely to own slaves and reap the financial benefits of slave labor. They also were the ones most likely to own and operate the toll roads and bridges, ferries, smithies, mills, gins, taverns, and stores. It was their cotton and livestock that went to market, and it was their money that built the fine homes. They were also the ones who spearheaded, except among the Creeks, the governmental innovations, wrote the constitutions, enacted the laws, and established the courts. They did these things, for the most part, because they were economically ambitious, but they also fully understood that their dreams could come true only in Indian country. The children of Indian mothers, the matrilineal societies of the southern Indians meant that they were linked by kinship in a far-flung pattern of life that bound them all together. If they were elites, they were Indian elites, and if their actions benefited themselves, they also usually benefited the rest of their people. The unique brand of incipient nationalism that characterized the southern Indian nations in the first quarter of the nineteenth century was, for the most part, their doing. And its purpose was clear – to stave off removal.

CRISIS IN INDIAN AFFAIRS

In the 1820s, the combination of rapidly growing American populations in the new states west of the Appalachians, Indian military weakness, successes, particularly in the South, of the "civilization" program, emerging Indian nationalism, and an increasing reluctance of Native leaders to sell more lands produced what Thomas L. McKenney, head of the Indian Office in Washington, called a "crisis in Indian affairs." It was a crisis that put the federal government and the states on a collision course that some feared could result in civil war. The issue was Indian policy, particularly the obligation the United States had incurred in past treaties and legislatively defined in the Trade and Intercourse Acts to respect the political sovereignty and territorial integrity of the Native nations and to protect them from its expansionist citizens. Short of violating its pledged word and ignoring its constitutional obligations, the United States could extricate itself from the crisis only by acting against its citizens, slowing its economic and territorial growth, winning the cooperation of the Indians, or making profound changes in its Indian policy. None of the solutions was easy, some were unpalatable, and all would take time to accomplish. One concept, the removal of the eastern Indians to country west of the Mississippi, emerged as the chosen way out of the dilemma.

President Thomas Jefferson first thought of the idea of moving eastern

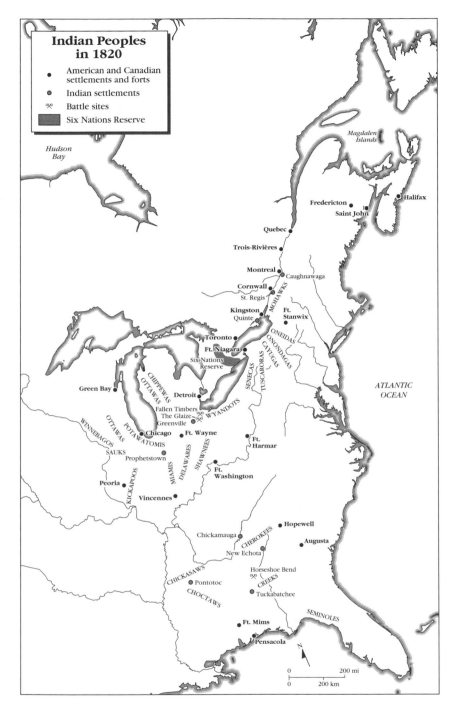

Figure 8.1. Indian peoples in 1820.

Indians across the Mississippi in 1803 as he contemplated the purchase of Louisiana from France. Over the next few years he suggested the notion to visiting delegations of Chickasaws, Choctaws, and Cherokees, but always as a recommendation to be considered at some future time. Only the Cherokees gave removal much thought. Groups of them had begun migrating into the Arkansas and White River valleys of present-day Arkansas in the 1790s and individual families and small groups continued to do so. Following the cessions of 1808 and 1810 the numbers of migrants to the West increased substantially. By the time of the War of 1812, some 2,000 Cherokees resided there. Some had gone as an act of resistance to the government's "civilization" policy, others had moved to exploit the rich land and constituted an Indian component of the larger westward migration of slaveowning cotton planters. Smaller numbers of Choctaws and Chickasaws, usually working as fur traders, also established small communities in the West.

Cherokee treaties of 1817 and 1819 directly addressed the question of removal. The 1817 document granted land on the Arkansas River for the Western Cherokees, recommended continued migration, and defined the means for paying the westerners a fair portion of the nation's annuity. The 1819 treaty repeated the encouragement to migrate and stipulated measures for compensating emigrants for their abandoned improvements. In both treaties the Cherokees sold large tracts of land in the East, and federal negotiators presented migration to the West as one of several options for those families living on the ceded lands. Another option was for each family to accept a 640 acre (259 hectare) reserve, to include their improvements, on which they would continue to reside as citizens of the states in which they were located. To the outrage of Tennesseans and North Carolinians, in whose states most of them lived, over 100 Cherokee families chose that option and attempted to achieve assimilation into local American society. For many, the harassment of neighboring Americans and discrimination at the hands of county and state governments proved too severe, however, and they abandoned their reserves to reenter the nation. But several families in western North Carolina that separated from the Cherokee Nation and accepted allotments held onto them. Being outside the jurisdiction of the Cherokee Nation, these Cherokees were exempt from the removal treaty of 1835 and remained behind when the others were carried west. Their community, isolated in the rugged Smoky Mountains, attracted other Cherokees who escaped the removal dragnet and together, on a land base formed by the allotments granted by the 1819 treaty and augmented later by purchase, they formed the Eastern Band of Cherokees who remain to this day in western North Carolina. The treaty of 1819 reminded southerners, however, that assimilation of Indians remained government policy. Then, in 1820, the Choctaws signed a treaty at Doak's Stand that contained provisions for a voluntary removal to the country between the Arkansas and Red Rivers. A small number of Choctaws made the move. One of the unintended results of these early migrations was that they siphoned off the people who might have been most inclined to negotiate land cessions and total removal and left in place those most opposed to moving west.

The removal articles in these early treaties reflected the political pressure that states of the South were able to apply in Washington. Responding to popular demand and heated resolutions passed by state legislatures, southern Congressmen and Senators engineered hearings and committee investigations, inundated the press, and pestered administrative officials for speedy action. United behind the goal of rapidly acquiring title to the vast tracts of land still in Indian hands, the southerners united as well on removal as the only acceptable solution to the problem of what to do with the Indians after their land was sold. Few regarded assimilation, the promise of the "civilization" policy, as acceptable. The Enlightenment view that culture, which could be changed, was the distinguishing feature of people increasingly gave way in the early nineteenth century to racism, which regarded a people's lifestyle as inherent and immutable. Most Indians were not "civilized" and never could be and thus could not live in American society, they believed, and those few who were "civilized" remained Indians and were thus racially tainted. George M. Troup, Governor of Georgia, announced that the best Indians residing in Georgia could hope for was a second-class status comparable to that of free blacks. Few southerners disagreed with him.

Removal thus emerged in the late teens and early twenties as an Indian policy alternative to the expansion-with-honor goals of the prewar years. The "civilization" policy had failed to convince Native Americans to part with their lands; the treaty system perpetuated the notion of tribal sovereignty that permitted a "civilized" Indian elite to block the desires of American expansionists, all the while growing rich at the expense of "uncivilized" Indian hunters.

To these arguments, simplistic if not absolutely untrue, Georgia added the further claim that the United States was legally bound to remove the

Native people from its borders. In 1802, when Georgia relinquished its charter claims to the country west of the Chattahoochee River, later to become the states of Alabama and Mississippi, it received from the federal government a cash payment and a promise that it would acquire for Georgia the Indian lands east of that river as soon as it could be done "peaceably" and on "reasonable terms." Purchases from the Creeks and Cherokees after 1802 had not completed the acquisition, however, and the treaties negotiated had actually obligated the United States to defend the rights of the Indians to the lands they retained. In the late teens, Georgia politicians began to argue that the United States not only had failed to live up to its 1802 bargain, it actually had strengthened Indian claims to lands within the state. The "crisis in Indian affairs" that worried McKenney in the mid-1820s was thus heightened, if not caused, by Georgia's heated demands. President Monroe's defense of government efforts emphasized the "peaceable" and "reasonable terms" provisions of the 1802 agreement and pointed out that if the Indian nations refused to sell, the United States could do no more than it had already done. Georgia insisted it could, however, by applying force.

This atmosphere of tension and the threat of civil conflict hung over the relations between the federal administration and the southern states in the mid-1820s and poisoned federal relations with the southern Indians. In hopes of calming the tension, Monroe accepted the recommendation of his Indian Office and embodied in his last State of the Union message, delivered on December 7, 1824, a plan for the removal of eastern Indians to the West. Followed the next month by a special report to Congress, Monroe explained his policy initiative by citing the demands of Georgia and the federal obligation according to the 1802 Agreement as well as his conviction that only removal could "shield [the Indians] from impending ruin." Believing that "in their present state it is impossible to incorporate them in such masses, in any form whatever, into our system," Monroe defined removal as a way to protect the Indians "against the dangers to which they are exposed" until such time as they could be "civilized" enough to function in American society. If the United States failed to act, he warned, "their degradation and extermination will be inevitable."[12] Thus Monroe expressed the twin arguments for removal that shaped the debate on the policy and justified its execution. Removal was necessary to accomplish the final acquisition of Indian-owned land east of the Mississippi, just as it

---

[12] James Monroe, Eighth Annual Message, Dec. 7, 1824, in Richardson, *Messages and Papers,* 2:261.

was necessary to save the Indians from the deleterious effects of association with Americans and their institutions. It also solved the problem of what to do with homeless Indians after their land had been sold.

Even as Monroe's Indian policy advisors put the final touches on his removal program, federal commissioners were in the Creek Nation attempting to negotiate a treaty that would send most of the Creeks west. Responding to Georgia's demand for the ouster of the Creeks, the commissioners opened talks for all their land east of the Chattahoochee plus as much west of that river as they would part with. In the face of a firm Creek rejection, the negotiations ended, only to be resumed privately with William McIntosh, an important Lower Creek chief known to be receptive to bribery. In January 1825 a deal was struck, and McIntosh and several Lower Creek associates signed a treaty at his Indian Springs tavern that conveyed to the United States all the Creek lands claimed by Georgia plus about two-thirds of their territory west of the Chattahoochee River within the limits of Alabama. McIntosh agreed to the cession despite a law enacted several years before by the Creek National Council that forbade any sale of the national domain without full Council authorization and consent. Failing to block ratification in the Senate, the Creek Council ordered the execution of McIntosh and his cronies. A specially appointed national police force carried out the order on May 1, 1825.

The execution of McIntosh is significant for two reasons. In the first place, it dramatized the changed thinking of the Creek National Council. The law McIntosh violated defined Creek lands to be national domain under the exclusive jurisdiction of the Council, thereby further undermining the traditional autonomy of the Creek towns. It was, in effect, a treason law, which suggests that the Creeks had evolved a national identity strong enough to imagine a crime against the nation. And with his execution the National Council demonstrated its willingness and its ability to act, through a national police force, to protect the nation and its domain. Although less formal than the governmental innovations of the Cherokees with their constitution, this series of events was no less remarkable as a watershed moment in Creek history.

McIntosh's execution was also significant in the history of worsening relations between the United States and Georgia. Georgia's Governor Troup interpreted the Council's action as a warlike act, mobilized the militia, and threatened invasion. John Quincy Adams, newly inaugurated President of the United States, was under treaty obligation to defend Creek borders from invasion. The president also believed that the Council's decision, while unfortunate, was perfectly legal as an act of the government of the sovereign Creek Nation. Thus the Adams Administration faced the likelihood of being drawn into armed conflict with Georgia to protect the Creeks. In hopes of avoiding this, Adams worked to mollify both Georgia and the Creeks and committed his administration to Monroe's removal policy. For much of the rest of his presidency, Adams struggled to keep peace in the South by continued negotiations with the Creeks and repeated recommendations to Congress to enact a removal law.

The turning point in Congressional consideration of Indian removal came with the 1828 election of Andrew Jackson to the presidency. Jackson's victory extended to the emerging Democratic party, which had its main support in the young states west of the Appalachians. A new majority entered Congress in 1829 that reflected a peculiarly western sense of national destiny, expansionism, economic opportunity, and the view that continued Indian occupation of western lands represented an important obstacle to progress. During the winter of 1829–30, few public issues commanded more attention than the question of Indian removal. Proponents of both sides of the issue bombarded Congress with memorials and petitions, editors exchanged claims, ministers preached sermons, essayists explored the issues, and Congressmen argued passionately (see Chapter 2).

Jackson had initiated this new and final phase of the debate over removal with his first State of the Union message, presented to Congress December 8, 1829. Directing his remarks most pointedly at the constitutional republic of the Cherokee Nation, Jackson announced that "their attempt to establish an independent government would not be countenanced" and they could have only two options: "to emigrate beyond the Mississippi, or submit to the laws of [Georgia and Alabama]." Because association with Americans will "doom [the Indians] to weakness and decay," the alternative of remaining in the East was, for their sake, unacceptable. Therefore, "justice and a regard for our national honor" insisted that removal was the correct course to take. But it was up to the Indians to decide. "This emigration should be voluntary: for it would be as cruel as unjust to compel the aborigines to abandon the graves of their fathers, and seek a home in a distant land." If they chose not to go, however, "they should be distinctly informed that, if they remain within the limits of the States, they must be subject to their law."[13]

[13] Andrew Jackson, First Annual Message, Dec. 8, 1829, in Richardson, *Messages and Papers*, 2:458–9.

This was the heart of the issue. Beginning in 1827 and continuing into the early 1830s, first Alabama and then Georgia, Mississippi, and Tennessee enacted laws to extend their civil and criminal jurisdiction into the regions within their boundaries that remained in Indian ownership. Indians living in those areas became subject to a body of law designed to prohibit the functioning of their governments, interfere with their economic and subsistence activities, and disrupt their societies. For example, Indians could not testify in court in cases involving Americans. This meant that unscrupulous persons could bring suits against Indian property owners on specious claims, win judgments, and enjoy the support of American sheriffs and posses to legally but unjustly confiscate their property. Native courts could not act in the defense of the Indians because the state laws disallowed their operation and provided heavy punishments to Indian judges who attempted to act.

Indian leaders petitioned, directly and through their agents, for federal protection against such state harassment. Arguing that the treaties guaranteed to the Indian nations the peaceful enjoyment of their lands free from the intervention of the states and citing provisions in the treaties and the Trade and Intercourse Acts that required the United States to defend them from the illegal actions of its citizens, Native leaders insisted that the Jackson Administration intervene on their behalf. Instead, Jackson defended the rights of the states to enjoy full sovereign powers over all the land and people within their boundaries. The treaties obligated the United States to defend the Indian peoples from private acts, not the sovereign exercise of state power, he explained. This interpretation obviously gave a very specific meaning to the options of removal or state citizenship that he held out in his address. Governor Troup had announced some years before that in Georgia, citizenship for Indians would be the second-class variety it offered free blacks. The laws extending state jurisdiction into Indian country simply defined the specifics of second-class citizenship. The state lawmakers, the Jackson Administration, Congressmen, the American public, and the Indians all understood the intent of the laws. As the Alabama legislature explained in early 1829:

It is believed that when they shall discover that the state of Alabama is determined upon her sovereign rights, and when they see and feel some palpable act of legislation under the authority of the state, that their veneration for their own law and customs will induce them speedily to remove.[14]

[14] Alabama House Journal, 1828–9, Debates (Jan. 21, 1829), 220–3.

If, with the connivance of the federal government, the states could make life for the Indians miserable enough, they would agree that removal was the best thing for them, sign removal treaties, and flee.

The debate in Congress that followed Jackson's message hung broadly on two arguments, constitutional and moral. Proponents followed Jackson's lead, citing the sovereign rights of the states, the general failure of the "civilization" policy to transform Indians into people capable of citizenship, and the necessity to isolate Native Americans in distant places in order to protect them from further "inevitable" decline, demoralization, and decimation. The failure of "civilization" was everywhere evident, they claimed, but no more so than in the refusal of Indian men to abandon hunting for agriculture. Refusing, as English and American men had always done, to credit agriculture by women as economically significant, they portrayed the matter as a contest between the needs of "savage" hunters and "civilized" farmers. God intended the land to be developed and used to support the masses, not to be left idle as a hunting preserve for the few. The "law of nature" should thus override whatever legal scruples one might erroneously have about treaty rights and guarantees. Southern Democratic Congressmen were most vociferous in these arguments, but they found important allies among northern Democrats and conservative churchmen.

Opponents steadfastly refused to believe Jacksonian assurances that removal would be voluntary and peaceful. Citing the treaties and the Trade and Intercourse Acts, they agreed with the Indians that the state jurisdiction laws were unconstitutional and that as long as they stood unchallenged removal could be nothing but involuntary and forced. The treaty system recognized the rights of the Native nations to govern themselves free from outside interference, the language of the treaties obligated the United States to protect that right, and the Constitution asserted that treaties, defined as part of the "supreme law of the land," were superior to state law. Indeed, United States honor was committed in the treaties and the refusal of the Jackson Administration to keep its word was both unjust and immoral. Furthermore, the opponents claimed, "civilization" had worked well if not completely, assimilation had been the implicit promise to "civilized" Indians, and to reject them now compounded the immorality of the removal scheme. In response to the natural law argument, Senator Theodore Frelinghuysen of New Jersey, one of the most outspoken opponents of removal, pointed out that American farmers did not need any more land from Indian hunters. At the current rate at which the United States sold its public lands to settlers, he figured it would take over 200 years to dispose of all the lands already purchased from the Indians. Opponents of removal tended to be political enemies of Jackson and the Democratic party, southern as well as northern, and included as well many of the Protestant churches most actively involved in Indian mission work.

In the spring of 1830, Congress enacted Jackson's removal bill. The margin in the House of Representatives was very close, 102 to 97, but in the Senate it was a more conclusive 28 to 19. President Jackson signed the bill into law May 28. By its terms the president was authorized to present the Indian nations with treaties that would offer land in the West in exchange for their eastern domains, provide a fee simple patent on request, and guarantee the country to be theirs "forever." Federal agents would appraise improvements left behind and pay for them, the United States would pay the costs of migration and provide subsistence in the West for one year, and after removal the government would protect the Indians in their new homes from any danger posed by western Indians or non-Indians.

First presented by the Monroe Administration as a viable policy solution to the mid-1820s "crisis in Indian affairs," removal became in 1830 the settled goal of the federal government. Successful expulsion west of over 100,000 eastern Indians would make way for the continued expansion of the booming United States. The execution of this policy would eliminate, for the first time since the establishment of the British Empire in America, Indians from the personal acquaintance and life experience of the vast majority of Americans. Native Americans would become aliens in America in fact as well as in law.

REMOVAL

The removal law of 1830 authorized the president to arrange by treaty the exchange of western lands for the holdings of all the Native nations east of the Mississippi. In fact, however, President Jackson was primarily interested in the removal of the five large southern nations – Choctaws, Chickasaws, Creeks, Cherokees, and Seminoles. Small groups such as the Catawbas, who lived on a reservation in western South Carolina and supported themselves by leasing their land to cotton planters, were outside the vision of the president. The planters wanted to own the land, however, and in 1840 the Catawbas agreed to sell. Their plan was to move in with the Cherokees in North Carolina, but before the decade was out mutual dissatisfaction caused the Catawbas to leave. Some went to Indian

Territory and lived with the Choctaws, others returned to South Carolina and purchased from the state a small fragment of their old reservation. But in the scattering the Catawba Nation became temporarily shattered and ceased to be an object of concern.

The official preoccupation with the removal of the southern Indians was partly due to the insistent demands of the southern states and partly in recognition of the overwhelming political support of southern voters. Thus Jackson notified northern political leaders that they would have to wait for the Indians to be removed from their areas until the removal of the southern Indians was well under way. Counting on the efficacy of the state laws that extended jurisdiction over the Indians, Jackson hoped for a quick and easy negotiation of removal treaties with Indian leaders eager to escape the legal and judicial harassment that awaited them. To that end his Secretary of War, John Eaton, invited delegations from all the nations except the distant Seminoles to gather in August 1830, at his home in Franklin, Tennessee, to finish the business. Jackson made plans to attend, and together he and Eaton expected speedy results.

Only the Chickasaws showed up. They drove a hard bargain with a demand that their country be surveyed into tracks to be allotted to each citizen in fee simple title. This would mean that each family would have control over the sale of its improvements and have a sum of money with which to begin life in the West. In addition, the Chickasaws insisted on both the right to select their new homeland and a clause that voided the arrangement if they failed to find an acceptable place. Jackson and Eaton agreed, but the deal fell through when a party of Chickasaw land rangers reported that they found nothing they liked. A second removal treaty, arranged in 1832 at Pontotoc in the Chickasaw Nation, repeated the allotment provisions of the first except on even more generous terms. Again, everything depended on the ability of the Chickasaws to locate a suitable region. Repeated failure to do so threatened to foil the efforts of the United States and Mississippi to oust the Chickasaws, despite the increasingly harsh application of Mississippi law. Finally, in January 1837, Chickasaw leaders purchased the right to settle among the Choctaws. Many Chickasaws sold their allotments at good prices, invested in slaves and livestock, and moved west during the summer and fall. They were never happy about being swallowed up in the Choctaw Nation, however, and in 1855 the two groups agreed to an amicable separation which led to the re-creation of the independent Chickasaw Nation.

Shortly after the Franklin talks, Eaton and a team of federal commis-

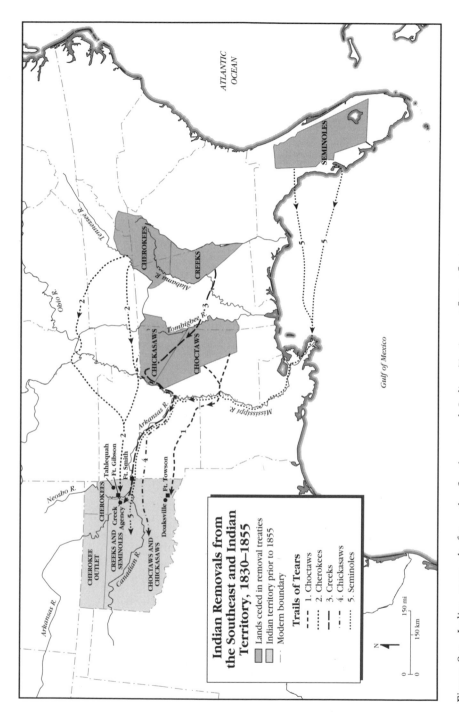

Figure 8.2. Indian removals from the Southeast and Indian Territory, 1830–1855.

sioners headed to the Choctaw Nation. The Choctaws already had western land, located between the Canadian and Red Rivers under the terms of the 1820 Treaty of Doak's Stand, and a small number of people had relocated there. Eaton's task in the fall of 1830 was to convince the rest of the people to sell their remaining holdings in the East, some ten million acres (4,040,000 hectares), and join them. But the Choctaw leaders were overwhelmingly opposed and repeatedly rejected Eaton's speeches. After a tirade in which Eaton threatened to declare war on the nation and invade, the talks broke down and many leaders left the grounds. Those who remained, led by Greenwood LeFlore and Moshulatubbee, then hammered out a treaty with Eaton. In return for a total land cession, the Choctaws accepted annuity payments, funds for the erection of schools and churches, and a promise to pay all removal expenses plus subsistence for one year in the West. Furthermore, the treaty contained a provision that extended substantial allotments to any Choctaw family wishing to remain as citizens of Mississippi. In violation of the spirit of this provision, however, Choctaw Agent William Ward made it virtually impossible for heads of families to register for allotments and only sixty-nine received one. Between 1831 and 1834, three groups of Choctaws trekked the 550 miles west to their new homes. The first of the mass removals, the Choctaw exodus was marked by government mismanagement, confusion, and fraud which imposed serious and unnecessary suffering on the people. As news trickled back of the hardships of the journey, which cost the lives of some 2,500 people, several thousand refused to go. Landless and homeless, they lived in marginal areas as squatters. In the late 1840s and early 1850s many of them finally left Mississippi. About 2,000 Choctaws never left, however. Their descendants remain in Mississippi on tribally owned land in and near Neshoba County.

Jackson was furious with the Creeks when they refused his summons to treat at Franklin. They made their choice to become Alabamians and submit to state law. Now, he warned, they could look after themselves. Intruders and swindlers, protected by Alabama law, made their lives miserable. At the same time, the Creek National Council tried to stave off removal by inhibiting those of its citizens who had decided it was best to get out and go west. Under the terms of the Treaty of Washington, concluded in 1826, the Creeks had a country in the West, north of the Choctaws between the Canadian and Arkansas Rivers, to go to. Initially, only the friends and supporters of William McIntosh fled there, but growing numbers of other Creeks, especially those from the Lower Towns who were required by the Treaty of Washington to vacate their lands claimed by Georgia, went as well. Believing that a trickle of voluntary migrants weakened the nation and its resolve to resist removal, the Council enacted laws and appointed police to keep the people at home. But over the winter of 1831–2, as the level of Alabama harassment increased and as the Jackson Administration continued its policy of refusing to enforce the protective provisions of the treaties, the Council caved in.

Under the guidance of Opothle Yoholo, de facto leader of the Creek Nation, the Council came up with a measure that might have met the interests of all the Creeks. Adopting the allotment concept written into the Chickasaw and Choctaw treaties, the Creek plan called for reserves to be allocated to every person. They were to be clustered, however, to perpetuate the towns. Creeks who wished to sell their allotments and move west could do so, but those who wished to remain in their homeland could preserve their town-based communal culture by contributing their allotments to the cluster that would represent their town. After the nation was surveyed, unallotted land would be available for sale to Alabamians. Acting on the assumption that the state of Alabama would never permit the scheme to work, the federal government accepted the Creeks' proposal and in March 1832 wrote it into a treaty.

Lewis Cass, newly appointed Secretary of War in Jackson's cabinet, had assumed correctly. Alabamians with and without state authorization descended on the Creeks. Land grabbers evicted them from their allotments, swindlers took them to court on fake charges, and grave robbers stole jewelry off the dead and buried. The Alabama legislature made hunting by Indians illegal, Creek women could not plant and harvest their crops in peace, and the people starved. In 1836, after four years of this, groups of young men struck out. The "Creek War" was hardly more than a few colorful but scattered incidents – a handful of warriors attacked and burned to the water line a steamboat on the Chattahoochee – but it was enough to provide Jackson, in a sharply contested election year, with an excuse to send troops. Claiming that the Creeks might make common cause with the Seminoles, the Army simply rounded them up and marched them off. Forced to abandon their allotments, improvements, and much of their movable property, the impoverished Creeks reached their new homes in the midst of one of the coldest, iciest, and snowiest winters on record.

The Seminoles, the next group to sign a removal treaty, were a nation of migrants and refugees. Attracted by fertile land, good hunting, and Spanish inducements, groups and towns of Lower Creeks began to move to

Spanish Florida in the early eighteenth century. Over the next several decades two groups augmented their numbers. One was composed of slaves escaped from South Carolina and Georgia plantations. Attracted by the isolation that Florida afforded them, growing numbers of these runaway slaves became attached to the Seminoles; some became intermarried kin, some were enslaved, and some established autonomous communities linked to the Seminoles by alliance. The other group to join the Seminoles arrived as defeated and displaced Nativist survivors of the Creek civil war. All found security in the Spanish colony and prospered.

After the War of 1812, Georgia planters who saw Florida as a haven for their runaway slaves launched a series of raids in hopes of breaking up their camps and recovering their human property. In 1818, Andrew Jackson led a force of Army troops and Creek warriors into Florida, ostensibly to smash Seminole military power. Jolted by the aggression, later termed the First Seminole War, in 1819 Spain sold Florida to the United States. United States–Seminole relations became formalized in 1823 with a treaty that relocated the Indians out of northern Florida onto a reservation in the peninsula. The unproductive land could not support their numbers, however, and Seminole hunting, trading, and grazing activities north of their reservation alarmed Florida settlers. They, like their Georgia and Carolina predecessors, also feared and resented the presence of people of African descent among the Seminoles. Thus they clamored for Seminole removal in the early 1830s, even though there was no settler demand for the Seminoles' sterile land.

Crop failure, hunger, the raids of slave catchers, and promises of a good life in the West with much government support drove many Seminole leaders to the conference table. On May 9, 1832 they signed the treaty that stipulated their removal. But like the Chickasaws, they included a proviso that called for a western tour by several headmen. The agreement to remove would be valid only when the leaders returned and reported that the land was good. The tour occupied much of the winter of 1832–3. In March the seven Seminole land scouts signed a document at Fort Gibson, an Army post on the Arkansas River, that expressed their satisfaction with the country. Despite the Seminole belief that they were to hear the reports and decide for themselves, the United States interpreted the Fort Gibson treaty as final.

In addition to the usual arrangement that the United States would pay all removal expenses plus subsistence in the West for one year, annuities, and compensation for abandoned improvements, the Seminole removal treaty required that they move onto the western Creek Nation. This prospect alarmed both the Creek civil war refugees who feared retribution and the black Seminoles who feared enslavement by Creek slaveholders. Thus the circumstances surrounding the western tour, the Fort Gibson document, and the federal interpretation of it generated heated controversy among the Seminoles, who repeatedly claimed that the land rangers had no authority to commit the nation, and thus they were under no obligation to remove.

Removal was to begin in January 1836. The month before, Seminole warriors killed the federal agent, Wiley Thompson, a leading pro-removal headman, Charley Emathla, and wiped out a column of U.S. troops. These acts began the Second Seminole War, which when declared over in 1842 had cost the United States 1,500 lives and over twenty million dollars. No one knows the number of dead Seminoles, but the war cost most of them their Florida homes. Removal occurred throughout the war. As groups of Seminoles surrendered or were captured, government officials loaded them on boats bound for New Orleans. There they transferred to river craft for the voyage up the Mississippi and Arkansas Rivers to Fort Gibson and the Creek Nation. By the time it was over, some 4,000 Seminoles and their allies of African descent had been relocated. About 500 remained in the swamps of southern Florida. In the mid-1850s those Seminoles tangled with some surveyors in what came to be called the Third Seminole War. As a result, 200 more were sent west. The rest persisted, and their descendants continue to live in Florida.

Just as the Chickasaws found living in the Choctaw Nation politically frustrating, so the Seminoles never reconciled themselves to being submerged into the Creek Nation. Controversies arose over land claims, political authority, and the rights of black Seminoles that were impossible to resolve. Finally, in 1856, the Seminoles purchased a tract from the Creeks and re-created their Nation.

While the Seminoles fought removal in the Florida swamps, the Cherokees waged their battles in the press, the halls of Congress, and the courts. Like the other southern nations, the Cherokees feared the operation of state law in their country, the implications of which became fully apparent in 1830 when one Cherokee man, Corn Tassel, killed another in the Cherokee Nation. Georgia authorities, claiming jurisdiction, arrested, tried, and convicted Corn Tassel for murder and sentenced him to be hanged. Cherokee chief John Ross had retained a Georgia firm to defend him and on his conviction sought out an attorney with a national reputation to handle the appeals. Ross's choice was William Wirt, a Baltimore lawyer who had served James Monroe and John Quincy Adams as Attorney General and had issued two opinions while in that office holding that Indian nations had independent sovereign status. Wirt quickly moved Corn Tassel's case through appeals to the U.S. Supreme Court. In December 1830, Chief Justice John Marshall ordered Georgia to appear before him to justify its jurisdictional claims. Instead, the Georgia legislature carried out Corn Tassel's execution. Wirt then filed a separate case, *Cherokee Nation v. Georgia.*

Wirt argued in the *Cherokee* case that the Cherokee Nation was a sovereign foreign nation over which Georgia could have no legal jurisdiction. The treaties between the Cherokee Nation and the United States and the Trade and Intercourse Acts all recognized Cherokee sovereignty, and the Constitution gave Congress sole authority under the commerce clause to conduct relations with Indian nations. Therefore, Wirt contended, the Court should strike down the Georgia laws as unconstitutional.

In March 1831 Marshall presented the Court's decision. The Cherokee Nation was not a foreign nation and could not bring suit against Georgia, he announced, and therefore dismissed the case. In *obiter dicta,* Marshall characterized the Cherokee Nation as a "domestic dependent nation" in a relationship with the United States that resembled that between a ward and a guardian. Privately, however, Marshall informed Wirt that he was sympathetic to the Cherokees and believed Georgia had no jurisdictional rights over them. If Wirt could bring a case the Court could hear, he would welcome it. Such a case was in the making.

Georgia law required all non-Indians in the Cherokee Nation who were not federal officials to register with state authorities and sign an oath of allegiance. Two of the many missionaries there, Samuel Worcester and Elizur Butler of the American Board of Commissioners for Foreign Missions, agreed to ignore the requirement in order to bring a test case. They were arrested, tried, and convicted in a Georgia court and sentenced to prison for four years at hard labor. Wirt brought the case, *Worcester v. Georgia,* on appeal to the Supreme Court, arguing again that Georgia had no jurisdiction in the Cherokee Nation and the law Worcester and Butler violated was unconstitutional and therefore null and void. The Court's decision, handed down in March 1832, agreed with Wirt and the Cherokees. In explaining the ruling, Marshall compared the relationship of the Cherokee Nation and the United States to that between a large and powerful state and a small and weak state. For reasons of its own, a small state could surrender various specific attributes of its sovereignty in return for particular benefits. Such surrenders did no more than the arrangement stipulated, however. The small state retained full sovereign rights and powers in all areas not specified. In the case of the Cherokee Nation, it had given up to the United States its sovereignty in such enumerated areas as foreign relations and trade with Americans but in all other areas it retained its sovereignty. In return for those surrenders the Cherokee Nation received from the United States its pledge of protection, including protection from American citizens. These guarantees, written into the treaties and affirmed by Congressional action, were superior to state law. Therefore, Georgia's legislation extending its jurisdiction into the Cherokee Nation was null and void.

The Cherokees, overjoyed by their victory, became despondent when they realized that the Court had no power to enforce its rulings. Georgia rejected the *Worcester* decision and proceeded with its policy to use its legal power to harass the Cherokees from their land. Chief John Ross launched another publicity blitz and desperately hoped that the 1832 election would turn President Jackson out of office. With the support of the vast majority of Cherokees, Ross's policy was to refuse negotiations with the United States and rely on the sense of justice of the American people.

A small number of well-educated and highly acculturated Cherokees came to believe that Ross was naive and his policy was doomed to fail. This view, articulated best by Elias Boudinot, John Ridge, and Major Ridge, held that American society was too deeply permeated by racism and economic ambition to care about the rights of Indians, that the political order was committed to removal, that the Cherokees were destined to be crushed by the onslaught, and that their only safety could be found in flight. Concluding that the essence of the Cherokee Nation was its people, Boudinot and the Ridges began to argue that it was wrong to sacrifice them in a futile effort to save the land. Motivated by the conviction that they knew what was best, despite the policy of Ross and the Cherokee national government, Boudinot, the Ridges, and about 100 like-minded Cherokees signed a removal treaty in December 1835 at Boudinot's home in New Echota, the Cherokee capital. Despite a petition circulated by the Ross government showing that virtually the entire Cherokee population opposed the treaty and in the face of clear evidence that the Cherokee signers had neither official standing nor authority to commit the nation to anything, the Senate ratified the document. Under its terms, the Cherokees were to be out of their eastern nation by the spring of 1838.

Boudinot, the Ridges, and the rest of the "Treaty Party" migrated in 1837. They joined the "Old Settlers" in the western nation north of the Arkansas River and together they numbered about 6,000. The bulk of the nation, under Ross's leadership, followed a policy of passive resistance. Ross remained certain that the American public would rise up in support of the Cherokees and somehow removal would not be forced on them. Thus when the June 1838 deadline arrived, the Cherokees had made no preparation to migrate. U.S. troops and Georgia militia entered the nation, rounded up the people, often at gunpoint, and herded them to temporary stockades built to hold them until they were shipped out. Suffering from exposure and a shortage of food and water, bereft of their possessions and in dire need, many people sickened and died in the camps. Ross then negotiated an arrangement with the United States by which the Cherokee government would organize and conduct its own removal. During the winter of 1838–9, under conditions so horrendous the Cherokees termed it the "trail where we cried," they struggled toward their new western homes.

The "National Party," as this group of some 15,000 Cherokees led by Ross called itself, was met with some trepidation by the people already in the West. The Old Settlers had been there for decades and had created social and governmental institutions that they wished to keep. The Treaty Party feared retribution. And the Nationals, representing the constitutional government and a majority of the people, expected to dominate affairs in the West. Tension became violent conflict in the summer of 1839 when Boudinot and the two Ridges were killed. Ross always claimed that the government had not ordered their execution, despite their having committed a capital crime, but their deaths precipitated civil strife marked by further bloodshed that lasted for seven years. Finally, in 1846, representatives of the three factions made peace and formed the basis for a united Cherokee Nation.

Except for the Cherokees' time of troubles, the southern nations adjusted to life in the West remarkably easily. The land proved to be unexpectedly fertile, and in most years the Indians grew large surpluses of corn which they sold on American markets. The Creeks contributed 100,000 bushels to help alleviate the Irish potato famine in 1846. The Indians also grazed large herds of quality horses and cattle and held sales that attracted buyers from throughout the Midwest. Planters who enjoyed the advantage of slave labor broke fields for cotton and entered the Little Rock and New Orleans markets. One Cherokee entrepreneur, Joseph Vann, purchased a steamboat to ply the Arkansas and Mississippi Rivers, and a Choctaw planter owned a fleet of river steamers. Missionaries followed the Indians west and built new school systems, organized new congregations, and continued their efforts in the name of "civilization."

Some Congressmen worried about the status of the removed nations. Treaties with western Indians, notably the Osages, had provided land titles to be signed over to the nations, but competition for land and resources threatened trouble. All the removal treaties included a clause that promised federal protection, but some thought more was needed. In 1834, Congress debated a bill to organize Indian Territory. It would be inhabited by Indians, mainly those removed from the East, would be governed by an Indian legislature and a governor appointed by the president, and would someday enter the Union as a state. The bill did not pass, to the relief of the removed nations, but the name Indian Territory stuck. In the absence of territorial government, the United States expanded its line of army posts, but it never invested enough in them to secure the safety of the Indians. Conferences involving various Indian nations held at Fort Gibson in the mid-1830s opened negotiations, if not altogether friendly relations, with the Pawnees, Kiowas, Comanches, and other southern Plains groups. These meetings were followed by a second series in the mid-1840s. The first hosted by the Creeks, the second in 1843 by the Cherokees, firmed up a pattern of tolerant amicability between the intruding southern nations and the resident Plains Indians that persisted for many decades.

By the time of these international councils, Indian Territory had become an increasingly complex place. Until the passage of the Kansas-Nebraska Act in 1854, the idea of Indian Territory embraced the region from the Red River boundary with Texas to the Platte River in the north. During the 1820s, the United States had granted the southern portion to the southern nations. The country north of the Cherokees, in Kansas, became the new homes for the Indian peoples removed from the northern states. Some Delawares, Kickapoos, and Shawnees had moved west of the Mississippi long before the passage of the removal bill and settled in present-day Missouri. Erected as a state in 1821, Missouri began to urge the expulsion of these Indians.

Indiana, Ohio, and Illinois joined the clamor for removal and beginning in the early 1830s, after its policy in the South was well underway, the Jackson Administration turned its attention northward. Ottawas, Potawatomis, Shawnees, and Miamis all sold their last holdings during

the 1830s and accepted new lands in eastern Kansas. The organization of
Kansas Territory in 1854 threatened their tenure, however, because it
removed the region north of the thirty-seventh parallel from Indian Territory. Some groups, such as the Miamis and bands of Shawnees and
Potawatomis, agreed to allot their lands in severalty and remain as citizens. But some bands of Potawatomis, Delawares, Shawnees, and others
resisted allotment. In a replay of the settler pressures that had driven the
eastern Indians to Indian Territory, the Indian groups relocated in Kansas
became, by the late 1850s, once again subjected to the demands of their
American neighbors that they vacate the country. The so-called "Senecas of
Sandusky," a mixed group in northern Ohio that included people from all
the Iroquois nations plus Wyandots and others, had sold out and moved
west in 1831. Their new home was south, however, in the tract east of the
Neosho River that was excluded from the Cherokee Nation. After the
Civil War, many of the northern peoples earlier removed to eastern Kansas
were sent into Indian Territory and several joined the Senecas in this small
northeast corner of the territory.

Most of the northern nations, like most of the southern, resisted removal but did so without resort to arms. On the Illinois side of the
Mississippi River, however, a militant band of Sauks led by Black Hawk
refused to surrender their homes quietly. The Sauks and their associates
the Foxes (Mesquakies) had controlled both banks of a stretch of the upper
Mississippi for generations. Patrilineal agriculturalists who, mounted on
horses, hunted buffalo on the western plains in the summertime, the
Sauks and Foxes represented transitional cultural patterns that linked
elements of Woodlands and Plains traditions.

In 1804, a handful of Sauk leaders on a mission to St. Louis signed the
first of the many Harrison treaties that surrendered title but permitted
continued use of the land sold. Through this cession the Sauks gave up
their title to western and northern Illinois. In the 1820s, in conjunction
with a lead mining rush into northwestern Illinois, the government called
on the Sauks to abandon their town on the Rock River and move across the
Mississippi. Many Sauks, persuaded by Keokuk, the leader of a faction
opposed to Black Hawk's policies, that retreat was the wise course, com-
plied. But several hundred others, guided by Black Hawk, persisted in
returning to their village each spring to plant their corn, arguing that the
1804 cession was unauthorized and invalid. Over the course of several
years, as the settler and miner population of the region grew, confrontations became sharper. Returning Sauks who found settlers living in their

houses and farming their fields became increasingly disgusted, while the terrified settlers demanded protection from Indians they claimed were intruders. Finally, in the spring of 1832, the Sauks ran into a force of mounted Illinois militia and shots were exchanged. With the Army close behind, militiamen and Sauk warriors fought a series of skirmishes in the Illinois-Wisconsin border area while Sauk women and children made their way to the Mississippi. A government steamboat armed with a cannon killed many of them while they crossed the river; Sioux warriors killed or captured most of the survivors. Black Hawk and his closest advisers fell into the hands of the Winnebagos, who turned them over to the Army for imprisonment. For the next dozen years the Sauks shared present Iowa with their Fox allies, only to be removed to Kansas in 1845. In 1869, to make way for American wheat farmers, the Sauks were relocated to Indian Territory on lands recently acquired from the Creeks. The Foxes, on the other hand, never fully cut the ties to their Iowa homeland. In 1856, the Iowa state legislature approved a Fox request that they be permitted to remain in the state. Beginning the next year the Foxes launched a land purchase program that led to the accumulation of about 4,000 acres (1,650 hectares) on the banks of the Iowa River, in Tama County, where they reside today.

In New York, the Iroquois nations owned large tracts of land reserved to them after the Revolution that attracted the interest of land companies and settlers alike. Each of the nations, from the Oneidas in the east to the Senecas and Tuscaroras in the west, faced similar problems of subsisting on reservations, reacting to the encroachments of settlers, dealing with missionaries, and staving off the recurrent demands that they sell out and remove. Handsome Lake's Good Words had helped many Senecas address the cultural implications of the myriad challenges, but most Iroquois, untouched or unresponsive to Handsome Lake's message, had to figure out for themselves how to survive.

Politics and religion became bound up with the pressures on the land and most reservations, by the 1820s, were more or less divided into competing factions. Some of the conflicts pitted Christian against non-Christian, others separated one Protestant denomination from another, and all worked to perpetuate disharmony at a time when the American interest in removal was growing.

The 1820s and 1830s were marked by a series of land sales that transferred most Iroquois land into the hands of Americans. In 1838, for example, a few corrupt Seneca chiefs sold all the Seneca reservations in western New York and agreed to remove to Kansas. The outcry of most of the Seneca people, utterly opposed to such an arrangement, was so great that in 1842 another treaty was negotiated to invalidate the first. The Senecas had to give up two reservations (Buffalo Creek and Tonawanda) but they held onto two (Cattaraugus and Allegheny) and were no longer required to emigrate. In 1846, a handful of Senecas decided to move to Kansas after all, but most sickened and died on route. In 1857 a portion of the Tonawanda reservation was bought back for the Senecas using money set aside for their removal to Kansas.

Unlike the Senecas, a faction of Oneidas became enthusiastic about removal. Led by Episcopal missionary Eleazar Williams, this group opened talks with Menominees in Wisconsin for the purchase of a tract of land. Apparently motivated by a desire to establish an isolated Christian haven for the Iroquois, Williams began leading his followers west in 1823 following the completion of the purchase. There they founded successful farming communities and managed a small logging operation. In the early 1840s, over 400 more Oneidas moved to land they had purchased near London, Ontario.

Removals depleted the Iroquois population in New York but did not eradicate it. Villages of all the Six Nations survived (the Mohawks at Akwesasne on the St. Lawrence had returned from Caughnawaga) despite the persistent efforts of federal and state governments, settlers, and land companies to get rid of them. Like other groups of eastern Indians overwhelmed by the tide of American settlement, they changed and adapted to repeated challenges but nevertheless retained their identities as Indians. Engulfed rather than isolated, outside the mainstream but subject to the pull of the current, the Iroquois, like the Catawbas, the Eastern Band of Cherokees, and the other groups that escaped removal, remained on their homelands and survived.

In Indian Territory, the peace and security the nations had tried so hard to achieve in the 1840s and 1850s came to an end in 1861. The cause was American civil strife, however, not intergroup warfare. Secession took the neighboring states of Texas and Arkansas out of the Union, the United States restationed western troops to the East, and Indian Territory was left to deal with the federal crisis on its own. Confederate agent Albert Pike stepped into the vacuum and during the summer of 1861 negotiated treaties with each of the five nations. The Choctaw and Chickasaw treaties reflected virtually unanimous support for the South, the Creek, Seminole, and Cherokee treaties obscured deep internal division which led, in the cases of the Creeks and Cherokees, to bloody conflicts between northern and southern factions.

The war years were difficult for everyone living in Indian Territory. With warriors in both armies and borders with Union Kansas and Confederate Arkansas, the Cherokee Nation was a crossroads of conflict. The Creek Nation, no stranger to the battlefield, was particularly devastated by gangs of terrorists and outlaws. Large percentages of people of both nations fled to neighboring Indian nations and states, sacrificing their property in hopes of saving their lives. Unionists went to badly managed refugee camps in Kansas, Confederates poured into the Choctaw Nation and Texas. When the war ended, the factions among the Cherokees and Creeks nurtured a level of hostility and mistrust that took decades to fade away.

United States policy toward the nations of Indian Territory in the reconstruction period rested on the assumption that they were defeated Confederate enemies who should be made to pay for their disloyalty. In a series of treaties dictated by the United States in 1866, the Creeks had to sell the western half of their country, the Seminoles lost all of theirs and received a small parcel from the Creeks, the Choctaws and Chickasaws gave up their western lands, and the Cherokees sold their holdings in Kansas. The nations also abolished slavery and agreed to extend full citizenship rights to their freedmen. Furthermore, each nation agreed to grant rights of way to railroads wishing to build across their lands. A literal foot in the door, the railroads brought corporate America and American citizens into Indian Territory with such speed and in such numbers that by the 1880s Native people were on the verge of becoming minorities in their own nations.

CANADA AT MIDCENTURY

During the first half of the nineteenth century, Canadian Indian policy was in fact the separate policies of the provinces conducted under the supervision of the British Colonial Office (full control was transferred to the Province of Canada in 1860). In the Maritimes, about 2,500 Micmacs, Maliseets, and Abenakis of Nova Scotia and New Brunswick continued to live in scattered communities on reserves or public lands under license from the governments. No land was set aside for Native people on Prince Edward Island before 1859. In Lower Canada (Quebec) fewer than 3,000 Indians (according to an 1844 census) lived in the seven reserves founded by the Jesuits in the seventeenth century. Huron, Mohawk, and Western Abenaki refugees from New England for the most part, they supported themselves mainly through farming and day labor. The Indians of Upper Canada (southern Ontario) numbered nearly 9,000. Half were descended from Iroquois, Ottawa, and Potawatomi refugees from the United States who lived at Grand River and a number of other reserves. The other half were Ojibwas who still controlled a great deal of land and who were under constant pressure from settlers and logging and mining interests to sell it. In 1850 the lands north of Lakes Huron and Superior were surrendered in two treaties negotiated by William B. Robinson in return for reserves, annuities, and fishing and hunting rights. These treaties provided a model for later ones that the Canadian federal government negotiated in western Canada. In 1862 the Ojibwa residents of Manitoulin Island were pressured into surrendering most of the land set aside as a reserve for them in 1836.

The Indian policy of Upper Canada remained conflicted between "civilization" and segregation. Efforts to develop some sort of centralized program got underway in the 1850s, however, as a result of a harshly critical report that surveyed the condition of mainly Upper Canada Indians and concluded that Canada had been woefully negligent in protecting Indian rights and achieving its goals of "civilization." Legislation enacted throughout the 1850s attempted to address the problem by stiffening rules for defending Native land rights and by developing a formalized system for assimilating "civilized" Indians into the Canadian mainstream. Known as "enfranchisement," the idea was to encourage "civilization" by permitting individuals to change their status from dependent Indians to fully equal Canadians. Ideally, this policy would ultimately do away with Canada's Indian problem by eliminating, through legislative fiat, its Indian population. All an Indian had to do was demonstrate that he was "civilized" enough to support himself. In place until recently, this policy found few takers. While Native people understood the need to adapt to changing times, and often took quite imaginative steps to do so, they tended to reject the notion that in the adaptation they must renounce their Indian heritage.

Further centralization occurred with the creation in 1867 of the Dominion of Canada; the federal government assumed responsibility for upholding British treaty obligations and for Indian affairs generally. The primary administrative focus lay in opening relations with the Native groups formerly the exclusive concern of the Hudson's Bay Company, however, and the importance of eastern Indians quickly became defined in terms of

Canada's western interests. For example, Canada needed more Ojibwa lands in order to open a safe and easy land route west (see Chapter 9). Indians remained wards of the government, reserves continued to house shrinking numbers of people subject to an increasingly debilitating governmental paternalism, and enfranchisement continued to be the goal officials held up for Indians to achieve.

CONCLUSION

Throughout the period between 1780 and 1880, eastern Native Americans continued the process of adaptation to Euro-American society that they had begun two centuries before. Buffeted by strange and deadly diseases, aggressive and violent people, missionaries dedicated to destroying their cultures, and patterns of economic dependency that demanded almost continuous adjustment, they somehow survived. While some institutions of Native life shattered and crumbled under the strain, others took on new shapes and strengthened. Each group found its own way to endure, shaped by the mixture of its unique culture and the experiences it faced, but a theme runs through many of their histories.

Indian communities had always been autonomous. They had traditions of facing and dealing with the problems of life as families of interrelated people who could act as they chose. Europeans and Americans recognized this power, respected it, used it if they could, often manipulated it, and frequently tried to undercut it. But they did not deny it. Rather, English colonists, Royal officials, and the independent United States shaped their Indian policies around the idea that Native polities, historically autonomous, were indeed sovereign nations. Finding in the diplomatic histories of both Europe and America well-established methods for managing the relations between sovereigns, English and American politicians in concert with their Native counterparts institutionalized the treaty system. A mixture of European and Indian ceremonial trappings, the treaties became crucial reminders of tribal sovereignty even as they entered American law. Frequently extorted, often broken, they nevertheless became the spine on which the body of relations grew. That is the history that gives this period meaning.

Congress ended the treaty system in 1871 with legislation that expressly denied the sovereignty of Native nations. The first in a series of post–Civil War policies designed to destroy, once and for all, the autonomous existence of Indian communities, the law was barely noticed. But in its action, Congress changed a history that was nearly three centuries old and opened a new period filled with new challenges which Native Americans also survived.

Sources abound for the history of eastern Native Americans during the century 1780–1880. Two volumes of the *Handbook of North American Indians,* William C. Sturtevant, gen. ed., contain essays that are particularly useful as introductions to the topics covered in this chapter: vol. 4, *History of Indian-White Relations,* ed. Wilcomb E. Washburn (Washington, D.C., 1988) and vol. 15, *Northeast,* ed. Bruce G. Trigger (Washington, D.C., 1978). Francis Paul Prucha's *The Great Father: The United States Government and the American Indians* (Lincoln, Nebr., 1984), 2 vols., is the classic history of the Indian policy of the United States. Helen Hornbeck Tanner, ed., *Atlas of Great Lakes Indian History* (Norman, Okla., 1986) contains excellent maps clearly described and explained.

Barbara Graymont, *The Iroquois in the American Revolution* (Syracuse, N.Y., 1972), remains the standard account of the important role of the Iroquois in the Revolutionary period. James H. O'Donnell III, *Southern Indians in the American Revolution* (Knoxville, Tenn., 1973), covers the southern theater. An important recent discussion of the Cherokee experience in the Revolutionary period is Tom Hatley, *The Dividing Paths: Cherokees and South Carolinians through the Era of Revolution* (New York, 1993). Colin Calloway, *The American Revolution in Indian Country* (Cambridge, 1995) offers a fresh perspective on the Revolutionary experiences of several Native groups.

The most complete discussion of post-Revolution U.S. Indian policy remains Reginald Horsman, *Expansion and American Indian Policy, 1783–1812* (East Lansing, Mich., 1965). L. C. Green and Olive P. Dickason, *The Law of Nations and the New World* (Edmonton, 1989), contains an excellent discussion of European international law and its applications to Native Americans. The standard source on Alexander McGillivray is John W. Caughey, *McGillivray of the Creeks* (Norman, Okla., 1938), supplemented by Michael D. Green, "Alexander McGillivray," in *American Indian Leaders: Studies in Diversity,* ed. R. David Edmunds (Lincoln, Nebr., 1980), 41–63.

Several scholars have studied the period between the Revolution and the War of 1812. The most valuable policy study of the period is Francis Paul

Prucha, *American Indian Policy in the Formative Years: The Indian Trade and Intercourse Acts, 1790–1834* (Cambridge, Mass., 1962), supplemented with Merritt B. Pound, *Benjamin Hawkins: Indian Agent* (Athens, Ga., 1951) and Bernard Sheehan, *Seeds of Extinction: Jeffersonian Philanthropy and the American Indians* (Chapel Hill, N.C., 1973). Developments in the North are surveyed in Richard White, *The Middle Ground: Indians, Empires, and Republics in the Great Lakes Region, 1650–1815* (Cambridge, 1991). The road to Fallen Timbers and Greenville is well marked by Randolph C. Downes, *Council Fires on the Upper Ohio: A Narrative of Indian Affairs in the Upper Ohio Valley until 1795* (Pittsburgh, Penn., 1940). Gregory Evans Dowd, *A Spirited Resistance: The North American Indians' Struggle for Unity, 1745–1815* (Baltimore, 1992) puts Fallen Timbers into a context that focuses on the roles of prophecy and spiritualism in Native America. His work accompanies that by Anthony F. C. Wallace, *Death and Rebirth of the Seneca* (New York, 1970), the story of Handsome Lake, and R. David Edmunds, *The Shawnee Prophet* (Lincoln, Nebr., 1983). Joel Martin's *Sacred Revolt: The Muskogees' Struggle for a New World* (Boston, 1991) argues that the Creek War of 1811–14 was a millenarian movement. Frank L. Owsley, Jr., *The Struggle for the Gulf Borderlands: The Creek War and the Battle of New Orleans, 1812–1815* (Gainsville, Fla., 1981) is the best recent history of the Creek War. R. David Edmunds, *Tecumseh and the Quest for Indian Leadership* (Boston, 1984) discusses the northern Indians in the War of 1812.

After the War of 1812, eastern Indians changed their cultures in response to new situations while the policy debate between civilizers and removers raged. Cherokee culture change is perhaps the best understood. See in particular Theda Perdue, *Slavery and the Evolution of Cherokee Society, 1540–1866* (Knoxville, Tenn., 1979) and William G. McLoughlin, *Cherokee Renascence in the New Republic* (Princeton, N.J., 1986). Michael D. Green, *The Politics of Indian Removal: Creek Government and Society in Crisis* (Lincoln, Nebr., 1982) and Duane Champagne, *Social Order and Political Change: Constitutional Government among the Cherokee, the Choctaw, the Chickasaw, and the Creek* (Stanford, Calif., 1992) concentrate on political change. R. David Edmunds, *The Potawatomis, Keepers of the Fire* (Norman, Okla., 1978) discusses the adaptation of that people.

Missionaries were central to the government's efforts to "civilize" Native people. For missionary work among eastern Indians, see especially Robert F. Berkhofer, Jr., *Salvation and the Savage: An Analysis of Protestant Missions and American Indian Responses, 1787–1862* (Lexington, Ky.,

1965) and two important books by William G. McLoughlin: *Cherokees and Missionaries, 1789–1839* (New Haven, Conn., 1984) and *Champions of the Cherokees: Evan and John B. Jones* (Princeton, N.J., 1990).

Many books discuss the debate over removal policy. Ronald N. Satz, *American Indian Policy in the Jacksonian Era* (Lincoln, Nebr., 1975) is extremely important. Francis Paul Prucha, ed., *Cherokee Removal: The "William Penn" Essays and Other Writings* (Knoxville, Tenn., 1981) and John A. Andrew III, *From Revivals to Removal: Jeremiah Evarts, the Cherokee Nation, and the Search for the Soul of America* (Athens, Ga., 1992) deal with one of the most active opponents of removal. Theda Perdue, ed., *Cherokee Editor: The Writings of Elias Boudinot* (Knoxville, Tenn., 1983) and Thurman Wilkins, *Cherokee Tragedy: The Story of the Ridge Family and the Decimation of a People* (New York, 1970) explain the proremoval faction of the Cherokees; Gary E. Moulton, *John Ross, Cherokee Chief* (Athens, Ga., 1978) discusses the antiremoval position of the Cherokee government. An interesting recent synthesis of the history of Indian removal is Anthony F. C. Wallace, *The Long, Bitter Trail: Andrew Jackson and the Indians* (New York, 1993). The Catawbas are covered in James H. Merrell, *The Indians' New World: Catawbas and Their Neighbors from European Contact through the Era of Removal* (Chapel Hill, N.C., 1989).

Grant Foreman's *Indian Removal: The Emigration of the Five Civilized Tribes of Indians* (Norman, Okla., 1932) and *The Last Trek of the Indians* (Chicago, 1946) remain the standard accounts of removal, although the tribal histories of many groups also contain material on removal. On life in Indian Territory after removal, see Foreman's *The Five Civilized Tribes* (Norman, Okla., 1934) and H. Craig Miner, *The Corporation and the Indian: Tribal Sovereignty and Industrial Civilization in Indian Territory, 1865–1907* (Columbia, Mo., 1976).

Indian armed resistance to removal is discussed in John K. Mahon, *The History of the Second Seminole War, 1835–1842* (Gainesville, Fla., 1967) and Anthony F. C. Wallace, *Prelude to Disaster: The Course of Indian-White Relations Which Led to the Black Hawk War of 1832* (Springfield, Ill., 1970). See Donald Jackson, ed., *Black Hawk: An Autobiography* (Urbana, Ill., 1955) for Black Hawk's account of events.

The history of the Indians of eastern Canada is discussed in Olive P. Dickason, *Canada's First Nations: A History of Founding Peoples from Earliest Times* (Toronto, 1992) and Edward S. Rogers and Donald B. Smith, eds., *Aboriginal Ontario: Historical Perspectives on the First Nations* (Toronto, 1994).

INDEX